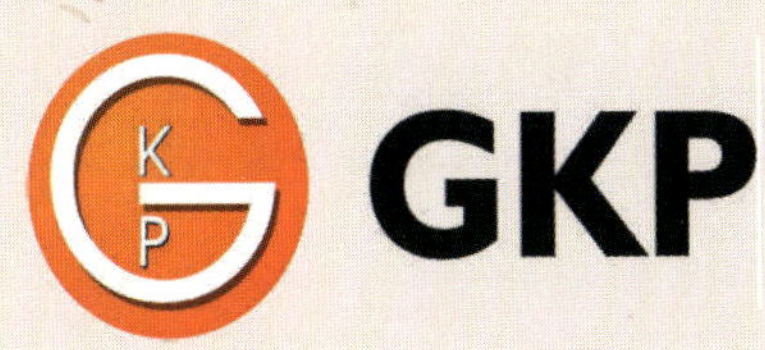

Unravelling

Indian Culture

The Essence of Bharat

— Ancient India —

MADHUKAR KUMAR BHAGAT

Title : Unravelling Indian Culture : The Essence of Bharat – Ancient India

Language : English

Author Name : Madhukar Kumar Bhagat

Typeset & Published by :

Career Launcher Infrastructure (P) Ltd.

A-45, Mohan Cooperative Industrial Area, Near Mohan Estate Metro Station, New Delhi - 110044

Marketed by :

G.K. Publications (P) Ltd.

Plot No. 63, Sector-27A, Near Sector - 28 Metro Station, Faridabad, Haryana-121003

ISBN : **978-93-56815-24-7**

Printer's Details : Printed in India, New Delhi.

Acknowledgements & Thanks

Government Departments, Museums and Art Galleries

- Department of Posts, Government of India
- Department of Tourism, Bihar
- Department of Tourism, Odisha
- Department of Tourism, Rajasthan
- Department of Tourism, West Bengal
- Directorate of Uttar Pradesh Tourism
- Karnataka State Tourism Development Corporation
- Madhya Pradesh Tourism Board
- Maharashtra Tourism Development Corporation
- Sangeet Natak Akademi
- Tamil Nadu Tourism Development Corporation
- Directorate of Archaeology and Museums, Government of Haryana
- Bihar Museum, Patna
- Chatrapati Shivaji Maharaj Vastu Sangrahalaya, Mumbai
- Government Museum, Chennai
- Nagpur Central Museum
- National Crafts Museum & Hastkala Akademi, New Delhi
- National Gallery of Modern Art, New Delhi
- National Museum, New Delhi
- Patna Museum, Patna
- State Museum, Bhopal
- The Government Museum, Bangalore

The Publishers

- **Vinod Bhan** – *Business Head*
- **Kannath Prakash** – *Editorial Coordinator*
- **Brijesh Jha** – *Text Layout & Design*
- **Bhagwan Das** – *Cover Design*

Dedicated to

Maa, Papa,

Bhaiya,

Garima,

Pranshu and Prabhav,

for family is

the fountainhead

of values and culture.

Preface

As I begin to pen this preface, I realise that it marks the culmination of a wonderful and long journey of more than three years, resulting in this work of three volumes on Indian culture. Endeavouring to capture the very essence of Indian culture and nearly 5000 years of its cultural history, was never going to be a straightforward undertaking. Indeed, it was audacious of me to even embark on this project and I am glad it could be completed. Accomplishing an arduous and challenging task is always satisfying. However, what brings me immense joy is that with this work, I could attempt to make a humble contribution, to foster an appreciation of the rich Indian culture. If to 'give' is a higher form of human fulfilment, then this work marks my modest, albeit gratifying offering to this quintessential element of Indianness.

The ambit of the subject is vast and complex. Ranging from the intriguing and advanced culture of the Indus Valley people to the simple folk culture of the present day, from the enlightening and complex Vedic philosophies like Advaita to the popular modern culture and its elements like Indian cinema; the work strives to encapsulate diverse elements of the all-encompassing nature of Indian culture. The three books also take the readers through the different cultural waves that have swept this vast land and its people, the confluence of certain contrasting sub-cultures and the emergence of the diverse, inclusive, dynamic and ever-evolving Indian culture. While an analytical appreciation of the different cultural phases is an integral element of this work, the various chapters also identify the macro and micro elements of Indian culture. These are expressed as tangible elements, like art, sculpture, architecture etc. and intangible elements, like religion, philosophy and others. The performing arts of music and dance, the visual arts of painting, sculpture and architecture and literary arts, besides other elements of culture, are covered in the three books, of the ancient, the medieval and the modern Indian culture.

It is said that a picture is worth a thousand words. Taking inspiration from this idiom, this work has included nearly 1500 photographs. These encompass different phases of cultural history and different subjects. Their span extends from the Harappan artefacts to modern-day festivals, from the ancient temples and sculptures to medieval monuments and modern-day crafts. Some of the images are sourced from the different state tourism departments and other government agencies. These are high-quality images taken by professional photographers. Many of the photographs are those taken by me over a period of several years. Some are also sourced from Wikipedia. These pictures are taken by common folks, and are thus, a contribution to this common cause of Indian culture. This wide gamut of photographs aids a clearer visual conception of the elements of culture and is expository of the very subject. They are indeed integral to the very concept of this project which is to offer the common person, a lucid understanding of the intricacies of the glorious Indian culture. The photographs also take these three volumes into the category of an illustrated work on Indian culture.

This book (volume 1) covers the cultural elements of ancient India and comprises seven chapters. The fundamentals of what constitute culture and it's interconnections with other salient institutions viz. religion, civilization and nationality, is a poignant feature of the first chapter. Besides, the various eras of cultural evolution beginning with the Indus Valley Civilisation phase, progressing to the Vedic phase, the arrival of Buddhism, Jainism and other Shramana traditions and the emergence of the Puranic culture, are also analysed. The second chapter on the Indus Valley Civilisation and Harappan culture dwells deeper into this mystifying civilisation. It identifies its salient elements, which, at its zenith was an unsurpassed culture of the ancient world. It also explores its town planning, arts, sciences, commerce, society, government etc., its mysterious yet undeciphered script and the possible causes of the decline of this civilisation. Also included is the gist of the exciting latest research which shed light on the food, the script, the life of the people, their DNA, their possible origin and the changing environment that adversely affected this advanced civilisation.

(Continued)

The subsequent three chapters on Hinduism, Buddhism and Jainism, highlight the essence of the grand philosophies of these ancient and living religions. These profound philosophies are intrinsic constituents of Indian culture and continue to guide the modern world. Also highlighted are their treatises, practices and belief systems which influenced the rulers and the people alike and shaped the numerous facets of culture of the entire region and overall social discourse in the ensuing centuries. Chapter 6 brings out the tangible and intangible cultural elements of the ancient world. They take us through the grand universities of this age, the intricate rock-cut architecture and the nascent free-standing temples. This kaleidoscope of ancient culture also offers a glimpse of the architecture, sculptures, and paintings of this age, of the path-breaking achievements in mathematics and medicine, of the treatises on numerous scientific disciplines, of the great literary classics of this golden age and of its myriad of achievements which bewilder and inspire pride. The last chapter on the grand ancient and medieval temples is a reflection of the culmination of the numerous disciplines of the ancient world. These include architecture and engineering, art and philosophy which in fusion with the religious fervour of the age, inspired beautiful and grand temples. These indeed were a marvel of the ancient world.

While India's culture has always been evolving and dynamic, it has also been inclusive and syncretic, which are traits inspired by the grand vision of the ancient seers who saw the interconnectedness of all beings. The Vedic verse, '*Udaracaritanam Tu Vasudhaiva Kutumbakam*', from Maha Upanishad, which means that for the generous-spirited, the entire world is a family, best exemplifies this inclusivity. This foundational cultural value also manifests in the aspirational hymn, '*Sarve Bhavantu Sukhinah*' of Brihadarnyaka Upanishad which prays for the happiness and well-being of all. The principle of universality, the desire to seek and understand the ultimate truth, the philosophy of goodness and interconnectedness and the highest urge of union with the supreme, have been some features of our cultural essence that have guided us in this evolutional journey of several millennia.

Indeed, over the span of centuries, our culture has not remained static or become an isolated mass of homogenous attributes. It has been pervious and dynamic, with fresh waves of socio-cultural influences sprouting diverse cultural milieus. In the numerous hues of culture and its diverse elements, these three books bring out some. Its chapters are akin to those windows in a large mansion, where each offers a unique glimpse of the outside world, with each glimpse through the windows representing a macro element of the grand Indian culture. No book on culture can claim to be comprehensive and nor does this. But it sincerely endeavours to bring out the salient elements of Indian culture and their essence.

I am thankful to the publishers for believing in this project from the very outset and sustaining their interest and hard work throughout these years. Special thanks are due to different state tourism departments and other government agencies who have contributed numerous photographs, and to the different museums across the country and their officials, whose guidance has been invaluable. Some of the unsung contributors whose photographs have found a place through the pages of Wikipedia, also deserve my thanks. And of course, a big thanks to you readers, for sparing your time in going through this book and evincing interest in this profound and yet fascinating subject.

Our family remains the repository of the social culture and the primary teacher and transmitter of values. I am thankful to my family. A special thanks to my father, who painstakingly went through the first draft of all the chapters and corrected them, as he has always done with me. To my wife and children who had to bear with me in these years, a thank you will not suffice. Above all, I pray to the Divine, to continue to bestow His grace as He has always done.

Om!

Madhukar Kumar Bhagat
December 2023
New Delhi

Contents

1

Culture Eras: Ancient India

> अयं निजः परो वेति गणना लघुचेतसाम् ।
> उदारचरितानां तु वसुधैव कुटुम्बकम् ।।
> *Ayam Nijah Paro Veti Ganana Laghucetasam*
> *Udaracharitanam Tu Vasudhaiva Kutumbakam*
> This is mine that is other's, such accounting is done by the petty-minded;
> For the generous spirited, the entire world is a family.
>
> **Maha Upanishad VI.71-73**

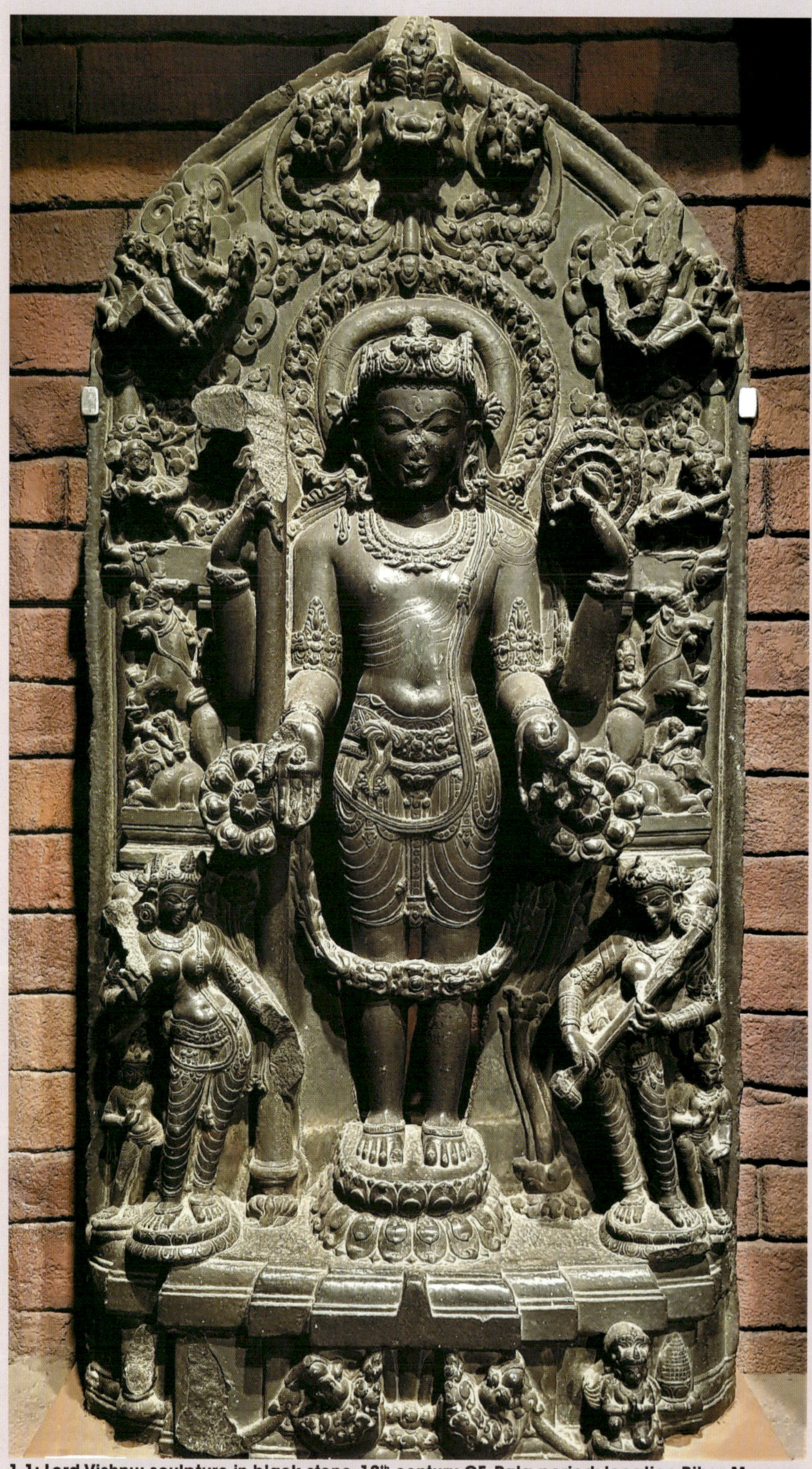

1.1: Lord Vishnu; sculpture in black stone, 12th century CE, Pala period; location Bihar Museum, Patna — photograph by Madhukar K Bhagat

INTRODUCTION

The term 'culture' is varyingly understood, often as encompassing different manifestations of human intellect and other expressions, particularly of ideas, beliefs, customs and social behaviour. At a more granular level, this conception incorporates different art forms, languages and literature, traditions and values and religious expressions and practices. At times, even urbane lifestyles and discerning tastes of material subjects are considered archetypal of what the term 'culture' embodies.

India, that is Bharat, with its near continuous history of more than 5,000 years as an evolving civilisation, has a dynamic and living culture. It is justifiably proud of this unique heritage, which is often considered a key element of its own national identity. However, there are questions as to what the true Indian culture is and which hue in this multitude of cultural chroma can be said to be the quintessential representative of Indian civilisation. But this begets some more queries as to what is civilisation, what is the broader domain of culture, how has it evolved in India, how inextricably is it linked to our religious thoughts and practices, and most importantly, what is nationhood itself. A brief perusal of these concepts would help in a better appreciation of the domain of culture and in capturing a glimpse of the vibrant Indian culture, which is the main endeavour of this work.

CULTURE: A MOSAIC OF COLLECTIVE INSTITUTIONS, INTELLECTUAL AND HUMAN KNOWLEDGE ELEMENTS

The connotation of the word culture is vast. It cannot be restricted to a singular definition. However, it can be understood as the collective values of a society manifested through its numerous institutions, as well as in the disposition, attitudes, and manners of its individual members. Those in turn find expression in various material objects, abstract ideas and beliefs of individuals and society.

Thus, culture includes certain aspects of **collective institutions**, such as morality, religion, spirituality, law, custom, art etc. which are not restricted to an individual and which are handed over from generation to generation. Evidently, the **institutional elements** of culture are evolutionary and dynamic.

Culture also includes **intellectual** and **knowledge elements** about languages, literature, human learning, social norms, customs and behaviour. **Human** and **social aesthetics** are another key aspect of culture, encompassing within it the numerous manifestations of **tangible** and **intangible** art forms, viz, music, dance, sculpture, painting, architecture etc.

The new-age theatre and cinema are as much a reflection of the modern culture as are the cave paintings of a prehistoric society, of which we know so little. The Bhakti and Sufi movements were the embodiment of the **spiritual elements** of medieval culture, as were the imposing forts and grand palaces of this age a reflection of its societal and corporeal cultural constituents. The Sangam literature was the manifestation of the **human intellectual and socio–ethical** elements of a culture at its zenith, nearly two millennia ago. Folk art and traditional lifestyles are also as much indicative of the culture of a society as is urban lifestyle and transient tastes. Thus, our habitat, cuisine, costumes, and physical objects, apart from performing arts and architecture, are all reflective of the **material** or **tangible elements** of **culture**, as are religions, customs, festivals, traditions, social practices and ethics, philosophy and law reflective of **non-material** or **intangible elements.**

But Culture in itself is never static or an isolated mass of homogenous attributes. It is pervious and dynamic, with fresh waves of socio-cultural influences sprouting pristine cultural milieus. **Inclusivity and evolution** are its inherent and integral traits. It is this very indispensable characterisitc which is reflected in Mahatma Gandhi's words, *"No culture can live if it attempts to be exclusive."*

But given its transient nature, what is that abiding essence which provides continuum and sustenance to a culture, to maintain its integrity over epochs? At the very core of the myriad cultural manifestations, lies the element of goodness of the civilisation and its people. It is the enduring element. Narrow canons of the self do not restrict it, nor is its domain limited to a specific society. It is all-encompassing and its ethos is best exemplified in the aspirational Upanishadic hymn, *sarve bhavantu sukhinah* (may all be happy).

Indeed, its universality extends even beyond the human dominion, to all the sentient beings and in its noblest manifestation, endeavouring even for the sustenance of the biotic world and the abiotic realm. Civilisations may somewhat assimilate this element as ethics and law, while religion may perceive it as

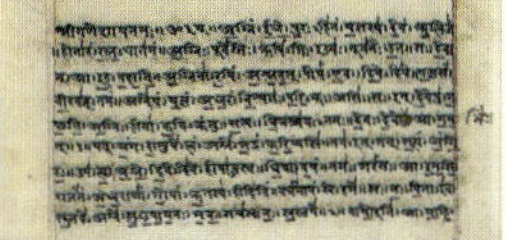

the principles of morality or the essence of spirituality. But goodness, irrespective of its classification, is the only and truly the eternal soul of any culture, bereft of which, its external trappings, no matter how seemingly glorious and glitzy, are a little more than a lifeless mass.

CIVILISATION: A MILESTONE OF HUMAN EVOLUTION

At times used synonymously with culture, the word civilisation is said to have its origin in the Latin word *Civitas,* meaning a city. Thus, it was originally meant to distinguish the human settlements, particularly the more complex urban settlements, from the nomadic, transitory or rootless people or those with a rudimentary society and negligible form of institutional governance. In the modern context, civilisation refers to a fairly advanced stage of human development of a people, which encompasses social, urban, technological as well as cultural development.

The presence of organised urban settlements, with diversity of human activity, hierarchical society, distinct forms of governance, social stratification, development of economic systems, technological growth, evolution of ethical traits and cultural elements, all can be said to be distinct features ascribable to an evolved civilisation. Thus, civilisation can truly be said to be a milestone of human evolution, encompassing within its fold all elements of growth and transformation of a society. The Indus Valley, Egyptian, Mesopotamian, and Chinese, were the earliest of ancient civilisations that prospered and left a mark on the sands of time.

Thus, cultural growth is an important albeit not the only factor to be reckoned for the characterisation of a society as a civilisation. Therefore, neither the two terms are analogous, nor mean even closely the same, although a developed culture may be considered a sine-qua-non for an advanced civilisation.

RELIGION AND ITS INTERCONNECT WITH CULTURE AND CIVILISATION

Religion generally refers to a socio-cultural system of faith, belief and worship which is usually integrated with a belief in god(s). Although there may not be any universally accepted definition of religion, there are indeed some identifiable features. Its core elements are invariably spiritualism, morality and ethics, with outward layers of customs, rituals, practices, sermons and other systems of veneration. Canonical texts, metaphysics, mythologies, rules of social and individual conduct such as at births, matrimony and funerary etc., are its other distinctive features. The existence of religious bodies and orders, priests and monks, sects and cults, festivals and ceremonies, along with associated cultural elements of literature, art forms, music and dance are other visible elements of religion.

Hinduism, Zoroastrianism, Judaism, Buddhism, Christianity, Islam and Sikhism are some of the extant world religions in the chronology of their emergence, which conform to all of these elements. But faiths like Jainism and Buddhism, which either denied the very existence of god or rejected the popular conception of a divine being with personal attributes governing the realms, are still very much accepted as complete religious orders, for they truly encompass the essence of a religion. Then what is that pith of the theological systems?

Dr. S. Radhakrishnan succinctly describes the very soul of religion in a few sentences. He says, *"Religion is not merely intellectual conformity or ceremonial piety; it is spiritual adventure. It is not theology, but practice. Religion is the fulfilment of man's life, an experience in which every aspect of his being is raised to the highest extent."*

Quiet appropriately, in the Indian context, the **seeking of truth and quest for eternal emancipating knowledge, along with righteous social and individual conduct, are considered as the cornerstones of religion.**

Neither religion nor culture can be said to be a sub-part of the other, although there remains a profound interconnect between them. From the perspective of religion, elements of culture are manifested often in the form of ceremonies, rituals, religious literature, art forms or other material and non-material religious practices. Thus, along with spirituality, morality, philosophy and other canonical beliefs, culture also aids religion in its objective, which is to find the real meaning and purpose of life. But culture also influences these elements of religion such as its philosophy, its religious text and even moral beliefs.

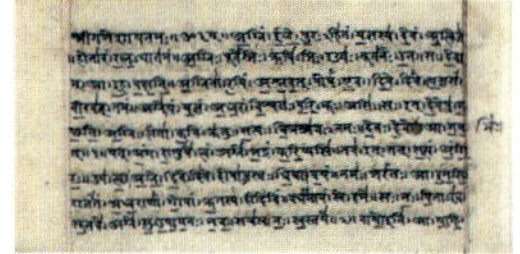

From the perspective of culture, the religious aspect of culture is one amongst many elements enriching it and indeed is an extremely vital one. Thus, that aspect of religion which is bereft of the external trappings and truly be characterised as its soul can also be said to be the very soul of culture, for culture without that element which defines the '**real purpose of life**' is akin to only a body bereft of life.

Put rather simplistically, **religion as well as culture are indeed distinct elements of human civilisation,** albeit all **have a deep interconnect.**

NATIONHOOD ITS ELEMENTS AND CULTURE: INTERCONNECT IN THE INDIAN CONTEXT

We often deliberate as to what is our true national culture and how has it evolved through the ages. A prerequisite to this discussion would be to understand what nationhood is and what its elements are. Are race, religion, and language and history essential elements of nationhood? Does culture have a significant bearing on the concept of nationality? How is Indian nationhood distinct and unique?

The modern concept of a nation and nationhood is only a few centuries old. Nationhood is usually understood as a large group of people domiciled in a geographical unit and united by a common political/ administrative order, law, culture, common history, economic order and language. Other uniting characteristics could be the commonality of race, religion, ethnicity etc. National flag, anthem and emblem could be some other symbolic elements of a national identity.

From the modern perspective, the intermingling of races and freedom of faith and belief has rendered race, religion and ethnicity meaningless as defining factors of nationhood. Similarly, a multitude of spoken languages in many modern nations does not make the commonality of a spoken/official language a necessary condition for nationhood.

Thus, modern-day nations can be recognised by their people domiciled out of free will, in a geographical area, united by legal/political order, culture, history and economic activity. However, exceptions and marginal variations would exist and a watertight definition may not be possible. Whereas in countries like the United States of America, language has been a common factor, for the European Union and many South Asian nations and India in particular, the same cannot be true.

Further, while countries like India, China, Japan, Egypt and Turkey boast of a long and common history, the nation-state of Singapore or Australia does not have this vital element to define its nationhood. Even the United States of America has a relatively lesser history of only a few centuries. Thus, even the conception of a well-defined political order has not been an enduring basis of national identity. History has witnessed such political orders to be transitory and at times even self-serving. The pre-independence India is certainly a case in this point. Perhaps it is the realisation of this limitation that prompted Tagore to observe thus about Indian nationalism, *"And the moment is arriving when you also must find a basis of unity which is not political. If India can offer to the world her solution, it will be a contribution to humanity".*

In the present context, India is a well-defined geographical entity with partly natural boundaries. The democratic constitution, the common history, economic singularity and its culture are the factors uniting the people which are otherwise characterised by different religions, languages, races, ethnicities and a multitude of other divergent factors.

The most important element of any national identity is its **People**. This is particularly true for India where a bewildering plurality is evident, almost beckoning the question as to what is the lifeblood of its national identity. Is it its unique national culture which is the bonding factor keeping it intact despite the seemingly disparate forces? And if yes, then what is this national culture?

Thus, Indian culture plays an important role in defining Indian nationhood. However, it has its own regional, social, linguistic and other variations too. Besides, Indian culture itself has never been static or an isolated silo of homogenous attributes. It has always been pervious, dynamic and evolving. Different waves of socio-cultural influences encompassed the Indian landscape leading to emergence of diverse cultural milieus, though unique to a time and space, but never singular and always sprouting.

Thus, any singular sub-culture no matter how brilliant and seemingly comprehensive, only offers a partial perspective of the all encompassing national culture. For it to appropriate the legacy of national culture would be akin to a part endeavouring to represent the whole.

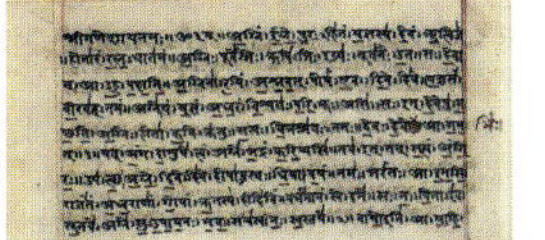

Indian culture has indeed played a defining role in shaping Indian nationhood. Over centuries, its numerous facets have created resilient bonds that have withstood the vagaries of space and time and overcome the ostensibly insurmountable differences and divergences. Be it the Vedic culture or the Sramana traditions, the Bhakti movement or the Sufism, the regional customs and social practices, the congruous economic orders and analogous social strata spanning numerous political domains, they all gave a cause for people to connect. But the most important element of cohesion was the ideal, of rising above the baser instinct of merely pursuing self-interest to the loftier philosophy of universal well-being, best exemplified in the *Upanishadic* hymn, *udaar charitanam tu vasudhev kutumbkam* (for the generous-spirited the whole world is a family).

As Tagore plainly puts it, *"Only those people have survived and achieved civilization who have this spirit of cooperation strong in them."* Thus, the basis of this integration was deep within, while the apparent differences were definitely without.

Call it the innate goodness, the ethics of society, the spirituality of religion, the all-pervading *Brahma* of the *Vedantist*, the conception of the divine of the theologian, or simply the spirit of service of the social minded, it is this immanent attribute of selflessness which has provided the deeper interconnect to our varied cultures. This spirit has further been manifested in the tenets of **inclusiveness, pluralism, vibrancy, evolution and mutual co-existence**, which are the all-pervading unifying forces of our culture. Indeed, these belief systems are the **cornerstones of Indian culture, which is also the hallmark of Indian nationhood**.

Bharat and India: A Cultural Unity

'India that is Bharat shall be a Union of States", says Article 1 of the Indian Constitution, recognising the two names of this ancient and diverse country. Over the several millennia of its unbroken cultural history, the land and its people have been known by many names, **Bharat, Bharatavarsha, Jambudweep, Aryavarta, Inde, Indica** and **Hindustan** among others. What is the origin of these names? Which of these emanated in the native Indian languages and within the region itself? How has the country been known in different phases of its long history? Do these names have any special cultural significance? Are the two names now in vogue representative of the different cultural ideas of the same country and its people? These are some questions that have arisen time and again, particularly since the days of India's independence.

Bharat, Bharata or *Bharatavarsha*, is perhaps the most ancient of the names with which this land and its people have been recognised. It is a name which is referred to in the ancient scriptures. Scholars believe that this name may trace its origin to the **tribe of Bharatas** referred to in the Rigveda and who emerged victorious in the 'Battle of Ten Kings' (Rigveda, *mandal*-7, hymns 18,33,83). The country could also have been named after the great **King Bharata**, the son of Dushyanta and Shakuntala, whose story is also referred to in the *Adi Parva* of the Mahabharata. He was a legendary emperor of the Chandravanshi dynasty (lunar dynasty), whose descendants were the Bharata tribes and also the Pandavas and the Kauravas. The region Bharat may initially have been referred to the Northwestern and Northern portion of the country and perhaps later to the entire subcontinent. The Hathi Gupha cave inscription of the 1st century CE in Udayagiri caves near Bhubaneshwar is often cited by scholars to support a limited connotation of the region of Bharat at one point in time in ancient India. In line 10 of the seventeen-line inscription, a reference is made to Bharatavarsha in the sense of a region in the North/Northwestern part of the country. However, many historians dispute such an interpretation.

Another possible origin of the name is said to be the name of **King Bharata** of the solar dynasty (*Suryavanshi*) who was the son of Rishabhadeva. Verses from various Puranas, in particular from the Vishnu Purana (verse 2,1,31) are cited in support of this. Some of these verses are as follows.

ऋषभो मरुदेव्याश्च ऋषभात् भरतो भवेत् ।
भरताद् भारतं वर्षं, भरतात् सुमतिस्त्वभूत् ।।

Rishabha was born to Marudevi and Bharata was born to Rishabha,
Bhāratavarsa arose from Bharata and Sumati arose from Bharata. (Vishnu Purana 2,1,31)

ततश्च भारतं वर्षमेतल्लोकेषुगीयते ।
भरताय यतः पित्रा दत्तं प्रतिष्ठिता वनम् ।। (विष्णु पुराण, 2,1,32)

This land is henceforth referred to as Bhāratavarsa since the times the father entrusted the kingdom to his son Bharata and proceeded himself as an ascetic to the forest.

Another verse from Vishnupurana describes the boundaries of Bharatavarsha. It says;

उत्तरं यत्समुद्रस्य हिमाद्रेश्चैव दक्षिणम् ।
वर्षं तद् भारतं नाम भारती यत्र सन्ततिः ।।

The country that lies to the north of the ocean and is in the south of the snowcapped mountains(Himalayas); it is known as Bharata where in live the descendants of Bharata. (Vishnu Purana 2,1,32)

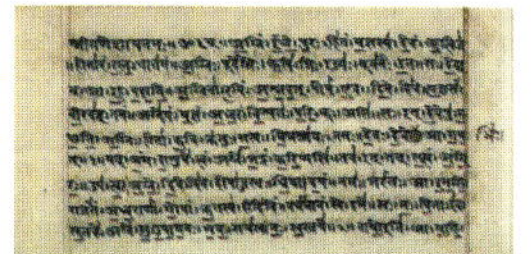

Some may also attribute the name to **King Bharata** of Ayodhya, the brother of Lord Rama and the son of King Dasratha. Thus, an undisputed attribution of this name may not be established. However, it is undisputed that the name *Bharat* originated in the Sanskrit language. Thus, it is an endonym, which is a name given by the people of the land to it. Its root word in Sanskrit is *bhr-* which means to bear or to carry. It is said to be cognate (a word with the same linguistic derivation as another) of the word 'bear' in English and *fero* in Latin. It was also a word to describe the qualities of 'Agni' which was the medium to bear and carry the oblation to the heavens and *devas*. Thus, it was an appropriate name for a land bearing rich natural resources, and for a civilisation and its people bearing a wealth of knowledge and deeply seeped in the quest for the divine and liberating knowledge.

Another ancient name with which this land was known is Jambudweep. This is also a name referred to in the ancient scriptures and in particular in the Puranas where Jambudweepa is recognized as one of the seven continents of ancient cosmology. This name is also said to be referred to in the treatise *Arthashastra* by Chanakya composed in around the 3rd century BCE. *Jambu* refers to the fruit *jambu/jamun* (berry) commonly found in the subcontinent and *dweepa* refers to an island. Hence the name alluded to the berry shape of the subcontinent, broader at the top and narrower at the bottom. Thus, the name had a geographical connotation and was also an endonym.

Aryavarta was yet another ancient name of this land which means, the land of the Aryas (Arya: people considered noble). Aryavarta was the land of the blossoming of the Vedic culture and the name was also an endonym. The name finds reference in the Dharma Sutras and the Dharma Shastras. Aryavarta is believed by scholars to have earlier referred to the northwestern and later to the entire Northern portions of the Indian subcontinent. However, with the Aryan influence and the Brahmanical faith expanding, the region of reference of Aryavarta also widened. As per the Baudhyayana Dharmasutra which is considered the oldest Dharmasutra (composed around 500 BCE or prior), the connotation of Aryavarta was limited to the areas between the Himalayas and the Vindhyas with eastern and western expanse limited by the Kalkavana and Adarsana. However, in the Vasistha Dharmasutra (500 BCE to 300 BCE), its western region is marked by the basin of the disappeared Saraswati River. Further, by the time of the composition of Manusmriti (200 BCE to 300 CE), the entire region from the Bay of Bengal in the east to the Arabian Sea in the west and from the Himalayas in the north to the Vindhyas in the south was included in the Aryavarta. Some scholars believe that Manusmiriti considered the entire Indian subcontinent as Aryavarta, with the Vindhyas cutting across it.

One of the great rivers of this land was the river **Sindhu** which flowed in the northwestern portion of the land and broadly formed the northwestern borders of the region. It demarcated the rugged mountains to its west and north from the fertile and thriving plains to its east. For the Persians, Greeks and other civilisations connected through trade and travellers, the river marked the gateway to the land of great bounties and richness. Hence the region and its people were recognized by the name of the river itself. The Sanskrit word *Sindhu* however took the form of *Indu/Inde* for the Greeks, and *Hindu/Hind* for the Persians and later Arabs.

The word *Sindhu* in classical Sanskrit refers to a river and also to a sea. Reference to the Sindhu (river) and Sapt-Sindhu (the seven rivers of the Northwestern region) is also found in the Vedas. The *'Nadistuti sukta'* contained in the 75th hymn (sukta) of the 10th book (Mandala) of Rigveda, is one such instance of the veneration of rivers wherein the first and the second verses highlight the glory of the river Sindhu (see inset box on 'veneration of rivers', later in the chapter). The river also lent its name to the ancient Sindhu kingdom which lay on the banks of river Sindhu, a reference to which is also said to be found in the Mahabharata and the Harivamsa Purana. Thus, the name Sindhu was an endonym referring to a mighty river and also to an ancient kingdom.

The word ***Indica/Indika/Inde*** was a Greek derivative of the word Sindhu. It finds the earliest reference in the works of Megasthenes, a Greek writer and ambassador to the court of Chandragupta Maurya. *Indika*, an account of the Mauryan empire and the region, of the late 4th century BCE is lost, but historians have constructed its parts from the accounts of other writers who have directly quoted from this work. Arrian, another Greek philosopher and military commander, also wrote 'Indica' in the 2nd century CE which draws from the 'Indika' of Megasthenese and also includes Arrian's account of the country. As per the reconstructed works of some modern writers (*J.W. McCrindle-1877* and *Stoneman 2022*), the work 'Indica' described the geography of India as that of a quadrilateral. As per it, India was a land bounded by the Great Sea in its east and its south and by the Indus River to its west. To its north was the mountain range of Emodus (which scholars describe as Hemodus) which referred to the combined mountain ranges of Hindu Kush, Pamir, and the Himalayas. The word *Hemodus* is also believed to be derived from the *Haimavata*, a Sanskrit word meaning 'covered with snow'. Thus, the word Indica, though an exonym, was a derivative of the name of a major river of the country which nurtured a civilisation and also formed its ancient identity.

The word **Hindu** was also a Persian derivative of the word Sindhu. Scholars believe that after the conquest of the Indus Valley by Darius I in the 6th century CE, the name Hindush, an Achaemenid equivalent of the word Sindhu, was used to describe the lower Indus basin region. Thus, the region and the people later came to be identified with this name in the Achaemenid, Persian and later in the Arabian empire and the regions of their conquest. The suffix *-stan* refers to a place in Persian, just as the suffix *-varsha* refers to a country/large region in Sanskrit. Thus arose the word Hindustan, the inhabitants of which were known as Hindus, a term which initially had a geographical connotation rather than any credal significance.

Al Biruni, a Persian scholar and polymath, wrote in the 11th century the *'Kitab Al-Hind'* (The book on India) which shows that the term **Hind** and **Hindu** had already come into vogue by the beginning of the 2nd millennium. This was how the country was addressed by the Persians and Arabs. With the establishment of the Delhi Sultanate in the 13th century and the emergence of the different Islamic dynasties later, the word **Hindustan** came to be in vogue within the country and described the land and its people. Abul Fazl, one of the prominent medieval authors in the court of Akbar, who

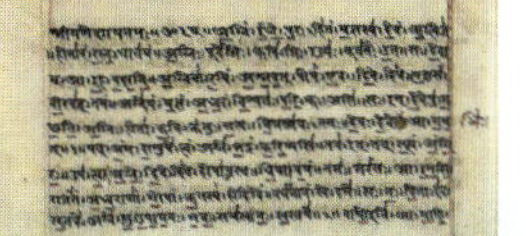

wrote the *Ain-i-Akbari*, describes the land/country as Hindustan. Therefore, in the medieval period, Hindustan became the name of the country by which the ruling establishments as well as some sections of people had started referring to it. Thus, while Bharat, an endonym, was the name of ancient India, its medieval name came to be established as Hindustan. This name was an exonym taken from the Persian language but had roots in the Sanskrit word Sindhu.

The changing times brought different colonial powers to the shores of **India**. By the latter half of the 18th century, the East India Company, and hence the British, had consolidated their political authority over a vast region. With the establishment of the new political regime, the country came to be known by a new name. India, the name of this country by which the British knew it, was a Latin derivation of the Greek term Indica. It was a name by which the country had been known to the European powers for centuries and the term India itself had been in currency perhaps since the early first millennium CE. However, like the term Hindustan, it became in vogue within the region, only when the political authority changed. British rule fully established the name of the country as India (then British India) within the country as well as in the international community. Like Hindustan, the name India, a derivative of the word *Sindhu*, was also an exonym.

With the independence of the country, the concurrent name **India** as well as the ancient name **Bharat**, both were adopted as the official names of the country, by our eminent leaders and framers of the Constitution. While the country continued to be addressed in English (and other foreign languages) as India, the name Bharat was adopted in Hindi and other Indian languages. The Hindi version of the Constitution states, *'Bharat that is India shall be a union of states'* ('भारत अर्थात् इंडिया राज्यों का संघ होगा' as written in Hindi in Devanagari script). Thus, emerged a practice, where depending on the language, the country is referred to by either of the two names with both names enjoying public acceptability.

Bharat and India have different meanings. One refers to the land of the Bharatas, or the land of the descendants of Bharat, and the other refers to the land beyond the river Sindhu (Indus). One is an endonym, while the other is an exonym that has roots in the Sanskrit word Sindhu. However, over a period of time, many of the derived words or exonyms such as Hindu and Hindi have also been fully assimilated into the indigenous languages and integrated with the culture of the people. At different points in history, the rulers have referred to this country by different names. In the current context, both **Bharat and India are representative of the same land and the same people**. At times, the word Bharat is said to allude to the indigenous, the ancient and the grassroots culture, and India, to the modern and urban. However, such differentiations and distinctions are largely perceptional. India also lives in its villages, while Bharat is modern and leaping towards the future. Attribution of separate cultural connotations to either of the two names would be misplaced, as India and Bharat are one. The integral constituent of a country is its land and its people. Its name-based identity is often temporal and over centuries, displays similar transience as its political identity. However it is the cultural identity that evolves and endures.

PHASES OF CULTURAL EVOLUTION AND CONFLUENCES

Over a period of 5000 years, Indian society has witnessed several phases of cultural evolution. Each of these had its distinct features. Many of these cultural phases overlapped with each other, resulting in a cultural confluence and leading to the emergence of new cultural traits. These cultural phases were **the Indus Valley culture, the Vedic and the Dravidian culture, the Buddhist and Jain cultural influences, the Puranic culture, the Bhakti movement, the Islamic influence and the Hindustani culture, the European influence and finally the modern Indian culture**. A snapshot of these phases and cultural confluences is captured below and in subsequent chapters.

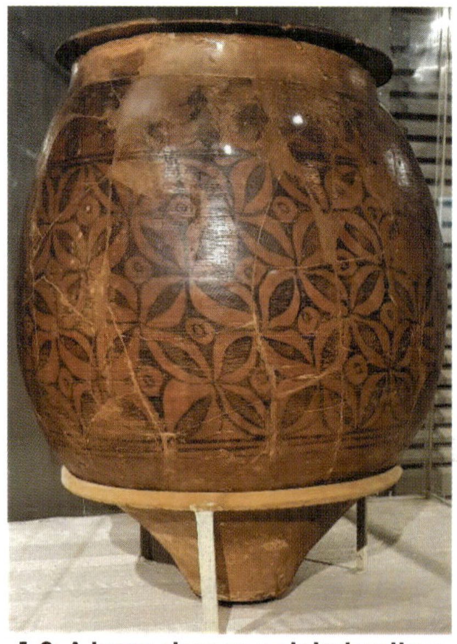

1.2: A large storage painted pottery with beautiful design; has a narrow bottom neck which was fixed in the ground; Mature Harappan period 2700-2000 BCE; National Museum, New Delhi — photograph by Madhukar K Bhagat

THE INDUS VALLEY CIVILISATION: THE FIRST PHASE OF CULTURAL EVOLUTION

Often referred to as the **harbinger of cultural evolution** in India, the Indus Valley Civilisation (IVC) was a distinct and foremost urban culture that flourished from 3500 BCE to 1800 BCE (Early and Mature Harappan phases). Its unique features included; an evolved town planning, modern cities, elaborate drainage system, walled citadel, extensive trade, developed script, evolved science and technology, growth of cotton and development of textiles, flourishing arts; of sculpture, bead and jewellery making, making of pottery, utensils, instruments and even weapons. According to Sir

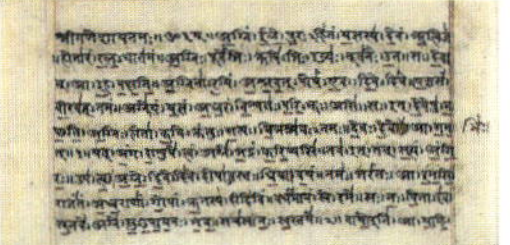

John Marshall (who oversaw the early excavations at Harappa and Mohenjo-daro), the standards of civilised life attained by people living in these cities were higher than that of Egyptians and ancient Babylonians and equivalent to that of Sumerians. At its zenith, spread over a large region of present North and North-West India, Pakistan and parts of Afghanistan, this advanced civilisation had a distinct and evolved culture. Further, recent research and discoveries in India have revealed some unique aspects of this civilisation, and in the process, also throwing light on their cultural practices.

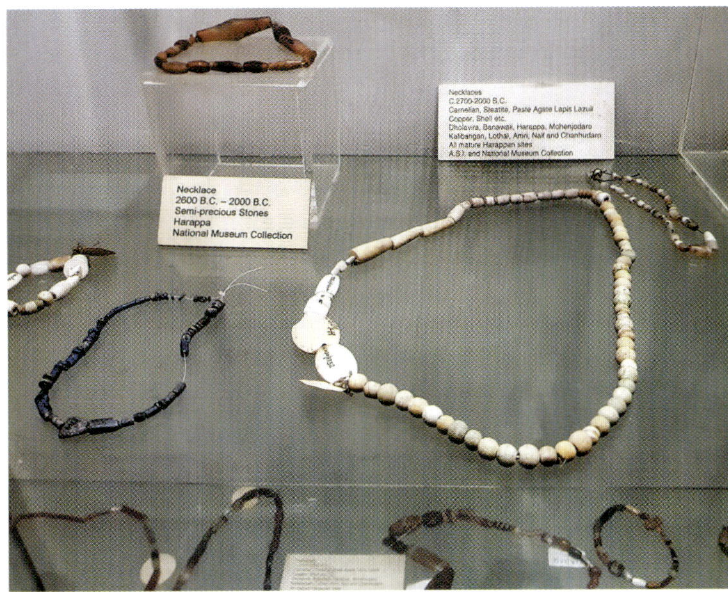

1.3: Necklaces with semi-precious stones and beads from different sites of Indus Valley Civilisation (IVC), beads and jewellery, an important export to other countries from IVC; National Museum, New Delhi — photograph by Madhukar K Bhagat

The larger settlements of Mohenjo-daro, Harappa and others reveal the extensive town planning, large and efficient drainage systems, network of streets and roads with iron grid layout, existence of walled citadels and lower towns built on burnt/sundried bricks, presence of sizable granaries, great baths and other public places, besides innumerable seals, potteries, weights, cherts and other artefacts. All of these are truly indicative of an efficient governance structure and municipal functions, organised labour and social stratification and well-defined rules of social intercourse and conduct. Besides, a flourishing commerce and trade, knowledge of engineering and sciences, and belief in socio-religious rituals, their art and aesthetics are also clearly evident from the findings over here and newly discovered settlements of this civilisation.

The existence of a tidal dockyard **at Lothal** (in Gujarat) with its **bead-making industry** has revealed a flourishing trade through the sea. The city was not only an important centre of production, but also a centre for overseas trade with far off cities in the Persian Gulf region. The channel-based **docking system** with a large man-made basin and a unique locking system is a reflection of advanced knowledge of hydraulics and engineering, besides that of extensive trade and commerce. Also known as the seafarers of Meluha in far Sumer, these people had extensive knowledge of seas, navigational astronomy and even winds and ocean currents to guide them over thousands of kilometres of perilous journeys.

Recent discoveries at **Dholavira** (Kutch, Gujarat), reveal extensive water conservation systems, including rock-cut channels and reservoirs for storage and efficient utilisation of water from nearby streams and rainwater. Research also indicates a change in the cropping pattern, to low water-requiring cereals such as millets, in response to the changing and drying weather system. Agricultural practices are also evident at **Kalibangan** (Rajasthan) where discovery has been made of a ploughed field that has a cross grid of furrows. Further, at Shortughai (Afghanistan), discovery of dryland farming has been made. Excavations here have also revealed an irrigation canal for fetching water. (see Chapter 2)

The discovery of **fire altars** at **Rakhigarhi** (Haryana) and **Kalibangan**, are indicative of the emergence of rituals and sacrificial practices. The cemetery and burial sites of Rakhigarhi where skeletons of the dead have been found with pottery and other items of daily use are indicative of the existence in belief in after-life and other funerary practices.

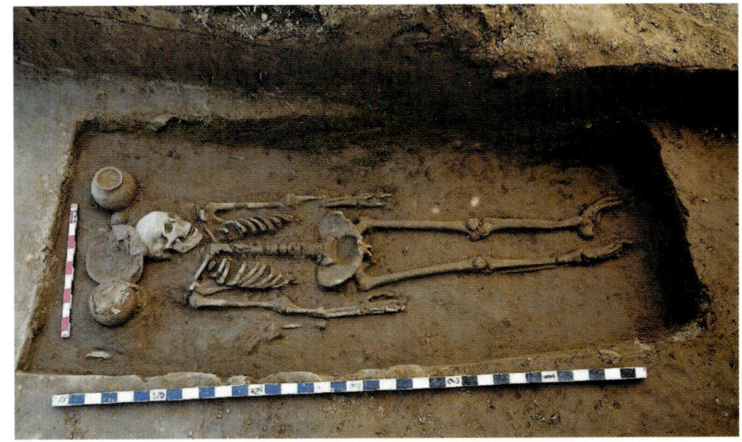

1.4: A skeleton in one of the graves at Rakhigarhi along with different types of pottery; an early example of the funerary practices of this civilisation — Courtesy, Directorate of Archaeology and Museums, Government of Haryana

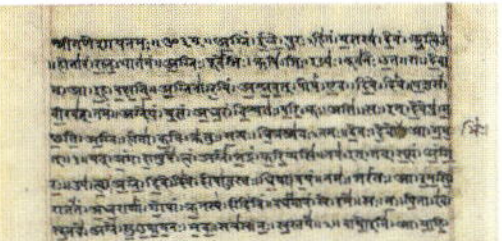

Apart from the above, a **bronze statue of a dancing girl, the bearded priest-king bust, the Pashupati seal, the Mother Goddess figurines** and several seals with animal and other inscriptions have been found. These succinctly reveal tangible elements of their culture, art and aesthetics, besides the existence of at least a rudimentary religious culture. The inscription on numerous seals and the Dholavira signboard (see Chapter 2) points to the evolution of a written script. Although un-deciphered as yet, the script is believed to be pictographic or logographic, implying that individual symbols represent things and concepts.

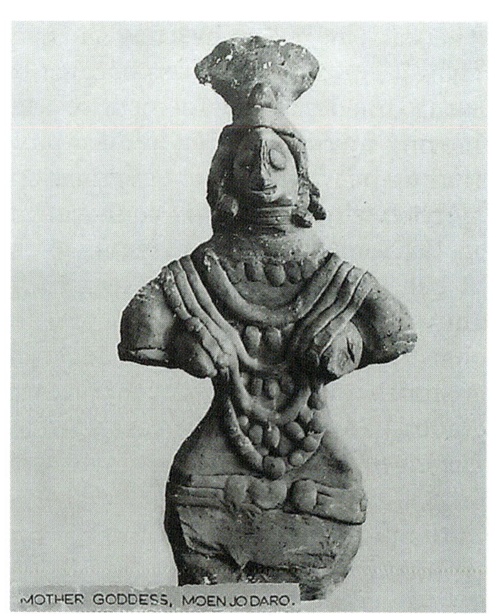

1.5: Picture of the Mother Goddess figurine — Wikimedia Commons

Thus, it is amply evident that the Harappan culture attained great heights and it truly rivalled the cultures of Mesopotamia and Egyptian civilisations of this age. It engendered an **unparalleled urban culture.** As a civilisation lasting nearly two millennia, it can truly be said have ushered a cultural wave heralding a neo-culture hitherto unknown to the human race. But an important question is, as to **why this civilisation did not survive; what was its enduring cultural legacy** (if any)? Did it have any material impact on the ensuing society or did the subsequent cultural phase remain totally disconnected from this first cultural wave?

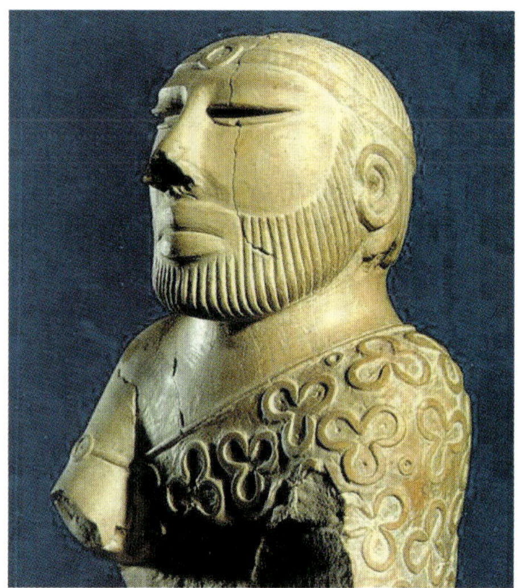

1.6: Priest-King statue — Wikimedia Commons

It is believed that Harappan culture did not have any perceivable cultural confluence with the Vedic culture which is said to have emerged around 1500 BCE. Experts earlier accepted the **'Aryan invasion theory'** (by Mortimer Wheeler) as the root cause of the decline of this civilisation. As such, a cultural disconnect between the Harappan culture and the succeeding Aryan culture was a natural corollary and a foregone conclusion.

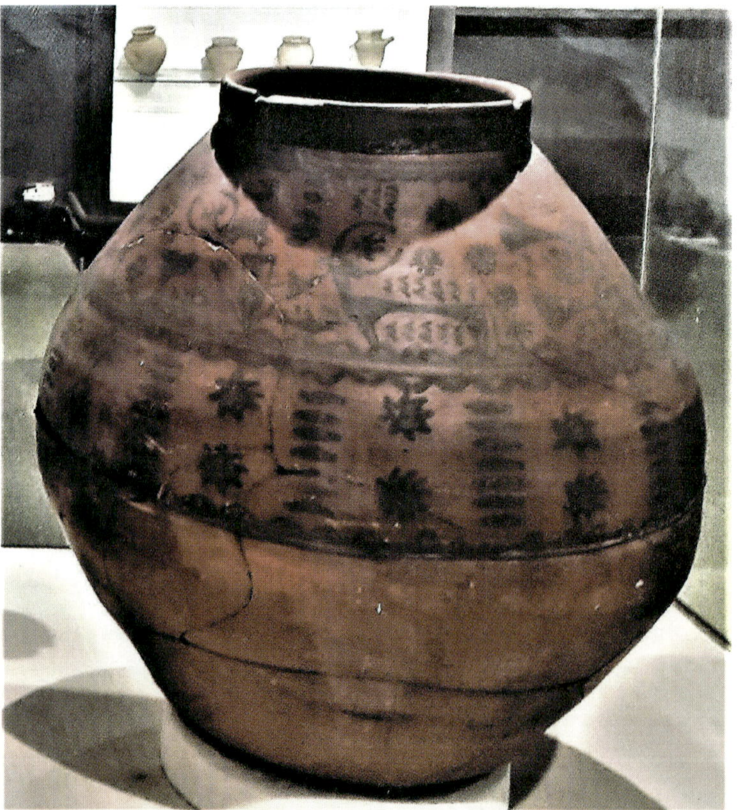

1.7: A burial pottery with painting from Cemetery H. Harappa, (2000-1900 BCE), depicting the image of cattle on a boat on a river (Vaitarani); considered analogous to early Vedic belief of journey of the soul after death; location National Museum, New Delhi — photograph by Madhukar K Bhagat

However, the latest researches reveal varying and largely **environmental factors as the cause for the decline** of many of these once-bustling cities. The Aryan invasion hypothesis as a cause of their destruction is largely discarded. While Mohenjodaro and Lothal were ravaged by floods, the changing weather pattern and the great **Megahalayan drought** which is believed to have lasted nearly 300 years (around 2000 BCE) and affected the global weather, was the root cause of the decline of Dholavira, Rakhigarhi and some other sites around this very period (see Chapter 2). The changing weather and dearth of water made such large city systems unviable eventually led to their gradual abandonment. **But what happened to the people and their knowledge?**

The current researches do not shed any conclusive light on the post decline aspect of this great civilisation. Some theories suggest their being pushed eastwards due to Aryan migration or because of environmental factors and resettlement in villages/rural setups. Some hypotheses also suggest their moving southwards and the **gradual merger and evolution of the Dravidian culture**. An archaeological finding in Tamil Nadu (Melaperumpallam near Poompuhar) in May 2007, shows pots with arrowhead symbols similar to that found on the seals of Mohenjo-daro. Similarly, a 2014 discovery in a cave in Kerala is believed to show 19 pictograph symbols similar to Indus writing. A deeper connection is believed to be seen in the Indus script with the Dravidian languages. Prof. Asko Parpola of the University of Helsinki, Finland (who has worked on deciphering the scripts since 1968) believes that the script may have been similar to the family of Dravidian languages (or its proto languages). A stone celt (axe-like structure) belonging to the 2nd millennium BCE, found in Mayiladuthurai (Tamil Nadu), had many more Indus period symbols. According to Prof. Iravatham Mahadevan, these represented a connection between the Indus script and early Dravidian languages. Whether these evidences are indicative of resettlement or contact due to trading for gold, is not fully established. But a semblance of cultural influence is quite noticeable.

A **cultural connect with the Vedic civilisation** is also possibly seen in the numerous figurines of a female figure, adorned in jewellery and imposing fan-shaped headgear. This is believed to be similar to that of the **Mother Goddess** of the subsequent Vedic culture. Similarly, a connection is also established by the seal depicting a figure seated cross-legged in a yogic posture with a horned headdress. The figure is surrounded by several animals and is considered to be a proto-Shiva or early form of **Pashupati/Rudra**. Seal of the **Swastika symbol** found in Harappa and other seals with animal motifs such as bull, elephant and tiger (*vahana* of celestial deities) which are revered in the Vedic culture, also indicate the cultural and religious influence.

The discovery of a burial pottery with a painting from Cemetery H. Harappa, (2000-1900 BCE), which also gives the name Cemetery H culture, reveals certain religious beliefs about the journey of the soul after death. The paintings on the vase are considered by experts to be akin to the subsequent Vedic belief, of the journey of the soul after death where it has to cross the river *Vaitarani*. Here the sacrifice of cattle like a cow/bull/goat is needed to cross the river. It is only then that the soul reaches the gates of the lord of Death where it faces the final judgement. The paintings on the large burial pottery from the late Harappan period (now kept in the National Museum Delhi) also depict similar images. Thus, could there be linkages of certain customs and practices associated with afterlife between the late Harappan and early Vedic periods?

At Lothal, one of the painted terracotta jars found was seen to be bearing the **image of 'the crow and the fox'**, believed to be depicting the story of the crow and the cunning fox, of the well-known fable. (This jar is on display at the onsite Archaeological Survey Museum at Lothal). Another jar is said to be carrying the image of the 'thirsty crow' dropping the pebbles. The discoveries, though seemingly innocuous, suggest that the fables have continued to be a part of folklore in the subsequent culture(s) and are popular even to this day. Could it be a reflection of a moderate intermingling and continuity of some folk cultural elements?

The evidence as of now can only be treated as tentative. In general, experts broadly believe that the Harappan culture did not have any substantial cultural confluence with the Vedic culture, which emerged as the next phase of cultural evolution in India.

THE VEDIC CULTURE: A NEW CULTURAL WAVE

The **Vedic age,** the next wave of cultural evolution, emerged around 1500 BCE, post the decline of the Indus Valley civilisation. The new civilisation and society it created dominated the Indian landscape for nearly 1,000 years and continued to profoundly influence it even beyond this period. It is generally believed that the advent of the Aryans from central Asia to the northern part of India and later to the eastern portion in the Ganga-Yamuna doab region heralded this cultural phase. However, there is no unanimity of experts as to the origin of Aryans or even of Aryan migration theory.

This period was characterised by the composition of four Vedas. These remain the chief source of information about this civilisation and its cultural practices, hence the name, the *Vedic culture*. The Vedic phase is further divided into the Early Vedic (1500 BCE to 1000 BCE) and Later Vedic phases (1000 BCE to 600 BCE). From an archaeological perspective, this period coincides with the **Black and Red Ware culture** period (1450 BCE to 1200 BCE) prevalent in the western Gangetic plain. The pottery found in this period was typically black and red coloured and was in the period of the late Bronze Age and early Iron Age. It

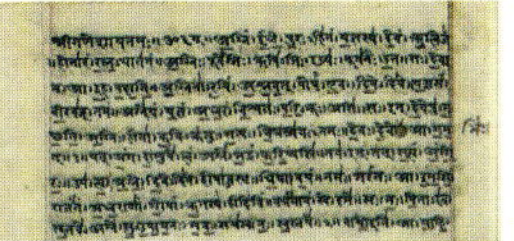

was succeeded by the **Painted Greyware** culture period. This was an Iron Age culture that was prevalent in the Ghagra–Hakra valley and the western Gangetic plain. (BRW culture is believed to be from 1500 BCE to 700 BCE or 1300 BCE to 500 BCE).

Organisation of the Vedic society

The early Vedic society was largely agrarian, with a dependence on agriculture as well as pastoralism. Larger cities like that of the Indus Valley Civilisation were absent in this phase. The administrative order was based on kingship (***rajya and rajan***), with ***sabhas*** and ***samitis*** as representative bodies being unique features of the socio-political setup in this age. The ***Jana*** (tribe), the ***Grama*** (village) and ***Kula*** (clan or family) were the fundamental units of social order. Pastoral lifestyle and cattle rearing (especially cows and bulls) were in vogue. Wheat and barley, and later rice, were the chief cultivated crops. Cotton and woollen fabrics were common. Copper, bronze and later iron, was actively used in the manufacturing of day-to-day items, utensils and weapons. The use of horses and chariots was known well in this age.

The **Varna system** provided the socio-economic order and division of labour and organised the society into four working classes. To begin with, it imparted an egalitarian social order with appropriate social mobility. Reference in Vedic texts is also seen of *Daas* and *Dasyus,* who were referred to as people outside the Aryan society and belief system (viz. not performing sacrifices and believing the commandment of the gods). Perhaps these were non-Aryan or aboriginal tribes (as believed by some historians). Vedic texts also indicate a greater respect for women as seen from the accounts of certain women poets and sages such as Lopamudra, Viswavara, Apala, Ghosha, Kadru, Savitri, Vak Ambhrini, etc. who are mentioned in Rigveda. Child marriages were unheard of, *swayamvara* as the right of women to select a groom was common, and monogamy was the order of the day with polygamy being largely restricted to the nobility and royalty classes. Widow re-marriages were also permitted.

Performance of *Soma* **sacrifice** and other *yagnas*/rituals by the king under the chief priest (*raj-purohit*) was another significant custom/religious belief-based cultural element of the society. Numerous references to it are seen, particularly in the Vedic texts.

The political orders based on kingship and clan/tribal identities were not bereft of conflicts and disputes. This is also evident from the Rigvedic account of '**Battle of Ten Kings'**. As per historians, this battle led to the eventual emergence of the earliest of the Vedic states, the 'Kuru dynasty'. The performance of *Ashwamedha yagna*, sanctioned by the Vedas to the 'powerful and noble kings', was another means by which kingship could be expanded to regions where the sacrificial horse wandered. This could lead to battles and conflicts or acceptance of the over-lordship and political hegemony. But it led to the consolidation and emergence of larger political units.

1.8: An early 19th century manuscript of Rigveda in Devanagari. The Vedic accent is marked by underscores and vertical overscores in red — Wikimedia Commons

The Battle of Ten Kings: The Emergence of the Kuru Dynasty

The Rigveda also contains the account of the 'Battle of ten kings' which took place on the banks of river Parushini (modern Ravi). Historians describe this as a battle among the different Vedic tribes. The tribe of Bharatas was led by their king/chief Sudas, who entered into a battle against ten tribes. The Bharatas lived in the upper regions of river Saraswati while another tribe of Purus, their western neighbour, lived in the lower regions, the remaining tribes lived northwest of Bharatas. In the ensuing battle, the Bharatas emerged victorious while the Puru chief Purukutsa was killed. Post war, the two tribes, the Bharatas and the Purus, merged into a new tribe, the Kurus. (*Rigveda, mandal-7, hymns 18,33,83*)

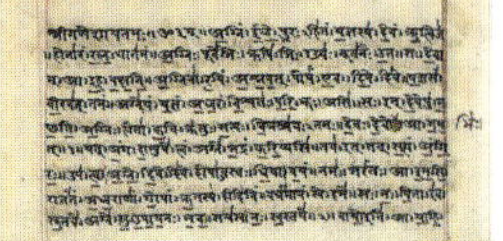

The Vedas: The text defining a cultural age

The word Veda is derived from the root word *'vid'*, meaning knowledge or wisdom. Thus, the Vedas were considered as the scriptures containing the total of the knowledge of the people. Further, the word *'vid'* also refers to the knowledge which could illuminate the path in the darkness (of ignorance), eventually leading to salvation. The Vedic texts comprise the **Rigveda,** the **Yajurveda,** the **Samaveda** and the **Atharvaveda**. The Rigveda is the oldest of all the Vedas and the most ancient of scriptures. A grand collection of hymns, it is also the most ancient Indo-European literary document.

The Vedas comprise four layers that include the **Samhitas** and the **Brahmanas,** the two former layers which together comprise the **Poorva Mimansa** or the *Karmakanda*. **The Aranyakas** and the **Upanishads** which emerged later as separate parts or layers of the Vedas, comprise the **Uttara Mimansa** or **Vedanta** (literally meaning the end of the Vedas), also referred to as the *Jnanakanda.*

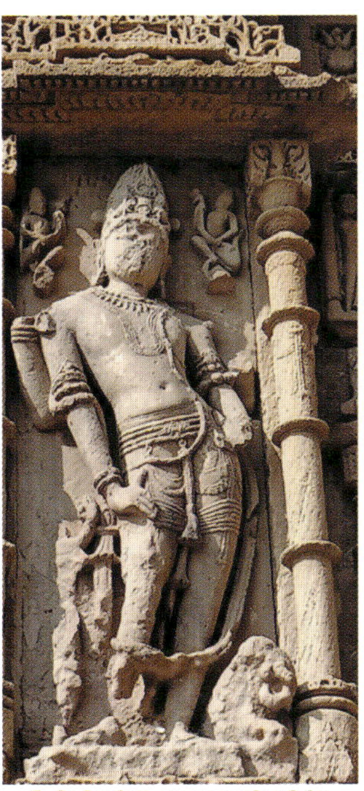

1.9: Indra, recognisable by his mount/vehicle, the elephant

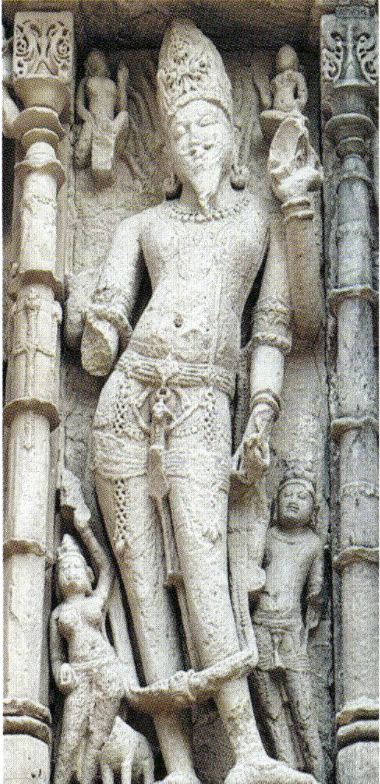

1.10: Agni, depicted as a priestly figure

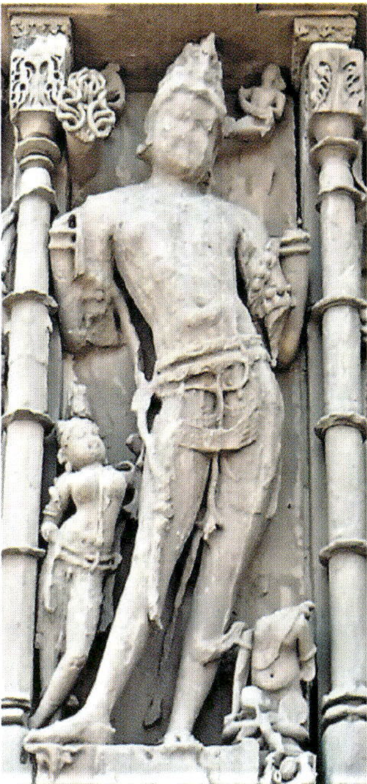

1.11: Varuna, depicted with his noose (*paash*)

The socio-religious and philosophical elements of culture of the early Vedic age is reflected in the philosophy of **Poorva Mimansa** (literally meaning former enquiry) as contained in the teachings of Samhitas and Brahmanas. It considers the Vedas to be eternal and infallible and emphasizes on *mantras* and rituals as prescribed therein in Vedas, as being of primary importance. This cultural philosophy is concerned more with **dharma** and **duties** of a person or **'***Karya***'** or *Karmakand*, rather than metaphysical knowledge.

Thus, a defining cultural practice emanating in this period was the performance the Vedic rites and *soma* sacrifices. Propitiation of elements of nature was an integral practice. These included rain, fire, earth, water, wind and the associated deities viz. **Indra, Agni, Soma, Prithvi, Mitra, Varun, Marut** etc.

As a religious-cultural practice, it was indicative of the very close integration of the daily lives of the people with nature and a profound connect with its constituent elements.

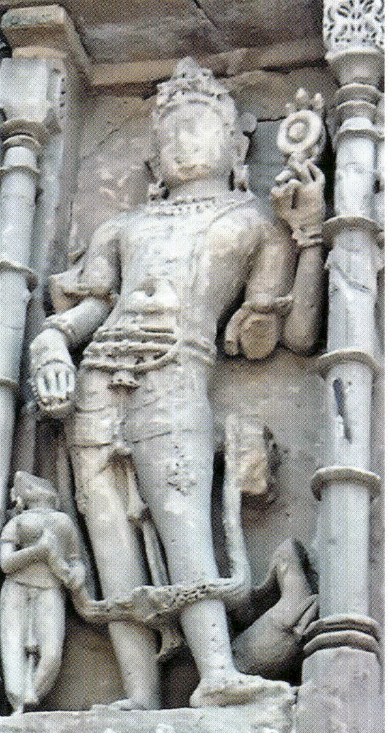

1.12: Vayu, with mount antelope at his feet

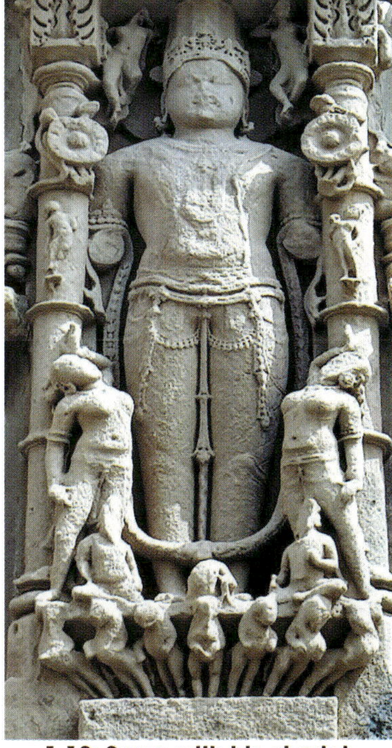

1.13: Surya, with his chariot, and with Usha and Pratyusha as consorts of Surya, and Aruna as charioteer

1.9 to 1.13: Early Vedic deities, reflecting the different elements of nature; pictures on the *gudhamandap* of Sun temple at Modhera (Gujarat), 11th century CE — photographs by Madhukar K Bhagat

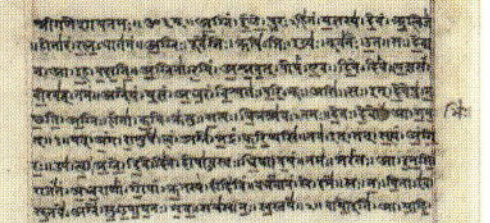

Indra was one of the most important early Vedic deities. Nearly 250 Rig Vedic hymns are dedicated to him. He was also the king of *devas*, whose different attributes are eulogised in the numerous hymns such as the killer of the *asura* Vritta (thus liberating the rivers), the breaker of the *vala* (a cave from which Usha was liberated) and the wielder of Vajra, the mighty one (*salwant*) and the one who is *Purandara* or the breaker of forts. Thus, he also epitomised valour in wars and his propitiation was perhaps seen as crucial for the victory of the Aryans in their onward spread. In a later period, he was also perceived as the god of rain and his propitiation was critical for an agrarian society dependent on the vagaries of rainfall.

Agni was a deity whose propitiation was essential in the performance of the numerous Vedic rites and *yagnas.* Nearly 200 hymns in his praise are contained in the Rig Vedic texts. He was the son of heaven, earth and water, who was worshipped as a god and offered sacrifices and oblations. Besides, he was also the medium that carried the oblations to the heavens and gods.

Varuna, the next important deity, is associated with *rta/rita* or the truth, and he is the protecter of *rta/rita* and thus the upholder of the natural order of the world. He is also perceived as the punisher of the sinners. In the later period he symbolised water and the mighty oceans.

The **Maruts** personified storms and the power of the wind. **Mitra**, another Aditya (son of Aditi), is often addressed along with Varuna (as *Mitravaruna*) and is also the protector of *rta*. **Parjanya** personified rains. **Usa/Usha** is the goddess of dawn who is closely associated with Surya (the Sun god). **Pushan** is a pastoral deity who wields a spear and a goad. **Soma** is a deity who is propitiated as well. It was probably a plant and its juice was offered to the gods in the ritual *yagnas*.

Vishnu, a later Vedic deity of great reverence, has only five hymns addressed to him in the Rig Veda. But he is known for the three wide steps in which he traverses the whole universe (a legend later associated with Lord Vishnu's Vamana avatar). His three steps are considered to be symbolic of the three divisions of the universe and is recognition of the great significance of this deity. **Rudra,** a relatively minor deity in Rigveda (with only three complete hymns dedicated), is the fierce god who is propitiated to be merciful and kind and is also associated with healing.

Veneration of Rivers: A Culture of Embodiment of Divinity in Nature

The Vedic culture flourished on the banks of mighty rivers and reference to the Sapt-sindhu (seven rivers in the Indian subcontinent) and others is often contained in the Vedas. The rivers were the givers of life and nurtured the civilisation and thus were venerated as a living deity. *Nadistuti sukta* contained in the 75th hymn (sukta) of the 10th book (Mandala) of Rigveda, is an important composition in the veneration of the rivers. In verses (rik/rk.)1, 2, 5, 7, 8 and 9 specific reference is contained of the mighty rivers.

(9) 75 (म.10, अनु.6)

ऋषिः सिन्धुक्षित् प्रैयमेधः छन्दः जगती देवता नद्यः

प्र सु व आपो महिमानमुत्तमं कारुर्वोचाति सदने विवस्वतः ।
प्र सप्तसप्त त्रेधा हि चक्रमुः प्र सृत्वरीणामति सिन्धुरोजसा ॥ 1 ॥
प्र तेऽरदद्वरुणो यातवे पथः सिन्धो यद्वाजाँ अभ्यद्रवस्त्वम् ।
भूम्या अधि प्रवता यासि सानुना यदेषामग्रं जगतामिरज्यसि ॥ 2 ॥
दिवि स्वनो यतते भूम्योपर्यनन्तं शुष्ममुदियर्ति भानुना ।
अभ्रादिव प्र स्तनयन्ति वृष्टयः सिन्धुर्यदेति वृषभो न रोरुवत् ॥ 3 ॥
अभि त्वा सिन्धो शिशुमिन्न मातरो वाश्रा अर्षन्ति पयसेव धेनवः ।
राजेव युध्वा नयसि त्वमित्सिचौ यदासामग्रं प्रवतामिनक्षसि ॥ 4 ॥
इमं मे गङ्गे यमुने सरस्वति शुतुद्रि स्तोमं सचता परुष्ण्या ।
असिक्न्या मरुद्वृधे वितस्तयार्जीकीये शृणुह्या सुषोमया ॥ 5 ॥
तृष्टामया प्रथमं यातवे सजूः सुसर्त्वा रसया श्वेत्या त्या ।
त्वं सिन्धो कुभया गोमतीं क्रुमुं मेहत्न्वा सरथं याभिरीयसे ॥ 6 ॥

Verse (*rik*) 1to 6 of the 75th hymn (*sukta*) of book 10 (*Mandal*-10) of Rigveda referred to as the *Nadistuti sukta*.

The first and the second verses highlight the glory of the river Sindhu and say as below.

The singer, O ye waters in Vivasvan's place, shall tell your grandeur forth that is beyond compare.

The rivers have come forward triply, seven and seven. Sindhu in might surpasses all the streams that flow. (verse 1)

Varuna cut the channels for thy forward course, O Sindhu, when thou rannest on to win the race.

Thou speedest o'er precipitous ridges of the earth, when thou art Lord and Leader of these moving floods (verse 2)

The fifth verse in a particular enumerates the 10 rivers including Ganga and says as below;

Oh Ganga, Yamuna, Sarasvati, Shutudri (Sutlej), *Parushni* (Iravati, Ravi), *follow my praise! O Asikni* (Chenab) *Marudvridha, Vitasta* (Jhelum), *with the Arjikiya* (Haro) *and Sushoma (Sohan), hear my call!* (verse 5)

(translation Ralph T.H.Griffith)

Another such composition in the Rigveda is ***Vishwamitra Nadi Suktam*** contained in hymn 33 of Mandal 3. It refers to the prayer of sage Vishwamitra (one of the seven Brahmarshi of the Vedic age) to grant a passage through the rivers *Vipas* (Beas) and *Sutudri* (Sutlej). The gist of the 13 verses of the *sukta* is as below.

Vishwamitra: *O' rivers, who come down from the mountains like two swift horses like, two shining cows that lick their calves. You move like chariots to the sea through the power of Indra. You are full of water and wish to unite with one another.* (Verse 1)

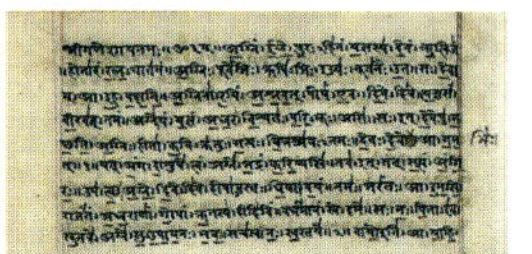

The rivers: *We who are full of water move along the path, the Gods have made for us. Once we start flowing we cannot be stopped. Why do you pray to us o' sage?* (Verse 4)

Vishwamitra: *O' sisters please listen to me, the singer who has come from a distance with his chariots and carts, let your water not rise above our axles so that we can cross safely.* (Verse 9)

The rivers: *We will listen to your prayers so that you can cross safely.* (Verse 10)

The conception of the universe

The early Vedic conception of the universe is not limited to the veneration of the elements of nature; rather it also extends to the entire cosmology and the very source of creation.

The 129th hymn (*sukta*) of the 10th book (mandala) of the Rig Veda contains the **Nasadiya Sukta** which is contemplative of the cosmology and the origin of the universe. It begins with the term '*na asat*', that is when the unreal/non-existent and the real/existent, were not in existence. Hence this *sukta* acquires the epithet of *Nasadiya Sukta* and is also referred to as the hymn of creation. It conceives of the state when existed; neither the real nor the unreal, neither the physical realm nor the realms beyond it, neither death nor immortality, neither the light nor the darkness. And then only existed the cosmological water (fluid) in which by force of heat (energy) the Supreme being came into existence. The verse further states that the Eternal being, the Brahma which emanated from the Supreme knowledge and Consciousness, had the desire to manifest and from which emanated the primal seed of creation.

It further ponders **as to who knows, how and whence the Creation came into being, for even the Gods of the universe were created after it.** It contemplates and concludes that perhaps the **mystery of creation is known only to that Eternal being, or maybe not even to Him**.

The verse, though inquisitive and at times assertive, does not provide a conclusive statement as to the creation/origin of universe. Its conclusion of that 'Supreme being the knower of the secret of Creation or even He may not be having this knowledge', may be seen as a sceptical inquiry or a humble statement of the seer's/composer's lack of knowledge of the secrets of Universe beyond a point. This *Sukta* is **reflective of the deep philosophical insight of the age which is contemplative, questioning, transcending any dogma** and almost akin to a secular scientific inquiry.

Nasadiya Sukta: the Hymn of Creation

नासदासीन्नो सदासीत्तदानीं नासीद्रजो नो व्योमा परो यत्।
किमावरीवः कुह कस्य शर्मन्नम्भः किमासीद्गहनं गभीरम् ।। 1 ।।

nāsad āsīn nó sád āsīt tadānīm
nāsīd rájo nó víomā paró yát
kím āvarīvah kúha kásya śármann
ámbhah kím āsīd gáhanam gabhīrám

Then even non-existence was not there, nor existence,
There was no air then, nor the space beyond it.
What covered it? Where was it? In whose keeping?
Was there then cosmic fluid, in depths unfathomed? (Verse 1)

न मृत्युरासीदमृतं न तर्हि न रात्र्या अह्न आसीत्प्रकेतः।
आनीदवातं स्वधया तदेकं तस्माद्धान्यत्र परः किञ्चनास ।। 2 ।।

ná mrtyúr āsīd amŕtam ná tárhi
ná rātriyā áhna āsīt praketáh
ānīd avātám svadháyā tád ékam
tásmād dhānyán ná paráh kím canāsa

Then there was neither death nor immortality
nor was there then the torch of night and day.
The One breathed windlessly and self-sustaining.
There was that One then, and there was no other. (Verse 2)

तम आसीत्तमसा गूहमग्रे प्रकेतं सलिलं सर्वाऽइदम्।
तुच्छ्येनाभ्वपिहितं यदासीत्तपसस्तन्महिनाजायतैकम् ।। 3 ।।

táma āsīt támasā gūhálam ágre
apraketám salilám sárvam ā idám
tuchyénābhú ápihitam yád āsīt
tápasas tán mahinājāyataíkam

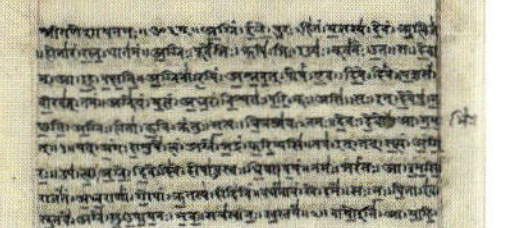

At first there was only darkness wrapped in darkness.
All this was only unillumined cosmic water.
That One which came to be, enclosed in nothing,
arose at last, born of the power of knowledge. (Verse 3)

कामस्तदग्रे समवर्तताधि मनसो रेतः प्रथमं यदासीत्।
सतो बन्धुमसति निरविन्दन्हृदि प्रतीष्या कवयो मनीषा।।4।।

kāmas tád ágre sám avartatādhi
mánaso rétah prathamám yád āsīt
sató bándhum ásati nír avindan
hrdí pratīsyā kaváyo manīsā

In the beginning desire descended on it -
that was the primal seed, born of the mind.
The sages who have searched their hearts with wisdom
know that which is, is kin to that which is not. (Verse 5)

तिरश्चीनो विततो रश्मिरेषामधः स्विदासीदुपरि स्विदासीत्।
रेतोधा आसन्महिमान आसन्त्स्वधा अवस्तात्प्रयतिः परस्तात्।।5।।

tiraścīno vítato raśmír esām
adháh svid āsīd upári svid āsīt
retodhā āsan mahimāna āsan
svadhā avástāt práyatih parástāt

And they have stretched their cord across the void,
and know what was above, and what below.
Seminal powers made fertile mighty forces.
Below was strength, and over it was impulse. (Verse 6)

को अद्धा वेद क इह प्र वोचत्कुत आजाता कुत इयं विसृष्टिः।
अर्वाग्देवा अस्य विसर्जनेनाथा को वेद यत आबभूव।।6।।

kó addhā veda ká ihá prá vocat
kúta ājātā kúta iyám vísrstih
arvāg devā asyá visárjanena
áthā kó veda yáta ābabhūva

But, after all, who knows, and who can say
Whence it all came, and how creation happened?
the gods themselves are later than creation,
so who knows truly whence it has arisen? (Verse 6)

इयं विसृष्टिर्यत आबभूव यदि वा दधे यदि वा न।
यो अस्याध्यक्षः परमे व्योमन्त्सो अङ्ग वेद यदि वा न वेद।।7।।

iyám vísrstir yáta ābabhūva
yádi vā dadhé yádi vā ná
yó asyādhyaksah paramé vyoman
só angá veda yádi vā ná véda

Whence all creation had its origin,
the creator, whether he fashioned it or whether he did not,
the creator, who surveys it all from highest heaven,
he knows — or maybe even he does not know (Verse 7)

Translation of A.L. Bhasham

Upanishads: The epitome of Vedic knowledge

The culmination of the Vedic cultural phase was indeed the conception of the Upanishadic philosophy also referred to as the **Vedanta.** This philosophy emphasized on *Jnana* (or knowledge) and explored metaphysical subjects and intriguing conceptions of the *Brahman* and *Atman* etc. While the former was equated with the cosmic being, the supreme creator, the primeval person and the infinite consciousness, the latter was described as the true-self or the soul of the sentient being. This doctrine laid greater stress on the acquisition of true knowledge and spiritual development, rather than on rituals and sacrifices. It propounded the enduring philosophy of unitism or monism as a part of the Vedantic thought which emphasised on the **unity** of the **Brahman** and the **Atman.** This unity enunciated as the ultimate **realisation of Brahman,** was hailed as the cardinal objective of a being's life.

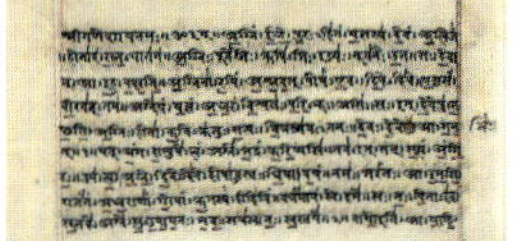

Thus the **doctrine of Vedanta** emerged in this age. This philosophy and its significance, is very succinctly described by Dr. Radhakrishnan in the book, 'The Hindu View of Life', where he states, "***Vedanta is not a religion but a religion in the most universal and deepest significance.***" Thus, the emergence of this profound and all-encompassing thought was indeed a marked departure from the early Vedic philosophy and led to the evolution of a totally new dimension and perspective of the culture in India.

Atman or the True Self: The Conversation of Prajapati and Indra

The concept of true self or *Atman* is well elucidated in the Upanishads, particularly in the *Chandogya*, *Mandukya* and *Katha Upanishads*. The *Chandogya Upanishad* (chapter 8. sections 7-12) recounts the explanation of the true self by Prajapati (the creator of the universe and a guru alike to *devas* and *asuras* who is also identified in the Puranas as Brahma). The gist of this metaphorical and illumining dialogue which dwells on the essential nature of the Atman is brought out here.

Prajapati announces *the Self (Atman) to be deathless, ageless and sinless, which knows no sorrow, hunger or pain. It is this Self which is worthy of seeking and worth all that is desirable and this Self must be known.*

Indra (king of the *devas*) and Vairochana (the leader of *Asuras*) approach Prajapati to reveal what is this *true-self*. But to be worthy of the divine knowledge, Prajapati asks them to do penance for 32 years. At the end of this period, Prajapati alludes to the physical body which one can see as the reflection of water, as the *true-self* (that is the self which can be known through the senses). Vairochana, satisfied with the explanation, advises his followers to serve and glorify the physical self. But Indra, though initially content with this elucidation, reasons with Prajapati as to how the physical body is the true self as it suffers sorrow and is prone to destruction and death.

Prajapati, to test Indra further, describes this *true self* to be the state of consciousness as we see ourselves in the dreams. Indra reasons that the self in dreams is a transient state and not an enduring one. Even this self is not immune to the suffering and pain that is experienced in dreams, so how can it be the *true self*?

Prajapati then alludes to the state of unconscious, in a dreamless sleep as akin to the *true self*. But this too fails to satisfy Indra. He reasons that such a state is a mere abstraction and the *self* in such a state is absolutely unconscious knowing and experiencing nothing and then how could it ever be the conscious and luminous one? Thus, though it does not experience the negative qualities associated with the physicalself, but squarely lacks the positive attributes postulated for the *trueself*.

Thus, after many years of yearning and inquisitiveness of Indra, Prajapati reveals what the *true self* is. He explains that *Atman* cannot be equated with the gross body, which is subject to decay and death, or the transient and ephemeral state of dreams. It is not even the unconscious state of oneself that does not have the knowledge or luminescence. *Atman* is beyond intellectual conception which is limited to physical senses and reason. *Atman* is the indestructible, self-embodied in the ephemeral physical or gross body. The body experiences the *doshas* or the attributes (viz. pain and pleasure) but *Atman* remains *nirdosha* or attributeless. Shackled by the body the *Atman* seems limited and restricted, but when freed from it, the Atman is again a part of the infinite and universal consciousness.

Varnashrama Dharma, a new socio-cultural and philosophical order

The Vedic period also saw the emergence of the philosophy of the **Varnashrama dharma**. This philosophy enunciated and integrated the concepts of social order and socio-economic concept of division of labour, with socio-cultural and ethical obligations and duties. These in turn were determined as per the stage and calling of life. The concept is said to be traceable to the ***Purusha Sukta*** of the Rigveda (*Mandal* 10, *sukta* 90). This *sukta* attributes the creation of the different varnas to the various parts of the body of the *Purusa*; the all-pervading cosmic being. Thus, this *sukta* brings out the cosmic connection between all the varnas. The different parts only symbolise their having different social duties. The concept later finds elaboration in the *Manusmriti* and the other *Dharmashastras*.

Purusha Sukta

पुरुष एवेदं सर्वं यद्भूतं यच्च भव्यम्।
उतामृतत्वस्येशानो यदन्नेनातिरोहति ।।1।।

The Purusha is verily all this (Creation,) that which existed in the past, or will exist in the future;

Everything is woven by the immortal essence of the great lord (Purusha);

by becoming food of which (i.e. by getting consumed in whose immortal essence through surrender) one transcends the manifest world and becomes immortal.

त्रिपादूर्ध्व उदैत्पूरुषः पादोऽस्येहाभवत्पुनः।
ततो विष्वङ् व्यक्रामत्साशनानशने अभि ।।4।।

The three parts of the Purusha is high above (in the transcendental realm),
and his one part becomes the manifest creation again and again;
There, in the manifest creation, he pervades all the living (who eat) and the non-living beings (which do not eat)

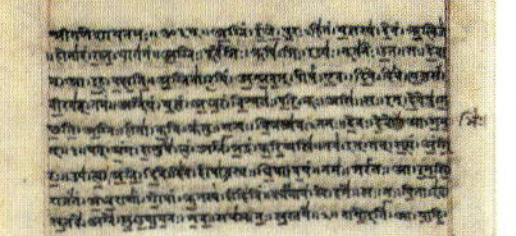

तस्माद्यज्ञात्सर्वहुत ऋचः सामानि जज्ञिरे।
छन्दांसि जज्ञिरे तस्माद्यजुस्तस्मादजायत ।।9।।

From the great offering of his yagna (i.e Virat who was born of the Purusha); was born the Rigveda and Samaveda the chandas (Vedic meters) were born from him, and the Yajurveda was born from him.

ब्राह्मणोऽस्य मुखमासीद् बाहू राजन्यः कृतः।
ऊरू तदस्य यद्वैश्यः पद्भ्यां शूद्रो अजायत ।।12।।

The Brahmanas were his mouth, the kshatriyas his arms,
the vaishyas were his thighs, and the shudras were his feet.

The word *Varnashrama Dharma* is composed of three distinct words. ***Varna*** (here referred to as the class), ***Ashrama*** (or stage/station in life) and ***Dharma*** (duty or obligation). Thus, based on *varna* (class) and *ashrama* (station) a person was obliged to discharge his duties. The *Shastras* identified four *varnas* and four *ashramas*. The four *varnas* are **Brahmans** (priests, preachers, teachers), **Kshatriyas** (kings, soldiers, warriors), **Vaishyas** (merchants, agriculturists, artisans etc.) and **Shudras** (labourers/service providers).

The four *ashramas* were ***Brahmacharya, Grihastha, Vanaprastha and Sanyasa. Brahmacharya*** was the first stage of life where the objective was to acquire knowledge and lead a life of discipline and celibacy. ***Grihastha*** or the stage of house-holder was the next, where one was to choose his occupation as per *varna*, marry and raise a family. ***Vanaprastha*** was the third stage, which literally means 'proceeding to the forest'. After fulfilling the duties of a house-holder, with the onset of age, a person could retire from worldly matters and spend more time in spiritual pursuits. ***Sanyasa*** was the final stage where a person was to detach himself from society and fully pursue the attainment of salvation or *moksha*. Depending on the *varna* and *ashrama*, a person was required to discharge his dharma, as an enunciated duty.

Thus, this cultural philosophy was to serve as the lodestar of the seeker through the journey of life and beyond. The *Atman* in its physical embodiment was to pass through the numerous stages of life. It would acquire various attributes including knowledge and material wealth. It would also undergo the experience of the worldly pleasures and sufferings. A seeker was not to remain mired in the worldly pursuits, but the true purpose of life was to seek the salvation through integration of the *Atman* with *Brahma*. The virtuous pursuit of appropriate worldly duties or the right *Karma* was the key to emancipation in this eternal cycle.

The Story of Nachiketa and the Discourse on the Nature of Atman and its Journey Beyond Life

The *Katha Upanishad* (or Kathopanishad) contains the story of Nachiketa and his conversation with Yama (the god of death), who reveals to him the secret of life after death, the nature of *atman* and other metaphysical concepts. The discourse is in the nature of a conversation between the two with Yama answering the incisive and unrelenting queries of the young boy.

Nachiketa's father Vajrashravasa performs a *yagna*, after which he donates his worldly possessions. But Nachiketa sees his father as offering what has little value, viz. old and barren cows. He attributes this to his father's poverty and thinking himself to be the most valued possession of his father, questions him as to whom would he be donated. Being repeatedly queried, the irritated father utters that he would be gifted to the *Yama*. As per the story, to honour his father's words, Nachiketa makes a journey to the abode of Yama. Unfortunately, he awaits Yama's audience for three days without even being offered food and water. Yama, on his appearance after this period, is remorseful for this sinful oversight and to atone for it, tries to conciliate Nachiketa by offering him three boons (wishes).

As the **first boon**, Nachiketa seeks to return to his home from the abode of Yama and also seeks acceptance by his father who has offered him to Yama. Most importantly, he also seeks as his first wish, his father's wellness and he being unresentful towards him on his return. Thus, he seeks the good of his father and unification with him. As his **second wish**, he seeks Yama's instruction on appropriate conduct of the fire-rituals which would grant one the passage to heaven; where there is no sorrow, hunger, fear, old age etc. Thus, he seeks to have the knowledge to secure wellness of all and their becoming free of misery and sorrow.

As his **third wish**, Nachiketa seeks to know as to **what lies and happens after death**.

Yama readily endows him first two boons but is reluctant to grant his third. At first, he tries to dissuade Nachiketa by expressing that the knowledge is too subtle even for *Devas* to fully comprehend. Later, he tries to allure Nachiketa with the prospect of granting him long age, material wealth and any other wish of his. But Nachiketa remains steadfast and rejects the latter offers of material wealth, long age etc. as all being ephemeral. Thus, having duly tested the yearning of Nachiketa, his resolve and his credential to be a recipient of this eternal knowledge, Yama goes to explain it.

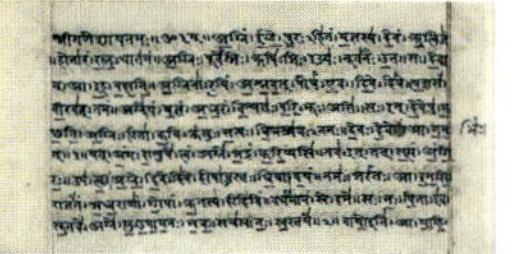

The story and its characters are all emblematic with Nachiketa being the deserving seeker and Yama being the celestial guru who is privy to life beyond death. What is relevant is the eternal concept of *Advaita* philosophy it propounds. The relevant parts and extracts of this conversation embodying the profound philosophy is briefly highlighted below.

Theory of *Preya* and *Shreya*: Yama first confers the knowledge of *preya* (dear or pleasant) and *shreya* (good, more appropriate and beneficial). He elucidates that the *preya* and *shreya* both approach a man but the wise distinguish and choose *shreya* over *preya*.

Thus, the first step to salvation was to make appropriate choice, of not the alluring but the more appropriate, beneficial and enduring. Expressed in verse (in *kathopanishad 1.2.1-1.2.2*)

अन्यच्छ्रेयोऽन्यदुतैव प्रेयस्ते उभे नानार्थे पुरुषँ सिनीतः ।
तयोः श्रेय आददानस्य साधुर्भवति हीयतेऽर्थाद्य उ प्रेयो वृणीते ।। 1 ।।

Yama says, 'one is shreya (good) while another is preya (dear or pleasant). These two, serving different ends, bind men; happiness (salvation) comes to him who chooses the shreya (good); whosoever chooses the pleasant forfeits the true purpose of life.'

श्रेयश्च प्रेयश्च मनुष्यमेतस्तौ संपरीत्य विविनक्ति धीरः ।
श्रेयो हि धीरोऽभिप्रेयसो वृणीते प्रेयो मन्दो योगक्शेमाद्वृणीते ।। 2 ।।

The Shreya (good) and the Preya (dear) approach the man,
The wise ponder over both and distinguish between them;
The wise choose the Shreya (good) over the Preya (dear),
The fool, bound by craving, chooses the Preya (dear).

Yama further instructs that the pursuit of shreya is difficult yet enduring and eternal while that of *preya* is pleasant and easy, yet transient.

The existence of Atman & the essence of Vedas: As per Kathopanishad (verses 1.2.14 through 1.2.22) the Atman or the true self does exist although invisible to our senses. It is primeval and enduring and recognisable by means of *yoga* (meditation and appropriate karma).

तं दुर्दर्शं गूढमनुप्रविष्टं गुहाहितं गह्वरेष्ठं पुराणम् ।
अध्यात्मयोगाधिगमेन देवं मत्वा धीरो हर्षशोकौ जहाति (Verse 1.2.12)

He (the Atman), difficult to be seen, full of mystery,
the ancient, primeval one, concealed deep within,
He who, by yoga means of meditation on his self, comprehends Atman within him as God,
He leaves joy and sorrow far behind.

The ultimate aim of the Vedas is to liberate a man from joy and sorrow, from his past and future and all his earthly bonds. This is possible through the right knowledge which liberates one from the darkness and ignorance pervading life and which leads to the realisation of *Atman* and *Brahman*. Further, the word *Om* is the reflection of *Brahman* which is the most elevated, the pure and the blissful within. Thus, the *Atman* itself was a reflection of the *Brahman*.

Nature of Atman: The true self of man, his *Atman*, is neither born nor dies, it is eternal, it is *Brahman*. Its nature is best expressed in the following verses of Kathopanishad. (verses 1.2.18 through 1.2.22)

न जायते म्रियते वा विपश्चिन्नायं कुतश्चिन्न बभूव कश्चित् ।
अजो नित्यः शाश्वतोऽयं पुराणो न हन्यते हन्यमाने शरीरे ।। 18 ।।

The Atman, is neither born, nor does it die,
It does not originate, nor does it become anybody,
Eternal and ancient, it remains eternal,
It is not killed, even though the body is destroyed.

अणोरणीयान्महतो महीयानात्मास्य जन्तोर्निहितो गुहायां ।
तमक्रतुः पश्यति वीतशोको धातुः प्रसादान्महिमानमात्मनः ।। 20 ।।

The Atman, subtler than the subtle, greater than the great,
is hidden in the heart of each creature;
one who is free from desire, free from avarice,
who has his mind and the senses composed, is peaceful and content,
he sees the supreme glory of Atman and is absolved from grief (attains salvation).

Further, the knowledge of *Atman* is acquired, not through textual knowledge of scriptures or discourses or reasoning. But it comes through self-realisation through meditation and appropriate conduct, through ethical living and a tranquil mind. Further, this knowledge eludes those who indulge in misconduct, live unethically and whose mind is not tranquil.

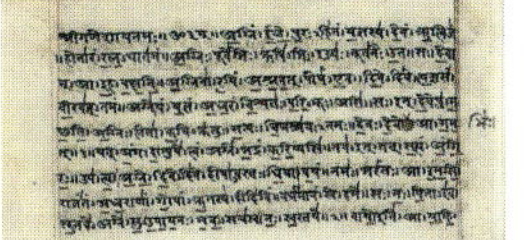

The allegory of Atman, mind, body and senses: The verses 1.3.3-1.3.4 of the Upanishad explain as to who can and who cannot attain the unison of the *Atman* and *Brahman*. Those who are unable to rein their senses through the powers of right reasoning, have their minds which are unbridled and they invariably remain entangled in the worldly life. But those who, through the right reasoning and power of intellect are able to harness the senses and rein the mind are the ones to attain liberation. Expressed in verse, it states;

आत्मानँ रथितं विद्धि शरीरँ रथमेव तु।
बुद्धिं तु सारथिं विद्धि मनः प्रग्रहमेव च।।3।।

The Atman is the rider in the chariot, and the body is the chariot,
the Buddhi (intellect and ability to reason) is the charioteer, and Manas (mind) is the reins.

इन्द्रियाणि हयानाहुर्विषयाँ स्तेषु गोचरान्।
आत्मेन्द्रियमनोयुक्तं भोक्तेत्याहुर्मनीषिणः।।4।।

The senses are the horses, whose objective is to travel the right paths,
Formed out of the union of the Atman, the senses and the mind, him they call the "enjoyer".

Unity and Plurality

The next verses explain that the understanding of 'the true self' is the grasping of inner knowledge and of Unity. This is the eternal knowledge of spiritual oneness. Thus, the knowledge of the oneness of *Atman* and *Purusha* or *Brahman* is the true eternal knowledge, signifying the unity of one with the All-pervading. This is the knowledge of *Advaita* (literally meaning 'no two') or **unitism**.

The knowledge of the external world on the other hand is the knowledge of plurality, where the self is separate from the external world and its subjects which are all transient.

Journey beyond the transient life: The verses in Katha Upanishad (verses 2.2.1 to 2.215) also describe what happens beyond death. It describes the *Atman* (soul) to be eternal and undying which exists even after the physical body perishes. The journey of soul further is defined by one's own *karma* as to whether it is liberated and becomes one with the *Brahman* or it takes a new life and form. Thus, these verses propound the '*karmic theory*' (described in verses 2.3.1 to 2.3.19) and that of the 'cycle of life and rebirth'. At the same time, they emphasise on the right knowledge and right *karma* for the emancipation of the soul and journey beyond.

योनिमन्ये प्रपद्यन्ते शरीरत्वाय देहिनः।
स्थाणुमन्येऽनुसंयन्ति यथाकर्म यथाश्रुतम्।।7।।

Some of these souls enter the womb and embody again as living beings,
others metamorphose unto what is Sthānu (immovable things),
according to their karma, and their shrutam (knowledge, learning). **(verses 2.2.7)**

Right knowledge and Yoga: The next few verses (in *adhyaya* 2, *valli* 3) prescribe the path of right knowledge and *karma* as means of knowing the *Atman* and its emancipation. This is achieved through the harnessing of senses with the mind (*manas*) and intellect/power to reason (*buddhi*). It is this unison which creates tranquillity (and not thoughtlessness). This is the path of Yoga and eventually leads to the unity of *Atman* and *Brahman*.

यदा पञ्चावतिष्ठन्ते ज्ञानानि मनसा सह।
बुद्धिश्च न विचेष्टते तामाहुः परमां गतिम्।।10।।
तां योगमिति मन्यन्ते स्थिरामिन्द्रियधारणाम्।
अप्रमत्तस्तदा भवति योगोहि प्रभवाप्ययौ।।11।।

When Manas (mind) with thoughts and the five senses is tranquil,
When Buddhi (intellect) does not waver, that is the highest state.
That is what one calls Yoga, the stillness of the senses, concentration of the mind,
It is not thoughtless heedless sluggishness, Yoga is creation and dissolution.

The last few verses describe, that the objective of life should be, acquiring this illumining knowledge and the instructions of Yoga by dint of which one can attain the Brahman. Thus, the treatise emphasises the right knowledge and action in this world itself and not any attainment in a yonder world.

The great treatise ends with a prayer of the student and the teacher seeking divine protection for any inadvertent faults of theirs in the course of receiving and imparting knowledge. It prays that the great lord may protect both by imparting the illumining knowledge and revealing the fruits thereof. Further, it wishes for the disciple and preceptor, to never hate each other, owing to blame incurred by them by improper recital or instruction due to oversight.

सह नाववतु। सह नौ भुनक्तु। सह वीर्यं करवावहै।
तेजस्विनावधीतमस्तु मा विद्विषावहै।।19।।

Let Him protect us both; let us exert together may what we study to be well studied; may we not hate each other.

ओं शान्तिः शान्तिः शान्तिः।।

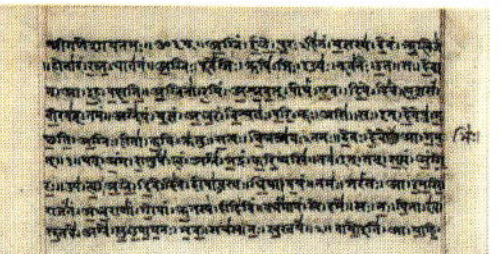

Varnashrama dharma and social mobility

As a basis for socio-economic order and division of labour, the Varnashrama system was egalitarian and flexible to begin with. The *Purusha Sukta* hymn sites the common origin of all *varnas* from the same cosmic entity the *Purusha*. Although some scholars believe this *sukta* to be a later addition to the Rig Veda, it is still a significant reflection of the conception of the ancient society of the spiritual unity of the cosmos and the inherent oneness of all emerging therefrom. Further, social mobility within the varnas was permitted as a matter of individual choice of occupation. The co-existence of different *varnas* in the same family is evident from the Rigvedic hymn;

I am a poet my father is a physician, my mother is a grinder;

earning livelihood through different means we live together (Rigveda IX.112)

Another Rigvedic hymn that elucidates existence of social mobility is hymn 3.43-5

O, Indra, fond of soma, would you make me the protector of people, or would you make me a king, would you make me a sage who has drunk soma, would you impart to me endless wealth.

Thus, the rigidities of birth-based *varna* do not seem to be existent as an early Vedic practice. But over the period of centuries, the **varna system** seems to have metamorphosed into a more stringent and rigid social system or the **caste system**. Varna was now determined by birth with the individual's choice in its determination altogether ceasing. Adding to it, there was the emergence of a dominant Brahmanical order of the priestly class, with an emphasis on rituals and sacrifices. Finally, with the marginalisation of the shudras in this socio-economic order, this system had ceased to be socially and culturally inclusive. The time was now ripe for a new thought to emerge and another cultural wave to sweep the land. This was provided by Buddhism and Jainism and their more inclusive philosophy.

Unitism and Vedanta: An enduring legacy of the Vedic age

From the perspective of cultural evolution, the Vedic age does not seem to have engendered an urban civilisation akin to the erstwhile Indus Valley Civilisation. It is only in the last phase of this period around 600 BCE that we see the emergence of bigger cities in *Mahajanapadas*. But the evolution of other tangible and intangible elements of culture, particularly of music and medicine, is indeed noticeable in the verses of Samaveda and Atharvaveda. Similarly, the growth of disciplines of mathematics, astronomy, metallurgy and other fields can be traced to developments in this period. However, the **Vedantic philosophy** and the concept of **unitism** are truly unique and enduring cultural heritages of this age. If the highest perspective of culture is it's that element, that seeks to understand the true meaning and purpose of life, then the **Vedantic philosophy was the pinnacle of cultural evolution** and which indeed left an enduring legacy for all the ages and cultures which ensued.

THE DRAVIDIAN CULTURE

The word *Dravida* in the Sanskrit language usually refers to the region in the southern part of India or the peninsular India. Thus, the culture of this region and the people domiciled therein are referred by historians as the Dravidian culture. As experts dwell on the elements of Dravidian culture and endeavour to define its contours, they invariably strive to identify, whether this culture was distinct from the Vedic culture? If yes, what were its unique features? Whether there was any confluence of these two streams? But the search for answers to the above queries also begets the question as to who were the Dravidian people.

The Dravidian People and their Origin

The origin of Dravidian people remains a subject of research and debate with many theories being proposed. The first being, that the **Dravidians were the Harappan people** who were pushed back to the eastern and southern parts of India because of the Aryan invasion. But with the Aryan invasion theory itself being discarded by experts, this notion too stands largely repudiated. Another hypothesis is that the Dravidians were the **aboriginal settlers**, who over the centuries, were pushed to the peninsular India, owing to the expansion of the Aryans. The contact between the two led to each influencing the language and culture of others. Historians and linguists point to the existence of many words in the Vedic texts that supposedly having origin in the Dravidian languages.

Another theory is that the **Dravidian** people could have indeed been the **Indus Valley settlers**, who abandoned the collapsing cities owing to the flooding of some of them and later because of draughts

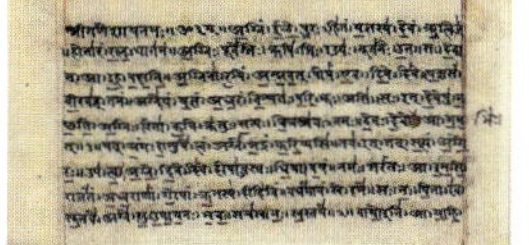

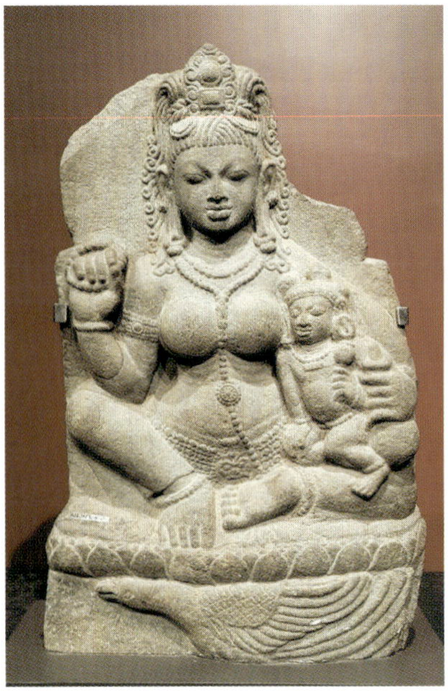

1.14: Brahmani

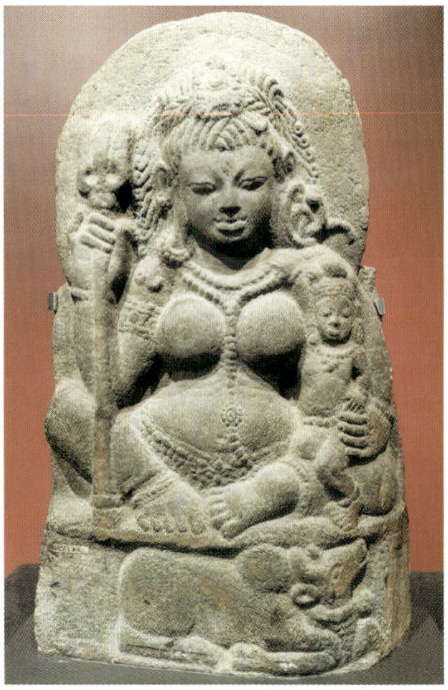

1.15: Maheshwari

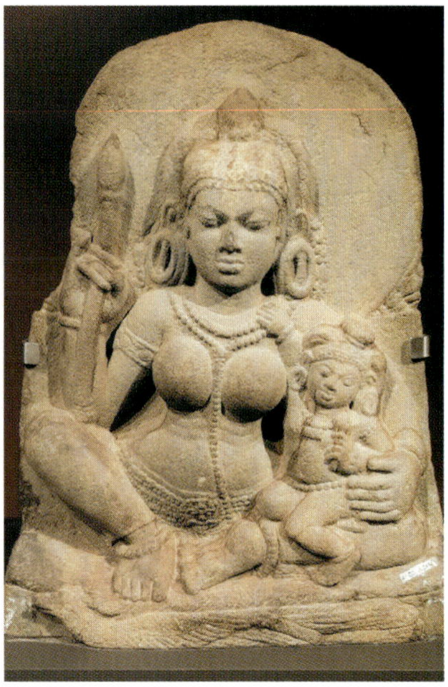

1.16: Kumari

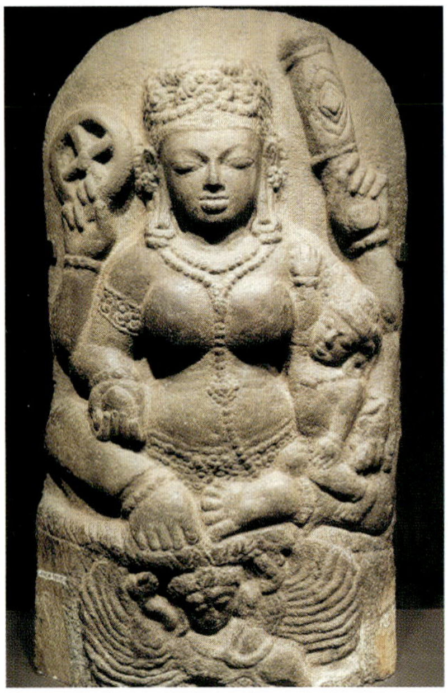

1.17: Vaishnavi

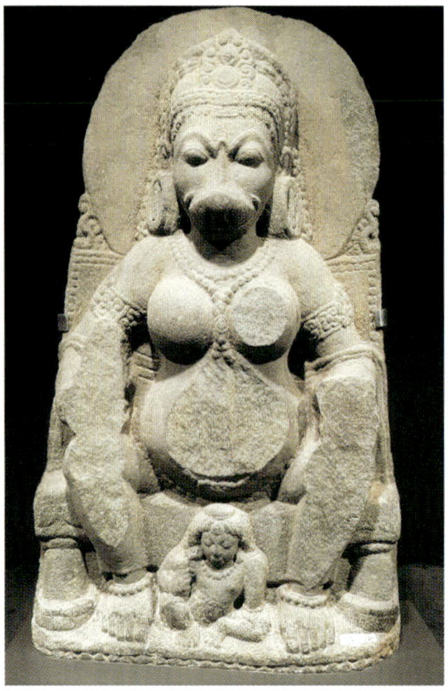

1.18: Varahi

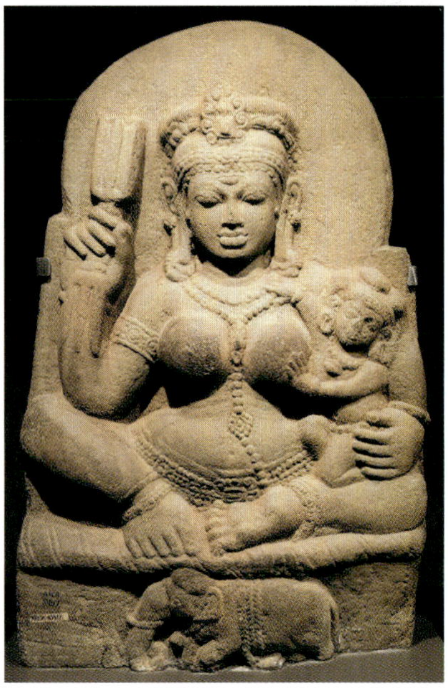

1.19: Indrani

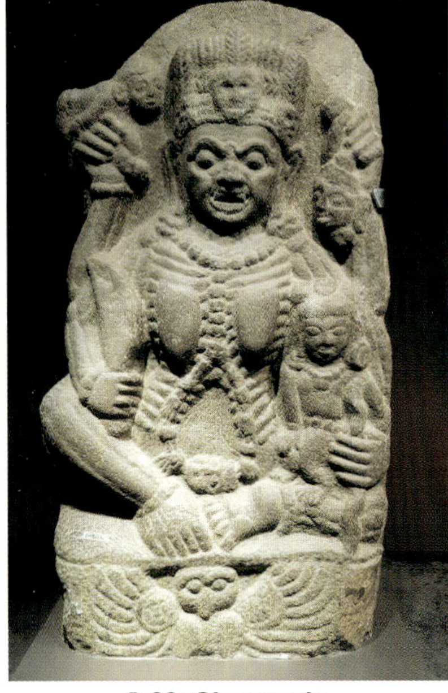

1.20: Chamunda

1.14 to 1.20: The *Saptamatrikas* having origin and strong presence in the Dravidian culture also had influence on the Puranic culture. Sculptures in grey sandstone from Saraikela from the 6th century CE; current location at Bihar Museum, Patna — photographs by Madhukar K Bhagat

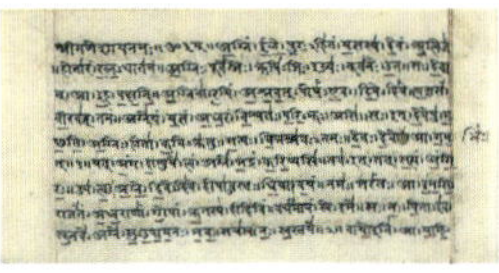

of several centuries (the Meghalayan drought 2000 BCE to 1800 BCE) (see Chapter 2). Eventually, they moved eastwards and later southwards and settled in the peninsular region. Prof. Asko Parpola and Iravatham Mahadevan are proponents of this theory. They believe of there being a strong evidence for a proto-Dravidian origin of the ancient Indus Valley civilisation. The existence of a stone celt found in Tamil Nadu having markings similar to Indus signs and other evidences are adduced to support this hypothesis. Recent studies of the DNA samples, of a female skeletal-remains, found from Rakhigarhi (of 2500BCE) suggest, that it had DNA that is largely in common with the current South Asian population (see Chapter 2). Thus, the genetic connect of the Indus people with the current South Asian population is intact. This has led further credence to the migration of Harappan people and their, later being identified as *Dravidas*. Some theories also suggest their West/Central Asian origin hypothesis. However, there seems to be no consensus as to any of these above theories and question of origin of the Dravidian people still remains shrouded in mystery.

Dravidian culture and its connect with Indus Valley Civilisation

Whether the Dravidian people were the Indus Valley settlers or not, remains not fully established, but the close contact between the two and the existence of the Dravidian civilisation prior to the Aryan culture establishing itself in North India, is duly accepted by the experts. Archaeological evidences, which suggest a close contact are; discovery of pots in Tamil Nadu with arrowhead symbols similar to that found on seals ofMohenjo-daro; pictograph symbols similar to Indus writing in a cave in Kerala; a stone celt belonging to the 2nd millennium BCE, found in Mayiladuthurai (Tamil Nadu) which is having many more Indus period symbols. The gold ornaments found in the Indus Valley had origin in the gold mines in southern India which suggests a possible trade between the two regions and cultural links. Discoveries at Adichanallur (in Thoothukudi district, Tamil Nadu), of an ancient burial site, indicate close similarity in practices of burial in urns and pots as found in some Indus Valley sites. Further, the Brauhi language spoken in parts of Baluchistan has a lot of words in common with the Dravidian languages.

Mutual influence of Dravidian and Aryan cultures

Whether the Dravida people got pushed because of an advancing Aryan culture, or whether they abandoned the Indus Valley cities due to extreme vagaries of nature, irrespective of the above, experts do agree that both cultures did come in contact with each other and the marks of this cultural influence on both is apparent.

The Sangam period literature remains one of the most important sources of information about the Dravidian culture and society. This literature also talks about the three *Sangams* or academies of seers and experts of different fields which took place in the ancient city of Madurai. These academies or *Sangams* took place in different periods and are variously dated. Some experts believe the oldest Sangam to be held around 2500 BCE or even earlier. But it is generally believed that the last occurred around 300 BCE to 250 BCE. One of these academies is said to have been led by sage Agastya who was a prominent Aryan preacher from northern India. Agastya is said to have spent a substantial period in the Dravida region preaching the Aryan philosophy and other disciplines. His work *Agathiyan* is said to have been the earliest treatise on Tamil grammar. Further, his twelve disciples are said to have composed a number of treatises on literature, grammar, music and dance which are themselves considered salient works of the Sangam period. One such treatise, *Tolkappiyam,* is purported to have been composed around 1000BCE, by his disciple Tolkappiyar, after the loss of *Agathian* in a great deluge (flood). *Tolkappiyam*, extant even today, lays the foundation of Tamil grammar and reveals about the culture and society. The dates of its composition and authorship remain disputed. However, from a cultural perspective, what is relevant is that sage **Agastya**, who finds mentions in Rigveda, is believed to be the **first composer of Tamil grammar** and is largely venerated in the Dravidian culture and his disciples authored seminal works of this culture.

Dravidian influence on the Aryan culture

The **Dravidian influence on the Aryan culture** is evident in the number of words incorporated in Rigveda from the Dravidian languages. These words and their usage become more in the subsequent Vedic layers after the *Samhitas.* The worship of **Shakti** (or mother goddess) is believed to have permeated the Vedic culture apparently from the Dravidian worship of the mother goddess which is also evident from the Dravidian practice of worship of ***Sapt Matrikas.*** This concept in the Puranic phase finds expression in the tradition of Shaktism and development of Puranic legends related to the different forms of the deity. The concept of **Rudra** and **Pashupati** in vogue in the Dravidian culture also seems to have merged into the Aryan god of Shiva/Mahadeva in the Later-Vedic period. Thus, the two cultures influenced each other over centuries and tended to have a greater confluence towards a culture that eventually emerged in the later Vedic period.

The Sangams and the Dravidian culture

Some of the literary works of the Sangam period which survive to this day, reveal a wealth of information about the people, society, the cultural evolution and the great height the Dravidian civilisation attained. Sangams usually refers to the **three academies** or **Sangams**, the first of which is said to have taken place in the ancient city of Madurai. The three Sangams include the head Sangam, the middle Sangam and the last Sangam. However, the first two Sangams are usually considered only legendary and it is only the last Sangam which is accepted as a historical fact and said to have occurred in the present Madurai. The Sangam period referred to by some experts spans the 6th century BCE to the 3rd century CE. The most important treatises of this period extant today are the *Tolkappiyam,* the *Pattupattu* and the *Ettuthogai.*

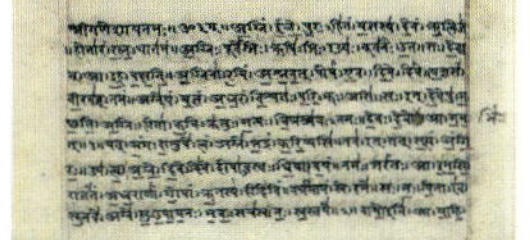

The original manuscripts of these treatises were lost for centuries and were rediscovered in a Shaiva monastery in Kumbakonam only in the 19th century.

The ***Tolkappiyam,*** the oldest surviving literary work is the most ancient work on Tamil grammar and also the oldest non-Sanskrit text. Some experts believe this to be a work from the second Sangam or around the 1st millennium BCE. However, most scholars do agree to a date of 2nd to 1st century BCE for its creation/compilation. The entire work is divided into three sections or books (*atikaram*). It has nearly 1612 sutras which provide the rules of etymology, phonology, orthography, sentence structure, semantics, prosody etc.

The ***Pattupattu*** which is a collection of 10 long poems can be said to be the earliest work of Tamil literature. The poems in the anthology range from 100 to 800 lines and are thus truly a substantive literary work. The most important of this collection is the *Nakkirars Tirumurukarrupattai* (A Guide to Lord Murugan).

Ettutogai, or the 'collection of eight', is another poetic literary work from this period, which along with the Pathupattu/*Pattupattu* forms the compilation of 18 ancient great literary works. These eight anthologies are a compilation of 2371 poems, each with 3 to 40 lines. These poems are attributed to nearly 470 poets whose names can be arrived at from their works. Among these, nearly 30 are believed to be women. These poets in themselves were from different parts of the region and engaged in different occupations. However, in nearly 100 stanzas the names of their authors cannot be worked out.

The poems of the Sangam period are broadly classified as *Akam* or *Agam or Aham,* meaning, 'inner' or 'love' and *Puram,* meaning 'outer' or 'public life'. These poems are of varied themes, including love and emotion, worship of deities, veneration of the king and his works and even on the theme of war. Thus, these grand literary works were truly a reflection of the intellectual and institutional elements of the society and its culture.

Another monumental Tamil work was the composition of the *Thirukkural* by the sage Thiruvalluvar. The celebrated treatise divided into three books and 10 chapters, contains 1330 kurals which are short couplets of seven words. Each of the kurals enunciates precepts to guide humanity to a noble living. The subjects of these couplets are broadly based on virtue (*aram*; dharma) wealth (*porul*; artha) and love (*inbam*; kama). These three are to have the objective of attaining salvation (*veedu*). Also referred to as the Tamil Veda or the divine book, the *Thirukkural* is believed to have been composed around 300 BCE to 500 CE. While some scholars believe the period of authorship to be around the end of the third Sangam period, others, based on linguistics, assign a later date of around 500 CE. Kural which is also one of the earliest of Tamil works containing the disciplines of metaphysics and epistemology is also considered among the greatest of works of ethics and morality.

Dravidian Society and Culture and Its Salient Elements

The Dravidian society, like the early societies, had agriculture as the substratum of socio-economic activity. As evident from the period's literature and archaeological findings, the industry of weaving and dyeing of cotton and woollen cloth, besides shipping was in vogue. The making of gold silver and other jewellery with stone inlays, ivory products making, metal works, making of leather products was well known. Trade with land and sea was established, particularly with many Southeast Asian regions in the Malaya peninsula. Maritime trade existed even with far of Egypt and the Roman empire, the coins of which have been found.

The society was centred around kingship with the king, a monarch (also called *Mannam, Ko, Vendan, Korravan*, *Iraivan* etc.) being the centre of administration. Social division of labour and different classes existed and were partly based on birth and choice of occupation. A rigid caste system does not seem to have been the order of the day. Many Dravidian societies were matriarchal, and social standing and respect of women was much higher.

The religious beliefs and practices seem to be of an early form of ***Shaktism*** and ***Shaivism***. The reverence to the mother goddess and Saptamatrikas is believed to have existed in this period. Shiva was worshipped as *Rudra* or *Pashupati*. **Murugan**, (also known as Skanda, Karthikeya and Subrahmanya), the warrior lord, was another revered deity of this period.

The Dravidian culture seems to have flourished into larger settlements and cities. Reference to an ancient city of **Madurai** is received where the first Sangam was held, while the second in **Kaptapuram** and third in present **Madurai**, after the earlier two cities were lost in the deluge. There was substantial growth in scientific disciplines as seen in irrigational practices and the building of dams etc. A **system**

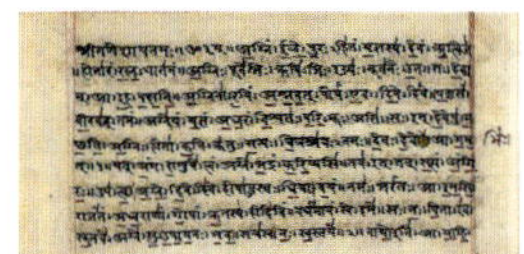

of calendars is known to be developed. A well-**developed script and language** with defined grammar and many **literary works** existed out of which only a few have survived. These are evident in the works of *Tolkappiyam*, *Pattupattu* and *Ettutogai*, whose manuscripts exist even today. The subjects and their depth are reflective of a literary and cultural evolution spanning multiple disciplines. Most importantly, the authors of these works were not a handful of seers, but many scholars including women distributed in the region, with works itself being indicative of the intellectual achievements of a society. Further, the **very conduct of these Sangams is reflective of a highly evolved culture** with excellence in different disciplines and great social respect for them.

EMERGENCE OF JAINISM, BUDDHISM AND SRAMANA TRADITIONS: THE AGE OF PLURALISM

With the emergence of **Buddhism, Jainism** and other **Shramana traditions** in the 6th century BCE, a cultural confluence of the Vedic, Buddhist and Jain cultures emerged. The latter were opposed to Vedic rituals, Brahmanical order, Varnashrama system, idol worship and animal sacrifices, which were some of the key features the Vedic system. This period from 600 BCE to 200 BCE was not only a phase of cultural confluence but also of socio-culture upheaval, as each faith vied for permeating in and occupying the socio-religious space. But what emerged from this social churning was a pluralistic and syncretic culture not bound by the dogma and capable of assimilating new thoughts and practices. Thus, **socio-cultural evolution and co-existence of multiple faiths** can truly be said to the characteristic of this age.

The doctrine of ahimsa or non-violence or non-injury to any sentient being was a defining socio-cultural and spiritual influence of this age. Although in vogue in the earlier Vedic systems too, the Jain doctrine followed by the Buddhist thought, brought the concept of ahimsa in centre stage of the religious and social life. The principle of ahimsa was the cornerstone of the Jain metaphysics, spiritual doctrine and its ethical conduct. It believed in the essence of life or soul to be existent in all sentient beings and thus there being a universal interconnect. Killing, or injury to such beings, meant a further entrenchment of the soul-body bondage, and further spiritual decay. Both Jainism and Buddhism strongly believed in the precept of Ahimsa and this meant **opposition to the Vedic sacrifices of animals**, a ritual accepted and practiced for centuries and even hallowed.

But most importantly, ahimsa was not just limited to the prohibitory precept of non-injury of any sentient being, but to the positive attribute of boundless and **loving compassion** for all. Termed as *metta* (*maitri* in Sanskrit), it was this attribute, which endowed **universalism** to the doctrine of ahimsa. This, in turn, was an integral element of *Panchamahavrat* in Jainism and *Tri-ratna* in Buddhism and thus it cast a profound social influence in this phase of cultural history. A few centuries down the chronology of time, we see the building of the colossal Mauryan empire by emperor Ashoka on the very foundation of ahimsa and universalism. This was an empire that in terms of the spread of political boundary reached a pinnacle and remained the most colossal of Indian empires even in the centuries to come. But more significantly, the essence of this philosophy and the socio-cultural-religious influence spread much beyond the vast boundaries of Bharatvarsha (India) and even to a significant part of the world, influencing it for the next two millennia and more.

Karma as the basis of salvation was also another spiritual concept emphasised by the two faiths. Although similar theories of karma were also propounded in the Upanishadic philosophy, what was significant was the singular emphasis by Buddhism and Jainism on karma and the rejection of ritualism as the basis of spiritual evolution. Even the concept of a **personal god** as the creator and the sustainer of the universe on whose grace the emancipation of the human soul was dependent or whose wrath was to befall on the vile, was completely rejected. The karma of the being was the basis of its salvation and its providence. The 'laws of the universe' were the sustainers of the cosmos. Thus, ritualism of appeasement, or the rites borne out of fear, had no role in the liberation of the soul and were summarily rejected. Hence, it shifted the complete onus of spiritual gain on the being and his/her endeavour.

Thus, emerged a heterodox school of thought that rejected the concept of a **personal god**, the infallibility of **ritualism in Vedas, (**which decried the **animal sacrifices)** and emphasized **universalism and ethical conduct**.

A new **inclusive social order** was clearly in the offing. The **Brahmanical supremacy** and orthodoxy were rejected. The Brahmins were not to be the only interpreters of the Holy Scriptures, and neither the spiritual education was to remain the exclusive preserve of a specific varna. The common folk irrespective of their birth and varna were all eligible to be a part of the religious order which included the Brahmins and Shudras alike. Thus, every being could strive and hope for salvation and spiritual evolution. The

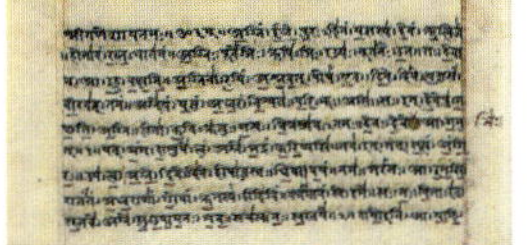

Sangha of Buddhism and the order of monkhood of the Jainism made no class or varna distinction in admittance of people in its fold. The only requisite was the belief in its doctrine and acceptance of its practices. Further, the concept of a particular *ashram* (stage of life) for renunciation was not necessary in the two faiths, and a person could adopt the life of monkhood at any stage.

While the members of the royal household like Rahul (son of Buddha) were accepted in the Sangha, so were Amrapali (a courtesan) and Angulimal (the reformed dacoit). While Sariputta the chief disciple of Buddha and Mahakashyap, another venerated disciple, were from the Brahmanical order, Upali, a barber, was entrusted the responsibility as the chief disciple in matters of Vinaya, and Sunita, a scavenger later on became an *arahant*.

Even **women** whose social status had been ebbing over the centuries were admitted in monkhood and referred to as the ***sadhvis*** (in Jainism) and ***theris*** (in Buddhism). Mahaprajapati Gautami was the first woman to be admitted to the Buddhist Sangha. They made significant contributions to the spiritual cause. ***Therigatha***, a class of scripture that was a part of the *Khudakka Nikaya* of *Sutta Pitaka*, was composed by the elder *bhikkhunis* and *theris*. Thus, there emerged a formal and inclusive **order of monks** which steered the evolution of *dharma* and the conduct of the monks and laity over centuries.

The **spiritual discourses were in the Prakrit languages** (Pali, Ardha-magadhi etc.) and not limited to Sanskrit, enabling the common folk to comprehend the message and be integrated in this quest for socio-spiritual elevation. Further, the followers of Buddhism, Jainism and other Sramana traditions were not restricted to the monks who had denounced the household but also included the house-holders and laity, for whom more benign social-spiritual conduct was acceptable rather than the strict codes of monkhood. The reliance on the spoken language of the masses also gave a fillip to the **education of the common folk** in the Jain, Buddhist and other traditions, thus creating a more inclusive social order, a far cry from the social segmentation of the Varna system.

A rational approach to spiritual and epistemological inquiry was another seminal contribution of this age. The basic premise of Jain and Buddhist doctrines was the theory of cause and effect. This is best captured in the words of Buddha in **Dhammapada** where he states;

"*Everything has a cause and produces an effect. This simple principle governs the whole universe, gods and men, heaven and earth. It is applicable not only to this vast universe stretching through boundless space, with its dazzling world systems and endless series of alternations of growth and decay but also to the events of human life and affairs of history. If we can detect and eliminate the cause of suffering, suffering itself will disappear.*" (*The Dhammapada* by Dr S. Radhakrishnan)

A similar approach is adopted by the Jain doctrine which considers the interplay of karma in the framework of the governing laws to be squarely responsible for our lives and their events. Further, both the schools decried blind faith and emphasised on the understanding of the reasoning to be essential in the appropriate adoption of the doctrine and its practice.

The conception of the Jain theological fundamentals is best exemplified in **Tattvartha Sutra,** an authoritative Jain scripture containing its philosophy. The spiritual discourse displays a unique **scientific enquiry** where in it explains the fundamentals, not just of the theory of karmic causation of the soul-matter bondage (*bandha*), *samvara* (its prevention) and *nirjara* (its elimination) from the province of the soul, but also elucidates the basics of the material world. It conceives matter (*pudgal*) to be composed of *paramanu* (atoms or the primary building blocks of matter) which aggregate together two or more *paramanus* in bonds called *skandhas* (akin to a molecule) and eventually build the simplest of matters to the *panch-bhoot* (the five elements) to the whole of the universe. Indeed, it is a sterling scientific theory that could withstand the test of modern scientific knowledge and enquiry. The theory further considers matter (*pudgal*) to undergo a change in its characteristics (transformation) but the fundamental substance (*paramanu*) remains the same and is indestructible.

The Jain treatises, like the Agamas, further dwell on a variety of topics ranging from **philosophy to mathematics to logic** etc. displaying an abiding **scientific and rational outlook to the spiritual conception**. This scientific and rational approach was further tempered with a sense of **individual inquiry**, thus eschewing any dogmatism and blind faith. This is best exemplified in the following words of Buddha to his disciples in the **Anguttara Nikaya** (fourth *nikaya* of the Sutta Pitaka).

"*This I have said to you O' Kalamas: but you may accept it not because it is the report, not because it is a tradition, not because it is so said in the past, not because it is given from the scripture, not for the sake of discussion, not for the sake of a particular method, not for the sake of careful consideration, not for the sake of forbearing with wrong*

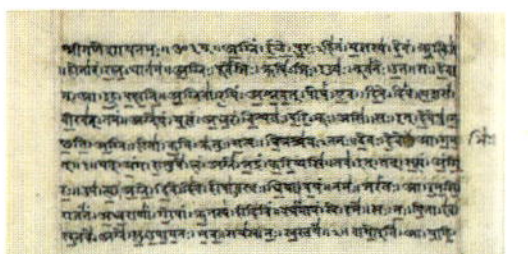

views, not because it appears to be suitable, not because your preceptor is a recluse; ***but if you yourself understand that this is so meritorious and blameless, and when accepted, it is for benefit and happiness, then you may accept it.***

The emergence of the **many sramana traditions** and **the plurality of faith** and belief systems was another salient aspect of this cultural phase. Literally, the word sramana refers to **'labour and toil'**. Thus, it implied the spiritual-toil of the class of seekers and ascetics. This phase oversaw the emergence of a number of faiths that professed its distinct philosophies at times radically different from the mainstream Vedic thought. Thus, the Sramana tradition began to refer to those schools of philosophy and spiritualism that were **non-Vedic and did not accept the infallibility of the Vedas.** They were also referred to as *nastik* or **heterodox schools** for rejecting the Vedic epistemology.

While Jainism with its emphasis on **Ahimsa** and ethical conduct and Buddhism eulogising the **middle path** and *Dhamma*, soon rose to prominence and had greater social acceptance than the rest, schools like the **Ajivika**, the **Carvaka**/Charvaka, the **Ajnana** etc., also arose around this time. Some of these existed even prior to Mahavira and Buddha and had a good following. But down the centuries they did not enjoy the same social acceptance as the other two faiths. However, they did contribute their unique philosophies to this age of **spiritual seeking**.

The *Ajivikas*, led by Makkhali Ghosal, were a **school of fatalists**, believing in the soul and consequences of nature and its laws. They professed asceticism akin to Jainism. However, they denied the existence of free will and role of karma in altering the predetermined course of our lives.

Ajita Kesakambli of the *Lokayata-Charvaka* school believed in **materialism**, and denied the philosophy of karma, after-life or rebirth etc. It believed that with death, humans disintegrated into the constituent elements and thus there were no fruits of good or evil deeds.

Ajnana **School** led by **Sanjaya Bellathiputta** was **agnostic and sceptic** disbelieving in the existence or non-existence of afterlife, good, evil, karma, soul etc. The **school of amoralism** propagated by **Purana Kasyapa** did not believe in inherent morality or immorality of any act.

However, the most important aspect of this phase was the questioning of the extant theology and breaking away from the dogma. The support these faiths enjoyed, particularly Jainism and Buddhism, is a clear indication of their social acceptance. Thus, there was the emergence of numerous doctrines that struck root in the socio-cultural soil and sprouted the saplings of **pluralism.**

Coexistence and tolerance of different faiths and their believers is another salient characteristic of this cultural age. Each of these traditions sincerely believed in its own correctness and at times were critical of the other, but all coexisted and competed for social and political acceptance. **Anekantvada**, a fundamental doctrine of Jainism on non-absolutism, talked of relative perspectives and coexistence of multiple aspects of the same truth. Thus, it was non-critical and accommodative of differing perspectives. Buddha himself preached to his disciples to be tolerant of critics.

Although political patronage was extended to these theologies, the professing of others was never prohibited or discouraged by the royalty or its administration. Bimbisara, a contemporary of Mahavira and Buddha is believed to have supported both faiths. Ashoka, one of the most important patrons of Buddhism, respected and supported other sects too. The Barabar caves were built by him for the Ajivikas as well as for the Buddhists. But the respect for all faiths is best exemplified in the rock edicts of Ashoka where he exhorts all to respect one's own as well as other faiths, thus proclaiming one of the greatest gospels of **peaceful coexistence based on** *Dhamma*.

Ashokan Rock Edicts: A Message of Plurality of Faiths and Peaceful Co-existence.

'The Beloved of the Gods, the king Piyadassi, wishes that all sects may dwell in all places, for all seek self-control and purity of mind. **(Major Rock Edict No.7, Girnar and Dhauli)**

'The beloved of the Gods, ***King Piyadassi, honours all sects*** *and both ascetics and laymen with gifts and various forms of recognition. But the beloved of the Gods does not consider gifts or honour to be as important as the advancement of the essential doctrine of all sects. This advancement takes many forms but its basis is control of one's speech, so as not to extoll one's own sect and disparage another's on unsuitable occasion, ...*

...For ***whosoever praises his own sect or blames other sects****; all out of pure devotion to his own sect, with the view of glorifying his own sect, if he is acting thus, he rather* ***injures his own sect very severely****. But concord is meritorious, (i.e.) that they should both hear and obey each other's morals. For this is the desire of Devanampriya (emperor Ashoka) (viz.) that all sects should be both full of learning and pure in doctrine. And those who are attached to their respective (sects), ought to be spoken to (as follows). Devanampriya does not value either gifts or honours so (highly) as (this), (viz.) that promotion of the essentials of all sects should take place.* **(Major Rock Edict No.12, Girnar and Dhauli).**

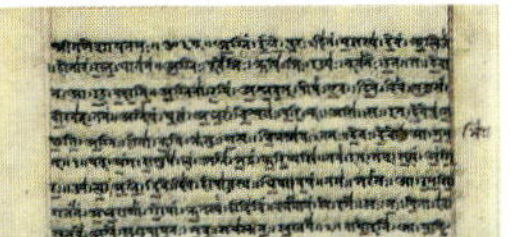

The Mutual Influence and Confluence

The mainstream theological belief systems and the Vedic culture though remained intact and flourished in this age but did not remain uninfluenced by these new thoughts. The concept of ahimsa permeated deep in the Vedic society too. The emphasis on ethics and spiritualism was reignited. Thus, *dharma* and *moksha* started to receive due significance as compared to *artha* and *kama* and the Upanishadic ideals too came into prominence as compared to the oft-emphasised ritualistic practices.

Down the centuries, new philosophical schools of thought emerged within the Vedic system viz. the Samkhya, Yoga and others which assimilated some of the views of the Sramana traditions. Rather, the emergence of these thoughts and the changes in the Vedic system brought a palpable influence on Buddhism too. The religion that decried idol worship became an inspiration for the Gandhara School of Art, which later saw sublime statues of Buddha. This influence was not limited to merely art and other tangible elements. Several aspects of the Vedic thoughts and the belief in a personal god were soon imbibed in mainstream Buddhism which is believed to have later given rise to Mahayana Buddhism. Soon, **Buddha** the heterodox, was to become the **divinity** he decried.

The Shad Darshanas and the Diverse Schools of Hindu Philosophy

The conception of the Shad-darshanas also took place in this period. These were the six branches of Hindu philosophy—*Nyaya, Vaisheshika, Samkhya, Yoga, Purva Mimansa* and *Vedanta*. Some scholars hold that the development of these philosophies took in the period of 200 BCE to 200 CE. These six philosophies are also referred to as the ***astika* philosophies** or the orthodox school, as they accepted the authority of the Vedas and believed in the validity of its doctrines, unlike the *nastik* or unorthodox schools of Buddhism, Jainism and others.

The **Samkhya** was a **rationalist school** whose philosophy revolved around the dualistic concepts of *Purusha* and *Prakriti*. While *Purusha* was the Supreme Consciousness, *Prakriti* implied nature whose bond with the *Purusha* created the *jiva* (the living being). Its belief system of the true knowledge being an emancipator of the *jiva* is considered a combination of rationalism and spiritualism. While *Nyaya*, a **realist school** of philosophy dealt with formal reasoning and logic, *Vaisheshika*, a **naturalist school** postulated the composition and functioning of the physical universe to the fundamental units called *paramanu* (atom). Thus, a spirit of logic, metaphysics and even other sciences were combined with spiritual seeking. The *Yoga* system of philosophy, propounded rationalism, analogous to the *Samkhya* but also expounded the virtues of *karma* (righteous action) as a means of salvation.

The other two schools comprised the **Vedic philosophy**. The former emphasised the rituals and practices and thus was a form of school of **philosophical realism**. The latter emphasised the right knowledge of *Advaita* philosophy or **non-dualistic monism** for salvation. Thus,

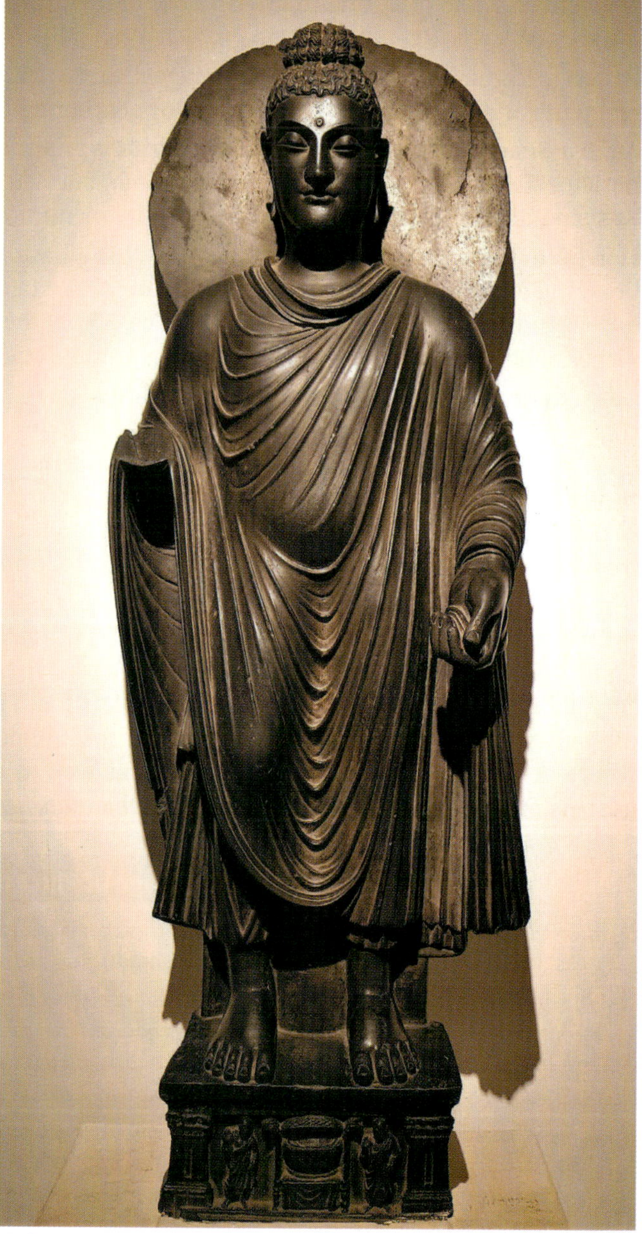

1.21: A sublime standing statue of Buddha from Gandhara School, personifying him as Godhead; location National Museum, New Delhi — photograph by Madhukar K Bhagat

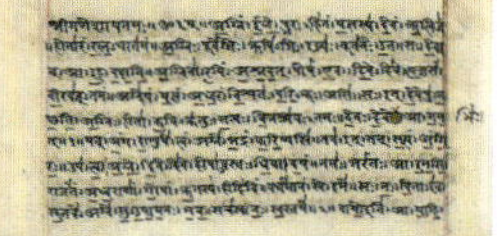

these diverse schools embodied a **liberalist and rational perspective of religious culture**, eventually laying the foundation of a **pluralistic approach to the seeking of the Divine**.

Overall, this was an **age of diverse thoughts and liberation from orthodoxy**, where numerous competing faiths emerged. At times, these multiple faiths exercised mutual influence; however, they did not converge to a singular belief system. Nor did it see the emergence of a predominant theology that could annihilate or subsume the others.

The tangible and non-theological cultural elements of this age were a marked departure from the erstwhile Vedic age. The socio-political administration saw the emergence of the **16 Janapadas** with Magadha amongst the most powerful of all. The **concept of a republic** also saw its birth in the Vajji Sangha of the Licchavis. However, **kingship** remained the main form of political administration. The emergence of Chandragupta Maurya who vanquished the Greeks and the Nandas, led to the emergence of a strong political establishment hitherto unseen. By the time the Ashokan regime ended, the **largest empire ever** whose boundaries covered the entire Indian subcontinent and even beyond, was founded. This influenced all elements of the socio-cultural life.

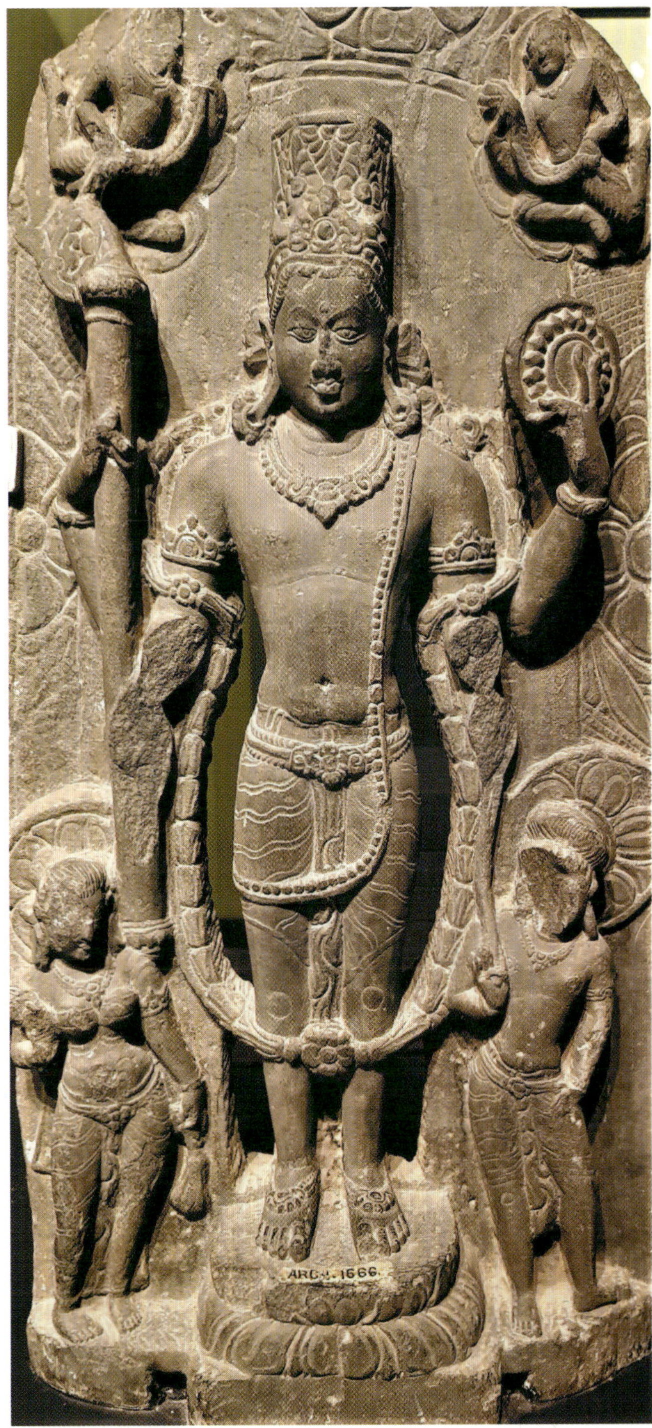

1.22: Lord Vishnu with consorts, the supreme deity in the Puranic age; sculpture in black stone, 12th century CE, Bihar Sharif, Pala period; location Bihar Museum, Patna — photograph by Madhukar K Bhagat

The emergence of **large human settlements and cities** were seen for the first time in more than a millennium (see Chapter 6). Agriculture, trade and commerce were much better organised and expanded. Political administration was diversified as seen from the appointment of officers/administrators for specific fields of work. This is best evident in Ashokan rock edicts where he proclaims the appointment of *mahamatras* (officers in charge for administration and justice) for *dhamma*, welfare of women, family, animals etc.

Stone as a building material gained prominence along with wood, with exquisite palaces such as Ashoka being built. New architecture was flourishing in chaitya, viharas and stupas. The stone pillars carrying Ashokan edicts with large capitals atop, weighing several tons and having mirror-like finish, and dexterous carving of petals, were **engineering and sculptural wonders** of this age. One such pillar at Sarnath, with a lion capital, has bequeathed an enduring legacy to the modern Indian Republic in the form of its **national symbol**. (see Chapter 6)

Literature and other intellectual elements too had a fair share of evolution. Seminal works such as *Shushruta Samhita*, a treatise on medicine and surgery; Panini's *Ashtadhyayi*, the earliest of works on Sanskrit grammar; *Arthashastra* of Kautilya which laid the rules of political-economic administration; *Panchatantra* by Vishnu Sharma and *Charak Samhita*, another fundamental work on medicine; all had birth in this phase. A range of non-canonical literature of Buddhists and Jains in the form of *Jatakas* and others

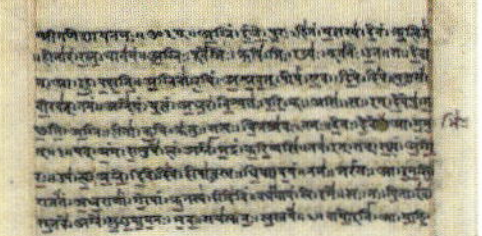

emerged. Schools of logic, mathematics and other sciences and important works in them developed. But most importantly, the emergence of the ancient university of **Taxila**, was truly the crowning glory of this **age of lore and reason**, reflecting the yearning for knowledge and education, of its people.

THE PURANIC AGE

The next cultural phase saw the emergence of **Puranic culture**. The ensuing 800-900 years are referred to as the **golden phase** of the Hindu religion. This also coincided with the emergence of the **Gupta empire**. **The composition of Puranas,** the seminal canonical literature defining this age took place. The Absolute or the Brahman, which was God without attributes, continued to be the core of the Vedantic philosophy, but there was also the emergence of the **personal god** who was the supreme manifest with attributes. The religious emphasis shifted from the Vedic gods who were elements of nature to the **trinity of Brahma, Vishnu** and **Mahesh**. Cults of Vishnu, Shiva and Shakti emerged. Brahmanism saw a revival. *Dharmashastras* or the various schools of personal law and social code and ethics emerged. This was also the **Classical Age** and the next **cultural confluence.**

Puranas: The Texts Defining an Age

The word *Purana* means old or ancient, or historical. The Puranas are a part of the Smriti texts and cover a vast repository of canonical literature. Reference to Puranas is also seen in some Vedic texts such as Atharvaveda where the word *Itihasa-Purana* is referred to in Shatapatha Brahmana, thereby reflecting their antiquity. However, it was only in this age (200 BCE to 700 CE) that they attained popularity and were compiled in the present form (around 400 CE) thus ushering in the **Puranic age**. Overall, 18 Puranas are said to have been composed, which are often recognised as the *Mahapuranas* (main Puranas) and 18 other *Up-Puranas* are also recognised. The *Mahapuranas* are categorised into six main groups in terms of the central deity around which the anthology of tales or the narration of eulogy is built. Thus, there emerged an **age of polytheism.**

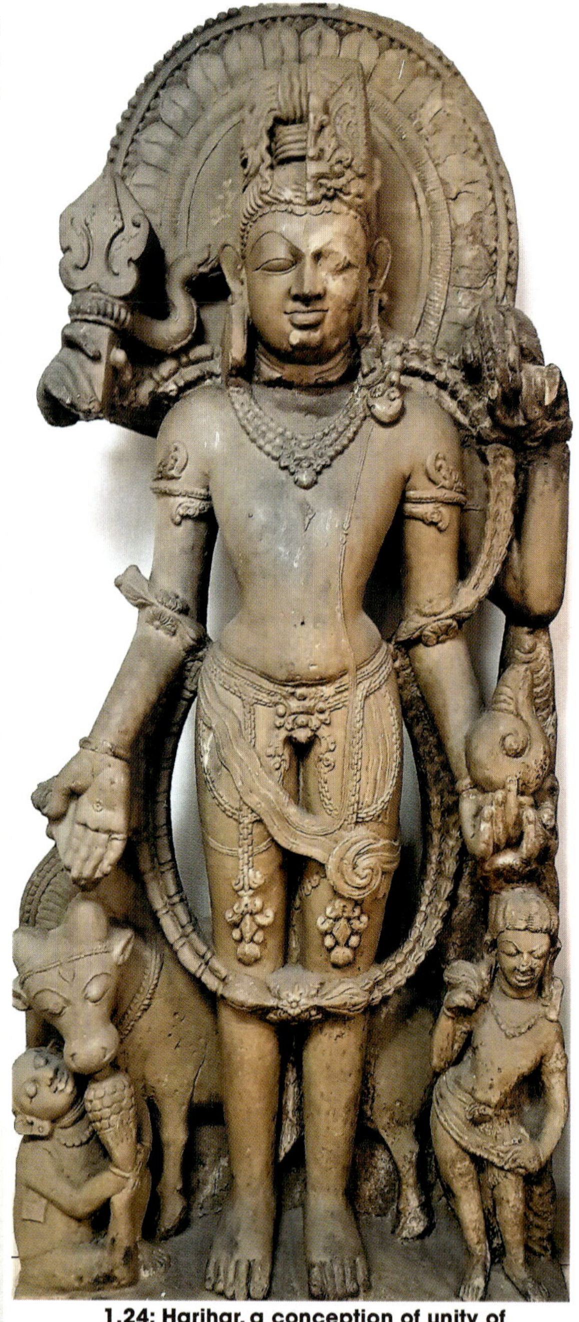

1.24: Harihar, a conception of unity of Vishnu (Hari) and Shiva (Hara). The right half depicts Shiva shown with a trishul (trident), left half depicts Vishnu holding a chakra (discus); sculpture 10th-11th century CE, Madhya Pradesh; location State Museum, Bhopal — photograph by Madhukar K Bhagat

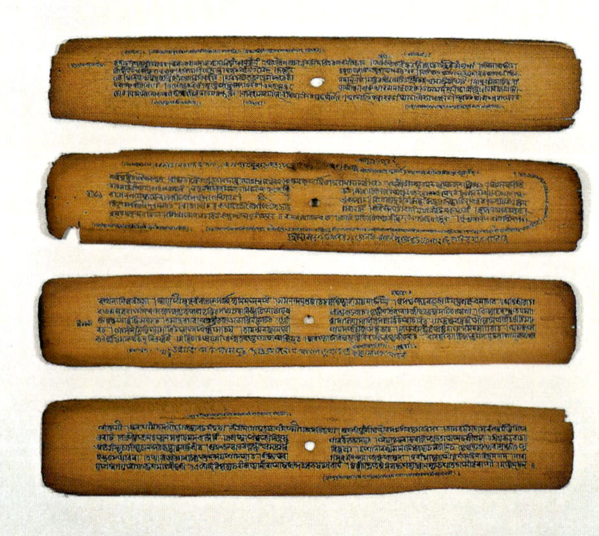

1.23: Bhagavata Purana, one of the Mahapuranas, manuscript on palm leaf, 16th century West Bengal; current location, Los Angeles, Museum of County Art — Wikimedia Commons

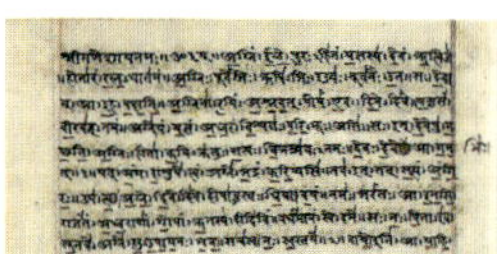

From Profound Monotheism to Vibrant Polytheism

While the Advaita philosophy and Vedic dharma continued to remain the cornerstone of the canonical belief, over a period of time there was a gradual assimilation of the popular beliefs, regional traditions and even local conception of divinity. The notion of the Brahman without attributes remained the pinnacle of the conception of the Supreme, but now the religion also recognised the personal god or the conditioned Brahman. Thus, the belief in divinity as Supreme consciousness expanded to include its physical manifestation. God with attributes became the mainstream thought. This God was perceived varyingly, as **Vishnu, Shiva, Shakti** etc. Further, the emergence of the divine trinity took place, which posited the three cosmological roles of the Supreme in the three physical manifestations of Brahma, Vishnu and Mahesh. The Vedic gods like Indra, Agni, Varun, Mitra, Soma etc. remained to be significant, albeit with the status of demi-gods or *devas* and not that of the cosmological creators. Hence, there emerged a religious tradition that harboured a **profound monism as well as a vibrant polytheism.**

A Syncretic and Assimilative Culture

The Puranic tradition was not only assimilative of divergent philosophical traditions that perceived the Supreme as that with or without attributes but also imparted a vast firmament under which the numerous sectarian traditions flourished and even integrated. The *Mahapuranas* were classified as per a central deity such as Brahma, Vishnu, Shiva, Shakti, Surya, Agni, Ganesh, Skanda etc. Thus, it recognised the extant traditions revolving around the different personal gods and accepted them as a part of the vast Puranic pantheon. Though the sectarian tradition of devotion as seen in Vaishnavism, Shaivism, Shaktism etc. found consonance in them, the Puranas in themselves were pluralistic. The union of **Shiva-Shakti** brought out in the Puranas, is incomplete without the cardinal conception of the female divinity. Thus, this very notion emphasises on integration and harmony of the seemingly diverse forces

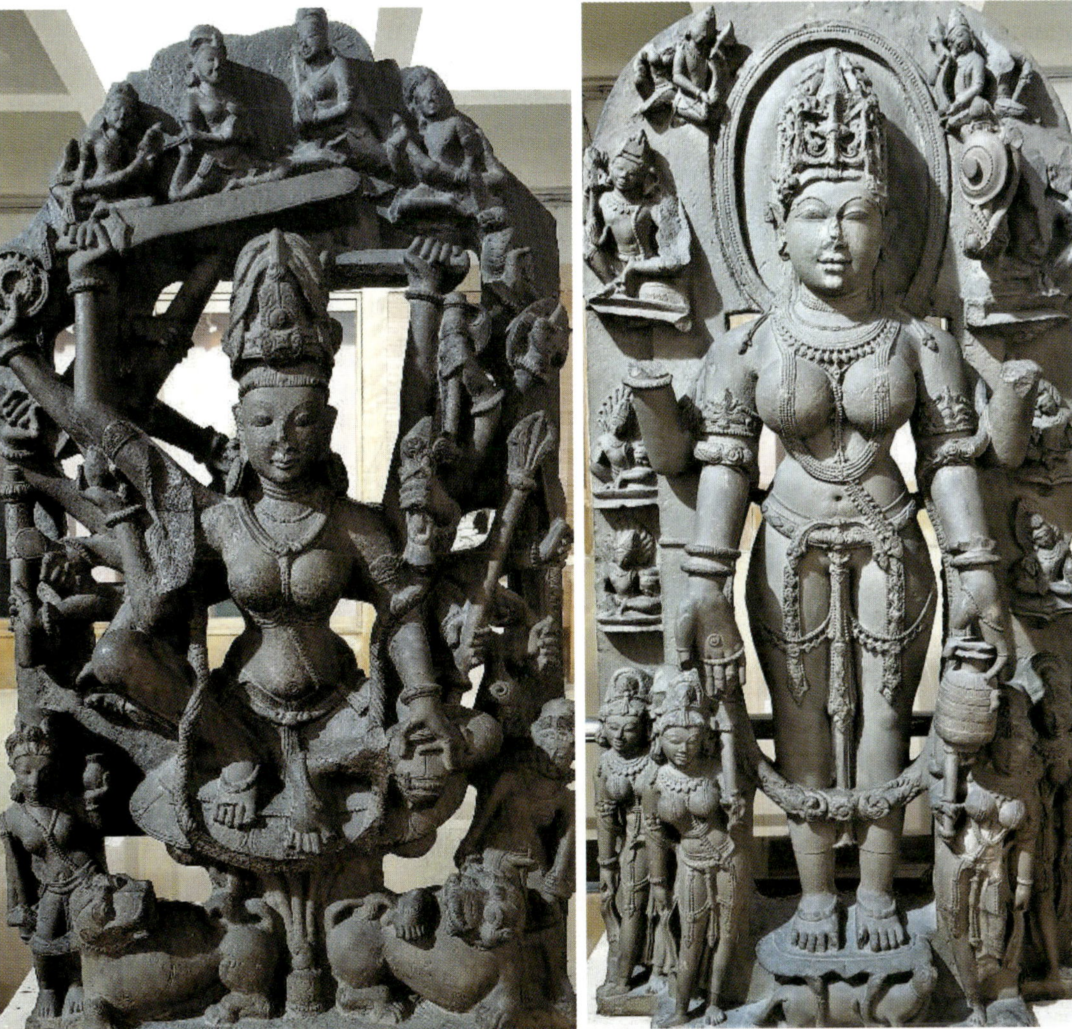

1.25 & 1.26: Goddess Durga (left) & and Goddess Gauri (right) the forms of Shakti and expression of female divinity in the Puranic age; whose worship was popularised by Markandeya Purana and Devi Mahatmya; sculpture 10th-11th century CE, Madhya Pradesh; location State Museum, Bhopal — photograph by Madhukar K Bhagat

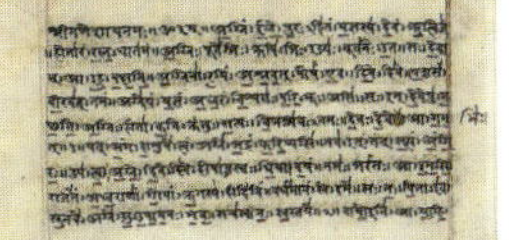

of the cosmos. Similarly, lord Shiva and lord Vishnu the godheads around which two distinct traditions flourished are considered often the manifestation of the same deity. Even the **trinity of Brahma, Vishnu and Mahesh** find a merger in one singular deity referred often as **Mahavishnu** or **Mahashiva**, thereby creating a convergence of the pantheon of Gods and believing in monism and Unity.

The Puranas encompassed the multitude of beliefs, seeing the Divine in all Its grand manifestations. They were not exclusionary or prescriptive as to corral the belief systems into a singular perspective or a dominant doctrine. As **Dr. Radhakrishnan** puts it in the book, *The Hindu View of Life*, '*Puranic Hinduism accepted the significance of different institutions of reality and the different scriptures of the peoples living in India, (sarvagama pramanya).*' Thus, it engendered a theistic pluralism and accommodative culture.

The cult and belief in the Dravidian conception of the ***Saptamatrikas*** and the pre-Vedic mother Goddess finds reflection in the worship of **Shakti** and her numerous manifestations. The concept of **Pashupati** of the pre-Vedic period and **Rudra** of the early Vedic period is integrated into the worship of **lord Shiva**. As per scholars, the legend of one of the chief Dravidian warrior-philosopher gods, **Murugan** or Subramanya gets integrated with the Kartikeya or Kumar in Puranic culture and his legends find expression in the Skanda-purana. While monism and convergence with the Vedantic philosophy remain the cornerstone of Puranas, their all-embracing outward manifestation, offered sufficient space for numerous faiths and belief systems to flourish and even integrate.

The Fountainhead of the Culture of Bhakti

While earlier Vedic traditions were centred on the ritualistic culture (*karma-kanda*) or the profound knowledge (*jnana*) based *Advaitic* spiritualism, the conception of a Supreme manifest with attributes, enabled the evolution of a tradition, centred around a **personal godhead**. Thus **Bhagavata-Purana** (*Srimada Bhagavata* or *Bhagavatam*), amongst the most important and well-known Puranas, is dedicated to the Bhakti (devotion) of Lord Krishna. Many other Puranas are dedicated to Lord Vishnu. **Shiva-Purana**, **Skanda-Purana, Markandeya-Purana, Linga-Purana** and other Puranas which capture the legends of the Lord Shiva, have formed the central tenets of Shaivism. The **Markandeya-Purana** which incorporates ***Devi Mahatmya*** has been the sacred scripture of Shaktism (worship of Goddess Durga and the numerous forms of female divinities). The conception of the ten incarnations of Lord Vishnu also came in vogue. Of these, the incarnations of Sri Ram and Sri Krishna were the most popular.

The Age of Smritis

The Puranic culture also paved the way for the popularity of Smriti texts such as **Ramayana, Mahabharata** and other traditions that were centred on the reincarnation of the Godheads. These Smritis by some accounts are said to have been compiled in this age, while some scholars believe them to be of much greater antiquity. However, there is a general acceptance that it was in the Puranic age that the Smritis of Ramayana and Mahabharata became popular. Along with these Smritis emerged a culture inspired by their values and ethics. These manifested in the canonical literature and **other tangible elements of this age**.

An Encyclopedic Account of a Civilisation

The Puranas were not just literature reflecting the theological beliefs of the age. They were indeed more than a treatise on the practice of devotion. Their extensiveness and the bewildering diversity of topics covered by them are truly encyclopaedic. Five key subjects referred to as the *panch-lakshanas* (five signs) are integral to Puranas. These include; ***Sarga***-the subject of the creation of the universe; ***Pratisarga***-their recreation after dissolution or secondary creation; ***Vansha***-the genealogy of gods and also of sages; ***Manvantra***-the creation of the human race and the account of the first human beings (*Manus)* in the numerous secondary creations and ***Vansanucharitam***-the genealogical and historical account of the solar and lunar dynasties. Thus, they functioned as a repository of cosmological hypotheses as well as a historical account of its age.

The **description of the various gods and their incarnations** is also an integral element of their composition. The **Bhagavata** comprising nearly 18000 shlokas (verses) describes the numerous *Avatars* of lord Vishnu (Sri Rama, Sri Krishna, Narasimha etc.), besides that of the *bhakta avatars* (incarnation of devotees) such as Prahalad, Narada, Kapila etc. The **Skanda Purana**, the longest of Puranas comprising a mammoth 81,100 verses, recounts the birth of Skanda (also known as Kartikeya and Murugan,) the son of Shiva and Parvati. It describes the narratives of him as the leader of the army of *devas*. The **Garuda Purana,** which centres around lord Vishnu is arranged as a dialogue between the deity (lord Vishnu) and his

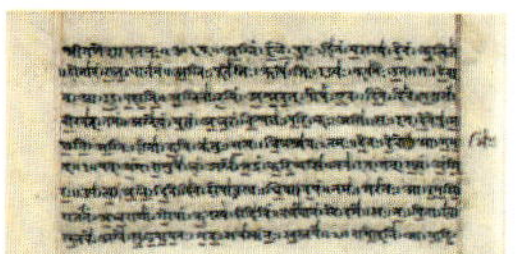

vahana (celestial vehicle) *Garuda*. This Purana covers an astounding range of topics including cosmology, numerous gods and their relationship, philosophies of *Yoga* and *Samkhya*, *moksha*, *karmic* cycles, rebirth and even the Upanishadic philosophy. The geography of *Bharatavarsha* (India), sites of pilgrimage, account of the salient rivers, diseases and medicines, astronomy, astrology and Hindu calendar system, architecture of homes and temples, rites of passage, different virtues to be emulated, duties of king and statecraft and even rules of grammar and genre of literature are some of the topics described in its wide array. Thus, the Puranic culture also engendered a tradition of repositing the diverse social knowledge for posterity.

The Golden Age

This was also the golden age of Hinduism. The Brahmanical religion staged a resurgence. Support of royalty from some of the Kushana rulers and later from the Gupta dynasty fuelled the growth of Hinduism for the next half a millennium and more. Although Buddhism and Jainism too remained in reckoning, the Brahmanical religion had again become the mainstream theology. The religious philosophy now incorporated not only the Vedantic thought and the Varnashrama dharma but also the tradition of personal god and devotion to the deity.

Another defining feature of the Puranic age was the conception of the **Dharmasutras** and the **Dharmashastras,** a genre of theological texts that prescribed the codes of righteous conduct, ethics and moral principles (*dharma*). These governed the discharge of individual and social duties for different classes (*varna*) in different stations (*ashramas*) of life, be it for *Brahmacharya* (student-hood), *Grihastha* (house-holdership), *Vanaprastha* (retirement from

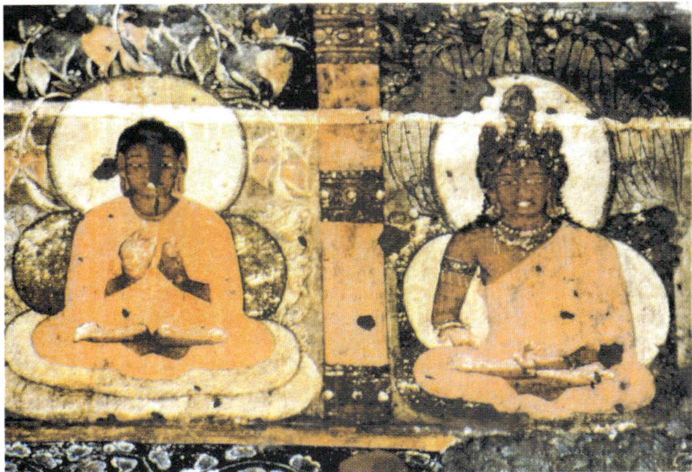

1.27: Buddha (left) and Maitreya Buddha (future Buddha) depicted in a painting on a door panel in cave no. 17 in Ajanta

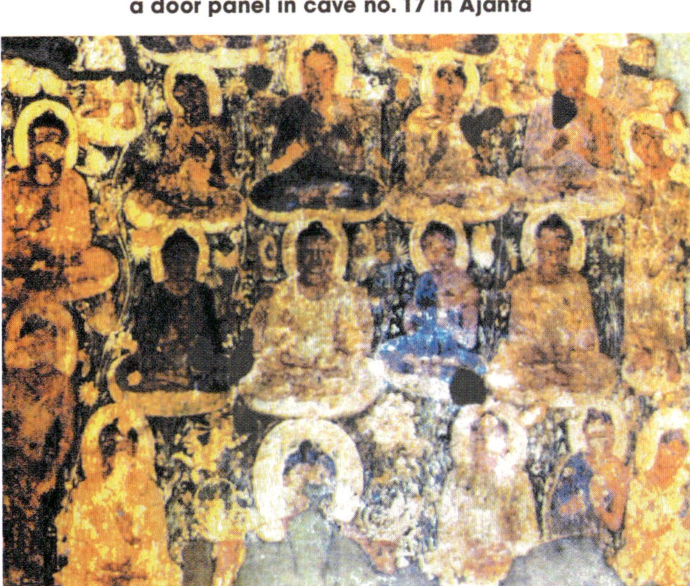

1.28: Painting in cave 1 in Ajanta depicting the anecdote of Mahapratiharya or the miracle of Shravasti. The story depicts one of the rare incidents where Buddha performs miracles. This was to affirm his spiritual powers before King Prasenjit of Kosala, in a challenge by six ascetics doubting his spiritual powers.

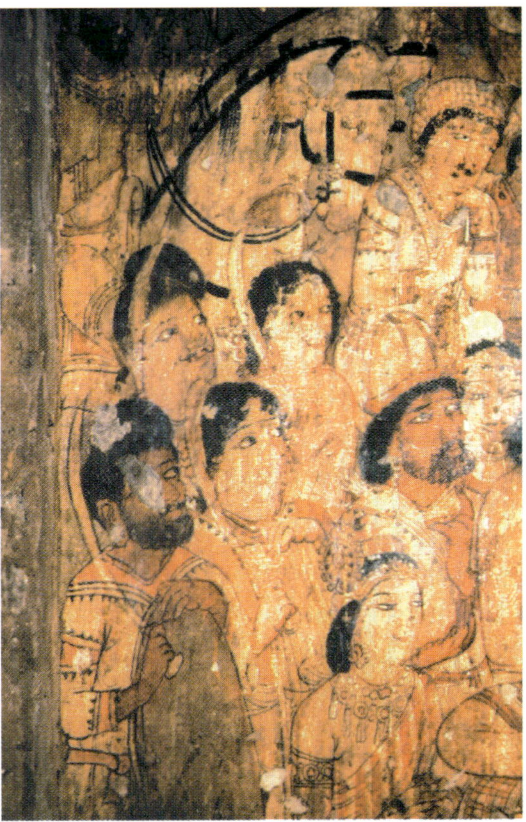

1.29: Painting in cave 17 Ajanta depicting people of different lands/non-natives listening to Buddha's sermon of Dharma on his descent from heaven

1.27, 1.28 & 1.29: Ajanta Paintings, an epitome of the tangible elements of ancient Indian culture — Courtesy, Maharashtra Tourism

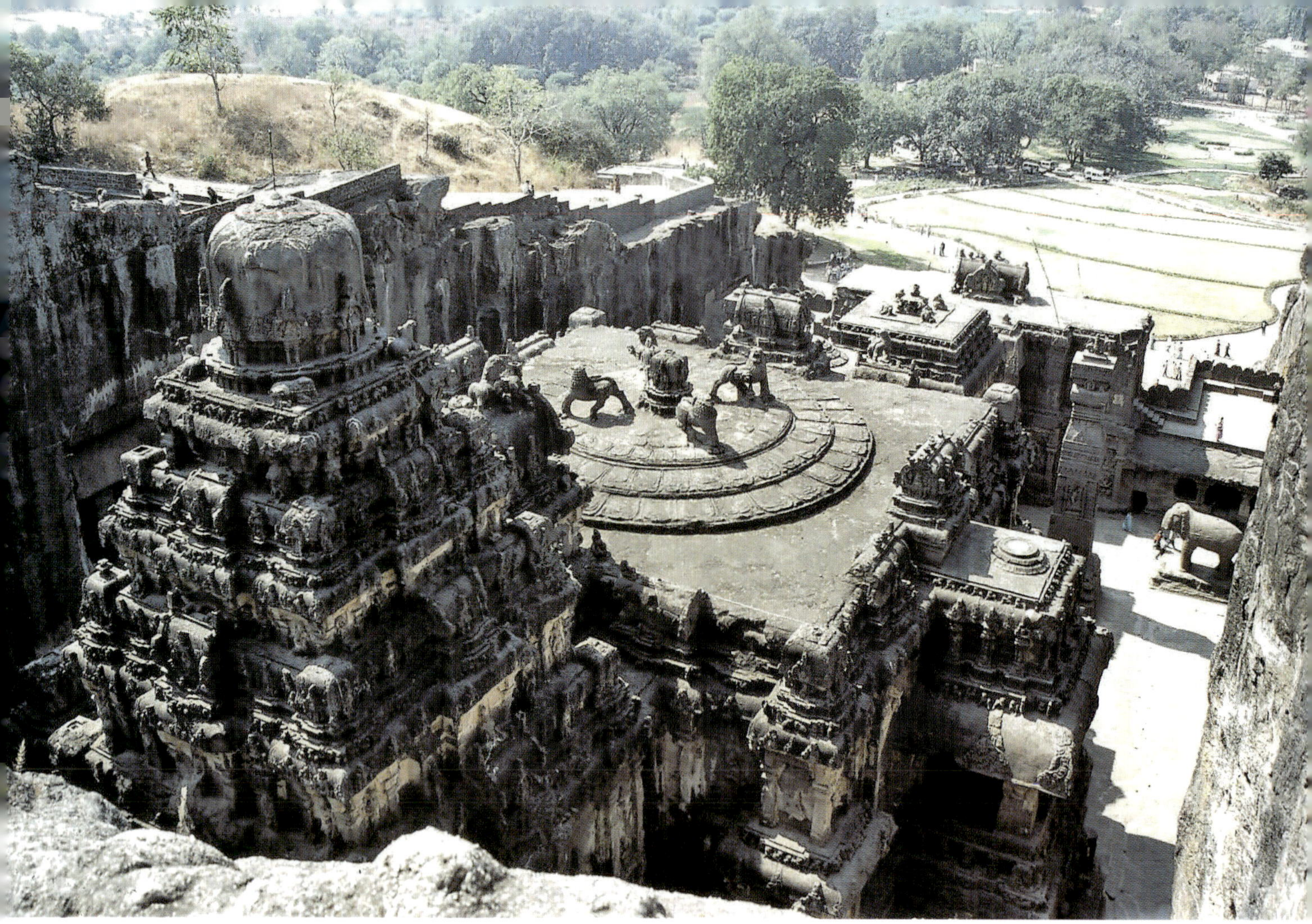

1.30: Rockcut Kailasa temple at Ellora Caves; largest monolithic temple, a wonder of ancient age — Courtesy, Maharashtra Tourism Development Corporation

social affairs) and *Sanyasa* (renunciation). The codes of ethics and duties of different sections, be it the kings or the brahmins etc. were all governed by these treatises. They also contained the rules of inheritance and the laws of civil and criminal justice for society.

The Dharmashastras are said to be many in number (between 18 and 100). They emanate from the Dharmasutras, which in turn are a part of the Kalpa *Vedanga*. While the Dharmasutras of Apastambha, Gautama, Baudhyayana and Vashistha have survived to this day, the Manu-smriti, Yajnavalkya-smriti, Narada-smriti and Vishnu-smriti are the extant Dharmashastras. Thus, through these treatises the codes of conduct and specific personal and social laws were codified, thereby integrating and providing a force of sustenance for the Aryan society. Since their conception in the Puranic age, the Dharmasutras and Dharmashastras have shaped the discourse of Hindu society for the next two millennia.

The Puranic age also encompassed the **golden period of Indian history**, besides that of Hinduism, particularly in the reign of the Guptas (320 CE to 550 CE). This was also **the Classical Age**, the period in which culture, art, sciences, philosophy, economy, literature, mathematics, astronomy, architecture, sculpture, agriculture, trade commerce administration and other pursuits of human life reached unsurpassed heights. The political stability and sovereignty over a large part of India coupled with an efficient and people-oriented administration heralded an age of prosperity and progress.

This was the age when the **Nalanda Mahavihara** was founded and flourished. Along with the other Mahavihara universities of this age, including the **Vallabhi** (Valabhi) in Gujarat and **Pushpagiri** in Orissa, the dawn of an age of learning took place. The world-famous murals of **Ajanta**, the rock-cut caves and sculptures of **Ellora, Elephanta, Udayagiri** and **Khandagiri** were the contributions of this age.

The field of sculpture saw the emergence of the indigenous **Mathura** and **Sarnath** schools of art which were worthy successors of the **Gandhara** and **Amaravati** schools which too flourished in the Puranic age. The beginning of **free-standing temples** as seen in the Dashavatara temple at Deogarh and Chaturmukhlinga temple at Nachna, marked the beginning of a new age of temple construction and architecture.

The Puranic age also witnessed the emergence of a range of canonical literature of Hinduism like Puranas, Smritis and Dharmashastras which were either composed or compiled. Buddhist Pitakas and

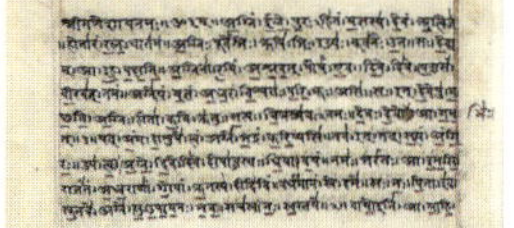

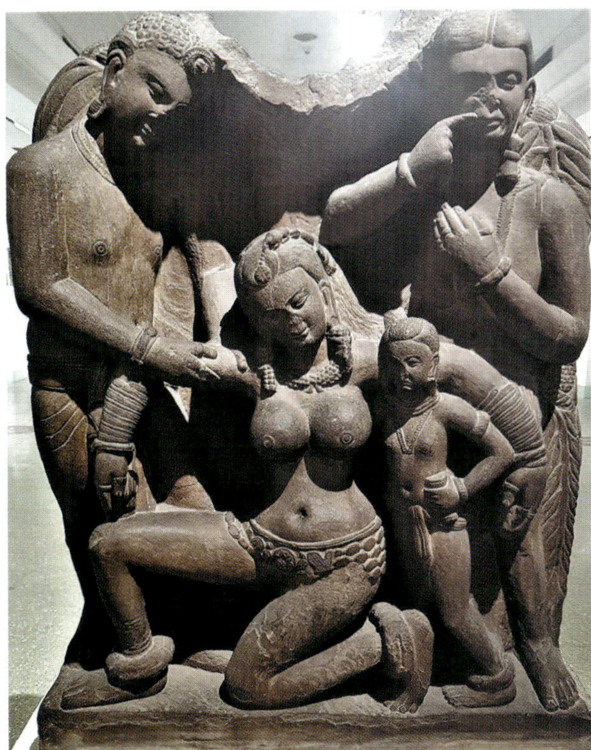

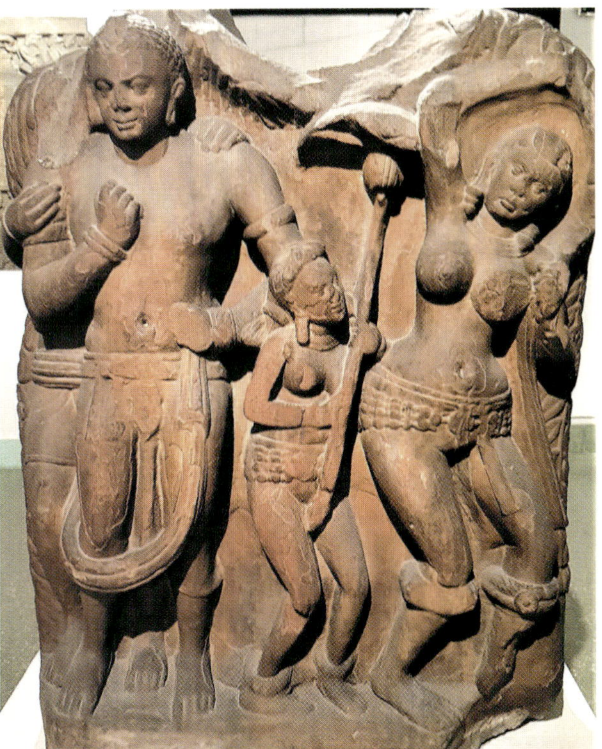

1.31 & 1.32: The sculpture of the 'The House of Courtesan, Vasantasena', a unique work with carving on both sides of the stone slab of a red sandstone, a work of Mathura school, Kushana period, 2nd century CE; location National Museum, New Delhi — photographs by Madhukar K Bhagat

Jain Agamas and sutras (like Tattvarthasutra) were the other canonical texts that were compiled in written form and widely propagated.

This was also the age of **classical Sanskrit literature**. Notable literary figures like **Bhasha, Sudraka, Ashvaghosha, Kalidasa, Bharavi, Bhatti, Magha, Vishakhadatta, and Dandin**, among others contributed richly to Indian literature. *Swapnavasavadatta* of Bhasa, *Mrichhaktika* of Sudraka, *Abhijnanashakuntalam* (and other texts) of Kalidasa, *Mudrarakshasa* of Vishakhadatta and many other literary creations of this age are considered all-time great classics.

This was an era of unprecedented growth of arts, science mathematics, astronomy, medicine and other disciplines. **Natyashashtra** of Bharata, a treatise on different art forms, Panini's **Ashtadhyayi**, a treatise on Sanskrit grammar, **Kamasutra** of Vatsayayana, **Yogasutra** of Patanjali, **Panchatantra** of Vishnu Sharma, **Aryabhatiya** of Aryabhatta, **Brihat-Samhita** of Varahamihira and many other singular treatises were composed in this period.

Approximation of the **value of (Pi)**, the concept of **earth rotating** on its axis, explanation of **solar and lunar eclipses** (by Aryabhata), concept of **planetary motion** (by Varahmihira), formal rules for **computing with zero** (by Brahmagupta), writing of numbers in the **decimal system** form, and the use of a circle for zero (by Bhaskara-1) were some such ground-breaking concepts which the European nations had to wait for another millennium to understand and discover.

It was an age of great prosperity for the **Dravida region** too, which saw similar progress in all realms of society; under the Vakatakas in central India and the Pallavas further south. The region also flourished in the reign of the Chalukyas and the other dynasties. The Puranic age also overlaps with the third of the Sangams which saw unprecedented progress and laid the cultural foundations of the society for the coming centuries. Treatises of the Sangam period extant today including the *Tolkappiyam*, the *Pathupattu* and the *Ettutogai* reveal the growth of language and literature. Trade and commerce with kingdoms in Srilanka, Burma (Myanmar) and Mainland Southeast Asia were established, eventually leading to the emergence of the maritime power of the Cholas in the ensuing centuries. The Brahmanical traditions also saw an upsurge in the region, and by the end of the Puranic age culminated in the Nayanar and the Alvar movements of Shaivism and Vaishnavism, which heralded the next epoch of the cultural evolution.

The Golden Prime of India: The Rule Under the Guptas

The cultural uprising was based upon the central idea underlying Dharma from early times. It predicated an unalterable faith in human endeavour, self-restraint (*samyama*) and self-discipline (*tapas*). Emphasis was laid on individual experience and becoming, rather than on belief and the scriptural word; it was reached only when a man could shed his limitations and become divine in this life. Running through a diversity of religious beliefs and social outlooks, it also laid an emphasis on the observance of the great vows— *mahavratas*—of non-violence, truth, non-stealing, continence and non-possession as essential steps in progress. All conduct, in order to be worthy of respect, had to be harmonised and regulated by ethical and spiritual values calculated to help the fulfilment of this ideal. The four Gupta emperors, (omitting, of course, the ignoble Ramagupta) in maintaining the ideals of a *chakravarty*, made the state at one and the same time powerful, stable, dynamic and happy. The age saw the speculative thought among others of Vasubandhu and the Nayanmars; the perfect lyric and drama of Kalidasa; the astronomical discoveries of Varahamihira; the iron pillar of Delhi; the beginnings of the structural temples; the beauty of the early Ajanta frescoes; the rise of Vaishnavism and Shaivism; the completion of the Mahabharata and the composition of Vayu-Purana and the Matsya-Purdnas. The empire was not merely based on conquests or administrative efficiency; its greatness lay in its integral outlook. Its strength was based as much on military strength as on internal order and economic plenty; the sap of its vitality was drawn from the roots of ancient tradition and race memory which they maintained, re-interpreted and replenished. The upsurge of the Kshatriya hierarchs of Madhyadesa and Magadha, loyally pledged to stability, constituted the steel-frame of the imperial structure. Nor was the splendour of the empire an isolated phenomenon surrounding the individuality of the rulers. The people, having discovered in their traditional way of life something noble and splendid, only saw it reflected in the greatness of their rulers.

...The Gupta emperors became the symbols of a tremendous national upsurge. Life was never happier, **our culture never more creative than during the Golden Prime of India.**

Dr. K.M. Munshi

(Excerpts from the foreword to the book,' The Classical Age'; A Bharatiya Vidya Bhavan publication)

The Enduring Legacy

The **Puranic age shaped the coming centuries like no other**. It left an enduring legacy in all walks of life, be it the emergence of the personal god, the cult of devotion, the popularity of the Smritis, the concept of incarnations, the codification of laws in the Dharmasutras, the emergence of grand universities, the free-standing temples, the literary classics, the scientific theories and mathematical concepts or the flourishing trade and commerce. But the most significant legacy of this culture was the **syncretic tradition** of devotion which encompassed even the seemingly divergent beliefs and which proved to be a **singular factor of integration** of the society for the coming millennium and more.

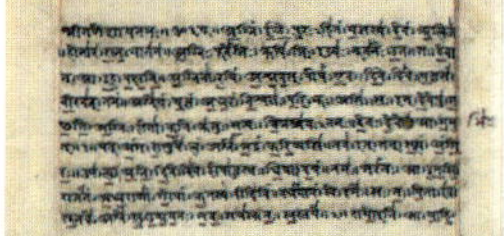

2

The Indus Valley Civilisation and Harappan Culture

> *If I were asked under what sky the human mind has most fully developed some of its choicest gifts, has most deeply pondered on the greatest problems of life and has found solutions, I should point to India.*

Max Mueller

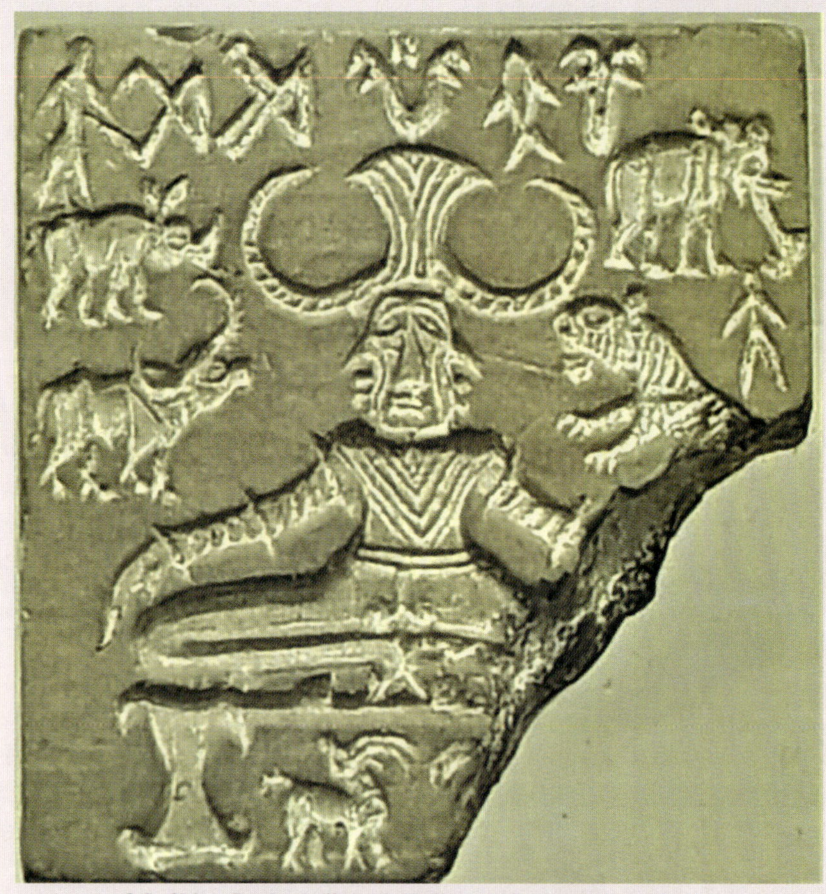

2.1: Shiva Pashupati seal; National Museum, New Delhi — photograph by Madhukar K Bhagat

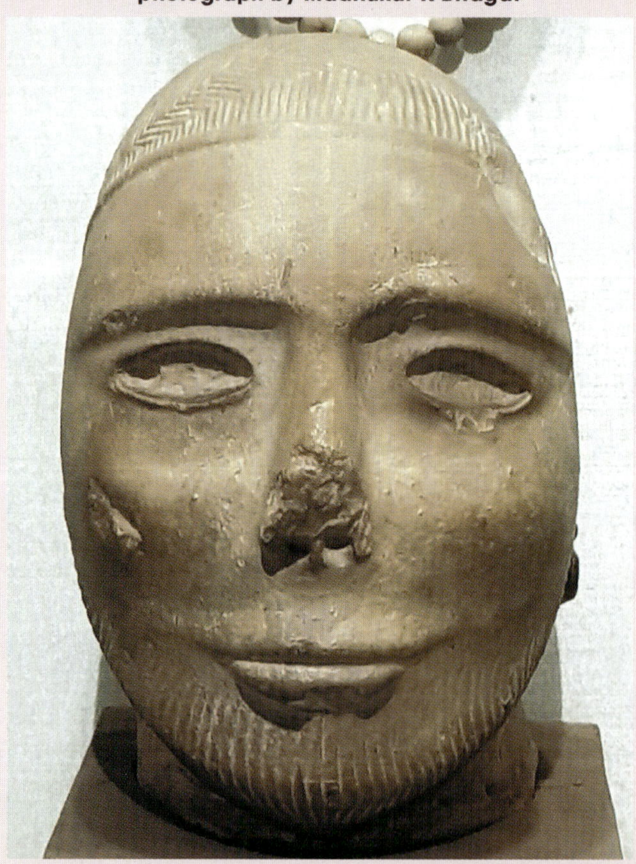

2.2: Head of Priest King; National Museum, New Delhi — photograph by Madhukar K Bhagat

WHAT IS THE INDUS VALLEY CIVILISATION?

The Indus Valley Civilisation dates back to nearly 4500 BP (before present) and is the earliest known urban culture in the Indian subcontinent. Among the many sites of this civilisation discovered so far, **Harappa** was the first site to be discovered in 1921, and hence the civilisation is also referred to as the Harappan Civilisation or the Harappan Culture.

In 1922, another great city of this lost civilisation, called **Mohenjodaro** (meaning 'mound of the dead') was discovered. A number of other sites such as **Dholavira, Rakhigarhi, Ganeriwala Lothal, Kalibangan, Chanhudaro,** etc. have subsequently been discovered. These sites are spread in a vast area, now located in present day Pakistan, Gujarat, Rajasthan, Punjab and Jammu regions in India, and even in many parts of Afghanistan.

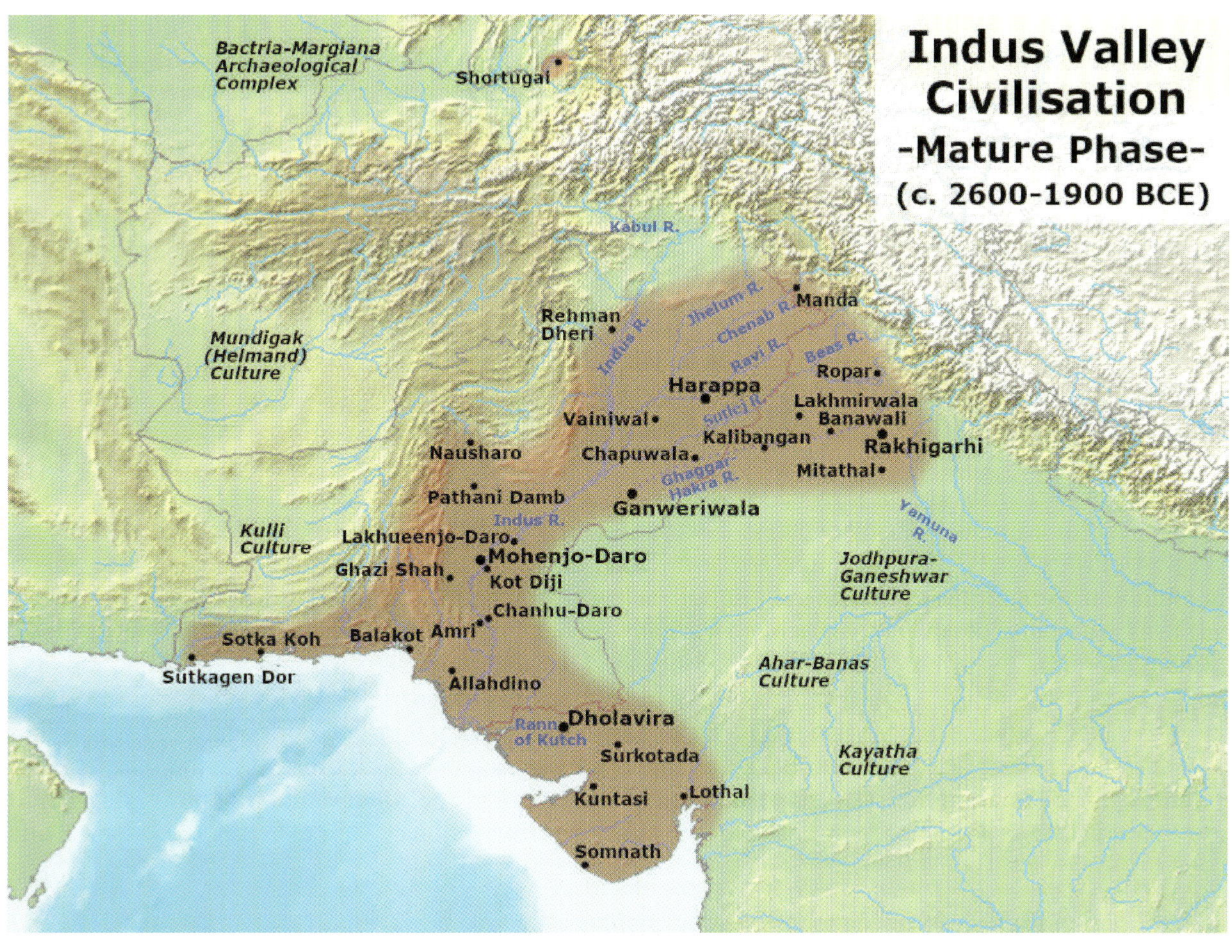

2.3: Indus Valley Civilisation (shaded region in brown) — Wikimedia Commons

Over 1000 such settlements have been discovered up till now in the valley of river Indus and the adjoining rivers and their tributaries (hence the name Indus Valley Civilisation). Out of these, nearly 100 sites have been excavated. The sites of Harappa, Mohenjodaro, Dholavira, Ganeriwala, and Rakhigarhi were found to be among the major urban centres.

PERIOD AND PHASES OF GROWTH

This civilisation is said to have flourished for nearly 2000 years between 3300 BCE to 1300 BCE. Thus, it was a contemporary of the Egyptian and Mesopotamian civilisations, the two other great civilisations of the ancient world. However, in terms of the geographical expanse, this was considered to be among the larger of the three. The phase of growth of this civilisation can be divided into three parts. The period 2600 BCE to 1900 BCE represents the Mature Harappan civilisation. This phase was preceded and succeeded by the Early Harappan and the Late Harappan phases. Archaeologists consider that the Early Harrapan and Mature Harappan cultures shared some common subsistence strategies. However, they were distinct cultures and there was even a break between the two. This is gathered from some large scale burning of Early Harrapan sites and even abandonment of some of these sites. Thus, the term Harappan Culture refers to the Mature Harappan phase of this civilisation.

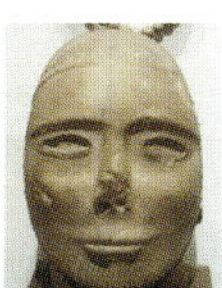

Archaeological Connotation of Culture

The term 'culture' is often used by archaeologists in the context of a civilisation and its archaeological findings. This is referred to as 'archaeological culture'. Here it connotes a **group of objects of distinctive style which have been found in a specific geographical area and in a specific period of time** that is representative of the civilisation and its people. In the Harappan context, it is the seals, beads, weights-stones, blades, baked-bricks and other archaeological objects and artefacts which reveal this culture. This culture was specific to a period of time viz. 2600 BCE to 1900 BCE (Before Common Era) representing the **Mature Harappan phase**. The preceding **Early Harappan phase** (3300 BCE to 2600 BCE) and succeeding **Late Harappan phase** (1900 BCE to 1300 BCE) are considered to be different cultures, but in the same geographical area. This geographical area comprised the basin of the Indus river system and of the seasonal Ghaggar-Hakra river systems, spread in Pakistan, parts of Afghanistan and north-western part of India.

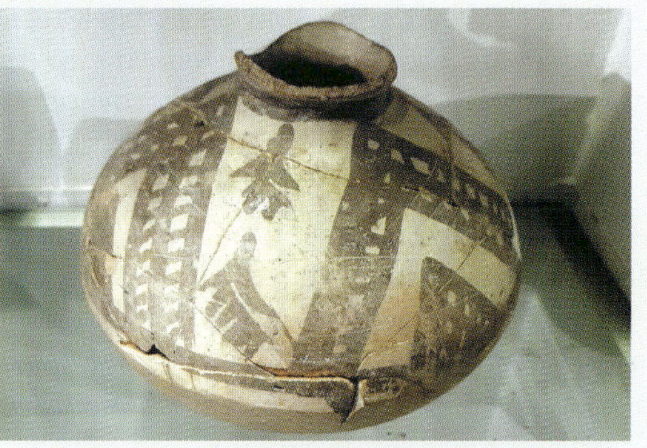

2.4: A storage pottery from a Pre-Harappan Period; National Museum, New Delhi — photograph by Madhukar K Bhagat

Archaeologists have identified different cultures in the Indian subcontinent in the Mesolithic period, Neolithic period, Harappan period, Vedic period and later. These cultures are named/classified on the basis of the region in which they flourished and also the type of pottery, the predominance of which was noted in the artefacts found and other characteristics. A prominent pre-Harappan culture was the **Bhirrana culture** dating to 7570 to 6200 BCE in the Saraswati basin region in Haryana, Punjab and Rajasthan. This is also reckoned as the oldest culture of the subcontinent. **Kot Diji culture** (3300-2800 BCE) in Sindh region, Pakistan, was another significant culture.

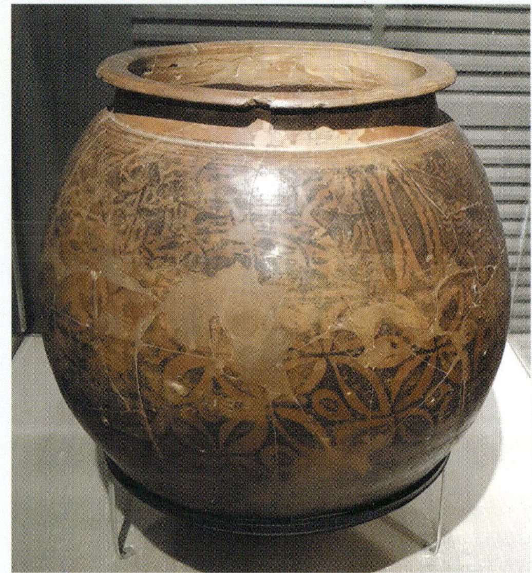

2.5: A large storage pottery of Mature Harappan Period 2700-2000 BCE; National Museum, New Delhi — photograph by Madhukar K Bhagat

In the post Harappan cultures, **Cemetery H culture** was one of the significant Bronze Age cultures which flourished in the Punjab region and north-western India from about 1900-1300 BCE. **Ochre Coloured Pottery culture** (OCP) (2000-1500 BCE) is another Bronze Age culture which flourished in the Indo-Gangetic Plain, eastern Punjab, northeastern Rajasthan and western Uttar Pradesh. The culture got its name from the excavated pottery, which gave off an ochre colour on the fingers of archaeologists when excavated. This culture shows similarities with the Late Harappan culture and the Early Vedic culture. This period also corresponds to the **Copper Hoard culture** (2000-1500 BCE). This culture developed in the Ganga Doab region in Western Uttar Pradesh and adjoining regions. The culture was characterised with findings of a large or small hoards of copper artefacts, including weaponry and different objects.

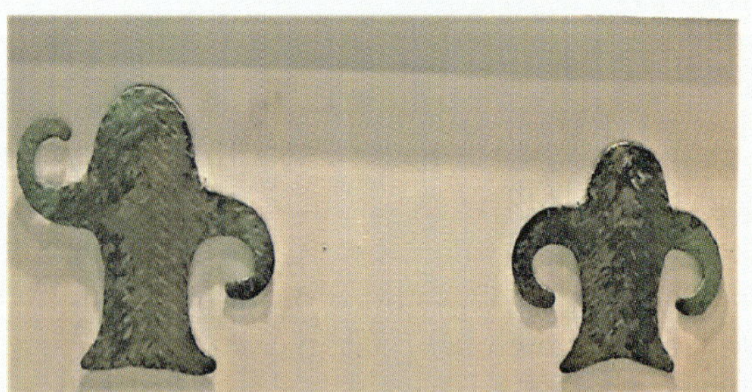

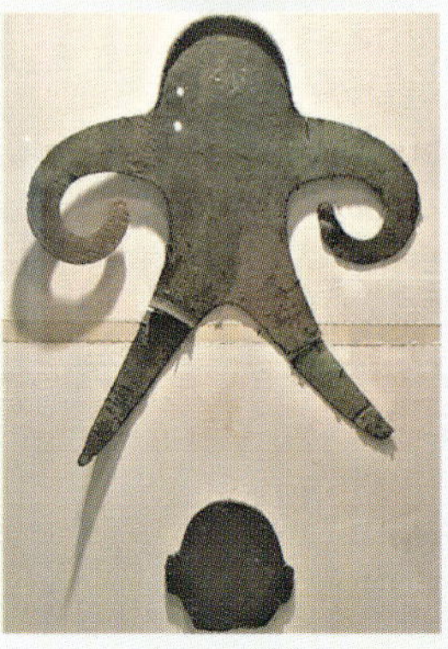

2.7: Anthromorphic images (around 2000-1500 BCE) from Copper Hoard culture; National Museum, New Delhi — photograph by Madhukar K Bhagat

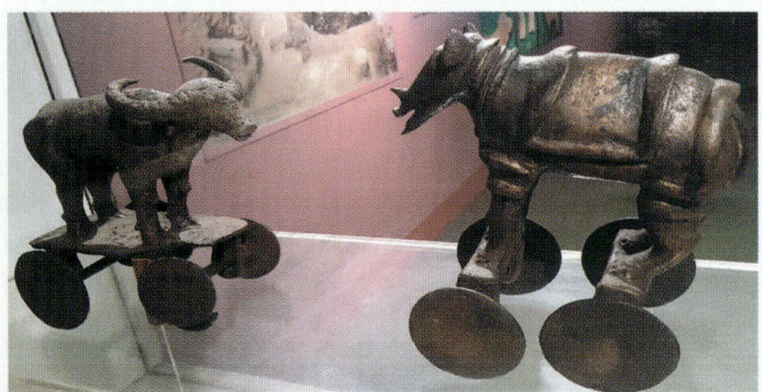

2.6: The bronze casting of Water Buffalo and Rhinoceros from the Daimabad Horde, considered by some experts to be of late Harappan culture or a subsequent Daimabad Culture; National Museum, New Delhi — photograph by Madhukar K Bhagat

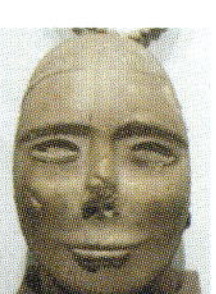

Among other prominent cultures in the **Vedic period** in the Indian subcontinent were the **Black and Red Ware culture** (1450-1200 BCE) in northern and central Indian subcontinent, (late bronze early iron age) and the **Painted Grey Ware** (1200-600 BCE) in Western Uttar Pradesh, Haryana, Eastern Punjab (Iron age). Besides these, other cultures in different parts have also been identified.

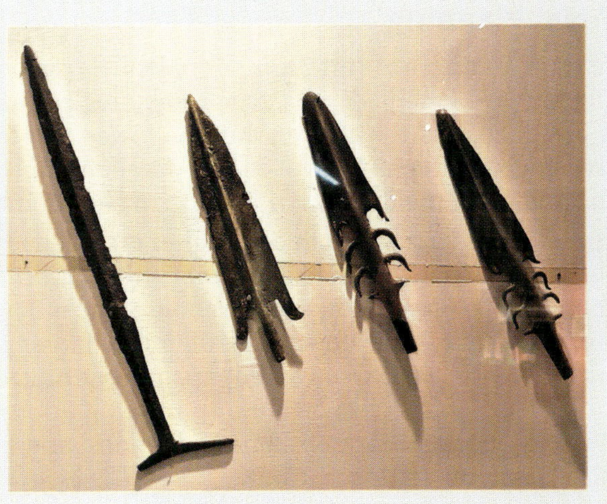

2.8: Double sided barbed harpoon (on right) and antenna sword (on left) from Copper Hoard culture (around 2000-1500 BCE); National Museum, New Delhi — photograph by Madhukar K Bhagat

SALIENT FEATURES OF THE HARAPPAN CULTURE

The Harappan culture is known for some of its very distinct features. These include the **development of urban centres, planning of towns, streets, sewage system, the great baths,** and **granaries**. The discovery of numerous artefacts, seals and statues, standard weights and measures which are unique to this culture, also throw light on the art, culture, science and technology, government, agriculture, religion, script, and other aspects of social life.

While the **dockyard at Lothal** signifies a stupendous engineering feat and flourishing trade and commerce, the tanks, reservoirs and water channels at Dholavira indicate the **water conservation systems**, which this civilisation adopted and adapted it to the changing environment. The **grid pattern layout** of its cities with elaborate **drainage and municipal systems** are an indication of not only a vibrant city planning, but also of advanced systems of governance. Its **Great Bath, warehouse, granary, walled citadels and lower towns,** suggest development of large community based societal systems. Its seals, potteries and other artefacts reveal a wealth of information about the people, their socio-religious beliefs, different art forms, trade with other world civilisations and even about the life in the individual settlements of its numerous cities. Its script, undeciphered as yet, continues to remain a challenge to modern day historians and scholars. Indeed, the Harappan civilisation served as a cradle to many later day city systems and is a true heritage of this world. The **UNESCO** has rightly recognised the archeological ruins at **Mohenjodaro** (1980) and **Dholavira** (2021) as **World Heritage Sites.**

Urban Growth

One of the most important features and achievements of this culture was the growth of urban centres and cities which flourished in this civilisation. After its extinction, such cities and urban centres emerged only a 1000 years later in the Indian subcontinent. The important urban centres discovered so far are Harappa, Mohenjodaro, and Ganeriwala in the present-day Pakistan, and Dholavira, Kalibangan, Rakhigarhi, Lothal and Ropar in India. Amongst these, the Harappan site is the earliest discovered, but the site of Mohenjodaro was better preserved. The latter reveals the excellent town planning and other features of this civilisation. Indeed, The Indus Valley Civilisation remains one of the earliest urban civilisations known to humanity.

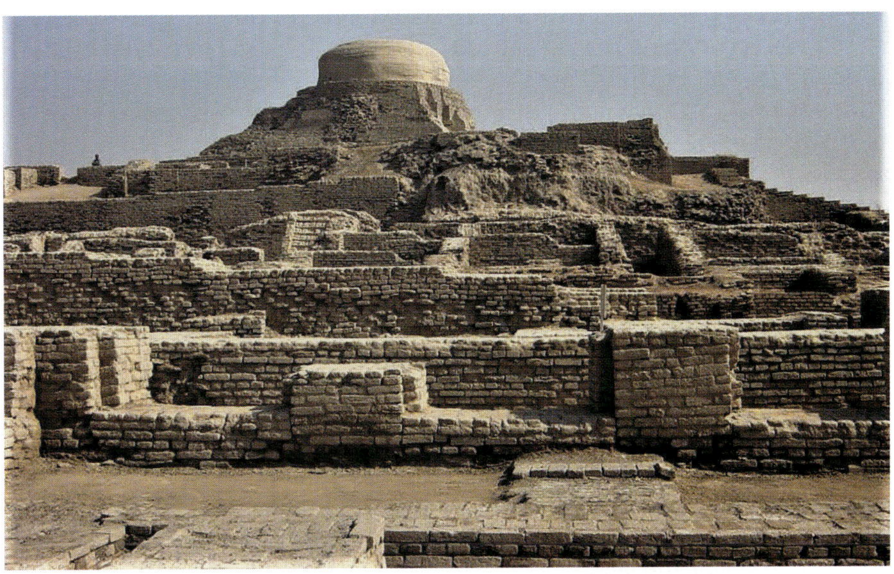

2.9: Archaeological ruins at Mohenjodaro — Wikimedia Commons

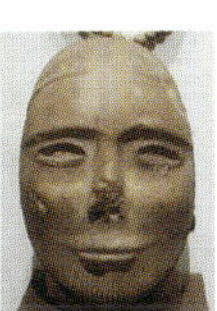

Town Planning

Town planning had certain distinct features which was common to many of the cities of this culture. The city of Mohenjodaro is seen to be divided into two distinct parts. The smaller, but higher portion is designated as the **citadel**, and the lower, but larger settlement, is referred as the **lower town**. Such division of settlement into a citadel/acropolis, and a lower town, is also noted in other urban centres, and also indicates the division of this urban society into two parts.

The citadel which was built on a higher ground had walls fortifying it from all the sides. The structures and houses were built on mud and sundried/burnt brick platform. These structures include many important ones like the **Great Bath, the warehouse, the pillared hall,** etc. which appear to have been used for public purposes. The lower town was of much larger area than the citadel, but built on a lower ground. Like the citadel, it was walled, apparently to keep the flood waters away. The houses and structures too have been found to be built on raised platforms made of mud and burnt bricks. The bricks were of standard size and ratio (of length, breadth, and height) and similar/standard bricks were employed in all settlements in this culture.

Streets and Town Planning

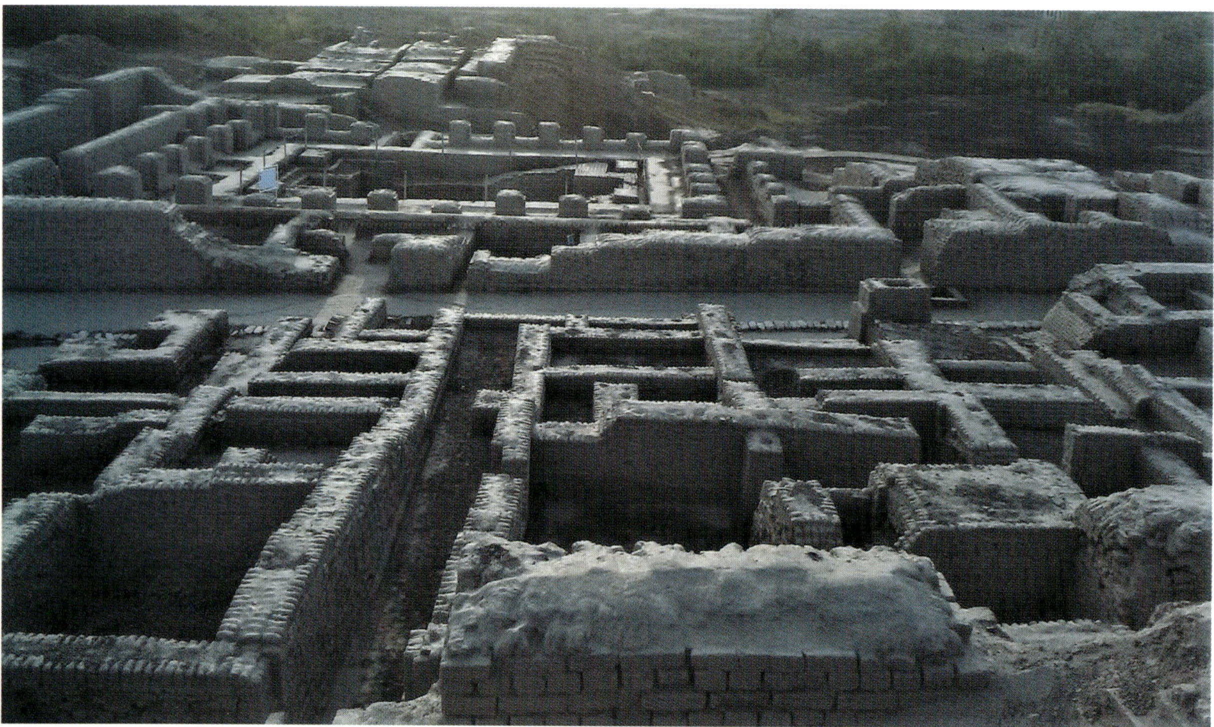

2.10: A view of the streets and buildings at Mohenjodaro indicating the advanced town-planning — Wikimedia Commons

The streets of the urban centres were constructed to run at right angles in east–west and north–south directions. It resembled a **grid pattern**, a layout often used in modern planned cities. These were as much as 30–35 ft. wide with corners rounded, making them suitable for wheeled and heavy vehicles like carts. They also had arrangement for **street lighting**. The streets along with the efficient drainage system seems to have been constructed first, and the houses built around them later, indicating existence of **advanced town planning** and **municipal system**.

The Drainage System

This civilisation had developed an advanced and efficient drainage system which was not found amidst other contemporary civilisations in the world. The drainage system along with urban town planning remains one of its most significant aspects, amongst many of its unique features.

Each house had its **private drinking well** and a **bathroom**. The water from them ran through **clay pipes** into **underground drains**, which then ran into **main drains**. These main drains were made up of bricks set in mortar and had large cross-sections to accommodate even a large waterflow. The house drains were first emptied into a cesspit or a sump in which the solid matter would first settle, allowing the water to drain in the main drain. The latter had sumps at regular intervals to enable its cleaning. The above arrangement indicates not only the advancement in city planning and municipal systems, but also the importance attached to social and personal hygiene, besides a good knowledge of brick-mortar construction.

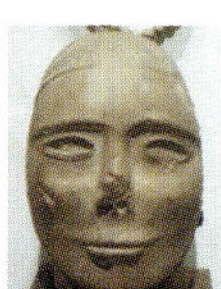

The Great Bath

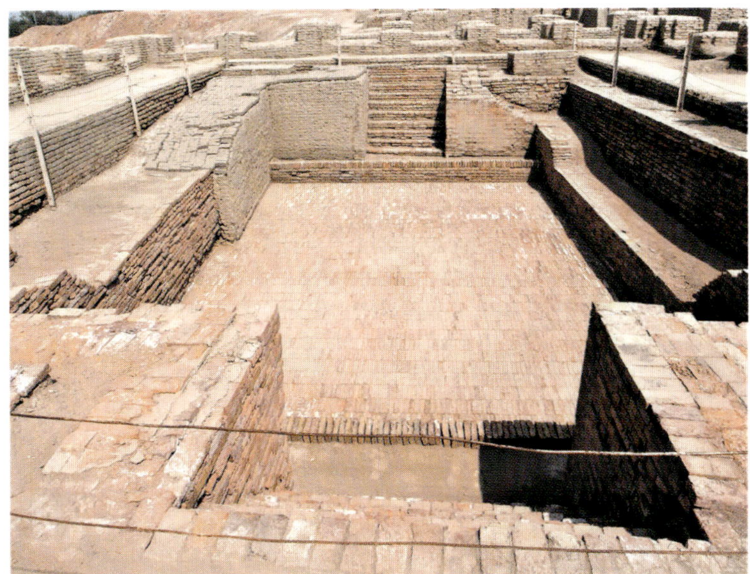
2.11: The Great Bath of Mohenjodaro — Wikimedia Commons

The Great Bath of Mohenjodaro is one of the most important finds of this civilisation. Located on the citadel, it was apparently used for ceremonial bathing purposes. The structure is rectangular in shape with approximate dimensions of 12 m by 7 m and depth of 2.43. It was accessible from two wide staircases, each on the northern and the southern side. The tank was **watertight**, as it was made of tightly fitting bricks with coating of mud and gypsum plaster. The pool had an **array of rooms** located on the three sides of it, with a **large well** located in one of the rooms, that was used for drawing water for the pool. The water from the tank ran into a **large drain**. To the north of the great bath and across a lane was a smaller building which had eight bathrooms. Historians believe that considering the elaborate arrangements, the uniqueness of the structure and its presence on the citadel, along with some other important structures, could have been used for ritual bath purposes.

The Great Bath is truly a reflection of the achievement of this civilisation in the field of engineering and construction technology. Besides, it also indicates the social significance attached to religious/ceremonial matters in public life.

Domestic House Planning and Architecture

The domestic house planning and architecture is evident in the lower town of Mohenjodaro. The houses were constructed along the roads and drains. Thus, it was the latter which were planned and constructed first and then the houses were built along them. Each of the houses is centred around a courtyard with rooms built around it. The courtyard could be the centre of household activities (viz. cooking, weaving, etc). The rooms and the walls on the ground level do not have any windows. The historians speculate that this could be apparently out of concern for privacy. Some houses also have remains of staircases to reach the roof of the second storey of the house.

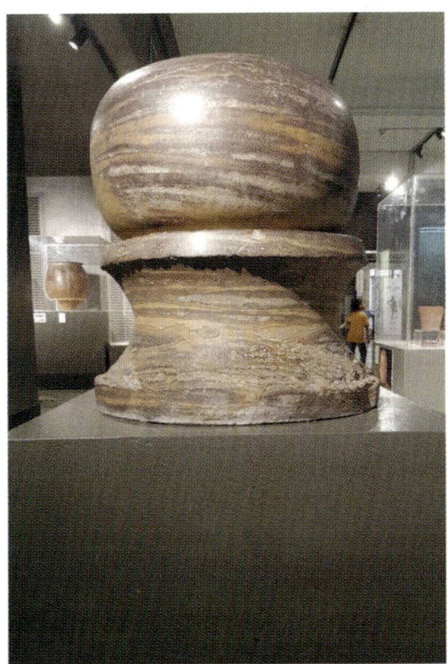
2.12: A part of a pillar and the base stone from Harappa; National Museum, New Delhi — photograph by Madhukar K Bhagat

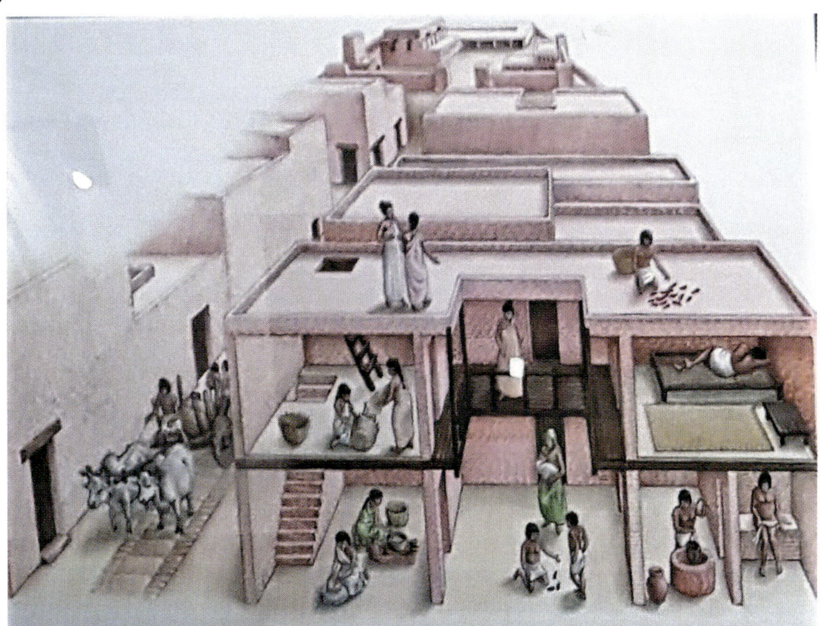
2.13: Pictographic representation of the house architecture in Indus Valley civlisation; image from Nagpur Central Museum — photograph by Madhukar K Bhagat

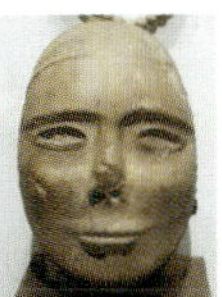

Each house had a separate bathroom, the discharge of which would run in the system of drains. Most of the houses had a well, and over 700 wells have been found in Mohenjodaro. Sometimes the wells were built in a room with access from outside, perhaps for allowing outsiders to access it.

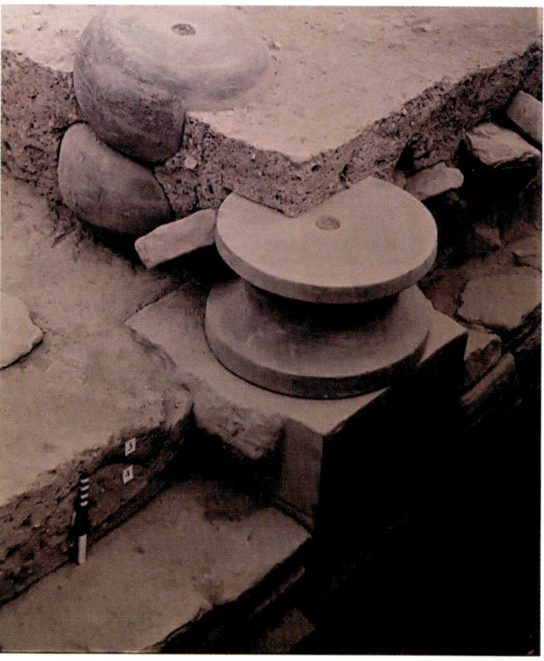

2.14: A picture showing arrangement of the pillar and the base stone; National Museum, New Delhi — photograph by Madhukar K Bhagat

Great Granary

Evidence has also been found of a large warehouse type structure at Harappa which is also referred to as the Great Granary. This mammoth brick structure (of nearly 2100 sq.m.), consisted of two blocks with six halls in each with a central aisle (7 meter wide) dividing it. Each hall (nearly 90 square metre in area) had three sleeper walls with air space between them (see picture 2.15). It is presumed that timber floors would have rested on these sleeper walls, with the spaces between the walls serving as air passages to prevent the grains from rotting. As a similar type of system was discovered in some granaries of ancient Rome, this structure too was believed to be serving a similar purpose. However, some historians contend this theory as no grain storage containers or clay sealings (for containers) have been found at the site. They therefore call them as public halls. However, with the discovery of more such structures in other sites, the general consensus of these structures being used as granaries has gained ground.

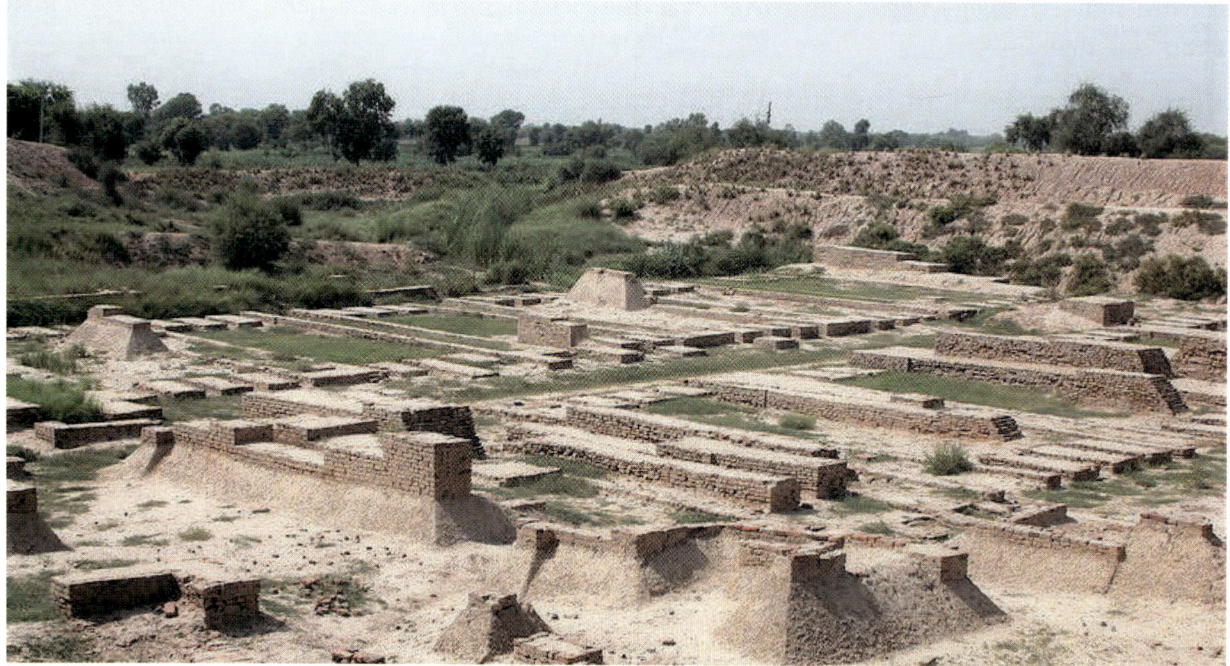

2.15: Archaeological site of Harappa with granary in picture — Wikimedia Commons

Dockyard at Lothal: An Ancient Engineering Marvel

The existence of a channel-based docking system at Lothal (literally meaning *Loth-Sthal*; or mound of dead) in the state of Gujarat, is an important and exciting find of the Harappan culture. This excavated site is as yet the only port-town discovered in the Indus Valley Civilisation. The tidal dockyard, with a huge basin (217 m by 26 m) was located along the Bhogava river (one of the tributaries of the Sabarmati). It was connected to the river through a channel through which boats could reach while following the tidal system. The dockyard had thick peripheral walls to withstand the pressure of tidal waters in this huge man-made basin. It had an inlet and a smaller outlet to maintain adequate water levels in it. The dock and the channel could be locked during a low tide with a wooden lock-gate system and unlocked during high tide. Thus it allowed navigation from this town to the Gulf of Khambat and further to

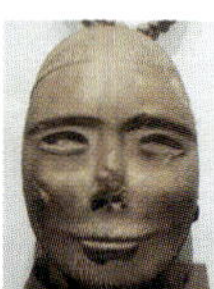

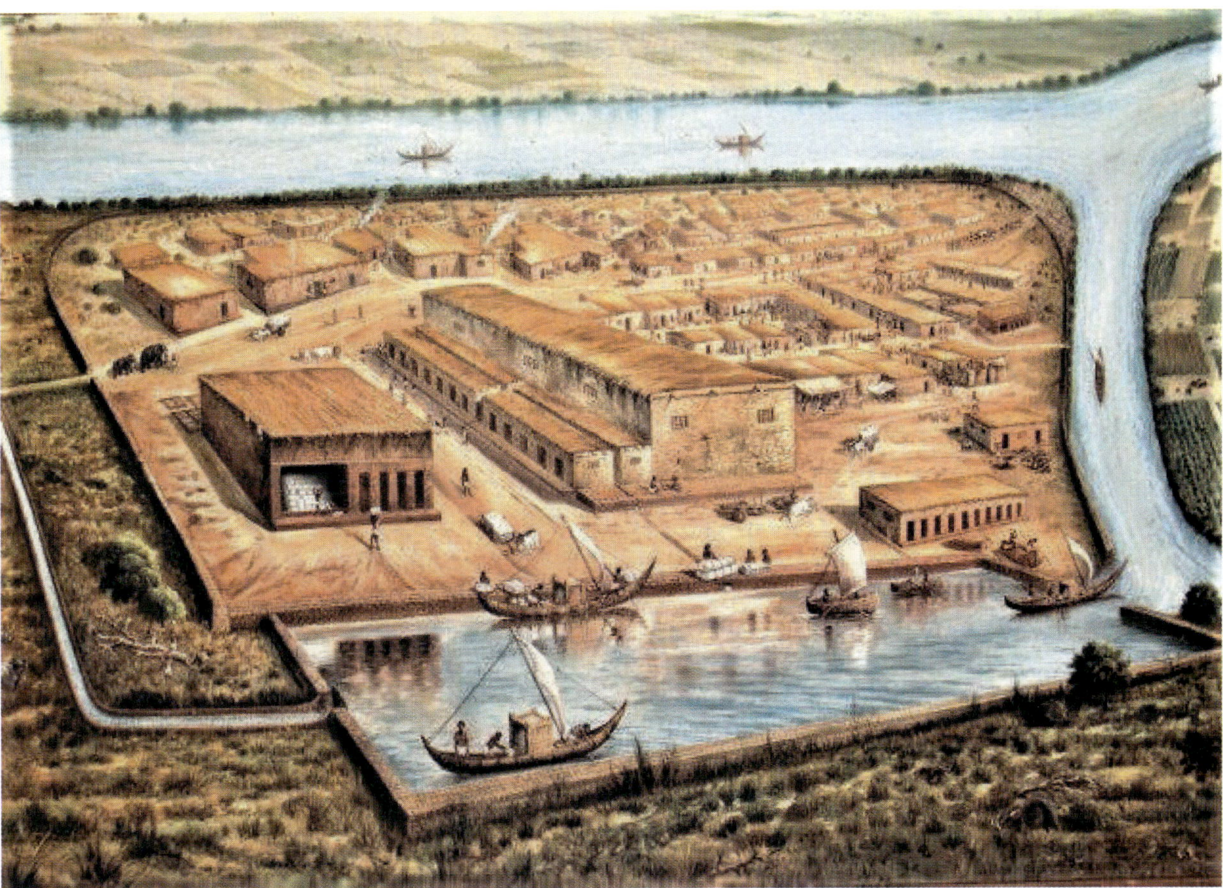

2.16: Pictographic image of Lothal dockyard at display at the museum in Lothal — photograph by Madhukar K Bhagat

other trading ports. The discovery of stone anchors, marine shells, sealings (the origin of which can be traced to the Persian Gulf) and a large warehouse, all confirm it to be a great ancient port and not merely a water storage system as contended by some experts earlier. The town also boasted of a citadel, or acropolis, and a lower town. Bead making, jewellery making and making of other metallurgical products flourished in this centre, which were the key items of export.

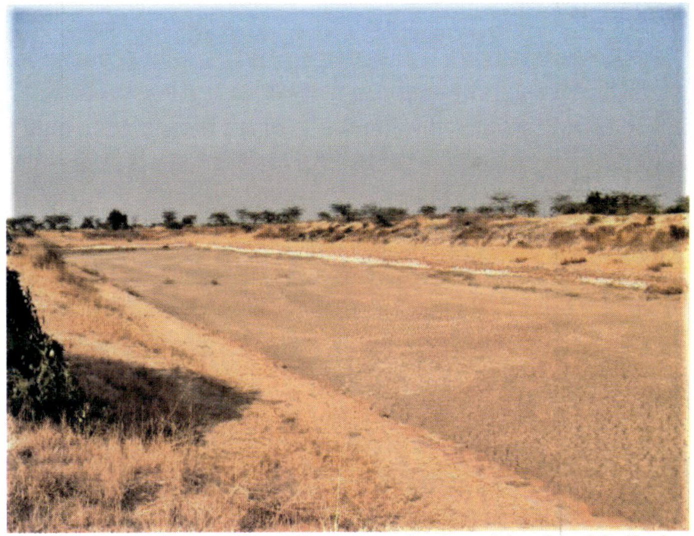

2.17: Present day site of the large dockyard basin at Lothal — photograph by Madhukar K Bhagat

Indus Script

The Indus script is an extremely interesting and enigmatic aspect of this ancient civilisation. The script which **has not been deciphered** as yet, is believed by some experts to have been a **pictographic** one. A large number of characters of this script (nearly 400) have been discovered so far, primarily on the numerous seals and ceramic pots excavated. Most of the inscriptions are short and the longest being of 26 signs, found in what is called a **sign board**, over a gateway structure in Dholavira. What is known is that the characters were written from right to left as in some seals/inscriptions. Many characters are seen to be squeezed for want of space towards the left end.

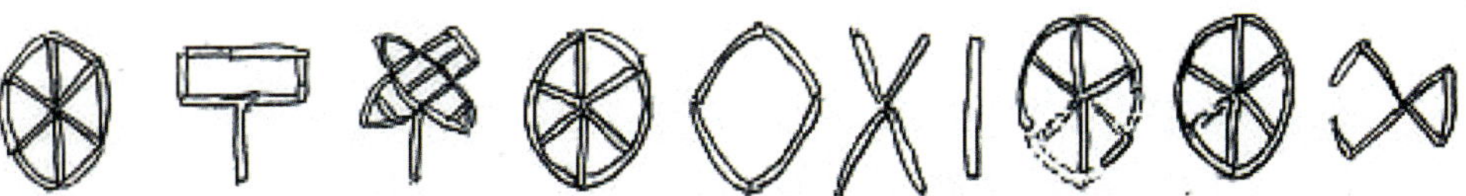

2.18: Ten Indus characters from the northern gate of Dholavira referred to as Dholavira signboard — Wikimedia Commons

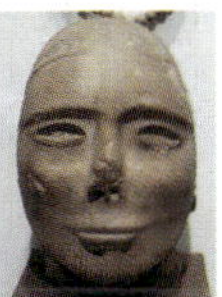

Does the Indus Script Really Represent a Language?

Despite over a 100 years having passed after the discovery of this advanced civilisation, archaeologists and experts have still not been able to solve the riddle this script represents. Most of the artifacts such as tablets, seals, ceramic-wares and metal objects, carry just four to five symbols. Along with it, the discontinuity of the Harappan traditions after the decline of the civilisation, has further added to the challenge of deciphering of the code. One tiny inscription which carries nearly 17 symbols is less than an inch long, while another long inscription the Dholavira signboard, which is 26 characters long are the best leads the experts have.

Most other ancient writings systems often have long writings, usually of more than 100 characters. The absence of any such discovery has led some experts to believe that these symbols may not have been a part of a structured language (Indologist Prof Michael Witzel) and they were perhaps used for economic transactions only, viz. controlling trade. (*Farmer, Sproat and Witzel in 2004*) The symbols were perhaps akin to the messages contained on modern days stamps, tokens and currencies which are used for regulating commercial transactions. But Prof. Asko Parpola, of the University of Helsinki, Finland (working on deciphering the scripts since 1968) believes that the script was very much linguistic and may have been similar to the family of Dravidian languages (or its proto languages). However, a 2009 study (*Rao et. al.* and some other scientists), compared the patterns of Harappan symbols with those of other forms of linguistics and non-linguistic systems. These included comparison with the highly ordered programming language codes and the randomly ordered DNA codes. Based on the entropy (randomness of the distribution of characters), it was found that the Harappan symbols indeed fell into the pattern of a spoken language.

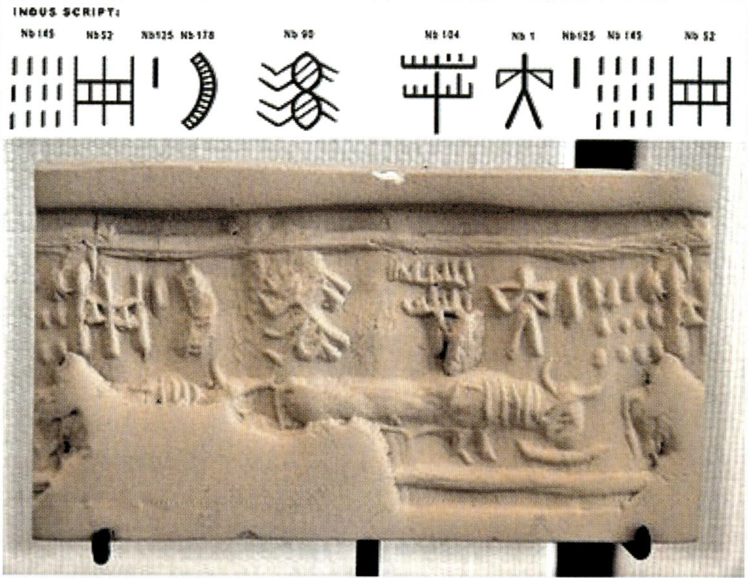

2.19: Impression of an Indus cylinder-seal (2600-1700 BCE) discovered in Susa (Iran) located in Louvre Museum, Paris. Numbering convention by Asko Parpola — Wikimedia Commons

Apart from the few symbols found in one place, experts attribute non- availability of a **Rosetta stone** – like artifact as another reason for the script not being deciphered. (Rosetta stone contained inscriptions in two languages, Egyptian and Greek, using three scripts, hierologlyphic, Demotic and Greek, and enabled the deciphering of the ancient Egyptian writings). However, some breakthroughs have indeed been made.

One such independent research by an Indian scientist (Bahata Ansumali Mukhopadhyaya), published in the journal *Palgrave Communications* in 2019, concludes that the Indus script was not phonetically written, i.e. the symbols do not represent speech sounds like in a modern language. However, they are largely **logographic**, implying that individual symbols represent things and concepts. She also opines that the existence of another parallel complex language cannot be ruled out, considering the advancement made by this vast and thriving civilisation. The other language could have been written in more perishable materials and destroyed in the ensuing thousands of years.

Thus, the only significant finding which experts do agree upon is that the characters were written from right to left. Till more discoveries, researches and convergence of expert opinion takes place this ancient script will continue to fascinate and mystify us.

Weights and Measures

The Harappan culture had also developed an accurate system of weights and measures. The weights were made of cubical pieces of stone,without any markings called **Cherts**. While the lower weights were binary in nature, (ratio of 1 : 2 : 4 : 8, etc.) the higher weights were of decimal base. The smaller weights are considered to have been used for measuring jewellery and beads. Even metal scales have been found to use for the weighment. At Lothal, an ivory scale (to measure length) was found showing smallest division of 1.704 mm. Historians consider this to be the

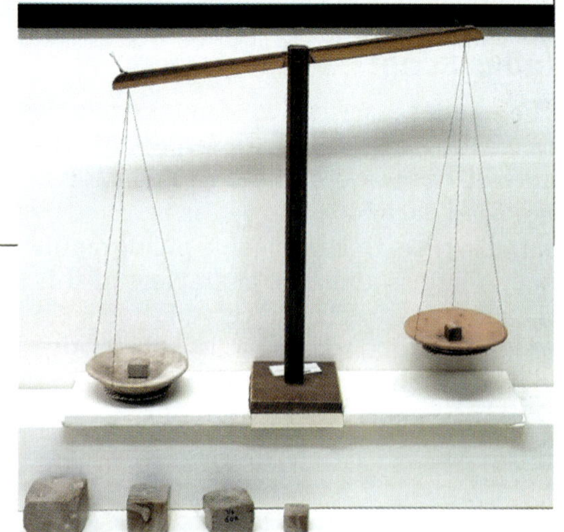

2.20: Harappan cubical weights (cherts) and scale (with reconstructed beam), Nagpur Central Museum — photograph by Madhukar K Bhagat

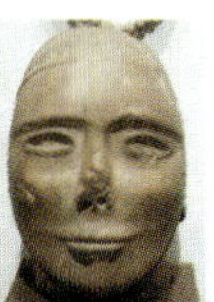

smallest division which was recorded in any civilisation in the Bronze Age. The use of accurate weights and measures categorically indicates advancement in science and mathematics and the growth of trade and commerce in this culture.

Seals, Pottery and Other Artifacts

A number of seals, pottery, jewellery, and other artifacts have been discovered which throw light on the art and craft of this culture. Chanhudaro (in Pakistan) was an important centre of such crafts which included bead making, metal works, making of seals and artifacts, pottery, and sheet cutting. A variety of stones, viz. steatite, quartz, and jasper crystal were used. Besides, terracotta, faience, and metals like copper, bronze, and even gold were used. This centre is considered to have been excusively devoted to such craft work. Lothal was another important centre of production of such beads and jewellery. To make such beads, special drills were used for piercing/cutting holes. Such drills/tools have been discovered at Chanuhodaro, Lothal and Dholavira. The above are indicative of high standards of craftsmanship, knowledge of metallurgy and foundry, besides flourishing trade and commerce.

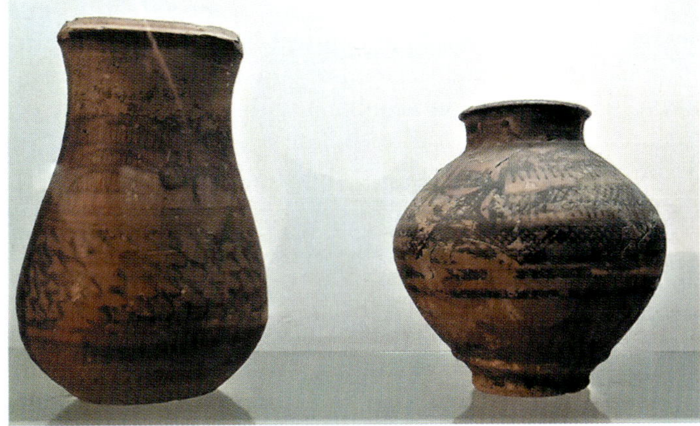

2.21: Pottery with design, (2800-2000 BCE) National Museum, New Delhi — photograph by Madhukar K Bhagat

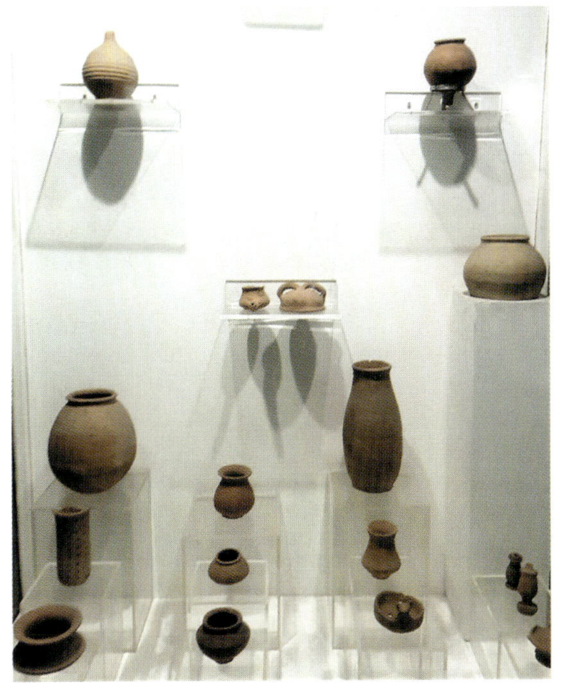

2.22: A variety of domestic clay pottery from Harappa, Mohenjodaro and Dholavira (2800-2000 BCE) National Museum, New Delhi — photograph by Madhukar K Bhagat

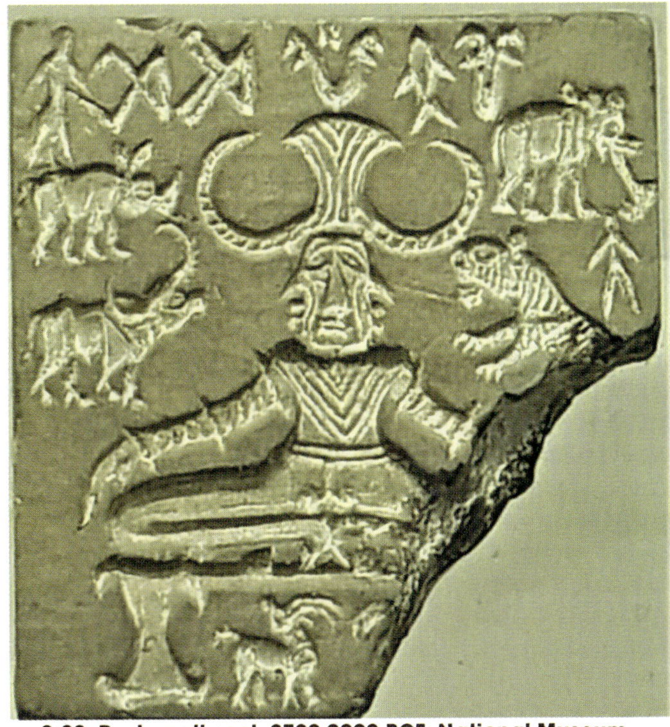

2.23: Pashupati seal; 2700-2000 BCE; National Museum, New Delhi — photograph by Madhukar K Bhagat

Important seals and artifacts

(a) ***Shiva Pashupati seal:*** The seal depicts a figure seated cross legged in a yogic posture with a horned head dress. The figure is surrounded by a number of animals (elephant, buffalo, tiger, rhinoceros, and antelope) and is considered to be a **proto-Shiva**, or early form of Shiva/Pashupati/Rudra venerated in later and contemporary Hinduism.

(b) ***Mother Goddess figurine:*** This is a terracotta figurine of a woman adorned with jewellery and imposing fan shaped headgear. Many such figurines have been found. They are considered to be a depiction of the Mother Goddess. The images of proto- Shiva and of the Mother Goddess indicate religious belief of people of this civilisation. Further, it could also indicate a link with the subsequent Hindu tradition and belief in similar/identical gods and goddesses.

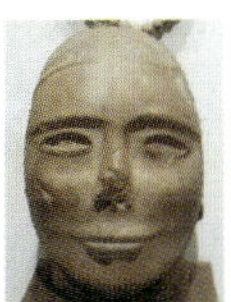

(c) ***Priest King statue:*** It is a famous stone (steatite) statue of a bearded man believed to be a priest king (as similar priest kings were existent in the Mesopotamiam culture). The bust (statue) has a fillet or a ribbon headband with a circular inlay ornament. A similar ribbon with fillet is found on the forearm. The figure is draped in a shawl with trefoil pattern. Similar other images were found in other Harappan sites, and also considered to be the statue of the priest king.

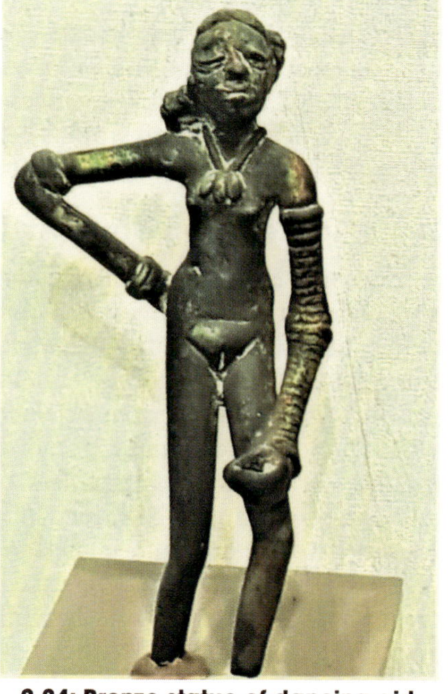

2.24: Bronze statue of dancing girl (height 10.5) cm; period 2700-2000 BCE; National Museum, New Delhi — photograph by Madhukar K Bhagat

(d) ***The Dancing Girl statue:*** This small bronze statue of a dancing girl found in Mohenjodaro is an excellent example of art and metallurgy of this period. The statue is dated to around 2500 BC. It depicts a naked girl striking a dancing posture with one hand on her hips. A number of bangles are seen in the other arm. She is also wearing a necklace. The arms are shown to be unusually long.

(e) ***The bull seal:*** This seal shows a humped bull and has good depiction of the features of the animal. A number of seals with animal depictions have been found. All this are indicative of knowledge of wild animals and hunting.

(f) ***The unicorn seal:*** It is another important seal depicting a unicorn which is a mythical animal (a horse with a single horn).

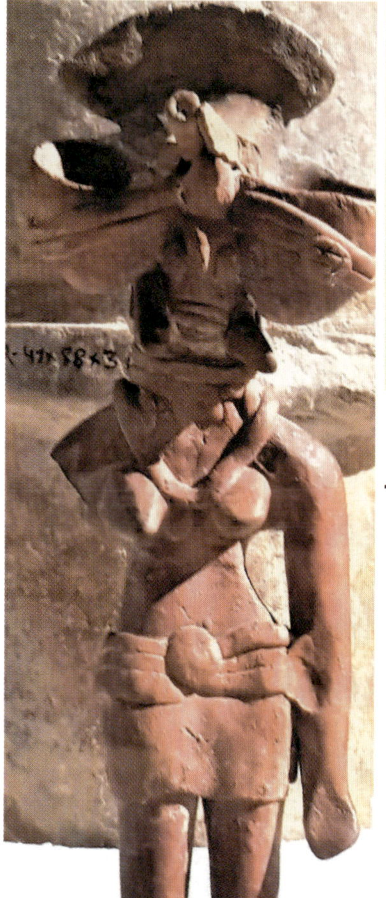

2.25: A female figurine considered as mother goddess; 2700-2000 BCE; National Museum, New Delhi — photograph by Madhukar K Bhagat

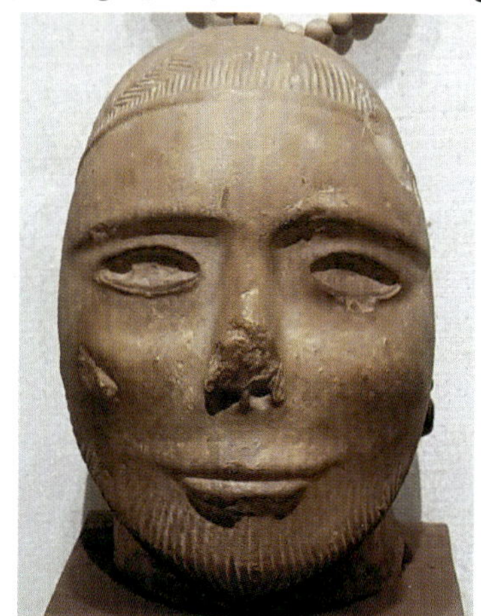

2.26: Head of a priest king 2700-2000 BCE; National Museum, New Delhi — photograph by Madhukar K Bhagat

(g) ***The male torso:*** This is another red sand statue depicting the male torso. The figure has socket holes in the arms and neck for attachment of arms and neck. The proportions of the male body (torso) are well shown. This statue is particularly relevant as to the accurate depiction of anatomical proportions and craftmanship, a feature of the much later Greek sculptures. However, some historians consider this to be of later date around the Gupta period. Another stellar statue is that of the torso of a male dancer in greystone. All of these represent the pinnacle of Harappan art.

Utility and significance of seals

Over 4000 seals and similar artifacts pertaining to the Harappan period have been discovered so far. The seals are believed to be used for sealing the consignment of goods and

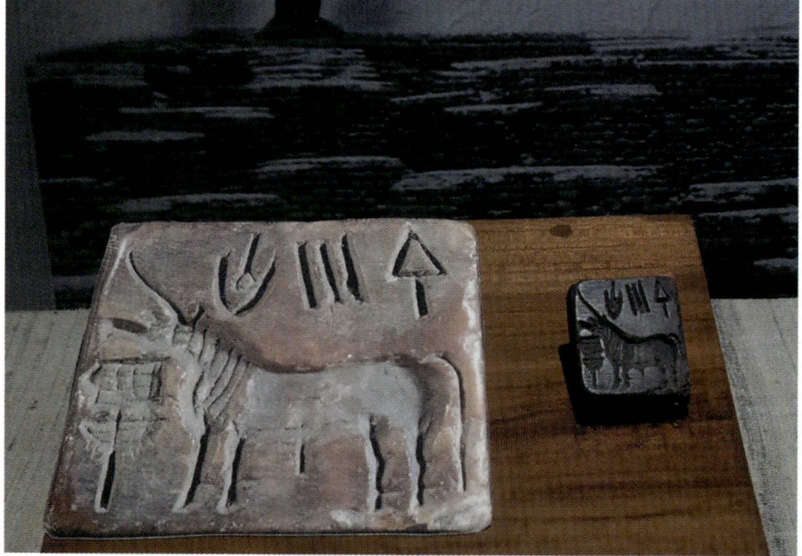

2.27: Unicorn seal at the Indian Museum, Kolkata — Wikimedia Commons

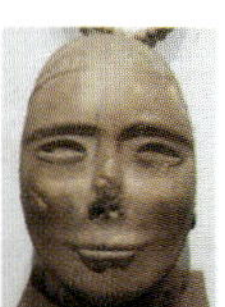

securing them (by placing a mark of the seal on the opening). The presence of an intact seal on the consignment at the destination was a sign of the goods being secure. Besides, the seals were also an indication of the identity of the sender. The discovery of a large number of seals at various sites is an indication of the flourishing trade and commerce and also of the fact that this urban civilisation was not just an agriculture dependent economy. The symbols on the seal indicate the existence of a script. The numerous figures throw light on the socio-religious and other aspects of the culture.

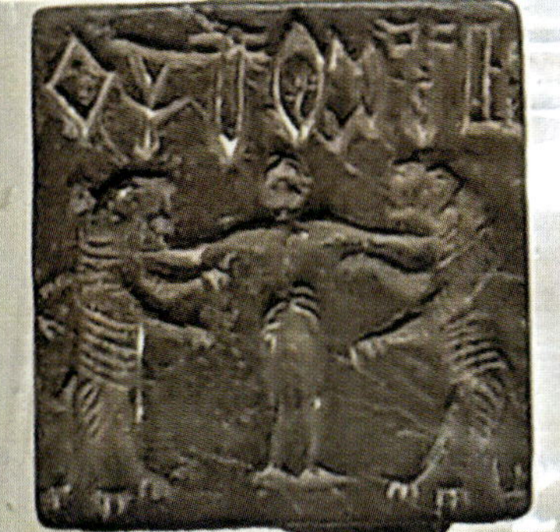

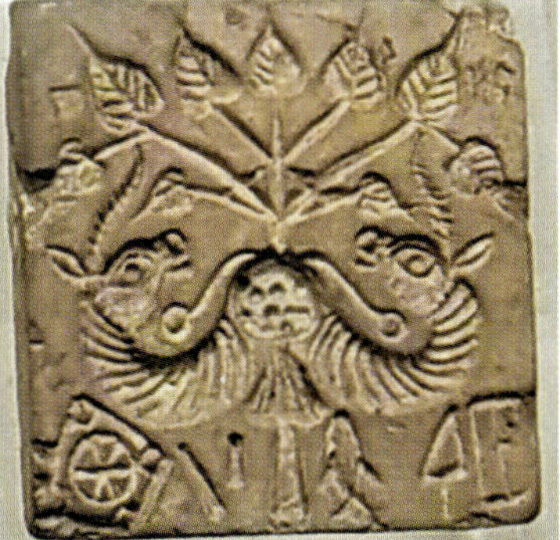

2.28: Two seals with different animal motifs 2700-2000 BCE; National Museum, New Delhi — photograph by Madhukar K Bhagat

Society and Government

From the archeological findings it is noted that the Harappan bricks, and seal weights etched uniformly, irrespective of not being produced in the same centre and being found in different places. The uniformity in bricks is especially noteworthy as they had common ratio of length, breadth, and height. Further, the existence of town planning, establishment of settlements near the source of raw material, etc., all point towards the existence of some kind of central authority. However, lack of discovery of large and distinct structures such as palaces (as found in Mesopotamian and Egyptian sites) suggests that the authority may not have been a monarch or a king. Thus, the society could have been egalitarian, with the distribution of power in the hands of many. Some historians even suggest that each of the various sites could have had separate rulers. However, the latter is less likely, considering the uniformity in weights and measures, bricks, and artifacts.

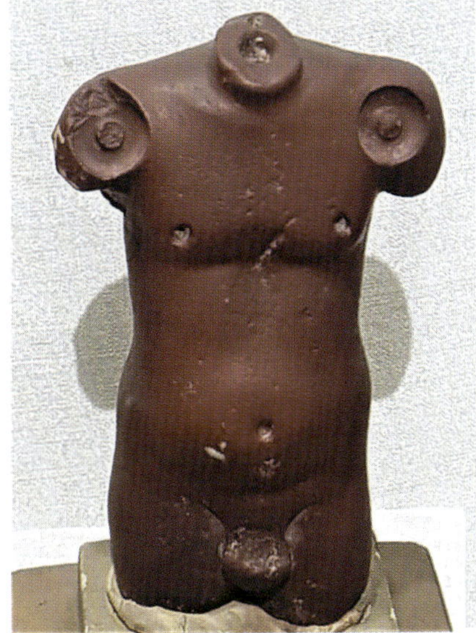

2.29: Small figurine of a male torso of red sandstone; National Museum, New Delhi — photograph by Madhukar K Bhagat

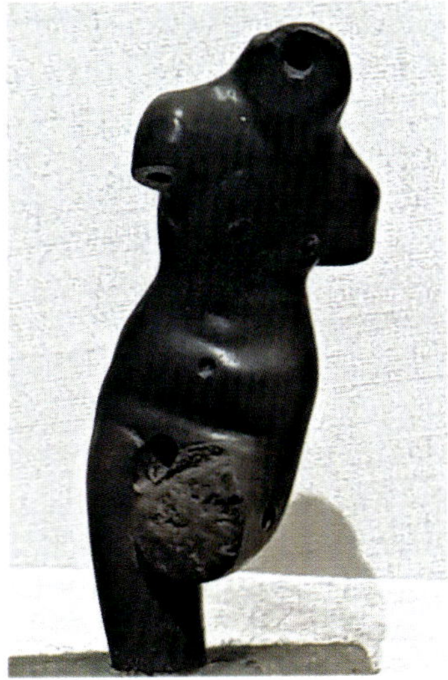

2.30: Small figurine of torso of a dancing male, greystone, 2700-2000 BCE, National Museum, New Delhi — photograph by Madhukar K Bhagat

Burials and Belief in Afterlife

The burial practices of a civilisation are a very poignant reflection of its socio-cultural belief systems. Evidences of such practices have been noted in several prominent settlements

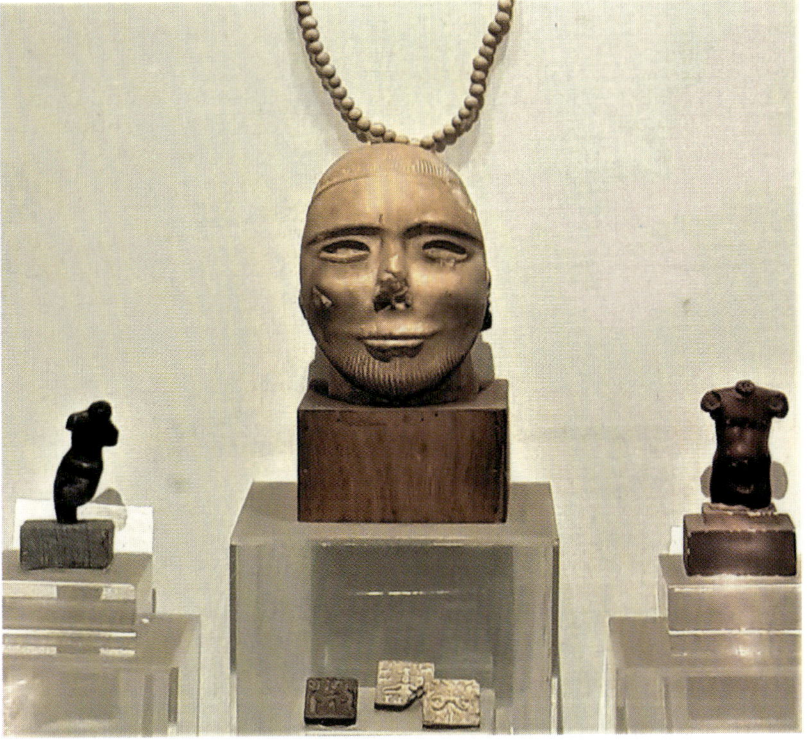

2.31: Bearded Priest King (centre) male figurines (left and right) Pashupati seal (bottom-centre) and other seals. A common picture of the artefacts revealing a relative perspective of their sizes; period 2700-2000 BCE, National Museum, New Delhi — photograph by Madhukar K Bhagat

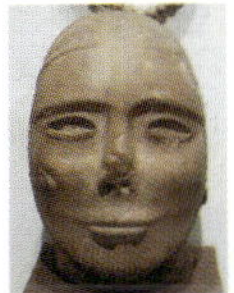

such as Harappa, Rakhigarhi, Kalibangan, Lothal, Dholavira and others. The usual mode of burial was **'pit burial'**. The pits were usually lined with bricks or occasionally with stones. In some cases, such linings were absent, indicating the existence of social differences and separate burial practices. The bodies were mostly placed in supine position with head northwards. Evidence of bodies in foetal position has also been found. Some burials with more than one body in it have also been discovered.

Pot burials were too in vogue where bodies would be in a foetal postion. Further, post cremation burial practices have also been noted in Rakhigarhi where funerary objects have been found in pots or rectangular/oval pits. Absence of any skeletal material in such burials suggests a distinct burial practice akin to a post cremation burial.

Burials were also accompanied with different kinds of pottery. Excavations also reveal jewellery and bangles in female skeletons. Household objects, microbeads, semi-precious stones and even copper mirrors have been found in some burials, all of these indicating to a possible belief in afterlife.

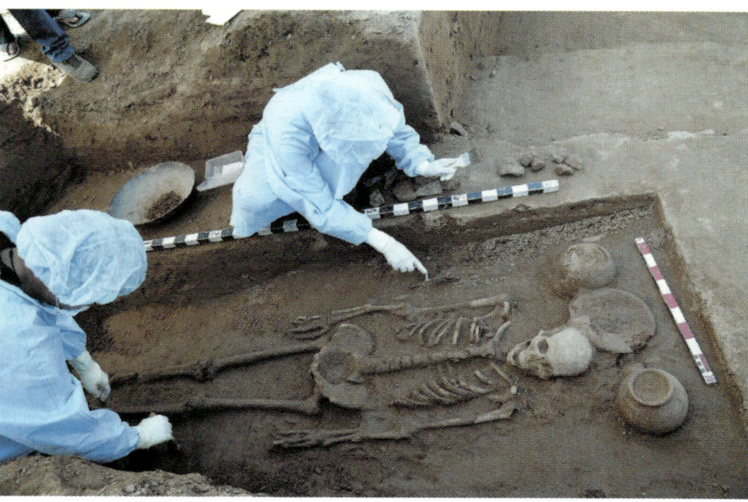

2.32: Experts from the Archaeological Survey at excavation work at the Rakhigarhi burial ground, mound RGR7, revealing burial practices — Courtesy, Directorate of Archaeology and Museums; Government of Haryana

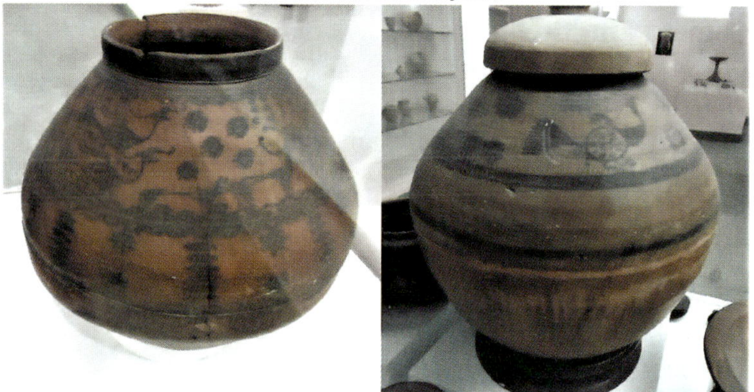

2.33: Some Cemetry H culture period pottery urns from Harappa — Wikimedia Commons

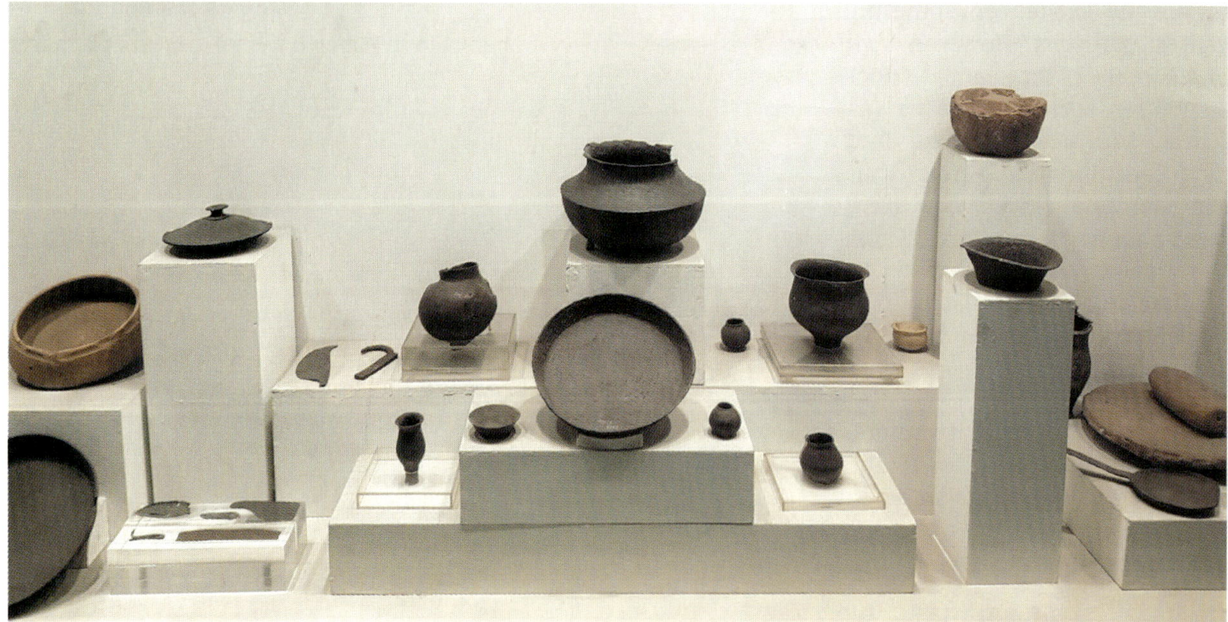

2.34: Copper objects, clay pottery and other domestic objects of clay and copper, period 2700-2000 BCE, National Museum, New Delhi — photograph by Madhukar K Bhagat

Trade and Commerce

Trade and commerce were an important sector of this culture's economy as evident from the numerous seals and artifacts. The raw material used in production were sourced from different places, viz. **copper from Oman** (as chemical analysis shows Omani copper and Harappan artifacts have traces of nickel, thus indicating common origin). Similarly, Harappan artifacts have been found at different sites too, viz.

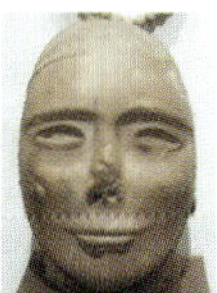

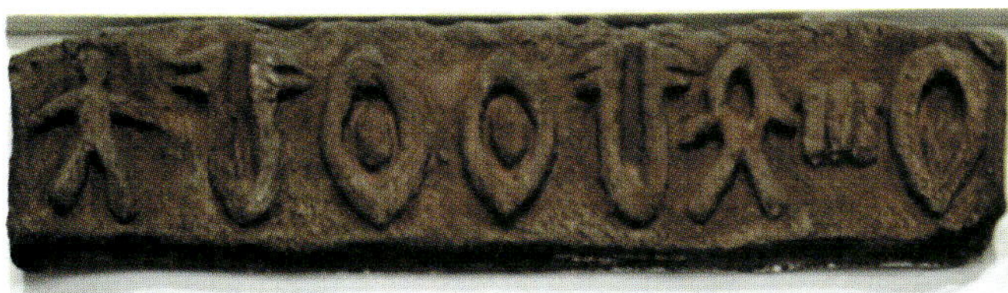

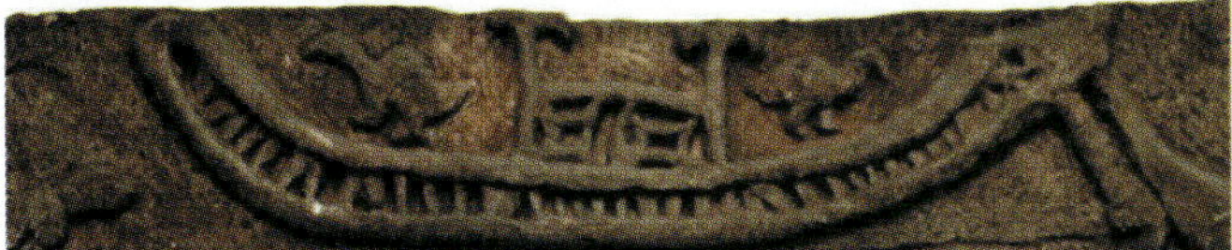

2.35: A Mohenjodaro seal with an image of a boat and direction finding birds on it (2500 to 1750 BCE); National Museum, New Delhi — Wikimedia Commons

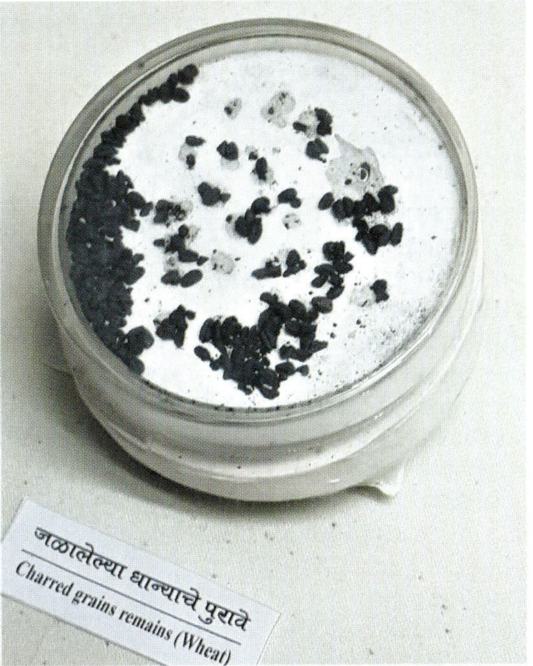

2.36: Charred grains of wheat from Indus Valley, Nagpur Central Museum — photograph by Madhukar K Bhagat

Harappan jars (pottery with a layer of black clay) have been found at Omani sites. The trade and commerce could have been carried through land or through sea. Seals depicting ships have been discovered beside the dockyard of Lothal which is further indicative of sea trade.

Agriculture and Food

Discovery of **charred grains** and **seeds** at some of the Harappan sites and **terracotta models of plough** found at Cholistan and Banawali (Haryana) point towards the prevalence of agriculture. Terracota figurines, statue and seals of bulls also suggest that oxen might have been used for ploughing. Evidence of **ploughed fields** has been found at Kalibangan (Rajasthan). Irrigation is thought to have been carried by use of wells or reservoirs which were found at Dholavira (Gujarat). Some traces of **canals** have also been identified at Shortughai, a Harappan site in Afghanistan.

Archeological findings indicate that **barley** and **wheat** were the major cultivated cereal crops. Besides, archaeo-botanists (specialists in ancient plants) have also found lentils, chickpea and sesame. In some sites of Gujarat, millets have also been found. But rarely has a cereal like rice has been found.

Bones of a variety of animals have been found which include cattle, goat sheep, buffalo and pig. These could have been domesticated. However, bones of animals like boar, deer and gharials indicate that their meat could have been a part of the diet. Besides, bones of fish and fowl also have been found indicating a consumption of a wide range of meat.

Dairy Production in Indus Valley Civilisation

As per a recent study published in the journal **Nature** (October 2020), evidence of dairy production was found in the Indus Valley Civilisation in a period as early as 2350 BCE. The study, was based on a research conducted by Kalyan Sekhar Chakraborty (a postdoctoral researcher at the University of Toronto, Mississauga) and team. They conducted a chemical analysis of residue in pieces of pottery from the archaeological site of Kotada Bhadli, (a rural settlement located in Gujarat). Through a process of isotope analysis, they could find presence of dairy lipids in 22 out 59 samples tested. These lipids were further identified to be from ruminants such as cows and water buffaloes, rather than goats and sheeps.

The researchers conclude that the above findings are a clear indication of large scale dairy production beyond regular household consumption. Archaeologists believe that this could be an important source of protein in the diet of these settlements, where animal protein could be consumed and accumulated without sacrificing the livestock. The above also takes the period of dairy production in the subcontinent to nearly 4000-4500 years BP, the earliest known period in South Asia for dairy product processing.

Ladoos of Multi Grain and Oilseeds in Harappan Diet

A recent excavation (2014-2017) in western Rajasthan (Binjor) site revealed the presence of large brown ball-like *ladoos* (food balls). The study was jointly conducted by the Archeological Survey of India (ASI) and Birbal Sahni Institute of Palaeo-sciences (BSIP), Lucknow and the report published in the **Journal of Archaeological Science** (in around March 2021).

The seven food balls were found along with two figurines of bulls and a hand-held copper *adze* (a tool similar to axe). These are dated to around 2600 BCE. The artefacts and the food balls survived because hard structure had fallen over them in a manner to act as a roof and thus saved them from being crushed. The *ladoos* were found to be made of wheat, barley, chickpea, pulses like moong, and a number of oil seeds. The archaeologists believe that the food balls could be a part of veneration to a deity or some kind of ritual offering. it also indicates common consumption of a variety of nutritious cereals, legumes and oilseeds by the population at large and their abundance in agricultural production.

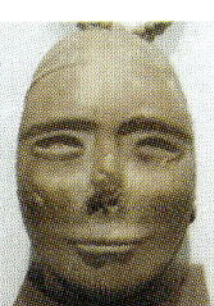

IMPORTANT HARAPPAN SITES AND THEIR SIGNIFICANCE

Mohenjodaro

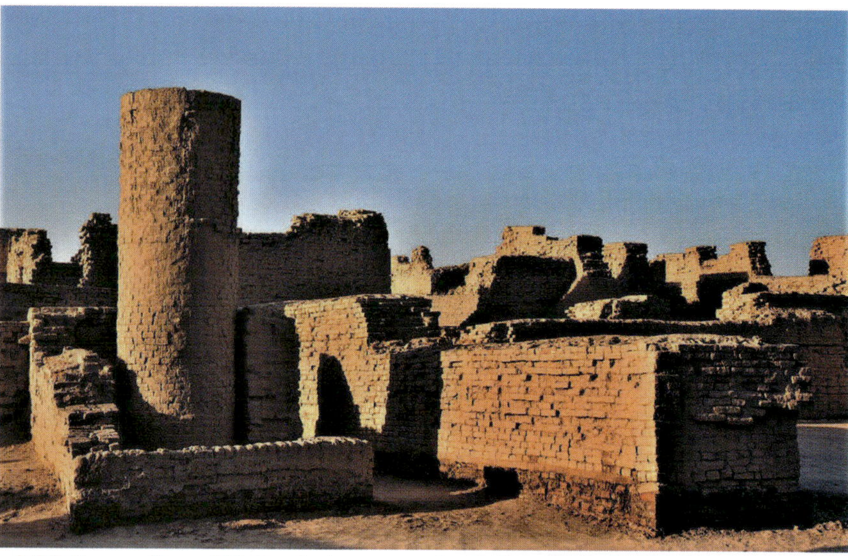

2.37: Excavation of Mohenjodaro revealed tall wells. Apparently, these were continually built and raised on account of constant flooding and rebuilding of the city, thus raising its street levels. — Wikimedia Commons

Mohenjodaro, or the mound of dead, was discovered in 1922 and is amongst the better-preserved sites of this civilisation. Located in the Sindh province, (near the banks of Indus River) in present day Pakistan, the site discovered so far, is spread in around 300 hectares. The city is estimated to have been built around 2600BCE. It is divided into two parts, the **Citadel and the lower town**. The Citadel, which is nearly 12 metres high, was made of mud brick platform with sundried or burnt bricks. It had the **Great Bath**, the large **pillared public halls**, granary/warehouse, planned roads running at right angles, large residential structures and an efficient **sewage system**. All of these are reflective of advanced urban planning and are symbolic of the Harappan civilisation.

Besides, the city also had a central market place. Public and private wells of which **over 700** have been discovered, appear to be the chief source of water. The citadel as well as the lower town, were fortified with walls. A number of important artifacts, including the **bronze statue of dancing girl, bearded priest king, Mother Goddess figurine, Pashupati seal,** were discovered here (see pictures earlier). These

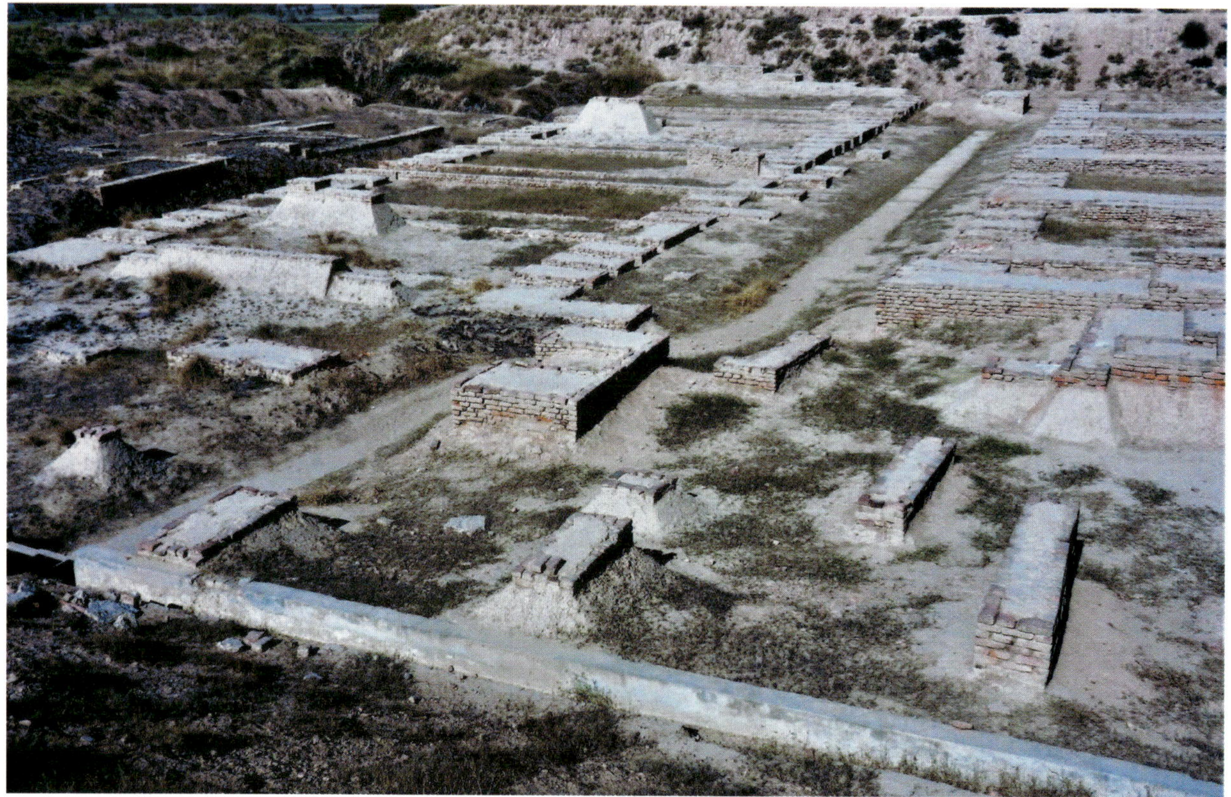

2.38: A view of granary and Great Hall in Harappa along with other ruins — Wikimedia Commons

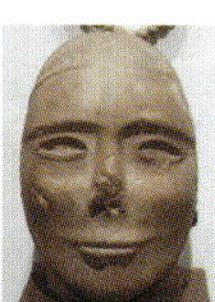

artefacts have helped the historians to understand the cultural practices of this civilisation. The city is believed to have been destroyed by several devastating floods in around 1900 BCE.

Harappa, discovered in 1921, was amongst the **earliest discovered sites** of the Indus civilisation and one of the **largest but much less preserved**. It is believed that a large part of the ruins was destroyed by the brick robbers and also used as ballast for laying railway tracks in the Lahore-Multan Railway, prior to its preservation. The site is spread in an area of 150 hectares (370 acres) considered fairly large for its time, and as per some estimates, had nearly 23500 residents. Besides **the Great Granary** (see picture earlier), a number of steatite (soapstone) seals, figurines, potteries etc. have been discovered here. The town planning has broad similarity to that of Mohenjodaro. The city is considered to have flourished from 2600 BCE to 1900 BCE in the Mature Harappan phase.

Lothal

Lothal, literally means *Loth-Sthal*; or the mound of dead. One of the biggest Harppan sites discovered in post-independence India (excavated in 1953-54 and later), Lothal flourished for nearly 800 years in the mature Harappan period (2400 BCE to 1900 BCE) and late Harappan period (1900 BCE to 1600 BCE).

The only port city of the civilisation discovered so far, it is unique for its tidal port (see picture earlier) with its advanced locking systems. The city also had a large warehouse, acropolis and lower town, bead making industry and was a prosperous centre of trade and commerce with cities as far as in Persian Gulf and Mesopotamia. Ships from the Gulf of Khambat could sail inland to this port town, enabling export of beads, jewellery and other shell objects, directly from the site of production.

A number of seals, terracotta figurines, items of gold jewellery, perforated jars and painted terracotta jars too have been found. One such jar bears the image of the crow and the fox, believed to be depicting the well known fable of the crow and the cunning fox. Indeed, this find is a highly exciting one, as the fable has continued to be a part of folklore till this day and hints at possible intermingling and continuity of cultures.

This ancient port town with its tidal navigation and control systems, bead making industry, and exports to far off cities in Mesopotamia, represents the zenith of the Indus Valley Civilisation. It is indeed a reflection of their knowledge of seas, navigational astronomy, hydraulics and civil engineering, besides of trade and commerce, art and craft as well the immaculate planning and efficient administration. The meandering of the river and repeated **heavy flooding**, (with the worst flood around 1900 BCE) are said to be the cause of its decay. For its embodiment of the above outstanding universal values of human advancement, this site is also nominated from India as a World Heritage Site and is in the tentative list of UNESCO.

Dholavira

Dholavira located in the Kutch region of Gujarat is amongst the largest five settlements of the Indus Valley Civilisation and even older than Lothal. The site was discovered in 1967, but major excavations only happened in the 1990s. Recent researches indicate that the site had been occupied for nearly 1800 to 2000 years, beginning from 3500 BCE, thus showing signs of all phases of the Harappan civilisation, from Early to Mature Harappan phase and Late Harappan phase.

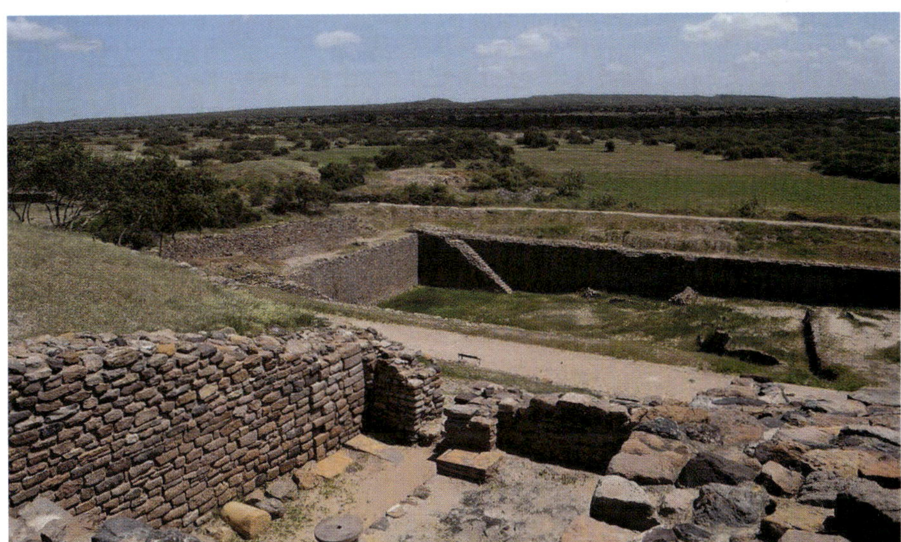

2.39: Ruins at Dholavira and water conservation tank — Wikimedia Commons

A unique feature of Dholavira has been the existence of a **middle town**, apart from the citadel and the lower town, with each having its own fortification walls, gateways, street systems, wells, underground drainage and even large open spaces. Interestingly, there is also a **castle** and a large **stadium**-like complex structure with seating arrangements.

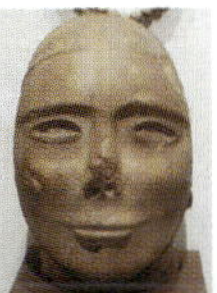

Dholavira : A UNESCO World Heritage Site

Dholavira was recognised by UNESCO as a World Heritage Site in 2021. Thereby, bringing out the significance of this ancient city and its importance to the world heritage.The UNESCO observed as below.

Dholavira: A Harappan City: *The ancient city of Dholavira, the southern centre of the Harappan Civilisation, is sited on the arid island of Khadir in the State of Gujarat. Occupied between ca. 3000-1500 BCE, the archaeological site,* ***one of the best-preserved urban settlements from the period in Southeast Asia****, comprises* ***a fortified city*** *and a* ***cemetery. Two seasonal streams*** *provided water, a scarce resource in the region, to the* ***walled city*** *which comprises* ***a heavily fortified castle*** *and* ***ceremonial ground*** *as well as streets and houses of different proportion quality which testify to a stratified social order. A* ***sophisticated water management system*** *demonstrates the ingenuity of the Dholavira people in their struggle to survive and thrive in a harsh environment. The site includes a* ***large cemetery with cenotaphs*** *of six types, testifying to the Harappan's* ***unique view of death. Bead processing workshops*** *and* ***artifacts of various kinds*** *such as copper, shell, stone, jewellery of semi-precious stones, terracotta, gold, ivory and other materials have been found during archaeological excavations of the site, exhibiting the culture's artistic and technological achievements. Evidence for* ***inter-regional trade*** *with other Harappan cities, as well as with cities in the Mesopotamia region and the Oman peninsula have also been discovered.*

A unique water conservation system

The most important feature of this settlement is a large and earliest known **water conservation system**, comprising **reservoirs and tanks** built of stones and rain water harvesting system. The reservoirs and wells were rock-cut and connected via huge stone drains to channel the storm water. The city also drew water from two seasonal streams (**Mansar** and **Manhar**), whose dry river beds exist even today, and were flowing in the northern and southern side of the city. There was a system of check-dams to channelise the water from the streams and to utilise water very efficiently. The discovery of a stone inscription (nearly three metres long) with several characters, near the northern gate of the castle, referred to as the **signboard,** is another significant find of this settlement.

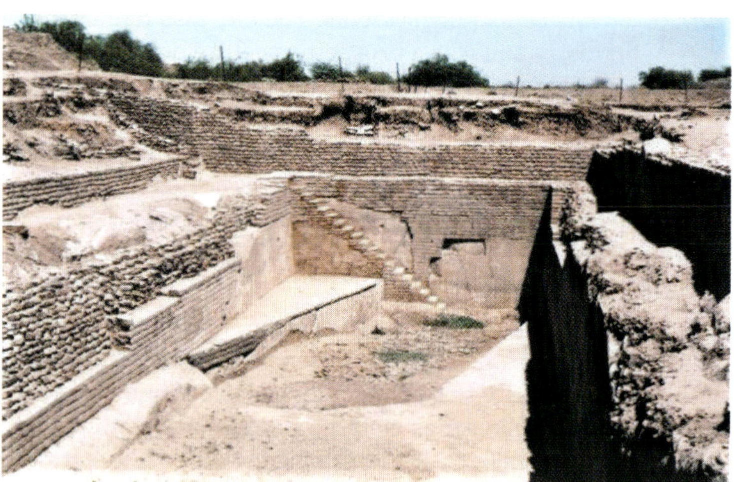

2.40: A large water stepped storage and conservation tank at Dholavira — Wikimedia Commons

What Isotopic Research Reveals About Dholavira Settlement

A recent research of IIT Kharagpur (led by Prof Anindya Sarkar of Geology and Isotope Geochemistry) published in *Wiley Journal of Quaternary Science* in 2020, indicates that a **Meghalayan drought** which lasted for nearly 300 years and affected the entire planet (2300 BCE to 2000 BCE) was the main cause of **decline** of this city. Research on oxygen isotopes (in fossils of snail mollusks, then found in this region) also indicates that this region was receiving **glacial melt water** fed from a river system, around 2700 BCE.

This is considered by some experts to be the **Vedic Saraswati river** system. The Isotope study further reveals that around the period 2300 BCE to 2100 BCE the glacial water feed substantially receded. The population initially adapted to it by development of extensive water conservation system and even changed the crop, apparently from rice to millets. But the changing monsoon and extremely long drought eventually sounded this settlement's death knell.

Thus, this settlement tells a great story of human survival; that of conservation and adaptation to the changing environment, indeed a lesson for all to remember especially in the present times.

Rakhigarhi

Rakhigarhi in Haryana is another fabulous and recent discovery (1997) where human settlements date back to pre-Harappan culture (4000 BCE to 2500 BCE). It also exhibits continuous settlements in the Early Harappan and the Mature Harappan phase (2600 BCE to 1900 BCE). Thus, it exhibits continuous human settlement for more than 4000 years.

The largest Indus Valley settlement

The site was discovered in the 60s and the excavation and the reporting on the discoveries have been recent and continues. With the excavation of two more mounds in 2014 (taking the total to nine mounds),

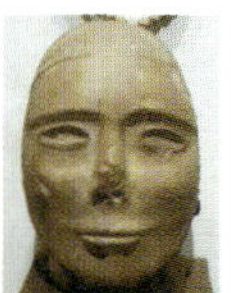

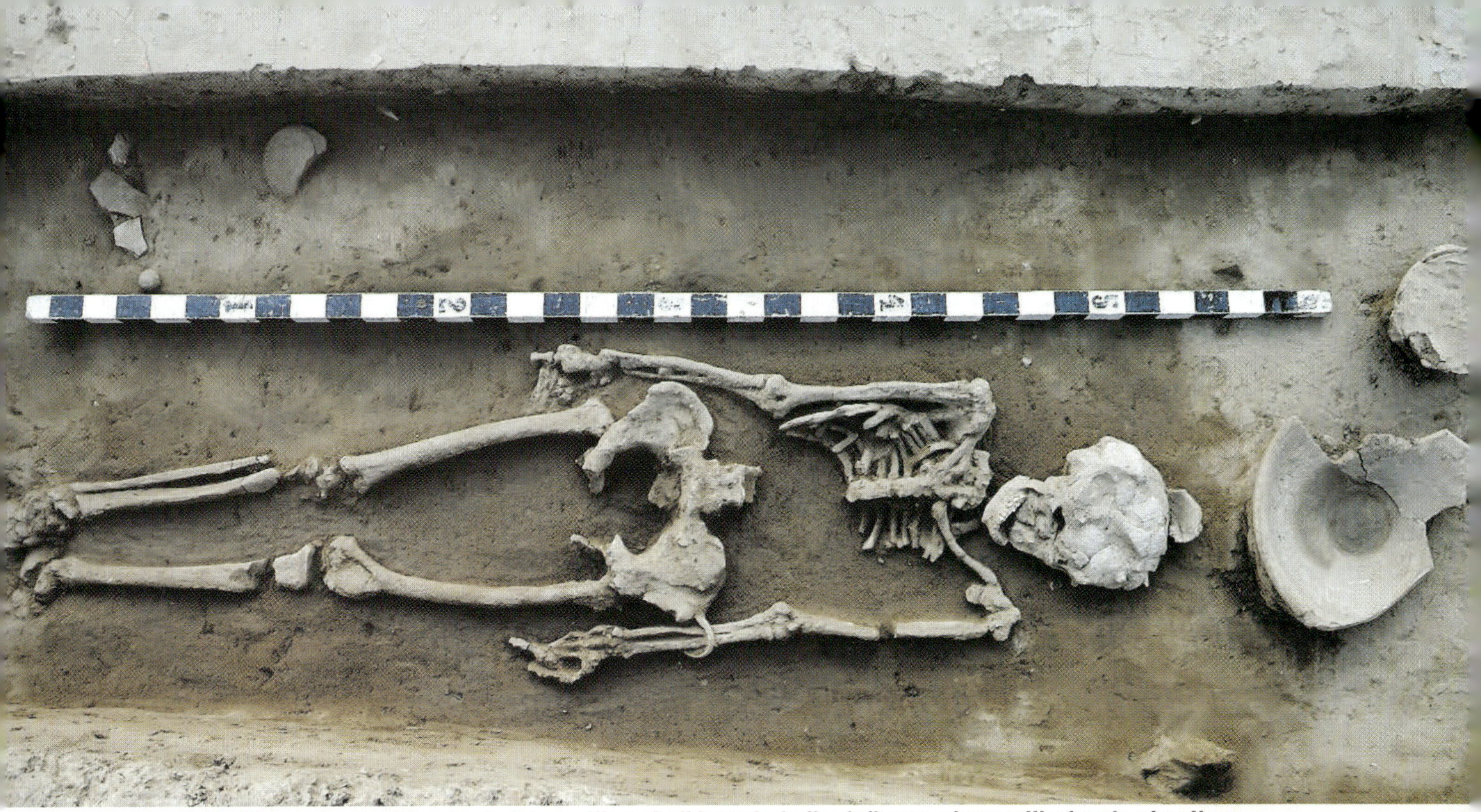

2.41: Discovery of a female skeleton with a shell bangle in the left arm, along with shards of pottery, at the site of Burial Ground RGR7 at Rakhigarhi — Pictures Courtesy, Directorate of Archaeology and Museums, Government of Haryana

Rakhigarhi is now the **largest discovered settlement in the entire Indus Valley Civilisation,** covering nearly 350 hectares and exceeding even Mohenjodaro (300 hectares). As per the latest reports emerging in 2020, a total of 11 mounds have been discovered, covering an area of 550 hectares, out of which only 5% has been excavated so far. Located in the Ghaggar–Hakra river plane (nearly 150 km from New Delhi), this is the north-easternmost settlement of this civilisation. This indicates the massive spread of this advanced culture, covering large parts of North India, Pakistan, parts of Afghanistan and even touching Iran.

The findings of Rakhigarhi reveal the existence of paved roads, numerous wells, efficient drainage system with pits and brick lined drains, a **granary** made of mud bricks, terracotta pottery, weights, seals, copper fish hooks, hunting tools and other artifacts similar to other Harappan sites. A unique discovery is of a **gold foundry with 3000 unpolished semi-precious stones,** along with foundry tools and even a furnace. Triangular and circular **fire altars**, certain apsidal structures and even pits for supposed animal sacrifices, have also been found, indicating rituals and religious practices of this culture.

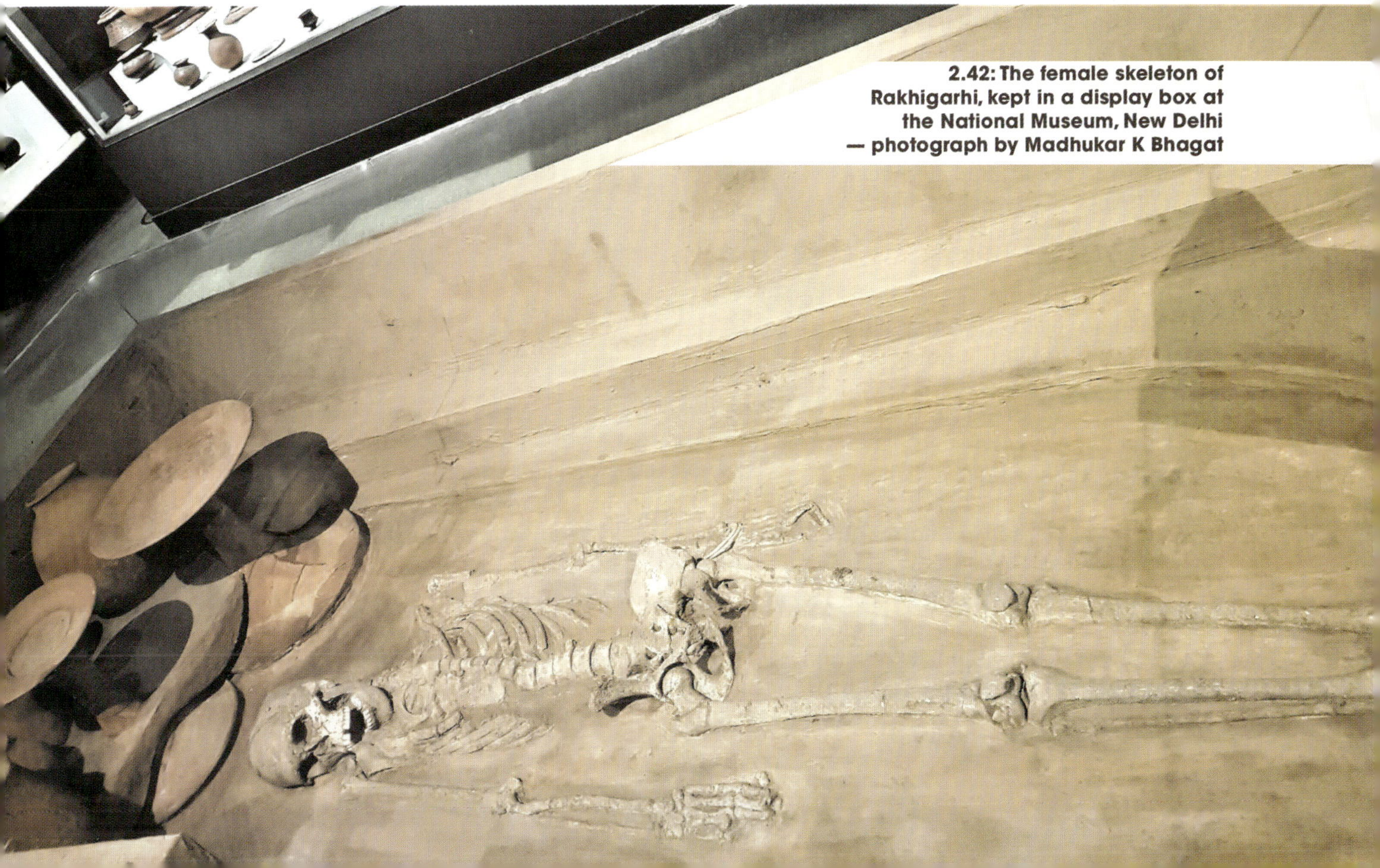

2.42: The female skeleton of Rakhigarhi, kept in a display box at the National Museum, New Delhi — photograph by Madhukar K Bhagat

Bhirrana near Rakhigarhi: The Oldest Pre-Harappan Settlement

An Archaeological Survey of India (ASI) report published in 2015 indicated the discovery of a settlement at Bhirrana or Birhana (in Haryana) dating to 7570 to 6200 BCE. This makes the settlement even older than Mehrgarh (6400 to 7000 BCE) in Pakistan. Thus, Bhirrana can be considered the oldest of pre-Harrapan settlements where agricultural communities got organised from the earlier nomadic/hunter gatherer communities.

Along with the finding of nearby Rakhigarhi being the largest of the Harappan settlements, historians, and archaeologists, consider that Rakhigarhi and adjoining regions could be the earliest of regions from where the Harappan civilisation emanated and perhaps then spread westward, as opposed to the earlier view of eastward migration from Mehrgarh region.

The discovery of a Mature Harappan period **cemetery** with over 50 **burial sites** and **preserved skeletons** has been an extremely significant find of this civilisation, which has revealed a wealth of information about burial and funerary practices of this population. The burials are of pit type, as well as burial chambers, which are lined with bricks. The skeletons are mostly found in supine position with head towards north. They are buried with pottery, filled with grains and other burial material. Female skeletons with shell bangles in left arm and one skeleton with even a gold armlet has been found.

Study of DNA Samples and Findings: What the Dead Reveal

Recently, studies of the **DNA samples** of a female skeletal remains found from Rakhigarhi were conducted. This was first of its kind DNA study of any Harappan civilisation's DNA sample. The study was conducted by a team led by Prof. Vasant Shinde (archaeologist, Deccan College of Pune), Vagesh Narasimhan, David Reich of Harvard Medical School (DNA experts) and others. The report was published in September of 2019 in a scientific journal, **"Cell"** under the title, *'An Ancient Harappan Genome Lacks Ancestry from Pastoralists and Iranian Farmers'.*

The **significant finding** of the **research** was that the gene pertaining to Iranian or steppe pastoral ancestry was missing in the female skeleton in Rakhigarhi. Further, the skeletal remains of the Rakhigarhi individual was from a population that is also the largest source of ancestry for South Asians.

The above finding implied that this Indus Valley population had no traces of ancestry of Iranian farmers and that it had a lot of genetic material in common with the current South Asian population. This, in turn, points to a genetic continuity and debunks the Aryan invasion theory. It even points contrary to the earlier proposition of the current South Asian population being of totally different genetic make than the Indus-Civilisation people.

Though the above propositions have been questioned by some experts, but it is for sure that further genetic studies and other researches would bring out more exciting results to the fore.

Kalibangan

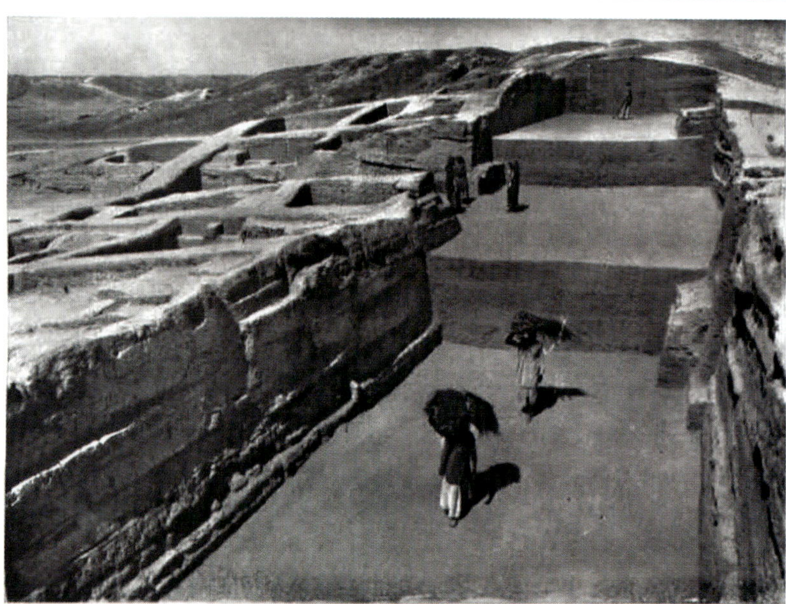

2.43: Kalibangan main street — Wikimedia Commons

Kalibangan is another prominent settlement of this civilisation, which is located in Rajasthan, (Hanumangarh district) in the Ghaggar-Harkra river plains. The name literally means 'black bangles', owing to apparently the discovery of a large number of fragments of terracotta black bangles found at the surfaces of the mounds.

The Kalibangan site is said to have been discovered by Luigi Pio Tessitori, an Italian Indologist, even prior to the discovery of the Harappan site. However, excavations were conducted here only after India's independence in the 1960s under B.B. Lal (Director General, Archaeological Survey of India). The discoveries of artifacts indicate early Harappan and **mature Harappan phases** of civilisation. The site also has remnants of a pre-Harappan settlement.

The excavations reveal a **grid-iron layout of this metropolis with mud brick fortification of a citadel.** The houses too were made of baked or sundried bricks. A variety of terracotta pottery, seals and other artifacts have been found. Excavations also reveal some **fire altars** indicating ritualistic practices of this civilisation. But the **most significant discovery has been of a ploughed field** which has cross grid

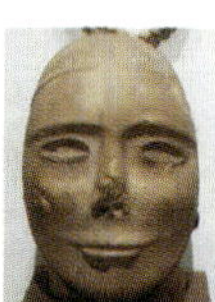

of furrows. This indicates the practice of cultivation of two crops. This is also one of the earliest discoveries of ploughing in this civilisation.

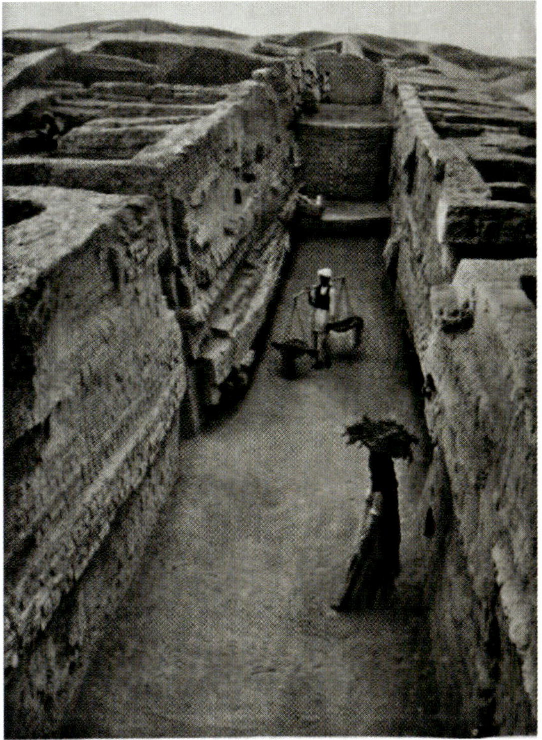

2.44: Kalibangan arterial thoroughfare — Wikimedia Commons

Cemeteries and burials

Cemeteries have also been found reflecting **three separate systems** of **burial practices**. These include burial in **oval pit** with head northwards. Other two practices include **burial in a pot** (urn), and in a **rectangular or oval pit with only pottery** and other funerary objects, but with no body/corpse in them (as no skeletal material has been found in them). Thus, the latter two types of burials were unique as these were a symbolic funerary practice or a post-cremation practice, which has not been noted elsewhere in the Harappan culture.

As per the archaeological findings, the early Harappan phase at Kalibangan came to an end because of a massive **earthquake in 2600 BCE.** This is also considered the earliest recorded archaeological evidence of an earthquake. The Mature Harappan settlement which flourished later, is believed to have ended in around 2000 BCE to 1900 BCE. As per **hydrological evidences,** this was caused due to drying up of the Ghaggar river (believed to be a part of the Saraswati- river system). This period also coincides with that of the end of other settlements such as Dholavira and is further corroborated with the recent Meghalayan drought theory.

Besides the above, Banawali (in Haryana), Surkotada (Kutch, Gujarat) Ganeriwala, Chanuhdaro and Kot-Diji in Pakistan are some other important sites. Shortugai in Afghanistan was perhaps the northern most tip of this civilisation and is known for **lapis-lazuli** mining and dry land farming. Excavations here have also revealed an irrigation canal for fetching water from a place called Kokcha at a distance of 25 kms. Suktagendor, (in Pakistan) near the Iranian border, was a smaller settlement with stonewalls and gateways, and marked the western border of this civilisation.

Harappan Sites and Significance — A Snapshot

Sites & Present Location	Significance and Archaeological Discoveries
Mohenjodaro (in Pakistan)	• Discovered in 1922, amongst the better preserved sites. • Existence of **citadel** and **lower town** • Discovery of **Great Bath**, pillared hall, granary planned roads, sewage system
Harappa (in Pakistan)	• Earliest discovered (in 1921), **one of the largest sites**, but less preserved as ruin—bricks were used for ballast for laying tracks in early British Rule and also lost due to theft. • The **Great Granary**
Lothal (in Gujarat)	• Existence of earliest **dockyard and acropolis** • Discovery of **weights and measures** • Flourishing centre of beads and gem making
Dholavira (in Gujarat)	• Discovery of large **water reservoirs** (built of stone) drawing water from channels and rivulets • One of the five large settlements of Harappan culture • Large **signboard** containing a number of characters • World Heritage Site
Rakhigarhi (in Haryana)	• Important and largest Harappan site • Discovery of artifacts 5000 years old (Early Harappan phase) • Paved roads, rain water collection, drainage system, granary, bronze artifacts, bangles, etc. • Discovery of **female skeletons** with shell bangles and gold armlet.

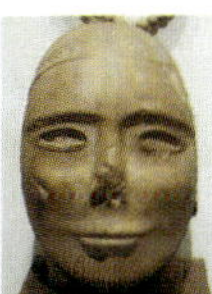

Kalibangan (in Rajasthan)	• Literally means 'black bangles', owing to discovery of a number of terracotta black bangles at this site. • Represents Early Harappan phase • Fortified settlement citadel and **fire altars** discovered • **Grid iron layout** of metropolis • Mud brick fortification of citadel. • Three systems of burial practices • Destruction due to earthquake
Kot Diji (in Pakistan)	• Settlement of Early Harappan phase • Existence of citadel and lower town • Discovery of defensive wall with a mud brick revetment with bastions
Ganeriwala (in Pakistan)	• Among the larger cities of Harappan civilisation (80 hectares)

Some Other Important Features of the Harappan Culture

Fabric and cloth

Cotton was commonly used as fabric for clothing, although wool could also have been used. Findings of spindles indicate that weaving and spinning was known. Needles and buttons have been discovered

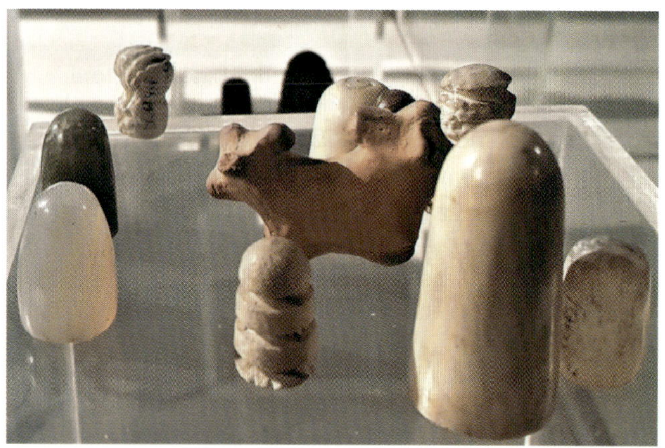

2.45: Small conical stones of jasper, chalcedony etc. found at Mohenjodaro. Scholars debate whether it could be representing lingas or whether they were used in board games. Location, National Museum, New Delhi — photograph by Madhukar K Bhagat

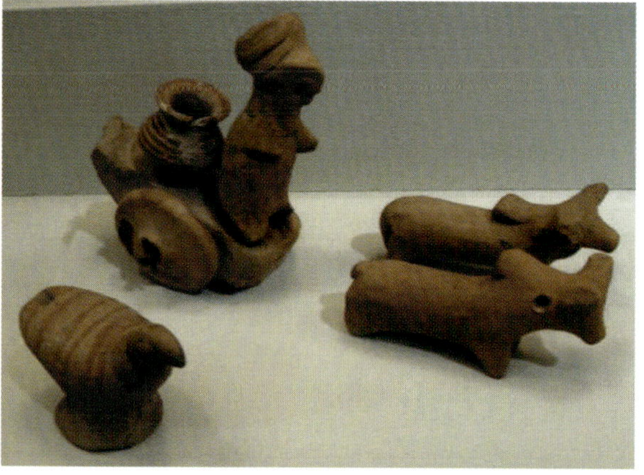

2.46: Clay figurines of an oxen pulled cart and chicken/domesticated jungle fowl — Wikipedia Commons

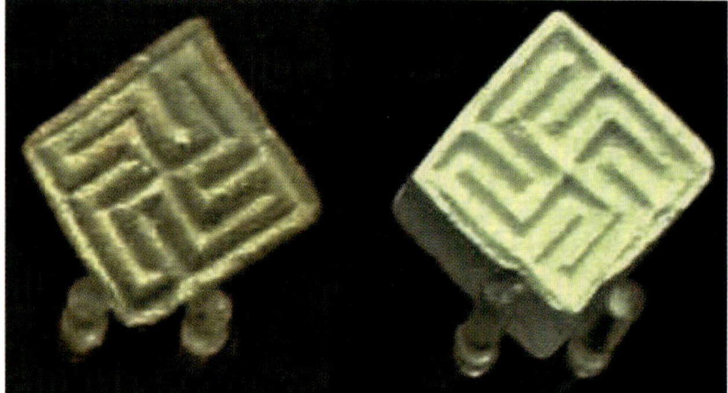

2.47: Swastik seals of Indus Valley Civilisation; British Museum. This symbol was considered auspicious in later Hinduism — Wikimedia Commons

indicating that perhaps stitching was also known. Dress, or fabric, has not survived, but statues and figurines suggest that two pieces of cloth were used by men and women. One piece resembled a dhoti covering the lower body. Other portion was worn over the left shoulder under the right arm.

Games, sports and entertainment

Objects similar to dice games and clay carts have been found. Hunting is believed to be common as seen from a number of seals carrying images of animals. Dancing and singing were popular as seen from the bronze statue of the dancing girl.

Religion

Discovery of the seal of Shiva Pashupati (proto-Shiva) and figurines believed to be of Mother Goddess, indicate presence of religious beliefs comparable to very early Hinduism. However, historians believe that religion does not seem to have a predominant influence on the society. The discovery of fire altars at Kalibangan and Lothal also suggests some kind of ritual practices were present in the society. A belief in

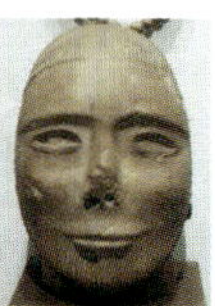

afterlife from the burial can be gathered; besides cremation practices are also noted. However, how much of this was integrated with the religious beliefs and whether a formal religion was practised as in the other contemporary civilisations is not as yet known.

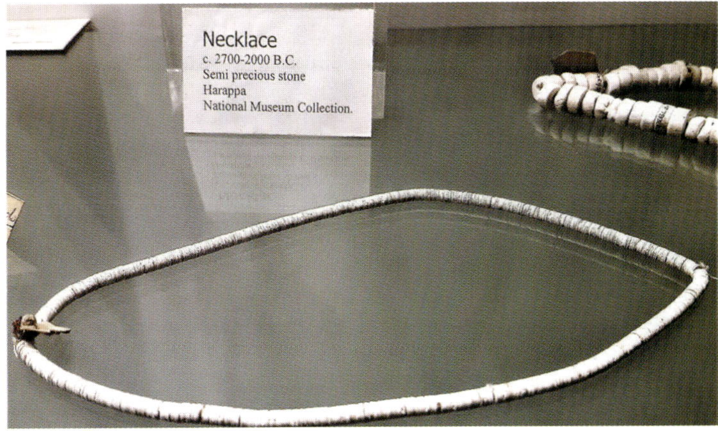

2.48: A necklace of very fine and over 400 beads made using specialised tools. National Museum, New Delhi — photograph by Madhukar K Bhagat

Craft production

Production of a variety of crafts was another hallmark of this civilisation. These included bead making, shell cutting, metal working, weight and seal making etc. Bead making in particular, was a highly advanced craft with centres like Chanhudaro (near Mohenjodaro) being exclusively devoted to it. Besides, Lothal and Dholavira were other important centres of bead making, where specialised drills and equipment used for this purpose, have been found. A variety of materials like stones of jasper, carnelian, steatite, quartz etc., copper, bronze, gold, shell, steatite and even terracotta were used for the bead production. These crafts were also important items of trade and export.

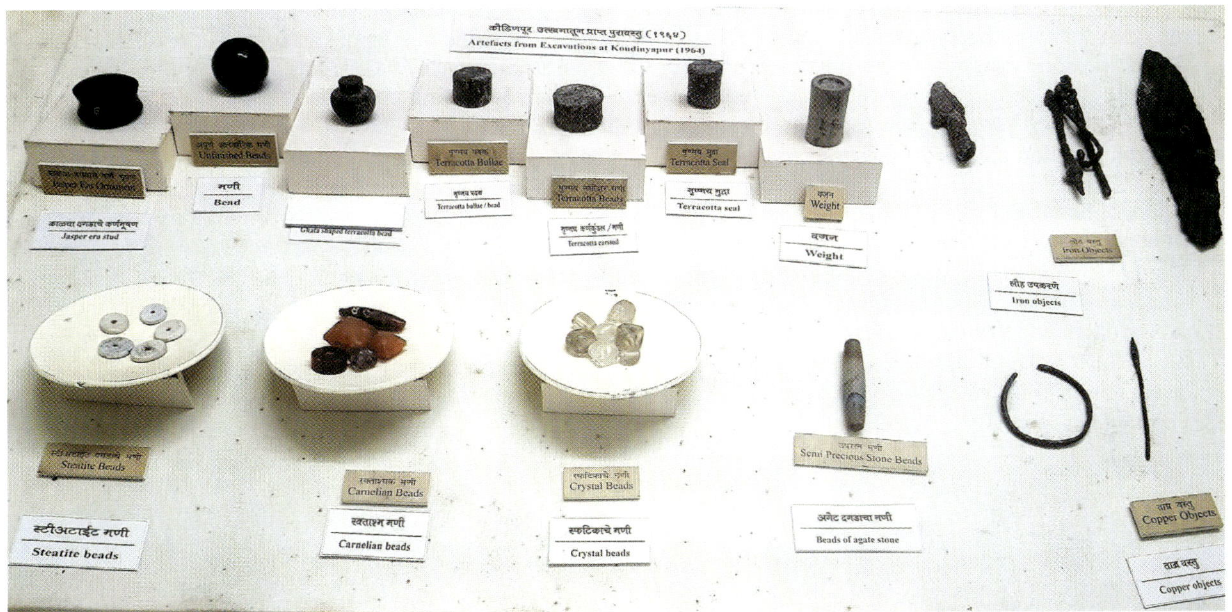

2.49: Beads, seals, copper objects — photograph by Madhukar K Bhagat

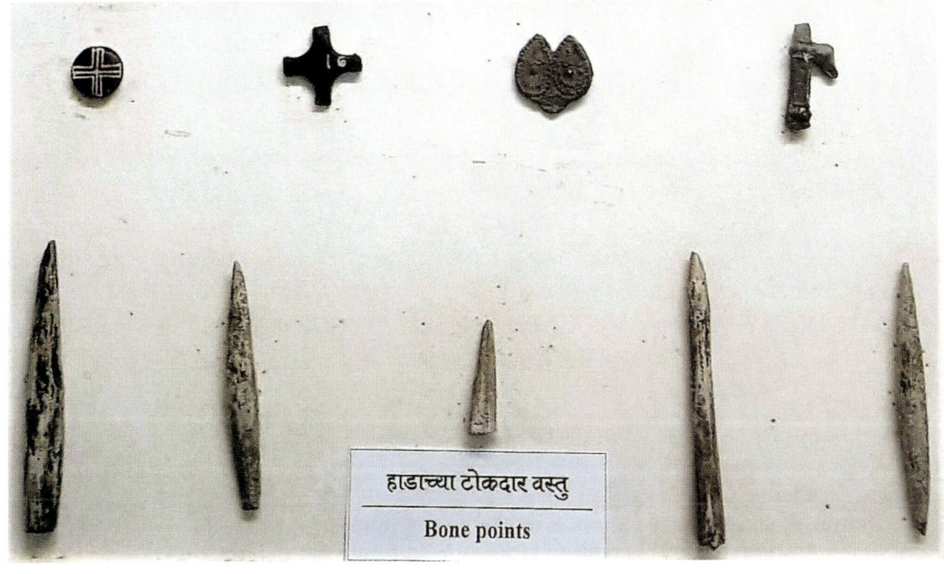

2.50: Bone points used as tools (lower image) 2700-2000 BCE, Nagpur Central Museum — photograph by Madhukar K Bhagat

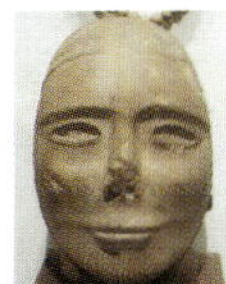

The Discovery of Sinauli and Whether it Represents a Harappan Culture?

Recent discoveries at Sinauli, an archaeological site in Western Uttar Pradesh, has added a new chapter to ancient Indian history. The site first came to be noticed in 2005-06 when certain artefacts including ancient pottery and human skeletons were found by local farmers during agricultural activities. Excavations were conducted in 2005-06 and also in 2018 in adjoining sites to the earlier ones. However, detailed analysis reporting was done in 2018. Carbon-14 dating of artefacts has indicated the period of this culture to be around **1865-1.550 BCE** and corresponding to Ochre Coloured Pottery culture and Copper Hoard culture.

A variety of artefacts have been unearthed which include copper objects, swords, copper shields, three complete chariots, copper helmets, large terracotta pots, red vases, grey ware pottery, coffins and burial sites with skeletons. Nearly **116 burials** have been found which are considered as the largest in South Asia. These are categorised into three types: The Primary or Coffin-burial with complete skeleton, the Secondary or Fragmented-burial with part skeletal remains, and Symbolic-burial with no skeletal remains. The coffin at burials were laid along the east and west axis. These coffins were four legged, were covered with lids which had thin plate of copper and were richly carved. These burials have a wealth of artefacts. Among these the most significant are the discoveries of **three complete chariots, two of which are found buried next to a coffin.** Besides, other salient discoveries **include copper antennae swords** and **female skeletons**.

This is considered as the first time where **archaeological discovery of chariots** has been made in the Indian subcontinent in a time period contemporaneous to Mesopotamian and Sumerian cultures. The wheels of these chariots are solid (and not spoked) and covered with triangular pieces of copper. The chassis of the carts is made of wood but covered with thick copper sheets. The seat is **semicircular /U shaped and the frame of the seat is made of copper pipes. A pipe for the attachment of the** umbrella is also seen. As per the chariots' design, it was meant for carrying two persons. Also, considering the nature and design of the chariots and a variety of swords, bows and arrows etc. found in the burial, a section of **archaeologists believe these to be war chariots which were drawn by horses.** However, this would imply a challenge to the theory of subsequent arrival of the horses with the Indo-Aryan population/central Asian tribes. Further, this theory would also impact the accepted belief of the origin of Indo-Aryan race in Central Asia and their being non-indigenous to the Indian subcontinent. However, historians like Asko Parpola opine that these chariots were drawn by oxen. Some historians consider that the solid wheels would make the chariots too heavy to be horse drawn and carts drawn by bullocks was in vogue in post Harrapan cultures.

The coffin burials also reveal skeletons of women wearing an armlet along with other artefacts including symbolic antenna sword, bows and arrows etc. Archaeologists consider this to be perhaps a **female warrior**, considering the nature of burial and artefacts found. If true, this would also be a first of its kind archaeological discovery revealing a completely new facet of this ancient culture.

The discovery of the hundreds of **antennae swords** of copper (and other swords) is also significant. The swords have wodden hilts which are copper wired. This is considered the first of its kind discovery of such swords in the Indian subcontinent and that too dating to nearly 3500 years ago.

Regarding the issue of which culture the Sinauli discovery falls into, archaeologists usually agree that it is late-Harappan or a post-Harappan culture and definitely not the Mature Harappan culture, as seen in the other sites of the Indus Valley Civilisation.

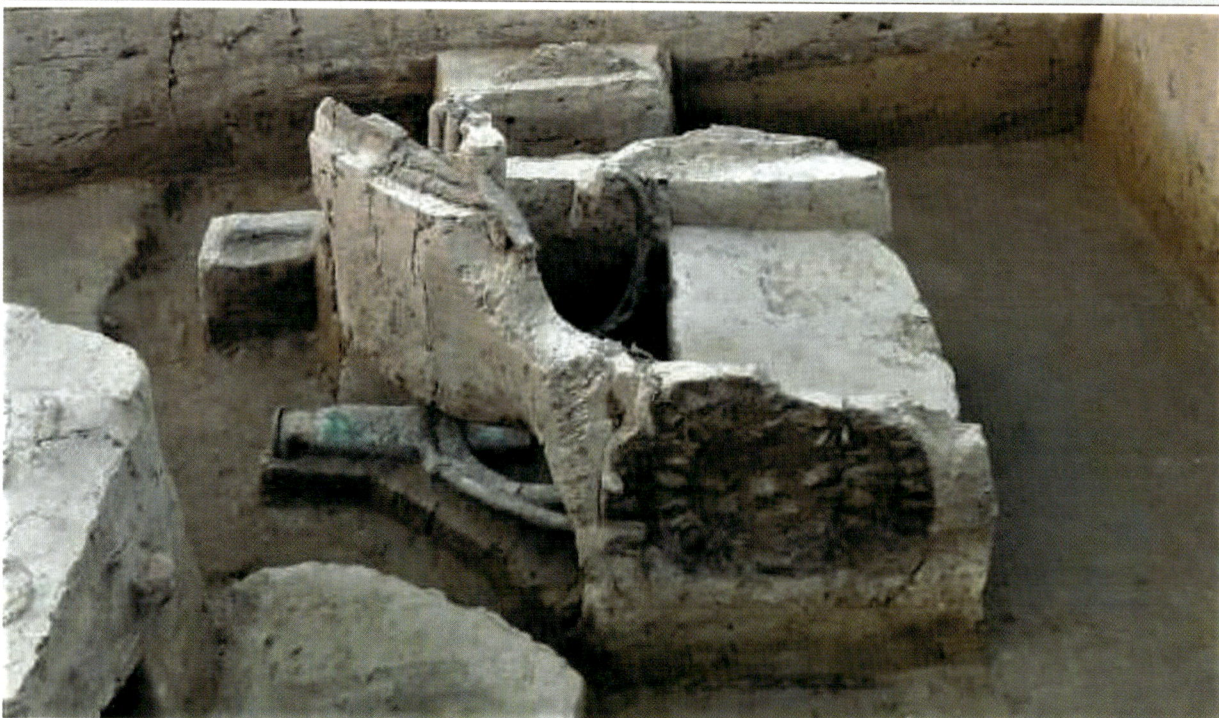

2.51: Chariot at Sinauli as discovered at the site of the burial; photograph of the Archaeological Survey of India — Wikimedia Commons

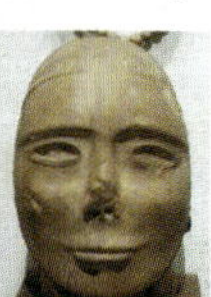

Hinduism: A Way and View of Life

> *Hinduism alone is by itself a vast and complex thing, not so much a religion as a great diversified and yet subtly unified mass of spiritual thought, realisation and aspiration.*
>
> Sri Aurobindo

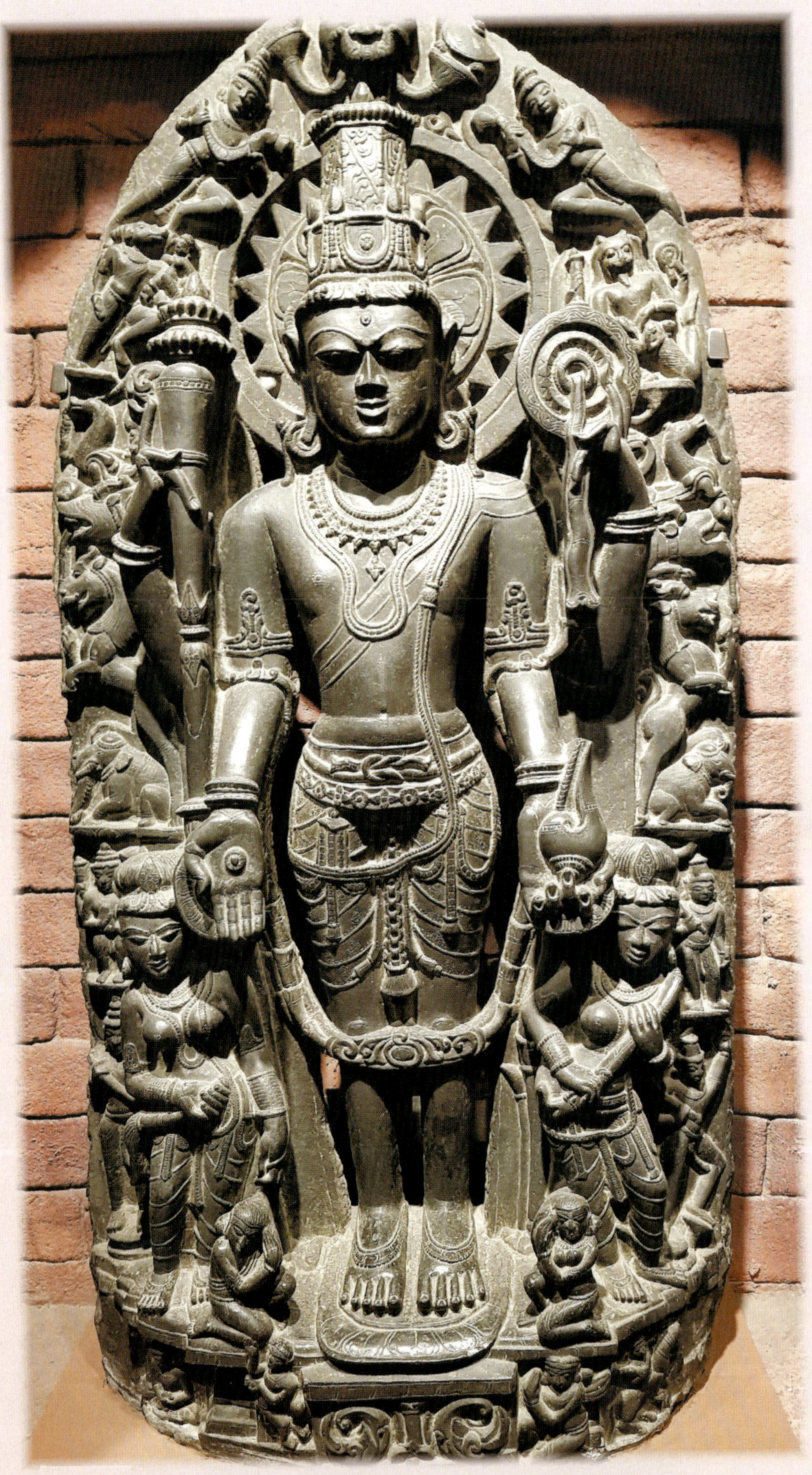

3.1: Lord Vishnu, 11th century CE, Pala period, Bihar Museum, Patna — photograph by Madhukar K Bhagat

AN INTRODUCTION

Hinduism is considered the oldest organised and living religion of the world. At present it has more than 1.1 billion followers which is roughly 15% of the world population. It is the third largest religion (after Christianity and Islam) in the world with wide geographical distribution of its followers. Believers of this faith are in majority in the demography of India, Nepal and Mauritius and are present in more than 100 countries including 35 of these with more than 100,000 population. However, over 98% of Hindu population is concentrated in South Asia (India; 1.05 billion, Nepal; 23.5 million, Bangladesh; 14.3 million, Pakistan; 3.62 million).

Hinduism as a religion does not have an origin at a single point of time, a singular religious preacher to whom it could own its genesis, a singular scripture to which its philosophy can be consigned, or a limited set of practises which can define it. It is a synthesis of beliefs, faiths, and philosophies. It is a religion which has grown over nearly 3500 years or even more. Numerous scriptures including the Vedas, the Gita, the Ramayana, the Mahabharata, the Puranas and others, bring out different manifestations of its philosophy. Many sages and reformers have contributed to its growth as it has evolved assimilating diverse beliefs and thoughts.

The very word 'Hinduism' is of later origin, referring to the people in the valley of river Sindhu (Indus) and beyond it. The coinage of the term 'Hindu' is Persian in nature, and over a period it acquired a religious connotation. In the early period of this growth, the faith has been referred to **Santana Dharma** (the eternal or universal religion), or **Varnashrama Dharma,** a faith based on fulfilment of duties based on *varna* (class) and *ashram* (stage of life), or a *vaidik dharma* (a faith based on principles of the Vedas).

The Genesis of the Word 'Hindu'.

The Hindu civilisation is so called, since its original founders or earliest followers occupied the territory drained by the Sindhu (the Indus) river system corresponding to the North-West Frontier Province and the Punjab. The people on the Indian side of the Sindhu were called Hindu by the Persians and the later western invaders. The term 'Hindu' had originally a territorial, and not a credal significance. It implied residence in a well-defined geographical area.

Dr. Radhakrishnan, in ***The Hindu View of Life***

A BRIEF HISTORY

Hinduism as a religion has its roots in the Vedic faith and texts which are said to be nearly 3500 years old. Over the period of centuries several waves of changes and evolution have swept it. Although the very core of its philosophy has remained unaltered, in form it has transitioned from a religion based on early Vedic ritualism to profound Advaitism, from Brahmanical orthodoxy to syncretic pluralism, from *varna* based social divide to Bhakti based centuries of social regeneration. The growth of the Vedic faith and the Hindu religion has been divided into several phases of development. These can broadly be said to be, the **early Vedic phase**, the **later Vedic phase**, the period of **Shramana tradition**, the **phase of Shad-Darshanas**, the emergence of **Puranic Hinduism**, the **Bhakti period** and phase of reforms and the phase of **modern Hinduism**.

The Vedic Phase

The period from 1500 BCE to 500 BCE is usually referred as the Vedic period. The four Vedas, the Rigveda, the Samaveda, the Atharvaveda, and the Yajurveda are said to have been composed in this period, the Rigveda being of the earliest origin amongst the four. The Vedic phase is further divided into the **Early Vedic Phase** (1500–1000 BCE) and **Later Vedic Phase** (1000–500 BC).

The early Vedic religion was closely integrated with the elements of nature which included the, rain, fire, earth, water, wind etc and the associated deities. Propitiation of these elements through rituals and practices formed the nucleus around which the religious philosophy and culture revolved. Over a period of time, the Vedic knowledge was organised into four Vedic layers, the Samhita, the Brahmana, the Aranyaka and the Upanishad. The former Vedic layers Samhitas and Brahmanas, which were also referred as the Karmakanda, defined the early Vedic Hinduism and dealt more with the conduct or rites and rituals.

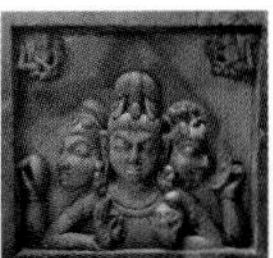

The Aranyakas and the Upanishads also referred as the Jnanakanda, were the final Vedic layers and were composed later, incorporating the knowledge and metaphysical elements to the Vedic religion. The philosophies of *Atman* and *Brahman*, their relationship and other spiritual concepts, had their genesis in this phase. This millennium also witnessed the evolution of the profound and diverse philosophies of **Vedanta** including that of Advaitavada (non-dualism), which is often considered the very soul of Hindu thought and philosophy. Besides, the Vedic period saw the emergence of Varnashrama Dharma, which determined the conduct and duties of the individual, thus enabling the Vedic religion to shape a social order for many centuries to come.

Buddhism, Jainism, Shramana traditions, Shad-darshanas and Their Influence

The advent of Buddhism and Jainism marked the next phase in the course of the Vedic religion (500 BCE to 200 BCE). This was a period of upheavals as there was opposition to the Brahmannical superiority, animal sacrifices and challenge to the authority of the ritualistic traditions of the Vedas by the two upcoming faiths. Besides, these two faiths brought to the fore a more inclusive social-religious philosophy, also combining reason with the culture of spiritualism. The Shramana tradition also emerged in this period, with its emphasis on asceticism, *ahimsa* and *karma*, while rejecting the infallibility of the Vedas. These competing influences did not annihilate the Vedic faith and culture. Rather, their key beliefs such as *ahimsa, karma* and other thoughts, itself permeated deep in the spiritual and religious mass of Hinduism and were analogous to some of the extant Vedic philosophies. However, they caused a relook at the caste rigidities, Brahmanical orthodoxy, excessive ritualism which had crept in the Vedic dharma and brought in a re-emphasis of the core Upanishadic teachings. Thus, this phase had a reforming effect on Hinduism, making its spiritual and cultural canvas more plural and enabling it to evolve further.

The conception of the Shad-darshanas: The six branches of Hindu philosophy—**Nyaya, Vaisheshika, Samkhya, Yoga, Purva Mimansa** and **Vedanta** came into vogue in this period. While *Nyaya* as a philosophy dealt with formal reasoning and logic, the Vaisheshika system incorporated metaphysical and philosophical elements and even dwelt on issues like nature of Parmanu. Thus, a spirit of logic, metaphysics and even other sciences were combined with the spiritual seeking. The Samkhya philosophy revolved around the concepts of *Purusha* and *Prakriti* and the belief system of the true knowledge being an emancipator, eventually leading to a combination of rationalism and spirituality. The Yoga system of philosophy, propounded rationalism, analogous to the Samkhya but also expounded the virtues of *karma* (righteous action) as a means of salvation. The other two schools comprised the Vedantic thoughts, with the former emphasising on the rituals and practices and the latter on the right knowledge of Advaita for salvation. Thus, these diverse schools embodied a liberalist and rational perspective of religious culture, eventually laying the foundation of a pluralistic approach to the seeking of 'real meaning and purpose of life'.

The Golden Period of Hinduism

The next 700 to 800 years, i.e., 200 BCE to 500 CE can be described as a **golden period for growth of Hinduism,** particularly the phase in history which coincides with the Gupta period. Under the patronage of the Gupta rulers, the Vedic religion and the Brahmanical order made a comeback and Hinduism expanded with a new vigour. This was the age of composition of the Puranas. This was also the age when scholars believe that the epics of Ramayana and Mahabharata in the present form were composed, or at least their tradition became dominant.

The emergence of Puranic Hinduism

The conception of the Puranas and the advent of the Puranic Hindu culture was the next significant landmark in the course of Hinduism. This was a period of assimilation of numerous and seemingly divergent thought processes. The concept of the personal God gained ground as against Brahman/the Universal/the *Purusha* without attributes. The personal God was invariably identified in the trinity of **Brahman** (the creator), **Vishnu** (the preserver) and the **Mahesh** (the destroyer) or their numerous manifestations. The early Vedic deities of Indra, Agni, Varun, Mitra etc, although were still venerated as deities/demigods/*devas* but were not considered as the all-powerful cosmic creators. The 18 Puranas, which were religious literature, were compiled in this period, with many of these devoted to a central deity. The writings in these are varyingly considered as mythological accounts of the religious beliefs and practices of the age.

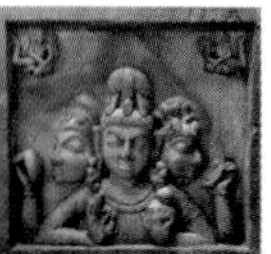

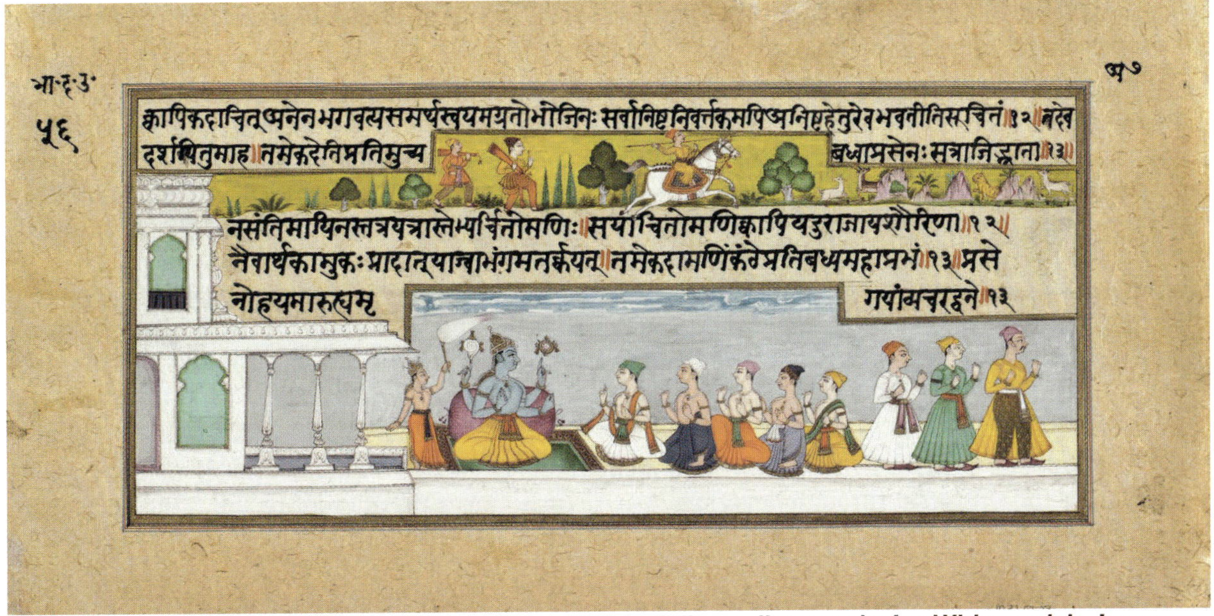

3.2: A page from the 19th century Purana manuscript depicting a discourse by Lord Vishnu; origin Jammu Kashmir region, current location, Los Angeles Museum of County Art — Wikimedia Commons

Although the central tenets of the Vedic religion continued to remain intact, the Puranic culture was accommodative of the regional/local/tribal religious beliefs and traditions. Incorporation of these in the mainstream religion created a polytheistic and assimilative Puranic Hinduism, which posited Vedic monism as a central tenet; yet it accommodated the pantheon of personal gods in its folds. Realisation of *Brahman* still remained the 'real purpose of life', but apart from the emancipating Vedantic knowledge and the 'rightful conduct' or practicing of 'Varnashrama Dharma', Bhakti, or devotion to the personal god, emerged as another appropriate means of attaining salvation.

The Harmony Between Monism and Polytheism of the Hindu Philosophy

Hinduism is the religion not only of the Vedas but of the epics and the Puranas. By accepting the significance of different institutions of reality and the different scriptures of the peoples living in India, (sarvagama pramanya), Hinduism has come to be a tapestry of the most variegated tissues and almost endless diversity of hues.

Hindu thought believes in the evolution of our knowledge of God. We have to vary continually our notions of God until we pass beyond all notions into the heart of the reality itself which our ideas endeavour to report.

Hinduism does not distinguish ideas of God as true and false adopting one particular idea as the standard for the whole human race. It accepts the obvious fact that mankind seeks its goal of God at various levels and in various directions and feels sympathy with every stage of the search. The same god expresses itself at one stage as power, at another as personality, at a third as all comprehensive spirit, just as the same forces which put forth the green leaves also cause the crimson flowers to grow. We do not say that the crimson flowers are all the truth and the green leaves are all false. Hinduism accepts all religious notions and facts and arranges them in the order of the more or less intrinsic significance.

The bewildering polytheism of the masses and the uncompromising monotheism of the classes are for the Hindu the expressions of one and the same force at different levels. Hinduism insists on our working steadily upwards and improving our knowledge of God.

- Dr S. Radhakrishnan, in *The Hindu View of life*

The Age of Adi Shankara, Advaita Vedanta and Other Vedantic Schools

Hinduism, in the latter half of 8th century CE, saw a wave of reform and revival with the emergence of Sri Adi Shankaracharya. His teachings were based on **Advaita philosophy** of Vedanta (non-dualism) emphasizing on the **unity of creator and creation.** He unified the various sects and streams of Hinduism, then in vogue, which were albeit disparate and at times even discordant. The founding of the four *mathas* (monasteries) in different geographical locations of the country (Sringeri, Dwarka, Puri and Badrinath) gave a much-needed formal structure to Hinduism, enabling it to emerge as a unified body and a formal religious order. His commentaries on the Vedas (*Brahman Sutras*) Upanishads and the *Gita*, form the bedrock of the core philosophies of Hinduism. The very concept of *Advaita*, implying the same universal force within all humanity and oneness with the Universal, heralded spiritual inclusiveness with a

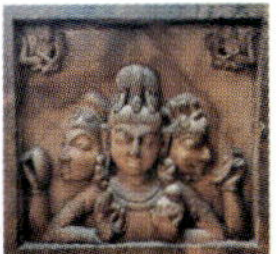

philosophy of reason, to revive Hinduism. This was especially significant, considering the existence of numerous competing faiths in the socio-religious landscape.

The **Vishishtadvaita** (qualified non-dualism) propounded by Sri Ramanuja in the 12th century CE and of **Dwaitvaada** (dualism) by Madhavacharya in the 13th century CE, were the next milestones in the history of evolution of the philosophical and spiritual traditions in Hinduism. Differing from the non-dualistic thoughts of Adi Shankaracharya, they provided competing philosophical alternatives in this vast firmament of assimilated and enriched spiritual lineage. They believed in the existence of the *Brahman*, but not as the only Reality. The *Atman* too was a real entity, distinct from the *Brahman*. Thus, the different interpretations of the Vedanta ushered seemingly divergent philosophies about the very nature of *Brahman* and *Atman*. But most importantly, the emergence and acceptance of these divergent views underlined a religious culture free from a rigid dogmatic outlook, open to questioning and interpretation of even the nature of the Absolute and its relationship with the Self. All these philosophies had their own space in a pluralistic culture of seeking, reasoning and understanding.

A unique feature of the **qualified-dualistic** and **dualistic** schools of philosophies was their emphasis on **realisation of the Universal through devotion**, thereby ushering a tradition of bhakti. Thus, emerged a movement which encompassed the spiritual landscape of the country for the next few centuries.

The Bhakti Movement

The Bhakti movement which encompassed the socio-religious milieu of the country in medieval period (15th century CE to 17th century CE) was another important epoch in the growth of Hinduism. Its origin is traceable to the earlier movements in the sixth century C.E when the Alvars (Vaishnavites) and the Nayanars (Shaivites) had emerged in South India. The teachings of Shankaracharya (Advaitavada) and in particular of Ramanujam (Vishishtadvaita) and Madhavacharya (Dwaitavada) provided the fundamental spiritual philosophies for their movement. It gained in prominence in the southern part of the country to begin with, but spread to the northern and eastern parts as well. **Ramananda, Vallabhacharya, Tukaram, Namdeva, Mirabai, Nanak, Kabirdas, Surdas, Tulsidas, Chaitanya,** etc. are all associated with it and ushered the Bhakti traditions in different parts of the country.

The movement brought to the fore the concept of **devotion to that Supreme as the means of salvation**. Ritualism and religious orthodoxy had little place this movement, and devotion and love were only the prerequisite of the *bhakta* (devotee). In a way, the Bhakti movement was also partly a response to the Brahmanical orthodoxy and rigidity in the caste system which permeated the Indian society. It endeavoured to provide an inclusive platform to the marginalized sections of society with its emphasis on equality of mankind and an all-inclusive philosophy. It provided hope for salvation to all including women, artisans, weavers, cultivators and untouchables. Thus, it appealed to a large underprivileged section of society. The decline of Buddhism and Jainism by this period and endowment of some political patronage (such as support by the kings to the Shaivite movement earlier) enabled the growth of Bhakti traditions.

But by the 14th century CE, sweeping socio-political and religious changes had taken place in India, with the advent of Islam. Its inclusive social philosophy and establishment of the Delhi Sultanate, under which the new Islamic faith prospered, created a socio-religious flux, challenging Hinduism and some of its orthodox traditions. Thus, there was a pressing need for fundamental changes and bringing regeneration in the Hindu society. The Bhakti movement ushered this essential reform in Hinduism from within. The core belief and Upanishadic thought remained its substratum, rather than there being emergence of any altogether new or disparate philosophy. The *Bhakti*, or the culture of devotion, had also branched into *nirguna* (devotion to formless god) or *saguna* (worship of specific gods and goddesses with attributes). Besides, it also incorporated religious traditions of different sects which were based on worship of different deities (such as Vaishnavism, Shaivism, Shaktism; Smartism) and other personal gods. Thus, it imbued the society in the spirit of devotion, faith, inclusiveness and traditions of service to mankind as fundamentals of socio-religious discourse.

The Modern Era and Phase of Reforms

The eighteenth and the nineteenth centuries saw another phase of reforms and revival in Hinduism through the Brahmo Samaj, Arya Samaj, Prarthana Samaj, Ramakrishna Mission, etc. Reformists like Raja Ram Mohun Roy, Dayanand Saraswati, Ishwar Chandra Vidyasagar, Vivekananda, and others endeavoured to purge it of many social events like *sati*, child marriages, untouchability, and caste systems, and base it on Vedantic philosophy and principles as laid in various scriptures and as per different schools of philosophical thought. The reforms of its practices and philosophical revivalism,

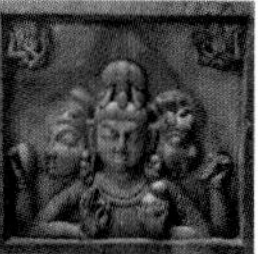

particularly the emergence of the **assimilative** and **harmonising** philosophy of **neo-vedantism**, are truly the defining features of modern phase of Hinduism.

Modern Hinduism, with its pantheon of gods and multitude of belief systems, may appear to have the form of a Puranic religion, but its substance truly lies in the universal and enduring philosophies of Vedanta. Over the centuries, it has assimilated the influences of Buddhism, Jainism, Sufism, Sikhism and other belief systems. It has been swept by centuries-long waves of *Bhakti* and decades of reforms of its practices. Today, it emerges as a **modern, syncretic and pluralistic faith**, albeit less of a classical religion based on a single tenet, but more of an evolving faith and a movement described appropriately as a **way and view of life**.

SCRIPTURES AND PHILOSOPHIES OF HINDUISM

Scriptures and philosophies of Hinduism are an integral element of its culture. Falling in the ambit of its vast canopy are the four Vedas with its several layers, the Ramayana and the Mahabharata comprising the Smritis, the Puranas, the Dharma-shastras and the philosophies of the Vedanta, shad-darshanas, varnashrama dharma, purusharthas etc. Each of these scriptures and philosophies are profound enough to merit a life time of study and comprehension. The endeavour here is to offer a peep in to this vast panorama of cultural and philosophical evolution.

Classification of Scriptures

The Hindu scriptures can broadly be classified into two categories the *Smritis* and the *Shrutis*. This classification is based on the purported origin of the scriptures.

The Shrutis

The word '*Shruti*' literally means '**what is heard**'. The *Shrutis* refers to the class of scriptures and texts which were 'heard' by the sages and seers in ancient times. They are believed to be of **divine origin**. Thus, these scriptures were purportedly revealed to them due to their divine knowledge and understanding and the sages communicated this knowledge to the world. The *Shrutis* comprise the most authoritative texts of Hindu philosophy and religion. These include the four Vedas.

The Smritis

These refer to the Hindu scriptures which are considered to be of human origin and can be attributed to a specific author unlike the *Shrutis* which were considered to be of primordial or non-human origin. *Smriti* means **what is remembered**. Thus, the composer of these texts recalled the occurrences of event and facts and captured them in the form of texts. The eighteen Puranas, authored by sage Veda Vyasa and the two epics Ramayana (by sage Valmiki) and Mahabharata (by sage Veda Vyasa) fall in this category. The epics are also referred to as **'Itihasa'**. The other Hindu scriptures would also fall in the category of *Smritis.*

IMPORTANT HINDU SCRIPTURES

The Vedas

The Vedas can be said to be the most important scriptures of Hinduism as they contain the central cannons of the Hindu philosophy. The word '*Veda*' is derived from the root word **'vid'** or **knowledge** or **wisdom**. Thus, Vedas were considered as scriptures containing the sum total of the knowledge of the people. Further, the word *vid* also refers to the knowledge which could illuminate the path in the darkness (of ignorance), eventually leading to salvation. Historically, they are said to have been composed between 1500 BCE to 600 BCE. However, recent researches particularly those based on astronomical dating of events described therein, attribute them to be of earlier origin although a formal compilation/categorisation could have occurred later. The six systems of Hindu philosophy — **Nyaya, Vaisheshika, Samkhya, Yoga, Purva Mimamsa, and Vedanta** (discussed later) —also accept the authority of the Vedas. The Vedas were composed in Sanskrit and their study was largely limited to the Brahmins.

The Atman and the creation of the world: Aitareya Upanishad

आत्मा वा इदमेक एवाग्र आसीत्। नान्यत् किंचन मिषत्।
स ईक्षत लोकान्नु सृजा इति।। 1.1.1 ।।

In the beginning this was verily the *Atman alone*. There was nothing else active, whatsoever living existed. He thought, '(now) verily I shall create the worlds.

(Shloka 1.1.1. Aiteraya Upanishad; Rigveda)

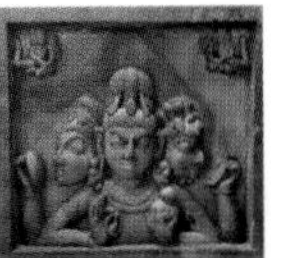

These are four in number; the **Rigveda,** the **Yajurveda,** the **Samaveda**, and the **Atharvaveda**. Each of these consists of and includes the Samhitas, the Brahmanas, the Aranyakas, and the Upanishads, as separate parts or layers of the Vedas.

Rigveda

The Rigveda is the oldest of all the Vedas. Thus, it is the most ancient of the Hindu scriptures. It is a collection of hymns or *suktas* (1028 in number) for propitiation of various deities. The earliest deities were the various elements of nature viz. Indra, Agni, Varuna, Soma, Surya etc.. The latter hymns deal with philosophical and metaphysical questions such as nature of God, origin of universe, *Brahman, Atman,* etc. The Rigveda is also referred to as the book of *mantras*. The main Upanishad incorporated in Rigveda is Aitareya Upanishad.

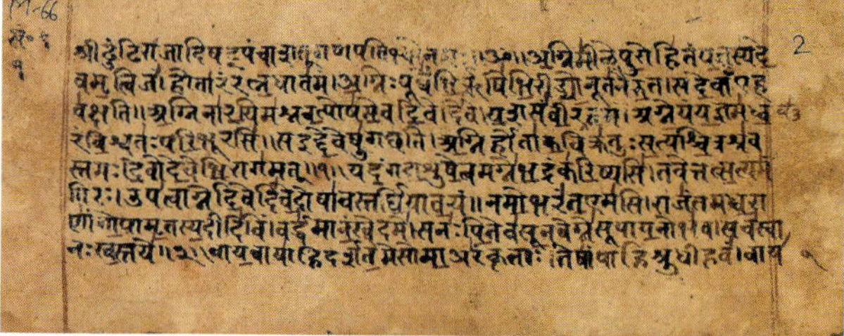

3.3: A page from the manuscript of Rigveda depicting Mandala1, Hymn (sukta1) Adhyaya, lines 1.1.1 to 1.1.9, manuscript period late 19th century; location, DAV College Library, Chandigarh — Wikimedia Commons

Yajurveda

The Yajurveda is a compilation of verses or mantras invoked or chanted in various rituals/offering by the priests. Thus, it prescribed the modalities for conduct of different *yajnas* and rituals. The earlier portion of Yajurveda (the *Samhita*) contains nearly 1875 *shlokas*. It also includes some important Upanishads, viz. the **Brihadarnyaka Upanishad, Katha-Upanishad, Isha-Upanishad, Tattireya-Upanishad,** etc.

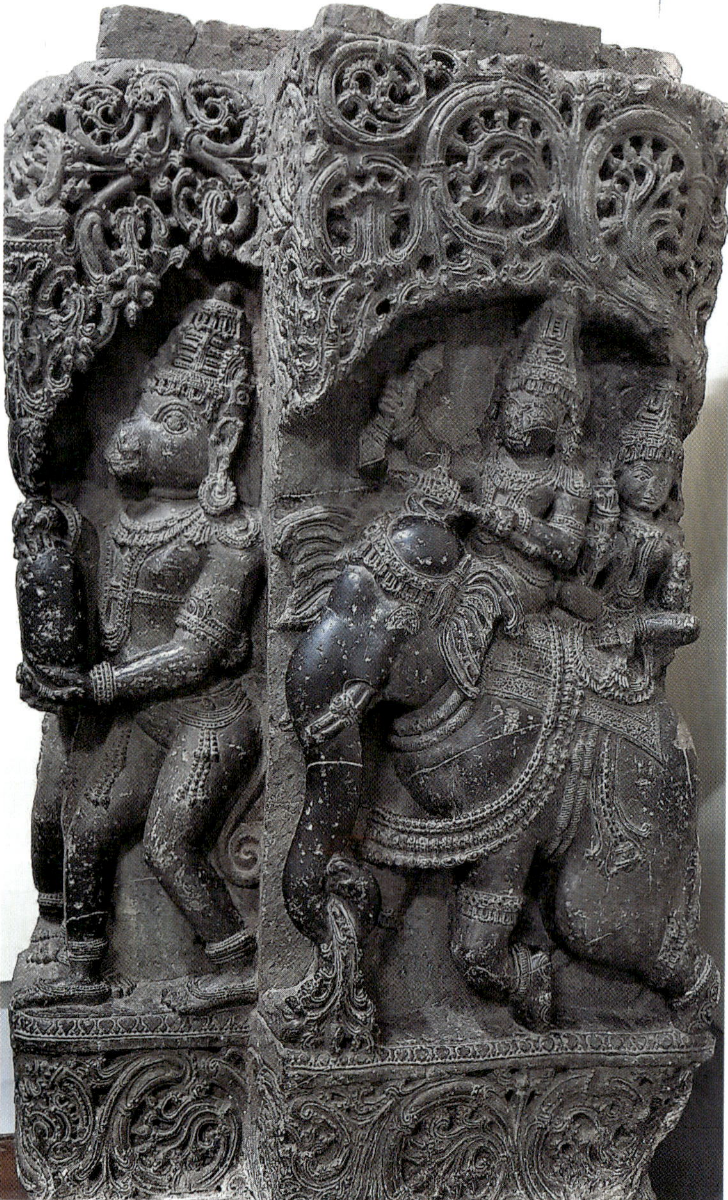

3.4: Indra, one of the most important of the early Vedic deities, seated with Sachi, on his mount Airavat. Indra is wielding a *vajra*. 12th century CE, Hoysala sculpture, temple column; Government Museum, Bengaluru — photograph by Madhukar K Bhagat

A Prayer for illuminating Knowledge in Brihadarnyaka Upanishad

ॐ असतो मा सद्गमय।
तमसो मा ज्योतिर्गमय।
मृत्योर्मा अमृतं गमय।
ॐ शान्तिः शान्तिः शान्तिः।।

Om asato maa sad-gamaya |
Tamaso maa jyotir-gamaya |
mrtyor-maa amrtam gamaya |
Om shaantih shaantih shaantih ||

Meaning:

Om, (O Lord), lead me from untruth to truth (from the unreality of ephemeral world to the reality of Eternal Self),

Lead me from darkness to light, (from ignorance of one's real self to the sublime spiritual knowledge of the Brahman),

Lead me from mortality to immortality (liberation from the mortal self through Self-Realization and unison with Brahman),

Om, peace, peace, peace

Shloka (1.2.28).Brihadaranyaka Upanishad, Yajurveda

A Chant of Fullness of the Supreme and Eternal Reality: Ishvashya Upanishad

ॐ पूर्णमदः पूर्णमिदं पूर्णात्पूर्णमुदच्यते ।

पूर्णस्य पूर्णमादाय पूर्णमेवावशिष्यते ।।

ॐ शान्तिः शान्तिः शान्तिः ।।

Om puurnnam-adah puurnnam-idam puurnnaat-puurnnam-udacyate |
puurnnasya puurnnam-aadaaya puurnnam-eva-avashissyate ||
Om shaantih shaanti shaanti ||

Meaning:

Om, that outer world (*Param Brahman)* is complete (replete with divine-consciousness - *poorna*). This inner manifested world is also complete (full with divine-consciousness -*poorna*). From the fullness of that divine-consciousness the world is manifested.

The *Param Brahman* is infinite and even after endowing fullness to the manifested world, it remains full and complete (poorna) Om, peace, peace, peace.

(Ishavasya Upanishad; Yajur Veda)

Significance: The Supreme Reality is complete, infinite, eternal and transcends the destruction of all, thus signifying the self-sustaining nature of the cosmos and the completeness of the universe. What is complete gives birth to something which by itself is complete. The *Param Brahman* is complete and from it is born our world, which again by itself is complete. If we take away fullness from fullness, fullness still remains, thereby incorporating the inexhaustible infiniteness of *Param Brahman*.

3.5: A page of manuscript from Vajasneyi Samahita of Shukla Yajurveda, period of manuscript, early 18th century — Wikimedia Commons

Samaveda

The Samaveda is a book of chants and hymns notated as melodies. It is the third Veda and shortest in terms of mantras, containing 1874 mantras in total. Many of its verses are derived from the Rigveda which are set in the form of musical notations. It has two major parts. These include melody collections in the first part (*Gana*) and the second part contains the verses (*Archika book*). The melody in the first part corresponds to the verse in the second part. Thus, the roots of Indian music and dance are contained in the Samaveda. It also contains the two important Upanishads — the *Chandogya Upanishad* and *Kena Upanishad.*

Atharvaveda

The Atharvaveda is the last of the Vedas. The name of this Veda is derived from the word **'Atharvanas'** implying procedures for everyday life. Thus, this Veda contained knowledge having application in daily life ranging from medicine to other physical sciences. However, it was earlier misinterpreted to be a book of magical spells or formulae.

3.6: A page from the manuscript of Samaveda, Sadavimsha Brahmana; period of manuscript mid-19th century; location, Varanasi Sanskrit College — Wikimedia Commons

The Basis of Eternal Knowledge : Kena Upanishad

तस्यै तपो दमः कर्मेति प्रतिष्ठा वेदाः

सर्वाङ्गानि सत्यमायतनम् ।। ८ ।।

tasyai tapo damaḥ karmeti pratiṣ ṭ hā vedāḥ
sarvāṅ gāni satyamāyatanam || 8 ||

Of the eternal knowledge in Upanishads (of *Atman* and *Brahman*), channelisation of the energies of the mind and the senses(*Tapas),* austerity and self-restraint (*damah*) and steadfast pursuit of one's duty (*karma*) are the foundations, the knowledge (Vedas) are its limbs; and Truth is its abode.'

Shloka 4.8 Kena Upanishad, Samaveda

This Veda has nearly 730 hymns and includes **Mundaka, Mandukya**, and **Prashana Upanishads** as a part of it.

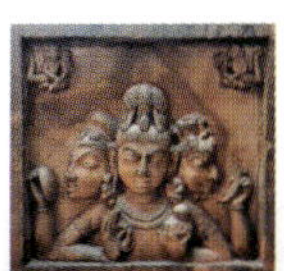

Truth Shall Prevail: Mundaka Upanishad

सत्यमेव जयते* नानृतं सत्येन पन्था विततो देवयानः।
येनाक्रमन्त्यृषयो ह्याप्तकामा यत्र तत् सत्यस्य परमं निधानम्।। 6।।

**satyameva jayate nānṛtaṃ satyena panthā vitato devayānaḥ |*
yenākramantyṛṣ ayo hyāptakāmā yatra tat satyasya paramaṃ nidhānam || 6 ||

Truth alone wins(prevails), not falsehood; by truth, the path of the good - (*Devas*) is widened, that by which the seers travel on, having nothing to wish for to where there is that, the highest treasure attained by truth.

(shloka 3.1.6 Mundaka Upanishad)

**The part of shloka, 'Satyameva Jayate' is incorporated as a part of the national symbol of India*

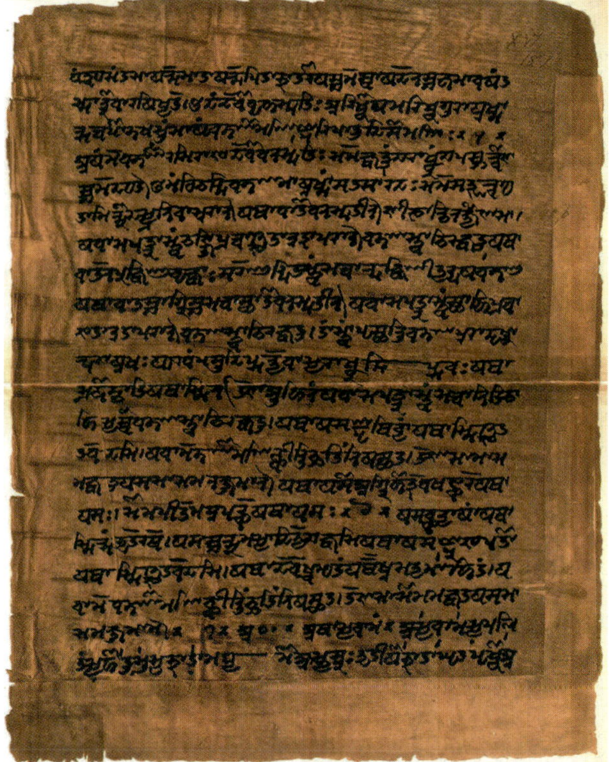

3.7: A page from a manuscript of Atharvaveda Samhita — Wikimedia Commons

Scriptures Comprising the Vedas

Samhitas

The Samhitas are the **first** of the four parts of the Vedas (also referred as the first layer). They are also referred as the **'*mantra*'** as they are a compilation of mantras, or sacred chants and incantations. These chants were invoked for propitiation of elements of nature and deities, and the latter were symbolic of the former. The Samhitas are also known by the Veda to which it belonged, viz. Rigveda Samhita or the 'Rig-Samhita'. As the Samhitas, along with the next part of the Vedas, viz. the Brahmanas, contain ritual instructions. They are together referred to as the ***Karma Kanda***, or literally the 'action portion' of the Vedas. In the Hindu school of philosophy, the Samhitas and Brahmanas put together contain the Purva Mimansa philosophy (literally meaning 'former inquiry').

Brahmanas

The **second part** (or second layer) of the Vedas is referred to as the *Brahmanas*. They are concerned with the various rituals and rites for propitiation of elements of nature and deities. They also offer explanation to the mantras as contained in the Samhitas. It is believed that with passage of time it became imperative to explain the meaning of the *mantras* which were becoming difficult to understand for the successive generations. Hence came the Brahmanas into existence, which elaborated upon their meaning and significance. Thus, they were concerned with the proper performance of rituals.

Important Brahmanas

- **Aitareya Brahmana** – dealing with Soma sacrifice
- **Kaushitaki Brahmana** – dealing with food sacrifice in Rigveda
- **Satapatha Brahmana** – the largest *Brahmana* in Yajurveda deals with Vedic rituals.

Aranyakas

The Aranyakas, the **third part** of the Vedas, mark a transition from a ritualistic to philosophical and metaphysical thoughts. They offer explanation to the various rituals from a philosophical and different perspective. They are the third part of the Vedas but are also considered by some as extension of or appendices to the Brahmanas.

The Aranyakas originates from Sanskrit word **'*aranya*'** meaning the forest. This book therefore was also called the 'forest book'. The Aranyakas are believed to have been composed by forest dwelling sages and seers, who eschewed the rituals and emphasised more on their spiritual and philosophical interpretation.

Important Aranyakas

- *Aitreya Aranyaka* and *Kaushitaki Aranyaka* of Rigveda
- *Taitreya Aranyaka, Katha Aranyaka* of Yajurveda
- *Chandoga Aranyaka, Kena Aranyaka* of Samaveda
- *Mundaka* and *Mandukya Aranyaka* pertaining to Atharvaveda

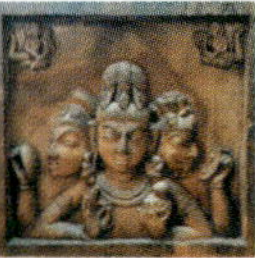

Upanishads

The Upanishads are the **final layer**, or the concluding part of the Vedas. In a way, they mark the highest point in the Vedic spiritual knowledge (referred as *Ved-shirsha*). They deal with numerous metaphysical and philosophical questions such as ***Brahman*** (universal god**),** ***Atman*** (soul), their nature, and relationship which are the focus of the Upanishads.

As they are the concluding portion of the Vedas, they are also referred as the **Vedanta** (or the end of the Vedas), and together with the **Aranyakas** they represent the ***'Jnana Kanda'*** or the knowledge portion of the Vedas. The Upanishads along with *Brahman Sutra* and the *Bhagavad Gita* encapsulates the **Vedanta philosophy**. Further, the branch of philosophy **'Uttar Mimansa'** (post analysis) is also based on the teachings contained in Upanishads.

The very word 'Upanishad' is derived from the word '*sad*' (or *satya*/truth). Thus, Upanishads were considered to be revelatory of truth or true knowledge. It is also thought to mean to sit close to a *guru* and to acquire knowledge. The Upanishads often present this knowledge in the form of a dialogue between a *guru* and *shishya* (master and disciple). The *shishya* raises queries about the philosophical and metaphysical issues (viz. nature of cosmos, *Brahma*, *Atman*, etc.) which the *guru* explains.

There are said to be 108 Upanishads of which ten Upanishads **Chandogya, Brihdaranyaka, Aitareya, Taittiriya, Kena, Isha, Mundaka, Mandukya, Katha**, and **Prashna** are considered to be more important or the principal Upanishads.

The Brahma-Sutra: The Essence of Vedantic Philosophy

The *Brahma Sutra* also referred as the *Vedanta Sutra* is one of the fundamental vedantic texts which captures the essence of the philosophical, spiritual and metaphysical elements of the Upanishads. Thus, it dwells on the subjects of, nature of reality, universe and human existence, the *brahman* and the *atman*.

As per the Indian tradition, Badarayana is believed to be the author of the *Brahma Sutra* while Vyasa is said to be the compiler, while some consider Badarayana to be Vyasa himself. It is believed that the *Brahma Sutra* was composed around 500 BCE to 400BCE while the *Brahma Sutra* text in vogue today could have been compiled around 400 CE to 450 CE.

The Brahma Sutra contain 555 *sutras* (aphorisms), divided into four chapters each with four sections. The concepts of the *Brahman*, the ultimate reality as discussed in the Upanishads is explained in the first chapter (*Samanvaya*; or harmony). The second chapter (*Avirodha*: or non-conflict) is a critique of the other competing schools of philosophy viz, Nyaya, Yoga, Vaishesika, Poorva Mimansa, Buddhism and Jainism, vis-a vis the Vedantic philosophy. (Hence the creation of Brahma Sutra is attributed to the post Buddha phase). In the third chapter (*Sadhana*, or the means), the path to ultimate emancipation is described. Thus, here the spiritual knowledge and principles of epistemology are captured. The last chapter (*Phala*, or the fruit) describes the significance of spiritual knowledge and the state that is achieved thereof.

The *Brahma Sutra* along with the principal Upanishads and the *Bhagavad Gita* forms the three fundamental treatises of the Vedantic thought and comprises the **Prasthana Traya** (or the three starting points or beginnings). While the Upanishads are referred to as the **Sruti Prasthana** (the beginning of the heard/revealed tradition), the *Bhagavad Gita* is the **Smriti Prasthana** (beginning of the remembered tradition). The *Brahma Sutra* forms the third pillar of this tradition the **Nyaya Prasthana** (the beginning of the logical tradition).

Over the centuries, different scholars and seers have studied the *Brahma Sutra* along with principal Upanishads and Bhagavad Gita and offered their commentaries (*Bhasya*) on them and on *Brahma Sutra* in particular. These interpretations and commentaries of *Brahma Sutra* have been the fountain head of the different vedantic schools viz. Shankara's *Advaitavada, Vishsista Advaitavada* propounded by Ramanuja and the *Dwaitavaada* school of thought enunciated by Madhavacharya. Thus, through the ages, their commentaries on *Brahma Sutra* (along with that of Nimbaka and Vallabhacharya) have been the chief source of interpretation of the *Brahma Sutra* and the Vedanta philosophy.

The Nature of Brahman

ऊँ जन्माद्यस्य यतः ऊँ।। 1.1.2

Om janmadyasya yatah om 1.1.2

That is Brahman from which (are derived) the birth etc. (of this universe)

verse II, section 1, chapter 1 Brahmasutra

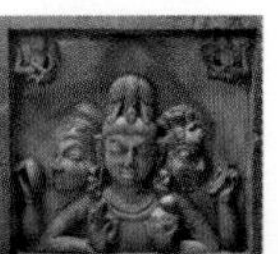

Itihasa

The word *Itihasa* is derived from the three words, *Iti-Ha-Asa* implying as it happened. Thus, the **Itihasa** texts are an account of historical events/history as it happened. **Itihasas** come under the classification of the *Smriti* scriptures. The two great Indian epics, the Ramayana and the Mahabharata are texts/scriptures falling under this category.

The Ramayana

One of the greatest epics to have been ever composed, the Ramayana, is also one of the holiest of Hindu scriptures. As a narrative, it gives an account of the crown prince Rama, (believed to be an incarnation of Lord Vishnu) and how he vanquishes Ravana and rescues Sita. But its social significance lies in the **ideals** and **standards** it sets for the society as to what an ideal king or a son or a brother or a husband etc. ought to be. This is personified in the very conduct of Sri Rama (who is also referred as *Maryada Purushottam*) as well as in the other central characters of this great epic. It also sets the standards for the ethics, human values and canons of human conduct to be adopted. Thus, to an extent, it lays the practical contours of ***dharma*** for the society at large. Even as a literary work, the storyline does not merely draw a historical account of the life of the crown prince Rama and his travails, but succinctly imparts a blueprint for the social, cultural, and philosophical elements worth emulation in a society. It wouldn't be incorrect to say, that innumerable societies transcending the geographical boundaries in the ensuing millennia, have perceived this ideological *Rama-rajya* as the gold standard of social governance worthy of being established or even aspiring for.

As a key and popular scripture of Hinduism, widely recognised and accepted across diverse societies in different ages, it has helped to coalesce the Hindu society with its multitude of sects and divergent practices. Over regions and centuries, it has almost served as the very face of Hinduism, embodying the values and philosophies with which this very religion could be identified. No wonder the story of Ramayana has been retold innumerable times in different versions and translations in South Asia, Southeast Asia and different parts of the world, for more than two thousand years.

3.8: Putrakamesthi-yagam, a masterpiece of a painting, depicting a scene from Valmiki Ramayana. Agni is seen appearing from the fire altar and bestows king Dasharatha a vessel with *kheer/payasam* as a boon for Dasharatha for being blessed with sons. (This was given to the three queens of Dasharatha who bore the four sons including Rama). The painting depicts king Dasharatha, sage Rishyashringa (performing the yagna), sage Vashistha and courtiers. Different characters bear different expressions ranging from gratitude to awe.
Oil on Canvas, Raja Ravi Varma; Government Museum, Chennai
— photograph by Madhukar K Bhagat

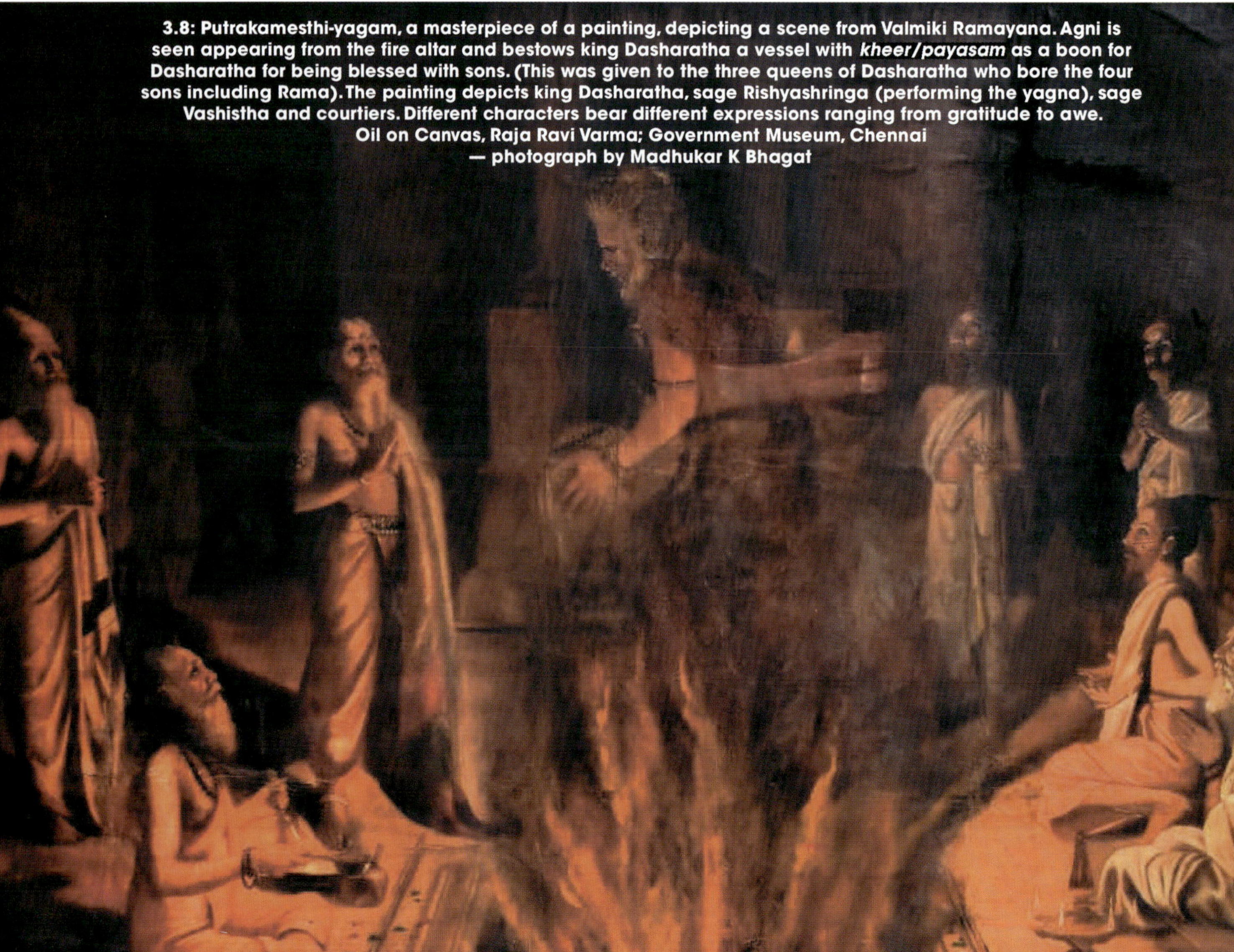

The Valmiki Ramayana

Although numerous versions of this great epic exist today, is accepted that the original version of Ramayana was written in Sanskrit verses by sage Valmiki. There is no unanimity regarding the exact date/period in which Ramayana was written. The generally agreed time frame given by historians is (1500 BCE to 600 BCE). However, some recent researches based on astronomic dating of events and *nakshatra* positions described in Ramayana suggest the story to be of older origin.

The epic is divided into seven chapters (*kanda*) and contains nearly 24000 verses making it indeed a great piece of ancient literature (*Aadi-kavya*). The six chapters (*kanda*) usually accepted to be a part of the original Valmiki Ramayana are; *Adi/Bala Kanda, Ayodhya Kanda, Aranya Kanda, Kishkindha Kanda, Sundara Kanda, and Yuddha Kanda. Uttara Kanda*, which is the last chapter of the extant version, is at times considered to have been incorporated later. The composition in Valmiki Ramayana is in *Anustubh* metre (found also in Vedic and classic poetry), with each verse being of four lines (*padas*) of eight syllable each.

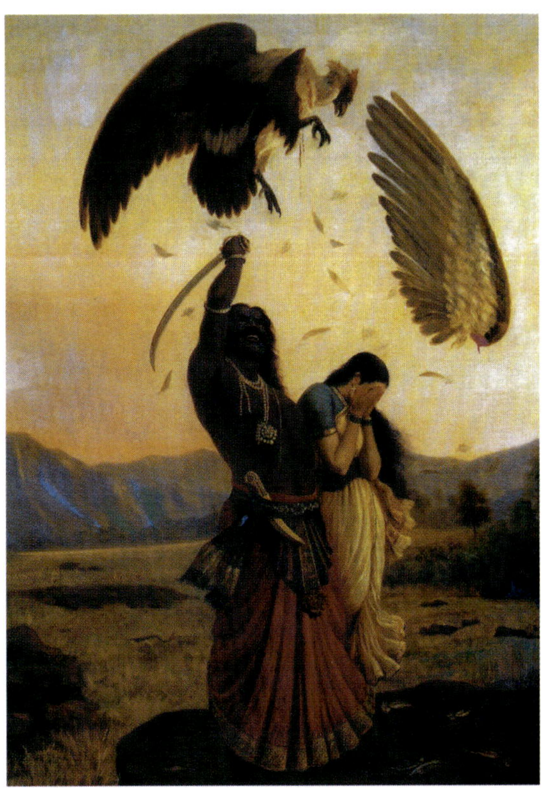

3.9: The fight of Jatayu and Ravana; a scene from Ramayana; painting by Raja Ravi Varma — Wikimedia Commons

A **critical edition** of the *Valmiki Ramayana* was compiled in 1975, after painstaking examination of over 2000 manuscripts and at least two major recensions (northern and southern and their subdivisions) of Valmiki Ramayana. These numerous versions existed in different parts of the country, in Sanskrit and other Indian languages and the **oldest of the manuscripts dated to the 11th century CE**. The objective was to bring out the most accurate or authentic version of the *Valmiki Ramayana* aas per the extant manuscripts. This mammoth project undertaken by Oriental Institute of Baroda, took nearly 15 years of continuous work by many eminent scholars, to culminate.

Sri Rama, an Epitome of all Virtues

When Valmiki inquired from the pre-eminent sage Narada, as to who amongst all in the three worlds possessed all the qualities of prowess, righteousness, gratitude, truthfulness, firmness in his vow, good conduct, knowledge of the lore, concern for all living beings, self-restraint, freedom from envy, conquest over anger, divine valour and thus truly could be said to be an epitome of all virtues, Narada describes to him the character of Sri Rama. These are described in the very opening verses of the Valmiki Ramayana and set the stage for this grand epic. Some of these verses describing Sri Rama and his divine qualities are highlighted here.

इक्ष्वाकुवंशप्रभवो रामो नाम जनैश्श्रुतः ।

नियतात्मा महावीर्यो द्युतिमान्धृतिमान् वशी ।। 1.1.8 ।।

People have heard his name as Sri Rama, who was born in the race of king Ikshvaku, having steady nature, possessing incomprehensible prowess, self-effulgent, self- commanding and subjecting senses under his control.

Verse 1.1.8 Valmiki Ramayana

धर्मज्ञस्सत्यसन्धश्च प्रजानांच हितेरतः ।

यशस्वी ज्ञानसम्पन्नश्शुचिर्वश्यस्समाधिमान् ।। 1.1.12 ।।

Pious, firm in his vows, he is ever intent on doing good to his subjects. He is, illustrious, wise, and pure at heart. He is obedient to elders (or accessible to those who are dependent on him) and ever meditating (on the means of protecting those who take refuge in him).

Verse 1.1.12 Valmiki Ramayana

स च सर्वगुणोपेतः कौसल्यानन्दवर्धनः ।

समुद्र इव गाम्भीर्ये धैर्येण हिमवानिव ।। 1.1.17 ।।

Sri Rama, bestowed with all virtues, sheer joy of Kausalya, He is like the sea in deportment and like Himavant in fortitude.

Verse 1.1.17 Valmiki Ramayana

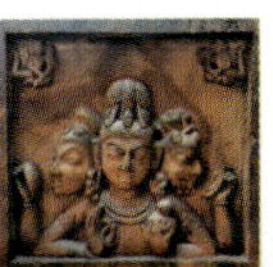

Numerous other shlokas of the *Valmiki Ramayana* too describe the qualities of Sri Rama. But the following shloka, equating Rama as the manifestation of *dharma* and lord of all worlds, is often considered to be unique for it is uttered by Maricha, a *rakshasa* (demon) and an enemy of Sri Rama. While Ravana commands Maricha to take the form of a golden deer, so as to lure away Sri Rama and thus help him abduct Sita, Maricha describing the many qualities of Sri Rama, implores Ravana to eschew enmity with Sri Rama, lest it brings the complete destruction of all rakashasa race.

रामो विग्रहवान् धर्मस्साधुस्सत्यपराक्रमः।

राजा सर्वस्य लोकस्य देवानां मघवानिव ।। 3.37.13 ।।

Rama is verily dharma incarnate. He is pious (sage like) and whose very strength is truth. He is king of all the worlds like Indra to the gods.

Verse 3.37.13 Valmiki Ramayana.

On Virtues and Duties of Kings and Administrators

The *Ramayana* incorporates many verses which succinctly bring out the virtues of a king and duties of an administrator, one of the gems of wisdom is highlighted here.

यथा दृष्टि श्शरीरस्य नित्यमेव प्रवर्तते।

तथा नरेन्द्रो राष्ट्रस्य प्रभवस्सत्यधर्मयोः ।। 2.67.33 ।।

The king is the source for protecting the truth and morality of a country like the eye which perpetually watches the welfare of the body.

Verse 2.67.33 Valmiki Ramayana

Truth as the Highest Virtue

On being exhorted by Jabali, a minister in the court of king Dasratha, to forsake his promise to Dasratha, abandon the fourteen years of exile and ascend the throne of Ayodhya, Sri Rama thus replies to Jabali, that truth is the very foundation of this world cannot be forsaken for material comforts or other gains.

सत्यमेवानृशंसं च राजवृत्तं सनातनम।

तस्मात्सत्यात्मकं राज्यं सत्ये लोकः प्रतिष्ठितः ।। 2.109.10 ।।

Truth and non-violence are the perpetual principles of kings. Therefore, a kingdom is based on truth. This world is firmly established in truth.

Verse 2.109.10 Valmiki Ramayana.

ऋषयश्चैव देवाश्च सत्यमेव हि मेनिरे।

सत्यवादी हि लोकेऽस्मिन्परमं गच्छति क्षयम ।। 2.109.11 ।।

Sages and gods all accept truth (as the supreme virtue). A truthful man of this world, attains the highest state (abode).

Verse 2.109.11 Valmiki Ramayana.

सत्यमेवेश्वरो लोके सत्यं पद्माश्रिता सदा।

सत्यमूलानि सर्वाणि सत्यान्नास्ति परं पदम ।। 2.109.13 ।।

Truth is God. The goddess of wealth always takes refuge in truth. Truth is the root of everything. It is supreme and there is nothing above it.

Verse 2.109.13 Valmiki Ramayana.

Dharma as the Essence of Human Pursuits

On entering the Dandaka forest, Sita implores Sri Rama who wields the great bow to follow dharma of ahimsa (non-violence) and benevolence and not to harm the animals and *rakshasas* with whom he has no personal enmity. To buttress her arguments, she quotes the following and other *shlokas*. Later, Sri Rama describes the entreaty of the sages of the forest to protect them from the wicked *rakshasas*, and his dharma (solemn duty) as a kshatriya as the reason for wielding his bow even in the forest and for offering refuge to the sages.

धर्मादर्थः प्रभवति धर्मात्प्रभवते सुखम् ।। 3.9.31 ।।

धर्मेण लभते सर्वं धर्मसारमिदं जगत्।

Following dharma (righteousness) brings wealth which in turn ushers happiness. Thus, dharma endows everything and in fact it is the essence of the world.

Verse 3.9.31 Valmiki Ramayana

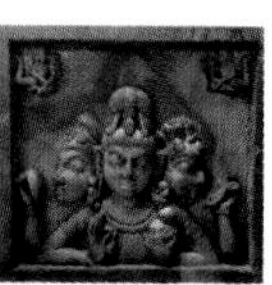

आत्मानं नियमैस्तैस्तै कर्शयित्वा प्रयत्नतः ।। 3.9.32 ।।

प्राप्यते निपुणैर्धर्मो न सुखाल्लभ्यते सुखम् ।

Dharma, which is the source of all happiness, can be attained even by a wise person, only after observing various disciplines for his own purification thus subjecting himself to great strain and stress. One cannot attain such dharma by leading a life given to the pleasures of the senses.

Verse 3.9.32 Valmiki Ramayana

Different versions and adaptations of Ramayana: Nearly three hundred versions of Ramayana, its recensions and adaptations, exist today in numerous languages and in different parts of the world. **Ramcharitamanas**, in Awadhi, composed by Goswami Tulsidas (16th century CE), is one of the most popular versions, particularly in North India. It is also highly acclaimed as a masterpiece of medieval poetry, which made the great Sanskrit epic accessible to the common folk in the extant language and thus ushered in a *saguna* (god with attributes) Bhakti tradition centred around Sri Rama as an incarnated god. (also see chapter on Bhakti movement for further details on Ramcharitamanas)

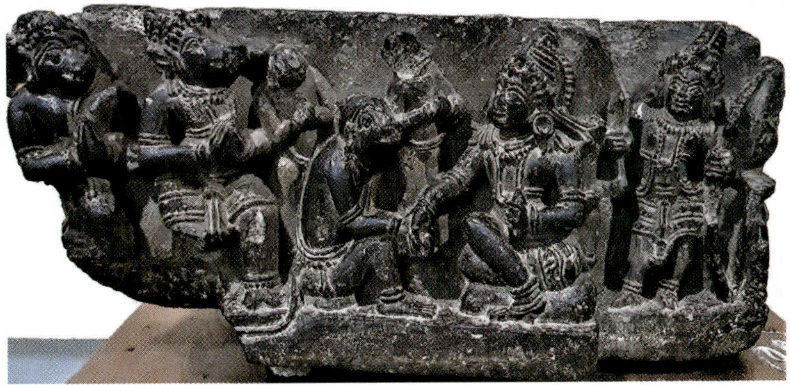

3.10: Sri Rama giving signets to Hanuman; Halebidu, Hoysala sculpture 12th century CE; Government Museum Bengaluru — photograph by Madhukar K Bhagat

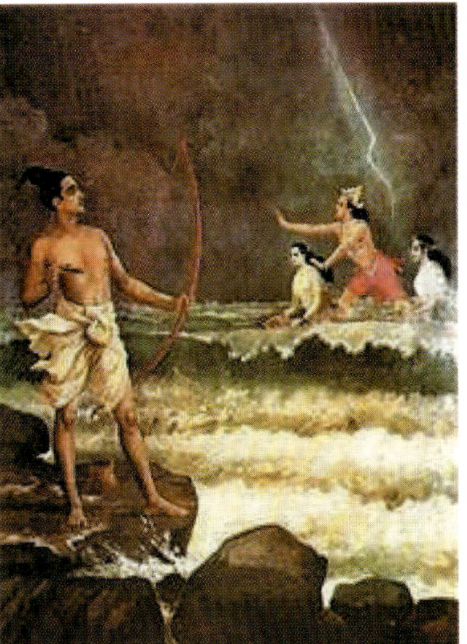

3.11: Sri Rama vanquishing Varuna, the god of sea; a scene from Ramayana, a painting by Raja Ravi Varma: — Wikimedia Commons

Sri Rama to Lakshmana; on virtues of service and benevolence

परहित सरिस धर्म नहीं भाई, परपीड़ा सम नहीं अधमाई II

(*Ramcharitamanas*)

There is not a greater virtue than service to others and not a greater sin than causing suffering to others.

The other important regional versions include; the ***Ramavataram*** in Tamil (12th century CE) also referred as the ***Kamban Ramayana***, The ***Ranganatha Ramayana*** in Telugu (14th century CE), the ***Krittivasi Ramayana*** in Bengal (15th century CE), ***Saptakanda Ramayana*** in Assam (14th century CE), ***Tulsi Kritta Ramayana*** in Gujarat (17th century CE); an adaptation of Ramcharitamanas, ***Bhavartha Ramayana*** in Marathi (16th century CE) by sant Eknath, ***Pampa Ramayana*** (12th century CE) and ***Kumudendu Ramayana***(13th century CE) in Kannada, the Odia ***Dandi Ramayana*** (14th century CE) and ***Vilanka Ramayana*** (by Sarla Das in 16th century CE) in Odisha, ***Ramayanu*** (11th century CE) in Goa, the ***Ramcharitam*** (12th century CE) and the ***Adhyatama Ramayanam Kilipattu*** in Malayalam (16th century CE) and ***Mappila Ramayanam*** (of Mappila Muslims) in Kerala, the ***Ramavatara Charita*** in Kashmiri. Thus, practically a version of this epic exists in almost all parts and languages in the country. The Persian version of it was commissioned by Akbar in the 16th century, and ***Pothi Ramayana***, an Urdu version, was composed in around 1776 CE. A unique feature of this great tale has been its acceptance and adaptation in Buddhist (***Dasaratha Jataka***), Jain (***Kumudendu*** and ***Pamapa Ramayana***), and Sikh traditions too.

A national epic and regional folklore

The story of Ramayana permeated other nations over a thousand years ago. The ***Khmer Reamker***, a Cambodian epic poem, which is based on the Sanskrit version of Ramayana, is said to trace its origin to 7th century CE, while the current manuscript is of 16th century CE. The old Javaneese (Indonesia) ***Kakawin Ramayana*** is believed to be written in the 9th century CE. The ***Ramakavaca*** is popular in Bali, and the ***Ramayana Swarnadip*** in Sumatra. The ***Ramakien*** has the status of national epic in Thailand and

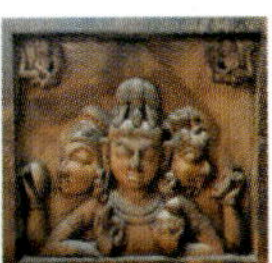

is based on the Budhhist ***Dasaratha Jataka***. The ***Phra Lak Phra Rama***, adapted from Valmiki Ramayana, is the national epic of the Lao people (Laos). ***Hikayat Seri Rama*** of Malaysia, ***Yama Zatdaw*** of Myanmar, ***Jankiharan*** in Srilanka, ***Siddhi Ramayana*** and ***Bhanubhaktako Ramayana*** in Nepal, ***Ramaenna*** *or* ***Ramaensho*** in Japan are some other popular versions of this epic. Besides, adaptations and versions have also been found in China, Thailand, Mongolia and Vietnam. The story has been a part of their folklore for centuries in these nations and has been depicted in folk theatres, dance dramas, paintings and sculptures.

A living cultural tradition

Culturally, Ramayana has inspired not only spiritual, ethical and values besides metric of social conduct, but several generations of art too. The story and incidents in the Ramayana have been depicted over years in different forms of folk theatres (such as Ramleela), murals, sculptures and paintings, many of which adorned the temples across India and Southeast Asia. In modern times, numerous plays, dance dramas, folk theatres, television cereals and movies have been made on its story. Thus, Ramayana in itself has served as a **living cultural tradition** of numerous civilisations across nearly two millennia and continues to do so.

The Mahabharata

The longest epic ever to have been composed, the Mahabharata is an encyclopaedic account of a civilisation, its culture, philosophy, religion, ethics, customs, administration, society and perhaps every relevant element of social discourse. No wonder it is often considered to be so significant to have been christened as the **fifth Veda** by its composer, sage **Veda Vyasa**. As a narrative, it climaxes towards the fratricidal war between the Kauravas and the Pandavas, while tracing the entire genealogy of the Kuru dynasty and the genesis of the war. The great battle which is said to have lasted 18 days, also embroils all of the remaining dynasties and kingdoms of the time, resulting in an unprecedented annihilation which marked the end of an epoch in the evolution of a civilisation.

The Mahabharata, as a poem and literary creation, is indeed considered one of the greatest ever. Its original and longer version is said to contain over 1,00,000 *shlokas* (verses), while the shorter version comprises 24000 *shlokas*. The structure of the *shlokas* is of couplets (*dohas*). As per estimates, the longer version would have contained nearly 1.8 million words and would be many times the combined length of Iliad and Odyssey and considerably longer than even the Ramayana. The book is divided into 18 *parvas* (books or sections) with *Bhishma Parva* (book 6) capturing the beginning of this great battle. The holy scripture, The Bhagavad Gita, a discourse by Lord Krishna to Arjuna on the eve of the battle, is itself a part of this very *Parva*.

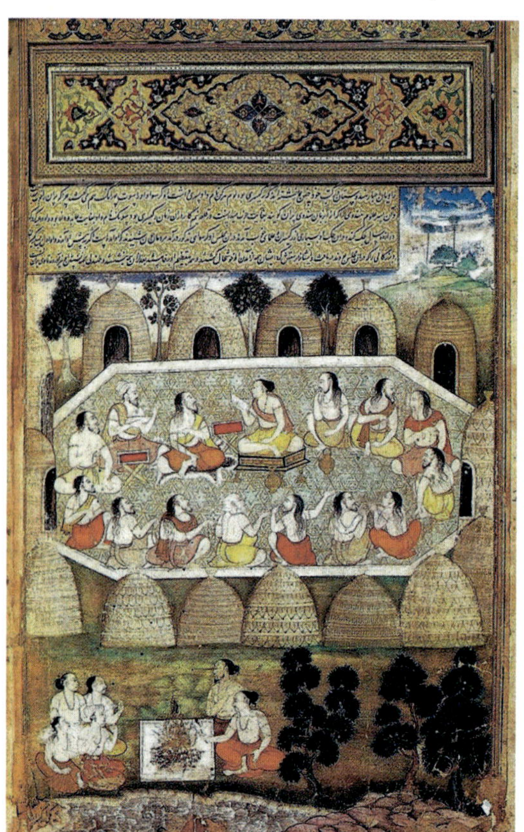

3.12: A page from the manuscript *Birla Razmanama* (dated 1605 CE). The miniature paintings depicting the first recital of the epic by rishi Vaishampayana and maharishi Saunaka on the occasion of Sarpayagna of king Janamejaya — Wikimedia Commons

Dating of Mahabharata

When did the Mahabharata war actually occur? The dating of the Mahabharata period has itself been a matter of many researches and great uncertainty. Historians suggest that this could have happened after the beginning of/in the Iron Age (around 1000BCE). In this period, the Kuru kingdom was in prominence (1200BCE to 800 BCE) and a dynastic conflict could have been the nucleus around which the story of Mahabharata was woven. The traditional belief of the date of Mahabharata battle, has centred around 3137 BCE, the estimate made by Aryabhata based on the beginning of the Kali age in 3102 BCE (captured in Aihole inscription). Of late, estimates based on astronomical analysis of the planetary positions described in the *shlokas* of Mahabharata manuscripts (similar to the discipline of archaeo-astronomy) have also shown the dating to be around this period itself. Historians also believe that even the compilation of this mammoth epic could have spread over hundreds of years and culminated around 400 BCE. The earliest reference to Mahabharata is found in the *Ashtadhyayi* (sutra 6.2.38) of Panini composed in the 4th century BCE. However, no general consensus as to what was the Mahabharata period has evolved as yet.

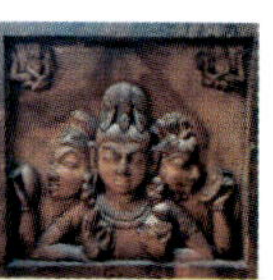

Different versions of Mahabharata

Just like Ramayana, different regional versions of Mahabharata, including several recensions and adaptations exist today. For working on the **'critical edition'**, of the Mahabharata (see inbox) the researchers collected as many as 1259 manuscripts found in different parts of the country, thus reflecting the popularity and spread of this great epic.

The story of Mahabharata has also been popular outside India, particularly in Southeast Asia. ***Kakawin Bharatayudha*** (written in ancient Java), popular in Indonesia, was composed in 11th century CE and later spread to Bali. ***Vayang wong,*** a Javanese dance drama and shadow puppet performance also draws from the stories and characters of Mahabharata (and Ramayana). Some *parvas* of Mahabharata have also been found in *Kawi* (old Javanese language) in Bali (Indonesia).

Over centuries, translations of Mahabharata into different regional and other languages have also been done. Prominent among these is ***Razmanamah*** (*Razm*: war; *Nama*: history or tale), a Persian translation of the epic commissioned by the emperor Akbar. A special feature of the book is the illustrations with numerous miniature paintings in Mughal school style of painting.

Like Ramayana, Mahabharata too has inspired a mass of ancient literature, art forms like sculptures, folk theatres, dance dramas paintings as well as contemporary arts, movies and TV cereals.

Critical Edition of Mahabharata

Standing tall amongst the literary projects of the 20th century was the compilation of the critical edition of Mahabharata. The project endeavoured to take into account the various extant versions of the epic and to compile an edition which could be considered the most accurate or authentic depiction of the tale of Mahabharata. The project was started in 1919 under the leadership of a noted Sanskritist, Sri V.S. Sukthankar and other eminent scholars at the Bhandarkar Oriental Research Institute in Pune and took nearly **five decades** of relentless effort to complete. Also called the Pune edition of the Mahabharata, this can be said to be the closest approximation to the earliest recoverable form of the epic.

The monumental work involved collection of nearly **1259 manuscripts**, depicting the numerous versions of the epic in Sanskrit. These were in vogue in different parts of the country, from Kerala to Kashmir and even in Nepal. The researchers' team then painstakingly studied all these versions, classified them as different adaptations, recensions and identified the common elements. They then documented the *shlokas* (verses) which could be considered to be depicting these common elements and were found in the maximum number of manuscripts.

The effort culminated in the **creation of an edition of Mahabharata running into 13000 pages, in 19 volumes and 89000 verses**. This was released in 1966 by the then President, Dr. S Radhakrishnan. A unique feature of the project has been the identification of the regional variations and differences, which have crept in the versions over the centuries. These have been documented in the footnotes and appendices to the main text.

A source of Itihasa and fountainhead of Indian mythology

The Mahabharata gives an in-depth account the entire genealogy of the Bharatavamsha; from Manu to the mighty king Bharata, to the Kauravas, Pandavas and their descendants. Thus, in a sense it is truly an *Itihasa* (a historical narrative). Many popular stories such as that of Dushyanta-Shakuntala, Nala-Damayanti, Savitri-Satyavaan, amidst others, categorised as mythology are a part of this great work. Further, various tales associated with Lord Krishna (particularly in the 19th *parva Harivamsha*) and even an abridged account of the Ramayana itself, are comprised in this epic. Thus, it is truly a fountainhead, or an all-encompassing repository of Indian mythological tales and characters.

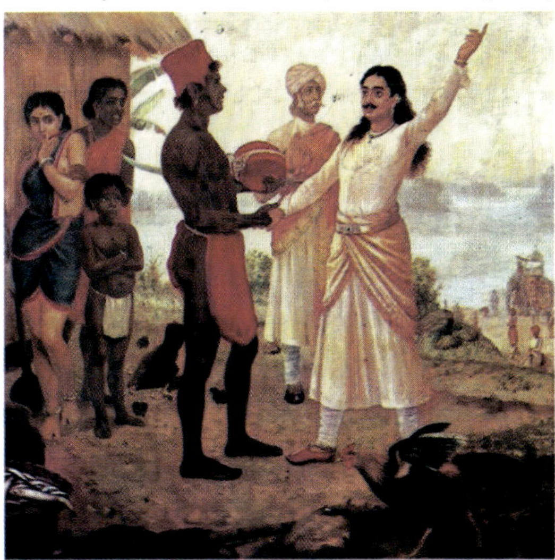

3.13: A vow of Bheesma to abdicate the throne and to remain celibate, a scene from Mahabharata; painting by Raja Ravi Varma — Wikimedia Commons

Complex plot, frame-tale narrative, realistic characters and storyline

A unique feature of this epic is its frame-tale style of narrative, with a story being told within a story. The first public recital of Mahabharata happens before King Janamejaya, the great grandson of Arjuna, in the *sarpayagyna* being performed. The recital is done by Vaishampayana, who is a disciple of sage Veda Vyasa, the composer of this epic. Vaishampayana recounts the events which led to the great battle, with many anecdotes in turn being retold by the characters themselves.

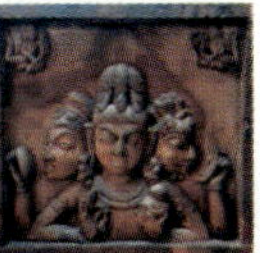

In fact, every relevant character in this epic has a story to tell of its own, underlining its relevance to the course of the events which ensue, and highlighting how significant even the seemingly mundane characters are to the storyline. The lovelorn Shantanu, the vow of Bhishma, the fate of Pandu, the erring of Kunti in giving birth to Karna, the spurning of Drupada by Drona, (leading to the former's humiliation by the Pandavas later, and eventual birth of Draupadi) and many others have a crucial bearing on the course of the very story itself.

A myriad of characters, a complex plot, with many branching story lines interconnected to the central narrative, are interwoven in this grand tale. The characters' depiction, albeit virtuous, is far from ideal. Even the most impeccable characters like Yudhishthira or Bhishma are not shown to be irreproachable. They are portrayed with their own human failings. Thus, in a tryst between realism and idealism, it is the latter which sees a sacrifice in the portrayal of characters, making them more life-like and the epic itself, a very real account of what and how it happened.

Substantially more than a narrative of a war

Although the Mahabharata does underline the inevitability of war to uphold justice, however it is much more than a story of just a war. The perils of war, the monumental loss that the society incurs and the dire need to make all possible efforts to avoid a war, are some crucial messages which resonate at numerous instances. The precept of the *purusharthas* (pursuits and duties of life), the need for upholding of dharma (social and personal duties, ethics and morality) and the quest for *nyaya* (justice) are integral to the narrative. The knowledge of diverse disciplines of a civilisation, ranging from tenets of kingship to rules of public administration, religious rites to ethical conduct, diverse armaments to warfare strategies, arts and architecture to material sciences, abiding virtues to human failings etc., are all documented in it for posterity. But most significantly, the deepest and the most encompassing philosophies of Vedanta and very essence of spiritualism are embraced in its soul the **Bhagavad Gita**.

The Shanti Parva: A Book of Enduring Wisdom

The *Shanti Parva* (the book of peace), the largest of the books (*parva*) comprising the Mahabharata, is described as veritable treasure trove of knowledge and wisdom. Set in the post Mahabharata war scenario, it includes the discourse of Bhishma Pitamaha to Yudhishthira on Dharma (duties law and rules of righteous conduct), *Satya* (truth) *Moksha* (salvation) etc. Post war, the remorseful Yudhishthira is encouraged by Lord Krishna to approach Bhishma (who is lying on the bed of arrows) and seek from him the gems of wisdom, before it is lost to the world.

The *Shanti Parva* (12th book of Mahabharata) contains over 12000 shlokas (in the critical edition) and is further sub divided into three sub-books (minor *parvas*). The first sub-book, *Rajdharma Anusasana Parva* describes the duties of a king. The next, *Aapaddharma Anusasana Parva* contains the rules of conduct in adversity. The last sub-book, *Moksha Dharma Parva* prescribes the path to be tread for attaining *moksha* (salvation).

As a treatise on kingship, it prescribes duties of king (*rajadharma*), principles of good and ethical governance, appropriate political conduct and administration, besides basis of revenue and taxation and other attendant disciplines. The **principles of crime and punishment**, viz. proportionality of crime to punishment and of a **benign tax collection**, are prescribed too. The examples of **bee harvesting honey** from flowers or the milk drawn from cow without depriving the calf or hurting the cow itself, are some enduring elucidations included. Thus, this book also serves as a study in ancient jurisprudence.

The parva also expounds on the *varna* arrangement (caste systems) whereby it describes it **as a product of differentiation in work with no rites of passage denied to any *varna*.** Rather, the merits of a person are not determined by his birth or claim of education but by virtues and actual conduct, thereby denying any inherent superiority of any *varna*.

On Truth:

There is nothing which leads so much to the success of kings as Truth, the king who is devoted to Truth enjoys happiness both here and hereafter. Even to the *rishis*, O king, Truth is the greatest wealth, Likewise for the kings, there is nothing that so much creates confidence in them as Truth.

Bhishma, Shanti Parva, Rajadharma anushasana parva,

Book xii.56.17-18

On Righteousness

Righteousness begets happiness as its fruit.
There is nothing superior to truth.
Everything is supported by truth, and everything depends on truth.
One should not take other's properties. That is an eternal duty.
A thief fears everybody, he considers other people as sinful as himself.
A pure hearted person is always filled with cheerfulness, and has no fear from anywhere.

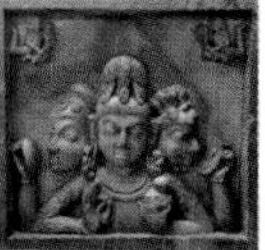

> Such a person never sees his own misconduct in other persons.
> A person should never do that to others, which he does not like to be done to him by others.
> Whatever wishes one cherishes about his own self, one should certainly cherish regarding another.
> The Creator ordained virtue, gifting it with the power of holding the world together.
> —*Bhishma, Shanti Parva,* Moksha dharma parva :
> ***Book xii.259.5-***

The Bhagavad Gita

The Bhagavad Gita, which literally means **'the song of the lord'** or **'the divine song'**, is considered to be the holiest of the Hindu scriptures. Although it is a part of the Mahabharata, owing to its philosophical and spiritual significance, it is often considered as a separate and a standalone scripture.

The Gita is a discourse by Lord Krishna to Arjuna, delivered on the battlefield of Kurukshetra. As the battle is about to commence, the greatest Pandava warrior and the mighty hero of Mahabharata is besieged with **moral dilemma** and despondency at the prospect of engaging in war with his *gurus*, cousins and dear ones. He beseeches Lord Krishna to explain as to how the prospect of winning the kingship of even this entire world could justify his slaying his revered elders and the members of family. When non-violence is a virtue, then how such a war and killing could be considered appropriate and as per dharma? He expresses his deep scepticism to the object of the war and deems it proper for him to abdicate the battle, renounce the world and even adopt the *karma* of an ascetic, rather than to be the cause of such violence and destruction.

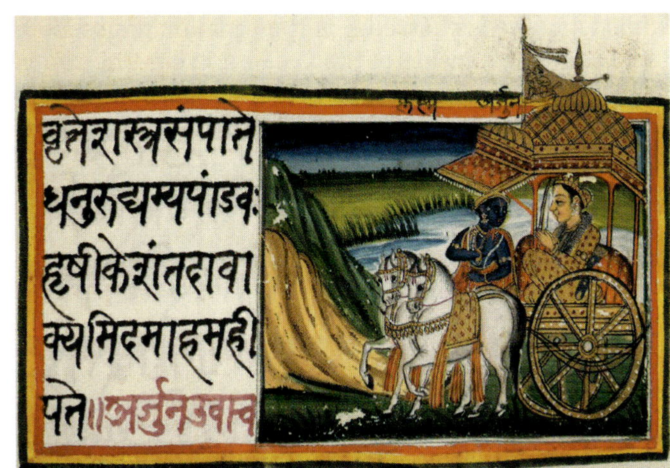

3.14: A 19th century illustrated manuscript of Bhagavad Gita. The folio contains a part of verse 20 and the beginning of verse 21 from the opening chapter of the Bhagavad Gita, depicting Arjuna's distress and dilemma; current location British Library, London — Wikimedia Commons

Initially, lord Krishna endeavours to dispel Arjuna's doubt by egging him to perform his bounden duty as a kshatriya and engage in a *dharmayuddha* (a battle for righteous objectives). But Arjuna's dilemma persists, and Lord Krishna reveals to him the profound and emancipating knowledge which forms the enduring philosophy of the Gita. Thus, rid of his predicament and with his qualms resolved, eventually Arjuna actively engages in the great battle.

Structure and origin

The discourse of the Bhagavad Gita is captured in **700 Sanskrit** ***shlokas*** (verses) arranged in **18 chapters** or sections. The *shlokas* are composed in different poetic metres, but the most frequent one is the *Anustubh Chanda* metre, where they are composed in form of *dohas* (couplets) each having two lines. These are further subdivided into two quarters, each with eight syllables. As a part of Mahabharata, its author is considered to be Veda Vyasa and the period of creation same as that of the Mahabharata. However, the presence of some elements of the *Shad-darshanas* (six system of philosophies) found in the Gita's philosophy, has made some experts propose that its composition could have been between 500 BCE to 200 BCE, or at least some portions of it could have been of latter origin and incorporated in this period.

Symbolism and universality

The backdrop of enunciation of this profound philosophy is the battlefield of Kurukshetra, with **Arjuna's despondency** and his weakness being the precursor (chapter 1 is often titled as 'Arjuna's despair'). However, these settings are often considered by scholars of the Gita, to be largely symbolic, with the domain of its profound knowledge and its pertinence being extremely wide. The Kurukshetra is symbolic of this world and the battle of life with all its attendant hardships and predicaments. The innumerable, who are gripped by ethical and moral dilemmas, are the Arjunas, uncertain of the appropriate course of action at many a vexing juncture. Lord Krishna is the embodiment of the divinity, while the philosophy of Gita so propounded is the emancipating knowledge, having abiding and universal relevance in all-encompassing circumstances.

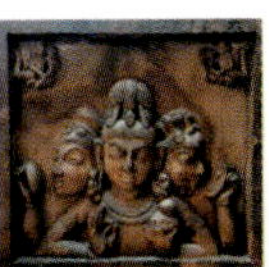

Bhagavad Gita: An Eternal Inspiration for Mahatma Gandhi

Taught by the blessed Narayana himself to Arjuna, compiled by Vyasa, the ancient seer, in the middle of the Mahabharata, I meditate on thee, O Mother, O' Bhagavad Gita, the blessed, of 18 chapters, the bestower of the nectar of non-dualistic wisdom, the destroyer of rebirth.

This famous *Gitasastra* is an epitome of the essentials of the whole Vedic teaching. A knowledge of its teaching leads to the realisation of all human aspirations.

I find solace in the Bhagavad Gita that I miss even in the 'Sermon on the Mount'.

When disappointment stares me in the face and all alone, I see not one ray of light, I go back to the Bhagavad Gita. I find a verse here and a verse there and I immediately begin to smile in the midst of overwhelming tragedies; and my life has been full of external tragedies and if they have left no visible, no indelible scar on me, I owe it all to the teachings of *Bhagavad Gita*.

M.K. Gandhi: *Young India* (1925)

Smriti Prasthana and synthesis of philosophical bases

In the Vedantic tradition, the Gita is considered to be one of the three fundamental canons of the Hindu philosophy or a part of the *prasthana-traya*. The Gita marks the ***Smriti Prasthana*** or the beginning of the 'remembered canonical tradition'. It is also considered to be the pinnacle of the Upanishadic knowledge, embodying the very essence of the Vedantic philosophy. However, scholars of the Gita do not consider it to be a mere extension of the Vedanta itself. The 700 verses also incorporate the elements of the *shad-darshanas* (the six systems of Indian philosophy) and in particular of Vedanta, Samkhya and Yoga. Thus, it is truly a synthesis of the different philosophical bases.

Harmonisation of Varying Religious Consciousness and Universality of Philosophy

The chief problem facing us today is the reconciliation of mankind. The Gita is especially suited for the purpose as it attempts to reconcile varied and apparently antithetical forms of the religious consciousness and emphasizes the root conceptions of religion which are neither ancient nor modern but eternal and belong to the very flesh of humanity past, present and future.

.... The teaching of the Gita is not presented as a metaphysical system thought out by an individual thinker or school of thinkers. It is set forth as a tradition which has emerged from the religious life of mankind. It is articulated by a profound seer, **who sees truth in its many sidedness**, and believes in its saving power. It represents not any sect of Hinduism, but Hinduism as a whole, not merely Hinduism but religion as such, in its **universality, without limit of time or space embracing within its synthesis the whole gamut of human spirit**.

The suggestions set forth in the Gita about the meaning and value of existence, the sense of eternal values and the way in which the ultimate mysteries are illumined by the light of reason and moral intuition, provide the basis for agreement in mind and spirit, so very essential for keeping together the world which has become materially one by the universal acceptance of the external source of civilisation.

Dr. S. Radhakrishnan; (in Bhagavad Gita, a commentary on the Gita authored by him)

Harmonisation of divergent paths to Moksha

The Gita does not prescribe any singular path of spirituality as the best fit for all. Neither, it deems any one path as superior or inferior to the other. Rather, it considers each to be converging to the same goal of *moksha* and unity of the *Atman* and *Brahman*. However, it duly takes into consideration the varying aptitude and abilities of human beings and even their varying approaches. These varying tendencies and temperaments also referred as the *gunas* (attributes), may manifest in one's yearning for knowledge, propensity for action, pursuit of devotion etc. Hence the Gita postulates ***Jnana-Yoga*** (salvation through the path of right knowledge), ***Karma-Yoga*** (salvation through appropriate duty or virtuous action) and ***Bhakti-Yoga*** (salvation through path of devotion to God), as the principal paths in pursuit of salvation. Thus, the Gita accepts and finds a harmony between the seemingly divergent paths of 'enlightenment-based renunciation', 'dharma-based household' and a 'personal god-based devotion'.

Nishkama Karma and Karma-Yoga

While the Gita rejects a life of indulgence, it does not support a path of extreme asceticism either, as the appropriate course for salvation (*moksha*). It propounds adoption of one's dharma (appropriate social and personal duties) and its rightful pursuit, as superior to inaction. Further, it does not consider even a common householder as unworthy of attainment of moksha, as compared to an ascetic or renouncer; or the former to be handicapped on account of being wrapped in worldly pursuits. Rather, it prescribes the doctrine of '*nishkama karma*' (detached pursuit of duties as the appropriate course of conduct). Thus, virtuous action and pursuit of one's rightful duties (*karma-yoga*) while remaining detached to the outcome of one's actions and devoid of the personal cravings and desires, is the path for salvation for the *karmayogi*.

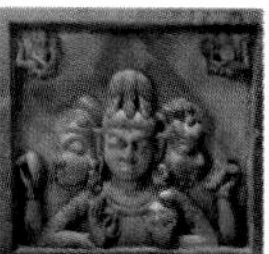

Nishkama Karma : A Unique Doctrine of the Gita

कर्मण्येवाधिकारस्ते मा फलेषु कदाचन।
मा कर्मफलहेतुर्भूर्मा ते सङ्गोऽस्त्वकर्मणि।। 2.47 ।।

Thy right is to action (duty-work) only, but never to fruits thereof. Let not the craving (attachment) for fruits of action be thy motive, nor let thy attachment be to inaction either.

(Verse 47, chapter 2, The Bhagavad Gita)

तस्मादसक्तः सततं कार्यं कर्म समाचर।
असक्तो ह्याचरन्कर्म परमाप्नोति पूरुषः।। 3.19 ।।

Therefore, without attachment, do thou always perform your dutiful actions which ought to be done (i.e. discharge your rightful karma); for by performing actions unattached, does a man attain the Supreme.

(Verse 19, chapter 3, The Bhagavad Gita)

मयि सर्वाणि कर्माणि संन्यस्याध्यात्मचेतसा।
निराशीर्निर्ममो भूत्वा युध्यस्व विगतज्वरः।। 3.30 ।।

Renouncing all actions in Me, with mind intent on the Self with a discriminating wisdom, free from any attachment, lust, despair or ego (free from expectations of results thereof) engage in this battle as your karma.

(Verse 30, chapter 3, The Bhagavad Gita)

त्यक्त्वा कर्मफलासङ्गं नित्यतृप्तो निराश्रयः।
कर्मण्यभिप्रवृत्तोऽपि नैव किञ्चित्करोति सः।। 4.20 ।।

Having abandoned attachment to the fruits of the action, ever content, depending on nothing, he does not do anything though engaged in activity.

(Verse 20, chapter 4, The Bhagavad Gita)

Emancipation through Jnana-Yoga

Comprehending the true knowledge of Self (*Atman*) and its relationship with the Universal (Brahman) has been described as one of the three paths to salvation in the Gita. The *jnana-yoga* emphasises on the realisation of One's true nature and the unity of the *Atman* and the *Brahman*. The path of *jnana-yoga* requires a much deeper understanding of the formless reality and the abstract, which are often beyond the superficial and sensory cognition. Thus, it is fraught with a slower progress and described to be better suited to those with yearning for knowledge and greater intellectual inclination.

The path of *jnana-yoga* is described in different shlokas and chapters of the Gita. In particular, the chapters 2 and 4, contain a fundamental exposition while other chapters contain an in-depth discourse on the specific and more minute concepts. In chapter 2, Lord Krishna describes to Arjuna the attributes of the indestructible, unchanging and eternal real self (the *Atman*) which is never born nor perishes but transmigrates into other human forms. He exhorts Arjuna to know this real Self and not limit his knowledge of Self to the identity of the mortal body or mind. In any case the death of this mortal body is not a cause for enduring grief for what is born is bound to perish. This marks the exposition to the knowledge of *samkhya*.

The Eternal Atman ; the Real Self

देहिनोऽस्मिन्यथा देहे कौमारं यौवनं जरा।
तथा देहान्तरप्राप्तिर्धीरस्तत्र न मुह्यति।। 2.13 ।।

As the soul experiences in this body infancy, youth and old age, so finally it passes into another. The wise have no delusion about this.

(Verse 13, chapter 2, The Bhagavad Gita)

न जायते म्रियते वा कदाचि
न्नायं भूत्वा भविता वा न भूयः।
अजो नित्यः शाश्वतोऽयं पुराणो
न हन्यते हन्यमाने शरीरे।। 2.20 ।।

It was not born; It will never die, nor once having been, can It cease to be. Unborn, eternal, ever-enduring, yet most ancient, the Spirit dies not when the body is dead.

(Verse 20, chapter 2, The Bhagavad Gita)

नैनं छिन्दन्ति शस्त्राणि नैनं दहति पावकः।
न चैनं क्लेदयन्त्यापो न शोषयति मारुतः।। 2.23 ।।

Weapons cut It not, fire burns It not, water wets It not, wind dries It not.

(Verse 23, chapter 2, The Bhagavad Gita)

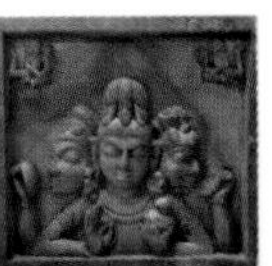

Different shlokas in chapter 4, capture the significance of the **true knowledge**. Lord Krishna explains to Arjuna as to how the eternal knowledge was revealed by Him (the Supreme God) to *Vivasvat* (the sun God) from whom to Manu, to Ikshvaku and henceforth (verses 4.1 and 4.2). In Shloka 4.24, he brings out the essential unity of the *Atman* and *Brahman* and enunciates that all is verily a manifestation of the *Brahman*. Further, he explains as to how this true knowledge liberates one from ignorance and redeems the soul.

On Manifestation of the Brahman and significance of true knowledge

ब्रह्मार्पणं ब्रह्महविर्ब्रह्माग्नौ ब्रह्मणा हुतम।

ब्रह्मैव तेन गन्तव्यं ब्रह्मकर्मसमाधिना ।। 4.24 ।।

For him, the sacrifice itself is the Brahman; the Brahman and the oblation are one; it is the Brahman, as its manifestation which is sacrificed in its fire (as it's another manifestation) and the man even in action is united with Brahman, since while performing his act, his mind never ceases to be fixed on Him.

(Verse 24, chapter 4, The Bhagavad Gita)

न हि ज्ञानेन सदृशं पवित्रमिह विद्यते।

तत्स्वयं योगसंसिद्धः कालेनात्मनि विन्दति ।। 4.38 ।।

Verily, there is nothing more purifying and sanctifying in this world like knowledge. He who is perfected in Yoga finds this true knowledge in the Self in time.

(Verse 38, chapter 4, The Bhagavad Gita)

तस्मादज्ञानसंभूतं हृत्स्थं ज्ञानासिनाऽऽत्मनः।

छित्त्वैनं संशयं योगमातिष्ठोत्तिष्ठ भारत ।। 4.42 ।।

Arise, O' Arjuna! with the sword of the knowledge (knowledge of the real Self) cut asunder the doubt of the self, which has sprung from your ignorance and resides in thy heart, and take refuge in Yoga (equanimity of mind and senses).

(Verse 42, chapter 4, The Bhagavad Gita)

Chapter 7 contains a discourse about the Inferior and Superior nature of the **true Self**. While the inferior nature (*apara prakriti)* has eight constituent elements, the ego-consciousness (*ahamkara*), the intellect (*buddhi*) and mind (*maan*) and the five grosser/root elements of earth, water, fire, air and ether, the superior nature (*para-prakriti*) is the true and the pure self. It is this self which is worth realising, as compared to the inferior self which causes bondage and pain and is misunderstood to be the real self. (Verses 7.3 & 7.4). Further, the all-shrouding *maya* is the root cause of this ignorance (verse 7.25), with people gripped by their delusion of likes and dislikes and trapped in the cycle of birth and death (verse 7.28)

The Real Self and the Delusion of Maya

अपरेयमितस्त्वन्यां प्रकृतिं विद्धि मे पराम्।

जीवभूतां महाबाहो ययेदं धार्यते जगत् ।। 7.5 ।।

This is the inferior Prakriti, O' mighty-armed (Arjuna); know thou as different from it, my higher Prakriti (Nature), the very life-element, by which this world is sustained.

(Verse 5, chapter 7, The Bhagavad Gita)

नाहं प्रकाशः सर्वस्य योगमायासमावृतः।

मूढोऽयं नाभिजानाति लोको मामजमव्ययम् ।। 7.25 ।।

Being enveloped by yoga-maya, I do not become manifest to all. This world in delusion does not know Me who am birthless and undecaying.

(Verse 25, chapter 7, The Bhagavad Gita)

इच्छाद्वेषसमुत्थेन द्वन्द्वमोहेन भारत।

सर्वभूतानि संमोहं सर्गे यान्ति परन्तप ।। 7.27 ।।

By the delusion of the pairs of opposites arising from desire and aversion, O' Bharata, all beings are subject to delusion at birth.

(Verse 27, chapter 7, The Bhagavad Gita)

The more detailed concepts of *Samkhya* and the hypothesis of the ***Purusha*** and the ***Prakriti*** are explained in chapter 13. Further, to satisfy the yearning of Arjuna, Lord Krishna also explains the qualities of an

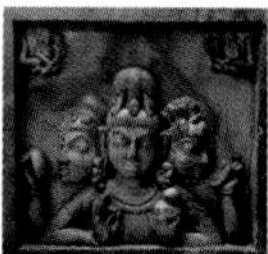

illumined person (sage) (in verses 13.7 to 13. 11) and three approaches of the path of realisation of the Self and emancipation (in verse 13.25). These paths include *Dhyana-yoga* (right mediation) *Samkhya-yoga* (right knowledge) and *Karma-yoga* (right action). The Lord then explains the unity of all life forms in the Brahman and realisation of that Brahman by comprehension of the true knowledge. Further, the three inherent qualities of Prakriti *(satva, rajas, tamas)* are described in chapter 14, how these *gunas* imbue different attributes to one and bind the soul to the body and how to liberate from them. The multiple qualities of the truly liberated person (a sage) is explained in the chapter 16. Thus, the gems of wisdom and true knowledge are strewn across the Gita in all its chapters.

Emancipation Through the Realisation of the Brahama

यदा भूतपृथग्भावमेकस्थमनुपश्यति।

तत एव च विस्तारं ब्रह्म सम्पद्यते तदा।। 13.31 ।।

He who sees the diverse forms of life all rooted in One and growing forth from Him, he shall indeed find the Absolute.

(Verse 31, chapter 13, The Bhagavad Gita)

क्षेत्रक्षेत्रज्ञयोरेवमन्तरं ज्ञानचक्षुषा।

भूतप्रकृतिमोक्षं च ये विदुर्यान्ति ते परम्।। 13.35 ।।

Those who with the eyes of wisdom, thus see the difference between Matter and Spirit, and know how to liberate Life from the Law of Nature, they attain the Supreme.

(Verse 35, chapter 13, The Bhagavad Gita)

Bhakti-yoga : The union through devotion

The third path to the spiritual salvation described in the Gita, is that of *bhakti*, or devotion to the Divine. This path underlines a loving surrender of one's thoughts and actions to a God with attributes and an implicit faith in this personal God as the redeemer from the *karmic* cycle of births and deaths. The teachings of *Bhakti-yoga* are largely contained in chapter 12 of the Gita. On being asked by Arjuna, as to the better path of salvation amidst those who meditate on the unmanifested and immutable Brahman vis- a-vis those who worship Him (God with attributes), Lord Krishna explains that both forms of worshippers may achieve salvation. However, the path of meditating on the unmanifested is replete with tribulations, as to focus on that formless, unmanifested, immutable Brahman, is difficult for the embodied beings. But for those who are devoted to Him (personal God), who surrender to Him and consecrate all their actions to Him, then He Himself becomes the redeemer of all such beings from this ocean of life and death. This brings forth the essence of the Bhakti Yoga.

Bhakti-yoga: Lord the emancipator of the Bhakta (devotee)

श्री भगवानुवाच

मय्यावेश्य मनो ये मां नित्ययुक्ता उपासते।

श्रद्धया परयोपेतास्ते मे युक्ततमा मताः।। 12.2 ।।

The Blessed Lord said Those who meditate on Me by fixing their minds on Me with steadfast devotion (and) being endowed with supreme faith-they are considered to be the most perfect yogis according to Me.

(Verse 2, chapter 12, The Bhagavad Gita)

ये तु सर्वाणि कर्माणि मयि संन्यस्य मत्पराः।

अनन्येनैव योगेन मां ध्यायन्त उपासते।। 12.6 ।।

तेषामहं समुद्धर्ता मृत्युसंसारसागरात्।

भवामि नचिरात्पार्थ मय्यावेशितचेतसाम्।। 12.7 ।।

As for those who, having dedicated all actions to Me and accepted Me as the supreme, meditate by thinking of Me with single-minded concentration only;

O' son of Prtha, for them who have their minds absorbed in Me, I become, without delay, the Deliverer from the sea of the world which is fraught with death.

(Verse 6&7, chapter 12, The Bhagavad Gita)

Lord Krishna advises Arjuna to fully immerse his consciousness in devotion to Him and fix his mind and intellect on Him. Thus, he would surely attain salvation. But if his mind wavers and such steadfast absorption of mind in Him is difficult, then through Yoga of relentless practice, he should try to be resolute

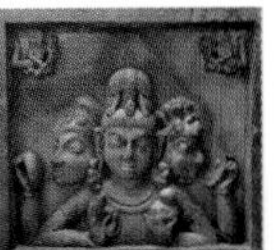

and attain Him. However, if this is also too difficult for him, then he should dedicate all his worldly actions to Him. He should discharge all his duties of *varnashrama dharma*, and all actions of the ephemeral and physical world, with the only intent of attaining Him. Thus, he should undertake all such actions on His behalf and thereby let go off his ego of him being the doer of any of these. But where even such dedication of all actions to Him is difficult, then one should practice discharging all one's *karma* unattached to the fruits thereof (*Nishkama Karma*).

The Manifold Path of a Bhakta

अभ्यासेऽप्यसमर्थोऽसि मत्कर्मपरमो भव।

मदर्थमपि कर्माणि कुर्वन् सिद्धिमवाप्स्यसि।। १२.१०।।

And if thou are not resolute enough to practise concentration (abhyasa yoga), then devote thyself to My service, do all thine acts for My sake, and thou shall still attain the goal.

(Verse 10, chapter 12, The Bhagavad Gita)

अथैतदप्यशक्तोऽसि कर्तुं मद्योगमाश्रितः।

सर्वकर्मफलत्यागं ततः कुरु यतात्मवान्।। १२.११।।

And if thou art too weak even for this, then seek refuge in union with Me, and with perfect self-control renounce the fruit of thy action.

(Verse 11, chapter 12, The Bhagavad Gita)

In the next few verses Lord Krishna describes the numerous qualities of his true and dear devotees, seeped in his Bhakti (stead-fast devotion). They are those who are, free from malice, unattached to possession, not caught in egotism, possessing equanimity, content, having self-control, compassionate, forgiving, free from fear and anxiety, have overcome desires, are unmoved by pleasure and pain, indifferent to worldly gains or sorrows, not a cause of strife or harm to the world or perturbed by its tribulations, internally pure, have intellect and mind resolutely focussed on Him and are fully dedicated in devotion to Him. Devotees possessing such qualities are dear to Him.

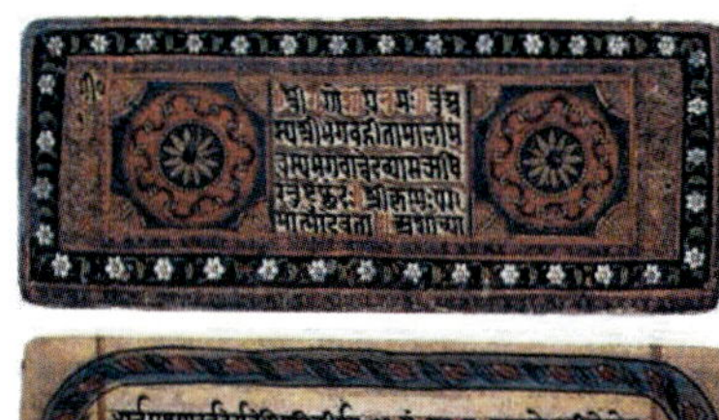

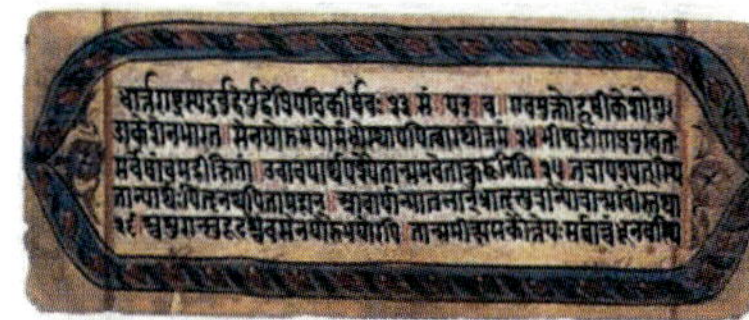

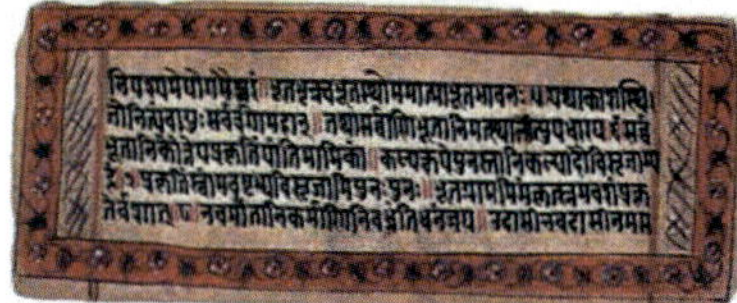

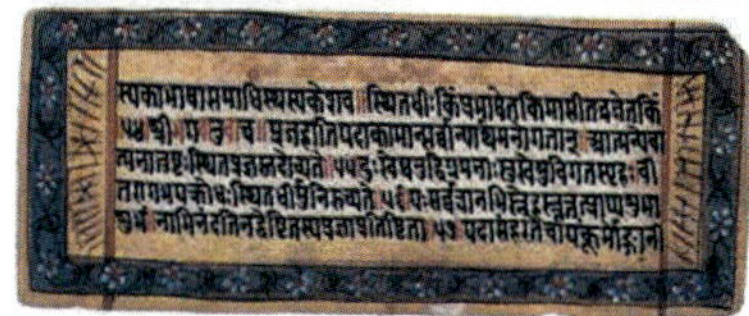

3.15: A 19th century paper manuscript of Bhagavad Gita with design of geometrical rosettes and floral ornamentation. Location, Library of Congress, USA — Wikimedia Commons

Numerous commentaries and interpretations

Since the time of Adi Shankaracharya, a number of interpretations and commentaries on Gita have been composed. While the classical commentaries include that of Adi Shankaracharya (800CE), Bhaskara (*Bheda Abheda* philosophy 10th century CE), Abhinavagupta (*Gitartha Sangraha* 11th century CE) Ramanuja (12th century CE), Nimbarka (*Gitatattva Prakashika* 12th century CE) Madhavcharya (*Gita Bhashya* 13th century CE), Vallabhacharya (*Sattvadipika* 15th century CE) and Chaitanya Mahaprabhu (*Acintya Bheda-Abheda* 15th century CE). Their interpretation of *Gita* as contained in *Bhashya* (commentary) composed by them or their immediate disciples, along with their interpretation of the other Vedantic canons (principal Upanishads and Brahmansutras) have formed the very basis for interpretation of Vedanta itself.

Shankaracharya interprets *Brahman* as described in the Gita, to be non-dual (*advaita*) and emphasises on the primacy of *jnana*. He propounds that with the right illuminating knowledge, *karma* (or action) loses its relevance and ceases to even exist. Thus, he lays the foundation of the non-dualistic tradition of interpretation of the Gita. Shankaracharya's *bhashya* is taken to be the earliest available interpretation of the Gita although he himself has referred to earlier commentaries on Gita (*bhashya*). However, these earlier ones seem to have been lost.

The interpretations of Ramanuja, which form the basis of *Vishishta Advaita* and that of Madhavacharya (*Dvaitavada*), emphasise on the path of devotion (*bhakti*) as central canon of the Gita. The interpretations of Vallabhacharya (contained in commentary *Sattvadipika*) prescribes the path of devotion while emphasising on the *Shuddha Advaita* (pure non-dualism) philosophy. The interpretations of Chaitanya form the basis of *Gaudyia Vaishnavism*. This school perceives Lord Vishnu as the manifested Brahman, prescribing the path of devotion to the Lord Krishna as an incarnation of Lord Vishnu.

Many modern interpretations and commentaries on the Gita have also been composed and these include those of Bal Gangadhar Tilak, Mahatma Gandhi, Vinoba Bhave, Aurobindo, Dr Radhakrishnan, Paramahansa Yogananda, Swami Sivananada, Swami Chinmayanada, Swami Prabhupada amongst

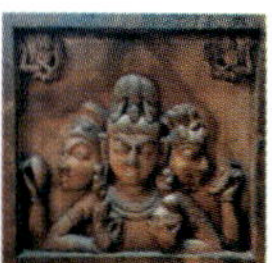

many others. Tilak in *Srimad Bhagavad Gita Rahasya*, emphasises on the primacy of Karmayoga as the central theme of the Gita. Mahatma Gandhi, in *Anasakti Yoga*, (his commentary on the Gita authored originally in Gujarati) emphasises on the performance of one's action unattached to the fruits thereof. He also emphasises on the ideal of *Sthitaprajna (sthita:* steady or established, and *prajna:* wisdom) as a key teaching of the Gita worth emulation. This concept is elucidated in chapter 2 (verses 55 to 70) and the qualities of such a Bhakta is also described in detail in chapter 12.

Paramahansa Yogananda identifies Rajayoga as a path of salvation highlighted in the Gita (in his translation titled, *God talks with Arjuna: the Bhagavad Gita*). The path emphasises on yogic techniques of meditation as the key to attaining salvation. The technique draws from the Patanjali's *Yogasutra*; the work which was interpreted and christened as *Raja-yoga* by Swami Vivekananda (in 1896). However, scholars often do not agree of *Raja-yoga* being any distinct path prescribed in the Gita other than the three, *Karma-yoga, Jnana-yoga* and *Bhakti-yoga*. Many other schools and tradition have also variously interpreted the Gita as largely emphasising on the Bhakti aspect as its key doctrine.

Over the years the Gita has also been translated into many Indian and foreign languages. These include, English translation by Sir Charles Wilkins (1785), translation into German Friedrich Schelgel (early 19th century), French translation by Emile Senart (1922) amidst others. While the Gita published by the Gita Press, Gorakhpur, has been translated into multiple Indian languages, the publication by Bhakti Vedanta Trust (part of ISKCON, founded by Swami AC Prabhupada) has been translated into nearly 56 non-Indian languages and purportedly published nearly half a billion copies worldwide.

Thus, transcending the boundaries of time and space and guiding innumerable societies and souls, the Gita serves as **a unique synthesis of pluralistic and universal philosophies, offering to humankind fundamental tenets and a practicable approach to spiritual evolution**.

Puranas

The word *Purana* literally means old, or ancient or historical. They are a part of the ***Smriti*** texts and cover a vast repository of religious literature ranging from legends and stories of various gods and goddesses, their incarnations, lesser deities, genealogy of kings, accounts of sages, certain elements of philosophy and even accounts of creation of the universe leading to its destruction. As an extremely diverse narrative, they are almost encyclopaedic and have had a profound influence on Hinduism, its beliefs and practices over the centuries. The tradition of bhakti, the practices and rituals associated with deity worship, festivals and religious ceremonies and innumerable cultural elements with which modern Hinduism as a religion is identified, owes its origin, preservation and continuity to the Puranas.

The Puranas and their origin

Composed in Sanskrit, there are 18 main Puranas or the *Mahapuranas*. Traditional belief has that sage Veda Vyasa was the compiler of these Puranas. This work was further entrusted by him to his disciple Lomaharshana and so on. It is also believed that originally there was one Purana, which over the years was segregated into many separate bodies.

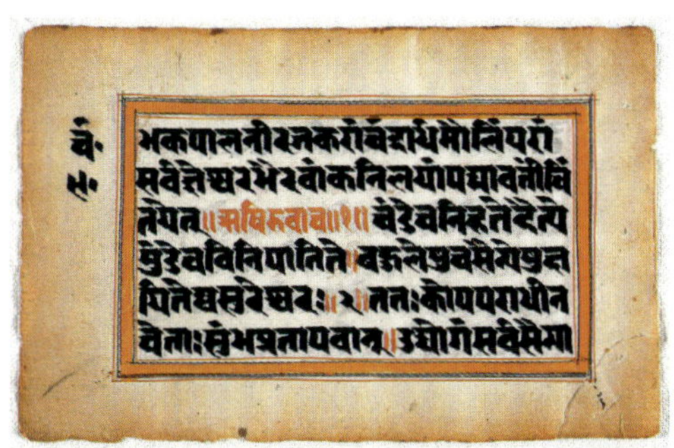

3.16: A page of text from a Bhagavata Purana of late 18th century, Kashmir region; current location of manuscript, Los Angeles, Museum of County Art — Wikimedia Commons

Historically, the specific origin of the Puranas remain uncertain. Owing to the oral tradition and having been passed through generations in the *guru-shishya* tradition, the Puranas may have been a part of the socio-religious discourse for centuries and different Puranas could have originated at altogether different points of time. However, the editions in vogue today are believed to have been compiled in written form around 4th to 6th century CE during the Gupta period or sometime later. Some historians believe that some Puranas could have been composed/compiled as late as around 1000 CE.

Mahapuranas

The main recognised Puranas which are 18 in number are also referred to as the *Mahapuranas*. Besides them, there are said to be 18 more puranas termed as *upapuranas* which are lesser known. Among the *Mahapuranas*, the **Bhagavata-Purana, Brahma-Purana, Vishnu-Purana, Shiva-Purana** and the **Markandeya-Purana** are considered to be the most important and well-known ones. These 18 Puranas are often classified in terms of the central deity around which the anthology of tales or the narration of

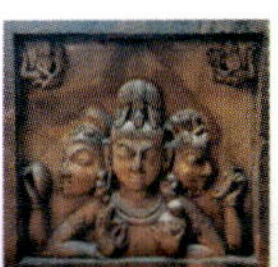

eulogy is built around (although cross referencing of the other main deities is invariably found in all the puranas). One such classification is as below.

Vishnu:	Bhagavata-Purana, Vishnu-Purana, Garuda-Purana, Narada-Purana, Varaha-Purana, Matsya-Purana, Vamana-Purana, Vayu-Purana
Brahma:	Brahma-Purana, Padma-Purana
Shaiva:	Shiva-Purana, Skanda-Purana, Markandeya-Purana, Linga-Purana, Kurma-Purana, Brahmannda-Purana
Agni:	Agni-Purana
Surya:	Brahma Vaivarta-Purana

Some sources also classify Puranas into three groups based on the principal *gunas* or attributes viz., *satva, rajas* and *tamas*, they are identified with. Some classifications are also as per those associated with the divine trinity of Brahma, Vishnu and Mahesha.

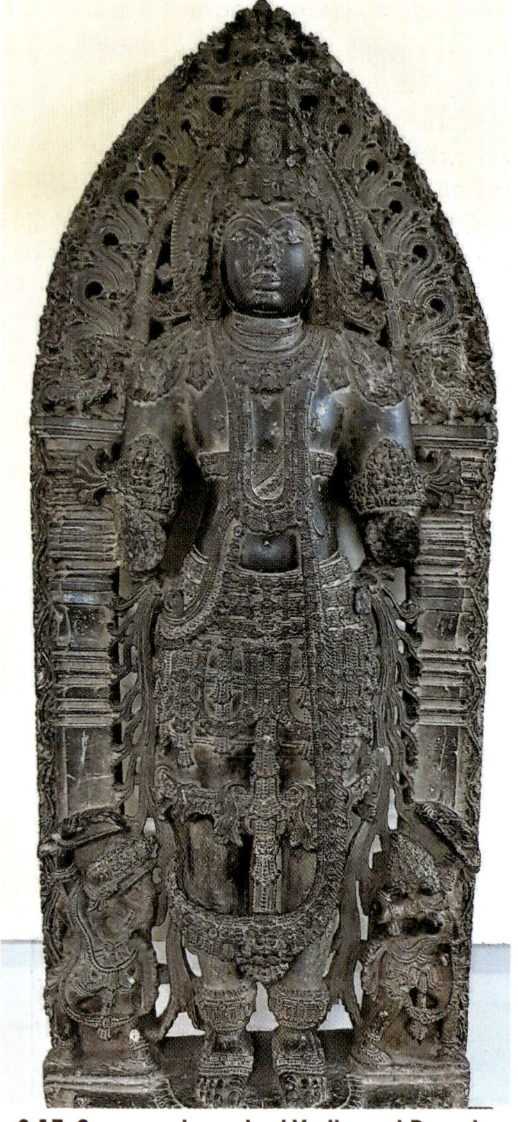

3.17: Surya, an important Vedic and Puranic deity. Usha and Pratiusha, consorts of Surya depicted in the bottom right and left of the sculpture. Hoysala, 12th century sculpture. Government Museum, Bangalore; — photograph by Madhukar K Bhagat

Structure, contents and significance

The Puranas, like other Vedic literature and smriti texts are composed in form of shlokas (verses) in Sanskrit. Some Puranas are found in regional languages and even some Jain Puranas are known to exist. Traditionally, Puranas are known to incorporate five key subjects referred to as the *panch-lakshanas* (five signs) which include;

(*i*) ***Sarga***: the subject of creation of universe

(*ii*) ***Pratisarga***: their recreation after dissolution or secondary creation

(*iii*) ***Vansha***: genealogy of gods and also of sages

(*iv*) ***Manvantara***: the creation of human race and the account of the first human beings (*Manus*) in the numerous secondary creations

(*v*) ***Vansanucharitam***: the genealogical and historical account of the solar and lunar dynasties

An inspiration for Bhakti

Most significantly, their contents invariably comprise, shlokas in veneration of a key deity/deities their life(s) and its narrative. Thus **Bhagavata-Purana** (*Srimad Bhagavata* or *Bhagavatam*), amongst the most important and well-known Puranas, is dedicated to the Bhakti (devotion) of Lord Krishna. It contains the description of the life of Lord Krishna as an avatar of lord Vishnu and includes tales of his birth, childhood, early life, and other stories which over the centuries have become folklore in the Hindu culture. But more significantly, elements of philosophy, ethics, path of moksha (liberation), devotion to the manifested God, restoration of the balance of the universe by the God, triumph of the good (incarnated god) over the evil, are some salient occurring themes of the narrative.

Over centuries, this Purana has been a key treatise of Vaishnavism and engendered the tradition of Bhakti centred around lord Krishna. It has also been an inspiration of many *bhakti sampradayas* (devotional sects) such as Gaudiya Vaishnavism founded by medieval saint in Bengal, Chaitanya Mahaprabhu. Similarly, the **Markandeya-Purana** which incorporates ***Devi Mahatamya*** has been the sacred scripture of Shaktism (worship of Goddess Durga and her numerous forms of female divinities). **Shiva-Purana, Skanda-Purana, Markandeya-Purana, Linga-Purana** and other puranas which capture the legends of the Lord Shiva, have formed the central tenets of Shaivism and over centuries have been the basis of movements like Nayanars and the entire Shaivite tradition.

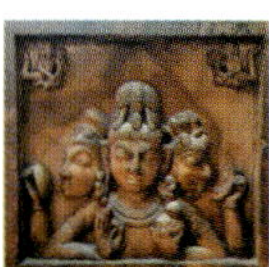

An encyclopaedic account

All the Puranas were more than a treatise on the practice of devotion, considering that the extensiveness of the work and the diversity of topics covered by them were truly encyclopaedic. The **Bhagavata,** comprising of nearly **18000 shlokas** (verses) describes the numerous avatars of lord Vishnu (Sri Rama, Sri Krishna Narasimha etc.), besides the *bhakta-avatars* (such as Prahalad, Narada, Kapila etc.) and various demons which were vanquished by these avatars (Hiranyaksha and Hiranyakashyapu; Ravana and Kumbhakarna; who are Jaya and Vijaya incarnate; Bali, Vritasura etc.). It also contains a detailed genealogical account of various dynasties.

The **Skanda Purana** is the **longest**, comprising nearly **81,100 verses**. It describes about the birth of Skanda who is also known as Kartikeya and Murugan, and is the son of Shiva and Parvati. It also contains the detailed narratives of him as the leader of army of *devas* in many important wars against the *asuras*. Thus, the sect of Bhakti centred around this deity in many parts of India and even in Southeast Asia, is largely attributed to this Purana. Skanda-Purana is also credited to contain a very detailed account of many pilgrimage centres, their geographical locations, their significance, worship practices besides stories and legends around them.

The **Garuda Purana,** comprising nearly **19000 verses**, primarily centres around lord Vishnu and is arranged as a dialogue between the deity, (lord Vishnu) and his *vahana* (celestial vehicle) Garuda. The Garuda Purana covers a bewildering range of topics including cosmology, numerous gods and their relationship, philosophies of *Yoga* and *Samkhya*, *moksha*, *karmic* cycles, rebirth and even other Upanishadic subjects. The geography of *Bharatavarsha* (India), account of the salient rivers, diseases and medicines, astronomy, astrology and Hindu calendar system, architecture of homes and temples, rites of passage, different virtues to be emulated, duties of king and statecraft and even the rules of grammar and genre of literature, are some of the topics described in its wide array.

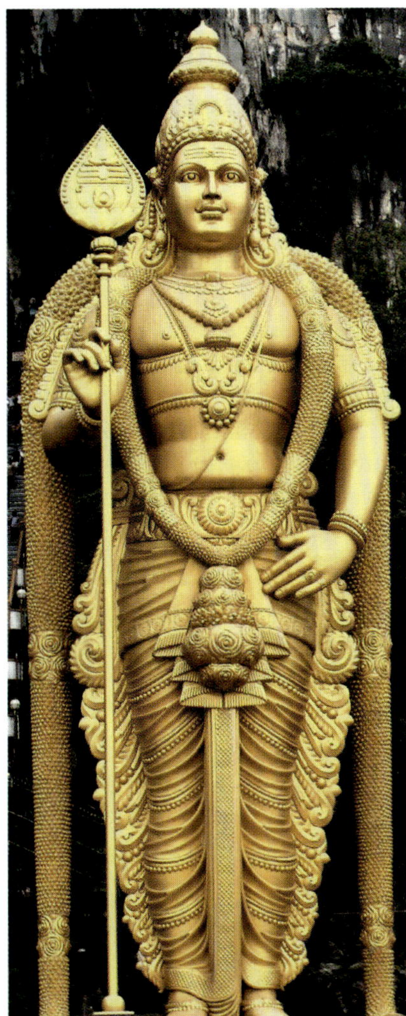

3.18: A large statue of Murugan at Batu Caves temple, Malaysia; a culture of worship of Kartikeya emanating from Skanda Purana and in practice in South and Southeast Asia. — photograph by Madhukar K Bhagat

Pluralism and syncretism

The organisation of different Puranas around different deities, incorporating their legends and mythological tales of eulogy, may have been the inspiration for movements of Bhakti such as Vaishnavism, Shaivism, Shaktism which were centred around the deities. However, the Puranas in themselves were pluralistic as well as syncretic. The Puranic tales while bringing out the virtues and deeds of the central deity, also had innumerable references and reverence to the other deities. Thus, veneration of Goddess Durga was not unique to Markandeya-Purana, but in many other puranas too. The union of Shiva-Shakti is incomplete without the female divinity and the very concept emphasises on integration and harmony of the seemingly diverse forces of the cosmos. Lord Shiva and lord Vishnu are considered often the manifestation of the same deity. Even the **trinity of Brahma, Vishnu and Mahesh** find a merger in one singular deity referred as **Mahavishnu** or **Mahashiva,** thus converging the pantheon of Gods and believes to monism and Unity.

The Puranas were not prescriptive as to cause people to believe about the appropriateness of a singular perspective or primacy of one believe system, but pluralistic and accommodative of the regional and even local beliefs. Thus, the cult and belief in the ***Saptmatrikas*** finds reflection in the worship of Goddess Durga and her various manifestations. The concept of ***Pashupati*** is integrated in the worship of lord Shiva. As per scholars, the legend of the one of the chief Dravidian warrior-philosopher god, **Murugan** or **Subramanya** gets integrated with **Kartikeya** or Kumar in Puranic culture, and his legends find expression in the Skanda-purana. While monism and convergence with the Vedantic philosophy remains the corner stone of Puranas, yet their outward manifestation offers sufficient scope for numerous faiths and belief systems to integrate and even flourish under its large canopy.

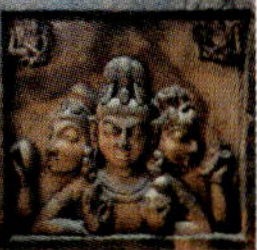

Manifestation of Hindu religion and culture

While the Vedantic culture embodies the spiritual and philosophical essence of Hinduism, the Puranic culture brought out the **tangible and manifested elements** of this religion. Thus, the pantheon of gods identified today with present day Hinduism, their legends and lore, the waves of **bhakti** which swept in the past and their numerous sects, are all attributable to the Puranas in one form or the other. The places of pilgrimages, numerous temples of innumerable deities, **rituals and practices of worship**, rites of passage, religious ceremonies followed today, owe their origin to the Puranas. Even the major **festivals** such as Holi, Dussehra, Deepavali which are based on certain legends, or those associated with the birth of principal deities, such as Ramanavami, Janmashtami, Mahashivaratri etc., are attributable to the Puranic culture. Many **religious art forms** such as Krishnaleela or *raasleela*, their music, dance and expression, temple architecture, sculpture, literature and folklore which emanated from the Puranas have been an **integral part of Hinduism and Indian culture** over the centuries. Even Jain and Buddhist belief systems were influenced later by the Puranic culture, thereby leading to emergence of legends of numerous demigods in their own fold.

Thus, the puranas are not just a source of manifested religious elements, but incorporated and preserved the elements of philosophy, ethics, rites of passage, art-forms and other disciplines of sciences, architecture, astronomy, medicine, literature, grammar etc. They were **syncretic** of the diverse social knowledge and various cultures and belief systems as well as. The knowledge of the past and the accruing knowledge was all integrated and preserved in this vast repository, transcending diverse geographies and the turbulent two millennium.

OTHER HINDU SCRIPTURES

Vedangs and Upvedas

Although strictly not a part of the Vedas, the Vedang (literally meaning 'part of the Vedas') and Upvedas (literally meaning 'subsidiary or sub-Veda') are considered to be auxiliary disciplines associated with the study of the Vedas.

Vedang

These are six separate and ancillary disciplines which were considered important in Vedic studies and aided in the comprehension of the Vedas. The *Brihadarnyaka Upanishad* considers them as key elements of the *Brahmana* layer of the Vedas. However, their studies flourished as independent subjects in themselves. Their authorship or even the period of their creation remains uncertain. Historians generally believe that their composition may have occurred around the end of Vedic age and most likely by the 5th century BCE. The Vedangs comprised ***Shiksha, Chanda, Vyakarana, Nirukta, Kalpa,*** and ***Jyotisha***. While *Nirukta* and *Vyakaran* were indispensable and common to the study of all Vedas, the others aided as well and developed into independent disciplines.

(*a*) ***Shiksha*** – This discipline incorporated the study of phonetics and pronunciation and documented their rules etc. Thus, the various alphabets, the appropriate method of their pronunciation, as to which part of the mouth, tongue, throat, pallet, teeth or nostril was to aid in the correct pronunciation, was a part of this study. Further, the common mistakes which occur in pronunciation, stress required in pronunciation, melody and the criteria for euphonic combination in recitation of the Vedic shlokas etc., were all integral to this discipline.

(*b*) ***Chanda*** – This *shastra* incorporated the study of verses and prosody. Thus, the various poetic metres, including those based on specific number of syllables per verse with specific rules of each, were included in its ambit. For instance, the *Anustubh Chanda*, which is usually employed in the Vedic shlokas, consisted of four quarter verses, each with eight syllables.

(*c*) ***Vyakarana*** – The study of *Vyakarana*, or grammar, was essential for the correct understanding of the Vedic shlokas and other compositions. All the rules of grammar and syntax which were essential for proper composition and understanding of the sentences and expression of ideas, formed a part of this study. This *Shastra* also analysed every word in its root or natural (*prakrit*) form and suffix (*pratyaya*). *Ashtadhyayi,* the treatise on grammar by Panini, is considered to the most authoritative work of ancient Sanskrit grammar.

(*d*) ***Nirukta*** – This *shastra* dealt with etymology and study of obscure phrases and words, and thus was crucial in proper understanding of the meaning of the of the Vedic *shlokas* and the *mantras*. Wherever the appropriate meaning of the word could not be deciphered using the *prakrit* (natural

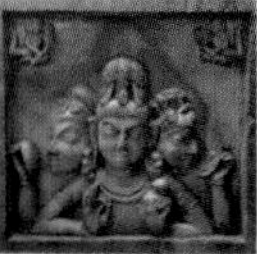

context) or the *pratyaya* (suffix form), then the aid of the discipline of Nirukta was taken in deciphering the appropriate meaning. However, Nirukta in itself was considered complementary to *Vyakarana*, and thus lower in significance to it.

(*e*) ***Kalpa*** –The ritual instructions associated with the various rites, religious ceremonies, and other events of life and *varnashrama-dharma*, were incorporated in the *Kalpa shashtra*. Thus, which Vedic ritual and mantra was appropriate in the events of birth, marriage, death etc. and what would be the appropriate conduct of an individual in the various stages of life would be the subject of this study. It was further divided into four auxiliary disciplines; *Shrutsutra, Grihasutra, Dharmasutra,* and *Shulbasutra.*

(*f*) ***Jyotisha*** – Based on the study of movement of celestial bodies, this *shastra* (astrology and astronomy) focussed on prescribing the appropriate time for conduct of the numerous Vedic rituals. As the preliminary layers of the Vedas were concerned with the *karmakanda,* which were discharged through the rituals and rites, the knowledge of the *kaal* or the auspicious and appropriate moment for the rituals, was essential, and thus the study of *Jyotisha* was integral to the Vedic knowledge.

Panini's Description of the Significance of the Vedangas

Maharishi Panini, in the treatise *Paniniya Shiksha* (in the shlokas 41 & 42), while extolling the significance of the Vedanga, gives the analogy of the *Vedangas* to be akin to the various parts of body of the Vedas.

छन्दः पादौ तु वेदस्य हस्तौ कल्पोऽथ पठ्यते,
ज्योतिषामयनं चक्षुर्निरुक्तं श्रोत्रमुच्यते।
शिक्षा घ्राणं तु वेदस्य मुखं व्याकरणं स्मृतम्,
तस्मात्सांगमधीत्यैव ब्रह्मलोके महीयते ।।

Chhandah padau tu vedasya hastau kalpoth pathyate,
Jyotisamayanam Chakshurniruktam Srotrammuchyate.
Shiksha Ghranam tu Vedasya mukha grammar smritam,
Tasmatsangamadhyatayava Brahmlok Mahiyate.

If the Vedas are imagined to be akin to a human body, then the *chhanda shastra* is the very feet of the *Vedas*, the *Kalpa Shastra* is its hands, *Jyotish* is the eyes, *Nirukta* is the ears, *Shikshaa* is like the nose and *Vyaakaran* is the mouth of the *Vedas*. Thus, each part has a unique role and significance in the whole, which are the *Vedas*.

Upvedas

There are five recognised *Upvedas,* each dealing with a separate discipline. These are believed to have originated from or branched out from one of the four principal Vedas. Their subjects incorporate different streams of human knowledge and elements of social wellbeing. Their domain was largely secular and not metaphysical, spiritual or even associated with rites of passage as in the Vedic domain. Thus, the *upvedas* were a significant and encyclopaedic contribution of a civilisation to the knowledge of humanity. The five Upvedas are;

(*a*) ***Arthaveda*** –The science of sociology, economics, and political systems are the subjects of *Arthaveda.* It is considered to be related to *Rigveda.*

(*b*) ***Dhanurveda*** – This *Upveda* incorporates the science of defence, arms, and armament. Its origin is attributed to *Yajurveda.*

(*c*) ***Gandharvaveda*** – The science of music, including singing and instruments are a part of *Gandharveda.* It is believed to have emanated from Samaveda.

(*d*) ***Ayurveda*** –Is the science of medicines, which is related to Atharvaveda. While the other three *Upvedas* are considered to have been lost, the fundamentals of Ayurveda are extant and available.

(*e*) ***Sthapathyaveda*** – This Upveda dealt with the science of architecture and is considered is related to Yajurveda.

Some traditions do not consider *Sthapatyaveda* to be an Upveda and recognise only the other four as the *Upvedas*, while some include *Sthapatyaveda* in this four, while excluding *Arthaveda* from this classification.

Dharma-Sutras and Dharma-Shastras: The treatises on Hindu law

The *Dharma-sutras* and *Dharma-shastras* are a genre of theological texts which prescribed the **codes of righteous conduct, ethics and moral principles (*dharma*),** governing the discharge of individual and social duties for different classes (*varna*) in different stations (*ashramas*) of life. Thus, these texts formed

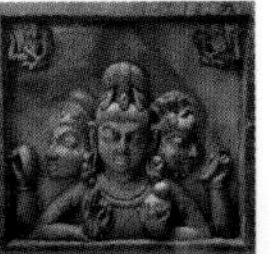

the basis of **ethics** and **law** which governed the very conduct at the individual and social levels for nearly two millenia. In the last 200 hundred years, and particularly in the British regime, they were taken to be the **source of the Hindu law**.

The *Dharma-shastras* are believed to be many in number (between 18 and 100). They themselves emanate from the *Dharma-sutras*, which in turn are part of one of the *Vedangas*. It is believed that towards the end of the Vedic era, as the Vedic texts became more archaic and difficult to comprehend, the emergence of the *Vedangas* took place. Later, from the ***Kalpa-vedanga*, the *Dharma-sutras* emerged**. But the *Dharma-sutras* in themselves were composed of highly condensed sutras with terse sentence structures, making them concise, but difficult to understand. These required higher skills of interpretation and led to the composition of the *Dharma-shastras* in *Anustubh* metre (four *chandas* each of 8-syllable verses) with lucid composition and easy comprehension.

Thus, both the category of texts are derivatives of the Vedic texts itself. However, unlike the Vedas which are believed to be of divine origin and categorised as *shrutis*, these texts are classified as *smritis* and have a human origin.

The Dharma-sutras

These treatises which emanated from the Kalpa-vedanga, provided the norms of conduct and social behaviour in the different *ashrams* (stations of life) be it *Brahmacharya* (student-hood), *Grihastha* (house-holdership), *Vanaprastha* (retirement for social affairs), and *Sanyasa* (renunciation). They prescribed the codes of ethics and duties of different sections, including those of the kings and the *brahmins* etc. They also discuss matters of personal law such as those related to marriage inheritance. Thus, they were akin to the personal, social, civil and even the criminal law which governed the society at multiple levels. Out of the many *Dharma-sutras* which are believed to have existed, only four are known to have survived to this day. These include the sutras of *Apastambha, Gautama, Baudhyayana* and *Vashistha*. These are believed to have been composed around the 5th to 1st century BCE.

Dharma-shastras

The Dharma-shastras were derivative texts of *Dharma-sutras* and were more elaborate in scope and lucid in meaning and comprehension. Although they claim to draw their authority from the Vedas as the ultimate source of Dharma, reference to these texts is not found in the Vedas. The earliest reference to them is observed in Katyayan's commentary on Panini's work in around the 3rd century BCE. Only four *Dharma-shastras* have survived to the modern times, these include, **the *Manu-smriti, Yajnavalkya-smriti, Narada-smriti*** and ***Vishnu-smriti***.

> **Gautama's Dharma-sutra and Testimony in a Trial**
>
> *The witness must take an oath before deposing.*
> *Single witness normally does not suffice.*
> *As many as three witnesses are required.*
> *False evidence must face sanctions.*
>
> **– Gautama Dharma sutras 13.2-13.6**

Among these, the *Manu-smriti* (2nd to 3rd century BCE) is the oldest and most well-known source of Hindu Dharma (law). The *Yajnavalkya-smriti* is often considered to the best composed and most sophisticated and more influential than even *Manu-smriti* as a text of legal theory. The *Narada-smriti* was more of a judicial text dealing with the judicial issues and matters rather than ethical conduct or rites. The last of these, the *Vishnu-smriti* (composed around 7th century CE) has more to do with the matters of devotion thus dwelling more on the bhakti tradition.

The *Dharma-shastras* traditionally have dwelled on three major areas *which include*;

- **(a)** ***Aachara***, which were rules of daily rituals and dharma of the four varnas
- **(b)** ***Vyavahara***, which were rules of substantive law and removal of doubts. These were categorised according to standard 18 titles of Hindu law.
- **(c)** ***Prayaschitta***, rules of penance and expiations in case of any violation of the laws (dharma).

The minor areas of exposition of Dharma-shastra includes the topics of,

(*i*) Sources of **dharma,** (*ii*) **Varna**, (*iii*) Consecratory or life-cycle, rites (***samskaras***), especially marriage, (*iv*) Orders of life, or life-stages (***ashramas***), (*v*) Five great sacrifices (***mahayajnas***), (*vi*) Rules for eating, (*vii*) Religious gifts (***dana***), (*viii*) Rules for renunciation (***sanyasa***), (*ix*) **Duties** of a king, (*x*) **Legal procedure,** (*xi*) Eighteen titles of law (***vyavaharapadas***), (xii) Categories of **sin,** (*xiii*) **Expiations** and penances, (*xiv*) **Karma,** (xv) Funerary and ancestral rites (***antyeṣṭi*** and ***shraddha***), (*xvi*) **Pilgrimage,** (*xvi*) **Vows**

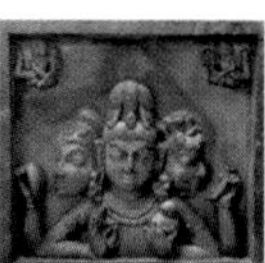

HINDU PHILOSOPHY

The Hindu philosophy is a collection of numerous philosophical doctrines ranging from the ***Shad-Darshan*** (six philosophical schools) propounded in ancient India, to the ***Advaita Vedanta*** (8th century CE), from ***Nirguna Brahman*** to ***Saguna Brahman***, and from ***Varnashrama-Dharma*** to ***Bhakti Yoga***. Each has enriched and added to the cumulative philosophical tradition. However, singularly, none can be said to represent the Hindu philosophy wholly. *Some of the important philosophical traditions are discussed below:*

The Shad-Darshanas

These refer to the six philosophical systems which emerged in ancient India between 6th century BCE to 4th century CE. They form the core of the Hindu philosophical system. These are **Nyaya, Vaishesika, Samkhya, Yoga, Purva Mimansa**, and **Vedanta.**

(*i*) *Nyaya*

The Nyaya school of philosophy is said to be founded in the 2nd century CE by sage Gautama. It deals with **formal reasoning, logic, epistemology, theology, and metaphysics.** *Nyaya-sutra* which is the foundational text of this school sheds light on sixteen topics pertaining to logic and reasoning. These are:

(*a*) **Pramana** - epistemology/proof

(*b*) **Pramey** - which is to be proven or ontology

(*c*) **Samasya** - doubt

(*d*) **Prayojana** - purpose

(*e*) **Drishtanta** - illustrations or case study

(*f*) **Siddhanta** - established doctrine

(*g*) **Avayavya** - premise of a syllgolism

(*h*) **Tarka** - logical deduction

(*i*) **Nirnaya** - conclusion

(*j*) **Vada** - discussion

(*k*) **Jalpa** - debates with view to defeat an opponent

(*l*) **Vitanda** - debate without interest in establishing a view

(*m*) **Hetvabhasa** - fallacious arguments

(*n*) **Chala** - unfair attempt to contradict a statement

(*o*) **Jai** - unfair reply to argument

(*p*) **Nigrasthana** - ground for defeat in a debate

(*ii*) *Vaiseshika*

This system of philosophy was founded by sage **Kanada** (in 1st century CE). It deals with philosophical as well as metaphysical issues. It postulates matter and objects in the physical world to be eventually made up of *Parmanu* (atoms). Earth, water, air, and fire are the four basic substances composing the physical world. These in turn are themselves of two types— 'atomic' (*Parmanu*) and 'composite'. A 'composite' in turn is divided into atoms, and atoms are indivisible, indestructible, and invisible.

However, beyond the metaphysical concepts, this school also postulates what is *Dharma* and that it is *Dharma* which leads to salvation. Its postulates are contained in the **'Vaisesika-sutra' of Kanada.**

(*iii*) *Samkhya*

The Samkhya school of philosophy is the **oldest** of the organised schools of Indian philosophy. The propounder of this school is said to be sage **Kapila.** This school developed independent of the Vedas and even finds a mention in the *Katha Upanishad* and the *Bhagavad Gita*. Some Jain texts too refer to this system. **Samkhya Karika** of **Isvar Krishna** (4th century CE) is the authoritative text of this philosophy.

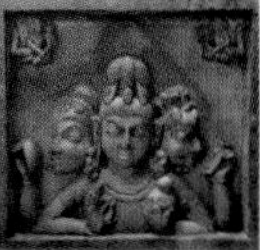

As per the Samkhya system, the universe comprises of two fundamental entities—the ***Purusha*** (consciousness-person) and ***Prakriti*** (matter, nature). The living being or *Jiva*, exists as a result of the bond between the *Purusha* and *Prakriti*. *Prakriti*, or nature, comprises the **three Gunas**

Sattva: based on knowledge, illuminance, goodness, compassion, positivity, etc.

Rajas: based on activity, passion, impulsiveness, and even chaos, and

Tamas: based on ignorance, inaction, negativity, lethargy, destruction etc.

All the three *gunas* are present in different proportions in different life forms. The *gunas* define character of a living thing and lead to pleasure or pain. With true *Satvic* knowledge does a being realise the distinction of *Purusa* from *Prakriti*, which eventually leads to the end of the cycle of **transmigration of soul**, or a state of complete freedom, or **Kaivalya**. This system does not base itself on the teaching in Vedas nor does it believe in a universal being or God. It is considered a **rationalist school** of Indian philosophy.

(*iv*) *Yoga*

The Yoga philosophy emanates from **Patanjali's *Yoga Sutra*** (4th century CE). The essence of this philosophy is also contained in the Bhagavad Gita. The Yoga philosophy quite like the Samkhya, does not derive its authority from the Vedas, and like the Samkhya it believes the cosmos to be a result of interaction between *Purusha* and *Prakriti* and that there is existence of the three Gunas. However, while in the Samkhya system, liberation is achieved by *Prakriti* (nature) enlightening the *Purusha* (which has a lesser proactive role), in the Yoga system *Purusha* is not a mere spectator, and by personal effort and practical action, *Purusha* can attain its own liberation. **The Ashtanga Yoga** as propounded by **Patanjali** is the means to such liberation. It consists of eight limbs which are:

Yama – comprising *Ahimsa*, eschewing *Asatya* (falsehood), *Aparigraha* (greed/envy), *Asteya* (acquisition), and practising *Brahmacharya* (sexual restraint)

Niyama – Discipline and observance of rules of simplicity, austerity, and purity

Asana – Physical postures and exercises

Pranayama – Control of breath and mind

Pratyahara – Withdrawal of consciousness/mind from sensory objects

Dharana – Concentration

Dhyana – Meditation

Samadhi – State of union of self with universe or *Kaivalya*

Yoga is recognised by the Hindu philosophy to be categorised as *Raja Yoga* (described in Patanjali's *Ashtanga Yoga* system), *Jnana Yoga, Karma Yoga, and Bhakti Yoga.*

(*v*) Purva Mimansa - The philosophy of Purva Mimansa or Mimansa is contained in the **Purva Mimansa Sutra** of **Jamini**. The words *Purva* (former) and *Mimansa* (enquiry) refer to the former part of the Vedas, i.e., to the *Samhitas* and the *Brahmanas* or the *Karmakanda*. Thus, this school of philosophy is based on the teachings of Vedas as contained in the *Samhitas* and *Brahmanas*. It considers the Vedas to be eternal and infallible, and **emphasises on *mantras* and rituals** as prescribed in Vedas as of being of primary importance, while the Upanishads were considered to be of secondary importance. Its philosophy concerns more with *Dharma* and duties of a person or '*Karya*', rather than metaphysical knowledge. This school also helped in development of philosophy of language, linguistics, and philology which influenced other schools.

(*vi*) Vedanta - The word 'Vedanta' literally means the 'end of the Vedas'. The philosophy of this school is based on the teachings as contained in the concluding portion of the Vedas, viz. the Upanishads. It is also referred as **Uttar Mimansa** (or latter enquiry) as opposed to Purva Mimansa.

The Vedantic philosophy is expressed in its classical form in the Vedanta Sutras or the **Brahma Sutras of *Badrayana*** (1st century CE) which is akin to a synopsis of the teachings of the Upanishads. It also finds expression in the teachings of the *Bhagavad Gita*. This philosophy emphasised on ***Jnana*** (or knowledge) and explored metaphysical subjects like *Brahman*, *Atman* (soul), etc. It laid greater stress on acquisition of true knowledge and spiritual development rather on rituals and sacrifices.

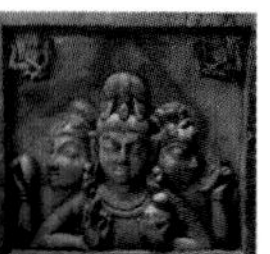

The Vedanta school branched out into separate sub-schools based on their philosophies of dualism to monism. Some of these schools are: **Advaita, Vishishta Advaita, Dvaita, Bheda-abheda,** and **Neo-Vedanta,** etc.

Branches of Vedanta

Advaita Vedanta

Advaita literally means **'no two'**, or sole, or unity. Thus, this school of philosophy is based on the principle of **monism** or **unitism** which says that all creation is a reflection of the supreme, which itself is without attributes (*nirguna*). Thus, it considers *Atman* (soul) not as a separate entity from the *Brahman*, but only its manifestation. **Sri Adi Shankaracharya** (8th century CE) consolidated the principles of Advaita Vedanta and structured the philosophy in a formal shape.

This school also believed that the **Brahman is the Supreme and the only reality** and this world itself was transient and illusory (a *maya*). With the knowledge of one's true self, one could pierce through this veil of *maya* which is the illusion of the world and of the *Atman* and Brahman being separate entities. Further, *Moksha* (liberation) could be achieved through the union of *Atman* and *Brahman*.

Vishishta advaita

This philosophy, also referred to as **qualified non-dualism**, was propounded by **Ramanuja** (11th century CE). Although it does consider *Jivatama* (soul-living being) to be a reflection of the *Brahman*, however, unlike Advaita school, it does not consider the *Brahman* to be without attributes. Thus, *Brahman* is *Saguna* (with attributes). *Atman* and *Brahman* were considered distinct entities but mutually inseparable. This philosophy and teachings of Ramanuja also laid the foundation of Vaishnavism.

Dvaita

Madhavacharya (13th century CE) was the propounder of this school of philosophy. Also referred as the *Bhedavada* or the *Tattvavada*, it considered *Brahman* (the Universal) and *Atman* (soul) to **be two distinct entities.** *Brahman* is also identified with **a personalised god with attributes** which was considered to be lord Vishnu with various incarnations. While Lord Vishnu was independent, the souls were dependent on him. It also emphasises on *Bhakti* as a means for salvation of the soul.

Bheda-abheda

This school of philosophy is known to have existed as early as 8th century CE. The word Bheda-abheda literally means 'difference and no difference'. It propounds that *Brahman* (universal/supreme) and *Jivatma* (soul-living being) are distinct and different, and yet not different from each other. **Bhaskara** (8th–9th century CE) and **Nimbarka** (13th century CE) were important teachers of this school.

Neo-Vedanta

This modern interpretation of Vedanta emerged in the 19th and 20th century. This is the result of thinkers and philosophers like Sri Ramakrishna, Sri Vivekananda, Sri Aurobindo, Dr Radhakrishnan and other philosophers and teachers. It is founded on the philosophy of **Advaita Vedanta of Shankaracharya**, but does not accept the concept of **universal illusionism** of this school. Rather, it propounds, the concept of **universal realism.**

Neo–Vedantism is also characterised by a synthesis of the traditional Vedantic thoughts of *Advaita* and *Dvaita* and bases its teachings on the practical realisation of the core Vedantic principles. Further, liberalism and rationalism are its key features. Thus, harmony of thoughts (amidst the different schools of philosophy, religious belief systems, people and society) and universality of faith (inclusion of all in its folds) are the cornerstones of this assimilative philosophy.

Brahman in Upanishads

What is *Brahman* and its comprehension, is an enduring theme in the Upanishads. The very concept of *Brahman* is considered to be one of the fundamental canons of the Hindu philosophy. Numerous shlokas in all the principal Upanishads describe the infinite facets of the *Brahman*. While in some of these treatises, the *Brahman* is perceived as the **Universal Spirit**, the **Unchanging Reality** and even the **Pure Consciousness**, it is also perceived as the **Ultimate Truth** or the **Truth of the Truth** (***Satyasya-satyam***). What all is seen, perceived or exists is *Brahman*, and at the same time *Brahman* is the 'Vital Force' which provides sustenance to the very world.

The *Kena Upanishad* describes *Brahman* as that which cannot be expressed in speech and words but rather the speech and words themselves find expression through *Brahman*. It attributes the knowledge of *Brahman* only through its

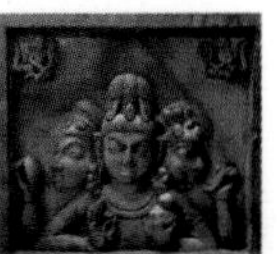

ultimate realisation and thus comprehension of *Brahman*, through the mere unaided intellect and finite senses may not be feasible. The expression ***'Neti Neti'*** (not this, not this) in Brihdarnayaka Upanishad is a negation of all known through senses, as even a mere description of the *Brahman*, which is held to be beyond attributes.

The concept of *Brahman* as very **consciousness**, is elucidated in the Aitareya Upanishad, while the doctrine of ***Aham Brahmasmi*** (I am *Brahman*) and ***Tat Tvam Asi*** (that thou art) or you are *Brahman*, are contained in Brihadarnyaka and Chandyogya Upanishads respectively. Thus, the living and non-living world is all but an expression of that 'Singular Reality'. Another expression of this doctrine, ***Ayam Atma Brahman*** or 'this self is *Brahman*', is contained in Mandukya Upanishad, while the mantra of ***So Ham*** (I am thee) is expounded in the Isha Upanishad. Thus, the Upanishads describe the essence of non-duality and monism.

Brahman is also considered to be without a second (***ekam evadvitiya***) while it is said to have innumerable manifestations (***ekam satya vipra bahuda vadanti***). *Brahman* is the ultimate reality. It is the source of all knowledge and knowledge itself. It is expressed in the minutest and yet is infinite and limitless. It is not bound in time and is ageless. *Brahman* is bliss or ***satchidananda***. *(sat: existence or reality; chit: consciousness; Ananda : bliss).* Some of these shlokas which capture a glimpse of the *Brahman* as contained in the Upanishads, are brought out here.

Aham Brahmasmi; Tat Tvam Asi : I and you as Brahman

(I) Aham Brahmansmi : The Brihdarnyaka Upanishad (in chapter 1, section 4,shloka 10) identifies one's own self with *Brahman*. It explains that the real self was the *Brahman* to begin with and therefore it indeed is *Brahman*.

ब्रह्म वा इदमग्र आसीत्, तदात्मानमेवावेत्, अहम् ब्रह्मास्मीति

Brahman vā idamagra āsīt, tadātmānamevāvet, aham brahmāsmīti

This (self) was indeed Brahman in the beginning. It knew only I, as 'I am Brahman. Therefore, It became all.

(1.4.10 Brihdarnyaka Upanishad, Yajurveda)

(II) Tat Tvam Asi: In Chandogya Upanishad (Samaveda), Uddalka Aruni, a Vedic sage, explains to his son Svetketu, the concepts of the Atman (true self) and *Brahman*. In the last shloka of the section, the father explains to his son that *Brahman* is the subtlest of all that can be perceived. While the world is in a state of constant change, that what does not change, which has that Existence or *Sat* as its Self, That is the Truth, the Reality or the *Brahman* and That is our real identity. Further, he too indeed is the manifestation of that *Brahman* and therefore the *Brahman* Itself. This concept is often quoted as, **'That thou Art'**.

(III) Ayam Atma Brahman: A similar concept of *Brahman* is contained in Mandukya Upanishad (Atharvaveda) where the very initial shlokas describe one's real self as the *Brahman* (shloka 1.2). It further describes the four states of self and equates it with the four parts of the celestial **Om** which signifies the *Brahman* itself. These four parts are the, **Visva** (the waking state), **Taijasa** (dream state), **Prājña** (*Sus.upti* or the state of dreamless sleep) and the fourth state of **Turīya** which is the same as *Brahman* or *Atman*. These four states are said to be symbolised by the three *mātrās* of *Aum* (*A, U* and *M* being the three *mātrās)* and the *amātra* of *Aum*. The fourth, also known as *amātra*, is without any corresponding letter, sound or description. This is *silence. It* symbolises the fourth state of self or the *Turiya*. *(Ātman* corresponding to *Turīya).*

सर्वं ह्येतद् ब्रह्मायमात्मा ब्रह्म सोऽयमात्मा चतुष्पात् ।। 2 ।।

sarvaṃ hyetad brahmāyamātmā Brahman so 'yamātmā catuṣpāt || 2 ||

All this is verily Brahman. This Atman is Brahman. This Atman has four quarters.

(1.2 Mandukya Upanishad)

(IV) Prajñānam *Brahman*: The shloka 3.3 of Aiterya Upanishad (Rigveda) describes the true knowledge to be *Brahman* itself (*Prajnanam Brahman ;* यप्रज्ञानम् ब्रह्म*).* Here Prajñānam refers to the highest form of wisdom which is obtained not merely through bodily senses, reasoning and inference thereof, but by the very realisation of the truth.

This shloka along with the three others cited above, are considered to be the four principal ***Mahavakyas*** of the Upanishads (*Mahavakya*: a great sentence signifying profound knowledge expressing the identity of the Self and the Universal). Thus, together they signify the fundamental premise of the Upanishadic Advaita Vedanta, i.e. non-duality of the Atman and *Brahman*. A similar meaning is also conveyed by other Mahavakyas of the Upanishads which are;

- ***Ekam Evadvitiyam Brahman*** - *Brahman* is one, without a second – (Chāndogya Upaniṣhad)
- ***So 'Ham*** - I am That - Isha Upanishad
- ***Sarvam Khalvidam Brahman*** - All of this is *Brahman* – (Chandogya Upanishad 3.14.1)
- ***Etad Vai Tat*** - This, verily, is That – (Katha Upanishad)

Satyasya Satyam

Chapter 2 of the Brihdarnyaka Upanishad contains a conversation between Ajatsatru the king of Kashi and Balaki Gargaya a brahmin. The anecdote reflects upon the true nature of *Brahman* emphasising about the unconditioned or *Nirguna* aspect of it.The brahmin approaches King Ajatsatru and offers to reveal to him the very knowledge of *Brahman*. The king happily agrees and even offers a *dakshina* (gift*)* of 1000 cows, similar to what the great and benevolent king Janaka would himself have given.

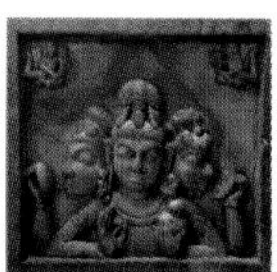

Balaki goes on to explain that he meditates upon that Being as *Brahman*, who is in the sun, the moon, the lightning, the ether (space, void), air, fire, in the looking glass (mirror, water), sound, shadow (external darkness), self etc. But the king Ajatashatru is not satisfied each of such a description of *Brahman*, which is only its physical manifestation or the 'conditioned *Brahman*'. He remarks that by knowing only that much, one could not claim to know the *Brahman* in entirety. The flummoxed brahmin in a reversal of roles, beseeches the king to explain what else the *Brahman* is. The king remarks that his offering of knowledge to a brahmin is contrary to the tradition but goes forth to explain the other aspect of *Brahman*. He asserts that what Gargya has recounted is indeed the manifestations of *Brahman* as perceived by senses (conditioned *Brahman*) but that is not the complete truth. He describes the true nature of *Brahman* with different analogies and as the 'Vital Force' and ultimately describes it as the *Satsya satyam* or the truth of truth (in verse 2.1.20).

स य एषोऽणिमैतदात्म्यमिदं सर्वं तत्सत्यं स आत्मा तत्त्वमसि श्वेतकेतो
इति भूय एव मा भगवान्विज्ञापयत्विति तथा सोम्येति होवाच ।। 6.8.7 ।।

sa ya eṣo'ṇimaitadātmyamidaṃ sarvaṃ tatsatyaṃ sa ātmā tattvamasi śvetaketo iti bhūya eva mā bhagavānvijñāpayatviti tathā somyeti hovāca || 6.8.7 ||

'That which is the subtlest of all is the Self of all this. It is the Truth. It is the Self. That thou art, O Śvetaketu.' [Śvetaketu then said,] 'Sir, please explain this to me again.' 'Yes, Somya, I will explain again,' replied his father.

(Shloka 6.8.7 Chandogya Upanishad)

स यथोर्णनाभिस्तन्तुनोच्चरेत्, यथाग्नेः क्शुद्रा विस्फुलिङ्गा व्युच्चरन्ति, एवमेवास्मादात्मनः सर्वे प्राणः, सर्वे लोकाः, सर्वे देवाः, सर्वानि भूतानि व्युच्चरन्तिय तस्योपनिषत्कृसत्यस्य सत्यमिति प्राणा वै सत्यम्, तेषामेष सत्यम् ।। 20 ।।

sa yathorṇanābhistantunoccaret, yathāgneḥ kśudrā visphuliṅgā vyuccaranti, evamevāsmādātmanaḥ sarve prāṇaḥ, sarve lokāḥ, sarve devāḥ, sarvāni bhūtāni vyuccaranti; tasyopaniṣat—satyasya satyamiti prāṇā vai satyam, teṣāmeṣa satyam || 20 ||

As a spider moves along the thread (it produces), and as from a fire, tiny sparks fly in all directions, so from this Self emanate all organs, all worlds, all gods and all beings. Its secret name (Upanishad) is 'the Truth of truth'. The vital force is truth, and It is the Truth of that.

(2.1.20 Brihdarnyaka Upanishad)

Neti Neti

The chapter 3 of this Upanishad further goes to identify the two forms of the *Brahman*, the gross and the subtle. It elucidates their characteristics, with the former being mortal, limited and defined. The subtle and unmanifested *Brahman* is not limited by the adjuncts of physical attributes. It is immortal, limitless and undefined. The last *shloka* of the chapter further elucidates the character of the subtle *Brahman* through different analogies and goes to assert that the reality or manifestation as comprehended by the physical senses does not describe the subtle *Brahman*. This unconditioned *Brahman*, which is independent of any limiting adjuncts, which cannot be described in terms of attributes such as name, or form, or action, or heterogeneity, or species, or qualities and does not bear any positive distinguishing characteristics that it is 'such and such', is described in terms of what it is not or cannot be and hence its best description is, ***Neti, Neti* or *"not this not this"***. *(shloka 2.3.6)*

तस्य हैतस्य पुरुषस्य रूपम् । यथा माहारजनं वासः, यथा पाण्ड्वाविकम्, यथेन्द्रगोपः, यथाग्न्यर्चिः, यथा पुण्डरीकम्, यथा सकृद्विद्युत्तम्य सकृद्विद्युत्तेव ह वा अस्य श्रीर्भवति य एवं वेदय अथात आदेशःकृनेति नेति, न ह्येतस्मादिति नेत्यन्यत्परमस्तिय अथ नामधेयम्कृसत्यस्य सत्यमितिय प्राणा वै सत्यम्, तेषामेष सत्यम् ।। 3 ।।

tasya haitasya puruṣasya rūpam | yathā māhārajanaṃ vāsaḥ, yathā pāṇḍvāvikam, yathendragopaḥ, yathāgnyarciḥ, yathā puṇḍarīkam, yathā sakṛdvidyuttam; sakṛdvidyutteva ha vā asya śrīrbhavati ya evaṃ veda; athāta ādeśaḥ—neti neti, na hyetasmāditi netyanyatparamasti; atha nāmadheyam —satyasya satyamiti; prāṇā vai satyam, teṣāmeṣa satyam || 3 ||

The form of that 'being' is as follows: Like a cloth dyed with turmeric, or like grey sheep's wool, or like the (scarlet) insect called Indragopa, or like a tongue of fire, or like a white lotus, or like a flash of lightning. He who knows it as such attains splendour like a flash of lightning. Now therefore the description (of Brahmann): 'Not this, not this.' Because there is no other and more appropriate description than this 'Not this.' Now Its name: 'The Truth of truth.' The vital force is truth, and It is the Truth of that.

(2.3.6 Brihdarnyaka Upanishad)

VARNASHRAMA DHARMA AND PURUSHARTHA

Varnashrama Dharma

The philosophy of Varnashrama Dharma finds reference in the various Dharma-shastras. The word *Varnashrama Dharma* is composed of three distinct words. *Varna* (here referred to as the class), *ashrama* (or stage/station in life), and *dharma* (duty or obligation). Thus, based on *varna* (class) and *ashrama* (station), a person was obliged to discharge his duties.

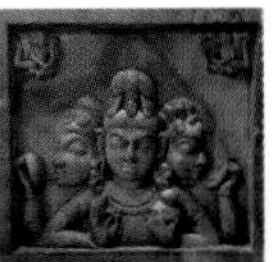

The shastras identified four *varnas* and four *ashrams*. The four *varnas* are **Brahmanas** (priests, preachers, teachers), **Kshatriyas** (kings, soldiers, warriors), **Vaishyas** (merchants, agriculturists, artisans, etc.) and **Shudras** (labourers/service providers).The four *ashramas* were **Brahmacharya, Grihastha, Vanaprastha,** and **Sanyasa.**

Brahmacharya was the first stage of the life where the objective was to acquire knowledge and lead a life of discipline and celibacy. **Grihastha**, or the stage of householder, was the next, where one was to choose his occupation as per *varna*, marry, and raise a family. **Vanaprastha** was the third stage, literally meaning 'proceeding to the forest'. After fulfilling the duties of a householder, with the onset of age, a person could retire from worldly matters and spend more time in spiritual pursuits. **Sanyasa** was the final stage where a person was to detach himself from the society and fully pursue attainment of salvation or *moksha*. But not all entered the last *ashrama*.

Depending on the *varna* and the *ashrama*, a person was required to discharge his dharma (duty) as enunciated in the Dharma-shastras. The *varna* system in later phases of Hinduism metamorphosed into the stringent caste system.

Purushartha

The *purushartha* has an important place in the domain of the Hindu philosophy as a beacon to human pursuits. The word 'Purushartha' is derived from the two words *purush* (human being) and *arth* (purpose). Thus, it literally means, 'the objective or purpose of a human being or his life'. This philosophy advocates four *purusharthas*, the pursuit of which should be the objective of every human being. These are **Dharma, Artha, Kama**, and **Moksha.**

Dharma refers to the social, moral, and ethical duties of a person. These duties would vary from person to person. Fulfilment/discharge of these duties is of prime importance for every person. It signifies the right conduct and appropriate way of living.

Artha refers to the material possessions, wealth, and other resources necessary for the physical existence. Thus, Artha signifies the means of physical sustenance of life.

Kama refers to desire and fulfilment of the sensory needs; be it emotional, aesthetics, or physical.

Moksha refers to the objective of liberation or emancipation of human soul from the Karmic cycle.

Thus, pursuit of the four *purusharthas* and ultimately *moksha* was the objective of human life. This philosophy also emphasised on the need for balance between the respective pursuits. In case of any contradiction or clash or disharmony, the pursuit of *dharma* was considered to be the most important, followed by *artha* and then *kama.*

Charvaka Philosophy or Lokayata School

This school of philosophy, also referred to as the ***Brahasptya***, is a philosophical school of materialism. Brihaspati is said to have laid the foundation of this school but Charvaka was the main propounder. The school denied the existence of *Brahman* (God) or *Atman* (soul) and denied that the objective of human life was salvation or unison of *Atman* with *Brahman*. Thus, it was an atheistic school. It emphasised on material pursuits and sensory enjoyment as an objective of human life and believed that the physical world as perceived by the senses is the only world and nothing beyond it exists.

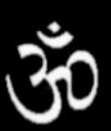

Om, the Symbol of the Eternal and the Essence of the Vedantic Philosophy

One of the sacred most symbols of Hinduism, ॐ (Om) is also amongst the most ancient of philosophical concepts having reference in all the Vedas and its four layers, in the Bhagavad Gita, in different Puranas and other holy scriptures. Om precedes the sacred mantras and is a revered *mantra* in itself. As an iconography, it is displayed as a mark of holiness in sacred texts and temples and also chanted as the key sound of meditation which is symbolic of the very Eternal. Whether it be the ritualistic traditions of Hinduism or the scriptural and spiritual domain, Om is all pervading. Most pertinently, Om signifies the **different states of consciousness** of the self as well as the **eternal state of the Self (Atman)** which is indeed a reflection of the Brahman itself.

Om is considered the primeval or the primordial sound of the Brahman and hence also referred to as ***Pranava*** (literally the fore sound). It denotes ***Omkar***, or the first source of sound, thus representing the very creation of the universe. It is ***Akshara***, or that which does not decay, the immutable and enduring in the otherwise transient world. It is also referred as the ***Udagitha***, the chanting of the Samveda or the song of the universe.

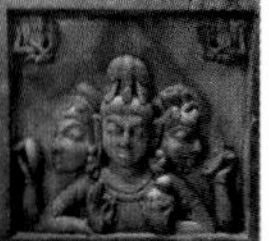

Reference to Om in Vedas

The ***Gayatri mantra***, revered in Hinduism which is contained in **Rigveda Samhita** (verse 3.62.10) is preceded by Om. Different Upanishads dwell on the spiritual and metaphysical significance of the word Om equating it with the Brahman.

Om in Chandogya Upanishad: The very opening verse of Chandogya Upanishad refers to Om as the *udgitha* or the most revered song of the universe and worthy of meditation as the Brahman itself.

ओमित्येतदक्षरमुद्गीथमुपासीत ।

ओमिति ह्युद्गायति तस्योपव्याख्यानम् ।। 1.1.1 ।।

omityetadakṣaramudgīthamupāsīta |

omiti hyudgāyati tasyopavyākhyānam || 1.1.1 ||

Om is the closest word to Brahman. One ought to recite Om as if one is worshipping Brahman. (treating Om as the symbolic of very Brahman). How to recite Om is elaborated herewith. || 1.1.1 ||

Chandogya Upanishad

Further in verse 2.23.3 of **Chandogya Upanishsad**, Om is considered as the essence of everything. The verse states;

तान्यभ्यतपत्तेभ्योऽभितप्तेभ्य ॐकारः सम्प्रास्रवत्तद्यथा शङ्कुना सर्वाणि पर्णानि ।

संतृण्णान्येवमोंकारेण सर्वा वाक्संतृण्णोंकार एवेदं सर्वमोंकार एवेदं सर्वम् ।। 2.23.3 ।।

tānyabhyatapattebhyo'bhitaptebhya ॐkāraḥ samprāsravattadyathā śaṅkunā sarvāṇi parṇāni saṃ tṛṇṇānyevamoṃ kāreṇa sarvā vāksaṃ tṛṇṇoṃ kāra evedaṃ sarvamoṃ kāra evedaṃ sarvam || 2.23.3 ||

*Prajāpati then meditated on three vyāhṛtis (**bhuḥ, bhuvaḥ, and svaḥ, the three worlds**)and from the vyāhṛtis, emerged Oṃ kāra. Just as in a leaf, its lattice of veins is spread all over, similarly, Oṃ kāra permeates every form of speech (hence everything). All this is verily Oṃ kāra. All this is verily Oṃ kāra. |||| 2.23.3 ||*

Chandogya Upanishad

Om in Mundaka Upanishad: In verses 2.2.2-2.2.4 of Mundaka Upanishad, Om is considered as the means by meditation of which the realisation of the true self and the union of *Atman* with the *Brahman* is possible. The verse 2.2.4 states;

प्रणवो धनुः शारो ह्यात्मा ब्रह्म तल्लक्ष्यमुच्यते ।

अप्रमत्तेन वेद्धव्यं शरवत्तन्मयो भवेत् ।। 4 ।।

praṇavo dhanuḥ śāro hyātmā Brahman tallakṣyamucyate |

apramattena veddhavyaṃ śaravattanmayo bhavet || 4 ||

The Pranava (Om) is the bow, the Atman (self) is the arrow and the Brahman is its mark. By the one who is unwavering and self-collected, this target is to be pierced. As the arrow attaches itself to the mark and becomes one with it hence the self is to become one with the Brahman. 2.2.4

Mundaka Upanishad

Om In Katha Upanishad: In Katha Upanishad, in the verses 1.2.15 and 1.2.16 the deity of death Yama describes to Nachiketa (see chapter 1 for the story of Nachiketa) that the goal of life as described by the Vedas is the attainment of Om (the symbol of Brahman). Implying thereby the union of Atman and the Brahman.

सर्वे वेदा यत्पदमामनन्ति तपाँ सि सर्वाणि च यद्वदन्ति ।

यदिच्छन्तो ब्रह्मचर्यं चरन्ति तत्ते पदँ संग्रहेण ब्रवीम्योमित्येतत् ।। 15 ।।

sarve vedā yatpadamāmananti tapāmॐsi sarvāṇi ca yadvadanti |

yadicchanto Brahmancaryaṃ caranti tatte padmॐ saṃgraheṇa bravīmyomityetat || 15 ||

The goal which is extolled by all the *Vedas,* which all acts of *tapas* (self-discipline, meditation and austerity) speak of and aspiring for which men lead the life of a *Brahmancharin*, (one who leads a life of purity and chastity) that goal I tell you briefly—It is this—***Om.***

Verse 1.2.16 Katha Upanishad

The next shloka describes the word Om as very Brahman; it states,

एतद्ध्येवाक्शरं ब्रह्म एतद्ध्येवाक्शरं परम् ।

एतद्ध्येवाक्शरं ज्ञात्वा यो यदिच्छति तस्य तत् ।। 16 ।।

etaddhyevākśaraṃ Brahman etaddhyevākśaraṃ param |

etaddhyevākśaraṃ jñātvā yo yadicchati tasya tat || 16 ||

This word is, indeed, Brahman, this word is indeed supreme; the knower of it attains whatever he aspires for.

Verse 1.2.16 Katha Upanishad

Om in Mandukya Upanishad: The very first verse in Mandukya Upanishad equates Om with the Universe itself and describes it as the three dimensions of time, the past present and future. Further even what is beyond the three dimensions is said to be Om. It states;

ओमित्येतदक्षरमिदं सर्वं तस्योपव्याख्यानं भूतं भवद्भविष्यदिति सर्वमोङ्कार एव द्य ।

यच्चान्यत्त्रिकालातीतं तदप्योङ्कार एव ।। 1 ।।

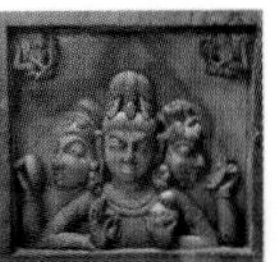

omityetadakṣaramidaṃ sarvaṃ tasyopavyākhyānaṃ bhūtaṃ bhavadbhaviṣyaditi sarvamoṅ kāra eva |
yaccānyattrikālātītaṃ tadapyoṅ kāra eva || 1 ||

Om! This imperishable word is everything. A clear explanation of it is as follows: What has become, what is becoming, what will become, all of this is Om. What is beyond these three states of time, that too, verily, is OM.

Verse 1.1 Mandukya Upanishad

Om and the four states of existence of Self

In the verses 1.2 and subsequent verses (1.3 to 1.7) of the Mandkya Upanishad Om is equated with the **four states of existence of self**. It is said to be composed of **four matras** which are the roots of the syllable Om. अ (A), उ (U) and म or ँ (M) while the fourth *matra* is called *amatra* for it being silent.

सर्वं ह्येतद् ब्रह्मायमात्मा ब्रह्म सोऽयमात्मा चतुष्पात् ।। 2 ।।
sarvaṃ hyetad brahmāyamātmā Brahman so 'yamātmā catuṣpāt || 2 ||

All this is verily Brahman. This Atman is Brahman. This Atman has four quarters.

Verse 1.2 Mandukya Upanishad

In the next few verses, the different states of existence of the self is described. The **first *matra* of Om** corresponds to the first state of the self which is ***Visva*** or the waking state. It is the state of worldly or physical consciousness. It is the physical plane of existence which we usually associate with and which most identify as the only world.

गरितस्थानो बहिष्प्रज्ञः सप्ताङ्ग एकोनविंशतिमुखः स्थूलभुग्वैश्वानरः प्रथमः पादः ।। 3 ।।
Jāgaritasthāno bahiṣprajñaḥ saptāṅ ga ekonaviṃ śatimukhaḥ sthūlabhugvaiśvānaraḥ prathamaḥ pādaḥ || 3 ||

The first quarter (Pāda) is Vaiśvānara the sphere of activity of which is the waking state. It is conscious of external objects, it has seven limbs and nineteen mouths and its experience consists of gross (material) objects.

Verse 1.3 Mandukya Upanishad

The description of seven limbs (*saptanga*) and nineteen mouths is symbolic. As per the *Śrutis*, the effulgent region or sky is its head, the sun its eye, the air its vital breath, the ether (*space*) the middle part of its body, the water its kidney/bladders and the earth its feet. The *Āhavanīya* fire (one of the three fires of the *Agnihotra* sacrifice) has been described as its mouth. Similarly, its nineteen mouths are the five organs of perception (*buddhindriyas*); the five organs of action (*karmendriyas*); the five aspects of vital breath (*prāṇa*, etc.); the mind (*manas*); the intellect (*buddhi*); egoity *ahaṃ kāra*); mind (*chitta).* These are, as it were, the mouths, *i.e.,* the instruments by means of which he (*Vaiśvānara*) experiences (objects).

The **second *matra*** उ (U) represents ***taijasa*** or the dream state. Thus, it is symbolic of our subconscious state or the mental and the astral plane of existence.

स्वप्नस्थानोऽन्तः प्रज्ञाः सप्ताङ्ग एकोनविंशतिमुखः प्रविविक्तभुक्तैजसो द्वितीयः पादः ।। 4 ।।
svapnasthāno'ntaḥ prajñāṃ saptāṅ ga ekonaviṃ śatimukhaḥ praviviktabhuktaijaso dvitīyaḥ pādaḥ || 4 ||

The second quarter (Pāda) is the Taijasa. Its sphere of activity is the dream. It is conscious of internal objects. It has seven limbs and nineteen mouths and it experiences the subtle objects.

Verse 1.4 Mandukya Upanishad

Thus, while in the state of the *viśva* one experiences consciousness associated with gross external objects; whereas, in *taijasa* (in the dream state), the object of experience is consciousness consisting of *vāsanās* which are the impressions caused by the past experiences. Therefore, this state is considered as the experience of the subtle.

The **third Matra** which is the म (M) represents **prājña** which is also referred as *susupti* or the state of dreamless sleep of which we are not conscious even when we are awake. It is a state of unconscious but inherent distinguishing knowledge and also associated with our innate spiritual consciousness.

यत्र सुप्तो न कञ्चन कामं कामयते न कञ्चन स्वप्नं पश्यति तत्सुषुप्तम् ।
सुषुप्तस्थान एकीभूतः प्रज्ञानघन एवाऽऽनन्दमयो ह्यानन्दभुक् चेतोमुखः प्राज्ञस्तृतीयः पादः ।। 5 ।।
yatra supto na kañcana kāmaṃ kāmayate na kañcana svapnaṃ paśyati tatsuṣuptam |
suṣuptasthāna ekībhūtaḥ prajñānaghana evā"nandamayo hyānandabhuk cetomukhaḥ prājñastṛ tīyaḥ pādaḥ || 5 ||

That is the state of deep sleep where there is no desire of any material objects nor experience of any dream. The third quarter (Pāda) is the Prājña sphere of which is deep sleep, in which all (experiences) become unified or undifferentiated, which is comprising of entire consciousness, which is full of bliss and which experiences bliss and which is the path leading to the knowledge (of the two other states).

Verse 1.1 Mandukya Upanishad

Thus, *prājna*, the state of deep sleep is without the experience of sensory inputs and where there is nothing to differentiate with consciousness and thus there is no consciousness of duality, desire or fear. *Prājna* being consciousness alone and at rest, the state is harmony and bliss.

The **fourth state** of self is ***turiya*** which corresponds to the *amatra* of the Aum which is silent. This symbolises our enduring self or the *Atman* in the pure state. This is the state of realisation of the self and its unison with the Brahman.

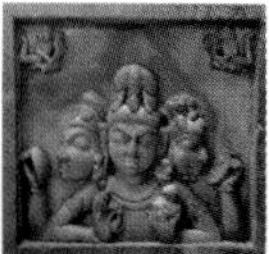

एष सर्वेश्वरः एष सर्वज्ञ एषोऽन्तर्याम्येष योनिः सर्वस्य प्रभवाप्ययौ हि भूतानाम् ।। 6 ।।

eṣa sarveśvaraḥ eṣa sarvajña eṣo'ntaryāmyeṣa yoniḥ sarvasya prabhavāpyayau hi bhūtānām || 6 ||

This is the Lord of all; this is the knower of all; this is the controller within; this is the source of all; and this is that from which all things originate and in which they finally disappear.

Verse 1.6 Mandukya Upanishad

Thus, Om represents the different states of existence of the self. It highlights the philosophy of our true self and that being the state of pure consciousness and oneness with the Brahman. **The concept of Om thus underlines the essence of Advaita monistic philosophy of the Upanishads.**

Om in the *Bhagavad Gita*

Om finds reference even in the Bhagavad Gita. In verse 9.17 Lord Krishna explains to Arjun as Him being the all and the essence of this universe including the sacred symbol of Om.

पिताऽहमस्य जगतो माता धाता पितामहः ।
वेद्यं पवित्रमोंकार ऋक् साम यजुरेव च ।। 9.17 ।।

I am the father of this universe, the mother, the dispenser of the fruits of actions and the grandsire; the (one) thing to be known, the purifier, the sacred monosyllable (Om), and also the Rigveda, the Samaveda and the Yajur-Vedas.

Verse 9.17 Bhagavad Gita

In verse 17.24 Lord Krishna expounds the significance of Om and highlights the significance of uttering of Om prior to sacrifices, charity and other holy practices. He states;

तस्मादोमित्युदाहृत्य यज्ञदानतपः क्रियाः ।
प्रवर्तन्ते विधानोक्ताः सततं ब्रह्मवादिनाम् ।। 17.24 ।।

Therefore, acts of sacrifice, charity and austerity as prescribed through injunctions, of those who study and expound the Vedas, always commence after uttering the syllable Om.

Verse 17.24 Bhagavad Gita

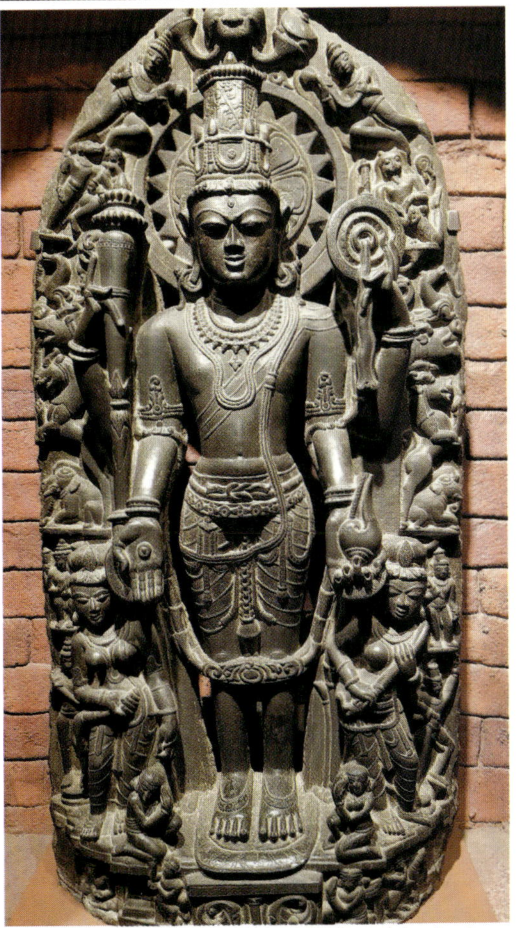

3.19: A sculpture of Lord Vishnu, black stone, 11th century, Pala Period, Bihar Museum, Patna. The sculpture depicts lord Vishnu holding the conch shell, mace, *chakra*. Besides, images of other avataras of lord Vishnu are carved in the side panel — photograph by Madhukar K Bhagat

Reverence in Other Religions

Om is also revered in Buddhism, Jainism and Sikhism. In Mahayana, Tibetan and other forms of Buddhism, the sacred *mantra* (*Om Manipadme Hum*) begins with Om and is dedicated to Avalokiteshwar, the Boddhisatva of compassion. In Sikhism, *Ik Omkara* is symbolic of the unity of the Divine and thus the essence of the Sikh faith of monism. It is also the first word of the *Mul Mantar* which is the opening verse of the holy Guru Granth Sahib. Om is also a revered symbol in Jainism where it is considered to be a condensed form of reference to *pancha paramesthi*, (the five supreme souls worthy of veneration).

SECTS OF HINDUISM

Over the period of centuries of evolution, several sects of worship have emerged in Hinduism. These are primarily distinguishable in terms of the central deity of veneration and the mode of worship adopted. Though at times disparate, these sects have invariably remained within the fold of the principal religion and owed their allegiance to the Puranic traditions. Although a watertight demarcation does not exist between different sects in Hinduism, however, depending on the primary deity being worshipped, there can be said to be three devotional sects in Hinduism. These are *Vaishnavism*, *Shaivism*, and *Shaktism*. Besides, *Smartism* is also considered a separate sect of worship.

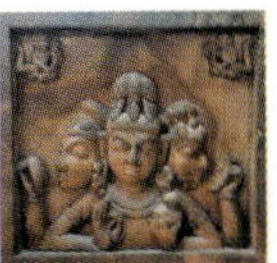

Vaishnavism

The **Vaishnava** sect worships lord Vishnu as the principal deity and also his many incarnations, the most important of which are that of Sri Ram and Sri Krishna. Vishnu literally means, the 'all pervading one'. He is also known as Narayana and Hari, and over a thousand different names are ascribed to him which elucidate his different attributes. He is also the Purushottama or the supreme *Purusha* described in the *Bhagavad Gita*. Lord Vishnu is also considered as the creator, sustainer, and destroyer of all the three worlds. Sometimes he is considered as the preserver in the trinity of *Brahman* (creator), *Vishnu* (preserver), and *Mahesh* (destroyer). He is perceived as formless (*nirguna*) or with form (*saguna*). There are many *sampradayas* (sub-sects) which fall under Vaishnavism, such as **Sri Vaishnavism** (associated with goddess *Laxmi*), **Ramanandi Sampradaya** (followers of Ramanand), **Swaminarayan Sampradaya** (followers of Swaminarayan), **Brahman Sampradaya** (followers of Madhava), **Rudra Sampradaya** (followers of Vallabhacharya), **Gaudiya Vaishnavism** (followers of Chaitanya), **Bhagavata sect** (followers of Sri Krishna), etc.

Dashavatara and Different Manifestations of Lord Vishnu

Vaishnavism is also intrinsically associated with the worship of the various incarnations of lord Vishnu, of which the most significant are the Dashavatara, literally meaning the 'ten incarnations' (*dasha*-ten; *avatara*- incarnation). Lord Vishnu, who is the considered to be the preserver of the cosmic order, is believed to incarnate from time to time in different epochs in different living forms, so as to restore the cosmic balance and to uphold truth and order. Although there are many minor *avataras* of lord Visnhu described in the various Puranas, it is the *dashavataras* which are considered to be the complete *avataras* of the lord and the most significant. These 10 *avataras* are **Matsya, Kurma, Varaha, Narasimha** (in Satyayuga); **Vamana, Parashurama and Rama** (in Tretayuga), **Krishna** (Dvaparayuga), **Buddha** (Kaliyuga) and Kalki *avatara* (Kaliyuga).

As a fish in ***Matsya avatara***, he steers Manu and other creatures of the world to safety in a boat (ark) when the *pralaya* (the great deluge) happens. He incarnates as a giant tortoise in the next; ***Kurma avatara***; and bears the weight of mount Mandara which is used by the *devas* and the *asuras* to churn the ocean so as to obtain the nectar. The ***Varaha avatara*** sees lord Vishnu incarnate as a giant boar whereby he defeats the *asura* Hiranyaksha and restores the Bhumi Devi (earth) sinking in the cosmic ocean. As ***Narasimha***, Lord Vishnu incarnates as half man and half lion, to save his beloved devotee Prahlada and to slay the *asura* Hiranyakashyapu, who is otherwise bestowed with the boon of being invincible to any human or animal. As the **Vamana** (dwarf) in his fifth incarnation, he humbles Bali the king of Asuras. The Vamana seeks alms of piece of land covered by his three steps. But he covers heaven and earth in his very first two steps itself. Bali, true to his promise, asks the Vamana (lord Vishnu incarnate) to place the third step on his head thus fulfilling his promise and also earning a place in Vaikuntha the abode of lord Vishnu (implying thereby *moksha*/ salvation). Lord Vishnu then incarnates as **Parashurama**, the axe wielding sage-warrior who slays the tyrannical *kshatriyas* many times and restores the balance on earth.

In the next *avatara* Lord Vishnu is born as **Rama** the prince, and later king of Ayodhya who battles and slays Ravana who has abducted Sita. As Rama, he puts an end to the tyranny of *rakshsas* (demons) on earth.

Krishna is the eighth *avatara* of lord Vishnu whereby as a teenager, he slays the cruel Kamsa. He as Krishna plays the role of a guru to the Pandavas in the battle of Mahabharta and as a divine yogi, bequeaths the spiritual knowledge of the Gita. The Krishnavatara is often considered the most complete of *avataras* of lord Vishnu, whereby he reveals to the world the deepest and most divine of philosophy through which humanity can transcend the mortal existence and attain salvation.

Buddha the sage is the 9th *avatara,* whereby he teaches to the world the value of compassion and ahimsa. Born in Kaliyuga, Buddha advocates the way to salvation from the bondage of birth and death through a path of neither indulgence nor of extreme asceticism.

Kalki is the 10th *avatara* which is yet to incarnate. He is depicted to appear on a white horse wielding a sword and blazing like a comet. He is prophesised to appear towards the end of the Kaliyuga and restore the balance between *satya* and *dharma.*

As per other traditions and different Puranas, Balarama the elder brother of Krishna, is the eighth incarnation while Krishna is the ninth. In some accounts Krishna may be considered as Lord Vishnu himself and not an incarnation, thus Balarama being the eight incarnation. Some scriptures may not consider Buddha as an incarnation. Besides, there may also exist other traditions whereby regional deities may be considered as lord Vishnu incarnate.

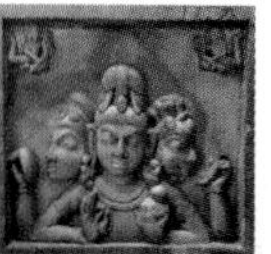

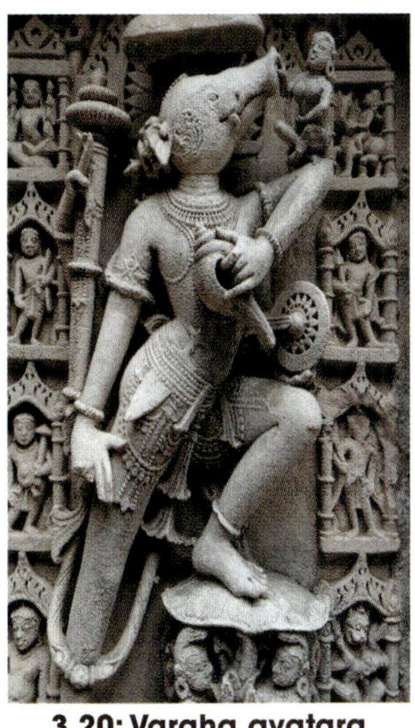

3.20: Varaha avatara

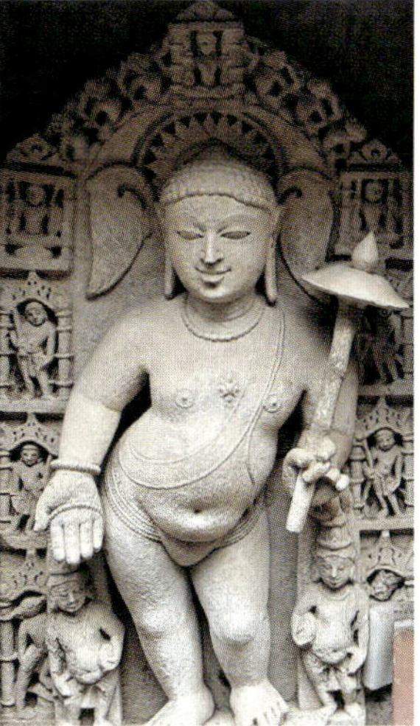

3.21: Vamana avatara

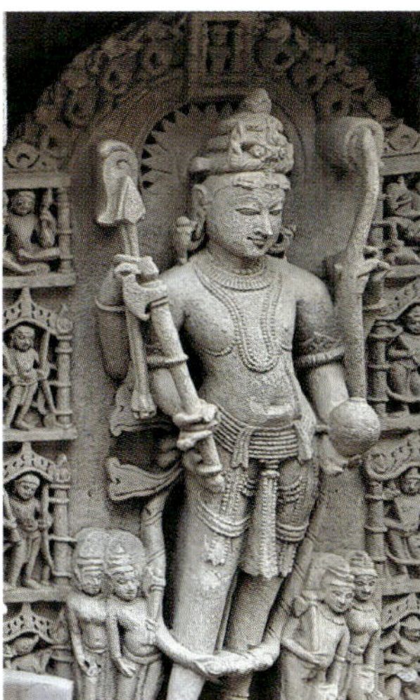

3.22: Rama avatara

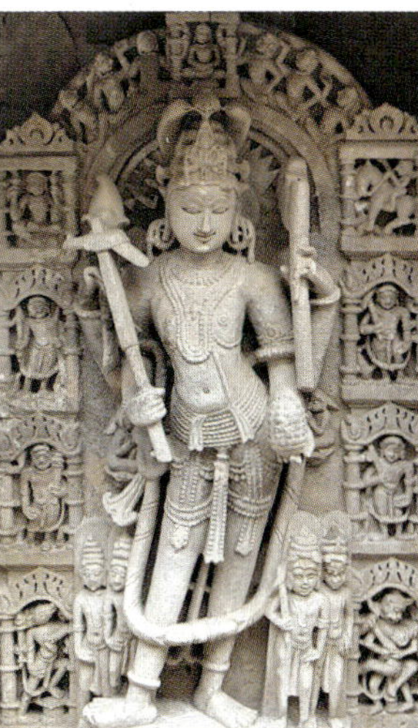

3.23: Balarama avatara

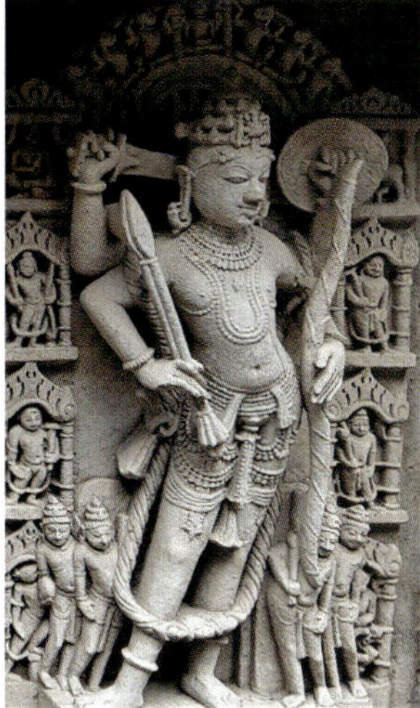

3.24: Krishna avatara

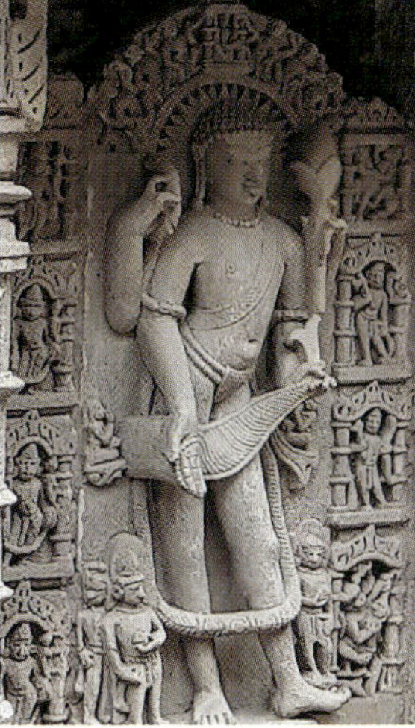

3.25: Buddha avatara

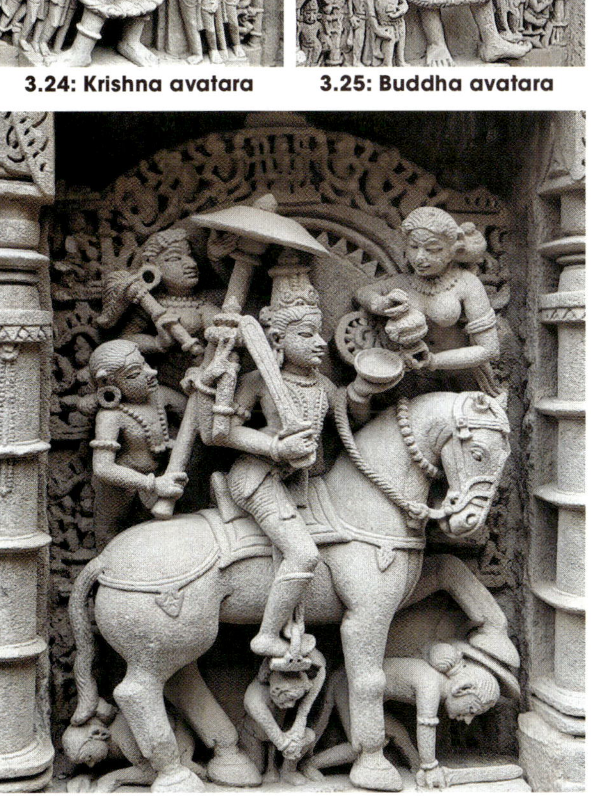

3.26: Kalki avatara

3.20-3.26: Panels of sandstone sculpture at Rani ki Vav (stepwell) Patan, Gujarat (mid 11th century CE) depicting some of the different avataras of lord Vishnu in the Dashavatara tradition — photographs by Madhukar K Bhagat

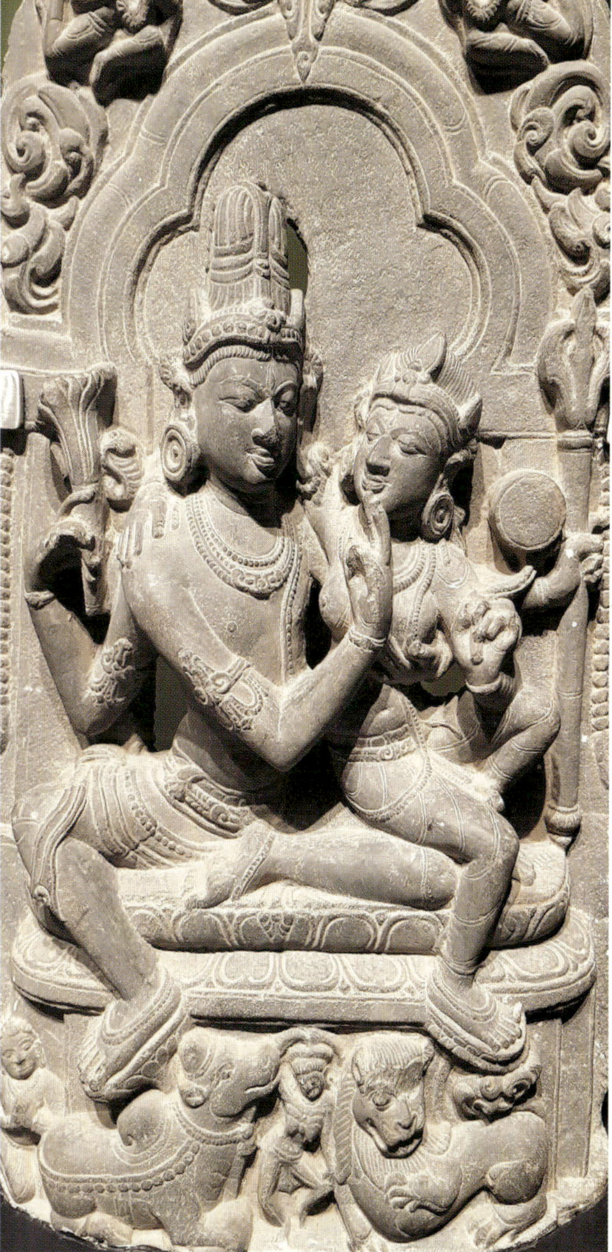

3.27: Uma-Maheshwar, signifying the unity of Shiva-Shakti, sculpture in blackstone, 11th century CE, Raxaul, Bihar Museum, Patna — photograph by Madhukar K Bhagat

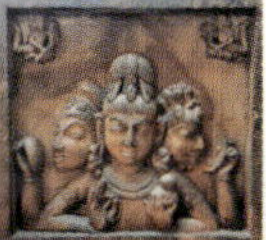

Shaivism

Lord Shiva is the prime deity of the **Shaivism sect.** Shaivism too sometimes takes the form of monism and sometimes dualism (the lord and the devotee are two different entities in dualism). It too has different Sampradayas such as **Pashupata Shaivism**, **Shaiva Siddhanta**, **Siddha Siddhanta**, **Lingayata, Kashmir Shaivism**, **Shiva Advaita**, etc. Many of the Puranas are dedicated to lord Shiva which also form the basis of Shaivism. Shaivism also draws from certain pre-Vedic traditions which assimilated later with the Vedic deity of **Rudra** and thus came under the Vedic Brahmanical fold. Like Vaishnavism, the Shaiva tradition also sees lord Shiva to be the creator, preserver and the destroyer. At times, he is identified with the third deity of the Trimurti and endowed with the cosmological functions of destructions. Shiva is also seen as a **divine yogi** from whom the various yogic traditions emanate and all of which are considered an integral part of Shaivism. This sect also integrates the tradition of worship of **Shiva-Shakti**, underlining devotion to the combined male and female godheads.

The Trimurti

The worship of the Trimurti of Brahma, Vishnu and Mahesh (Shiva) is a singular feature of the polytheistic dimension of Hinduism. At times, it is this poignant element with which the very religion is closely identified with. Though, broadly this holy trinity encompasses the three significant perspectives of worldly existence viz. the creation, the preservation and the eventual destruction, the symbolism and the significance of Trimurti runs much deeper.

In the Trimurti of gods, **Lord Brahma** is perceived as the **creator**, the one divine father of all worlds and diverse beings. **Lord Vishnu** is considered the **preserver** of the worlds, who through his numerous manifestations and *avataras*, brings succour to the worldly beings and the oppressed. **Lord Shiva** is attributed the **powers of destruction**, which encompass destruction of the evil, cessation of time and the three worlds, thus enabling the beginning of the next cycle of worldly creation.

Evolution of the concept of Trimurti: While the very essence of the Vedanta lies in the philosophy of the non-dualistic monism or the unity of the *Brahman* and the *Atman*, the concept of conditioned polytheistic godhead of the *Trimurti* appears to be incongruous with it. However, the syncretic evolution of Hinduism has enabled different layers of philosophies and perspectives grow around its core philosophy and integrate it with the seemingly inconsistent. Thus, has emerged the concept of ***ekam-bahulam***, i.e. god being one as well as many. While the unconditioned Brahma remains the Ultimate Reality, the growth of Hinduism over centuries saw the interweaving of the broader believes, with the very Divine being attributed with *gunas*. The attribute-less Brahma was hence worshipped as *Ishwar*, the Divine lord or the Supreme self, which was also physically manifest with all the conditioned attributes (*saguna*). Thence numerous sects and extant faiths identified their personal Gods with this Supreme being. Some saw this God to be Mahavishnu, while some considered Him to be Mahashiva. But with passage of time the concept of three supreme Gods emerged. Each was attributed with a distinct form, divine attributes, had specific cosmological roles but all were conjugate in upholding the Dharma and the sustenance of the worlds. The theological prominence of Trimurti is said to have happened in the Puranic age. With the passage of time the tradition of worship of Lord Vishnu and Lord Shiva gained greater acceptance while that of Lord Brahma became more of an exception.

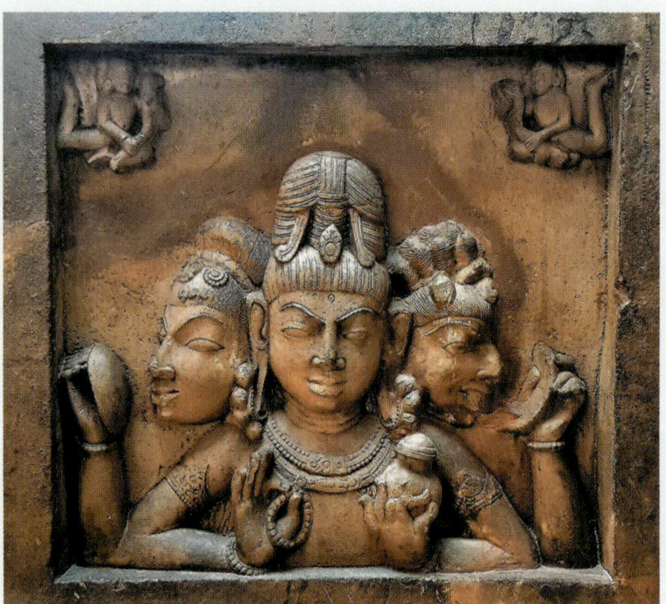

3.28: A stone sculptural panel depicting Trimurti; 10th century CE, Morena, Madhya Pradesh, present location, State Museum, Bhopal — photograph by Madhukar K Bhagat

However, during the earlier **Vedic age**, the reference to the Trimurti is not seen to be so pronounced. Even the significance of the three gods seems to have changed since the Vedic age. The reference to Brahma in the Vedas is seen in the form of **Prajapati**, who is the teacher and ruler of all beings. He is also the father of all, be it the *devas* (gods and demi gods), the *asuras* (demons) or *manvas* (humans). He is venerated by all alike. The Vedic reference to **Vishnu** is considered by the scholars to be of one of the twelve **Adityas** (solar deities). He is also recognised as the **Vamana**, who straddles the three worlds with his three steps. **Shiva** is considered to be **Rudra** in the Vedas. He and lord Vishnu finds reference in the Rigveda and other Vedas. Some minor Upanishads are also classified as Vaishnava and Shaiva Upanishadas in the *muktika* anthology of 108 upanishads. For instance, in the Maitreya Upanishad (a minor Upanishad), reference to the three Gods and to Lord Shiva in particular is also seen. In verse 2.1.1 of this Upanishad, Lord Shiva while endowing the true knowledge says, *"The body is said to be a temple. The Jīva (soul) in it is verily the Shiva. Having given up all the cast-off offerings of ajñāna (ignorance), one should worship Him with the thought So'ham (I am He).*

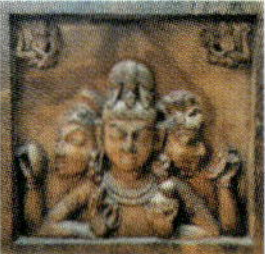

However, the invocation of lord Vishnu and lord Shiva is lesser as compared to the prominent Vedic gods. The deities which are chiefly venerated in the Vedas, particularly in the early Vedic period are those representing the elements of nature viz. the *devas* Indra, Agni, Varun, Mitra, Soma etc.

It is in the age of the **Puranas** that the recognition of the Trimurti gets fully crystallised and so does their significance and veneration. The 18 Puranas and other 18 *Up-puranas* are often classified on the basis of the principal deities around which they are centred. While Bhagavata-Purana, Vishnu-Purana, Garuda-Purana, Narada-Purana, Varaha-Purana, Matsya-Purana, Vamana-Purana, are among those which recognise Lord Vishnu as the supreme lord, Shiva-Purana, Skanda-Purana, Markandeya-Purana, Linga-Purana are some of the Puranas which are dedicated largely to lord Shiva. Among the group of Puranas dedicated to lord Brahma are the Brahma-Purana, and the Padma-Purana. Thus, by the Puranic age the departure from the worship of the early Vedic gods to that of the Trimurti was complete and later the sects around lord Vishnu and lord Shiva evolved.

However, the essential unity of these three deities as a singular divine god is also highlighted in many of these Puranas which often emphasise on Brahma, Vishnu and Shiva not being distinct from each other, but a reflection of the same Supreme. In particular, Kurma Purana has specific reference to the Trimurti while emphasising on the essential unity of the three Gods.

The Trimurti, Iconography, Attributes and Symbolism

The Puranic phase imparted specific attributes, iconography, symbolism and cosmological roles to each of the godheads. The iconography of **Lord Brahma** is that of a venerated deity having white appearance with **four heads** (each overseeing a cardinal direction) and having **four hands**. In one of the hands, he is holding the **Vedas**, in another, a **rosary**, in the third, a **lotus flower**, and in the fourth, the **ritual ladle** (*kamandal*). All of the above being symbolic of the cosmological functions associated with him. He is creator of the world, the originator of all knowledge, he lays the laws of the worldly order and he is also the God to whom the rituals and sacrifices are offered. The female divinity Saraswati, the goddess of great learning is his consort and the white swan is his vehicle. ***Satyalok*** is his abode and he is the wielder of the ***Brahmastra***.

Lord Vishnu, the **preserver**, is the god of love and compassion who responds to the cries of devotees. Through his numerous incarnations, he has always relieved the world from tyranny and evil, re-established worldly order and the faith in *dharma*. He is also considered the god who is the emancipator from the cycle of life and death and in whom the devotees seek salvation or ***moksha***. His abode is **Vaikuntha** in the *ksheer sagar*, the mythical ocean (symbolic of the primeval ocean of milk). Here he lies resting on the bed of coiled mighty serpent ***Shesh Nag*** or *Adishesh* (symbolic of the endless cycle of time). His appearance is blue as the clouds and the sky. In his four hands he holds the ***chakra*** (disc), the **conch shell**, a **mace** and a **lotus flower**. Goddess **Lakshmi** the female divinity of wealth and material wellbeing also equated with *maya*, is his consort. **Garuda**, the king of birds is his vehicle. He is the wielder of ***Sudarshana Chakra***.

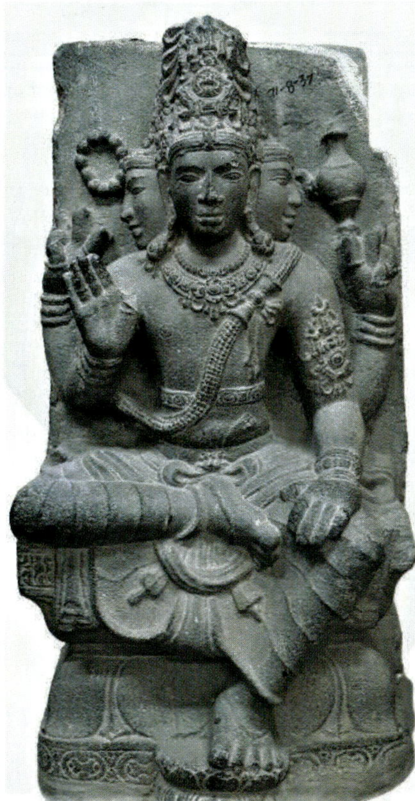

3.29: Pallava period (9th century CE) sculpture of Lord Brahma; black granite stone; Government Museum, Chennai, — photograph by Madhukar K Bhagat

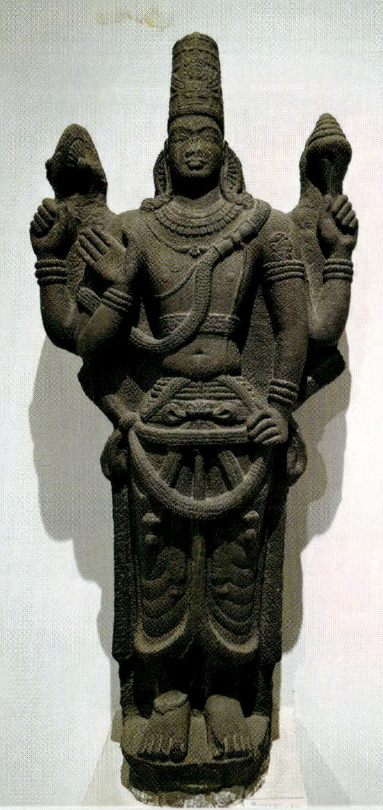

3.30: An early stone sculpture of Vishnu depicted holding *shankh* and *chakra*, 7th century CE, Pallava dynasty, National Museum, Delhi — photograph by Madhukar K Bhagat

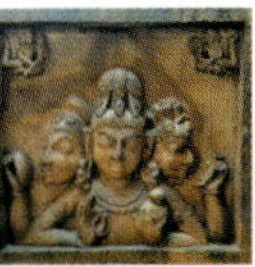

The conch shell called ***Panchajanya*** is shown as a spiral and symbolizes interconnectedness of cyclic existence. The ***Sudarshana chakra*** represents him as the wielder of the divine weapon, by dint of which he annihilates the evil, thus restoring the cosmic equilibrium. The ***gada*** (mace-club) called *Kaumodaki* symbolizes authority and power of knowledge. While the **lotus** symbolizes purity and transcendence.

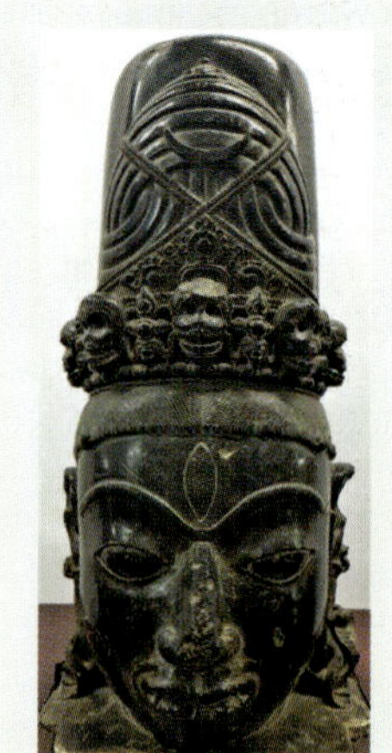

3.31: Shiva represented as mukhalinga, 12th century CE, Narsinghpur, Madhya Pradesh, Nagpur Central Museum, — photograph by Madhukar K Bhagat

Lord Shiva is portrayed as the ultimate **yogi**. His abode is on the snowy **Kailash** Mountain, where he resides with his consort goddess **Parvati** and his numerous disciples which are ascetics, *gandharva*, *kinnar* and other fierce beings. His family also includes the mighty **Kartikeya** (leader of the army of the *devas*) and the wise **Ganesh** who are other two venerated deities of the Hindu pantheon. The sacred bull **Nandi** is his vehicle.

He is represented as a god with not very appealable physical countenance. He is smeared with ashes and draped only in tiger skin. He wields the ***trishul*** (trident), has long locks from which the holy **Ganga** (river Ganges) emanates, a **snake**(cobra) is coiled around his neck and the crescent **moon** is seen rising from the locks. He has a third (vertical) eye between his forehead which causes annihilation when opened. In one of his hands he holds the *damru* from which emanates the cosmic beats.

As the ***Maharudra***, he is the fierce one who has within his powers to bring an end to the cycle of time, destroys the worlds, dissolve them and thus enables the creation of new worlds. He is also seen performing the cosmic dance *Tandava* which brings an end to the world.(see chapter 11 for symbolism of *Tandava*).

Lord Shiva is often depicted as engrossed in deep meditation. He is the god of healing and sickness, the protector of animals (as the **Pashupati**) the bestower of the spiritual knowledge. He is a divine yogi. He is the benevolent god who easily bestows boons on the devotees. It is he who swallows the venom emitted by Vasuki the king of serpents at the time of *samudra manthan* (churning of the ocean) and thus protects the worlds from its lethal poison. He stores it in his throat which turns blue thus giving him the epithet of *neelkantha* (one with blue throat).

As the *Maharudra*, he is the fierce one who has within his powers to bring an end to the cycle of time, destroys the worlds, dissolve them and thus enable the creation of new worlds. He is also seen performing the cosmic dance *Tandava* which brings an end to the world.

Shiva's Tandava

Lord Shiva is also known as Nataraja, literally meaning the Lord (king) of performers (dancers). He is often depicted in sculptures and paintings as performing a dance called *Tandava*. As a form of dance, *Tandava* is considered to be of two types; ***Ananda-Tandava*** and ***Rudra-Tandava***. While the *Ananda Tandava* is a dance of joy and bliss, the *Rudra Tandava* is reflective of lord Shiva's violent and fierce form. It is the latter dance form that the word *Tandava* is usually associated with.

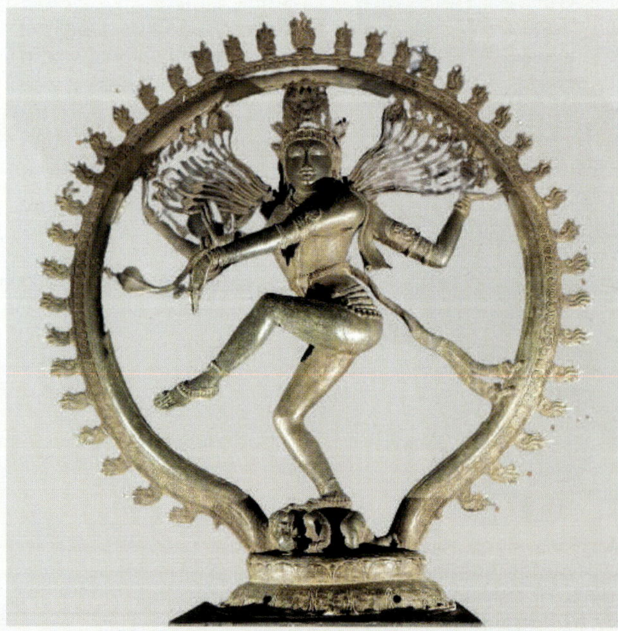

3.32: Natesa or Nataraja, 11th century CE, Chola bronze idol depicting Lord Shiva's Tandava; Government Museum, Chennai — photograph by Madhukar K Bhagat

As per legends, Lord Shiva performed this dance while suppressing the indomitable demon **Apasmara**. While as per another legend, on the occasion of death of Sati at the *yagna* of Daksha, lord Shiva performed this dance bringing almost an annihilation of the world. The different elements of the imagery and different gestures of the *Rudra Tandava* are all considered symbolic of certain profound philosophical elements.

In *Rudra Tandava,* Lord Shiva is depicted in a specific dance posture while balancing on one of his two legs and also suppressing a demon with it. He is shown with four hands in one of which he holds a *damru* and from the other flames are seen to be emanating. Two other hands are seen in specific posture of benediction. His hairlocks are seen to be flowing out. The entire image is also portrayed to be surrounded by a flame.

Lord Shiva's leg is suppressing the demon **Apasmara** which represents ignorance. As per some accounts, Apasmara is said to represent bond caused due to innocence, ignorance and ego. Thus, the Tandava itself is considered symbolic of the **suppression of ignorance and ego** the primary impediments to salvation of the soul.

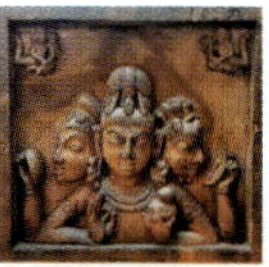

His left leg is raised and is seen to be kicking away (in *bhujangatrasita* stance). This symbolises pushing away of the ***maya*** (illusion cast by the ephemeral world) from the mind of the devotees and thus enabling them to grasp the divine knowledge.

His main right hand is in ***abhaya mudra*** bestowing protection to devotees from ignorance and fear. His upper left arm carries a flame which is said to purify the soul while the other left arm is held in *dola hasta* and connects with right arm in *abhaya mudra* (*abhaya hasta*). The image is seen surrounded by a flame representing the entire cosmos. The upper right hand holds *damaru* from which emanates celestial beats and which symbolises the next cycle of life and death. In a way, the imagery represents the path of salvation and freedom from the conditioned existence.

Overall, the *Tandava* is considered to be a **cosmic dance** which also symbolises the end of the physical world and the beginning of another.

Shaktism

Shaktism refers to the worship of *Shakti* or the divine mother as the Supreme being. She is represented in various forms such as **Durga Kali, Saraswati, Laxmi, Parvati,** etc. As Durga, she is seen as **Mahadevi** or the unified form of the female energy which is also the destroyer of the demons. As **Kali**, she is the fierce one and annihilator of the evil. **Parvati**, the consort of Shiva, is a pristine form of divinity which is also the granter of boons to the devotees. **Saraswati** (consort of Brahma) is the endower of knowledge and wisdom while **Lakshmi** (consort of Vishnu) is the goddess of wealth and material well-being. The female divinity is also seen as the supreme **Maya** and integral to lord Vishnu in Sri Vaishnavism. Further, in the Shaiva traditions, *Shiva* and *Shakti* are often considered to be the two forms of the Supreme and complementary cosmic forces. Thus, Shaktism is a **singular tradition** which venerates the divine mother as the primordial creator of the universe and which makes the polytheistic theology of Hinduism indeed unique.

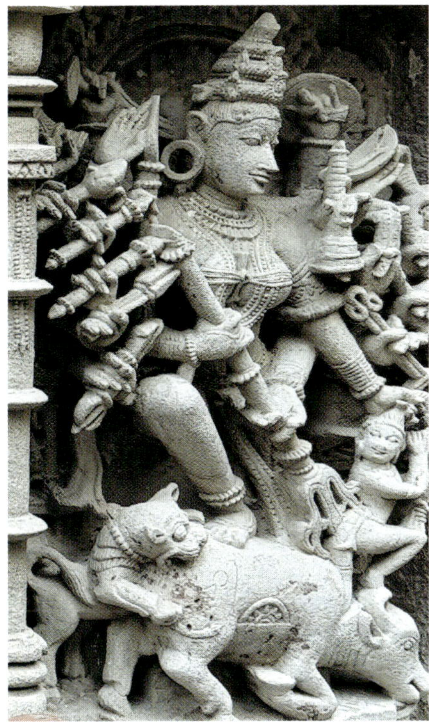

3.33: Durga as Mahishasura Mardini, sandstone panel carving, Rani ki Vav, mid 11th century CE — photograph by Madhukar K Bhagat

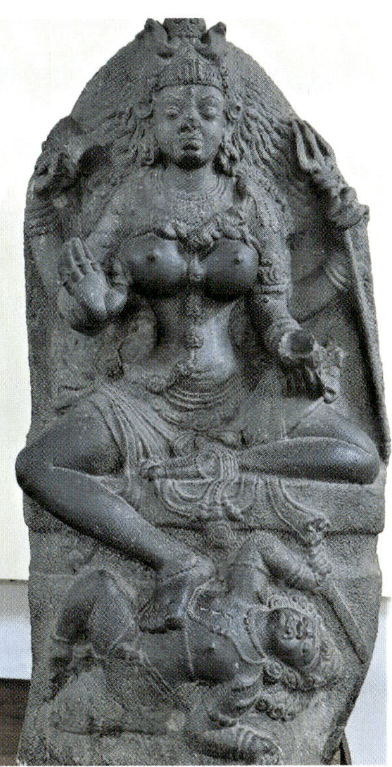

3.34: Sculpture of Goddess Durga suppressing a demon, 10th century CE, from Avani region, Ganga period, black sandstone; Government Museum, Bangalore — photograph by Madhukar K Bhagat

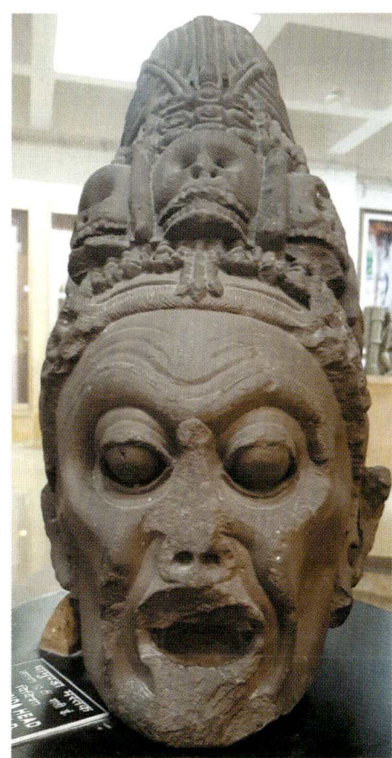

3.35: The head of Chamunda; 10th century CE Vidisha, present location State Museum, Bhopal — photograph by Madhukar K Bhagat

The **origin** of the tradition of female divinity is considered to be pre-Vedic. Reference to the worship of Mother Goddess is also noted in figurines of Harappan civilisation. Along with Shaivism, it is also considered one of the oldest forms of Hinduism. The Vedic reference to Shaktism is seen in the Rigvedic verse (10.125), also referred to as the *Devi Shuktam*, where she is described to be the eternal and infinite consciousness of the universe. The several **Shakta Upanishads** (a set of minor Upanishads) are also an important source of the Shakta traditions. These include the Devi Upanishad, the Saraswati Rahasya Upanishad, Saubhagya Lakshmi Upanishad, the Sita Upanishad, the Tripura Upanishad, Bhavana Upanishad etc.

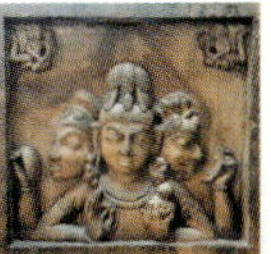

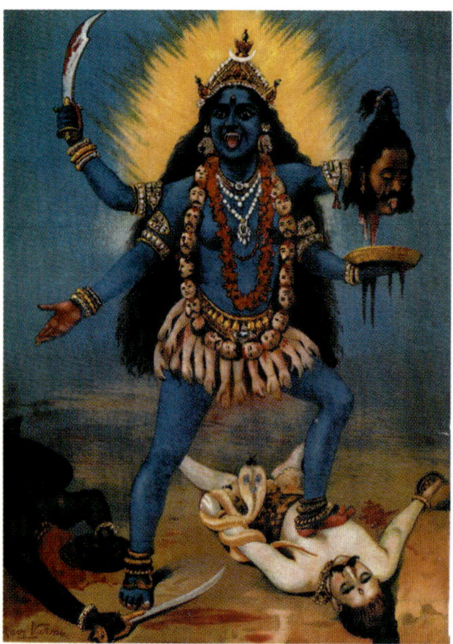

3.36: Goddess Kali, the fierce form of Shakti; a painting by Raja Ravi Varma, late 19th century — Wikimedia Commons

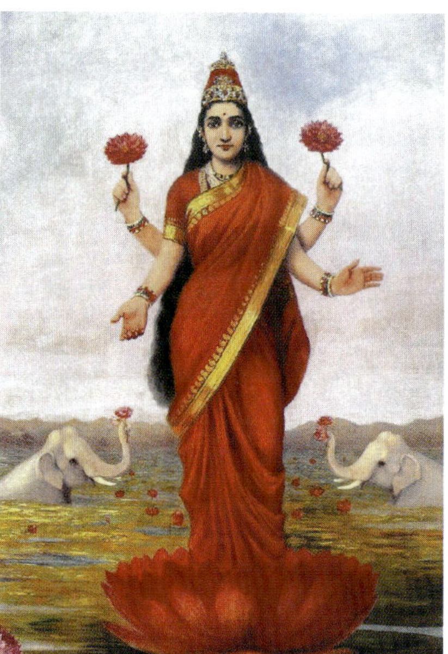

3.37: Goddess Lakhmi on lotus; the goddess of material wealth; a painting by Raja Ravi Varma, late 19th century — Wikimedia Commons

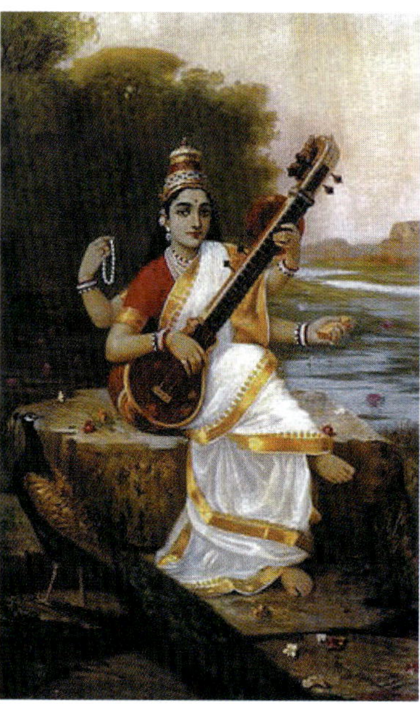

3.38: Goddess Saraswati, the endower of knowledge, a painting by Raja Ravi Varma, late 19th century — Wikimedia Commons

The *Devi Bhagavata Purana*, a major Purana, and *Devi Mahatmya*, a part of the Markandeya Purana, are considered as the most significant canons in the Shaktism tradition. Brahmanda Purana and Skanda Purana are also considered as Shakta Puranas. Besides, all major Puranas contain sections which eulogise the female divinity.

The tradition of worship of Devi is specially popular in the eastern and north eastern parts of the country where it is also manifested in the festivals of Navaratra and Durga Puja. The sub-traditions of Tantra and Kundalini Yoga are also associated with Shaktism.

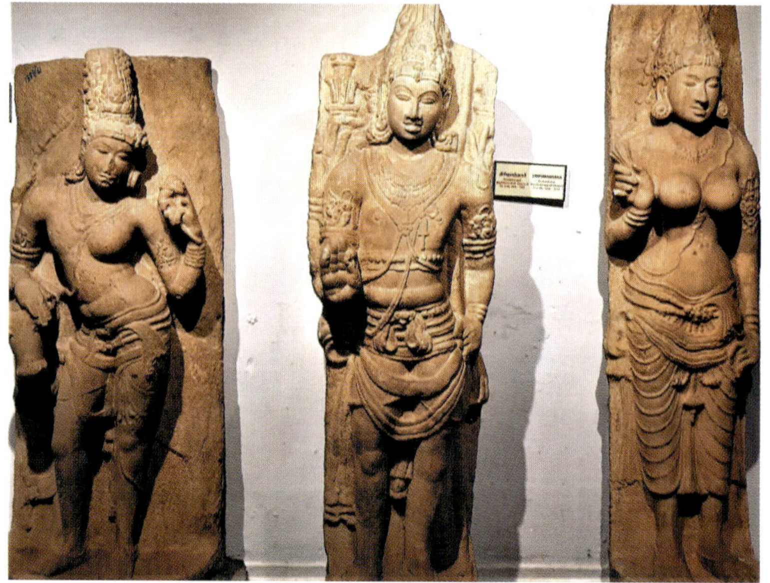

3.39: Lord Shiva (central sculpture), Goddess Tripurasundari, his consort (sculpture to the left of Shiva's sculpture) and Ardhanarishwara (on right) which combines the elements of Shiva and Shakti. Sculptures 10th century CE, Government Museum, Chennai. — photographs by Madhukar K Bhagat

Devi Suktam, a Vedic Proclamation of the Female Divinity

The Rigveda 10th Mandala and 125th verse, contains *advaitic* expression of the unity of the creation where the **Adi Parashakti** or the divine mother is expressed as the Supreme cosmic force. The composition of the hymn in eight stanzas is attributed to ancient seer **Rishiki Vak Ambhrini**, daughter of a great seer Ambhrina. Realising the highest truth, she expresses herself as the supreme creator, the strength of all the gods, the very breath of life and the essence of the universe. Some of the verses are described here.

ॐ अहं रुद्रेभिर्वसुभिँश्चराम्यहमादित्यैरुत विश्वदेवैः ।

अहं मित्रावरुंणोभा बिंभर्म्यहमिन्द्राग्नी अहमश्विनोभा ।। 1 ।।

I proceed with the Rudras and with the Vasus, I wander with the Adityas and the Vishwadevas.

I support both Mitra and Varuna, and also Indra and Agni and the twin Ashwins. 1

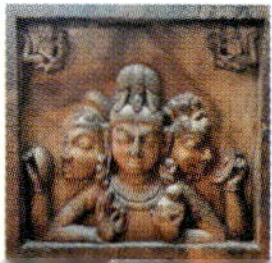

अहं सोमंमाहनसं बिभमूर्यहं त्वष्टारमुत पूषणं भगम्।

अहं दंधामि द्रविंणं हविष्मंते सुप्राव्ये ए यजंमानाय सुन्वते।। 2।।

I uphold the Soma, which accords delight to the Gods. I am the supporter of Tvaṣṭar, Bhaga and Pushan who vanquish the foes. I am the bestower of the fruits of the sacrifices and oblation, to the institutor of sacrifices and to the performer of the sacrifices. 2

अहं राष्ट्री संगमंनी वसूनां चिकितुषी प्रथमा यज्ञियानाम्।

तां मा देवा व्यंदधुः पुरुत्रा भूरिंस्थात्रां भूर्य वेशयन्तीम्।। 3।।

I am the sovereign queen of the entire existence, the one who collects all the treasures (viz.one who is the sovereign of material wealth), full of wisdom,(the knower of all), foremost worthy of worship through the ritual yajna. It is me, the devas have incorporated in different, places, directions and homes for me to enter and abide in.(viz. to take all forms and enter the conditioned bodies as the consciousness or the atman)

मया सोऽअन्नंमत्ति यो विपश्यंति यः प्राणिंति य ईं श_णोत्युक्तम्।

अमन्तवोमान्त उपंक्षियन्ति श्रुधिश्रुंत श्रद्धिवं ते वदामि।। 4।।

By my power and through dint of me alone that one eats, sees, breathes and hears the spoken word. (viz. the very energy of life).

Though not aware of me, yet one dwells in me alone (viz. pervading all life).

Listen with concentration, hearken those who can hear! for, I tell you what is worthy of belief (that what is the eternal truth). 4

अहमेव स्वयमिदं वंदामि जुष्टं देवेभिंरुत मानुंषेभिः।

यं कामये तं तंमुग्रं कृंणोमि तं ब्रह्माणं तमृषिं तं सुंमेधाम्।। 5।।

It is I who determine and declare as to what are pleasing to gods and men. It is I who chose to make the man dear to me mighty in strength, a knower of the Brahman, a sage, a learned scholar, or a wise one, as I please. 5

अहं रुद्राय धनुरातंनोमि ब्रह्मद्विषे शरंवेहन्त वा उं।

अहं जनाय समदं कृणोम्यहं द्यावांपृथिवी आविंवेश।। 6।।

It is I who bend the bow for Rudra so that his arrow may slay the tormentors of the knowers of the sacred wisdom(devotees and followers of dharma thus protecting dharma and order).

I rouse the people and make them strive.(viz. the energy of all).

I pervade the earth and the heaven and everything. 6

अहं सुंवे पितरंमस्य मूर्धन् मम योनिंरप्स्व (अ) ९न्तः संमुद्रे।

ततो वितिंष्ठे भुवनानु विश्वो तामूं द्यां वर्ष्मणोपंस्पृशामि।। 7।।

I bring forth the father of this sky (implying being the creator of the god of the sky).

My genesis is in the waters of the cosmic oceans, thence I permeate all living beings and with my vertex, I touch that sky (heavens). 7

अहमेव वातंऽइव प्रवाम्यारभंमाणा भुवंनानि विश्वा

परो दिवा परएना पृंथिव्यै तावंती महिना सम्बंभूव।। 8।।

I breathe like the wind and tempest, generating from it all living beings and all the worlds. I hold together the entire existence – beyond this, earth the heavens and time. So grand is my encompass! 8

ॐ शान्तिः शान्तिः शान्तिः।।

Smartism

Smartism is another recognised sect of Hinduism where the followers may worship more than one of the chief deities. Thus, they may worship any or all of the deities such as Vishnu, Shiva, Durga, Brahman, Surya, Skanda, Ganesha etc. as *istadevata* (deity of choice) and not just consider Lord Vishnu or Lord Shiva as the only primary deity worthy of veneration as in Vaishnavism and Shaivism respectively. Thus, Smartism does not recognise theistic sectarianism, but is a synthesis of the extant Vedic and Puranic traditions. Usually, Smartism is associated with *panchayatan puja*, or the worship of five venerable deities which include Vishnu, Shiva, Shakti, Surya and Ganesh. However, in some forms of Smartism, Brahma and Kartikeya (Skand or Kumar) are also included in this fold.

Literal meaning of Smart is that is what is derived from the Smritis and thus it is based on the Smriti and the traditional Hindu beliefs. Smartism is said to have its origin due to the efforts of Adi Shankaracharya who unified the various sects. However, some scholars also attribute an earlier genesis of Smartism. Its philosophy is drawn from the Vedas while it also believes in the legends of the various gods as brought in the Puranas. Smartism recognises the *nirguna Brahma* or the unconditioned attribute-less god which represents the pure consciousness and the power of creation as enshrined in the Vedas. It also believes in the above prime deities being the god with attributes, or *saguna Brahma*, and being the epitome of

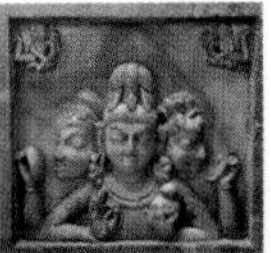

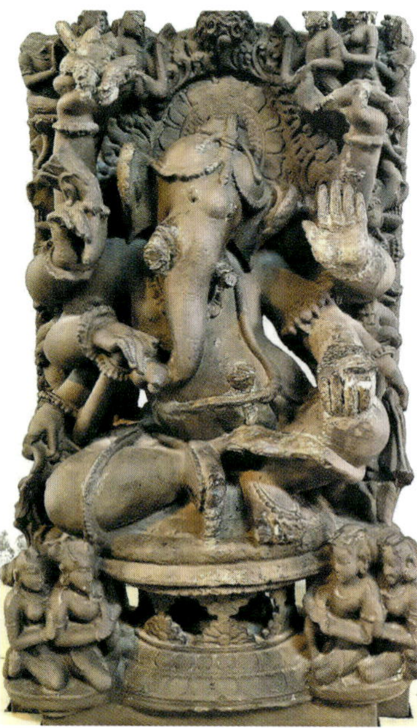

3.40: Ashtabhuji Ganesh, 11th century CE, Jabalpur; State Museum, Bhopal; — photograph by Madhukar K Bhagat

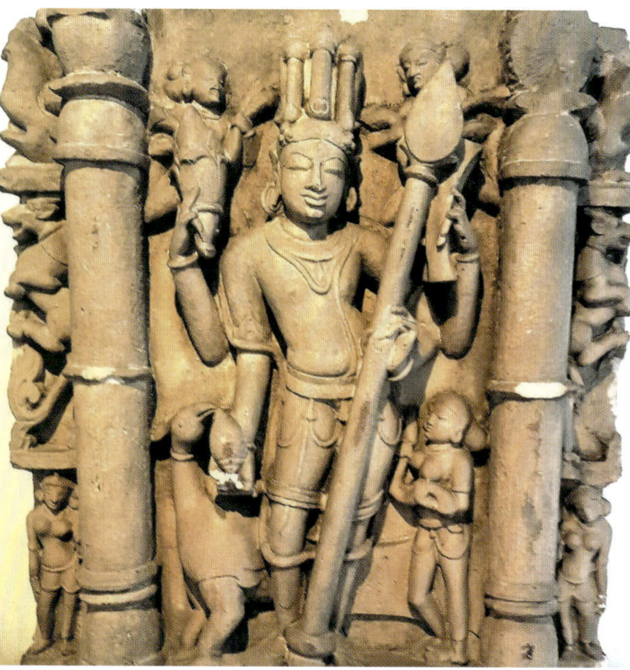

3.41: Kartikeya, 12th century CE; Morena, current location State Museum, Bhopal — photograph by Madhukar K Bhagat

love, compassion and upholder of justice and cosmic order. Thus, in the evolutionary realisation of God it considers the conditioned Brahma to be a step earlier to the realisation of unconditioned Brahma.

Hinduism and Holy Ancient Cities

The thousands of years of evolution of Hinduism has seen it flourish in different parts of the country and beyond. However, some of the cites have special place in this journey and are considered among the holiest of Hindu sites. Of these the most renowned are the *saptapuri* (seven sities). These find reference even in the Garuda Purana and are considered be to doorways to salvation (*moksha*) on account of their intrinsic association with deities like Sri Rama and Sri Krishna and also on account of their spiritual significance. The shloka states

अयोध्या मथुरा माया काशी काञ्ची अवन्तिका।
पुरी द्वारावती चैव सप्तैते मोक्षदायकाः।।

Ayodhya Mathura, Maya (Mayapuri or Haridwar) Kashi(Varanasi), Kanchi (Kanchipuram), Avantika (Ujjain) and Dwaravati (Dwarka). These seven cities are endowers of moksha (liberation).

While Ayodhya is considered the birth place of Sri Rama, Mathura and Dwarka are associated with Sri Krishna. Varanasi and Ujjain are holy cities where one of the 12 *Jyotirlingas* are located. Haridwar is the place where descent of the holy Ganga in the plains takes place and is sacred to both the Shaivas as well as Vaishnavas.

Among these, Varanasi is considered one of the holiest of cities, which is also considered one of the ancient most continuously inhabited city of the world. Located on the bank of river Ganga (also confluence of Varuna and Assi tributary rivers of Ganga) where the river takes a northwardly turn in its hitherto easterly flow, the city is truly emblematic of the great river Vedic culture. The Brihadanyaka Upanishad also contains reference of king Ajatashatru of Varanasi who imparts the knowledge of unconditioned Brahma to Gargeya (a brahmin). As per legends, Raja Harischandra had to undergo a severe test of his truthfulness by serving as lighter of funeral pyre at its *ghats* (river bank). Kasi was one of the 16 Mahajanapadas in later Vedic period. Sarnath, near Varanasi was the place where lord Buddha delivered his first sermon. Adi Shankaracharya is said to have established Varanasi as a seat of worship of lord Shiva (Shaivism). Many medieval saints like Ramananda, Kabirdas, Vallabhacharya, Ravidas and Tulsidas have composed their spiritual verses and great works on the banks of Ganga here. Indeed, for thousands of years it has been a cradle of Vedic learning and the very epicentre of Hinduism.

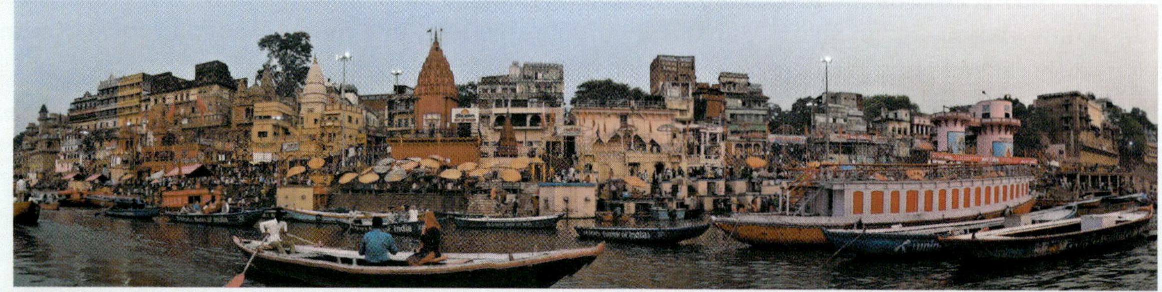

3.42: Panoramic view of Ganga ghats,Varanasi; a cradle of Vedic dharma — photograph by Madhukar K Bhagat

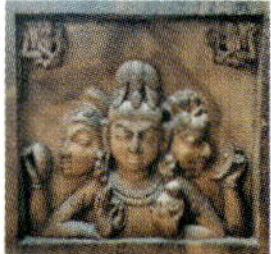

Even today, it's a firm belief of many followers of Hinduism that a death in this city and cremation at its ghats imparts salvation from the cycle of births and deaths, and the continuous ritualistic cremation and the burning of funeral pyres at its ghats (Manikarnika and Harischandra ghats) have never abated since ancient times. Its many temples dedicated to lord Shiva, lord Hanuman, goddess Durga, *Ganga aarti* (veneration of river Ganga) are testimony of the essential monotheism and vibrant polytheism of Vedic philosophy and Hindu religion.

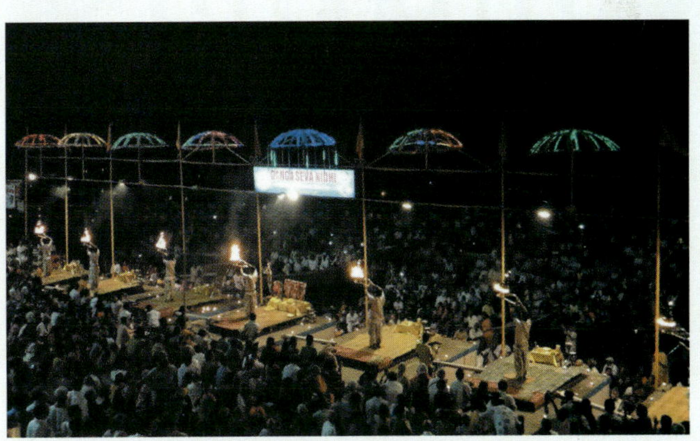

3.43: The Ganga aarti, Varanasi, a living tradition of veneration of the holy river — photograph by Madhukar K Bhagat

Well Being of All; an Enduring Philosophy of Hinduism

A prayer for universal well-being in Brihadarnyaka Upanishad

ॐ सर्वे भवन्तु सुखिनः
सर्वे सन्तु निरामयाः ।
सर्वे भद्राणि पश्यन्तु
मा कश्चिद्दुःखभाग्भवेत् ।
ॐ शान्तिः शान्तिः शान्तिः ।।

Om Sarve Bhavantu Sukhinah
Sarve Santu Niraamayaah |
Sarve Bhadraanni Pashyantu
Maa Kashcid-Duhkha-Bhaag-Bhavet ||
Om Shaantih Shaantih ||

Meaning:

Om! may all be happy,
May all be free from illness.
May all see what is auspicious,
May no one suffer.
Om! peace, peace, peace!
(Brihadarnyaka Upanishad)

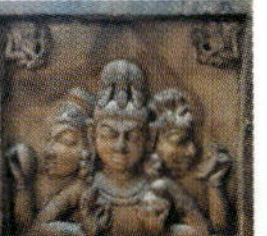

PICTURE GALLERY

Hinduism, a polytheistic religion is known for its expression of divinity in diverse material forms. Stone sculptures of the 1st millennium are a tangible manifestation of this element of Puranic Hinduism. These sculptures are a reflection of the change within Hinduism; from its profound monotheism to vibrant polytheism; as well as a testimony to the evolution of the art of sculpture-making, its aesthetics and intricacies, over a period of hundreds of years. The picture gallery is a compilation of some of the stone sculptures of Hindu deities from museums in different parts of the country.

BRAHMA

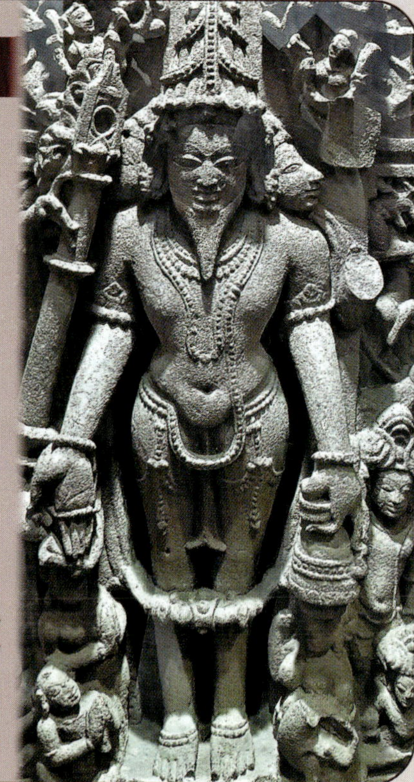

3.44: Brahma; among rare sculptures of the deity; 12th century, Chandarpur, Maharashtra; Nagpur Central Museum — photograph by Madhukar K Bhagat

VISHNU

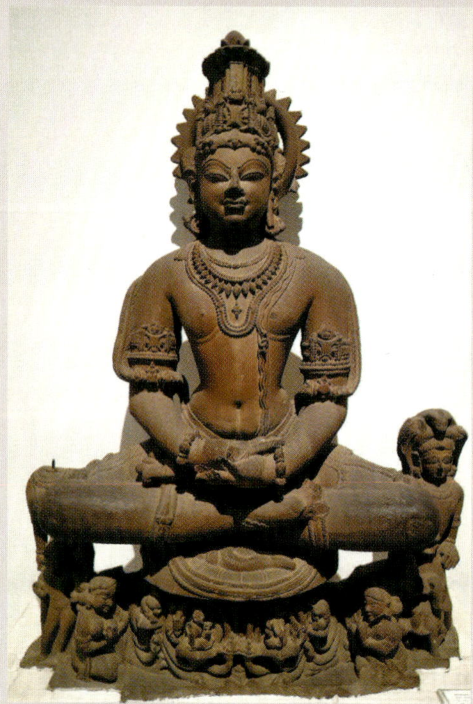

3.45: Yoganarayana; lord Vishnu as a yogi seated in *dhyana mudra*; Shesh Nag (the coiled serpent on which lord Vishnu is seated) is seen on his left. Sculpture in stone, 10th century, Chandela dynasty, Khajuraho, Madhya Pradesh; National Museum, New Delhi — photograph by Madhukar K Bhagat

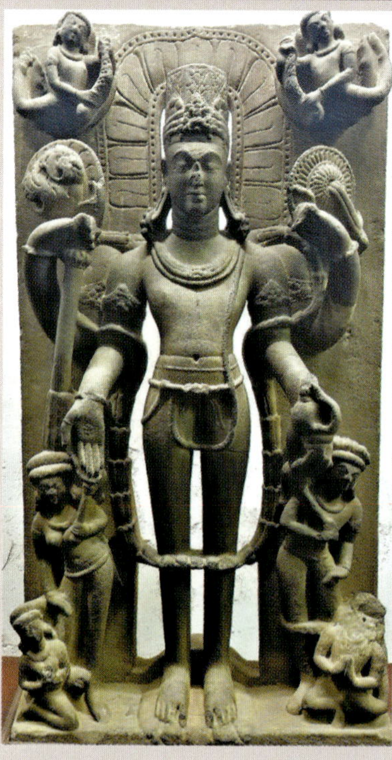

3.46: Vishnu, 8th century CE, Majhgawan, Madhya Pradesh; Nagpur Central Museum — photograph by Madhukar K Bhagat

Vishnu ... (*Continued*)

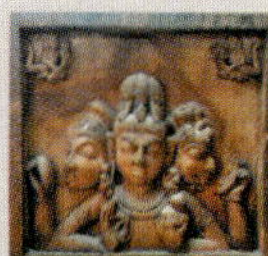

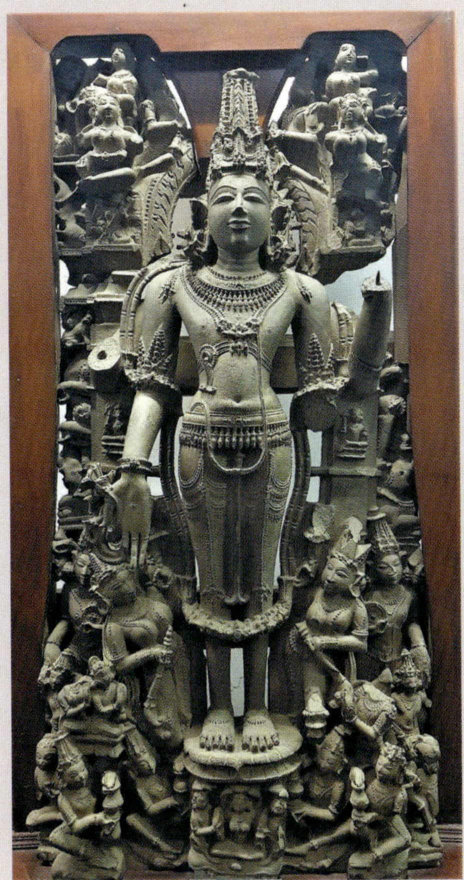

3.47: Vishnu, 11th century, Seoni, Madhya Pradesh, Nagpur Central Museum — photograph by Madhukar K Bhagat

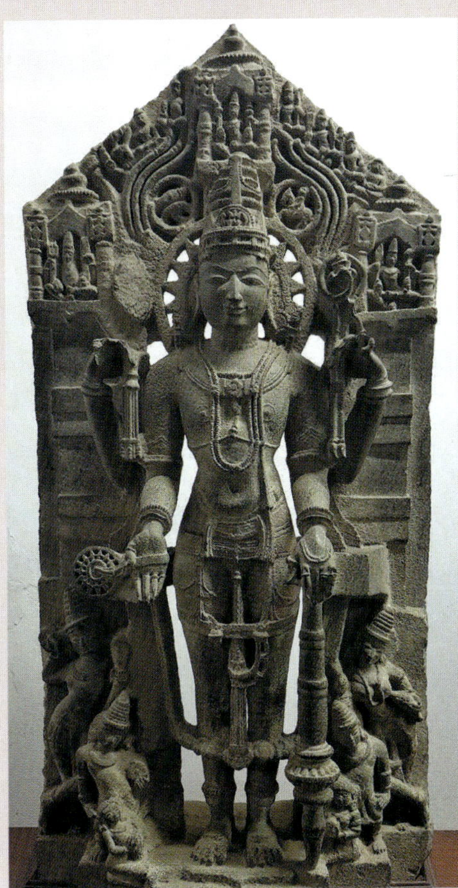

3.48: Vishnu, 11th century, Wardha, Maharashtra; Nagpur Central Museum — photograph by Madhukar K Bhagat

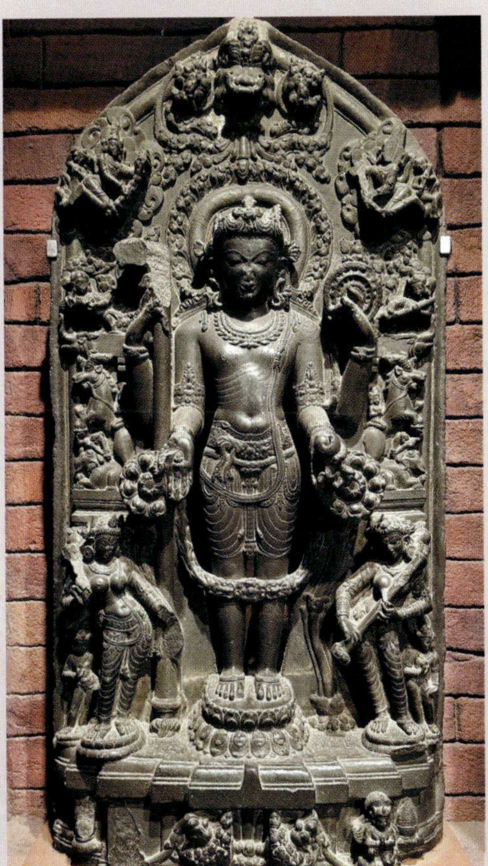

3.49: Vishnu, 12th century, Pala period; Bihar Museum — photograph by Madhukar K Bhagat

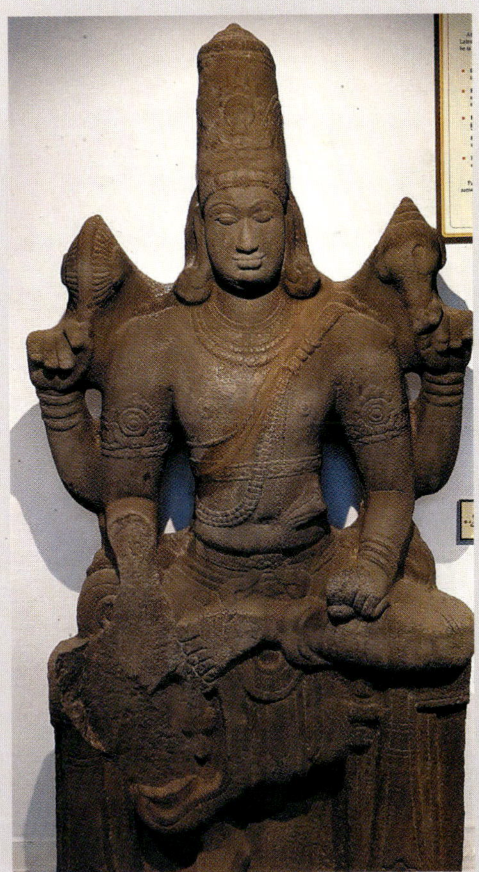

3.50: Vishnu, a Pallava period sculpture; Government Museum, Chennai — photograph by Madhukar K Bhagat

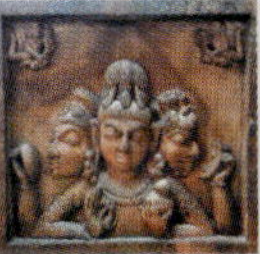

KRISHNA

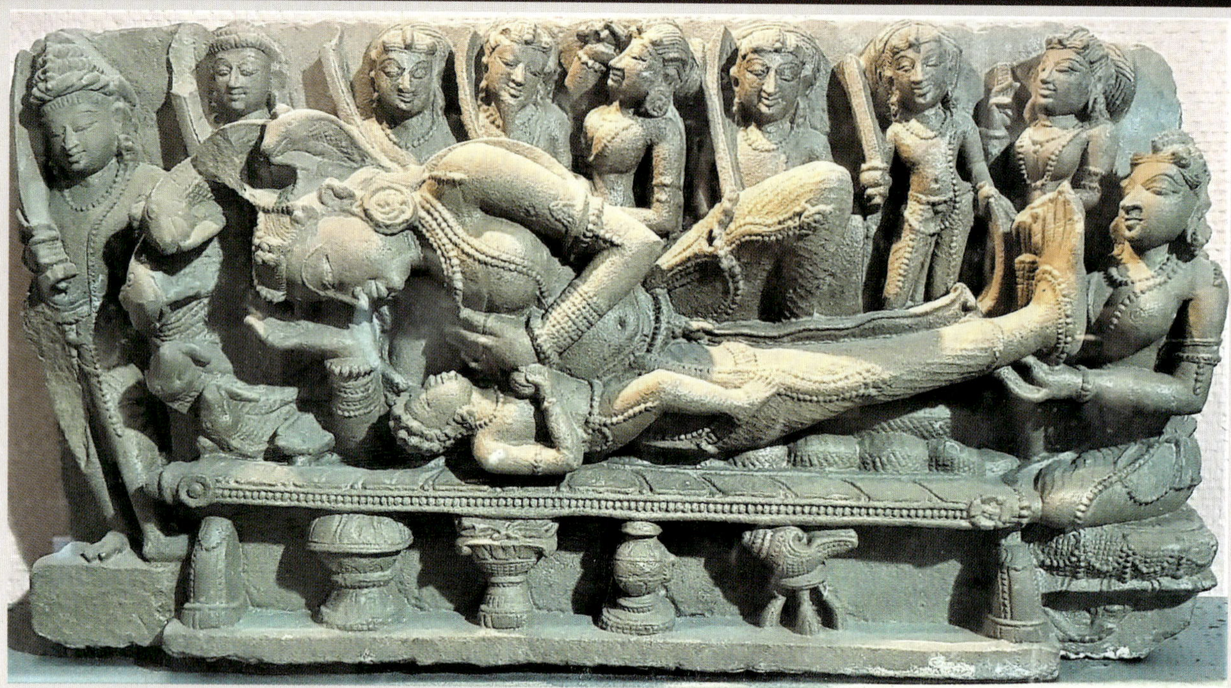

3.51: A sculptural panel depicting the birth of Sri Krishna, the eighth incarnation of Lord Vishnu; Shahdol, Madhya Pradesh; State Museum, Bhopal — photograph by Madhukar K Bhagat

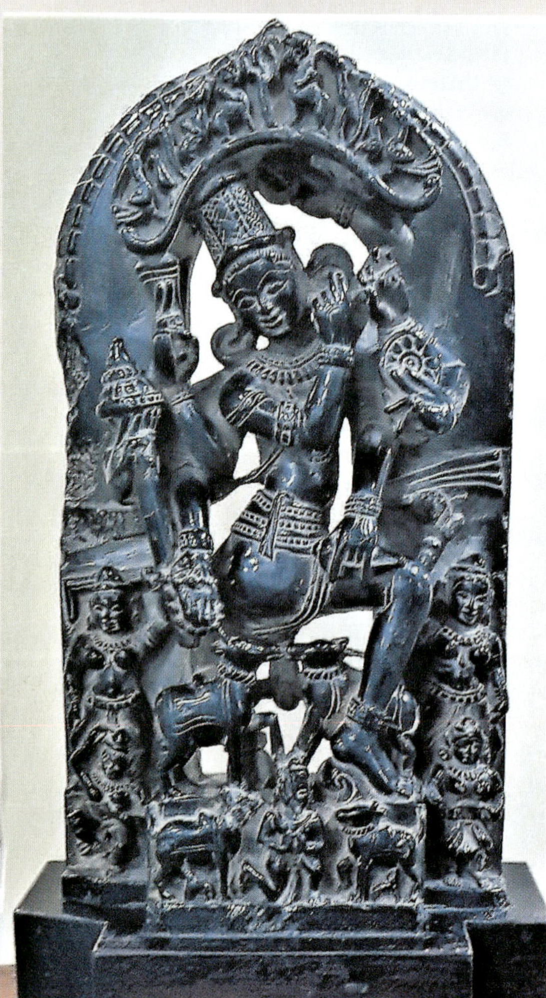

3.52: Govardhandhari Krishna, 12th century Blackstone sculpture, Chalukya dynasty; Kalyan, Karnataka; Government Museum, Bangalore — photograph by Madhukar K Bhagat

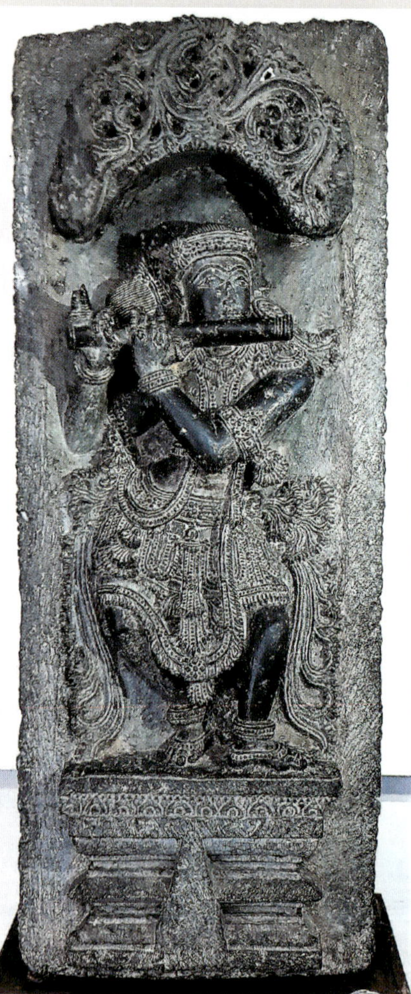

3.53: Venugopal (meaning: Sri Krishna the protector of cows as the bearer of flute), 12th century, Hoysala sculpture, Halebidu; Government Museum, Bangalore — photograph by Madhukar K Bhagat

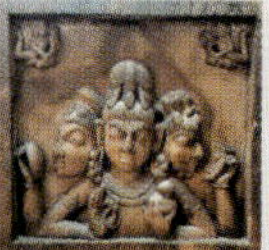

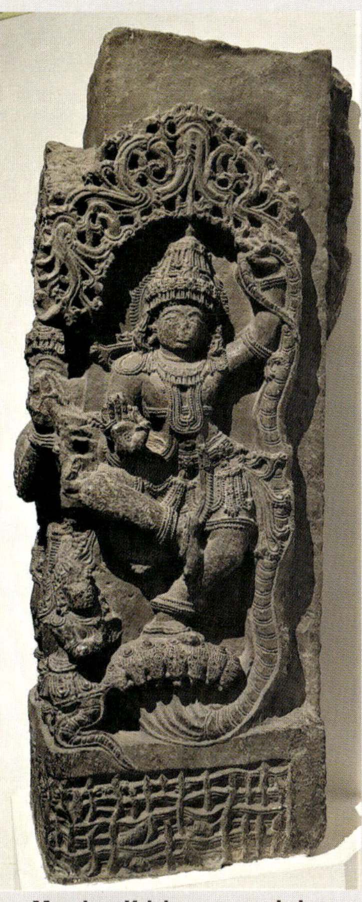

3.54: Kaliya Mardan Krishna; a sculpture on a stone column depicting Krishna subjugating the serpent Kalia; 11th century Halebidu, National Museum, New Delhi — photograph by Madhukar K Bhagat

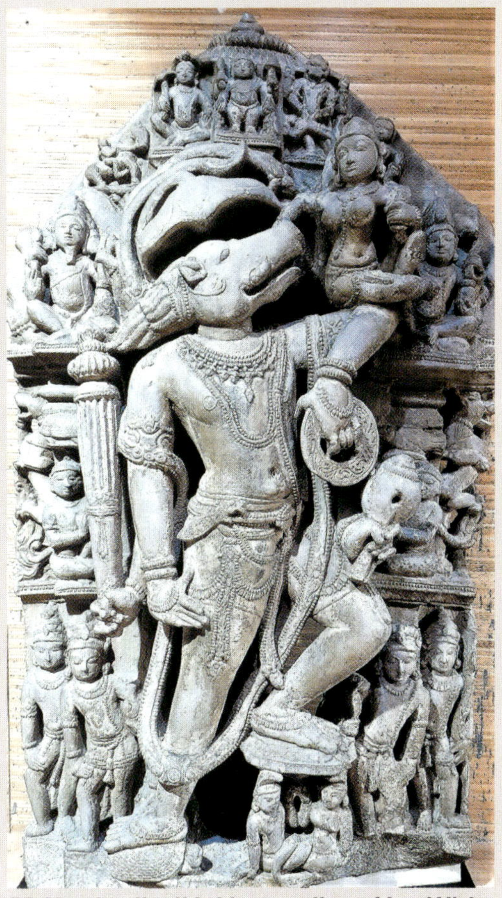

3.55: Varaha, the third incarnation of Lord Vishnu, a sculpture of 9th to 10th century, Mandsaur, Madhya Pradesh; State Museum, Bhopal — photograph by Madhukar K Bhagat

SHIVA

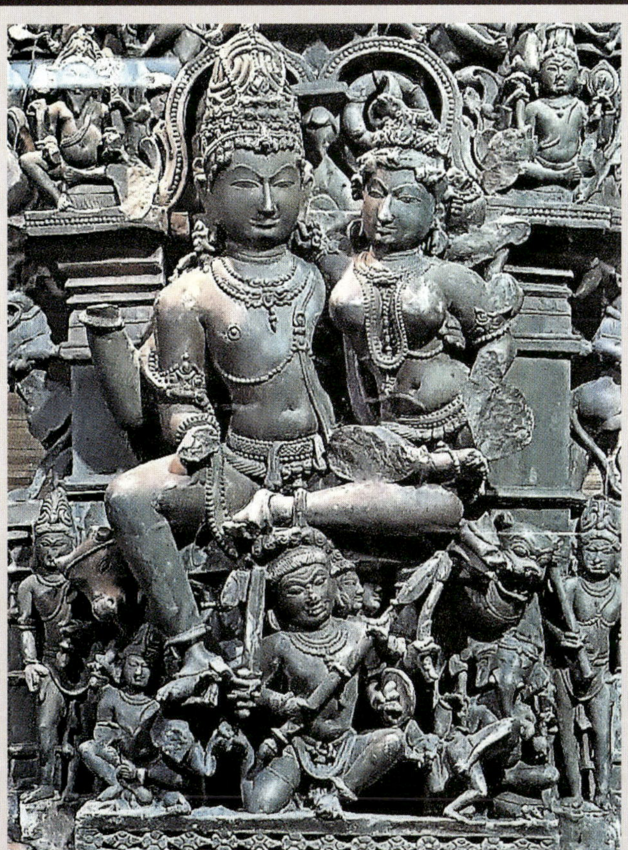

3.56: Ravananugraha, a sculpture panel depicting the anecdote of Ravana trying to uproot Mount Kailash. Lord Shiva seated with Parvati then presses the toe of his foot down, trapping Ravana beneath Mount Kailash. Ravana then sings hymns in praise of Lord Shiva, who then releases him and bestows an invincible sword. 11th century sculpture panel, Mandsaur, Madhya Pradesh; State Museum, Bhopal — photograph by Madhukar K Bhagat

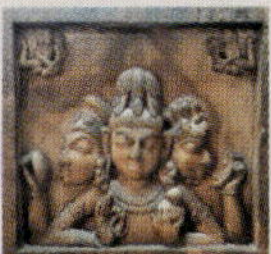

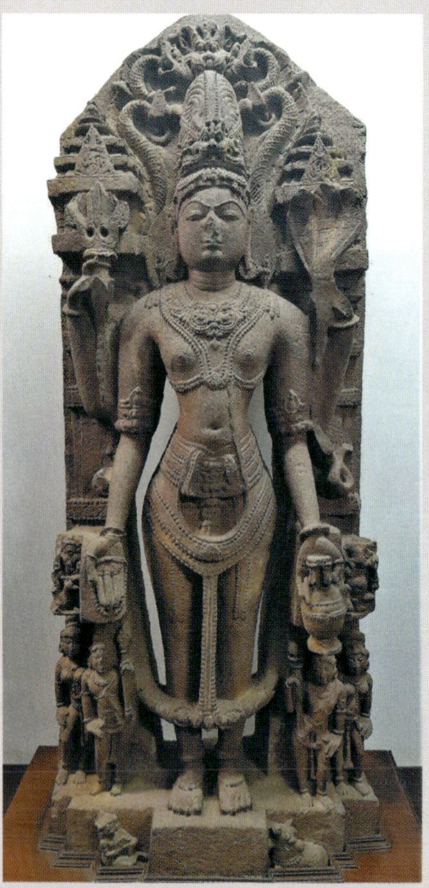

3.57: Lord Shiva, 11th century, Gondia district, Maharashtra; Central Museum, Nagpur — photograph by Madhukar K Bhagat

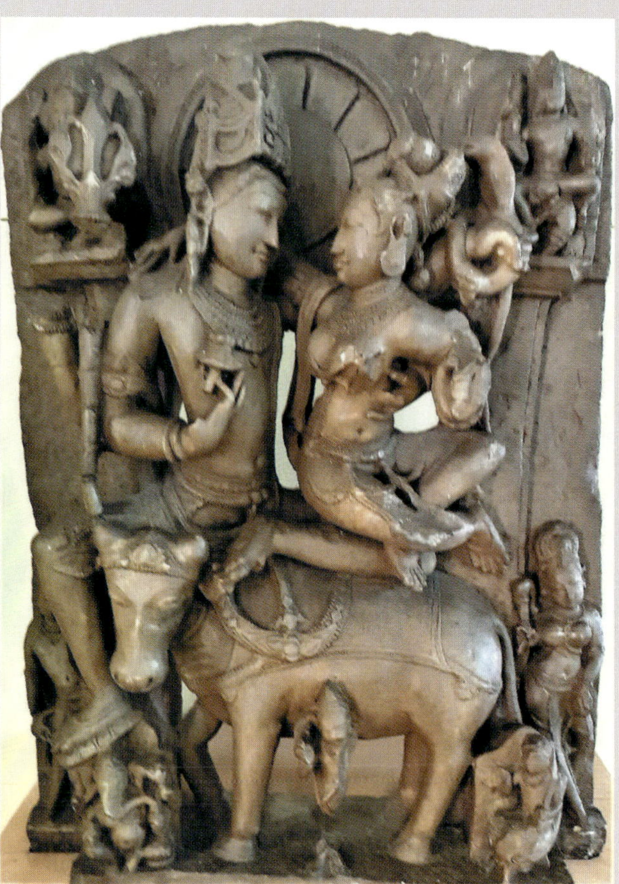

3.58: Uma Maheshwar, 11th-12th century, Hinglajgarh, Madhya Pradesh; State Museum, Bhopal — photograph by Madhukar K Bhagat

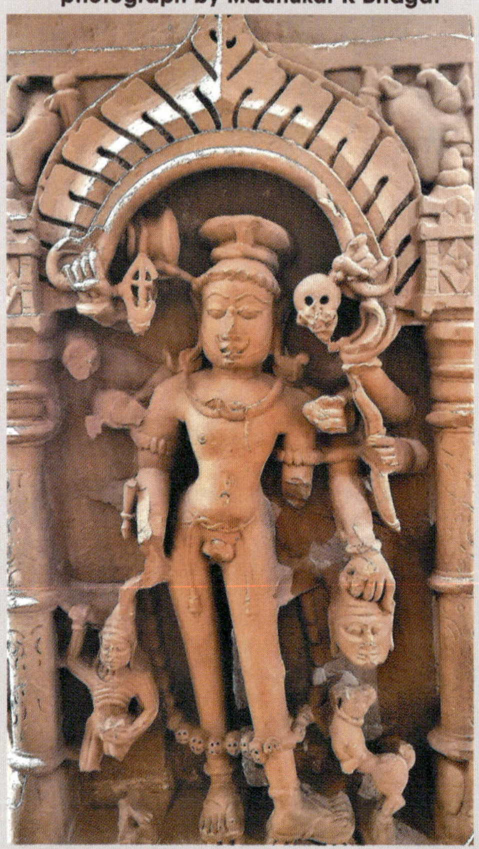

3.59: Bhairava or Kala Bhairava, a form of lord Shiva associated with death and annihilation, sculpture 11th century, Mandsaur, Madhya Pradesh; State Museum, Bhopal — photograph by Madhukar K Bhagat

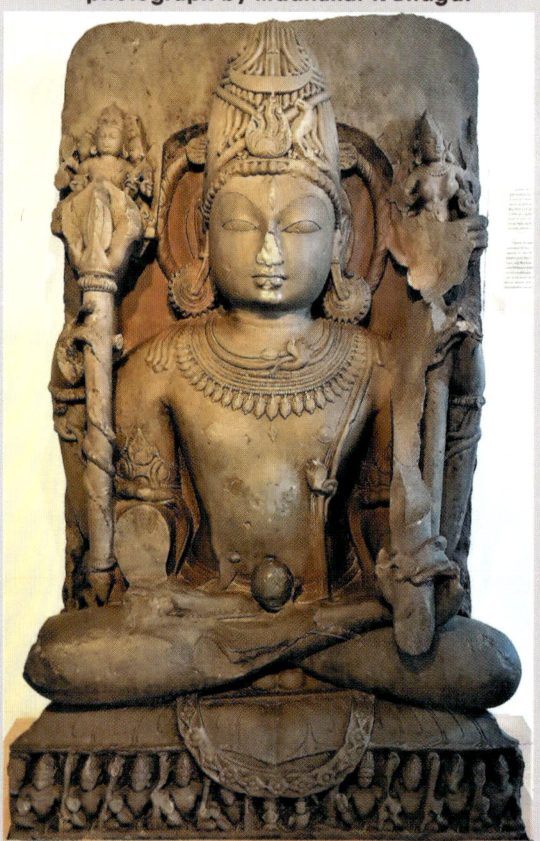

3.60: Lakulisa (literal meaning: the lord with staff or mace), considered the 28th incarnation of Lord Shiva and the propounder of the Yoga system, a sculpture of 10th century, Mandsaur, Madhya Pradesh; State Museum, Bhopal — photograph by Madhukar K Bhagat

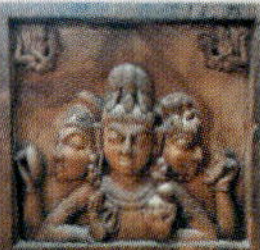

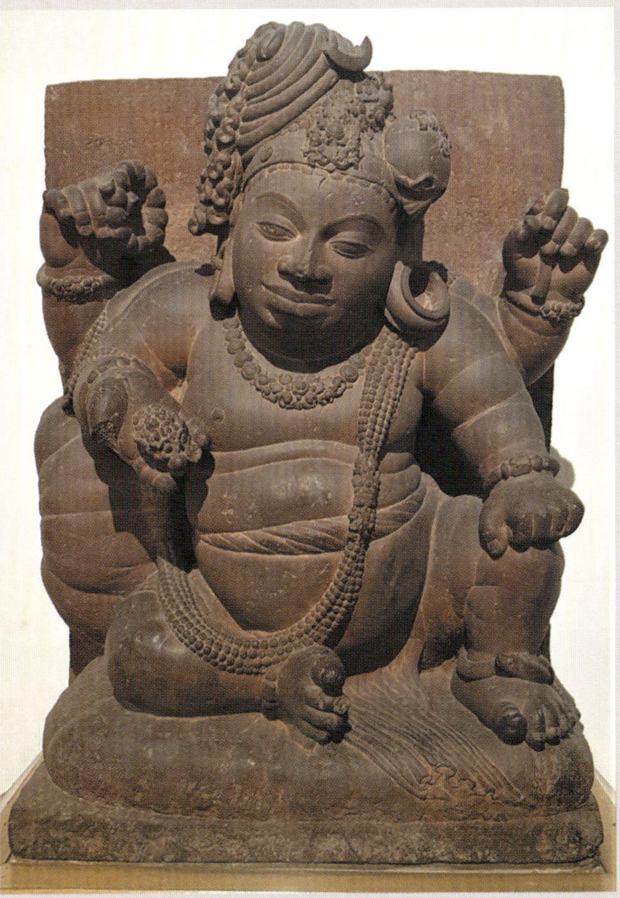

3.61: Shiva Vaman, a unique stone sculpture (height 83 cm) depicting lord Shiva as a Vamana (dwarf), 5th century CE, Vakataka dynasty, Mansar, Maharashtra; National Museum, New Delhi — photograph by Madhukar K Bhagat

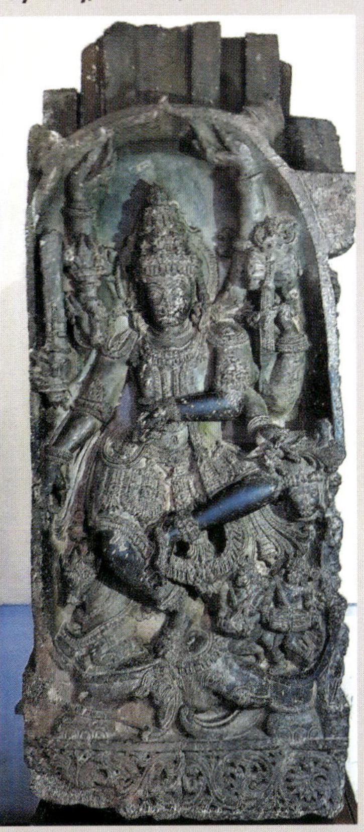

3.62: Gajasura Samhara; Shiva as the slayer of the elephant demon; an eight-armed Shiva is shown as trampling the head of the demon elephant; 12th century blackstone sculpture, Hoysala dynasty, Halebidu; Government Museum, Bangalore — photograph by Madhukar K Bhagat

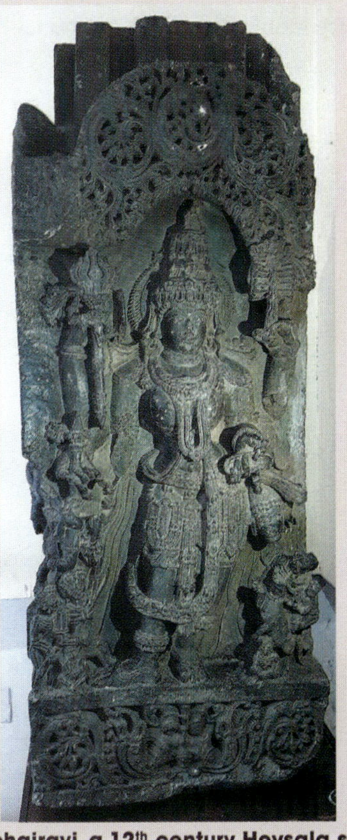

3.63: Kalbhairavi, a 12th century Hoysala sculpture, the reverse part of the temple column in which the Gajasura Samhara Shiva sculpture was built (the two sculptures are two sides of the same column); Halebidu; Government Museum, Bangalore — photograph by Madhukar K Bhagat

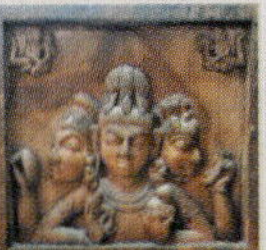

SHAKTI AND HER FORMS

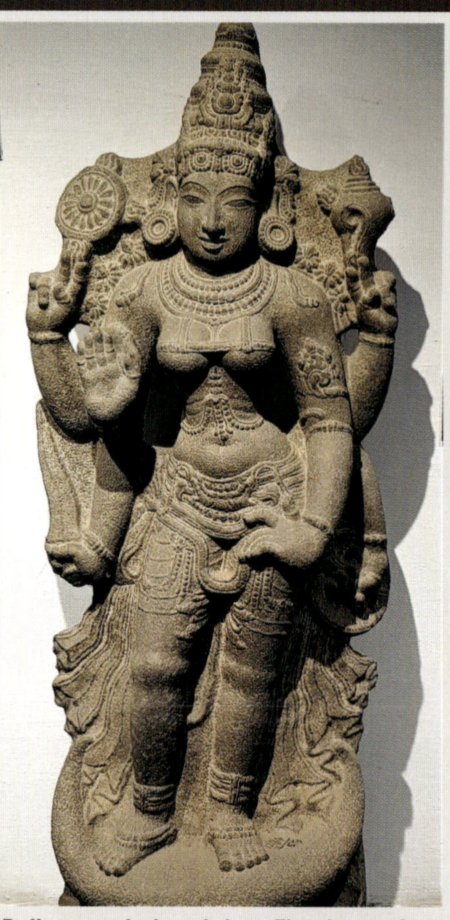

3.64: Mahishasuramardini, Pallava period sculpture, Thanjavur; Government Museum, Chennai — photograph by Madhukar K Bhagat

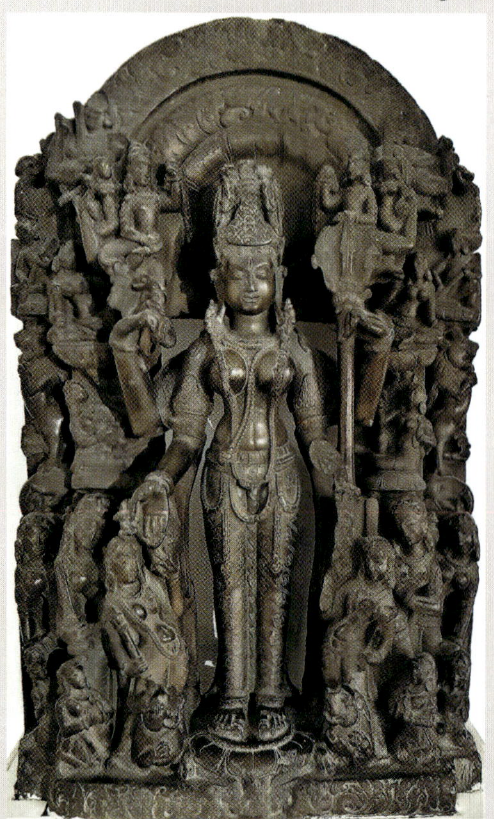

3.65: Parvati 11th century, Pratihara dynasty, Baijnath, Himachal Pradesh; National Museum, New Delhi, — photograph by Madhukar K Bhagat

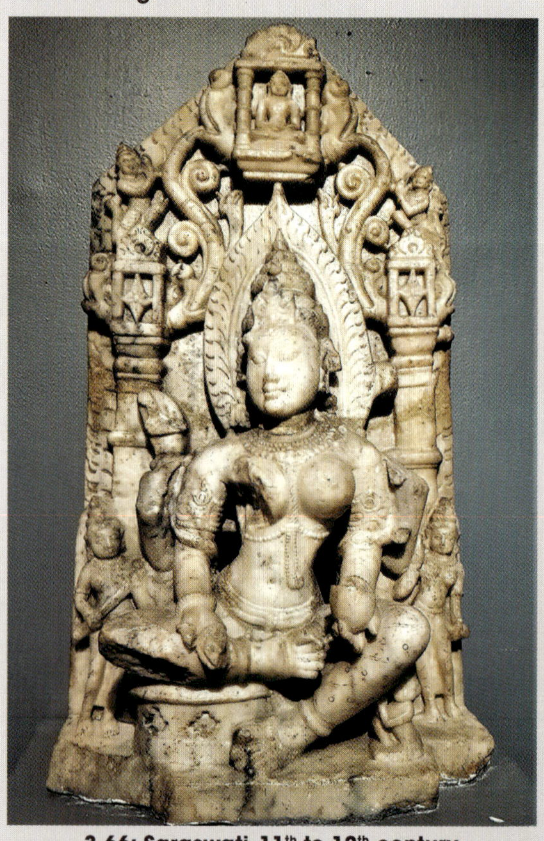

3.66: Saraswati, 11th to 12th century, Rajasthan; National Museum, New Delhi — photograph by Madhukar K Bhagat

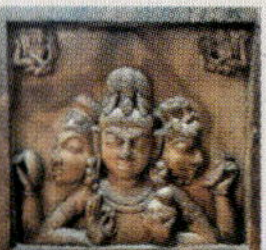

SURYA

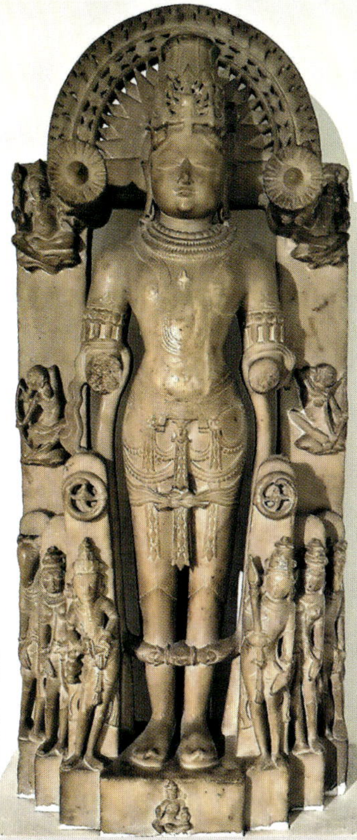

3.67: Surya with consorts, 12th century; Gahadwal, Rajasthan, National Museum, New Delhi — photograph by Madhukar K Bhagat

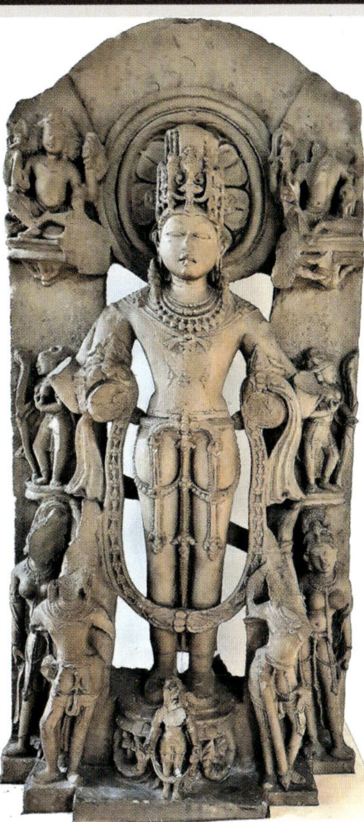

3.68: Surya with charioteer Aruna (in the bottom of sculpture) and other consorts, Mandsaur, 11th century Madhya Pradesh; State Museum, Bhopal — photograph by Madhukar K Bhagat

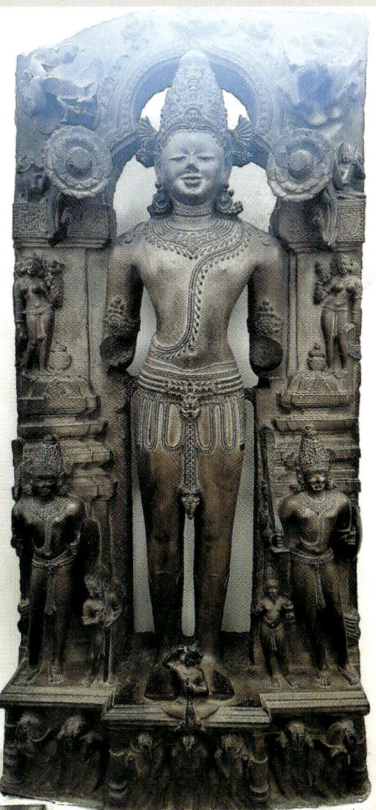

3.69: Surya with charioteer Aruna and other consorts, 13th century, Eastern Ganga dynasty, Konark, Odisha; National Museum, New Delhi — photograph by Madhukar K Bhagat

OTHER DEITIES

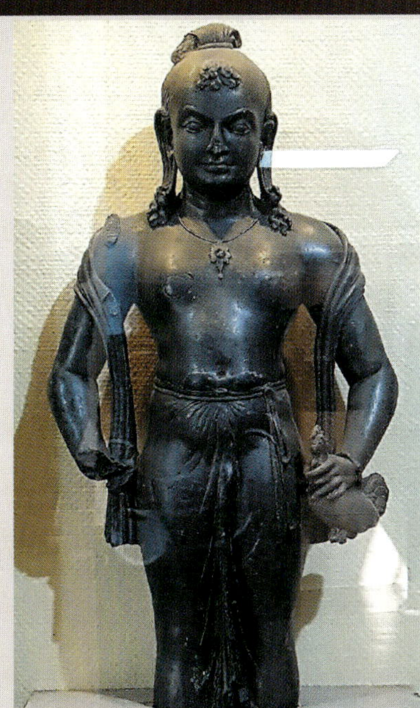

3.70: A unique stone sculpture of Kartikeya where the deity is depicted without the iconographies of holding a spear (weapon), seated on a peacock (mount), or as a god with six heads. 3rd - 4th century CE, Mandsaur, Madhya Pradesh; State Museum, Bhopal — photograph by Madhukar K Bhagat

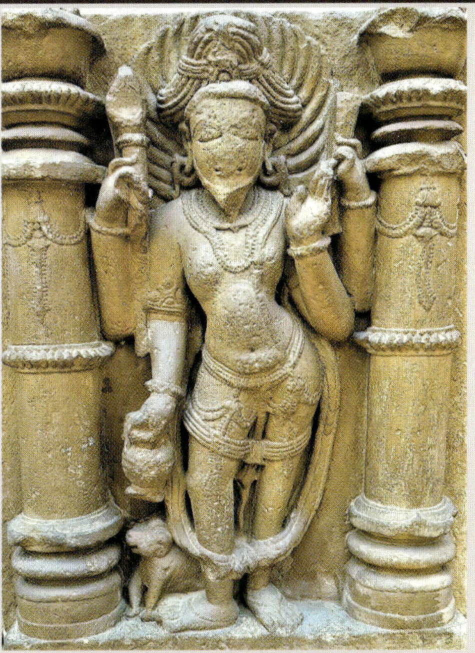

3.71: Agni, 10th century, Shivpuri, Madhya Pradesh; State Museum, Bhopal — photograph by Madhukar K Bhagat

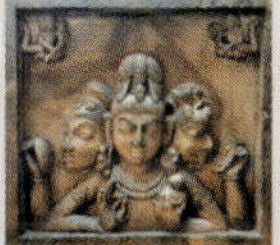

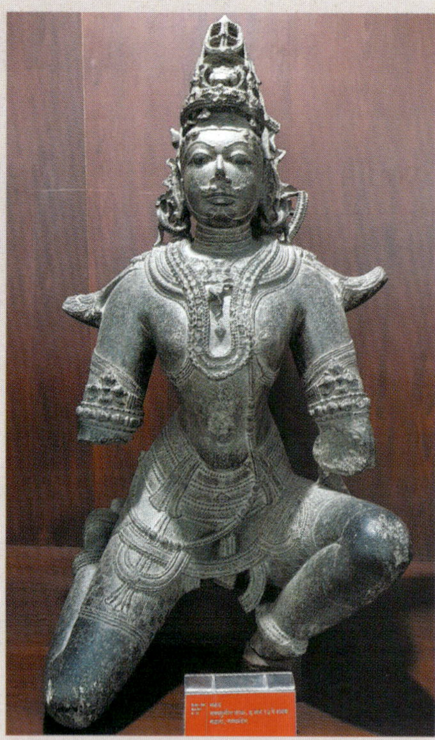

3.72: Garuda, the vehicle of Lord Vishnu, stone sculpture, 13th century Mandala, Madhya Pradesh; Central Museum, Nagpur — photograph by Madhukar K Bhagat

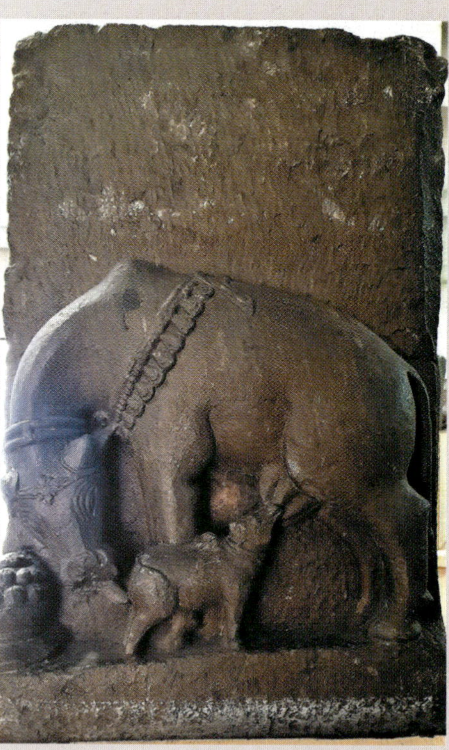

3.73: A sculptural panel depicting Kamadhenu and her calf. Kamadhenu also known as Surabhi, is the bovine goddess and the endower of plenty. A sculpture on stone, 12th century, Mandsaur, Madhya Pradesh; State Museum, Bhopal — photograph by Madhukar K Bhagat

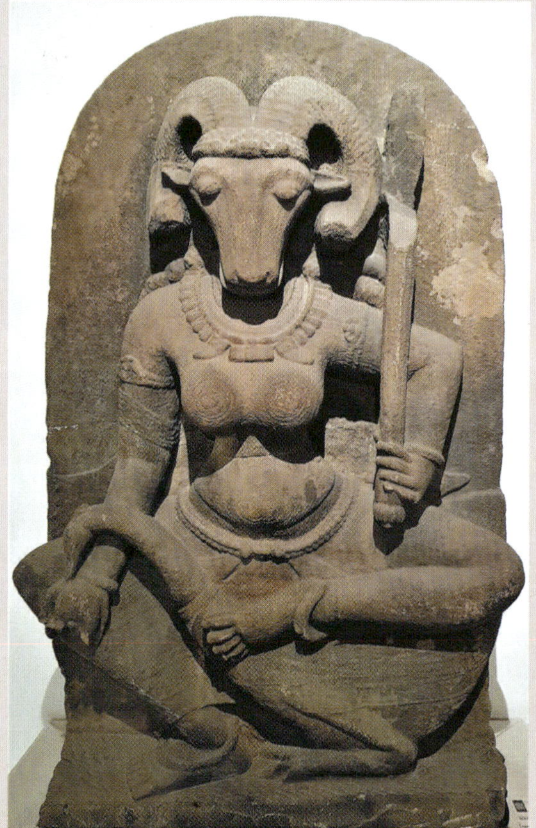

3.74: Yogini Vrishanana, 10th-11th Pratihara dynasty, Banda, Uttar Pradesh, National Museum, New Delhi — photograph by Madhukar K Bhagat

Yoginis are female divinities, a part of the yogini cult that emanated between the 6th to 10th centuries CE, with 64 such yogini divinities. They may also be depicted in animal forms with human figures and animal heads. The Vrishanana Yogini (buffalo-headed Yogini) is depicted seated in '*lalitasana*', holding a club in the left hand and a '*bilva*' fruit (bael or wood apple) in the right. The representation is plain and bereft of the ornamentation usually associated with the deities.

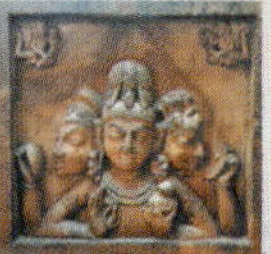

4

Buddhism: The Middle Path

> *"From craving springs grief, from craving springs fear, for him who is wholly free from craving, there is no grief, much less fear."*
>
> **Dhammapada Verse. 216**

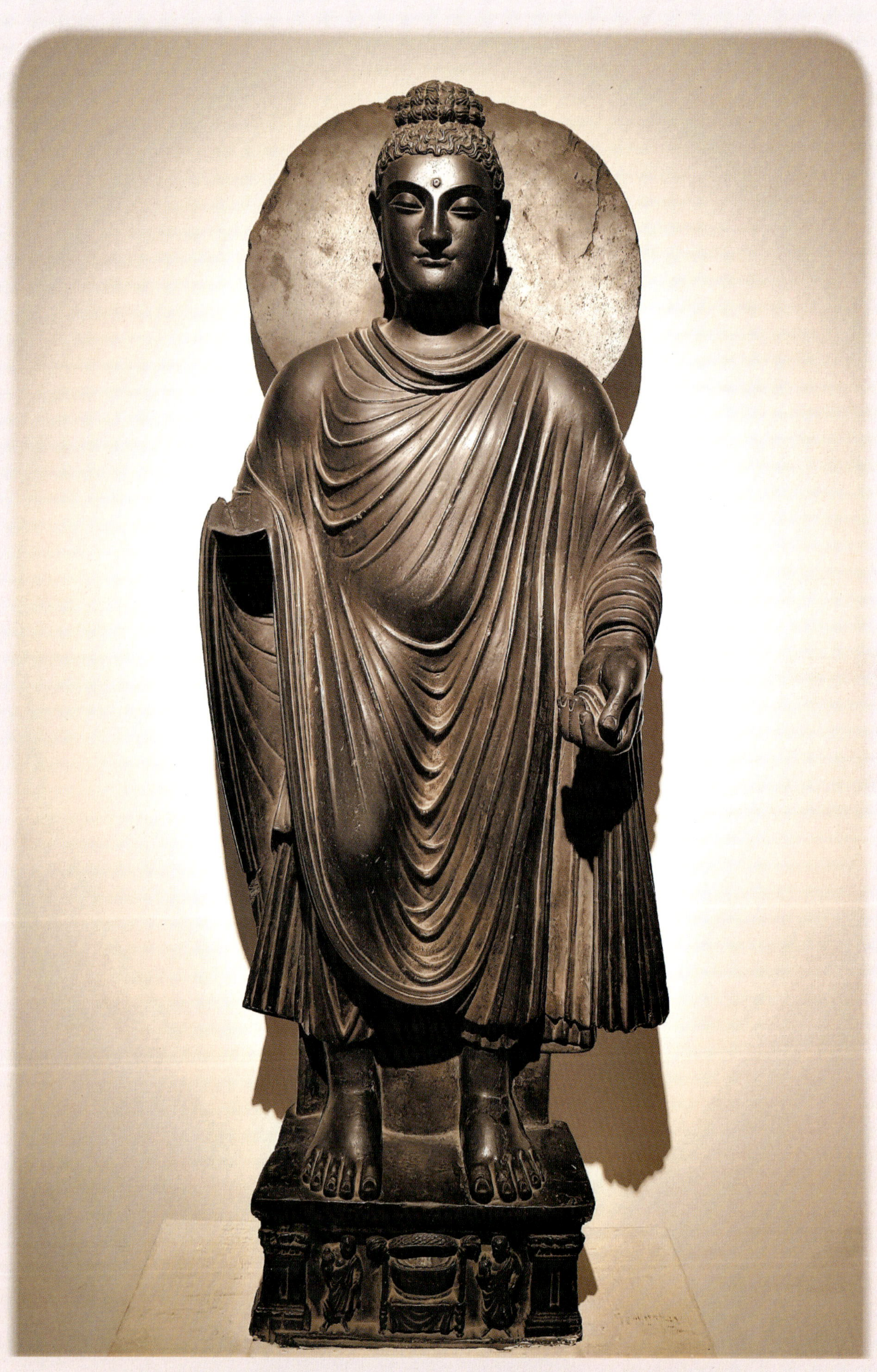

4.1: A serene standing Buddha in meditation, a sculpture in schist, Gandhara School, 2nd century CE, National Museum, New Delhi — photograph by Madhukar K Bhagat

AN INTRODUCTION

Buddhism is the fourth largest religion in the world having nearly 500–550 million followers (7%–8% of the world population). It is concentrated largely in Asia, with the maximum Buddhist presence in China in terms of absolute numbers (24.5 million followers, i.e nearly 18% of the country's population. However as a percentage of a country's population, Cambodia (97.9%) Thailand (94.5%) Myanmar (87.9%) Bhutan (75%) Sri Lanka (70.2%), and Japan (69.8%) are countries having a majority Buddhist presence.

Buddhism as a religion was founded by Gautama Buddha in the 6th century BCE in India. It has a history of more than 2500 years, making it one of the oldest living religions in the world along with Hinduism, Judaism, and Jainism It is divided into numerous sects, viz. Mahayana, Hinayana, Vajrayana, and Theravada. It has a rich philosophy captured in the Tripitakas and other Buddhist scriptures. These texts also throw light on the history of the religion and the regions, indicating the profound impact on art, culture, and other social aspects of the countries where Buddhism had flourished.

A BRIEF HISTORY

Origin of Buddhism

The history of Buddhism falls under the category of recorded history (unlike early Hinduism). Events and occurrences have been found to be recorded in the various Buddhist texts and accounts of travellers and writers like **Faxian** and **Xuanzang**. Further, inscriptions and edicts of emperor Ashoka and other kings which survive to this day on stupas, chaityas, and other rock inscriptions serve as an important source of information about Buddhism.

As per the accepted historical account, Buddhism originated in the teachings of Buddha (also referred as **Gautama, Siddhartha, Shakyamuni,** and **Tathagata**). He was born in 563 BCE to King Suddhodhana (a Sakya ruler/head of Sakya clan of Kapilavastu) and Mayadevi, in Lumbini (in present day Nepal). He was named Siddhartha, with Gautama being the family name. After the death of his mother (seven days after his birth), he was raised by his foster mother Prajapati Gautami (younger sister of Maya devi) to whom king Suddhodhana got married. It is said that owing to the predictions of seers, that he would either become a great king or a great sage, his father restricted his life to the comforts of the palace. He was married to Yashodhara and had a son Rahul.

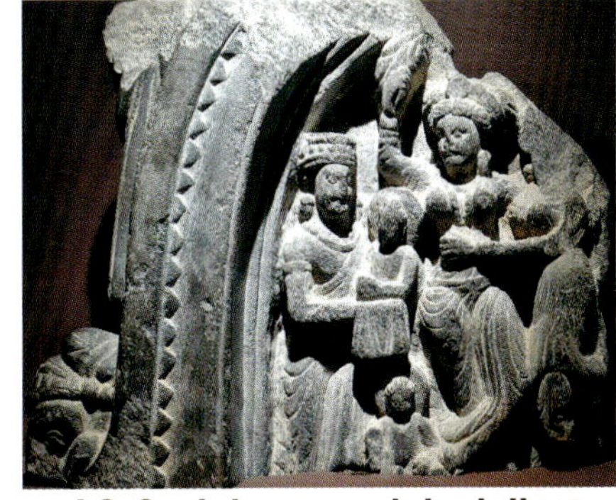

4.2: Sculpture panel depicting the birth of Buddha at Lumbini; Mayadevi is depicted standing while holding the branches of a sal tree; Chhatrapati Shivaji Maharaj Vastu Sangrahalaya, Mumbai — photograph by Madhukar K Bhagat

Once in a venture outside the palace, the sight of a sick man, an old man, a corpse, and a monk (referred to as the **'four sights'**) deeply influenced him. With the first three sights, came the realisation of existence of sorrow, impermanence of material world and its pleasures, the inexorable nature of life and the universal ailments of humanity. The fourth, personified to him the possible means to overcome the sorrow and suffering, and to attain calm and peace. These four sights urged him to give up his worldly life, family and kingdom in pursuit of the truth, which could emancipate one from its sufferings and impermanence. This was the **Great Renunciation** and the second important event of his life (the first being his birth).

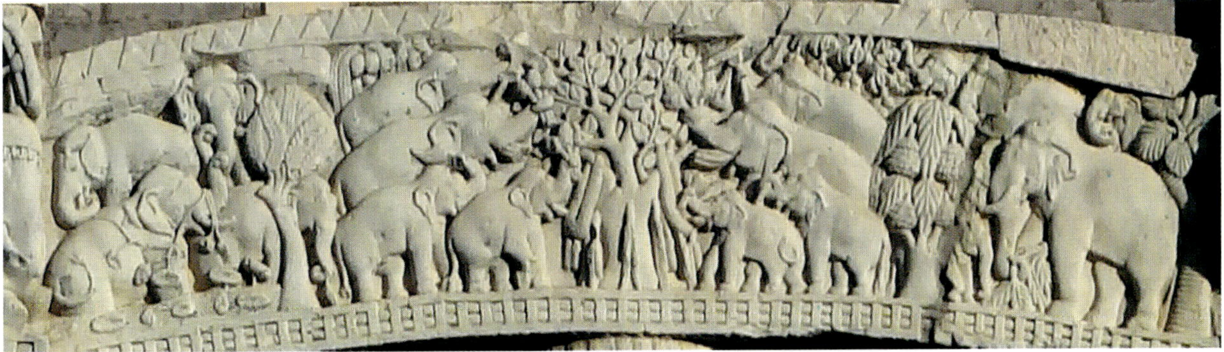

4.3: Gateway panel frieze, Sanchi stupa, representing Buddha's enlightenment — photograph by Madhukar K Bhagat

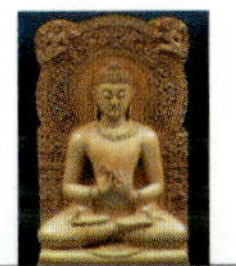

Buddha is said to have renounced the world at the age of 29. After nearly six years of relentless asceticism and meditation, Gautama attained enlightenment in Bodh Gaya (presently in Bihar State, India) under a pipal tree (called the Bodhi tree) and hence became Buddha—one who is enlightened. This was the next of the most important events of Buddha's life.

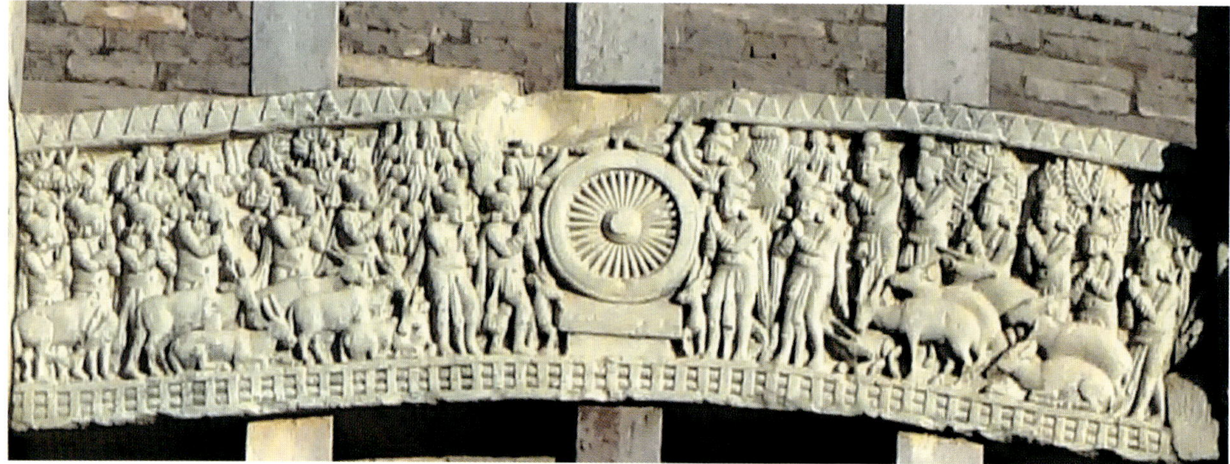

4.4: Gateway panel frieze, Sanchi stupa, representing dharmachakra pravartana — photograph by Madhukar K Bhagat

He delivered his first sermon to his five disciples at Sarnath (Varanasi), an event called the *Dharmachakra Pravartana* or the 'turning of the wheel of law' (the fourth of the important events). This marks a formal beginning of the Buddhist religion. This was also the beginning of the Sangha (or the order of monks).

Buddha spent the rest of his life in preaching in different parts of the country—largely in Magadha and Kosala Mahajanapadas. At the age of 80, he attained Mahaparinirvana (the last of the important events) at Kusinagara (in present day Uttar Pradesh).

Spread of Buddhism

Buddhism soon spread in India and in different parts of South Asia and Southeast Asia. The factors existing in the Indian society, viz., excessive emphasis on ritualism, Brahmanical superiority and caste system on one hand, and simple teachings of Buddhism with emphasis on ahimsa, equality, compassion, and ethics etc. on the other, which endeared it to the masses, helped in its growth. Further, patronage and propagation by several emperors and kings also enabled it to spread far and wide. Emperor Ashoka and his missions to Sri Lanka, Southeast Asia, China, patronage of Buddhism by Menander-I (a Bactrian king in the 2nd century BCE), by the Kushanas, particularly emperor Kanishka, (1st century CE), by Pala Kings, and by emperor Harsha (6th century CE), were important factors for its spread far and wide. However, with the decline of royal patronage beyond the reign of Harsha, and with rejuvenation and consolidation of Hinduism as a result of efforts of Shankaracharya (8th century CE) and other Hindu religious leaders, Buddhism suffered a decline in India, although it continued to spread in other countries outside it.

The Buddhist Councils and a Structure of Religion

Although the Buddhist Sangha came into existence during the lifetime of Buddha, the four Buddhist councils which were held much later, helped in better organising the Sangha and the Buddhist texts, structuring them and spreading the teachings of Buddha.

Ancient Buddhist Councils

The **first Buddhist Council** took place in 483 BCE in Rajgriha after Buddha's death. It was presided by **Mahakashyapa**, a disciple of Buddha, and took place under the **patronage of king Ajatashatru of Magadha**. The **Vinaya Pitaka** (book of monastic rules and discipline) was compiled under the supervision of disciple Upali and the **Sutta Pitaka** (sermons/teachings of Buddha under disciple Anand) was compiled in this council.

However, some scholars question the veracity of this council ever having taken place. Another school of thought believes that just after Buddha's death, the compilation of the *Vinaya Pitaka*, *Sutta Pitaka* and *Abhidhama Pitaka* (book of Buddhist philosophies) was done at Vesali (Pali for Vaishali, which is near modern Patna) by a group of senior monks.

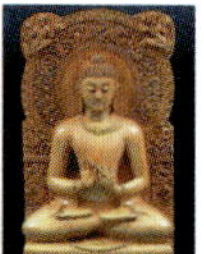

The **second Buddhist Council** took place in **Vaishali (Bihar) in 383 BCE** around 100 years after the death of Buddha, where schism between **Sthaviravadins** and **Mahasamghikas** took place. It is generally agreed by the scholars that this council indeed took place and was a historical event. The second council was held during the reign of king Kalasoka (of Shisunaga dynasty) and was presided over by monk Sabkami.

The points of debate in this second council were pertaining to relaxation of rules of monastic order as enshrined in the *Vinaya Pitaka*. It is said that there were around ten points of deliberation for the council, chief among them was the acceptance of money (gold and silver) as donation by the *bhikshus*. While the group which rejected any changes was called **Sthaviravadin**, the other group was **Mahasanghika**.

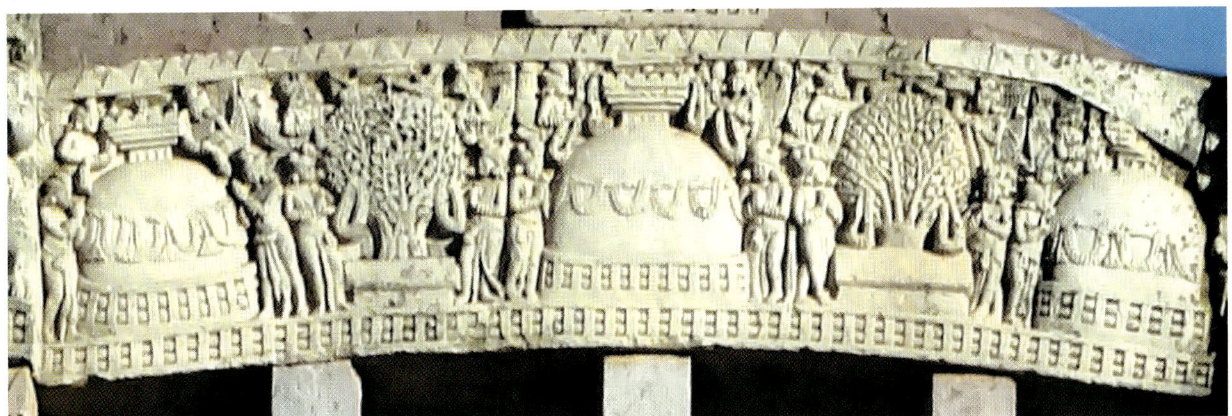

4.5: Gateway panel frieze Sanchi stupa representing *Mahaparinirvana* — photograph by Madhukar K Bhagat

The third council took place under the patronage of emperor Ashoka in 247 BCE in Pataliputra and was presided by **Moggaliputta Tissa**. This council helped in the revision of the Buddhist scriptures and consolidation of their teachings.

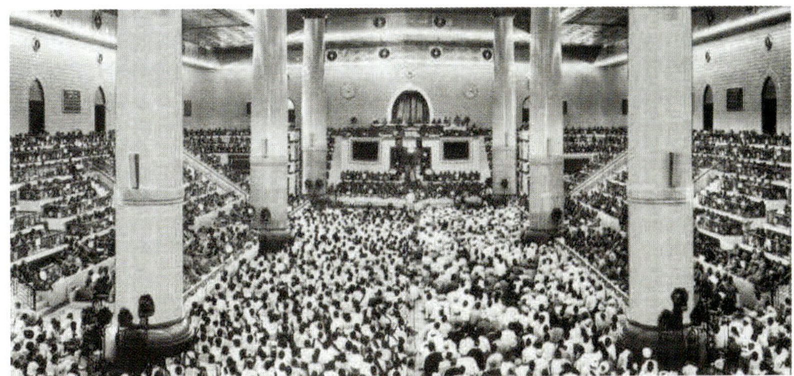

4.6: The Sixth Buddhist Council in Rangoon — Wikimedia Commons

Different accounts of this council exist in different schools, with a possibility of several third councils. But there is agreement that it did take place in Pataliputra under the patronage of king Ashoka.

Apart from consolidation of the teachings of Buddhism, one of the objectives was to purge the Sangha of some opportunistic monks who were lured by the prospect of the patronage of the royal court. As per some accounts, this council also brought out differences and led to the emergence of **Vibhajyvadins** (believer of the doctrine of analysis) and **Sarvastavadin** (believers in the doctrine of 'all is real')

The **fourth and last of the ancient councils** took place during the reign of emperor Kanishka in Kashmir and was presided by **Asvaghosa** and **Vasumitra**. Here, the division of Buddhism into **Mahayana** (larger vehicle), and **Hinayana** (smaller vehicle), took place.

For this council also, different accounts are in vogue as per different schools of Buddhism. As per one view, the council took place under the patronage of King Kanishka in 73 CE in Kashmir. The council was attended by nearly five hundred monks, who, over a period of 12 years, compiled over three lakh verses and translated the canonical documents from Prakrit to Sanskrit. The **Sarvastivada** school no longer in existence now, was henceforth inherited by the Mahayana Buddhism.

An account of another fourth council of Theravada school, having taken place in Sri Lanka, is also available. This Council is said to have taken place in Alu Vihara in Sri Lanka around the 1st century BCE. At that time, a severe famine in the country had resulted in the deaths of several monks. As the scriptures in Pali canon were existent in oral tradition till then, it was decided to consign it to writing, lest many of those were lost to the future generations.

Modern Buddhist Councils

The **fifth and sixth** councils took place in modern times under the patronage of Theravada Buddhist school. The fifth council in 1871 in Mandalay, Burma, was attended by over 2400 monks. The objective was to examine and approve of the entire **Tripitakas**. A joint recitation of the scriptures is said to have

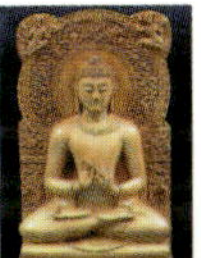

taken for nearly five months, post which, the inscription of the **Tripitakas** was done in over 729 marble slabs to preserve them for posterity.

The last and the sixth council in 1954 was also under the Theravada school and took place in Yangoon, formerly Rangoon (Burma). It commemorated 2500 years of Lord Buddha's **Parinibbana**. The objective of this council was also to affirm and preserve the canons of Vinaya and Dhamma Pitakas. The entire canons were read in this Council also.

BUDDHIST TEACHINGS AND PHILOSOPHY: A PERSPECTIVE OF SPIRITUAL RATIONALISM

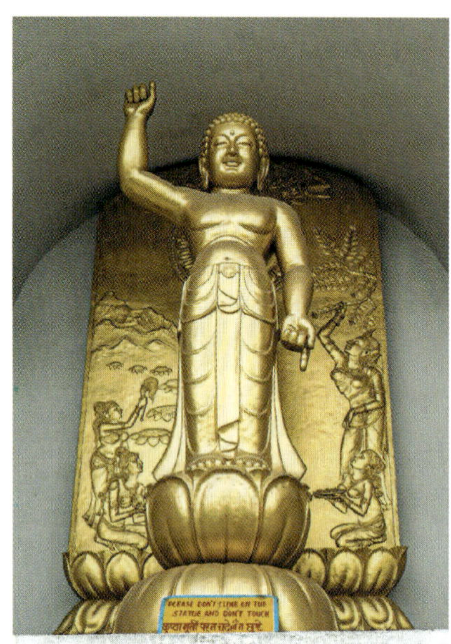

4.7: Buddha proclaiming the truth, Vishwa Shanti Stupa, Vaishali — photograph by Madhukar K Bhagat

The core of the Buddhist teachings is found in the scriptures called the Pitakas and in particular the *Sutta Pitaka*. The foundation of the Buddhist teachings and philosophies is contained in the principle of the Middle path, the recognition of the Four Noble Truths and practices of the Eight-fold path.

The Middle Path

The principle of the Middle Path emphasizes on a life of neither self-indulgence nor of extreme ascetism. Buddha himself relinquished the worldliness and its pleasures for the search of the emancipating truth. His earlier worldly life of gratification of senses and fulfilment of bodily desires could not endow him the Truth he was yearning for. But despite the severest of penances and ascetic practices for many years, the Truth still eluded him. Having given up self mortification, eventually Buddha acquired the true knowledge while meditating under the Bodhi tree in Bodh Gaya. Thus, Buddha's own attainment of the true knowledge is a testimony to avoiding of either extremes and following the principle of the middle path.

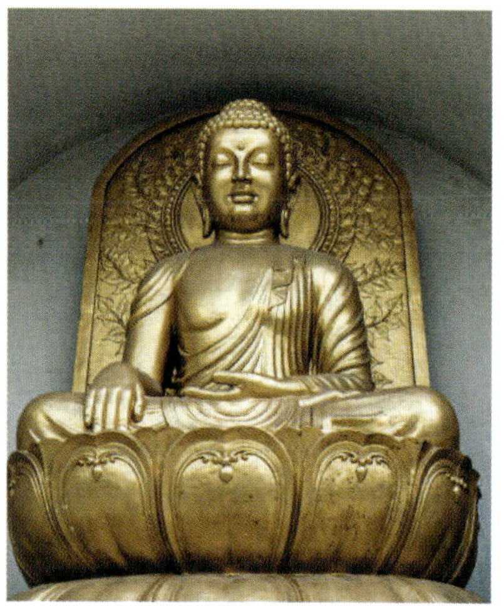

4.8: A meditating Buddha in Bhumisparsha Mudra; Vishwa Shanti Stupa, Vaishali — photograph by Madhukar K Bhagat

The Four Noble Truths

'Chatvari Arya Satyani' (in Sanskrit) or **Ariya-sacca** (in Pali) or 'The Four Noble Truths', can truly be said to be the nucleus of the Buddhist philosophy. Expressed simply, these truths are;

(I) **The world is transient and impermanent (Anicca)** and human existence is not eternal **(Anatta)** and is **filled with sorrow (Dukkha)**. All are subject to birth **(jati)**, and consequently to decay **(jara)**, disease **(vyadhi)**, and finally to death **(marana)**. No one is exempt from these four inevitable causes of suffering.

(II) **Desire** (craving) **or attachment (trishna** in **Sanskrit** and **tanha** in **Pali) is the root cause of sorrow**. It is this desire (craving), gross or subtle, that leads to repeated births in **Samsara** (manifested world) and makes one cling to all forms of life and thus experience the **Dukkha**.

The Philosophy of the Middle Path and the Tale of Sujata

The principle of the Middle Path and the story of Sujata are both inextricably linked and central to this Buddhist philosophy. Gautama, having decided to discover the emancipating truth, initially sought the divine knowledge from two learned sages of that age, **Alara Kalama** and later from **Uddaka Ramaputta**. But despite having realised the highest form of techniques of concentration in the company of the venerable masters, Gautama was far from satisfied, for it did not reveal the ultimate truth he was yearning for. Having parted their company and treading the path of austerity, Gautama eventually reached a forest grove near the town of Uruvela (near present day Bodh Gaya). He immersed himself in the highest form of asceticism whereby he was reduced to mere skin and bones. And yet the ultimate truth eluded him. Here he was closely followed by five sages, who seeing the extreme austerity practised by him, believed in his eventual success of discovering that redeeming truth.

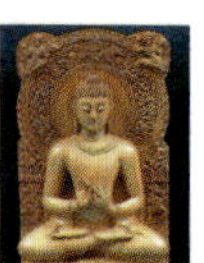

Sujata, the daughter of the chief of the local milkman tribe, who had prayed for a virtuous husband and a son to a 'tree spirit' and had been granted both the boons, had come to offer her obeisance to the tree spirit. But observing the emaciated Buddha, she believed him to be the living tree spirit **(deva)** and offered him **kheer** (porridge of milk and rice).

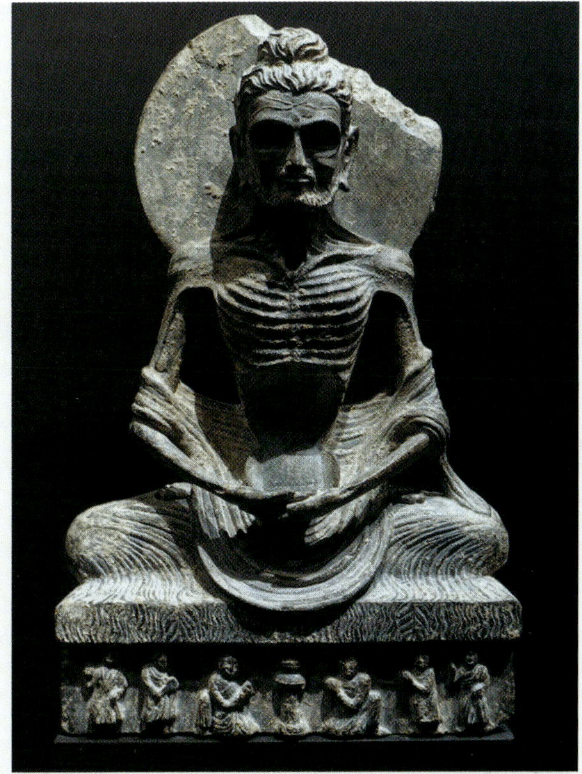

4.9: The fasting Buddha, receiving the gift of Sujata in the bottom relief (Gandhara, 2nd century CE) Linden-Museum, Stuttgart, Germany — Wikimedia Commons

Gautama, whose physical frame was devoid of any energy, sapped by the severe penances, accepted the offering and experienced a new wave of thought and energy flowing in himself. Thus, he ended six years of extreme austerity which could not bestow upon him the true knowledge. However, disappointed by his renouncing of the path of asceticism, the five disciples distrusted his ability to discover that emancipating truth and eventually abandoned his company.

However, Gautama realised the futility of severe penances (which made his being weak) and consciousness too feeble, to discover the path of salvation. Henceforth, he tread on the Middle Path, of avoiding either extremes and eventually attained the true knowledge, thus becoming a Buddha.

The story of Sujata has however many versions. In one, she offers the porridge which is accepted by Buddha. In another, while Buddha is lost in meditation, she prays in a local song, the words of which mean that let not the strings of **veena** (a stringed instrument) be too taut lest it breaks, or it be too loose, for then it may not play. Thus, it underlines the message of Middle Path.

In another parable, Sujata offers Buddha the **kheer** in a golden bowl. Buddha, having partaken the **kheer**, resolves to tread the Middle Path. He throws the golden bowl in the middle of a river, saying that if he is to succeed in his endeavour, then let the bowl float upstream. The bowl indeed flows upstream and in the middle of the river, signifying the golden Middle Path which was against the extant/current belief of both asceticism and material indulgence.

Having become Buddha, Tathagata delivered his first sermon at deer park Sarnath, to the very same five disciples who had abandoned him. The event is referred as the **Dharmachakra Pravartana** or setting in motion the 'wheel of law'.

(III) To end sorrow, one must control desire. By elimination of all forms of cravings and renouncing all worldly attachments, one can attain **Nibanna (Nirvana)** and then there can be cessation of suffering.

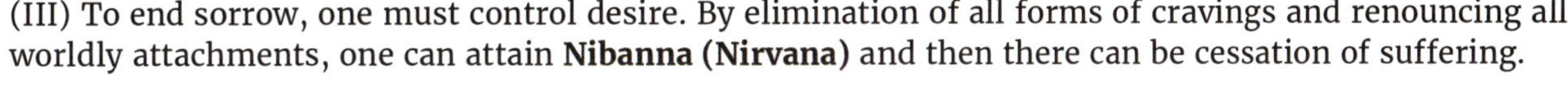

(IV) To control desire, one must follow the Eightfold path.

In certain texts the four noble truths are also summarised as; existence of sorrow or **dukkha**, cause of sorrow or **samudaya**, the removal of sorrow or **nirodh**, and the way leading to it or **marga**.

Desire, the Fountainhead of Grief: Second Noble Truth

"From craving springs grief, from craving springs fear, for him who is wholly free from craving, there is no grief, much less fear."

Dhammapada Verse. 216

The Victory Over Mara

Buddha's victory over the demon 'Mara' (referred also as Mara Vijaya) is a poignant theme in Buddhist philosophy, scriptures and art, symbolizing the Buddha's vanquishing of those negative forces which are an impediment to acquiring true knowledge and enlightenment. In essence, it represents Buddha's own tryst with and overcoming of the elements of negativity, attachment and bondage, which result in the cyclicality of life and thus are a cause of suffering (dukkha).

The word 'Mara' is derived from the Sanskrit word *mar* or *mrit*, meaning death, decay or destruction, and again rebirth. Thus, the demon Mara represents death and the destruction of true knowledge, causing the sentient being to be trapped in the relentless cycle of birth and deaths and experience decay and destruction in the process.

Reference of Mara is first found in *Padhana Sutta* of *Samyutta Nikaya* of the *Sutta Pitaka* and also detailed accounts are contained in Jataka commentaries. In the Buddhist mythology, Mara is a celestial demonic king, who represents death and temptation. He is also referred as Namuchi (one from whom no one can escape) and Vasavatti (one, who rules all). He is an antagonist to enlightenment and is also considered a tempter for the seekers of true knowledge, dissuading them by evil means of allurement, attachment, greed, fear and other vicious measures.

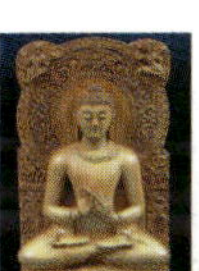

As per the traditional Buddhist legend, Gautama, while contemplating under the Bodhi tree is attacked by tenfold armies of Mara comprising fearsome and loathsome demons. This army represents aversion, hunger, thirst, craving, sloth and torpor, cowardice, doubt, hypocrisy and stupidity, false glory and conceit. Mara himself directs his armies in his four forms. (as per some texts it is five forms). These forms are; *Maacumara* or *Mrityumara* (representing death and destruction); *Skandhamara* or *Khandamara*, who represesnts conditioned existence and the five aggregates, *rupa* (form), *vedana* (feeling), *samajana* (perception), *samskara* or *sankara* (volition) and *vijnana* (consciousness); *kilesamara* or *klesamara*, representing impure emotions of greed, hatred lust etc. and finally *Devaputra-mara* or *Devaputta-mara*, who represents the sensuous realm or *kama*.

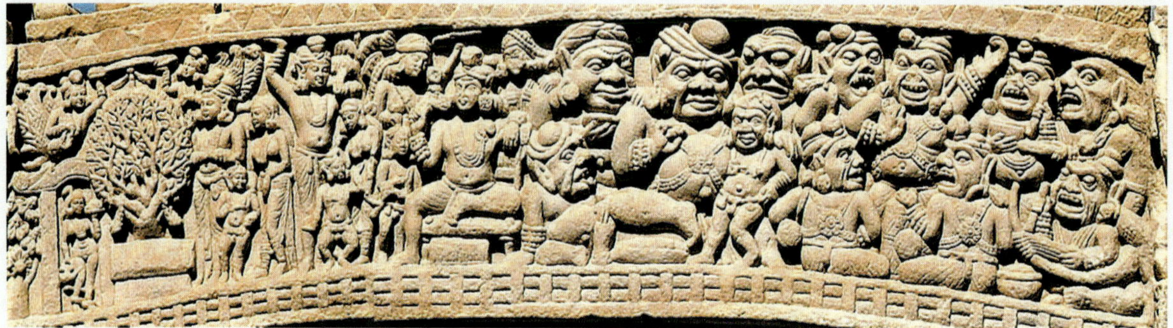

4.10: A frieze at northern gateway, Sanchi Stupa; Temptation of the Buddha; Mara and his daughters and other demons attacking Buddha — photograph by Madhukar K Bhagat

Despite the vicious attack of the fearsome demons, Buddha remains completely unperturbed. His serenity and spiritual aura simply repel all the attacks. He, as Boddhisatava in previous births, had acquired 10 *paramis* (paramita) or perfections which annihilate each fold of Mara's army. These *paramis* are *dana* (generosity), *sila* (morality), *nekhamma* (renunciation), *panna* (wisdom), *viriya* (energy), *khanti* (forbearance), *sacca* (truthfulness), *adhitthana* (resolution), *metta* (compassion, loving kindnesss) and *upekkha* (equanimity).

Having thus lost to Buddha, Mara then unleashes his three daughters on him, who, through sheer sensuousness, try to entice Buddha. These daughters are *Tanha* (craving), *Arati* (discontentment and aversion) and *Raga* (attachment, desire, greed and passion). But their onslaught is utterly futile as Buddha does not even take note of them.

As per the legend, Mara then questions the authority of Buddha to be seated in the place he was contemplating (symbolic of questioning Buddha's overcoming of the earthly bonds and attaining enlightenment) and asks him to vacate the seat for Mara. To this, Buddha asks the Earth (as he had no other witness), to bear the testimony of his having overcome all the negativity and of attaining enlightenment. This, Buddha does by touching the earth by his middle finger while in contemplation (referred to as Bhumisparsha mudra). The earth bears the testimony to his being a Tathagata (one who is beyond the worldly-transitory phenomenon). Hearing this the world resounds in his victory (celestial being who witnessed this victory).

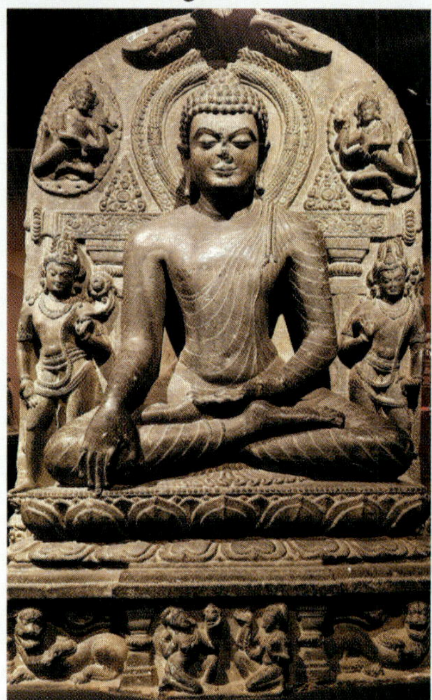

4.11: Buddha in Bhumisparsha Mudra, medieval period, Bihar Museum — photograph by Madhukar K Bhagat

Essence of Mara's Conversation with Buddha

Another perspective on the Mara Vijaya is the conversation of Buddha with Mara contained in Buddhist scriptures. While performing severe penances, Gautama was drained of his energy, reduced to a mere skeleton and on the brink of death of his mortal body. At this juncture he was approached by Mara. The conversation of Mara (his enticement) and Buddha's rebuffing of such inducements, is described in the **Padhana Sutta** in Pali canon and is as below.

Mara to Buddha:

"You are lean and deformed. Near to you is death. A thousand parts (of you belong) to death; to life (there remains) but one. Live, O good sir! Life is better. Living, you could perform merit. By leading a life of celibacy and making fire sacrifices, much merit could be acquired. What will you do with this striving? Hard is the path of striving, difficult and not easily accomplished."

Buddha's response to Mara:

"O Evil One, kinsman of the heedless! You have come here for your own sake.

Even an iota of merit is of no avail. To them who are in need of merit it behoves you, Mara, to speak thus.

Confidence (saddha), self-control (tapa), perseverance (viriya), and wisdom (panna) are mine. Me, who am thus intent, why do you question about life? Even the streams of rivers will this wind dry up. Why should not the blood of me who am thus striving dry up? When blood dries up, the bile and phlegm also dry up. When my flesh wastes away, more and more does my mind get clarified. Still more do my mindfulness, wisdom, and concentration become firm.

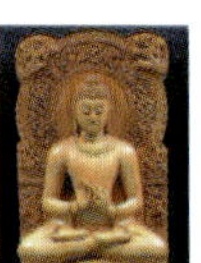

While I live thus, experiencing the utmost pain, my mind does not long for lust! Behold the purity of a being! Sense-desires (kama) are your first army. The second is called aversion for the holy life (arati). The third is hunger and thirst (khuppipasa). The fourth is called craving (tanha). The fifth is sloth and torpor (thina-middha). The sixth is called fear (bhiru). The seventh is doubt (vicikiccha), and the eighth is detraction and obstinacy (makkha-thambha). The ninth is gain (lobha), praise (siloka) and honour (sakkara), and that ill-gotten fame (yasa). The tenth is the extolling of oneself and contempt for others (attukka sana-paravambhana).

This, Namuchi, is your army, the opposing host of the Evil One. That army the coward does not overcome, but he who overcomes obtains happiness.

*This Munja*do I display! What boots life in this world! Better for me is death in the battle than that one should live on, vanquished!*

Some ascetics and brahmins are not seen plunged in this battle. They know not nor do they tread the path of the virtuous.

Seeing the army on all sides with Mara arrayed on elephant, I go forward to battle. Mara shall not drive me from my position. That army of yours, which the world together with gods conquers not, by my wisdom I go to destroy as I would an unbaked bowl with a stone.

Controlling my thoughts, and with mindfulness well-established, I shall wander from country to country, training many a disciple. Diligent, intent, and practising my teaching, they, disregarding you, will go where having gone they grieve not."

**Munja is grass crest, worn by warriors on their head or banners signifying that they will not retreat from the battlefield.*

The Eightfold Path

While the four noble truths form the philosophical base of Buddhism, the Eightfold Path or the Noble Eightfold Path (*Arya Ashtanga Marga* in Sanskrit, or *Ariya Atthangika Magga* in Pali) forms the core of the Buddhist practices and lays the foundation for ethics, morality, appropriate thought, knowledge and conduct. Each of these paths is prefixed with the word *samma* (in Pali), or *samyak* (in Sanskrit), which signifies right, proper or most appropriate. The word *arya*, or noble, is not descriptive of the paths, rather it is of the people who tread them. Thus the eightfold path was the way of noble men. The eight spokes in the Dharma Chakra (wheel of law) symbolize this set of Eightfold path.

(a) Right Understanding or Right View (Samyak Drishti or Sammā Ditthi): The right understanding means having a comprehension of the right or appropriate knowledge which is the understanding of the four Noble truths. Thus, the understanding of the reason for sorrow, the role of karma in the cycle of birth and death and the path to be tread for liberation, was the first milestone in this journey of emancipation or Nibanna. Eventually, it is the right knowledge which brings forth clarity of thought and leads one to the second factor of the Eighfold path, 'the Right Thoughts'.

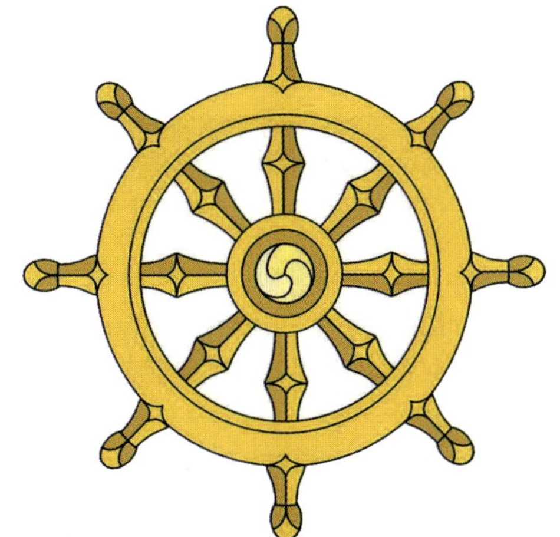

4.12: Buddhist Dharmachakra with eight spokes — Wikimedia Commons

(b) Right Thoughts (Samyak Samkalpa or Samma Samkappa): Also referred as to Right Intention or Right Resolve, this is the next of the paths to be adopted. Once a person has the correct understanding of the Truth and a clarity of vision of the world,

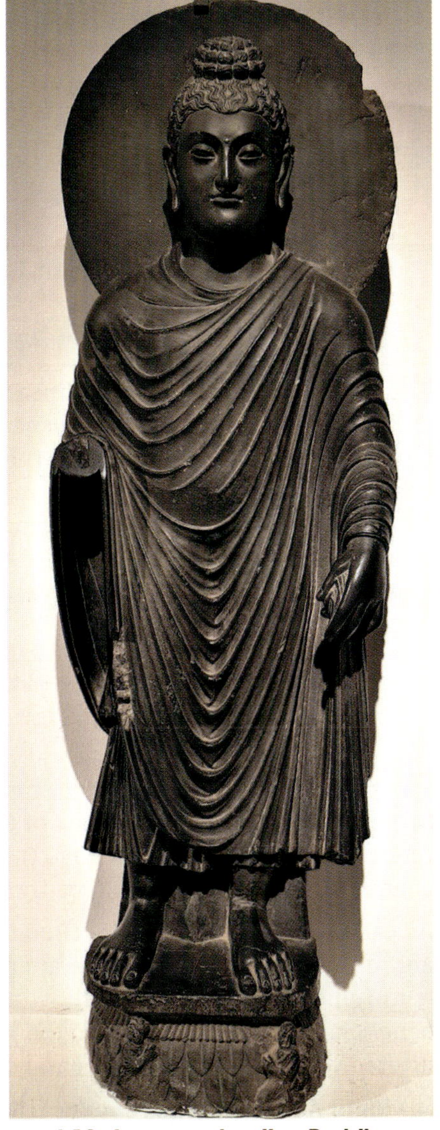

4.13: A serene standing Buddha with eyes half open, 2nd century Kushana period, Gandhara school, National Museum, New Delhi — photograph by Madhukar K Bhagat

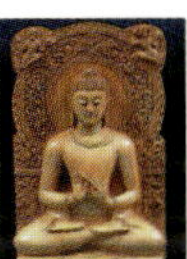

then the next step is to inculcate the right thoughts. Thoughts define as to who we are, determine our karma and enable us to adopt the right recourse for emancipation. Developing right thoughts implies inculcating the positive thoughts while eschewing the negative ones.

This path is also identified as a **three-fold step**. The initial step being renunciation of worldly pleasures, cravings, selfishness, and self-possessiveness (also referred as **Nekkhamma** in Pali). This begins with adopting the path of monkhood or similar pursuits of a renunciate.

The next step (referred as **Avyapada** in Pali) is inculcation of loving-kindness, goodwill and benevolence, as opposed to hatred, ill-will, or aversion. While the term **Vyapada** refers to the negative traits of anger, ill-will and hatred, the term **Avyapada** which literally implies non-enemity, has a positive connotation. It stands for the word **metta** (**maitri** in Sanskrit). Thus, kindness and goodwill are the positive connotations of this step.

All That We Are is the Result of Our Thoughts

manopubbangama dhamma, manosettha manomaya,
manasa ce padutthena, bhasati va karoti va,
tato nam dukkham-anveti cakkam va vahato padam

Dhammapada* verse 1

The (mental) natures are the result of what we have thought, are chieftained by our thoughts, are made up of our thoughts. If a man speaks or acts with an evil thought, sorrow follows him as a consequence, even as the wheels follow the foot of the drawer that is the ox which draws the cart.

manopubbangama dhamma, manosettha manomaya,
manasa ce pasannena, bhasati va karoti va,
tato nam sukham-anveti, chaya va anapayini.

Dhammapada verse 2

The (mental) natures are the result of what we have thought, are chieftained by our thoughts, are made up of our thoughts. If a man speaks or acts with pure thoughts, happiness follows him in consequence like a shadow that never leaves him.

**Dhammapada* is a part of *Khuddaka Nikaya of Suttapitaka,* containing sayings/ teachings of Buddha.

The final of the three steps is **Ahimsa** (**Avihimsa** in Pali), implying compassion, (**Karuna**) and harmlessness as opposed to cruelty and callousness. Thus, the concept of Ahimsa is not merely abjuring violence or harm to others, but encapsulates the positive quality of the tender compassion. This compassion was to be boundless, unceasing and not restricted to domains of identity (viz. **sangha**, **grama**, **janapada** etc). Sensitivity to the need and suffering of others and sacrificing one's own comfort, or even oneself, for others sake, were essential traits of the principle of compassion (**karuna**). Buddha's life and the story of Boddhisatvas (Budhha's prior lives) as contained in the Jataka tales embody this very virtue.

Our Thoughts: A Doorway to Emancipation or Suffering

There is no fire like lust, no grip like hate, there is no net like delusion, no river like craving.

Dhammapada verse 251

(c) Right Speech (Samyak Vacha or Samma Vacha): From right thoughts arises the right speech. This is refraining from a lie or falsehood (untruthful words) slandering, abusive words or frivolous words (idle chatter). One's speech should be truthful, polite and benficial.

As per **Abhyasutta**, Tathagata (Buddha) spoke the truth which was beneficial, words which were polite, and only at times which were appropriate. Thus, one's speech must stand the tests of beneficence, truthfulness, politeness and timeliness. An untruth was to be totally eschewed. But even a truth not beneficial and not connected to the goals was also to be avoided. However, an unpleasant truth could be uttered where it was beneficial and connected with the objective, but at the appropriate moment.

(d) Right Action or Right Conduct (Samyak Karmanta or Samma Kammanta): Right conduct exhorts the follower of the path of Dhamma of abstaining from certain negative conducts. Abstinence from killing, stealing and sexual misconduct are the 'three negatives' which must be eschewed. These misdeeds in turn emanate from craving and anger which are further fuelled by ignorance. Thus, with right knowledge and purity of mind these blemishes can be completely erased.

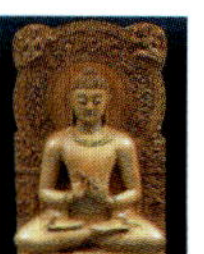

The first precept on abstaining from killing applies not just to human beings, but to all sentient life forms (having consciousness) including animals and other creatures of lower forms (except plants which are not considered to fall in this category). Thus, in a way, this precept is a practical extension of the all-encompassing principle of **ahimsa** (non-violence and non-injury) and **karuna** (compassion to all beings).

The second precept of prohibition from stealing exhorts the followers of Dhamma from not taking intentionally anything which is not offered voluntarily by the person to whom it belongs. Acquisition of anything by stealth, deceit, fraud or force is completely unworthy of a pursuer of Truth. Here the intention of a person is considered as important as the actual conduct.

The prohibition of sexual misconduct, the third of the precept, meant a complete sexual celibacy of those pursuing the strict monastic order. However, for others, this meant not having sexual conduct with someone unmarried (who is under protection of parents, guardians etc.), or married to another person (adultery) or someone prohibited by **dhamma** (viz. nuns, relatives etc.)

(e) Right Livelihood (Samyak Ajiva or **Samma Ajiva):** This precept prohibits a follower of **dhamma** from practising five kinds of trades or livelihoods. These include, trading in arms (**sattha-vanijja**), practising slavery or trading in human beings (**satta-vanijja**), trading in animal flesh (**mamsa-vanijja**), i.e. breeding animals for slaughter, trading in intoxicating drinks (**majja-vanijja**), and trading in poison (**visa-vanijja**). This precept thus extended the principle of Ahimsa into the practical realm by prohibiting any livelihood which could cause injury, suffering or killing of any sentient being.

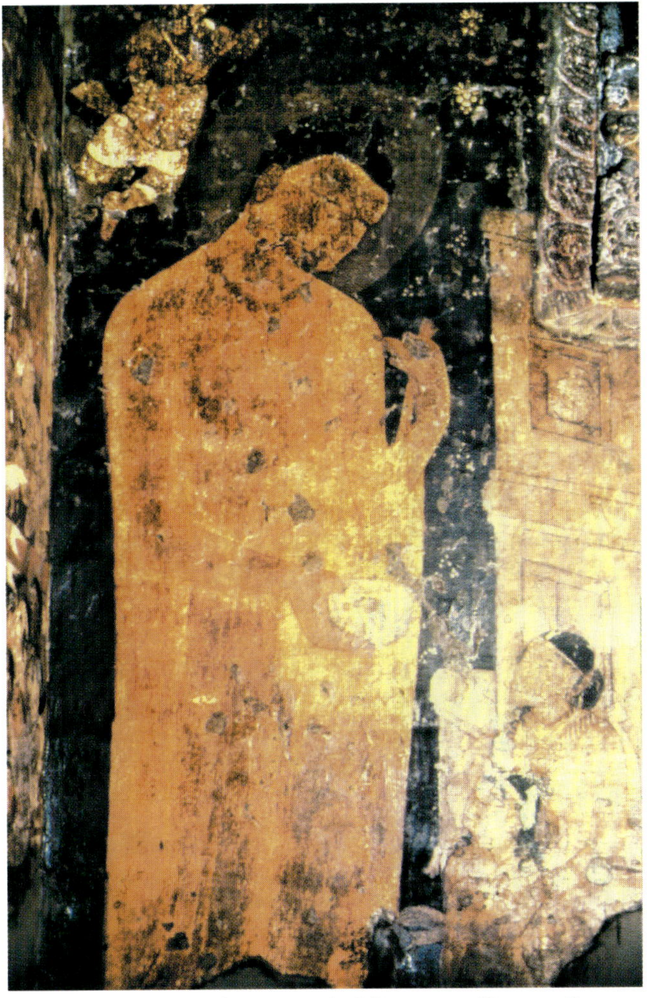

4.14: Living on alms, a part of the monastic practice of Vinaya. Buddha seeking alms from Yashodhara and Rahul; a painting in cave no. 17, Ajanta caves — Courtesy, Maharashtra Tourism Development Corporation

Rules from the *Vinaya Pitaka*: A Life of Austerity for the Monks

When a new felt (blanket/rug) has been made by a *bhikkhu*, it is to be kept for (at least) six years. If, after less than six years, he should have another new felt (blanket/rug) made, regardless of whether or not he has disposed of the first, then – unless he has been authorised by the *bhikkhus* – it is to be forfeited and confessed.

In case a *bhikkhu*, arriving at a family residence, is presented with cakes or cooked grain-meal, he may accept two or three bowlfuls if he so desires. If he should accept more than that, it is to be confessed. Having accepted the two or three bowlfuls and having taken them from there, he is to share them among the bhikkhus.

For a lay disciple, right livelihood involves abstaining from the five wrong livelihoods. But for those in the monastic order, this also meant living on alms/charity of the householders, not accepting everything donated and only keeping that what was strictly needed.

(f) Right Effort (Samyak Vayama or Samma Vayama): Right effort is a crucial precept in the path of salvation. It exhorts the seeker to endeavour for deliverance through one's own effort rather than by merely seeking refuge in others or in prayers. Simply put, right effort is prevention of evil/unwholesome states from arising, or their elimination, if they already exist. Further, it incorporates strengthening of the good existing within, and cultivation of the good which is desirable. Thus, it is composed of four steps, which are;

(*i*) the effort to discard evil/unwholesome state that has already arisen,

(*ii*) the effort to prevent the arising of un-arisen, evil/unwholesome state,

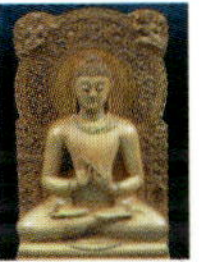

(*iii*) the effort to develop un-arisen good wholesome state, and

(*iv*) the effort to promote the good/wholesome state which has already arisen.

The guarding of senses (**indriya samvara**) and their control through conscious effort, is considered as the key to right effort. This effort also aims at overcoming the five hindrances **(panch-nivarana)** which includes, ill-will, sensual thoughts, doubts about the path to deliverance, restlessness, laziness/drowsiness. The first two hindrances are considered of more serious nature requiring a greater effort in their overcoming. While sensual thoughts emanate from desire and require restraint of the senses, ill will arises from aversion, hatred and anger. As such, control of mental faculties is essential for its subjugation.

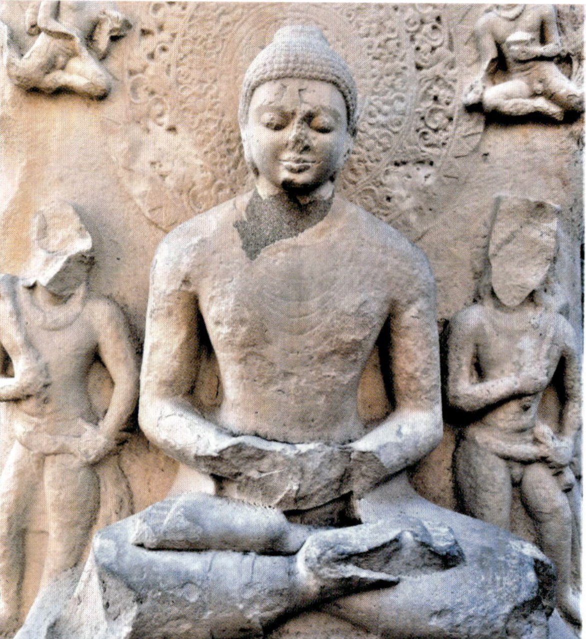

4.15: Meditating Buddha panel, depicting Buddha in Dhyan Mudra; Sanchi stupa — photograph by Madhukar K Bhagat

(g) Right Mindfulness (Samyak Smriti or Sammā Sati): With right effort comes right mindfulness. This precept enjoins the seeker to be mindful of four objects; one's body (*kayanupassana*), one's feelings (*vedananupassana*), one's thoughts (*chittanupassana*), and one's mind objects (*dhammanupassana*). Thus, right mindfulness is being attentive to all one is doing and one's different states.

The word *samyak smriti* (in Sanskrit), or *samma sati* (in Pali), originally implied appropriate memory or ability of retention. Thus, the original context of the term could have been to be retentive of/or mindful of the dhamma (the teachings). However, this mindfulness was limited not only to an absorbed state of mind akin to that in a yogic practice, but to mindfulness of the four states.

This mindfulness in turn enables the seeker to realise the transient and impermanent nature of things and to lessen their cravings. Thus, right mindfulness tends to eliminate the misconceptions with regard to desirability of objects (*shubha*), material happiness (*sukha*), permanence of worldly things (*nicca*), and immortality of being/soul (*atta*).

(h) Right Concentration or Right Samadhi (Samyak Samadhi or Samma Samadhi). The last of the eight precepts is only attained with right effort and right mindfulness. Right concentration refers to a state of single pointedness of mind. The word *samadhi* refers to the act of bringing together. Here it implies the bringing together or collectiveness of the consciousness and the faculties associated with it. Another connotation of the word *samadhi* is the word *Samatha*, which implies calmness. Thus, right concentration is a reference to the process and state of attaining singular focus of the consciousness and its concomitants on that one single object/objective.

Right concentration is also understood as going through the four stages of *dhyana*; the final stage of which is *samadhi* where the awareness and consciousness is without any object focus, and unto nothingness.

Rationality, Reasoning and Realism: The Fundamentals of Buddhist Precepts

Buddha encouraged his pupils to accept things not for the sake of mere acceptance, or for the sake of reverence for him, or because it was a stated position, but to do so if they comprehended it fully to be so, and sincerely believed in it. Thus, a rational understanding emanating from reasoning and self-belief was the cornerstone of perceiving and practising the Buddhist thoughts, evolving into a spiritual rationalism. The above perspective is best exemplified in the following words of Buddha in the *Anguttara Nikaya* *.

"This I have said to you O' Kalamas: but you may accept it not because it is the report, not because it is a tradition, not because it is so said in the past, not because it is given from the scripture, not for the sake of discussion, not for the sake of a particular method, not for the sake of careful consideration, not for the sake of forbearing with wrong views, not because it appears to be suitable, not because your preceptor is a recluse; but if you yourself understand that this is so meritorious and blameless, and, when accepted it is for benefit and happiness, then you may accept it."

**Anguttara Nikaya* is the fourth of the five *Nikayas* (collections) in the *Sutta Pittaka*.

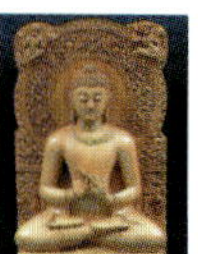

SOME SALIENT ASPECTS OF BUDDHISM

Transmigration, Karma and Nirvana

Buddhism believes in cyclicality of life and rebirth in different living forms. This conception is at the very core of the organic whole of the Buddhist philosophical system. Buddha himself recounted the stories of his previous births in human as well as in animal forms, which are compiled in the *Jatakas*, a compendium of tales of enduring values recounting Buddha's previous births.

Rebirth as sentient beings was considered an integral reality of the **Karmic** cycle and a product (the effect) of one's own actions (the cause). While **tanha** (**trishna**) or attachment, was the root cause of our clinging to the mortal form, our emancipation was possible by giving up this attachment/craving. It believed that human desire of clinging to the transient or impermanent was also the cause of our sorrow (**dukkha**) and an obstacle to one's liberation from the cycle of birth and death. Thus, **Dukkha** is not merely sorrow or suffering as understood commonly in a worldly sense. Rather, **Dukkha** here embodied the impermanent state of unsatisfaction and imperfection which eluded bliss. To overcome the **Dukkha** and attain salvation or **'Nibbana'** (**Nirvana**) which literally means extinguishing of the ego and desire, the Buddhist philosophy emphasised on righteous thought, ethical action and wisdom.

Buddha's Word on Enlightenment

The following verses of the *Dhammapada* bring out Buddha's utterance on attaining enlightenment, succinctly highlighting the root cause of dukkha, rebirths and the way of emancipation.

I have run through a course of many births looking for the maker of this dwelling (earthly form) and finding him (the cause of it) not; painful is birth again and again.

-verse 153 Dhammapada

Now are you seen, O' builder of the house (tanha or attachment), you will not build the house again. All your rafters are broken, your ridgepole is destroyed, your mind, set on the attainment of nirvana, has attained the extinction of desires.

-verse 154 Dhammapada

The eternal soul

Although Buddhism believed in the rebirths and the karmic cycle, but quite unlike some other extant belief systems, it did not believe in an eternal unchanging human soul and hence its transmigration. Its core doctrine of *anatta*, i.e. no eternal or permanent self, did not recognize the entity 'soul', which was believed by other philosophies to be enduring, the real self and the vehicle of rebirth. As to what provided the continuum from one sentient life form to another, the Buddhist conception believed in *vijnana*, or a person's consciousness, to be the basis for the cyclicality of life. This consciousness ever evolving as per the *karma*, underwent rebirth in another body and mind, experienced the attachments of life and its results thereof and the eventual death.

Milinda Panha: Rebirth Without the Transmigration of the Human Soul

The Buddhist text *Milinda Panha*, dating to 200 BCE to 100 BCE contains the conversation between the Indian- Bactrian King Milinda and the sage Nagasena. The conversation, captured as questions of King Milinda and responses of the sage, cover a diverse range of subjects, one of which is the paradox of rebirth without the soul. The sage explains as to how the body and mind is the bearer of one's deeds and is reborn without the vehicle of a soul.

King Milinda: When there is no transmigration of soul, O', venerable Nagasena, does rebirth take place?

Sage Nagasena: Yes, O' king.

King Milinda: How can that be? Give me an illustration.

Sage Nagasena: Suppose, O' King, a man was to light a lamp from another lamp, would the one lamp have transmigrated over to the other lamp?

King Milinda: Certainly not sir.,

Sage Nagasena: In the same way, O' king, does rebirth take place without anything transmigrating.

King Milinda: Give me a further illustration.

Sage Nagasena: Do you remember, O' king, having learnt, when you were a boy, some verse or other from your teacher of poetry?

King Milinda: Yes, indeed sir.

Sage Nagasena: O' king, did the verse pass over to you from your teacher?

King Milinda: No sir.

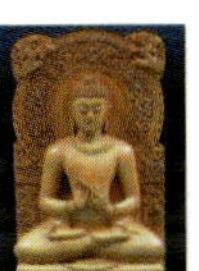

Sage Nagasena: In exactly the same way, O' king, does rebirth take place without anything transmigrating.

King Milinda: Venerable Nagasena, then what is it that is born into the next existence?

Sage Nagasena: It is mind and body that is born into the next existence.

King Milinda: Is it the same mind and body that is born into the next existence?

Sage Nagasena: O' king, it is not this same mind and body that is reborn, but with this mind and body, one does a deed which may be good, or evil. It is by reason of this deed that another mind and body is born into the next existence.

King Milinda: If it is not this very mind and body that is born into the next existence, is one not freed from one's evil deeds?

Sage Nagasena: If one were not born into another existence, one would be freed from one's evil deeds but, O king, in as much as one is born into another existence, therefore one is also not freed from one's evil deeds.

The Buddhist Concept of God

Buddha did not believe in an eternal god as a creator of the universe, nor did he consider a personal god as essential for governing it. Rather, Buddhism emphasized on the impermanent nature (**Anicca**) of the entire world and even of human existence. However, Buddhist texts do not either contain explicit denial of existence of god, as is the unambiguous postulate of non-existence an eternal, unchanging soul. Regarding the conception of an absolute God, Buddha is said to have maintained a silence, neither affirming nor unequivocally refuting the said extant belief systems. He expounded the concept of **dhamma (dharma)**, the eternal law comprising truth, righteousness and ethics, to be governing the empirical world and beyond. It is in the framework of **dhamma** that the interplay of cause and effect determines and shapes all the worlds and our lives. The following words of Buddha in **Dhammapada** best explain the causation concept in the domain of the universal law of **Dhamma**.

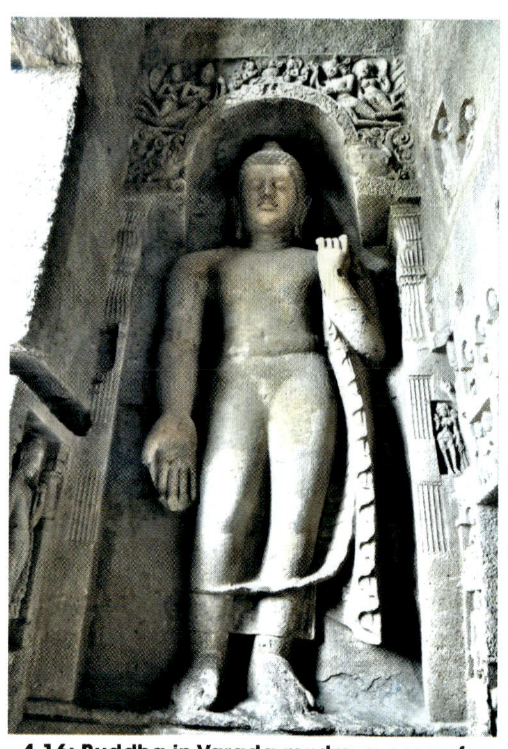

4.16: Buddha in Varada mudra, a pose of benediction; a large rockcut sculpture of Buddha at Kanheri caves, Mumbai — photograph by Madhukar K Bhagat

"Everything has a cause and produces an effect. This simple principle governs the whole universe, gods and men, heaven and earth. It is applicable not only to this vast universe stretching through boundless space, with its dazzling world systems and endless series of alternations of growth and decay, but also to the events of human life and affairs of history. If we can detect and eliminate the cause of suffering, suffering itself will disappear."

Thus, an omnipotent, personal God, was not essential in Buddha's conception of the universe or in the process of attaining of nirvana. Rather, it was replaced by the Universal law which governed the worlds.

Personal God in Buddhism

"The Buddha learnt from life around him that men never use the powers they possess to advance the good in life so long as they wait upon some agency external to themselves, to do the work they are responsible for doing. They expect the exercise of divine magic for a sudden transmutation into a higher kind of nature. Dependence on an external power has generally meant a surrender of human effort. The Buddha did not deny the existence of the popular gods, but he treated them as angels who belonged to the empirical order and needed instruction themselves. By precept and example, he was an exponent of the strenuous life. The whole course of the universe is governed by law. It is unnecessary to make the divine creator responsible for the strange disproportion in mens' lives. The Buddha rejects the conception of God as a personal being who takes sides in our struggles or a supernatural tyrant who interferes with the process of the universe. Theistic emphasis seemed to him to deprive man of his independence and make him an instrument for the realization of ends that are not human."

Dr. S. Radhakrishnan in his work **'The Dhammapada'**

Interpretation of Buddha's Silence

Many schools of thoughts debate on the issue of this conception of God and Buddha's perspective on it. While some sections assert Buddha's silence to be denial of a personal God, some even speculate as to his knowledge of the Absolute. Another school believes that the Buddha's crucial emphasis was on the

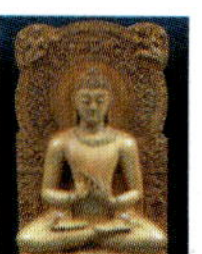

self-realization of the truth through personal effort and through the path of righteousness as the means for emancipation. This school believed that the concept of God as a super being, (where emphasis is on surrender of the personal will) undermined the crucial aspect of personal effort. This was detrimental to individual striving and an impediment to the ultimate goal of nirvana.

Another possible reason attributed by a school of thought to his silence on the conception of the Absolute, is the belief that though the Supreme God can be realised and experienced, but it cannot be described. Our senses and intellect fail to determine or describe the attributes of the Absolute which is beyond the senses and hence considered attribute-less. This is akin to the Vedantic concept of Brahma expressed as *Neti-Neti* (not this, not this) or 'That which cannot be described'.

But most importantly, the Buddhist philosophy was concerned with the process of attaining nirvana, and not in theistic conceptions, which it did not consider to be of much material consequence in advancing the very cause of emancipation.

Buddha's Perspective of Certain Theistic Conceptions Being Infructuous

The *Majjhima Nikaya* (2nd of the five *Nikayas* of the Sutta *Pitaka*, which contains the medium length discourses of Buddha), contains the anecdote of a disciple Malunkyaputta, who, desirous of advancing his emancipation by leaps, questions Buddha about his conception of certain speculative problems, as to whether the world is eternal or not and whether the world is finite or infinite. He threatens to discontinue in the order of monkhood if he does not get an answer to it. He even taunts Buddha as to say so if he does not have any conception of these issues, it would be the upright thing to say.

Buddha maintaining his calmness, counter questions the erring monk, as to whether his joining the order of monkhood was conditional upon the solution to such conceptions. The monk replies in the negative to this. Then Buddha goads the *bhikkhu* not to fritter his time and energy in matters not conducive to the moral progress and further explains to him as below.

"Whoever, Malunkyaputta, should say, 'I will not lead the holy life under the Blessed One until he elucidates these questions to me' – that person would die before these questions had ever been elucidated to him. It is as if a person were pierced by an arrow smeared with poison and his friends and relatives were to get a surgeon, and then he was to say. 'I will not have this arrow taken out until I know who was the person who wounded me, the nature of the arrow with which I was pierced, etc. That person would surely die, before this would ever be known by him. In exactly the same way whoever should say, 'I will not lead the holy life under the blessed one until he elucidated to me whether the world is eternal or not eternal, whether the world is finite or infinite...' that person would die before these questions had ever been elucidated by the Accomplished one.

"If it be the belief that the world is eternal, will there be the observance of the holy life?

In such a case – no! If it is the belief that the world is not eternal, will there be the observance of the holy life? In that case also – no! But, whether the belief be that the world is eternal or that it is not eternal, there is birth, there is old age, there is death, the extinction of which in this life itself I make known.

Malunkyaputta, I have not revealed whether the world is eternal or not eternal, whether the world is finite or infinite. Why have I not revealed these? Because these are not profitable, do not concern the bases of holiness, are not conducive to aversion, to passionless, to cessation, to tranquillity, to intuitive wisdom, to enlightenment or to Nibbana. Therefore, I have not revealed these.

However, in the decades and centuries which followed, the subsequent Buddhist thoughts were not completely impervious to such theistic conceptions. This perhaps eventually lead to the deification of Buddha himself. The latter forms of Buddhism, particularly Mahayana sect, believed Buddha himself to be an eternal god, and the other five Buddhas to be ruling the heavens and other realms of world (viz. **Amitabha, Vairochana, Akshobhaya, Ratnasambhava,** and **Amoghasiddha**). As such, Buddhism in the extant form is often not considered an atheistic religion in a strict sense.

Ushering Spiritual and Social Transformation

Ritualism, idolatory and equality

At a social level, Buddhist teachings were against **ritualism, idolatry, animal sacrifices, caste system** and even **Brahmanical orthodoxy**. It did not believe in the Vedic rituals or **karma-kanda** as a means for emancipation or **Nibanna**. The exclusive preserve of the Brahminical class over imparting of true knowledge, was completely rejected by it. The admission of women in the Sangha as **Bhikkhunis**, asserted the Buddhist philosophy of women being fully capable of achieving that exalted state of a knowledgeable one. In a way, it endowed them, equal social rights and status within the Buddhist realm. Once in the Buddhist Sangha, the caste and class distinction too were obliterated and inclusiveness and equality prevailed. Thus, it questioned the extant social status quo and its relevance vis– a vis spiritual progress, social well-being and individual goodness.

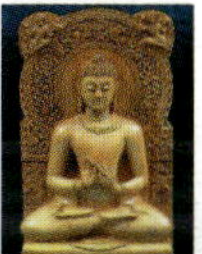

Emphasis on ahimsa

Buddhist teachings also emphasised on **Ahimsa** or non-violence, both at the individual and social realm. The practice of animal sacrifices at yagnas was completely rejected and the principle of Ahimsa coupled with Karuna (boundless and loving compassion) formed the very basis of ethical conduct. The guiding precepts of Right Action and Right Livelihood, forming the key tenets of ethical conduct (*sila*–morality) in the Eightfold Path, embodied this very principle. However, Buddhism was more moderate as compared to Jainism in the extent and strictness to which Ahimsa and its edicts were to be implemented or even asceticism was to be adopted.

Sangha and Entry of Women

The Sangha, or the religious order of Buddhist monks, did not initially permit the entry of women in its fold. However, on request and mediation of Ananda, one of the chief disciples of Buddha, women were allowed in the Sangha. The women were referred to as the **Bhikkhunis**. Buddha's foster mother **Mahapajapati Gotami** was the first woman to be initiated in the order. Many of the women in the order later became **Theris**, women who had attained liberation and were thus respected. **Therigatha**, a compilation of verses composed by elder Bhikhunnis and Theris is also a part of *Sutta Pitaka* and is contained in the *Khuddaka Nikaya*. In Pali canon it contains 73 poems.

Social inclusiveness

Most significantly, Buddhism brought to the fore a more **inclusive social philosophy** as well as its actual practice. Its unwavering belief in equality of all and their potential redemption, offered hope of emancipation to its followers. While the Sangha accepted Mahaprajapati Gautami (Buddha's foster mother), Rahul (Buddha's son) and other members of the royal family in its fold, it also accepted Amrapali (a courtesan) Upali (a barber who was entrusted the responsibility of chief disciple in matters of **vinaya**), Sunita (a scavenger who later became an *Arahant*) and even Angulimala (the dreaded dacoit and murderer who was reformed by Buddha) in the order of monks. Thus, the founding of an egalitarian order and emphasis on one's own Karma, as the only determinant of one's salvation, were truly redeeming aspects of Buddhism. Over a period of time, it influenced even the extant Hinduism, ushering a change in the mainstream thought process towards a more inclusive society.

BUDDHIST SCRIPTURES: THE BASKETS OF KNOWLEDGE

The Buddhist doctrines and canons like other scriptures of that age, were transmitted through the oral tradition to begin with. These were composed in the group of languages called Prakrit, which was spoken by the common folk at that time. The Pali language was a part of this set of Prakrit languages. Many of the initial Buddhist texts preserved to this day, particularly of Theravada Buddhism, are consequently in Pali. This set of Buddhist texts is accordingly referred to as a part of the Pali canon. Similarly, Buddhist texts of the Sanskrit canon, Mahayana Buddhism, Chinese, Tibetan, Mongolian, Japanese canon etc. exist to this day, with a broad similarity amongst them.

While the initial practice of oral rendition and group chanting enabled the preservation and accurate transmission of these texts, it is believed that the first writing of these scriptures happened in the Fourth Buddhist council in Sri Lanka in First century BCE., when a long famine had hit the region. The consequential death of may monks threatened the oral tradition and the prospect of these texts being lost forever, necessitated their being consigned to writing.

Buddhist Teachings

The Buddhist teachings are in form of sutras (verses) which are organised in **Nikayas** (in Pali canon) which are further contained in the **Pitakas** (the baskets), a compilation of **Nikayas**. Earliest Buddhist works which are also preserved in the Sanskritic and Chinese tradition are categorised into **Agama** (literally meaning 'sacred work' in Sanskrit) which is analogous to the **Nikaya** (a collection) of Pali tradition.

The Pali canon

The most important of the Buddhist philosophy in this canon is contained in texts referred as the **Tipitaka** (Tripitakas in Sanskrit). It literally means the three **baskets** (of knowledge and teachings). These were written in Pali and include the **Vinaya Pitaka**, the **Sutta Pitaka** and the **Abhidhama Pitaka**.

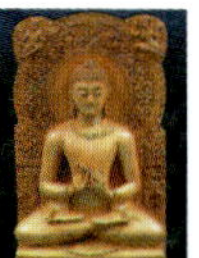

The Vinaya Pitaka

It contains the rules and regulations of the monastic life and functioning of the Sangha. It is divided into three parts comprising nearly 227 rules, including incidents from the life of Buddha and circumstances which led to the promulgation of these rules as well as exceptions to it.

The first part, **Suttavibhanga**, comprises these community rules and circumstances of origin. The second book called **Khandhaka**, incorporates the accounts of spiritual awakening of Buddha and 10 principal disciples. Besides, it also contains the accounts of the first two Buddhist councils. The third book **Parivara**, contains an analysis of the rules laid in the first two books.

The Sutta Pitaka

This Pitaka contains the main teachings of Buddhism and the sermons of lord Buddha.

In turn, it is divided into five *Nikayas*.

The first of these is the **Digha Nikaya** which contains the long teachings. The corresponding Agama in the Sanskritic tradition is *Dirgha Agama*. This Nikaya in turn is divided into many sutras, some of which are, **Mahaparinibanna Sutta** (containing the sermons of the final days of Buddha) and **Sigalovada Sutta** (containing Buddha's discourse on ethics for lay followers).

The second of the five is the **Majjhima Nikaya**. This has around 152 medium length discourses of Buddha and his chief disciples. It corresponds to the **Madhyama Agama** of the Sanskritic tradition.

Jatakas: Tales of Many Lives and Enduring Values

The *Jatakas* are a set of stories from the previous births of Buddha, who as per Buddhist legend remembered the accounts of his several prior incarnations. This literature is in Pali canon as well as in Sanskrit. In the stories, Buddha (in previous births) whether in human or animal form, embodies various qualities and virtues. In Theravada Buddhism (Pali canon), the *Jatakas* are a part of the *Khudakka Nikaya* (shorter collection) of the *Sutta Pitaka*. These stories are in form of 547 verses corresponding to separate stories. 34 of these stories are also compiled in *Cariyapitaka*, another of the texts of *Sutta Pitaka*. These shorter set of tales were used for didactic purposes. Many of these stories are also illustrated in the Ajanta paintings, temple of Borobudur and other Buddhist structures. Among the well known Jatakas are:

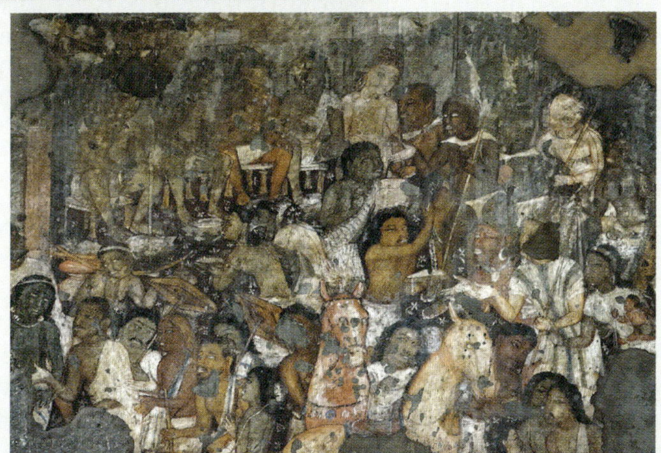

4.17: A scene from Vessantara Jataka in Ajanta Paintings — Wikimedia Commons

The **Vessanatra Jataka**, where Vessantara (Buddha in his previous life) gives away everything including his children displaying extreme generosity.

Dasaratha Jataka, which captures the story of Dasaratha and Sri Rama with the latter as a previous reincarnation of Buddha. However, there is a major variation; of there being no Ravana or abduction of Sita by him, or battle of Sri Rama with Ravana.

Jataka of King Sibi, who to uphold his dharma of protecting his subjects, which in the story was a mere pigeon, offers his own flesh instead to the falcon.

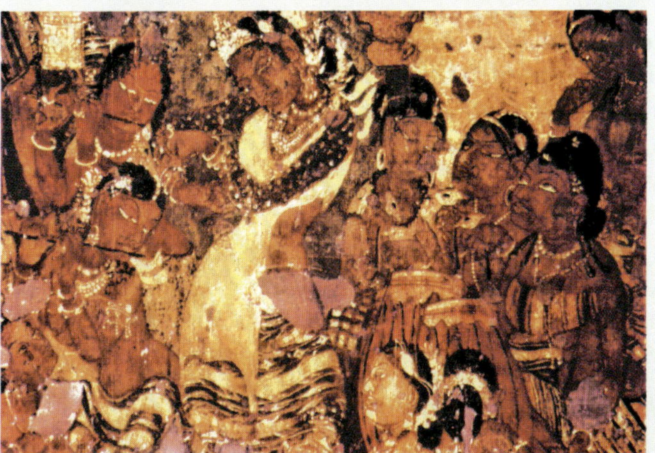

4.18: People celebrating the coronation of King Mahajanaka, a picture showing King Mahajanaka, queen and others; a scene from Mahajanaka Jataka in Ajanta painting in cave 1, Ajanta — Courtesy, Maharashtra Tourism Development Corporation

'The ass in the lion's skin' (*Sihacamma jataka*), 'The cock and the cat' (*kukuta jataka*), The crab and the crane', 'The monkey king' (*Mahakapi Jataka*), are some of the other famous Jataka tales. Many of these tales are also a part of *Panchatantra*, another regional folklore. Some like 'The swan with the golden feathers (*suvannahansa jataka*) are found in Aesop's fables with some variations.

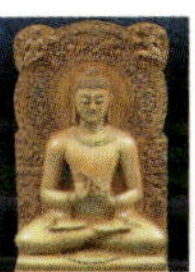

Avadana: The Compilation of Karmic Cause and Effect

Avadana (Sanskrit) or *Apadana* (Pali), meaning 'legends', are a set of Buddhist literature, containing stories and explanation by Buddha of the events of one's life based on the virtues and deeds of the previous life. Apadana are a part of the *Khuddaka Nikaya* of *Sutta Pitaka*. The *Vessantara Jataka* is amongst the most important of the Apadana stories. These are also a part of the Sanskrit canon which includes Mahasamghika's **Mahavastu** (The Great Book), Sravasitvada's *Avadanasatka* (The century of legends) and **Divyavadana** (The Heavenly Legends). Such stories are also included in the **Vinaya Pitaka**.

Groups of shorter teachings according to certain common topics is compiled in **Samyutta Nikaya**. This corresponds to the **Samyukta Agama** of the Sanskritic tradition. The word **samyukta** implies 'connected', hence referring to the connected issues captured in these discourses. Some of the important topics discussed in it include, 'the theory of causation', 'the five aggregates of clinging' and 'the six sense bases'.

A collection of discourses arranged as per subjects is compiled in the **Angutta Nikaya**. This Nikaya contains several thousand discourses attributed to Buddha and his disciples. This Nikaya corresponds to **Ekkotara Agama** (increased by one discourse) in the Sanskritic tradition.

Khuddaka Nikaya, the last of this set, is a collection of a variety of shorter texts in verse and prose. The word Khuddaka literally means, 'small', thus signifying this collection to have lesser number of verses as compared to the other **Nikayas**. It is generally believed that this **Nikaya** was composed after the other four, and those discourses not captured in the erstwhile **Nikayas** found place here. This **Nikaya** corresponds to the **Ksudraka Agama** of the Sanskirtic traditions. It is further divided into two strata. While **Sutta Nipata, Itivuttaka, Dhammapada, Therigatha (Theragatha), Udana** and **Jataka** belong to the first stratum, the next stratum includes **Khuddakapatha, Vimanavatthu, Petavatthu, Niddesa, Patisambhida, Apadana, Buddhavamsa** and **Cariyapitaka**.

Among these, the **Dhammapada** is perhaps the most studied and translated particularly by the western scholars. This text captures the quotes of Buddha in the form of 423 verses compiled in 26 chapters. Spoken by Buddha on different occasions, it is often considered as a treasury of knowledge.

Abhidhama Pitaka

The higher metaphysical concepts and philosophy of Buddhism are contained in this Pitaka. The very word *Abhidhama*, consisting of **Abhi**; higher, **Dhama**; doctrine/teaching, (implying higher teaching), is indicative of the significance of this text. It is generally believed that amidst the teachings of Buddha contained in the *Suttas*, a scholastic analysis and summary, suitable for more advanced study by spiritually advanced monks was compiled here. Further, this text lends coherency and has better organization of the otherwise dispersed teachings of Buddha. This *Pitaka* is also significant for it being recited at special occasions, festivals and funerals.

Abhidhama Pitaka is further divided into seven chapters which are, **Dhammasangini, Vibhanaga, Dhatukatha, Puggalapannati, Kathavatthu, Yamaka** and **Patthana**. While **Dhammasangini** is akin to a manual of monks, **Vibhanga** (classification or division) has 18 chapters on different issues. **Dhatukatha**, literally meaning 'the discussion of the elements', contains discourses on issues such as five aggregates, 12 bases and 18 elements. The next chapter, **Puggalapannati** (classification/designation of persons) describes the various characteristics of persons at the different stages of evolution as per the Buddhist conception. **Kathavattu**, or points of controversy, identifies nearly 200 points of debate and discussions on certain doctrines, such as the existence of the soul. The next chapter **Yamaka**, literally meaning a pair, has ten chapters dealing with different topics. Broadly it deals with, roots, origin-arising and understanding of various issues. The last chapter **Patthana** deals with activation of causes and comprises various cause and effect theories.

The Sanskrit canon

The Buddhist scriptures are said to have been compiled in written Sanskrit texts, in the fourth Buddhist council which took place in India in the first century BCE, during the reign of emperor Kanishka. Like the Pali canon, it also traces its origin to the sermons of lord Buddha and has a similar form as well as content. These texts include; **Vinaya Vaibasha** which are the monastic rules, **Sutra Vaibhasha** – the Dharma, with the five *Agamas* corresponding to the five *Nikayas* of the Pali Canon, and the **Abhidharma Vaibasha**, the scholarly philosophical analysis. However, this text has some difference with the corresponding sections of the Pali Canon.

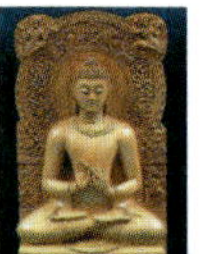

Besides the Tripitakas, the **Dhammacakkappavattana Sutta** (discourse on turning of wheel of law), the **Dhammapada** (treasury of truth), **Mahasatipattha Sutta** (four foundation of mindfulness), etc. are some important Buddhist scriptures which are also considered significant as stand-alone scriptures.

Ancient Chinese Travelers and Their Quest for Buddhist Texts

Faxian (Fa- Hien), an ancient Chinese Buddhist monk, travelled to India in the fifth century CE (399 CE to 412 CE), performing a perilous journey on foot of thousands of miles over treacherous mountains and icy deserts. His objective was visiting the sacred Buddhist places to collect sacred Buddhist texts. His travelogue, A "Record of Buddhist Kingdoms" serves as an important source of information of Buddhism and its influence in India and neighbouring countries.

Faxian also visited a number of prominent cities like Pataliputra, Mathura and Kannauj. His records throw much light on the religion, culture and other aspects of life, including wealth and prosperity during the Gupta period and also established a cultural link between India and China. He returned via Sri Lanka (Ceylon) and Java.

Xuan Zang (Hieuen Tsang) was another Chinese Buddhist monk who came to India in search of Buddhist manuscripts from Nalanada Mahavihara (particularly **Yogacharyabhumi-Shastra** a discourse on the stages of Yogic practices). His travails too were indeed very challenging and the travelogue equally rich.

He came to India in around 627 CE during the reign of King Harsha and travelled far and wide from Taxila, Nalanda and Tamralipti in East to Kancheepuram in South. His travel accounts of nearly 17 years is documented in his work, **"Records of the Western Region Visited During the Great Tang Dynasty".** This gives an account of various kingdoms, cultures and in particular of Kannauj, a flourishing city at the pinnacle of emperor Harshavardhana's rule.

Triratna and its Significance

Literally meaning 'the three jewels', Triratna (**Tiratna** in Pali) is a Buddhist concept implying the 'triple refuge' of the acceptor of the Buddhist faith. The Triratna comprises the **Buddha**, the **Dhamma**, and the **Sangha**, While Buddha is the enlightened teacher of the path to nirvana, the Dhamma is the doctrine encapsulating the appropriate moral and ethical pursuit, and the Sangha is the order of the monks.

The chant of accepting Buddhism incorporates this triple refuge as; **Buddham Saranam Gacchami** (I seek refuge in Buddha), **Dhammam Saranam Gacchami** (I seek refuge in the Dhamma), **Sangham Saranam Gacchami** (I seek refuge in the Sangha), thus implying the acceptance of the principles as laid out in the Triratna.

Buddhist inscriptions, sculptures and manuscripts represent this symbol with a trident. At times, the symbol incorporates a lotus flower within a circle, an anand chakra (a wheel), and a trident, with the three arms of the trident representing the triple refuge.

SECTS IN BUDDHISM

Over a period of 2,500 years, Buddhism has divided into several sects and schools of thought assimilating diverse ideas and practices within its fold. The earliest of these divisions occurred in the ancient times (during the reign of emperor Ashoka) into *Sthaviras* (elders) and the *Mahasamghikas* (the greater community). From the *Sthaviras*, a number of other sects arose later, which includes the Sarvastivada school. This school believed in the doctrine of 'all is real' and it became popular in North-west regions and Kashmir. The Vibhajayavada was another school emerging from the Sthaviras and believed in the 'doctrine of analysis'. The Theravada, which spread in South India, was another prominent sect to arise from the Sthaviras. After the fourth Buddhist council, the emergence of the Hinayana and Mahayana, the two main forms of Buddhism, took place. Some of these significant schools and their doctrines are briefly given here.

a. Hinayana

Literally meaning the **smaller vehicle**, Hinayana emerged as a separate form of Buddhism after the fourth Buddhist council (during the reign of emperor Kanishka). This was the orthodox sect that emphasised on individual salvation by following the original teachings of Buddha (ethical conduct, discipline, and right knowledge). In this sect, unlike in the Mahayana sect, Buddha was not considered as eternal or a god, nor making of his statutes or worship was encouraged. In Hinayana sect, Buddha and events of his life were represented symbolically. This school of Buddhism does not exist to this day and is believed to have been absorbed in other sects from which Theravada later emerged.

b. Mahayana

Literally meaning the **larger vehicle**, this sect believed in **universal salvation** rather than merely the salvation of individuals. They also followed the concept of **Bodhisattvas**, such as Avalokiteshwara,

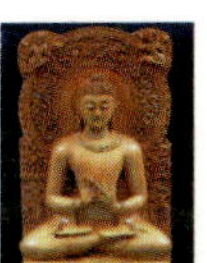

Vajrapani, Kshitigarbha, and Visvapani. These were venerated souls who had generated *bodhichitta*, or had attained personal salvation, but took birth on this earth to enable the salvation of other souls. Thus, the concept of personal salvation as in that of an *Arhat* (Arahant in Pali) believed in the Hinayana school was valued less in Mahayana Buddhism. Further, Mahayana sect also accepted making of statues of Buddha in human form and **believed Buddha to be an eternal god**. This sect was propagated by emperor Kanishka and later spread far and wide.

In India, two major Mahayana traditions developed, referred as the **Madhyamika** (the Middle Way) and **Sunyawada** (the Emptiness school). Philosopher Nagarjuna was an important proponent of the latter. Yogacara and Vijnapatavada were other schools of Mahayana. Outside India, Buddhism spread in China as per the Mahayana tradition. This school has its own Mahayana Sutras which are preserved in the Chinese Buddhist canon. Many other Buddhist forms such as Zen, Pure Land and other sects which spread further to Japan, Korea, Vietnam and other countries, arose from the Mahayana school and is also called East Asian Mahayana or East Asian Buddhism.

c. Theravada

This literally means the **doctrine of elders**. Like Hinayana, it emphasised on attaining of individual 'nirvana' through mental discipline, appropriate knowledge, and right conduct. It is among the only major non-Mahayana schools which have survived to this day. This school is said to have emanated from the Sri Lankan Mahavihara sect, which in itself was a branch of the South Indian Vibhajayvada school.

This school has its own set of Buddhist texts, which is the Pali canon, and does not recognise the Mahayana texts as true **Buddhavacana** (Buddha's words). This is also the only complete Buddhist canon which is surviving in an Indian language. The school's communications are also done in Pali, which is considered as a sacred language. The school also has a different sect which emphasise on different aspects of the Buddhist philosophies and canons, particularly on the practices as prescribed in the *Vinaya Pitaka* or *Visuddhimagga* (literally meaning the 'path of purification', a text of Theravada Abhidhamma composed by Buddhaghosha in Sri Lanka in the 5th century CE).

This sect has a sizeable presence in South and Southeast Asia, particularly in Sri Lanka, Cambodia, Myanmar, Vietnam, Thailand and Nepal and is often referred as the Southeast Asian Buddhism.

d. Vajrayana

A new form of Buddhism emerged in Bengal and Bihar during the Pala rule under the influence of tantric sects of Hinduism. This sect worships Buddha, Bodhisattvas, and female divinities like Tara. A distinguishing feature of their practice was the use of Mantra, Mudras and Mandalas etc., which were unique only to this school. This sect was essentially a derivative of the Mahayana Buddhism but which also assimilated some of the practices of the tantric sects, the Siddhas and Naths (hathayogis) etc.

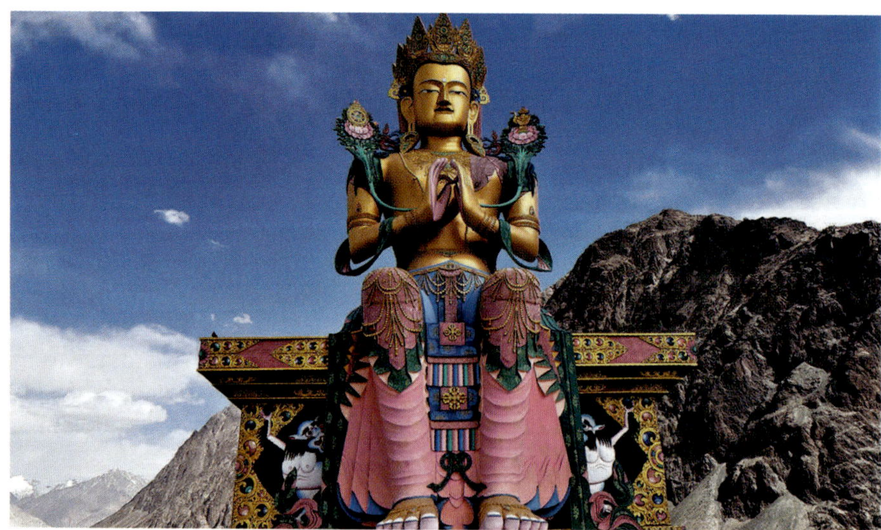

4.19: A large statue of Maitreya Buddha at Diskit Gompa (monastery), Nubra valley, Ladakh, which is in the tradition of Vajrayana Tibetan Buddhism — photograph by Madhukar K Bhagat

The term 'Vajra' literally means 'the thunderbolt' and 'Yana', a vehicle. Thus, Vajrayana symbolised the indestructible form of a religion or which brought out the indestructible and absolute real element of human beings.

This sect spread later in the Himalayan region. Tibetan Buddhism, Mongolian Buddhism, Shingon Buddhism (a sect in Japan), Chinese Esoteric Buddhism and Newar Buddhism (a sect in Nepal) are some of its derivative forms.

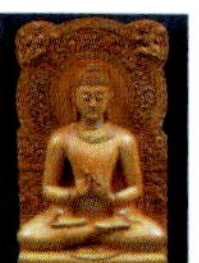

Bodhisattva and Maitreya

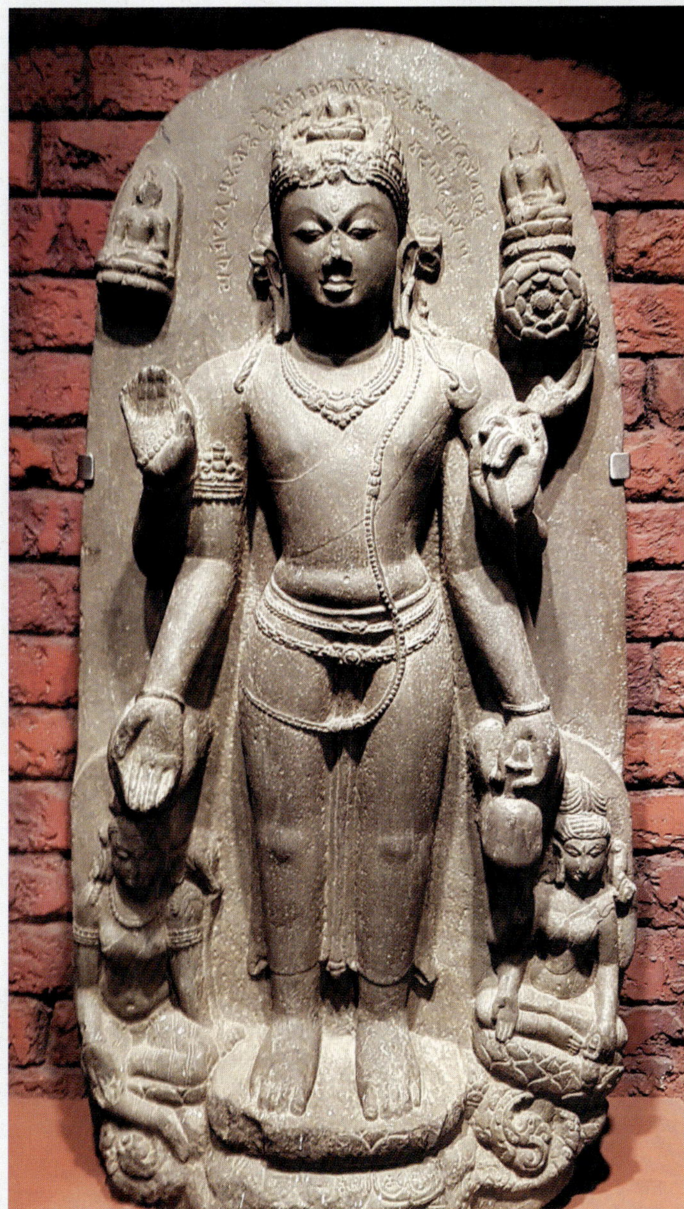

4.20: Four armed Avalokiteshwara, 10th century, Pala period, Kukrihara, phylite stone, Bihar Museum — photograph by Madhukar K Bhagat

The word 'Boddhisatva' is composed of the two words 'Bodhi' and 'Sattva'. In Buddhism, the word **'Bodhi'** refers to the attribute of **enlightenment**, while **Sattva** refers to a sentient being. In early Buddhism, the term was in reference to **previous incarnations of Buddha**, where he was on path to Buddhahood but had still not fully overcome the **dukhas**, viz. birth (**jati**), decay (**jara**), disease (**vyadhi**), and death (**marana**). Thus, the Bodhisattva concept referred to a sentient being possessing the qualities of Buddhahood and on way to Buddhahood.

In Mahayana Buddhism, this concept was further associated with **Buddhachita**, or those venerated beings having the attributes of Buddhahood and attained their personal salvation, but took birth or continuing their existence in this world to help the others on their paths of salvation.

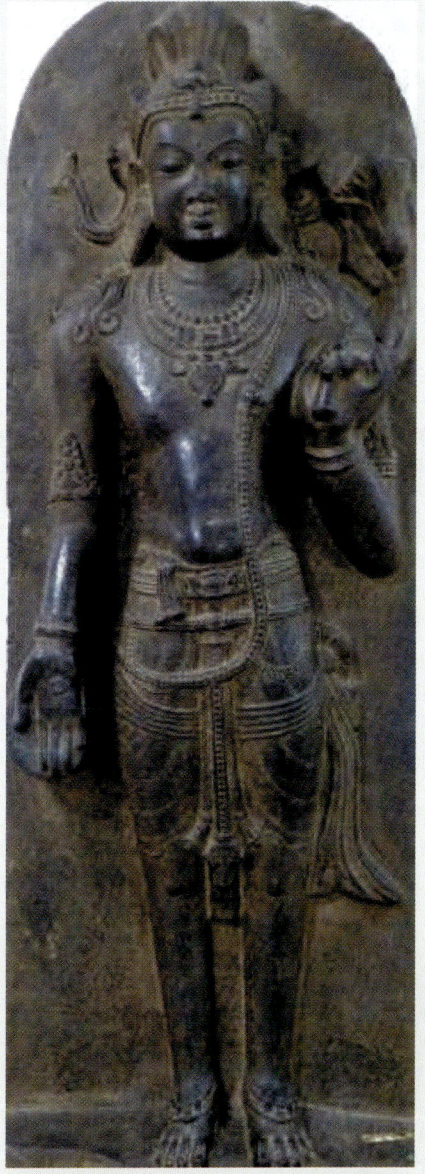

4.21: Manjushri, 10th century CE, — Courtesy, Patna Museum

In Theravada Buddhism, the concept is associated with a venerated being who possesses the attributes of Buddhahood, has resolved to become a Buddha and also receives a confirmation from a living Buddha as to his indeed becoming a Buddha.

The above concept is in consonance with the story of encounter of Gautama Buddha as Boddhisatva (in his previous births) with **Dipankara**, the living Buddha in that age. Gautama, as Boddhisatva, had resolved to become a Buddha in his earlier life and also received the blessing and confirmation of Dipankara of his becoming so.

The many Bodhisattvas: Different scriptures in Mahayana and Vajrayana Buddhism recognise many Bodhisattvas. While the Lotus Sutra cites four main Bodhisattvas, there are as many as 25 main Bodhisattvas in some other schools (viz. Pure Land Buddhism). Each of these are associated with different positive attributes and represented in the paintings and sculptures accordingly. Unlike the very plain appearance of the Buddha in such art forms, viz, shown with a simple robe, like a mendicant monk, the images of the Bodhisattvas are richer,

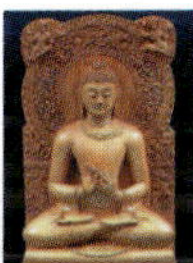

having flowery robe and ornaments etc. Their appearance is almost royal like, alluding to erstwhile royalty of Buddha.

The most important and widely recognised Bodhisattvas are:

Avalokiteshawara, who is also referred as Padmapani (one who holds a lotus in hand) is the Boddhisatva of compassion. He is recognised as Guanyin in the Chinese canon and Kannon in Japan.

Manjushri, literally mean, 'a youth', and is associated with *prajna* (transcendent wisdom). In Chinese canon he is referred as Pinyin.

Samantabhadra, or one who is considered 'universally worthy', is associated with the attribute of practice and meditation. Like the other Bodhisattvas, he too is recognised in Chinese canon, Japanese and other Mahayana Buddhist schools.

Kshitigarbha literally means 'earth's womb'. This Boddhisatva is depicted in yellow (or green) colour usually as a monk. As per his vow, he would not attain Buddhahood till the hell is cleared of all the sentient beings and thus till all attain deliverance.

Vajrapani, or one who wields the *vajra*, is one of the earliest recognised Boddhisatva. He is considered a protector of Gautama Buddha and thus is a dharmapala. He also manifests the power of all the Buddhas and the five Tathagata Buddhas (see Eternal Buddhas).

Maitreya (literally meaning mitra, or a friend) is considered to be a Bodhisattva who is a future Buddha. As per the prophecy of the scriptures, when there is decay and annihilation of the dhamma, which has been forgotten by the sentient beings, then Maitreya would appear on earth, attain enlightenment and again teach and restore the dhamma. In different sutras (viz. *Amitabha Sutra* and *Lotus sutra*) he is also known as Ajit. He is one Boddhisatva who is recognised in Mahayana as well as the Theravada Buddhism.

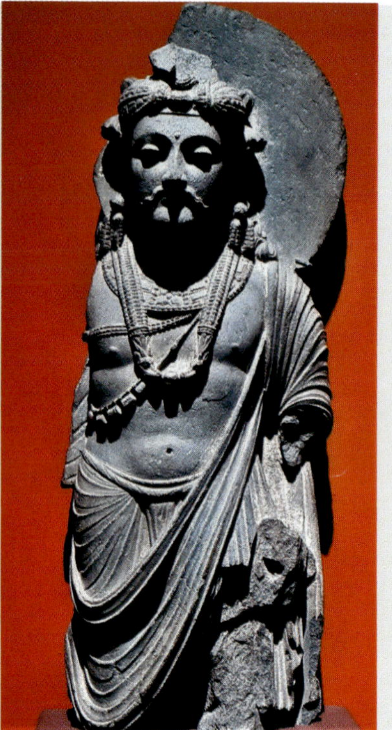

4.22: Maitreya Boddhisatva Gandhara School, 3rd century CE, location Chhatrapati Shivaji Maharaj Vastu Sangrahalaya, Mumbai — photograph by Madhukar K Bhagat

EVENTS AND SYMBOLS IN BUDDHISM

The Buddhist art, sculptures, and architecture is replete with symbols which are representative of important events in the life of Buddha. These events often are the **birth** of Buddha, his **renunciation** in search of truth, his attaining of **enlightenment**, his delivering of the **first lecture** (or **Dharmachakra Pravartana**), and his death (**Mahaparinirvana**). As early Buddhism eschewed any representation of Buddha in the form of statues or human images, the tradition of his symbolic representation and depiction of events through symbols started around 4th to 3rd century BCE, while the human imagery came in practice a few centuries hence. Some of these symbols preceded the human embodiment of Buddha and continued to remain in vogue even later. Their meaning and significance are brought out here.

Lotus

This represents the birth of Buddha, as the lotus is traditionally associated with emergence of knowledge and purity; for it retains its beauty while floating over muddy waters. Some interpretations also consider the lotus to be a symbol of Buddha's enlightenment.

Pipal/Bodhi Tree

It represents attainment of enlightenment by Buddha. It was while meditating under the bodhi tree that he attained enlightenment.

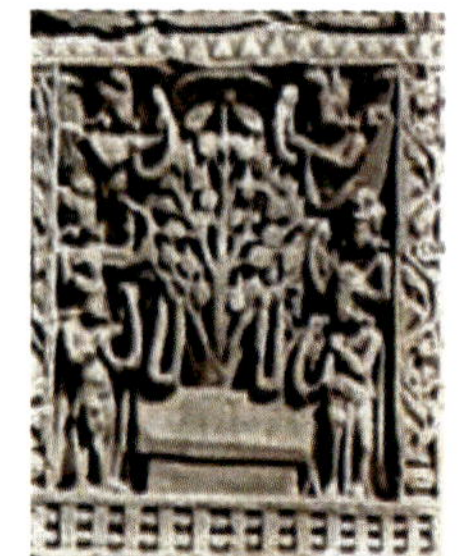

4.23: Pipal/Bodhi tree — photograph by Madhukar K Bhagat

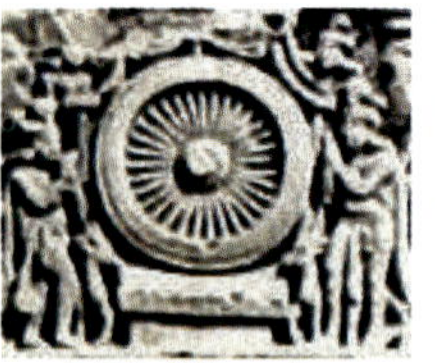

4.24: Wheel — photograph by Madhukar K Bhagat

Wheel

This represents the delivering of the first sermon by Buddha at Sarnath or *Dharmachakra Pravartana* or turning of the wheel of law. The eight spokes of the wheel represent the Eightfold path of Buddhism.

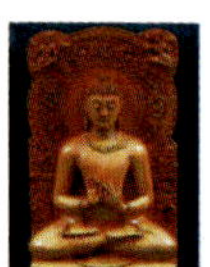

Stupa

This represents the Mahaparinirvana of Buddha. Sometimes, it also refers to an enlightened Buddha.

4.25: Stupa — photograph by Madhukar K Bhagat

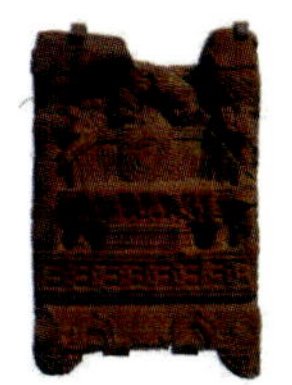

4.26: Empty Throne — Wikimedia Commons

Empty Throne

This represents the Buddha himself and it is also a reference to his royal ancestry. At times, it also signifies the Buddha in meditation.

Lion

This symbol traditionally represents strength, power, and royalty and it is also representative of Buddha. His exposition of the Dhamma was akin to the fearless roar of a lion.

Footprints

It is representative of the footprints of the Buddha and his holy presence.

Three jewels (Triratna)

The triple gems represent the **Buddha**, the **Dhamma** (**Dharma** or his teachings), and the **Sangha** and symbolize the 'triple refuge'.

Deer

It is a reference to Buddha's first teaching at Deer Park at Sarnath or the **Dharmachakra Pravartana**.

Elephant: It represents valour, strength, and wisdom, qualities of Buddha himself.

Ashtamangala*

Besides these early symbols, with the advent of Mahayana Buddhism some more symbols came in vogue, of which the **Ashtamangala** or the 'eight auspicious symbols' are the most recognized. This includes;

i) **The lotus** symbolising knowledge, purity and enlightment.

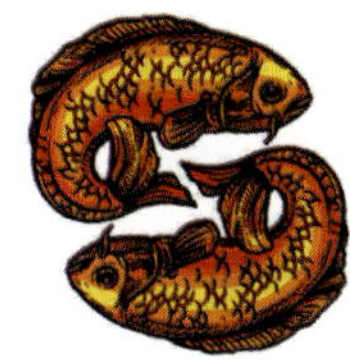

4.28: Golden fish pair

ii) **The Wheel of Dharma** represents the Dhamma with the **Ashtanga Marga** being symbolized by its eight spokes.

iii) **Parasol** (like a large umbrella) is considered a sign of royalty and thus representing Buddha's royal lineage, born in the clan of Sakya rulers. But this lineage is also considered to be the royal lineage of Bodhisattvas. Besides, it also epitomises the shelter from suffering and craving which the Dhamma offers.

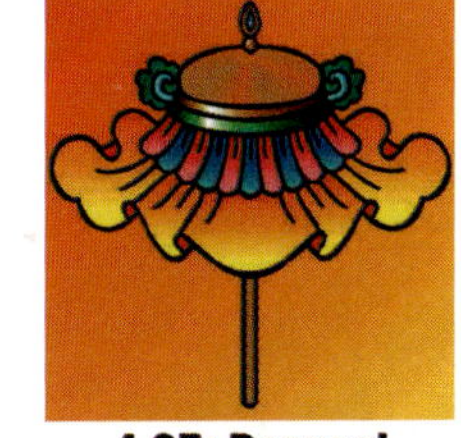

4.27: Parasol

iv) **Golden fish pair** is symbolic of good luck and happiness. They are also said to represent the ability to swim freely in the 'ocean of suffering and craving' towards **nibanna**.

v) **Endless knot** or the **mandala**, with its intertwining lines represents the interconnectedness of the numerous facets of life, particularly of virtues like wisdom and compassion. It is also said to represent eternal harmony.

4.29: Endless knot

4.30: Dhvaja

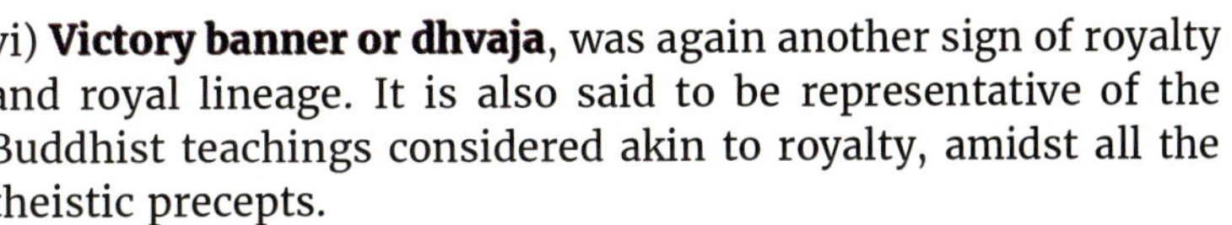

vi) **Victory banner or dhvaja**, was again another sign of royalty and royal lineage. It is also said to be representative of the Buddhist teachings considered akin to royalty, amidst all the theistic precepts.

vii) **Treasure vase**, or the urn of wisdom, is symbolic of the eternal wisdom and particularly of the Dhamma.

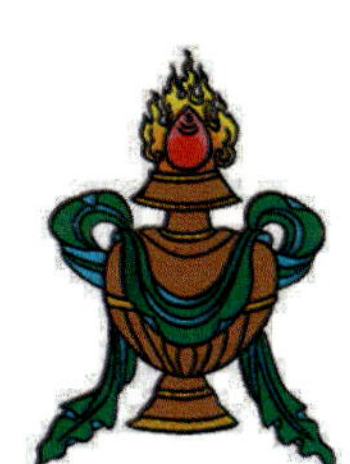

4.31: Treasure vase

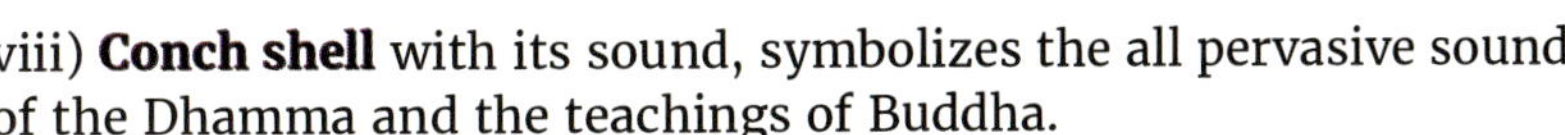

viii) **Conch shell** with its sound, symbolizes the all pervasive sound of the Dhamma and the teachings of Buddha.

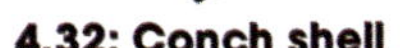

4.32: Conch shell

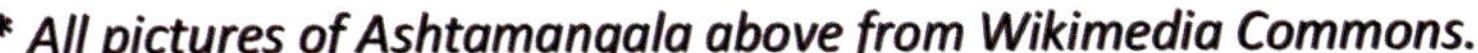

** All pictures of Ashtamangala above from Wikimedia Commons.*

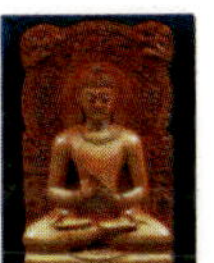

Buddhist Symbolism and its Misinterpretation

An appropriate understanding of the numerous symbols has often been a key to understanding of the meaning endeavoured to be conveyed by Buddhist art and architecture. However, a lack of knowledge of it may also lead to a possible misinterpretation, as was in the case of James Fergusson, the famous art and architecture historian of the mid19th century. On seeing the inscriptions of numerous trees and serpants in the newly discovered Sanchi Stupa, Fergusson erroneously believed it to be an earlier centre of tree and serpent worship. Understandably, with little Buddhist literature having being translated by then in western languages, he may not have been aware of their significance of numerous symbols in Buddhism.

While the Bodhi tree was representative of Buddha's enlightenment, the serpent is also venerated. It is believed that when Buddha was about to reach enlightenment, a fierce storm and rain lashed. The snake with its hood over Buddha, protected him under the shelter of the Bodhi tree from this tempest.

MUDRAS IN BUDDHISM

In early Buddhism, the representation of Buddha was done just through symbols. It was only in the first century CE with the emergence of the Mahayana Buddhism that anthropomorphic images of Buddha started emerging in the Gandhara, Mathura and other schools of art. In these schools, Buddha was shown in seated or standing pose with various hand gestures called the **'mudras'**. These mudras, in turn, were symbolic of different attributes such as knowledge detachment, benediction or even various states of mediation. Some of the important ones are described below.

(a) **Dhyana Mudra** – This is among the most common of mudras in which Buddha is depicted. He is shown to be seated in lotus posture while both his hands are placed on the lap. The palm is open and facing upward, with fingers stretched. The right palm is over left and the eyes are closed in **meditation**.

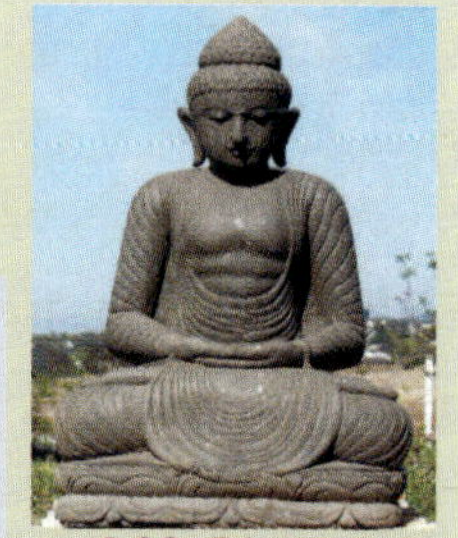

4.33: Dhyana Mudra — Wikimedia Commons

(b) **Abhaya Mudra** – This is a posture of **fearlessness and also blessing**. The right arm of Buddha is shown to be elevated and bent slightly. The palm is facing outward and fingers are extended upwards. This mudra is also a common one showing a peaceful Buddha in benediction.

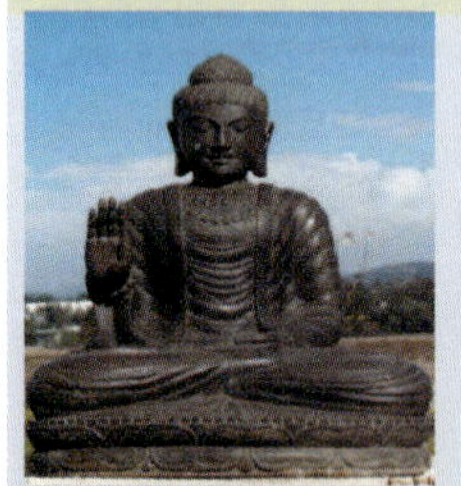

4.34: Abhaya Mudra — Wikimedia Commons

(c) **Bhumisparsha Mudra** – Buddha is shown to be seated in lotus posture **(Padmasana)** with his right palm hanging on the right knee and the fingers touching the earth. The left hand rests on the lap with palm upwards. It symbolises Buddha calling the earth to be his witness to his **victory over Mara** (Mara is a demon representing passion trying to entice Buddha into worldly pleasures).

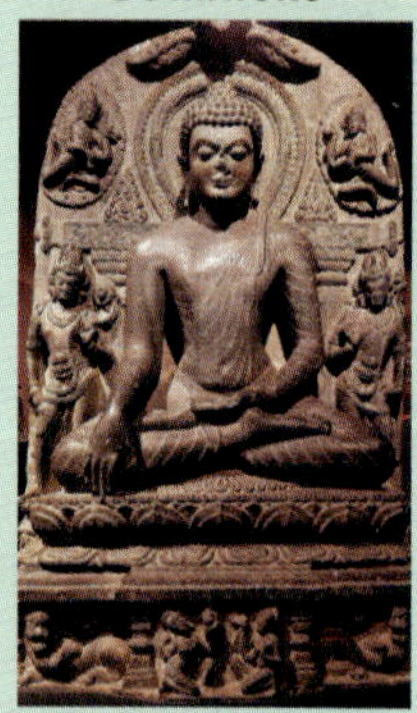

4.35: Bhumisparsha Mudra — photograph by Madhukar K Bhagat

(d) **Varada Mudra** – In this mudra, Buddha is shown to be **conferring his grace or blessings**. The arm is shown extended all the way down with the palm facing outward. Buddha is usually depicted in a standing position in this mudra.

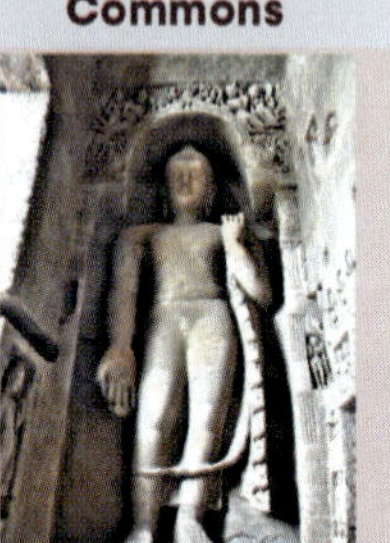

4.36: Varada Mudra — photograph by Madhukar K Bhagat

(e) **Shraman Mudra** – The hand points downward and away from body and is symbolic of Buddha's **renunciation of worldly pleasures**.

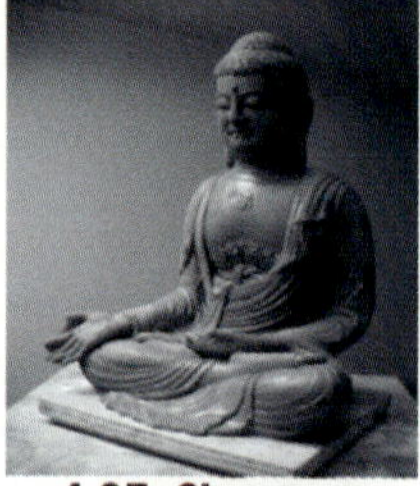

4.37: Shraman Mudra

(f) **Chin Mudra** – This mudra is symbolic of spiritual understanding. The thumb and index finger are touching and forming a circle, appearing as if grasping a fine object (as a grain of truth). The three remaining fingers are gently stretched outwards.

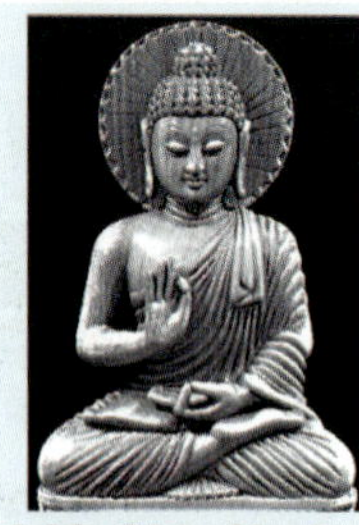

4.38: Chin Mudra

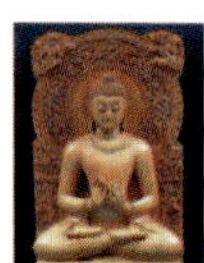

The Eternal Buddhas

The Mahayana Buddhism, and in particular the Vajrayana, enunciated the concept of the five eternal Buddhas, who were Vairochana, Akshobhaya, Ratnasambhava, Amitabha and Amogsiddhi. These are also called also called the 'Five Tathagatha', 'Knowledge Buddhas' and at times the 'Dhyani Buddhas' (meditating Buddhas). They represent the five self-born Buddhas, who are celestial and exist from the very beginning of time. They are often depicted in the Vajrayana mandala on the four sides, and atop the stupas and other sculptures.

Each is said to exist in a different realm, represents different qualities of Buddhahood, is associated with different seasons, colours and even identified with separate sound syllables. Each also represents one of the five *skandhas* (the mental and physical aggregates) viz. rupa, i.e. physical form, matter and body, *vedana*, i.e. feelings, *sanna* i.e perception, *samskaras* i.e. mental formation and attributes and *vijnana* i.e. consciousness. Together, they constitute the individual as well as the very cosmic existence. At times, each is also associated with a female deity.

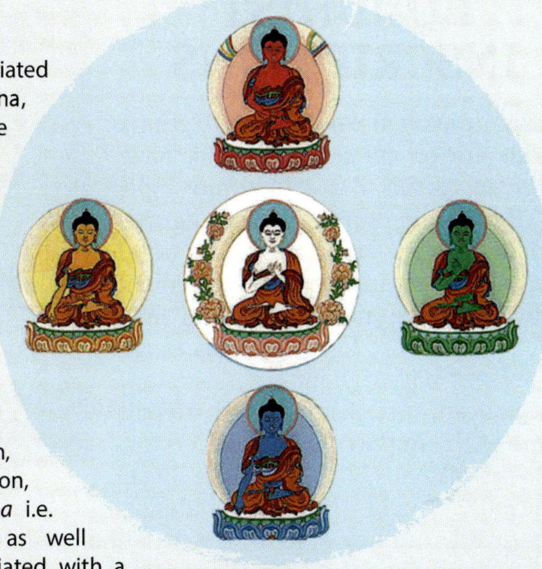

4.39: Five Buddhas

Vairochana is the central deity and epitomizes the teaching of dharma and attribute of meditation. His representative colour is white, and symbolizes the aggregate rupa (form).

Akshobhaya is depicted in blue(water), resides in the eastern realm, is the deity of Vijnana or consciousness and is the endower of the ability to reflect.

Depicted in golden-yellow(earth), Ratnasambhava is the lord of south, is associated with vedana (feeling) and is endower of equanimity.

Amitabha is shown in red (fire), rules the western realm, is associated with sanna (perception) and is endower of wisdom of observation.

Amoghasiddhi is depicted by the colour green, represents the northern direction, is the deity of Samskara (mental formation) and is associated with the attribute of perfect practice.

The attributes of Buddhahood, namely *vajra, ratna, lotus* and *karma* are also respectively associated with them. Together, they represent the *dharmakaya*, or the body of the dharma, which is the principle of enlightenment in Buddhism.

BUDDHIST STRUCTURES AND THEIR SIGNIFICANCE

The Buddhists constructed a number of viharas, stupas, and chaityas. Their purposes and significance is briefly explained.

- **Viharas** – These were monasteries or the places of residence of the Buddhist monks where wandering monks took shelter, particularly during the rainy season. Owing to a large number of viharas in the erstwhile Magadh region, it was also called Bihar (a land of viharas)
- **Chaityas** – These were Buddhist shrines which were prayer halls with a stupa at one end of the hall. It had pillars on the side of the pathway which led to the stupa. The purpose of these chaityas was to offer a community place of worship for a large number of Buddhists. Many chaityas were rock-cut structures. Some of the famous ones surviving to this day are chaityas of Ajanta caves, Bhaja caves, and Kanheri caves.
- **Stupa** – A stupa is a hemispherical (mound shape) construction which contains holy relics or cremated remains of Buddha or other monks. Apart from the hemispherical structure, most of the stupas also have a fence around it which serves to separate the sacred space of the stupa. Later, stupas had a balcony atop and a mast also.
- **Gompas** – Gompas refer to a Buddhist temple (place of worship) or a monastery which is in vogue particularly in the Mahayana form of Buddhism. The structure has a central prayer hall with a statue of Buddha. It usually also houses places of residence of the monks. A large number of gompas exist in Tibet. In India, such structures abound in the Ladakh region.

Origin of Stupa

As per the Mahaparinibbana portion of *Sutta Pitaka*, at the time of death of Buddha (Mahaparinirvana), Ananda and his disciples asked him as to what should be done to his remains. However, Buddha did not want any honour for his remains. But being pressed by Ananda further, Buddha asked for a stupa to be constructed over them which would accord peace to those paying obeisance to it.

It is believed that Buddha's cremated remains were divided into eight portions and a stupa was built in the eight kingdoms associated with the life of Buddha. It is said that later, emperor Ashoka dug up the stupas and distributed the relics in 84000 portions, building stupas over them in different parts of world.

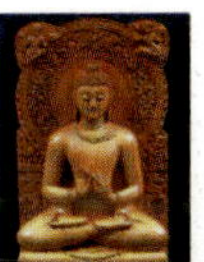

BUDDHIST INSCRIPTIONS

A large number of Buddhist inscriptions which are on pillars and rocks have survived to this day and throw light on Buddhism, the existing regime, and the society at that point of time. Many of these inscriptions are edicts of king Ashoka (pillar edicts and rock edicts). These are found in areas as far as present day Afghanistan, Pakistan, Bangladesh, Sri Lanka, and Nepal. Some of the important pillar edicts are those at Vaishali (Bihar), Sarnath (Uttar Pradesh), Sanchi (Madhya Pradesh), Amaravati (Andhra Pradesh), Kaushambi (Allahabad district of Uttar Pradesh), Lauriya Nandangarh (Bihar), and Kandahar (Afghanistan).

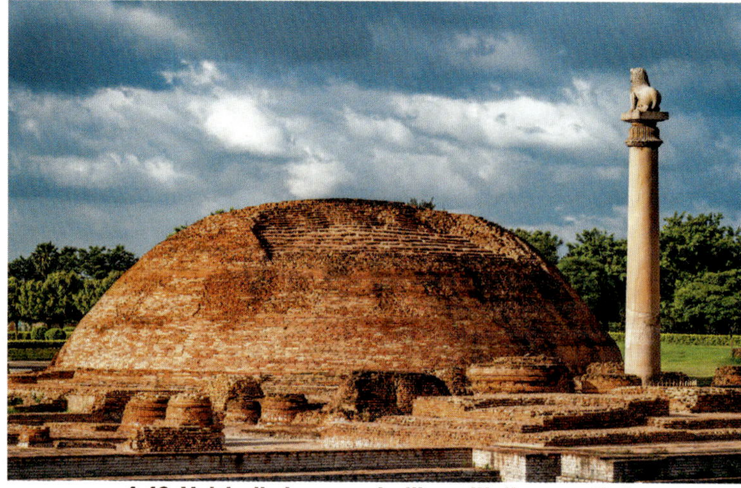

4.40: Vaishali stupa and pillar with lion capital — photograph by Madhukar K Bhagat

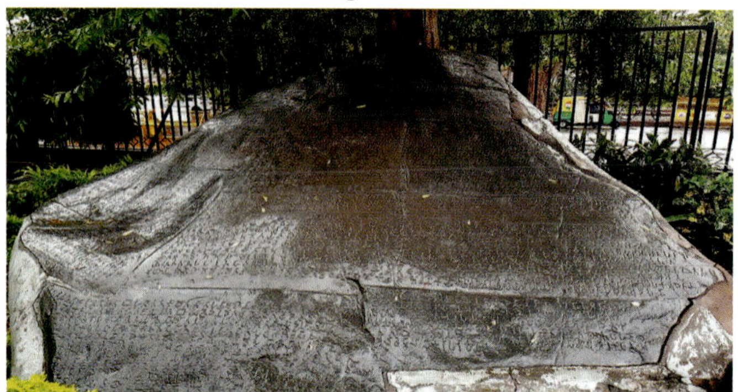

4.41: The replica of the Ashokan rock edict at Girnar, placed at the National Museum, New Delhi — photograph by Madhukar K Bhagat

The Lion Capital of Ashoka with four lions at Sarnath is also adopted as a national symbol of India.

Rock edicts have been found at Girnar (Gujarat) and Junagadh (Gujarat), besides Nepal, Pakistan, and Afghanistan. These edicts give the moral precepts (Dhamma) of emperor Ashoka and are based on the teachings and philosophy of Buddhism. It exhorted people to follow the word of Buddha and emphasised upon right behaviour, benevolence among people, kindness to prisoners, respect for animal life, etc.

Mandala: An Aid to Meditation

In Vajrayana and other forms of Mahayana Buddhism, a sacred mandala is often a ubiquitous and important aid for the purposes of meditation. Literally meaning a circle, a mandala is often constructed in the form of geometric configuration of symbols and patterns with numerous colours deployed to distinguish different elements. The mandala represents the entire cosmos, or a microcosm of the universe. It is also said to represent the very circle of life, wholeness, intricate relationship existing in the structural design of the world and the entities therein.

Several thousands of mandalas are known to be common in the Vajrayana Buddhism. One popular form of mandala gives the cosmological representation of the universe with the mythical mount Meru at the very centre of it. Another common mandala depicts the five eternal Buddhas, each embodying different attributes of enlightenment. In a way, all mandalas are representative of the essence of some significant aspect of the teachings of Buddhism.

The Thangka paintings (also referred as Tangka or Tanka) which are painted as scrolls of silk or cotton, and common in Tibetan Buddhism and even Nepal, also contain mandala as the main image. Sometimes the Thangkas also contain the images of Buddha or the important scenes from his life.

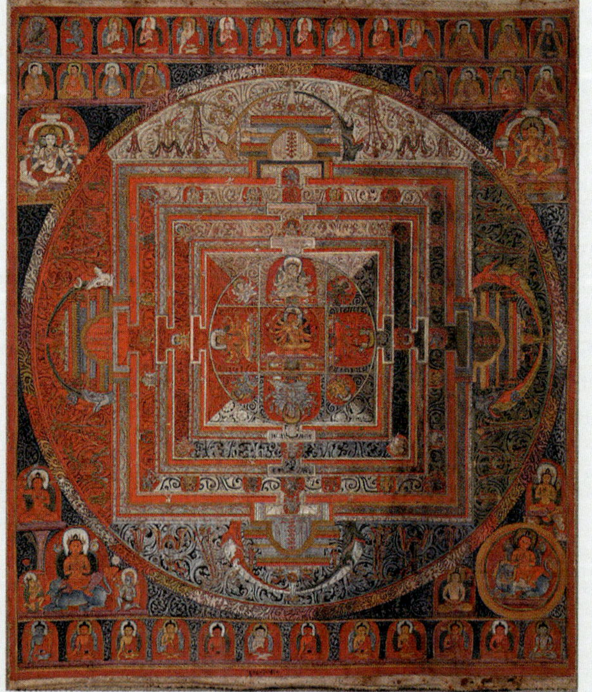

4.42: Mandala — Wikimedia Commons

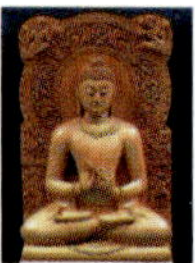

Laughing Buddha: The Metamorphosis of a Conception?

The image of a monk, wearing a simple robe who is plump, bald and pot- bellied, is often found in the Mahayana temples and other religious places, in China, Japan and Thailand. The monk is in different postures, seated on a tortoise, holding gold coins but always laughing. Popularly known as the 'Laughing Buddha', the image is associated with a Chinese monk Budai/Hotei of the 10th century CE, who as per tradition was believed to be a Maitreya (future Buddha). However, the laughing image of the monk gave it a name of the Laughing Buddha. He is also referred as the 'Fat Buddha' in the western world. As per Fengshui and popular belief, rubbing the pot belly is associated with good luck, besides different poses and images are associated with success, overcoming hardships, removing negative energy etc. As per another school of belief, a similar image in the Indian Mahayana tradition is associated with the Yakshas, who were protectors or guardians always adorning the four entrances of stupas and other religious places, thus symbolizing the four directions. They are seen to be plump, pot belied with hands held upwards (in a similar gesture as that of some of the laughing Buddhas), each bearing different expression (laughter, anger, frown etc).

4.43: Laughing Buddha

This image could have metamorphosed or been an inspiration in the Chinese Mahayana tradition, which later became popular as the Laughing Buddha.

However, as per the current belief system, there is little connect between the two, and the image of the Laughing Buddha is associated with the Chinese monk Budai, a Maitreya.

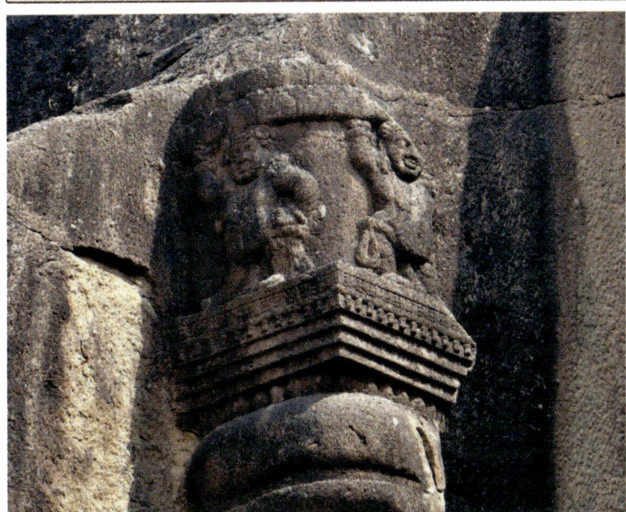

4.44: Yakshas atop a pillar in Kanheri caves — photograph by Madhukar K Bhagat

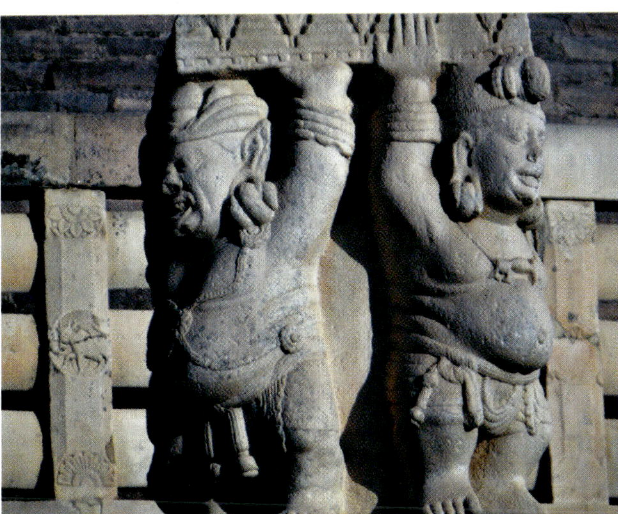

4.45: Yakshas on Sanchi stupa gateway — photograph by Madhukar K Bhagat

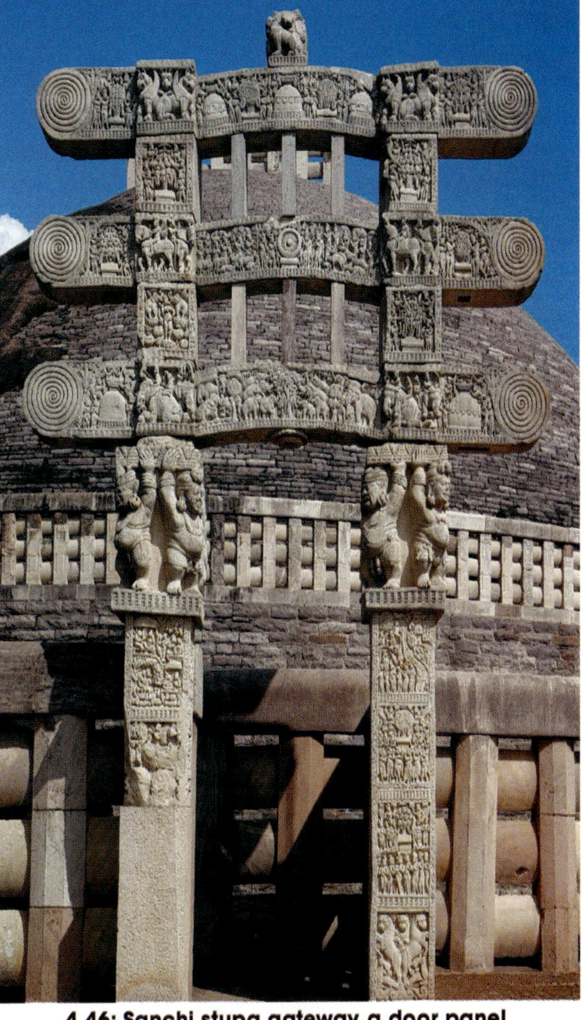

4.46: Sanchi stupa gateway, a door panel depicting the confluence of the changing Buddhist beliefs and intricate artwork — photograph by Madhukar K Bhagat

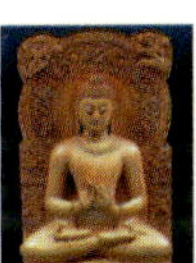

Shalabhanjika Motif

The change within Buddhism and evolution of its art

This motif is the figure of a Yakshi woman found in Sanchi Stupa, on the edge of a gateway shown to be holding on to a tree and swaying. This beautiful and sensuous motif is apparently in contradiction of the early Buddhist teachings of renunciation and simplicity. It is believed that the image represented Shalabhanjika (literal meaning, one who is breaking the branch of Sala tree), a woman whose touch caused trees to bear fruits and was thus considered auspicious. The motif also depicts the influence of extant social norms and culture on Buddhist beliefs and the change it brought in Buddhism. Earlier, Buddhist art and architecture were limited to only depiction of Buddha and that too, only symbolically. Further, this motif also indicates dexterity of the evolving art forms in Buddhism.

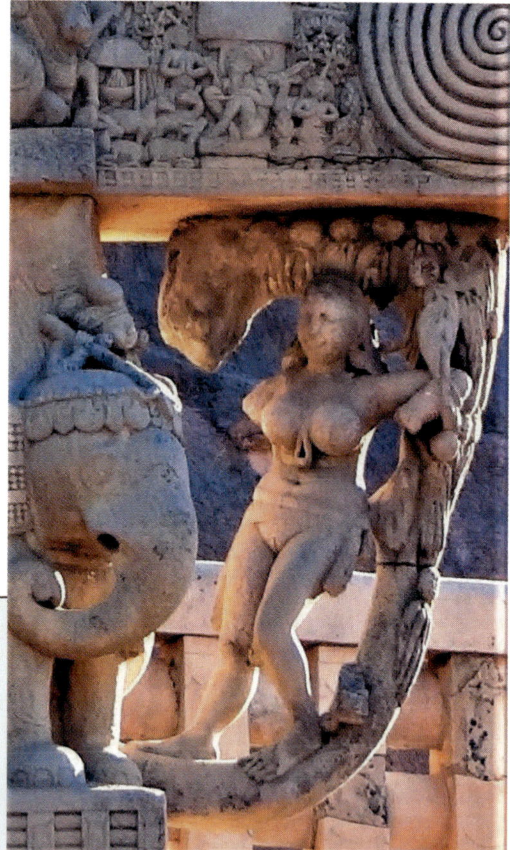

4.47: Yakshi woman, Sanchi stupa — photograph by Madhukar K Bhagat

Appo Deepo Bhava

The *Mahaparinibanna Sutta* which is a part of *Digha Nikaya* of *Sutta Pitaka*, contains a detailed account of the last few months of Buddha. It describes the travel of Buddha in his 80th year; from Rajgir in Magadha to Pataligrama (later called Pataliputra), crossing the Ganges, travelling to Vaishali, interaction with the Lichhavis, accepting the meal of Amrapali, his discourse to her and his eventual onward journey to Kushinagara (Kusinara in Pali), where he attains **Parinibanna**. Besides, it contains many other anecdotes, discourses to his disciples etc. One of the most significant and enduring messages of Buddha in his last days is, **'Appo Deepo Bhava'**. Having fallen ill, very weak on his way to Kushinagara, Buddha, through his spiritual will, holds his physical self and recovers. Ananda, his constant companion and disciple, expresses relief and happiness at Buddha's overcoming the disease, for he feared that Tathagatha may depart without giving a last instruction to the community of Bhikkhus. Although Buddha maintains that he has disclosed all what was esoteric or exoteric and never been close fisted, he asks Ananda to gather all his disciples. His words **Appo Deepo Bhava** is an instruction to Ananda on this occasion.

Commonly and literally interpreted as 'be a lamp to yourself' or be a light unto yourself, it's a message to Ananda (who had not attained salvation by then) and others to be a guide to your own-self, or tread the path towards knowledge or emancipation through your own effort. For, a teacher shows the path, but the disciple has to tread on his own, thus emphasising on the karmic spiritual principle of Buddhism.

The Pali cannon, however interprets the word 'deep' as an island (the word **dweep** or **deep** in Sanskrit and Pali is also an island). The Pali texts quote the following words of Buddha.

"Therefore, Ananda, be islands unto yourselves, refuges unto yourselves, seeking no external refuge; with the Dhamma as your island, the Dhamma as your refuge, seeking no other refuge. And how, Ananda, is a bhikkhu an island unto himself, a refuge unto himself, seeking no external refuge; with the Dhamma as his island, the Dhamma as his refuge, seeking no other refuge?

When he dwells contemplating the body in the body, earnestly, clearly comprehending, and mindfully, after having overcome desire and sorrow in regard to the world; when he dwells contemplating feelings in feelings, the mind in the mind, and mental objects in mental objects, earnestly, clearly comprehending, and mindfully, after having overcome desire and sorrow in regard to the world, then, truly, he is an island unto himself, a refuge unto himself, seeking no external refuge; having the Dhamma as his island, the Dhamma as his refuge, seeking no other refuge." Thus, irrespective of the semantics and differences in literal translation, the message of Buddha was unequivocal, 'seek refuge within'.

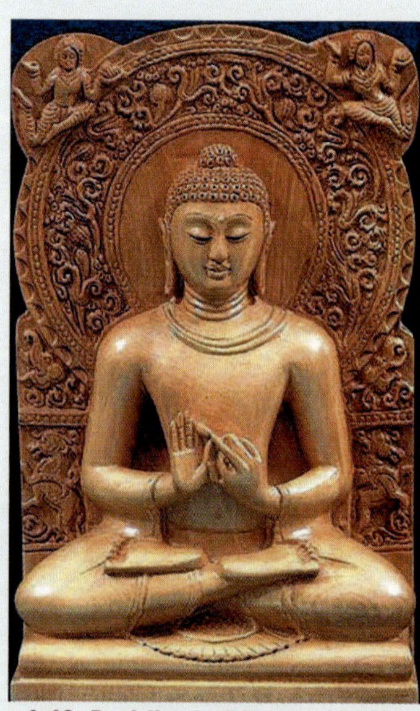

4.48: Buddha in Dharmachakra pravartana mudra — photograph by Madhukar K Bhagat

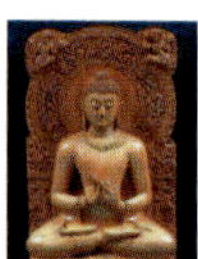

PICTURE GALLERY

Buddhist Stupas

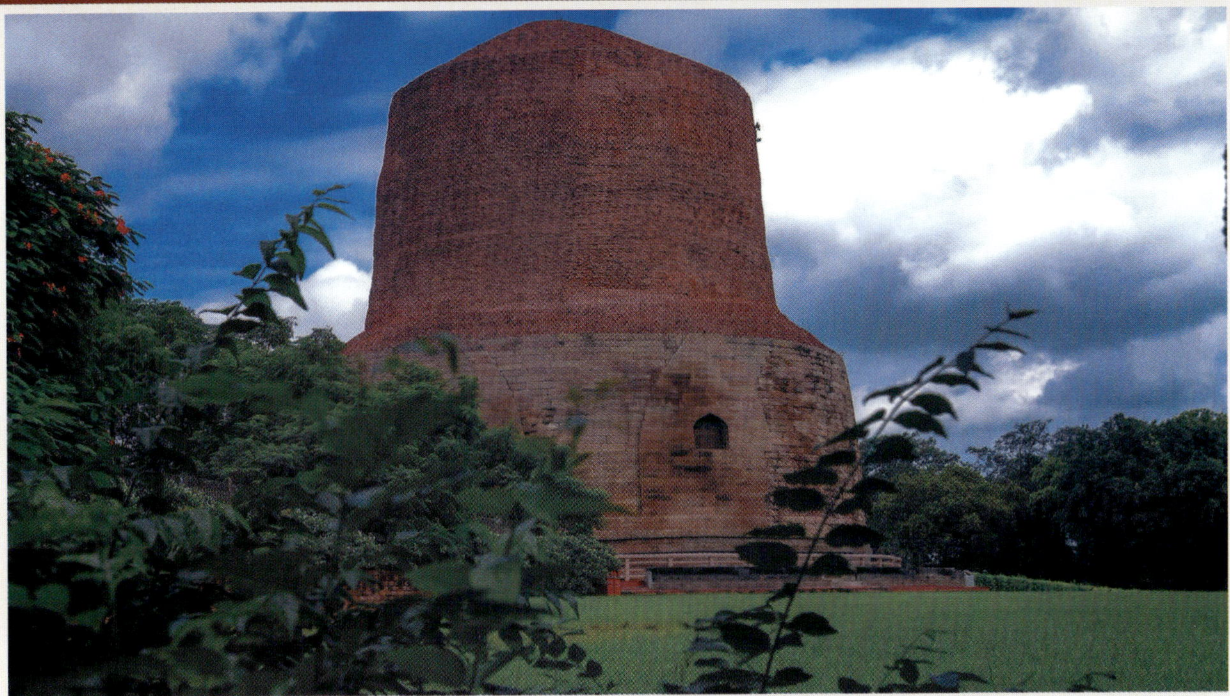

4.49: Dhamek Stupa, Sarnath, which is the location where Lord Buddha delivered his first sermon marking the Dharma Chakra Pravartana. Also, it was one of the eight original stupas where the ashes of Lord Buddha was placed. — Courtesy, Directorate of Uttar Pradesh Tourism

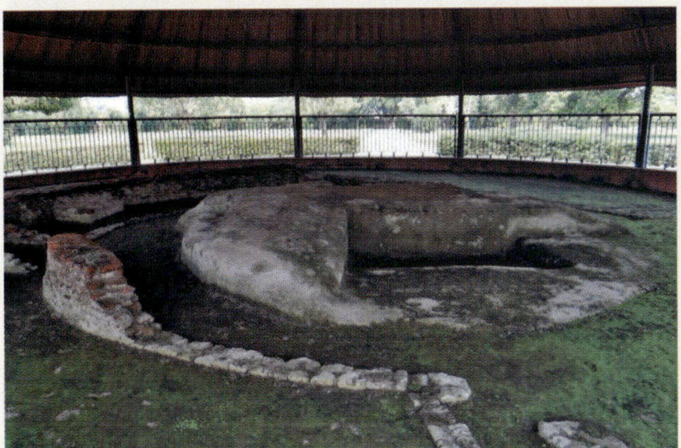

4.50: Buddha's Relic Stupa at Vaishali; considered another of the eight original stupas where the ashes of Lord Buddha were buried — photograph by Madhukar K Bhagat

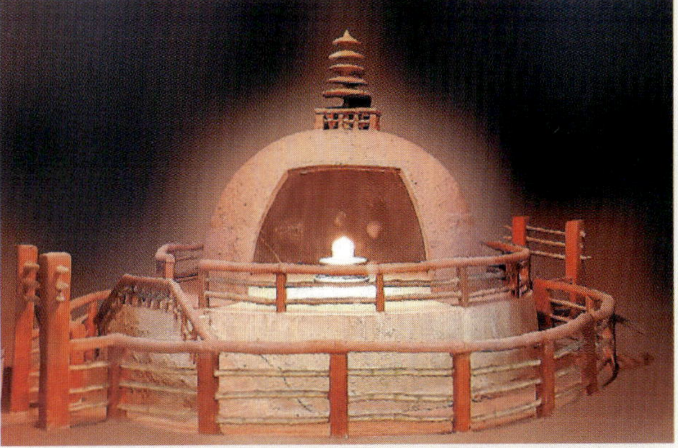

4.51: The casket of holy ashes of Lord Buddha along with other relics from the Vaishali Relic Stupa, kept in Patna Museum in a small clay replica of the Vaishali Relic Stupa — photograph by Madhukar K Bhagat

As per the Buddhist traditional belief, after the Maha Parinirvana of Lord Buddha, his body was cremated by the Mallas of Lichhavi with royal honours befitting a universal king. The mortal remains were distributed among eight claimants. These included the Lichhavis of Vaishali, King Ajatashatru of Magadha, the Sakyas of Kapilavastu, the Bulis of Alakappa, the Koliyas of Ramagram, a Brahmin of Vethdweep, and Mallas of Pava and Kushinagara.

The Vaishali Stupa was originally a small mud stupa (around 8.07 metres in diameter). Later in the Sunga and Kushan periods, it was encased with bricks, and in four phases further enlarged to a diameter of 12 metres.

In 1958, this site was excavated by Kashi Prasad Jayaswal Research Institute and an extremely significant discovery was made of a small relic casket of stone partly filled with ashes, a small conch, two glass beads, a small piece of gold and a copper punched marked coin. These are believed to be the items buried in the casket along with the ashes of Lord Buddha.

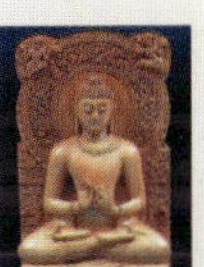

Modern Buddhist Stupas: A Glimpse

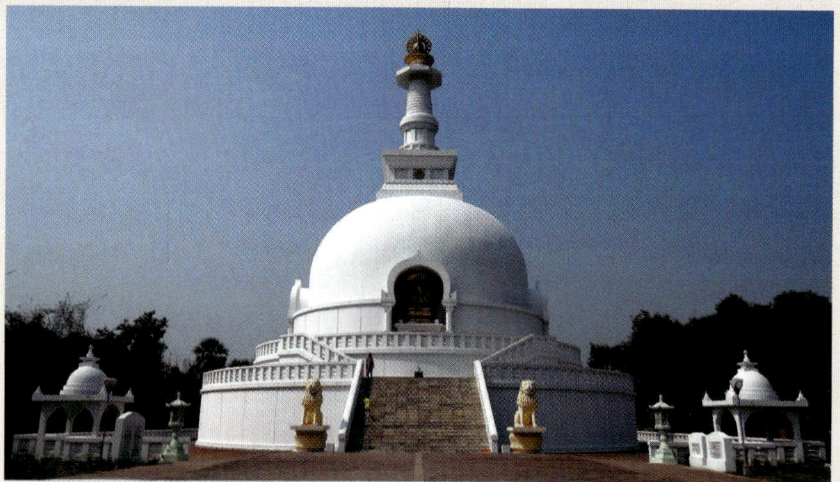

4.52: Vishwa Shanti Stupa at Vaishali — photograph by Madhukar K Bhagat

This modern stupa at Vaishali was built by Nipponzan Myhoji and Rajgir Buddha Vihar Society, through the contribution of devotees in India and Japan. It was part of an endeavour to build several stupas around the world by Venerable Nichidatsu Fuji Guruji, after World War II and post the humanitarian tragedy caused by the atomic bombs in Hiroshima and Nagasaki in Japan.

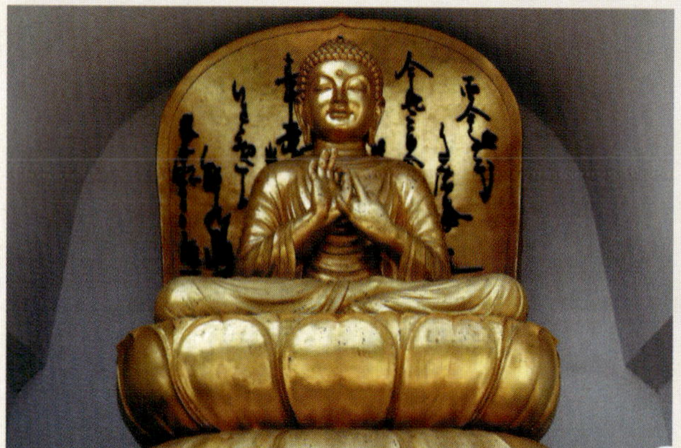

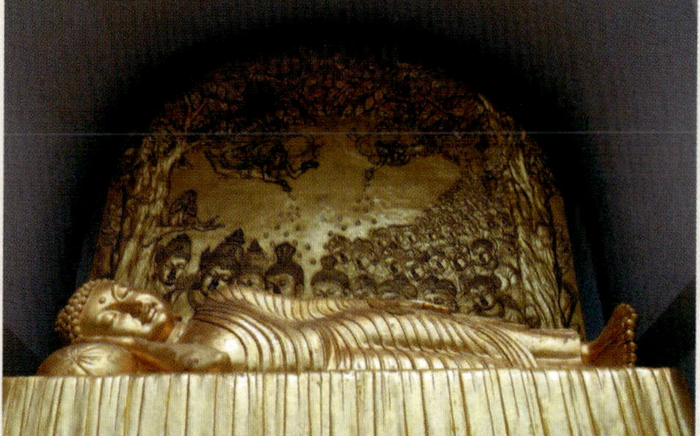

4.53 & 4.54: Buddha in Dhammachakra Pravartana Mudra (left) and Buddha Mahaparinirvana (right) depicted in the niches at Vishwa Shanti Stupa, Vaishali — photograph by Madhukar K Bhagat

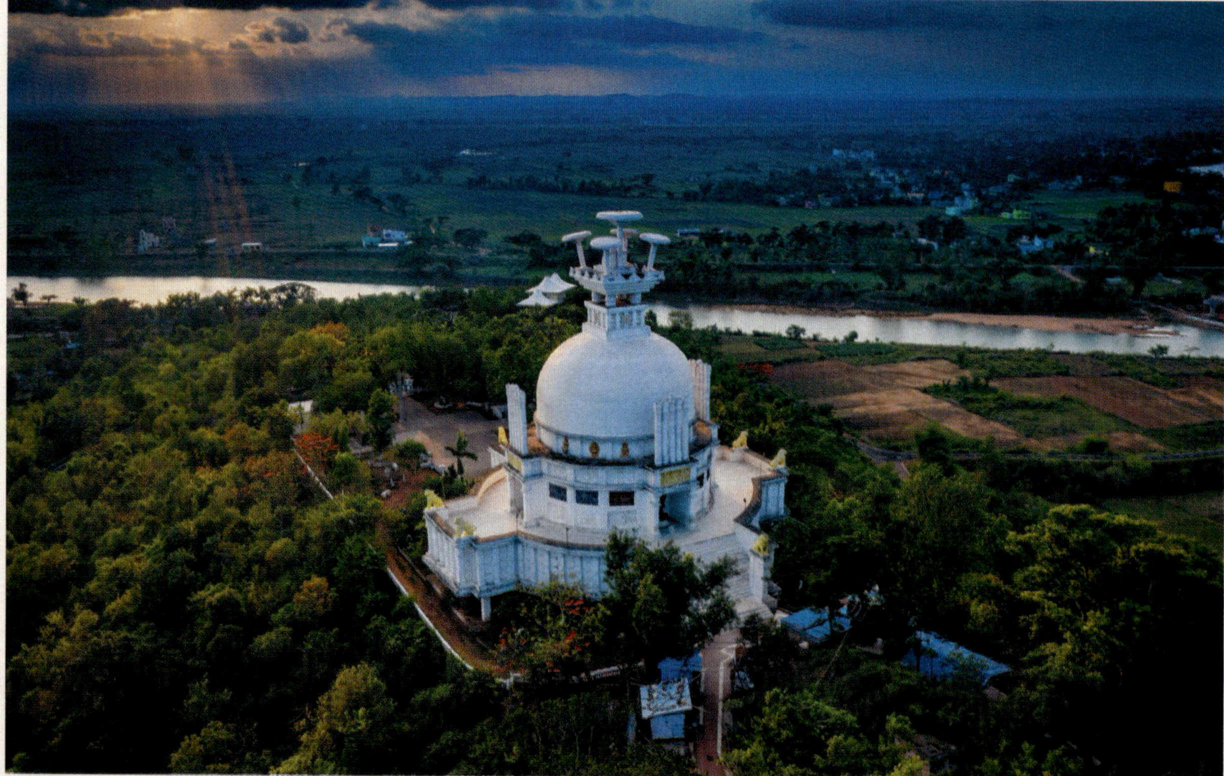

4.55: An aerial view of Shanti Stupa at Dhauligiri, near Bhubaneshwar in Odisha; another of the modern stupas whose construction was assisted by Venerable Nichidatsu Fuji Guruji — Courtesy, Department of Tourism, Odisha

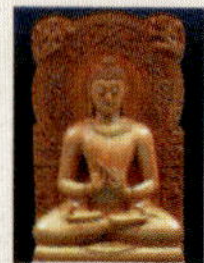

5

Jainism: The Theology and Practice of Ahimsa

> *Have benevolence towards all living beings, joy at the site of virtuous, compassion and sympathy for the afflicted, and tolerance towards the indolent and ill behaved.*
>
> Tattvartha Sutra

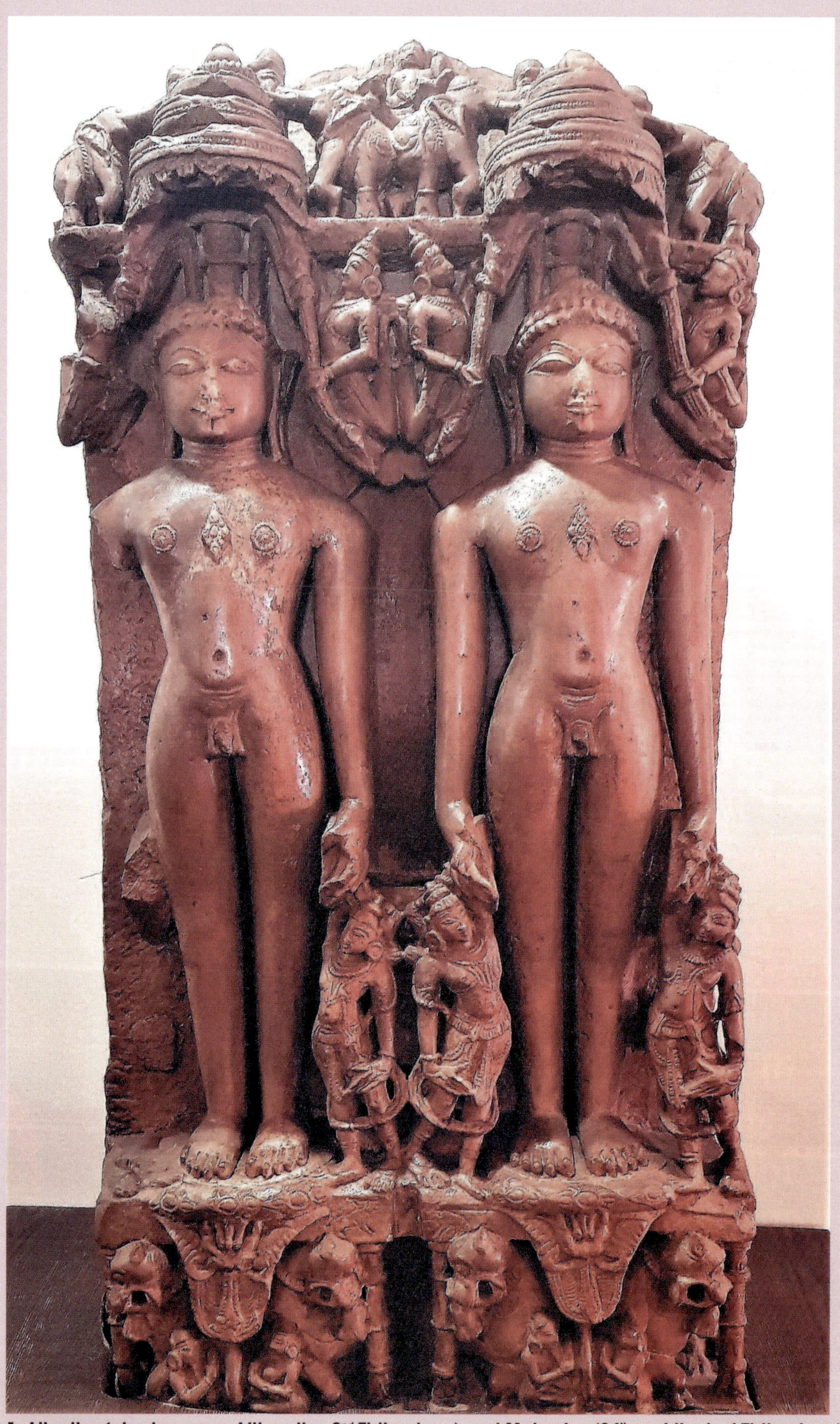

5.1: Ajinatha (also known as Ajitanatha, 2nd Tirthankara) and Mahavira (24th and the last Tirthankara) in standing meditation posture (*Kayotsarga*); stone sculpture 12th-13th century; Shivpuri, Madhya Pradesh; current location, State Museum Bhopal — photograph by Madhukar K Bhagat

AN INTRODUCTION

Jainism, along with Hinduism and Buddhism, is among the oldest of all existing religions. This faith is said to have been propounded by Mahavira in the 6th century BCE. At present there are 4.5 to 5 million Jains in the world and the followers are mostly concentrated in India. However, within India, the followers are spread in almost all the states and Union Territories. As a community, despite the small numbers (less than 0.5% of the Indian population), it enjoys a great deal of prosperity and high standards of literacy. Today, it is considered to be a separate religion distinct from Hinduism, and has been accorded a minority community status in India.

A BRIEF HISTORY

The philosophy of Jainism is based on the teachings of 24 Tirthankaras. Rishabhanatha was the first Tirthankara and Mahavira was the 24th and the last Tirthankara. As such, Mahavira is not considered a founder of the Jain traditions, but indeed one of the most influential, albeit the last teacher in the long tradition. As a philosophy, Jainism is as old as Vedic Hinduism, with Rishabhanatha, Arishtanemi, and Ajinatha (Tirthankaras) being referred to in the Vedas. Rishabhanatha (also known as Adinatha) is also considered as an incarnation of Lord Vishnu in the Puranas. Considering the long tradition of the Tirthankaras, some scholars consider the Jain tradition to be even older than the Vedic traditions. However, scholars generally recognize only Mahavira and Parshvanatha, (the immediate predecessor of Mahavira who is said to have lived around 7th to 8th century BCE) as historical figures.

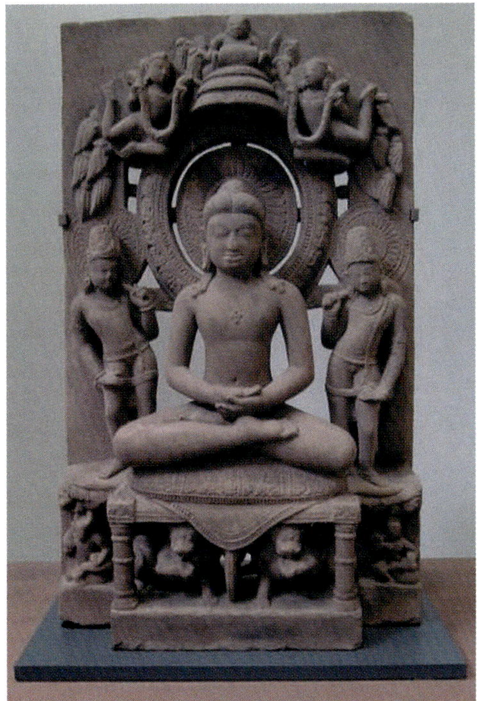

5.2: Rishabhanatha in meditating posture; location, Victoria and Albert Museum, London — Wikimedia Commons

Jainism flourished as a separate religious philosophy only after the advent of Mahavira, the last Tirthankara. The excessive ritualism, animal sacrifices, etc. which were opposed by the Jain teachings, along with its emphasis on ahimsa, compassion, morality, ethics, and other precepts, enabled it to spread in the country. Like Buddhism, it too received royal patronage. It is believed that king Bimbisara and king Ajathashathru, the Magadhan rulers of the 6th century BCE, were supporters of Jainism and lay followers of Parshvanatha. (support to Buddhism by the two rulers is also contained in Buddhist texts). King Chandragupta Maurya who founded the Mauryan dynasty in the 4th century BCE, is said to have converted to Jainism and later even become a Jain monk. In

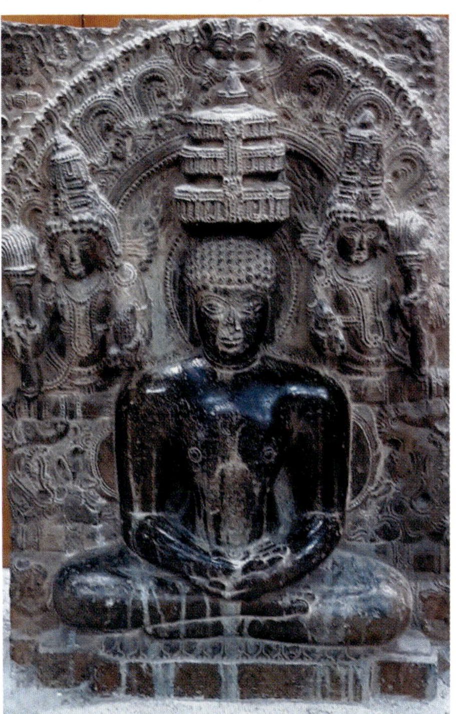

5.3: Ajinatha, the second Tirthankara 12th century, polished black granite sculpture, 12th century CE, Karnataka, Government museum, Chennai — photograph by Madhukar K Bhagat

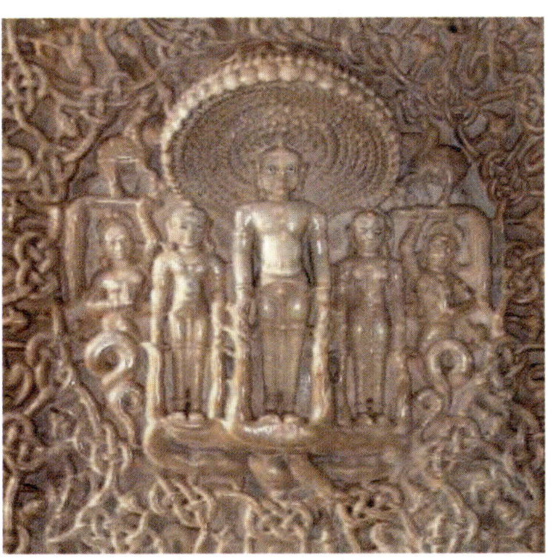

5.4: Parshvanatha with 1008 serpent-heads, a carved panel in marble at Jain temple, Ranakpur, Rajasthan — photograph by Madhukar K Bhagat

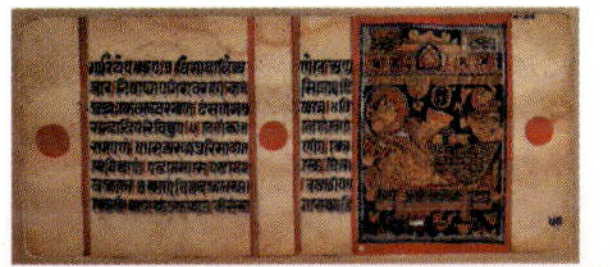

South India, and particularly in the present region comprising the state of Karnataka, Jainism received royal patronage from the Ganga dynasty (3rd to 11th century CE) and later from the Rashtrakuta (8th to 12th century CE) and the Hoysala (11th to 14th century CE) dynasties.

Centuries later, with the regeneration of Hinduism (in the 8th century CE), Jainism was pushed to the social fringes and to the states of Gujarat, Rajasthan, and southern India, where the community still has a good presence even today.

The 24 Tirthankaras

Literally, the word 'Tirthankara' means one who could show a fordable passage across the sea. Thus, Tirthankaras were those great souls who had themselves overcome transmigration of the soul and could guide others across the sea of this life of continuous births and deaths. They also referred as *kevalins*, or those who have acquired *keval gyan* or omniscience, *arihants*, or those who have overcome their inner passions and destroyed their karmas, *jinas* or those who have conquered their inner enemies etc.

As per the Jain belief, the Tirthankaras are born in each time cycle, which are *utsarpini* or the ascending time cycle, and the *avasarpini*, the descending time cycle, which is the current one. In the current time cycle, 24 Tirthankaras have been born with Rishabhanatha as the first and Mahavira as the last.

5.5: Sambhavanatha 3rd tirthankara and Neminatha 22nd tirthankara; sculpture 12th-13th century CE, Shivpuri; present location, State Museum, Bhopal — photograph by Madhukar K Bhagat

Rishabhanatha is believed to have been born nearly 86400 years ago. His first son was Bharata, a *chakravarti* king, after whom the land is named, and the last was Bahubali, an eminent sage. Among the 24 Tirthankaras, Rishabhanatha, Neminatha, Parshvanatha and Mahavira are the most revered ones. Neminatha is also said to be a cousin of Sri Krishna. The 19th Tirthankara, Mallinatha, is believed by the Shwetambaras to be a woman, while Digambaras believe her to be a man.

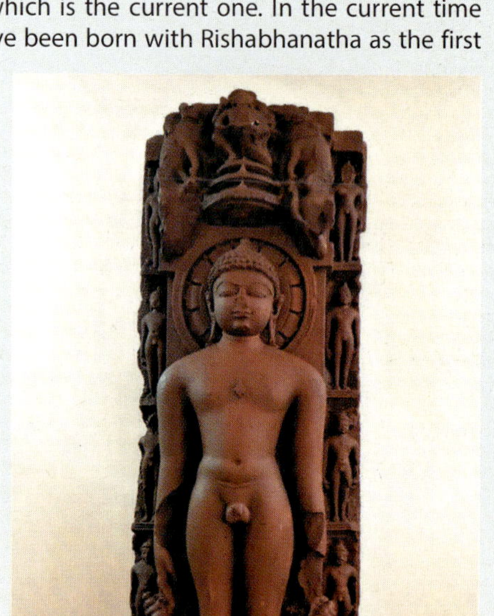

5.6: Chandraprabha, 8th tirthankara; sculpture 10th-11th century CE, Vidisha; present location, State Museum, Bhopal — photograph by Madhukar K Bhagat

As per the Jain tradition, each of these great spiritual teachers is associated with an emblem. Their name, in order of chronology and emblems are as below.

5.7: Suvratnatha, 20th tirthankara; sculpture 12th century CE, Shivpuri; present location, State Museum, Bhopal — photograph by Madhukar K Bhagat

1. Rishabhanatha (bull)
2. Ajitanatha (elephant)
3. Sambhavanatha (horse)
4. Abhinandananatha (monkey)
5. Sumatinatha (heron)
6. Padmaprabha (red lotus),
7. Suparshvanatha (swastika)
8. Chandraprabha (crescent moon)
9. Pushpadanta (crocodile)
10. Shitalanatha (kalpavriksha)
11. Shreyansanatha (rhinoceros)
12. Vasupujya (buffalo)
13. Vimalanatha (boar)
14. Anantanatha (falcon)
15. Dharmanatha (vajra)
16. Shantinatha (antelope)
17. Kunthunatha (goat)
18. Aranatha (fish)
19. Mallinatha (kalasha; water-pot)
20. Munisuvrata (tortoise)

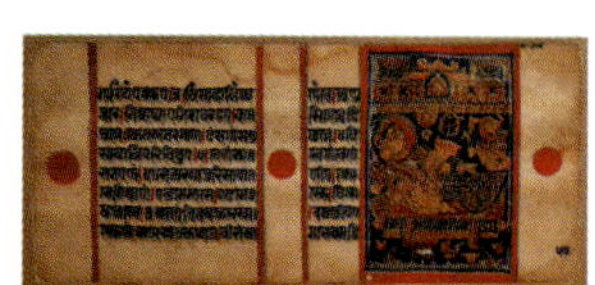

21. Naminatha (blue lotus)
22. Neminatha
    (shankha-conch shell)
23. Parshvanatha (snake)
24. Mahavira (lion)

As per the legends, 20 out of the 24 Tirthankaras and many other saints attained Nirvana at the Sammed Shikhara or Shikharji. This is is one of the most revered Jain holy place and is located on a hill top of Parasnath hills (Giridih district in Jharkhand)

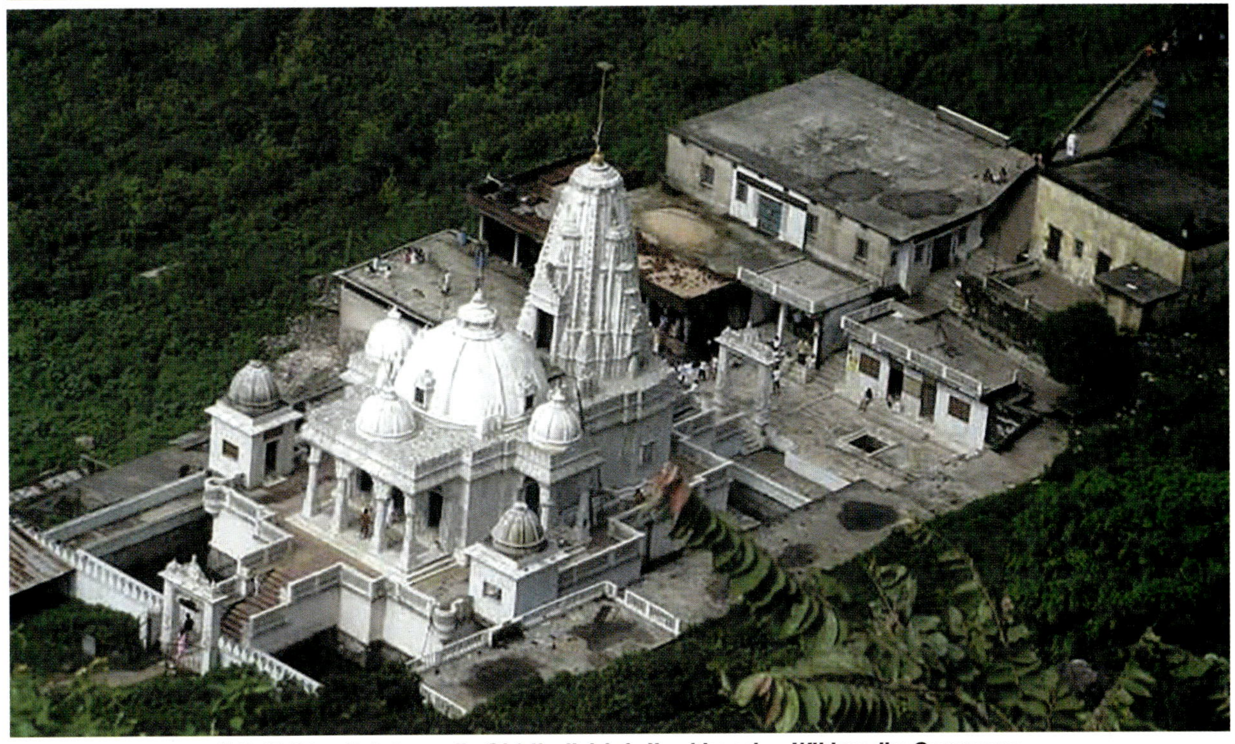

5.8: Shikharji Jalmandir, Giridh district, Jharkhand — Wikimedia Commons

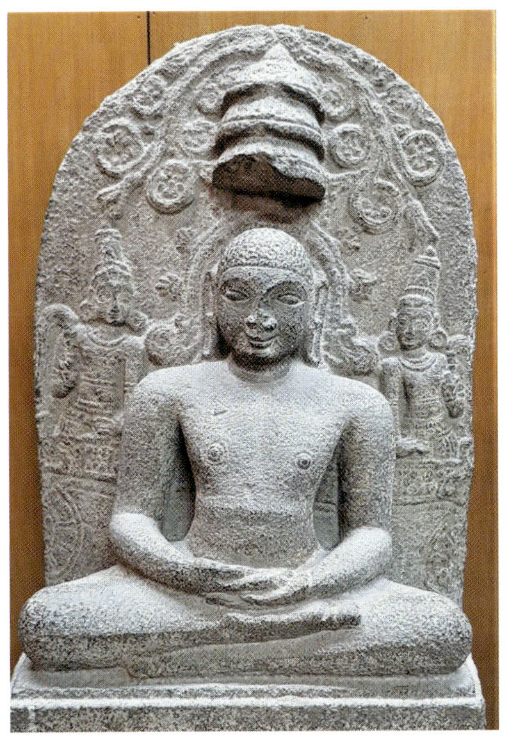

5.9: Mahavira in meditating posture, granite sculpture, 10th century CE, Government Museum, Chennai — photograph by Madhukar K Bhagat

THE LIFE AND TIMES OF MAHAVIRA

Vardhaman (Mahavira) was the son of King Siddhartha (the chief of Jnatrika clan of Ikshavaku dynasty) and queen Trishala (Licchvi dynasty). They are also believed to have been lay followers of Sri Parshvanatha. Vardhaman was born on the thirteenth day of Chaitra month in 599 BC in Kundagrama (Vaishali, in present day Bihar). As per the Svetambara texts, he is said to have married Yashoda and even had a daughter Priyadarsana. However, as per the Digambara traditions, he had refused to marry despite the insistence of his parents.

At an age of 30, he renounced his family and kingdom including all worldly possessions, even his clothes, and set out in search of the truth. After 13 years of wandering as an ascetic and performing severe penance and meditation, on the 10th of Vaishakha, he eventually found true knowledge while meditating under a *sal* tree on the banks of river Rijupalika, near Jrimbhikagrama. Thus, he became *Jina* (or the conqueror), or *Mahavira* (the great one). He was also referred to as *Nigrantha* (or Nigantha), literally meaning, 'without any knots' or 'one who is free from attachments and vices'.

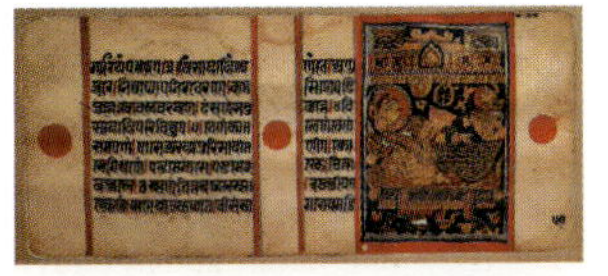

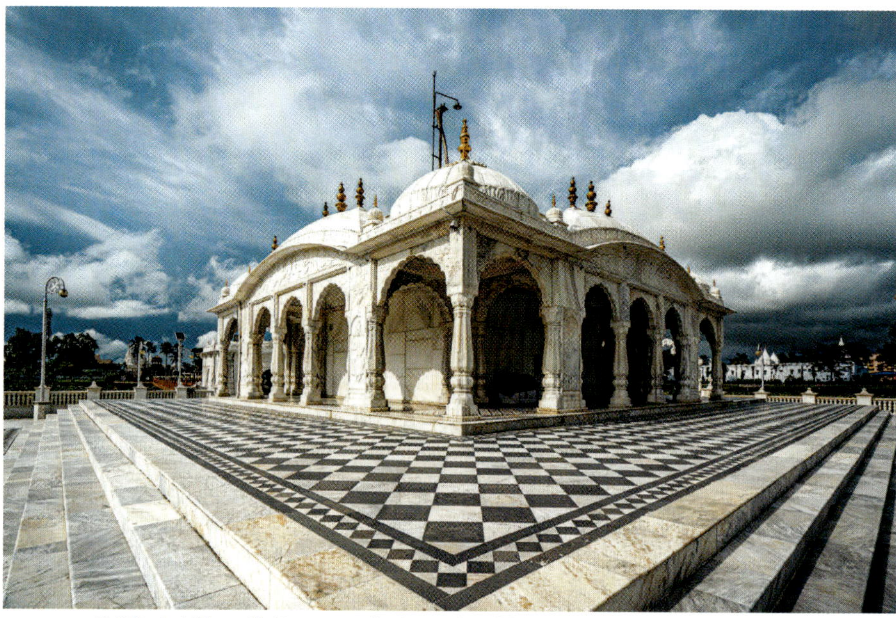

5.10: Jal Mandir Pawapuri where Lord Mahavira attained Nirvana — Courtesy, Bihar Tourism

After attainment of *Kaivalya* (also called *kevala gyana* or enlightenment—true knowledge) he preached for nearly 30 years. As per *Kalpasutra* (a treatise containing the hagiography of Parshvanatha and Mahavira), Mahavira had 11 brahmins as the first set of followers. These were also called the Ganadharas, and Indrabhuti Gautama was their leader. The Ganadharas, who were the principal pupils, are said to have remembered the teachings of Mahavira. These were orally transmitted by them after his death and later consigned in writing in the scriptures called *Agamas*.

At the age of 72, lord Mahavira attained Nirvana at Pavapuri (Bihar).

Lord Mahavira and His Previous Births

Jainism, like the extant Hinduism and later Buddhism, believed in the karmic philosophy, transmigration of soul and rebirth in human and non-human forms. Jain texts like *Mahapurana* and *Tri-shakti shalak-purusha charitra** also recount nearly 26 previous births of Mahavira. As per the texts and Jain philosophy, *Samyak Jnana* (gyana), or the right knowledge, is essential for liberation of the soul from the cycle of reincarnations. Mahavira, in his earlier incarnation as Nayasara, who was a village headman, had acquired the *Samyak Jnana* (*samyaktva*; right perception also considered as partial enlightenment). He also had many incarnations prior to being born as Nayasara, but after acquiring the *Samyak jnana*, there were 25 more births, before attaining Kevalya in his 27th incarnation as Mahavira.

As per the legends he was also born as Marichi, the grandson of Rishabhadeva, the first Tirthankara and son of king Bharata, a *chakravartin*.

* *Tri-shakti shalak-purusha charitra,* which literally means "The lives of the sixty-three illustrious People", is a Sanskrit epic poem written by Hemachandra in the twelfth century CE.

TEACHINGS AND PHILOSOPHIES OF JAINISM

The Jain philosophies are based on the teachings of the Tirthankaras compiled in the scriptures called *Agamas*. These teachings emphasise on a universal view of life based on the salient principles of *ahimsa*, *anekantavada* (non-absolutism) and the ethos and practice enshrined in the *Triratna*. Triratna incorporates the three jewels (Tri-ratna) of *samyak darshana* (right faith) and *samyak jnana* (right knowledge) and *samyak charitra* (right conduct). The concept of *samyak charitra*, or the right and ethical conduct, through the *panch maha vratas* (five great vows) emphasises on the principles of ahimsa, truth, non-stealing, non-possession and celibacy, thus imbuing it with the spirit of simplicity, austerity and piety. The karmic theory of cause and effect of one's actions (karma) as the basis of transmigration of soul and overcoming of the attachment and other negative bonds by means of asceticism, for attaining *kaivalya* (liberation) are other integral elements of the Jain philosophy and practices.

Ahimsa: A Central Tenet of Belief and Practice

Ahimsa, as non-violence or non-injury, is a restraint which exhorts one to abjure killing or violence in any form. It is one of the central tenets of Jainism and a very poignant aspect of its ethical conduct, bereft of which the very spiritual conception is rendered meaningless. The teachings of ahimsa, though in vogue in the other contemporary theological systems like Hinduism and Buddhism, is perhaps the most pronounced and emphasized in philosophy and the practice in Jainism, which distinguishes the latter

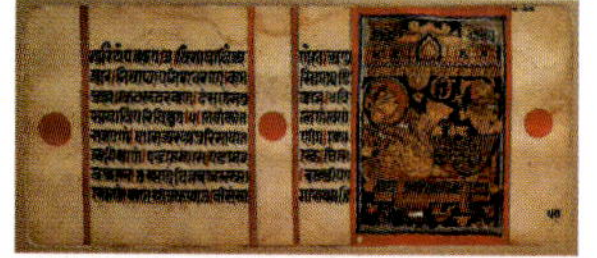

from other religions. Jainism considers *ahimsa* as a key tenet of the *Panchmahavrata*, with the principle of *satya* and *ahimsa* complimenting each other and the other *vratas* also incorporating and manifesting the very principle of *ahimsa*. Thus, *asteya* or non-stealing, is a restraint on violating the properties of others, while *brahmacharya* (celibacy) prohibits sensory violation, and *aparigraha* (non-possession/ non-attachment) is a restraint on material violation. Even the philosophy of Anekantavada exhorts the follower to adopt a more plural theological perspective and avoid violence in speech and thought.

Universal perspective of ahimsa

The ambit of *ahimsa* in Jainism is not just limited to humans and to the other sentient beings, but to even lower life forms like insects and plants, which have limited sensory perception. Further, as per certain schools of thought, Jainism considers that the whole world as animated (having life) and therefore it forbids even its purposeless destruction (viz. pollution of water bodies and environment). Thus, the perspective of *ahimsa* encompasses the biotic and even abiotic world and has an extensive and universal view.

Ahimsa in thought and conduct

Jainism exhorts the follower of the dharma to eschew violence in all forms and against all beings. As per its theology, not only killing or harming other beings is incorrect, but even causing to kill or consenting to such violence is against the religious doctrine. Further, violence is to be abjured, not only in action or conduct but also in speech and even thought. Thus, an intention to harm is also violence. Further, an act of harm, bereft of compassion and carried out intentionally, becomes more violent.

Compassion integral to ahimsa

While non-violence is a restraint of negative attribute of thought and conduct, the positive manifestation of ahimsa is compassion. Karuna (compassion) should be universal and boundless, with *maitri*, *kshama* and *abhay* as its essential layers. While *maitri* refers to universal friendliness, *kshama* is the attribute of universal forgiveness. *Abhay* refers to quality of universal fearlessness which the follower is imbued with. Thus protecting, sharing and serving, all fall within the domain of compassion and the larger perspective of *ahimsa*.

Karma as the basis of ahimsa

As per the Jain doctrine of *ahimsa*, compassion as a virtue, the need for coexistence of living creatures and preventing harm to animated world, are not the only basis of *ahimsa*. The karmic precept enunciates that any violent act produces negative and unwholesome karma, which is then acquired by the soul and must be reaped. Thus, violence adversely affects the very spiritual progress of the soul, impeding its journey towards *kaivalya*. *Ahimsa* is therefore a necessary and a continual discipline in thought and action for the seeker of salvation.

Thus, the Jain philosophy deems *ahimsa* to be integral to the universal well-being and individual salvation and pivotal to coexistence and spiritual emancipation, embodying the very precept of *ahimsa parmo dharmah* (non-violence is a sacred duty or the most exalted dharma).

Practice of ahimsa in daily life

The life and conduct of Jainas or seekers in the monastic order and even the lay followers is often shaped by non-violence. Vegetarianism is essential to their conduct, as consuming non-vegetarian food means killing of animals. While consumption of milk is permitted, (lacto-vegetarianism) some modern practitioners and strict followers of Jainism follow the vegan principle on account of injury and cruelty caused to animals by modern dairy practices. Even plant products like roots/tubers (viz. onion, garlic, potato etc.) are avoided for they have the ability to spring life despite being uprooted. Further, the uprooting is also believed to cause injury to the tiny creatures inhabiting the soil. Even having food after sunset is prohibited, lest small creatures get ingested with the food in dark, thus involuntarily causing to kill them.

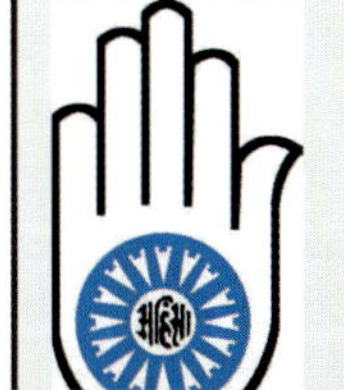

Call for Ahimsa

"One should not injure, subjugate, enslave, torture or kill any living beings including animals, living organism, and sentient beings. This doctrine of Non-Violence (Ahimsa Dharma) is immaculate, immutable and eternal."

Mahavira (Acharanga Sutra)

Strict followers of Jainism travel only on foot and do not travel by vehicles as it could trample insects. Further, they cover their mouth with a white cloth (*mukhvastrika*) so as not to accidentally ingest. They also use a broom (of fine thread called *ogho* or *rajoharan*) to sweep where they sit, lest they kill any insect.

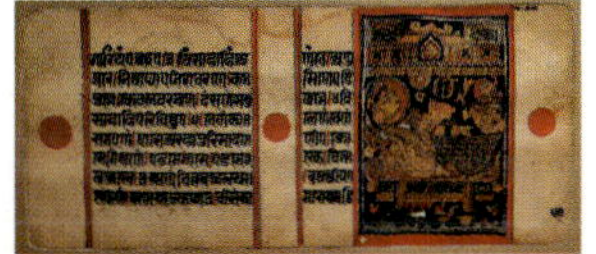

Karma and Transmigration of the Soul

The karmic philosophy and the doctrine of transmigration of soul (the rebirth in different living forms) are the principal theological conceptions of the Jainism which shapes its remaining spiritual doctrines. As per the *Tattvartha Sutra* and other Jain scriptures which elucidate this doctrine, the soul is eternal and has the attributes (Guna) of *chaitanya* (conception, perception knowledge), *sukh* (bliss), *virya* (energy). In its nascent form, when the *atman* (soul) is not associated with *ajeev* (lifeless matter) and specifically with *pudgal* (tangible matter), it is pure, has unlimited energy and bears an infinite capability. But in the mortal form, it acquires *karma* and experiences *bandha* (bondage).

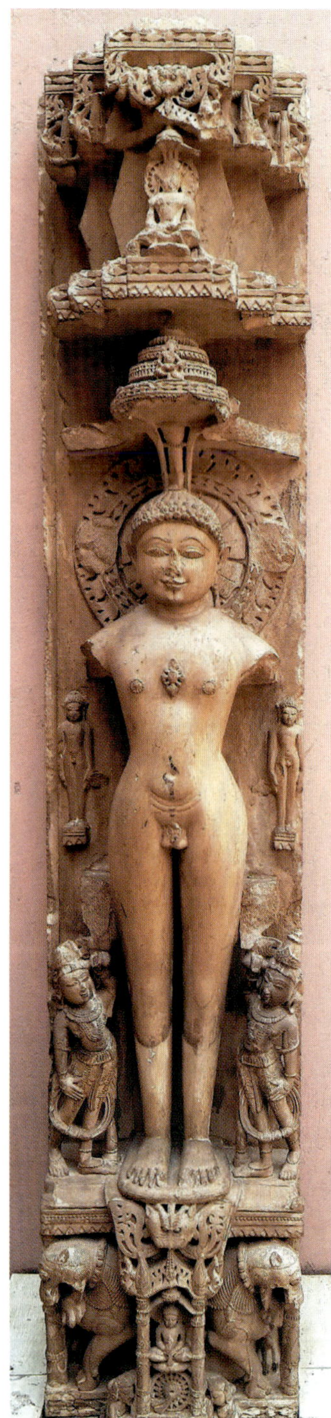

5.11: Shreyanshnatha, 11th tirthankara, sculpture of 11th-12th century CE, Shivpuri, Madhya Pradesh; current location State Museum, Bhopal — photograph by Madhukar K Bhagat

The attachment of karma is explained through the concept of *Aasrava*, (literal meaning; incoming or ingress) *raag* (attachment) and *dwaish* (aversion). As per *Tattvartha Sutra, aasrava* is the realm of soul (*pradesh*) through which the karma attaches to the soul. As per this theory, the exercise of mental, physical and other faculties (viz. speech) creates a *yog* (union or attachment) through which the *atman* interacts with the bodily organs and the material world. When this interaction is laced with *raag* (attachment) or *dwaish* (aversion) in their various manifestations, then it becomes a cause of *aasrava*, allowing the karmic particle to cling to the atman. The emergence of *karma* causes *bandha* (bondage). This in turn causes the transmigration of soul, till there is *samvara*; (prevention of entry of karmic particle), *nirjara*; (eradication/removal of the karmic matter already entered in soul) and *moksha*; (liberation due to attaining a state where no karmic matter remains attached to the soul).

Thus, the above doctrine encapsulates a 'cause and effect' theory, where there is centrality of the karma of the being, which is producing the cause of attachment thus causing the cycle of births and deaths. The *karma* itself can be wholesome (meritorious) and unwholesome (negative) with the latter causing the *kashaay* (defilement of soul) leading to the karmic bondage. The degree of *kashaay* determines the duration and intensity of bondage while the *yog* (bodily interaction of the soul) determines its category and plentitude.

Thus, *karma* remains the principal basis of *kashaay*; defilement of soul, its consequential transmigration and also the key to its emancipation. *Moksha* as per this theology, is not a result of beneficence or endowment by any external supreme being, but the product of the karmic endeavour of the sentient being. Further, to attain *kaivalya* (moksha), one must practice the right *karma* by following the principles of *triratna* of right conduct, right faith, and right knowledge.

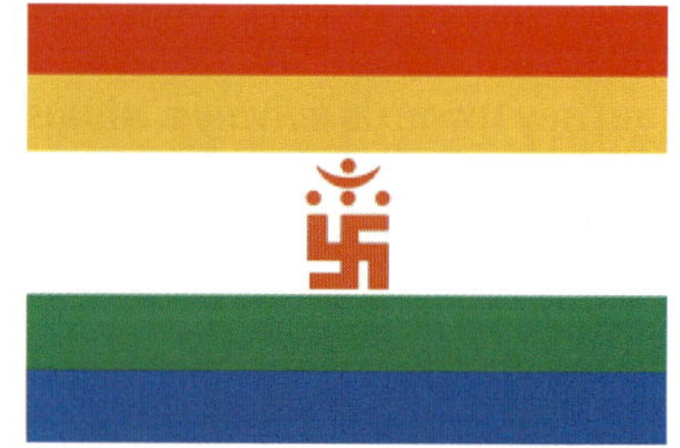

5.12: The Jain flag with the three dots above the swastika symbolising the ratnatraya or the 'triple gems' — Wikipedia

RATNATRAYA

Ratnatraya, or the **Triratna**, literally means the triple jewels, referring to *samyak darshana*, *samyak jnana* and *samyak charitra*. As per the very first shloka of *Tattvartha Sutra*, the three doctrines together constitute the path of moksha (liberation). ***Samyak darshana*** refers to the right perception, or right faith. It implies the faith which arises within, from the perception of the fundamental truths. ***Samyak jnana*** is the right knowledge which in turn is classified as of five kinds depending on how it is acquired. The last of the three, ***Samyak charitra***, refers to the right conduct which is the practical application of the right faith and right knowledge. All the three doctrines complement each other and are integral to the attainment of *kaivalya*.

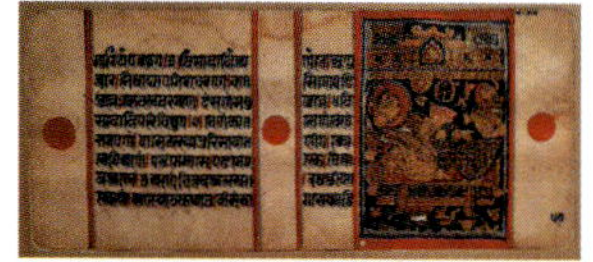

Samyak Darshana: Perception of the Truth

The right faith which arises from the perception of the enduring truth is the principal step for embarking on the journey for *kaivalya*. As per *Tattvartha Sutra*, the right faith can be inborn or may be acquired through the endeavor of self. *Samyaktva* or right faith, when inborn by birth is often the result of the effort of previous lives. Thus, the appropriate discernment is available to the being from his very birth. But the correct perception can also be acquired during one's life time though knowledge and conscious effort. But what is this right perception?

The right faith, or *samyak darshan*, implies to understand the true nature of substance and to have faith and firm belief in it. To do this, one must have faith in the teachings of the Tirthankaras, which enables a person to distinguish between the right and wrong *karma*. As per this philosophy, a person ought to believe in seven *tattvas* (also referred to as reality), which are *jiva, ajiva, aasrava, bandha, samvara, nirjara* and *moksha*. Having a clear and comprehensive knowledge of this 'reality' (*Tattvas*) and other philosophies is *samyak jnana* or right knowledge.

What is Samyak Darshana and How it Arises

तत्वार्थश्रद्धानं सम्यग्दर्शनम् ।। 1-2 ।।

Tattvarthashraddhanam Samyaggarshanam.

The faith in essential truths is the right perception.

verse 1-2 Tattvarthasutra

तन्निसर्गादधिगमाद्वा ।। 1-3 ।।

Tannisargadadhigamdva.

The right perception arises naturally or by acquisition.

verse 1-3 Tattvarthasutra

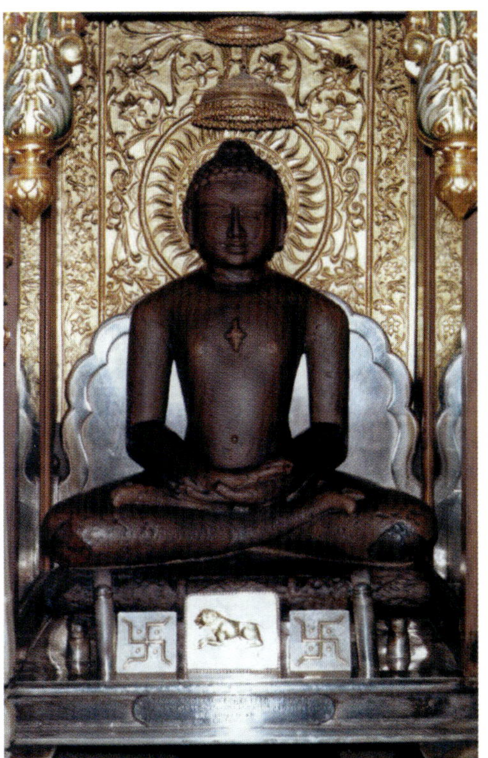

5.13: Statue of Mahavira meditating in the lotus position at Shri Mahaveer Ji, Rajasthan, India — Wikimedia Commons

Ratnatraya

सम्यगदर्शनज्ञानचरित्राणि मोक्षमार्गः ।। 1-1 ।।

Samyagadarshanagyancharitrani mokshamarga

Right perception, right knowledge and right conduct constitute the path of liberation.

Verse 1-1 Tattvartha Sutra

The Seven Truths

जीवाजीवाश्वबन्धसंवरनिर्जरामोक्षास्तत्वम

।। 1-4 ।।

Jeevajeevashravabandhasamvaranirja-ramokshastatvam

Soul (*jiva*), lifeless matter (*ajiva*), incoming of karma (*aasrava*), bondage (*bandha*), prevention (*samvara*), eradication of bondage (*nirjara*) and liberation (*moksha*) constitute the seven category of truths.

verse 1-4 Tattvarthasutra

While the Digambara tradition considers this 'reality' to comprise the above seven elements, the Shwetambara tradition considers it to be nine, and includes *paap* and *punya* as distinct elements. However, as per the former doctrine, the two are not separately reckoned, but implicit in the concept of *aasrava*.

THE SEVEN TRUTHS: THE CONCEPTION FOR LIBERATION

The knowledge of the seven truths, or *Tattvas*, is the fundamental conception of the Jain doctrine and is considered imperative for faith in the philosophy and its eventual practice. Further, to understand the entire theology including the principle of *karma* and the basis for omniscience, the knowledge of the 'seven truths' is considered essential.

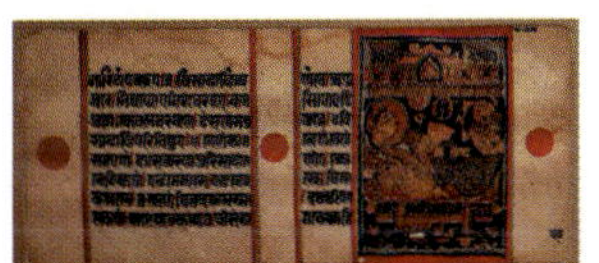

Jiva

Jiva refers to the soul, which is said to exist since time immemorial, possesses consciousness and is immortal. It is the sentient element amongst the seven elements and one of the two most important of the elements. The attributes (*guna*) of *chaitanya* (consciousness, perception, knowledge), *sukh* (bliss), *virya* (energy) characterize the soul. It is pure when not smeared with karmic particles and has infinite potential. But as an embodiment of a being, and not conscious of its own true self and potential, it interacts with tangible matter in pursuit of its perceived happiness, thereby creating a karmic bondage. Thus, the soul experiences transmigration and repeated cycles of births and deaths.

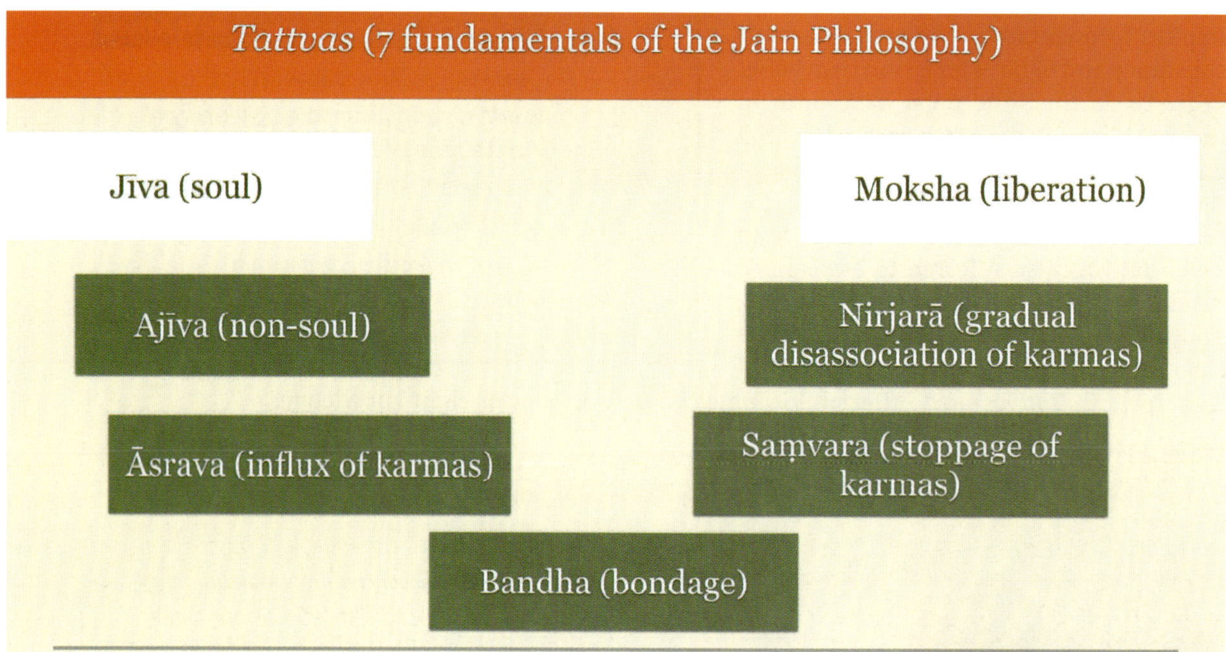

The conception of *jiva* in the Jain metaphysics ascribes to it the attributes of it being the knower (*jnatra*), actor (*kartra*) and the enjoyer (*bhoktra*), endowing it with the triple qualities of cognition, conation, affection/ emotion. Thus, it draws parallel with the Vedantic conception of the atman, but is much wider than the Samkhya conception, where the purusha has a meagre role as the doer, although it is the knower and the enjoyer.

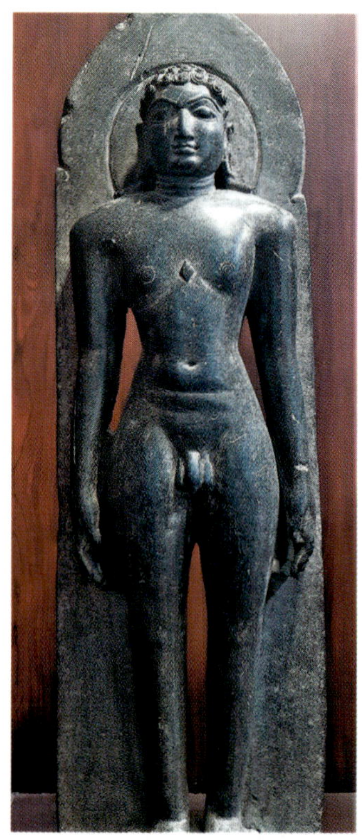
5.14: Shantinatha, 16th tirthankara, sculpture, 11th century Akola; current location, Central Museum, Nagpur — photograph by Madhukar K Bhagat

The states of soul

The detailed philosophy of a sentient being further describes the different categories of living beings (*jiva*), their modes, sense organs, objects of senses, types of bodies life spans etc. For instance, the classification based on the sense organs recognizes the organisms as *ekandriya*, that is having only one sense organ, viz. plants (having only sense of touch), *dvindriya* (having two sense organs viz. worms) to *panchendriya* i.e. having the five senses, such as the animals. At the highest level, is the human beings, having all the five senses as well the *manas* (the mind). Further, five different modes of souls are identified by the doctrine. These are suppressive, destructive, mixed, operative and intrinsic. The modes indicate the changing states of the soul depending upon the influence of different types of karmas.

Those having the right perception and right conduct are categorized as the suppressive souls. In this mode, called *aupashmik* (suppressive mode) the *karmas* remain suppressed like settled impurities in still water. But they have the potential to resurface in case of turbulence. Thus, the suppressed *karmas* can also become operative in this mode. Among the numerous category of *karmas*, the deluding *karma* which prohibit the soul from perceiving its true nature is considered the most destructive. Other defiling *karmas* include, the perception obscuring, the knowledge obscuring and the obstructing karmas.

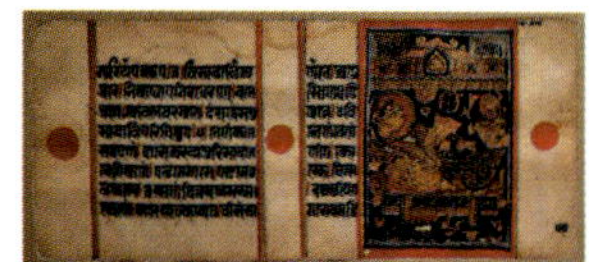

In the destructive (*kshayik*) mode, the lasting purity of soul can happen with the complete destruction of the *karma.* But in this state the soul can acquire new *karma* as well and has to bear its effects. The next mode is the mixed mode (*kshayopasmik*), where the *karma* may be partly in a suppressive and partly in destructive mode.

In the operative mode (*audayik*), the soul may not be in any of the three states or some of its different karmas may be in different states. Thus, this state refers to emergence or rise of karma. The fifth classification intrinsic mode (*parinamik*) refers to the innate characteristics of the soul that are, consciousness, worthy or unworthy of liberation. Therefore, it does not relate to any situation per-se.

Soul and its Capacity to Know

उपयोगो लक्षणम् ।। 2-8 ।।

Upayogo Lakshanam.

The innate capability of the soul to know, is its essential characteristics.

verse 2-8 Tattvarthasutra

The innate capacity to know (*upayog*) is a salient characterisitic of the soul. This is an exclusive attribute of the soul (*jiva*) which is absent in all other insentient elements and is also a key to its emancipation. This ability is further characterised as *sakar upayog* (knowledge) and *nirakar upayog* (perception).

Ajiva

Non-soul refers to the matter or material that is without soul and lacks consciousness and the ability of knowing. In the larger domain of the *ajiva*, it is the *pudgal* (tangible matter) which has the potential to interact with the soul. This is the second of the 'two most important' of the seven elements, as it is the interaction of *jiva* with *ajiva* that produces the karmic bondage. Understanding *ajiva*, and in particular, *pudgal*, is crucial to understand the essentials of its interaction with the soul, hence the cause of the bondage, prevention of this interaction and its eventual eradication.

The *ajiva*, or insentient matter, is further classified as *dharma*, *adharma*, *akaash* and *pudgal. Ajiva* is also considered to be indestructible and hence exist forever.

The doctrine of dravya

Together with the *jiva* (sentient) the the ajiva (insentient) that is *dharma*, *adharma*, *akaash* and *pudgal*, constitute a group called *dravya*. They are also referred to as *panchastikaya*. Here *asti* means existence, and *kaya* means volume, implying what is capable of spatial relationship. As per some schools of philosophy, *kala* (time) is also considered a *dravya*, thus constituting the six entities in the category of *dravyas*.

5.15: A tirthankara in meditation, 12th-13th century CE, Shivpuri; current location, State Museum, Bhopal — photograph by Madhukar K Bhagat

The *dravyas* are characterised by *gunas* or properties and *paryayas* or different forms in which they may exist. Thus, each of the *dravyas* have unique and distinct properties. There is disappearance of one *parayaya* and appearance of the other, but the substance remains the same. Thus, though the form of the *dravyas* may change, they themselves continue to exist and hence are considered indestructible.

Pudgal refers to all tangible objects which are visible or invisible. These are the only entities in the category *dravya* which have form. The word *pudgal* is composed of *pud* meaning 'coming together or to aggregate' and gal or 'coming apart or to disaggregate'. Thus, it literally means that which is capable of influx and reflux. All objects capable of sensory perception are considered as *pudgal*. They are also associated with the attributes of odour, colour, taste and touch. Thus, it is analogous to *maya* in Vedanta and *prakriti* in Samkhya philosophies. As entities, they are considered to be divisible and said to be composed of smallest indivisible and indestructible units called *parmanu* (a concept analogous to elementary particles) which is even smaller than *anu* (atom). However, some schools of thought equate *parmanu* with the smallest unit or atom. Further they are capable of aggregation through bonds and such aggregation are called

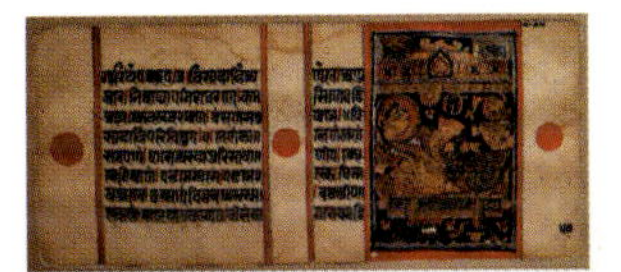

skandha. A *skandha* may be of merely two *parmanus* or it may be the most important and the biggest aggregate constituting the entire universe. The *pancha bhuta* or the five elements, are the aggregates of *parmanus* and hence a *skandha*. The *parmanu* being very minute cannot be perceived by ordinary senses.

Similarly, *kala* (time) is also composed of smallest units (*kaal parmanu* or *samay*) and has the property of being unidirectional, with before and after constituting the time series, with no possibility of simultaneous movement in same time.

The *jiva* along with *pudgal* is considered as the principle dravyas and also referred to as the *sakriya dravya* or *dravya*, which are capable of acting, while the others viz. *dharma*, *adharma*, *aakash* and *kaal* are nishkriya dravya.

Aakash implies the infinite space as is commonly understood. It is further classified as *lokakasha*, or the cosmic space (world space), and *alokiakasha* (para-cosmic space), the latter being much larger than the former but empty. Thus, the *jiva*, *pudgal* and other dravyas fall within the *lokakasha*.

The doctrine of dharma dravya and adharma dravya

The *jiva* and *ajiva* together constitute the *dravya*. However, this doctrine is in a way unique, for in this doctrine of *dravya*, *dharma* and *adharma* do not have the meaning as taken in general parlance, which is the religious or ethical duty and its antonym. Here, *dharma* refers to the principle of motion, and conversely, *adharma* is the principle of rest. Both *jiva* (soul-sentient being) and *pudgal* have the attributes of motion and rest and the medium of their motion or rest is provided by *dharma* and *adharma*. Further, the *dharma* and *adharma*, or the principle of rest and motion, pervade the entire universe. But they find existence only in the *lokakash* or the physical universe itself and not beyond it in the *alokiakasha*. For instance, for a fish to swim, the causative factor for swimming is within it, but the medium is water. Similarly, for a bird to fly, the medium is air. For every movement there is a medium of movement, and conversely, for rest or for movement to stop, the principle of *adharma* comes into play. Without the two principles of *dharma* and *adharma*, there would not be any definite structure of the world and the cosmos would disintegrate into primordial atoms (*parmanu*), thus the *lokakash* would cease to exist.

Aasrava

In the 'seven truths' comprising the *Samyak Darshana*, the concept of *aasrava* is next in order of significance to *jiva* and *ajiva*. *Aasrava* refers to the influx of auspicious and evil karmic matter in the soul. As a result of indulgence in the attachment *(raag)* and aversion *(dwaish)* which arise periodically, the karmic particles are caused to penetrate the realm of the soul and attach to it. This penetration in the realm of soul is *aasrava*, or the ingress of the karma. Sometimes the realm of soul or the opening/ gateways through which the penetration of karma takes place is also referred to as aasrava.

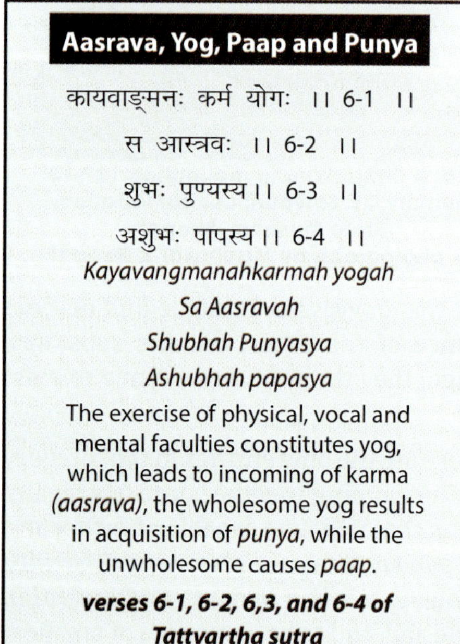
Aasrava, Yog, Paap and Punya

कायवाङ्मनः कर्म योगः ।। 6-1 ।।

स आस्त्रवः ।। 6-2 ।।

शुभः पुण्यस्य ।। 6-3 ।।

अशुभः पापस्य ।। 6-4 ।।

Kayavangmanahkarmah yogah
Sa Aasravah
Shubhah Punyasya
Ashubhah papasya

The exercise of physical, vocal and mental faculties constitutes yog, which leads to incoming of karma *(aasrava)*, the wholesome yog results in acquisition of *punya*, while the unwholesome causes *paap*.

verses 6-1, 6-2, 6,3, and 6-4 of Tattvartha sutra

Origin of aasrava

The concept of *aasrava* is integral to the karmic theory and hence liberation. The very first few verses of chapter 6 of *Tattvartha Sutra* elucidate the concept of *aasrava* and the reasons for their origin. It mentions that it is the exercising of the physical, vocal and mental faculties which create a *yog*. The body organs through which these faculties are exercised, are in themselves insentient, and in absence of the soul, lack the capability to exercise these faculties. Thus, the exercise of these faculties is the cause of *yog* (a form of connect or union) causing the interaction of the soul with the sense organs. This results in the emanation and acquisition of karma.

The interaction or *yog* would continue till the soul thrives in the mortal body. However, only those interactions where there is undue exercise of the faculties, viz. interactions which are laced with attachment (*raag*) and aversion (*dwesh*) are the root of the karmic matter and hence a cause of the aasrava. The exercise of the faculties may be wholesome and may lead to meritorious *karma* or *punya*, or it may be unwholesome, causing unmeritorious *karma*, termed *paap*. This doctrine also takes into account the intentions of the person. Thus, activities performed with positive intentions like charity, help, worship etc. are considered

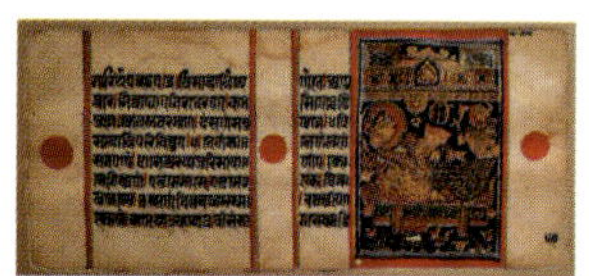

wholesome, while those with negative intentions viz. violence, stealing hatred etc. are unwholesome.

Activities in themselves may not be entirely wholesome or absolutely unwholesome, but may contain traits of both, with difference in degrees of constituting wholesomeness and unwholesomeness. Further, certain category of activities or certain manner of exercise of faculties results in defilement of soul called *kashaay*. Anger, pride, deception and greed are examples of defilement causing exercise of faculty. Such activities are referred as *saamparayik karma* thus causing *saamparayik aasrava*. They affect the very purity of soul and the karma acquired has a stronger impact and a longer attachment. However, where the karma is acquired due to innocent exercise of the faculties, it is relatively weaker and not long lasting (*iriyapathik karma* and *iryapathik aasrava*).

The doctrine further elucidates the four causes of the *saamaparayik aasrava*. These are, the absence of the five restraints which are *ahimsa* (non-violence), *satya* (truth, not lying), *asteya* (non-stealing), *aparigraha* (non-possession) and *brahmacharya* (celibacy). *Kashaay*, or instincts that defile the mind (thought), is the next cause of *iriyapathik aasrava* and emanates from *raag* and *dwesh*. The third factor is non-dispassionate use of sense organs, viz., the senses of touch, taste, sound, sight and odor. This results in attachment or aversion getting instilled in the worldly soul. The last of the causes is a certain category of activities such as violence, which results in the most defiling *aasrava*.

Thus, the nature of activity, intention of the doer, the intensity of the act etc., all have an important bearing on the *aasrava*, its quantum and its duration of attachment within the soul.

Bandha

Once the *aasrava* takes place, the karmic matter is able to bind to the soul. This bondage caused by intermingling of the karmic particle and the soul is referred as the *bandha*. The duration of the karmic attachment is determined by the intensity of the indulgence in attachment or aversion.

मिथ्यादर्शनाविरतिप्रमादकषाययोगा बन्धहेतवरू।। 8-1 ।।
Mithyadarshaviratipramaadkashaayyoga bandha-hetava
Wrong perception (*mithyaa darshana*) absence of restraints (*avirati*) indolence (*pramaad*) defilement (*kashaay*)and undue exercise of faculties cause the bondage (*bandha*).
Verse 8-1: Tattvartha sutra

5.16: Aranatha, 18th tirthankara, 12th century Narasinghpur current location, Central Museum, Nagpur — photograph by Madhukar K Bhagat

Tattvartha sutra (chapter 8) explains in depth the concept of the *bandha* its causes and categories. It states that wrong perception, absence of restraints, defilement, undue exercise of faculties and indolence are the five causes of bondage.

Wrong perception, *mithyaa darshan*, implies lack of understanding of the right perception *(samyaktva)*. It further arises due to a delusional believe of the worldly occurrences and affairs being true and enduring. This is akin to a person caught in a dream believing the pleasure and pain experienced therein to be true and ignorantly pursuing it.

Avirati is the lack of the five restraints. This in turn is caused due to misguided belief in the worldly happiness as the enduring truth and the sentient being failing to exercise restraint in the course of pursuing it.

Pramaad is the failure to exercise vigour. It is the indolence which is caused due to lack of firm belief in the true faith. If not for it, the being would exercise vigour and restraint in pursuing the right faith.

Kashaay is the defilement of soul which occurs due to *raag* and *dwesh*. These cause the being to respond without equanimity to worldly occurrences in pursuit of its perceived worldly happiness. Thus, the situations apparently favourable to the sentient being, engender a yearning *(raag)* and unfavourable ones give rise to *aversion (dwesh)*. These in turn lead to emergence of defilements of anger, arrogance, deception and craving.

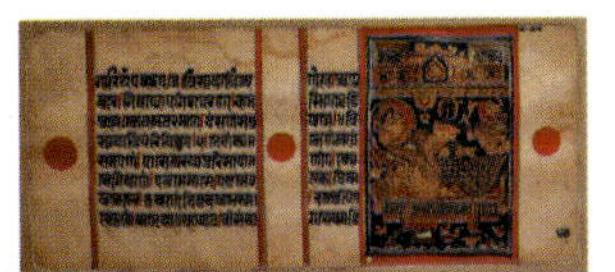

Yog is caused due to undue exercise of the faculties, causing the interaction of the soul and the organs of senses. This is prompted as the sentient being remains in pursuit of the ephemeral happiness on account of ignorance and delusion.

The doctrine of *bandha* further elucidates the four crucial aspects of *bandha*, which are type, duration, intensity and plentitude. Further, it also identifies eight broad categories of *karma*. These *karmas* are; *jnanavarniya* (knowledge obscuring), *darshanavaraniya* (perception obscuring), *vedaniya* (that which generate comfort or discomfort to the soul), *mohaniya* (deluding), *ayushya* (life span determining), *nam* (physique and physical features determining), *gotra* (societal status determining), *antaray* (causing obstruction to objectives). Of the above, *jnanvarniya*, *darshanavarniya*, *mohaniya* and *antaray* are considered to be defiling karmas, while the other four are deemed non-defiling *karmas*.

Samvara

The restraining of the inflow of karmic matter into the soul is referred as *samvara*. The karma which arises on account of *yog* and undue use of faculties leads to the karmic particles entering and defiling the soul. This is compared to accumulation of dust in a house. The first step to clean this house would accordingly be to prevent the entry of this dust in the rooms, for which the doors and windows would have to be shut. Similar to this analogy, the doctrine of *samvara* aims at prevention of the entry of the karmic matter. This is to be done by exercise of due restraint, thus preventing the soul from being defiled any further and ascending the spiritual ladder. The doctrine further explains that *samvara* can be achieved through the observation of the steps of *gupti*, *samiti*, *dharma*, *anupreksha*, *parishahjay* and *chairitra*.

The Constituent Elements of Samvara

स गुप्तिसमितिधर्मानुप्रेक्षापरीषहजयचारित्रैः ।। 9-2 ।।

तपसा निर्जरा च ।। 9-3 ।।

Sa Guptisamitidharmanupreksha parishahjaycharitraih. 9-2

Tapas Nirjara cha 9-3

It consists of gupti, samiti, dharma, anupreksha parishahjay and chairitra. Observance of tapa also leads to Nirjara.

verses 9-2, & 9-3 of Tattvartha sutra

Gupti refers to restraining of the mental faculties *(manogupti)*, vocal faculty *(vachangupti)* and physical faculties *(kayagupti)*. Though restraint of the faculties is essential for prevention of the karma to arise, nevertheless, the very existence in the mortal form necessitates the use of these faculties. The seeker of *kaivalya* must be watchful in our daily lives in such circumstances. This is referred to as *samiti*, which is being vigilant while moving *(iryasamiti)*, while speaking *(bhasha samiti)*, while accepting articles *(eshana samiti)*, while placing objects *(nishkep samiti)* and while disposing waste *(utsarga samiti)*.

Dharma refers to the inculcation and observation of the attributes of forgiveness *(kshama)*, mildness *(mardav)*, straight forwardness *(arjav)*, purity *(sauch)*, truth *(satya)*, self-restraint *(samyam)*, austerity *(tapa)*, renouncement *(tyaaga)*, eschewing possession *(akinchanya)* and celibacy *(brahmacharya)*. The above 10 attributes constitute the highest form of religious (spiritual) observation and also referred to as the *dashlakshana dharma*.

Anupreksha refers to contemplation about the transitory nature of the world, ephemeral pleasures which sentient beings seek, and the experience of sorrow which the being experiences in the various cycles of birth and death and other spiritual truths. The doctrine specifies *anupreksha* to include contemplation about helplessness, worldliness, aloneness, otherness, impurity, incoming of karma, its prevention, eradication, nature of universe, rarity of right guidance and tenets of the lord.

Parishahajay is the principle of forbearance, which exhorts the seeker to bear the hardships and discomforts patiently so as not to waver from the right path and thus to eradicate the bondage of *karma*. These hardships could be, hunger, thirst, cold heat, insect, bite, unclad state, disease, despise, seduction, moving about, reproach, injury, seeking alms, thorny pathways, rough bed, dirt etc.

The last in doctrine of *samvara* is *charitra*, which implies putting the precept into practice. This is to be done by following of the monastic order. The first stage of this monastic order (through which the *samvara* precepts are put into practice) is equanimity *(samyik)*. This is followed by initiation in the monastic order *(chhedopasthapan)*. At the next stage is the practising of purity *(parihar vishuddhi)*. This leads to a stage where only finer defilements remain *(sookshma samparay)*, while the grosser ones are removed. The seeker is then able to achieve total detachment *(yathakhyat)*.

Nirjara

While *samvara* is the practice of prevention of the entry of the new karmic matter in the realm of soul, *nirjara* is the next spiritual step of eradication of the existing/old karma and or separation/dissociation of

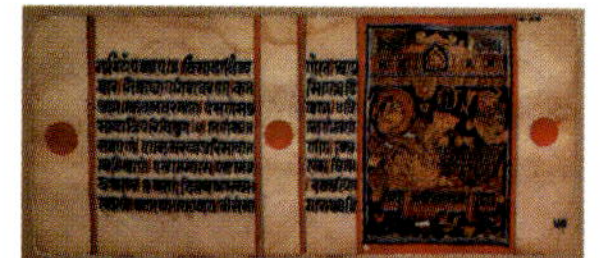

karmic bondage. This is to be achieved through *tapa* or the practice of austerity. The austerities also help in prevention of new karma from being generated, hence they are also considered as a *samvara.*

Broadly, the austerities are classified as external and internal. The austerities which operate at the physical level are classified as external austerities. These include *anshan* or *upvas*, or fasting, *avamaudarya*; eating lesser quantities, *vrittiparisankhya*; reducing the variety of articles, particularly food articles, *raasparityag*; giving attachment for tastes, *viviktashyashan;* living in forlorn spaces and occupying minimum space and *kayaklesh;* bearing physical discomfort.

The internal austerities are not externally visible and entail conditioning and disciplining of the mind. These also include six broad categories, which are *prayaschita* (repentance), *vinay* (modesty), *vaiyavrita* (service), *swadhyaya* (self-study), *vyutsarga* (remaining unperturbed by physical and mental concerns) and *dhyana* (meditation).

Moksha

Also referred as *kaivalya*, *siddhi*, or *mukti*, *moksha* is the ultimate state of liberation of the soul, where it is completely dissociated from the karmic matter. As per the doctrine of *kaivalya*, the soul in its nascent state is pure and has infinite capabilities. But in its worldly embodiment, it is oblivious of its true nature. The undue exercise of faculties resulting in *yog*, leads to *aasrava* and defilement of the soul with karmic particles, thus causing *bandha.* This bondage persists and is the cause of transmigration of soul into any of the four *gatis* (states) viz. *devas* or divine beings, *naras* or human beings, *narakas* or denizens of hell, and *tiryakas* or the lower animals and plants. Thus, the soul experiences innumerable birth and death cycles till the soul is eventually liberated. But liberation happens only when the prevention of the karmic particles *(samvara)* and their ultimate eradication *(nirjara)* has taken place. The attainment of this karma-less state is *kaivalya* or liberation.

Moksha: Destruction of All Karmas

मोहक्षयाज्ज्ञानदर्शनावरणान्तरायक्षयाच्च केवलम् ।। 10-1 ।।

Mohkshyajjnandarshanavaranantaryakshyachcha kevalam.

Omniscience is manifested by the annihilation of the delusive karma, the knowledge and the perception obscuring karmas and the obstructing karma.

Verse 10-1: Tattvartha sutra

बन्धहेत्वभावनिर्जराभ्याम् ।। 10-2 ।।

Bandhhetvabhavnirjarbhyam

Karma are destroyed by prevention of the very cause of bondage and by their elimination (of ingressed karma).

Verse 10-2: Tattvartha sutra

कृत्स्नकर्मक्षयो मोक्षः ।। 10-3 ।।

Kritasnakarmakshayomoksha

Complete extermination of all the karmas is moksha (liberation).

Verse 10-3: Tattvartha sutra

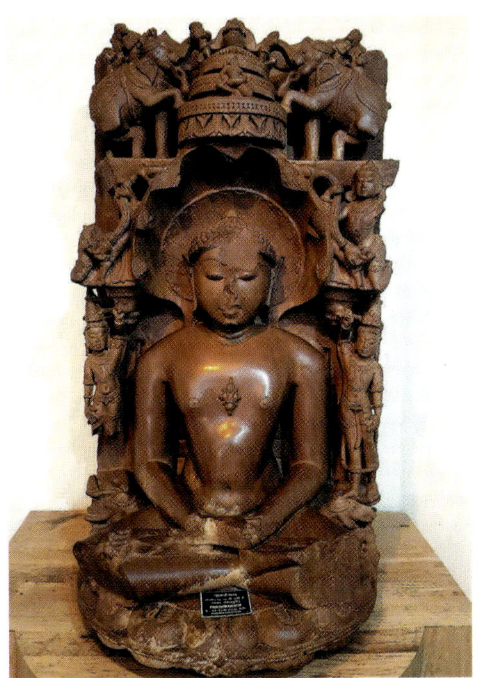

5.17: Parsvanatha, 23rd tirthanakara, 12th century CE, Shivpuri; current location, State Museum Bhopal — photograph by Madhukar K Bhagat

The doctrine further states that *kaivalya* is manifested by the annihilation of the delusive-*karma*, the knowledge-obscuring and perception-obscuring *karma* and the obstructing-karma. The above types of *karmas cause* the defilement of soul and their destruction eventually leads to omniscience or *kaivalya*.

Samyak Jnana

The second of the *ratnatraya*, *samyak jnana* is the right knowledge which is essential for the sentient being and a precursor to the right conduct. The two elements, *samyak darshan* and *samyak jnana* are interdependent and complimentary to each other. While *samyak darshana* is to have the correct perception of the true faith and the 'reality', the *samyak jnana* is the correct and complete knowledge of the soul and the 'reality' viz. the 'seven elements'. Without the true faith and knowledge, the adoption of the right course of conduct may not be possible or the seeker may eventually waver in its conduct. Like other elements of the Jain philosophy this theory of *samyak jnana* is also fairly developed with detailed classifications.

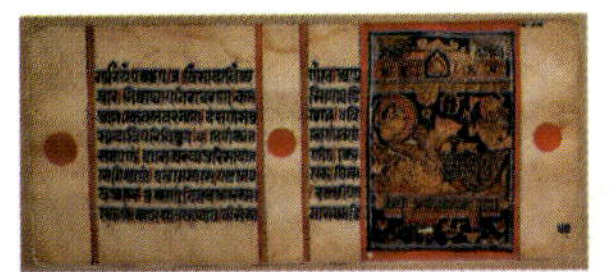

Samyak Jnana: The Modes of Knowledge

मतिश्रुतावधिमनः पर्यायकेवलानि ज्ञानम् ।। 1-9 ।।

Matishrutavadhimanahparyaykevalani jnanam.

Matijnan (intellectual knowledge), srutijnan (scriptural knowledge) avadhijnan (clairvoyance), manahprayayjnan (telepathic knowledge) *and kevaljnan* (omniscience) are the five types of knowledge.).

Verse 1-9: Tattvartha Sutra

As to how the true knowledge is gained, the Jain scriptures classify *samyak jnana* into five types, depending on the mode of its acquisition. These are *matijnana* (intellectual knowledge), *srutijnana* (scriptural knowledge) *avadhijnana* (clairvoyance), *manahparyaya jnana* (telepathic knowledge) and *kevaljnana* (omniscience). These forms of knowledge are also referred to as *pramanas* or instruments of knowledge. The first two category of knowledge viz. *matijnana* and *srutijnana* are acquired through the sensory perception and faculties *vide* means of intelligence, rationality, scriptures and books, teaching and discourses etc. Accordingly, these are deemed as external and considered as indirect *(paroksha jnana).* These are also the common forms of knowledge. The other three categories of knowledge arise by virtue of inner purity of the seeker and thus are considered to be internal and direct *(pratyaksha jnana).* This philosophy also states that the first three categories of knowledge (*mati*, *sruti* and *avadhi*) may be misleading at times, as the person may be lacking vivek or discernment, to fully distinguish what is right and what is not. Hence the last two are the forms of *jnana* which are trusted and most valued.

Matijnana is the knowledge acquired through the human faculties and senses (sensory knowledge) which are gathered by means of intellect, memory, recognition, reasoning and deduction. Thus, it is the knowledge acquired through the ordinary process of sense experience which is conditioned by the sense based perception and inferential knowledge.

This knowledge is said to arise in four stages which are *avagraha* (apprehension), *iha* (faint perception), *avaya* (comprehension) and *dharana* (imprint). The mere knowledge of existence of something is said to be *avagrah* when the person has some faint idea of its existence, but is unable to distinguish it clearly vis-a-vis others (viz. distinction of a rope from a snake) then it is termed as iha. When the conception of the object and its distinction vis-a-vis others becomes clear, then it is the stage of *avaya*. Finally, when even in the absence of the object the conception remains very clear, it is called *dharana*. Each of these can be sub-categorised as to how the knowledge is gained, viz through sense of sight, hearing, touch, taste, smell or faculty of mind.

Srutijnana is acquired through two sources, *viz.* hearing of oral instructions and discourses, and through reading of scriptures and texts. The emphasis in Jain philosophy is on the latter. The scriptures themselves are said to be revealed by the sarvajna (omniscient). The scriptural texts of the Jains include the *Agamas, Acharangasutra, Tattvartha sutra* and *others.*

Avadhijnana refers to clairvoyance or extrasensory perception. This is the ability to see in time and space much beyond the limits of normal faculties. This is said to arise in heavenly and infernal beings *(bhavapratyaya avadhi)* and in human being by means of internal purity and pacification of karma *(gunapratyaya avadhi).* This is further divided into six categories depending on the degree and steadiness of the avadhijnana.

Manahprayay refers to the telepathic knowledge, *vide* which the thoughts and mind of the others can be read. This also arises by attainment of internal purity. While the internal purity is lower, then this ability is limited and is (referred to as *rijumati*) which can be even lost. When the purity is higher, the ability (referred as *vipulamati*) is enduring, and continues till attainment of omniscience.

Kevaljnana is the the highest form of knowledge which arise at the pinnacle of the spiritual pursuit. This is a stage where the *jiva* has become completely bereft of all past karmas. This is the stage of omniscience.

Samyak Charitra

The last of the triple jewels, *samyak charitra* is the practical application of the *samyak jnana* in the domain of the day-to-day life of the follower. Without translation of the knowledge to practice, the former is rendered meaningless, hence the interdependence and interconnect of the two. *Samyak charitra* operates in the two key areas of the seven truths, viz, *samvara*, that is the prevention of the arising of new karma, and *nirjara*, which is the eradication of the existing karma from the domain of the soul. When the twin objectives are fully met in practice, then only the state of omniscience is attained. Thus, the daily conduct of the follower has to be in sync with the philosophy of prevention and elimination of the karmic matter.

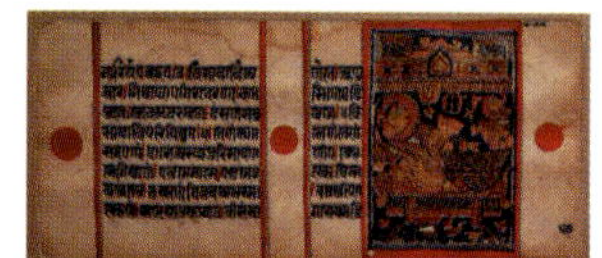

But what are the stated practices? Broadly, *Samyak charitra* can be considered as the observation of six essential practices and five *mahavratas* and other subsidiary vratas. These practices themselves draw from the principles of *ahimsa* (non-violence, compassion), *anekantanvada* (non-absolutism and multiplicity of viewpoints) and *asteya* (non-attachment to and limiting of material needs).

The daily essential practices of the Shwetambaras comprise: *samayika* (equanimity), *pratikraman*, which is to repent, reproach and reflect upon one's past wrong deeds and thoughts, *pratyakhyana*; taking vows of renouncing certain activities and certain types of food for self-discipline, *chauvisattho*; to pray and appreciate the virtues of the 24 tirthankaras, vandana; devotion and service to ascetics, *kayotsarga*; practices to develop non-attachment to body and of meditation.

The Digamabara tradition is also similar and incorporates devapuja; respect and appreciation of virtues of the tirthankaras, *gururpasti*; devotion and service to ascetics, *swadhayaya*; studying of scriptures by oneself, *sanyam* (self-restraint), *dana* (charity) and *tapa* (austerities and penance).

But beside the above, the *panch mahavrata* (the five great vows) the three guna vrata (merit vows) and the four *shiksha vrata* (disciplinary vows) form the bedrock of *Samyak charitra*.

The Panchamahavrata: The Bedrock of Samayaka Charita

हिंसानृतस्तेयाब्रह्मपरिग्रहेभ्यो विरतिव्रतम ।। 7-2 ।।

Hinsanritsteyabrahmaparigrahebhyo virativratam.

Refraining from violence lies, stealing, sensuality and accumulation constitutes the restraints.

Verse 7-2: Tattvartha Sutra

The Panchamahavrata: The five great vows or the panchmahavrata (major restraints) include *ahimsa*, *satya*, *asteya*, *brahmacharya* and *aparigraha*. While the ascetics and monks are to observe these restraints fully and in their true spirit, for the laity (lay followers) complete observation of ahimsa and other vratas in totality may not be feasible in the worldly life. Jainism permits their partial observance which is referred to as *anuvrata* (minor vows). Further, each of the restraints are also associated with five aspects, which assist in the observation of the restraints and are referred to as bhavana, which are akin to a monastic code.

Violence, a Source of Distress and Evil

हिंसादिष्विहामुत्र चापायावद्यदर्शनम् ।। 7-4 ।।

Hinsadishvihamutra chapayavadarshanam

Distress in the world and evil beyond are inherent in violence and other faults.

Verse 7-4: Tattvartha Sutra

Ahimsa or non-violence or non-injury, is one of the fundamental precepts of Jainism and the most crucial of the restraints. *Satya* (truth) and *ahimsa* are considered complimentary and interdependent on each other, for there can be no *ahimsa* without truth and vice-versa. The concept of *ahimsa* is expansive and universal, and is based in compassion for sentient being (and even includes the abiotic world). Besides, it is integral to the karmic principle. The *bhavanas* which are associated with *ahimsa* are observation of vigilance in making any movement, moving any object, acceptance of object, mental thoughts and activities, consuming any food and water. These are considered essential to avoid killing or injury to even insects or lower forms of life. Besides, violence should not emanate even in our thoughts, for which it is considered important to be vigilant of even our thoughts.

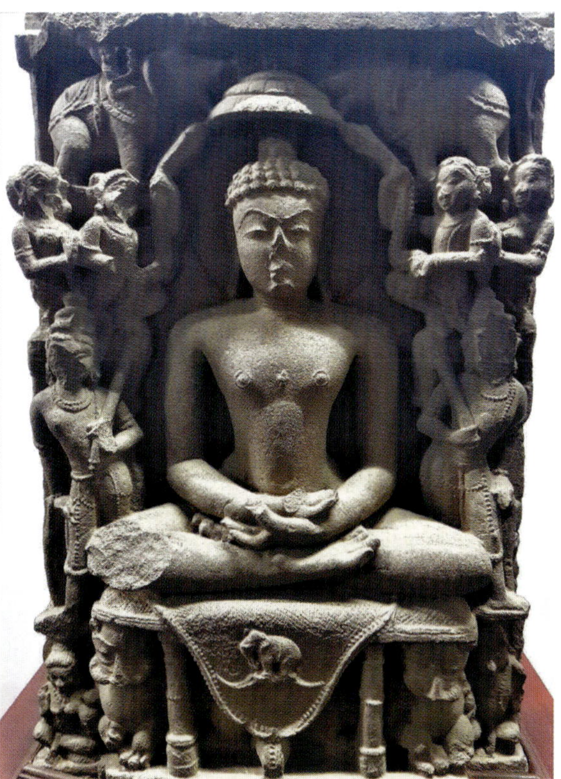

5.18: Ajinatha, 2nd tirthankara, in a posture of meditation; sculpture, 10th century Narasinghpur, Madhya Pradesh; current location, Central Museum, Nagpur — photograph by Madhukar K Bhagat

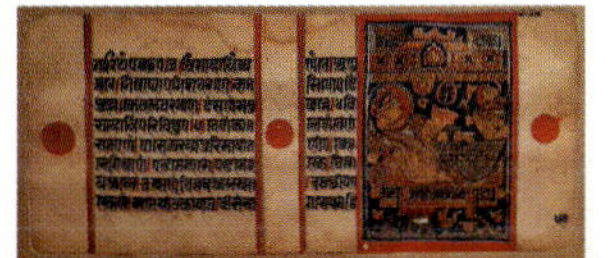

Satya is the practice of speaking the truth or restraint from uttering a lie. Even making a statement which is not commendable is to be restrained. *Tattvartha sutra* elaborates that denying any fact or thing which has been done, or stating anything contrary to the facts, is lying. Besides, it covers untrue contemplation as well. The *bhavanas* associated with this restraint are exercise of vigilance while speaking, and avoidance of anger, greed and mocking laughter. The influence of above factors may incite a person to lie or even to violence.

Asteya refers to non-stealing and exhorts the follower on restraining himself from appropriating what is not his. *Tattvartha sutra* considers taking anything which is not given as akin to stealing. Thus, taking or getting anything not offered by the appropriate owner is improper and amounts to stealing.

Defining Untruth

असदभिधानमनृतम् ।। 7-9 ।।

Asadbhidhanam anritam

Lie consists of uttering what is not true

Verse 7-9: Tattvartha Sutra

Brahmacharya, as per the usual interpretation is considered to be observation of celibacy. However the doctrine of *brahmacharya* has a larger connotation and implies not just non-indulgence in any sexual activity, but also restraining from sensual indulgence of any kind. Thus, this philosophy considers every type of sensual pleasure as negation of celibacy. As with the concepts of *ahimsa* and *satya*, compliance to *brahmacharya* is not only to be implemented in conduct, but even in thoughts.

Aparigraha is generally understood to be the principle of non-accumulation of possessions. This is essential to reduce the multiplicity of dependences of followers and enabling him to cultivate a sense of worldly detachment. However, a more comprehensive interpretation of *aparigraha* implies non-attachment to material objects and possessions. Thus, not only thc worldly needs are to be limited but even the attachment to material objects are to be eliminated. A latter connotation of the concept of *aparigraha* enables the detached use of material objects for the benefit of others.

Gunavrata and Sikshavrata: Besides the *pancha-mahavrata*, the doctrine of *samyaka charita* exhorts the followers to follow seven more subsidiary *vratas*. These are the three gunavrata and the four *shikshavrata*. These are to be complied with, by the monks as well as the lay followers. However, the latter may comply them with modifications/partially in form of *anuvrata*.

The ***gunavrata*** (merit vows) comprise the *digvrata* which is restriction in movement with regards to the direction; *bhogopabhogaparimana*, which is limiting the use of consumable and non-consumable articles and *anartha-dandavirati* which is refraining from purposeless violence, activities and occupations which are harmful.

Deshvirati is the first ***shiskhsavrata*** which stipulates restricting the areas of operation for a certain period of time. *Samayik* is a vow to maintain equanimity. This is also considered as a vow to practice meditation, daily for a specific period of time. *Atithisamvibhag* refers to serving/offering food and other articles to the monks and needy. The last, *pausadhaupavas* refers to observation of the monastic code. For the laity, this implies observing such monastic rules viz. fasting etc. for a day or longer.

ANEKANTAVADA

A Doctrine of Non-Absolutism

Also known as the philosophy of non-absolutism or of relative pluralism, *Anekantavada* is among the core and distinguishing doctrines of Jainism. The very word 'anekant', implies 'many sidedness' or 'not one sided' (vada: doctrine) underlining the many-foldedness and multiplicity of perspectives of the metaphysical truths. As per this philosophy, "although the truth is one, but owing to different perspectives, different people perceive the same truth differently". Thus, truth can be approached in different ways. This is so, as every substance has infinite attributes. Thus, truth as we perceive, may not be taken as absolute, rather it is even relative.

The doctrine traces its origins to comments and teachings of Mahavira as contained in the Jain *Agamas* particularly in his hypothesis that finite and infinite depend on one's perspective. However, the first comprehensive discussion of the philosophy is contained in the *Tattvartha sutra* by Acharya Umaswami (1st-2nd century CE). The concepts of *Syadvada* or 'conditional view points' and *Nayavada* or 'partial viewpoints' are believed to have further developed from *Anekantavada* in the subsequent centuries.

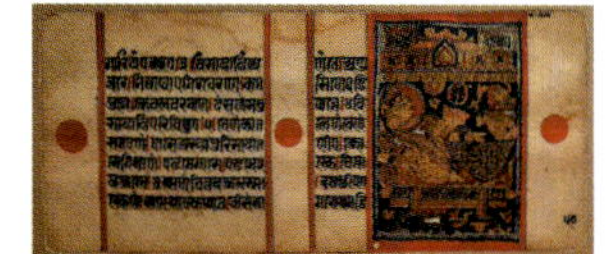

The Different Perspectives or Naya

नैगमसंग्रहव्यवहारऋजुसूत्रशब्दा नयाः ॥ 1-34 ॥

Naigamsangrhavyavaharrijusutrashabda naya.

There are five viewpoints (naya); common view, linear view practical view, verbal view, and literal view.

Verse 7-4: Tattvartha Sutra

The fundamental premise of *Anekantavada* is that though the absolute reality can be experienced, its description by means of human faculties remains only partial. As such, to attribute completeness to any singular perspective would not be proper. This leads to the concept of relative perspectives *(naya)* and conditioned viewpoints *(syad).* It is only a *kevalin* (omniscient) who has the ability to perceive the truth in its entirety.

The doctrine recognises the existence of different perspectives or point of views or *nayas*. It broadly classifies the nayas into two main categories, *nischaya naya* or absolute point of view, and *vyavahar naya*, implying a practical point of view. The perspective of an object in its true intrinsic form is referred to as the nischaya naya. Thus, considering the soul as pure and spotless with infinite capabilities is an absolute perspective. But considering the soul to be smeared with karma is a worldly or practical viewpoint or *vyavahar naya*. Thus, considering both the perspectives as reflection of the same truth and accepting both as partial perspectives, is the trait of this doctrine.

The doctrine of *Anekantavada* is applied by Jainas in religion, philosophy, and all fields of life. Thus, it encourages free thinking and helps in reconciliation of different perspectives. At the same time, it also forewarns us not to be too dogmatic or a stickler to one's own viewpoint as the perceived aspect of truth may not be absolute. Thus, it promotes tolerance of views and reconciles with the philosophy of *ahimsa*, by eschewing violence even in our thoughts and perspectives.

Other Salient Aspects of Jain Philosophy

Austerity and asceticism

Jainism lays special emphasis on renunciation, austerity and asceticism with these being completely integrated in the practice of the monks and partially even with the lives of the laity. These in turn are driven by the principles of *ahimsa* and the codes of *mahavrata/anuvrata* with the objectives of prevention of ingress and eradication of the karmic matter. These practices of the monks, viz. strict vegetarianism, travel only by foot, discarding of all material possessions including clothes, fasting and even subjecting to physical mortification are some of the unique and salient physical elements of Jainism and its spiritual practices. *Samayika*, or brief periods of meditation, too finds a significant place in its code of practices, but with the objective of attaining equanimity and prevention of karmic ingress. *Kayotsarga*, or meditation in standing, lotus, or other specific postures, for hours or days with complete disregard of the body and its physical elements is another of its challenging ascetic practices. *Sallekhana* (not in vogue in modern times), a voluntary abdication of food and even water as a process of renunciation of the mortal life was another unique practice of Jainism. But overall, all these practices were integrated with the principles of ahimsa and truth and a very simple and austere way of life.

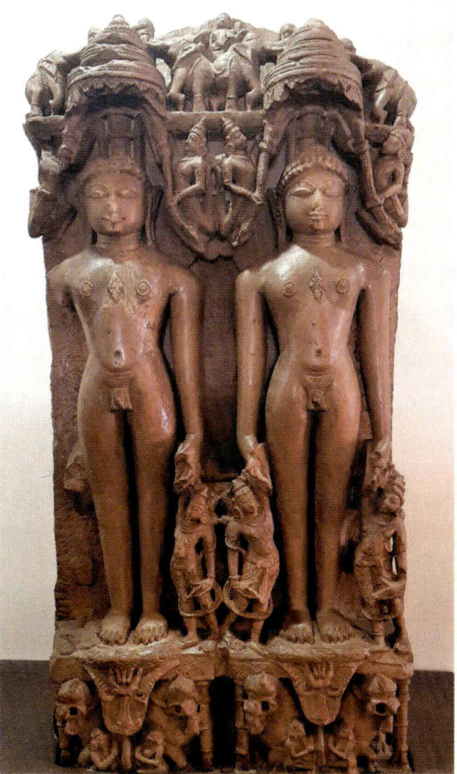

5.19: Ajinatha and Mahavira in standing meditation posture (Kayotsarga); sculpture 12th-13th century; Shivpuri Madhya Pradesh; current location, State Museum Bhopal — photograph by Madhukar K Bhagat

Co-existence, equality and social inclusion

Jainism was opposed to ritualism, animal sacrifices. The latter was in complete violation of the principle of *ahimsa*. Jainism was amongst the earliest of spiritual faiths which emphasized on *ahimsa*, compassion and coexistence of all sentient beings as a measure of universal well-being.

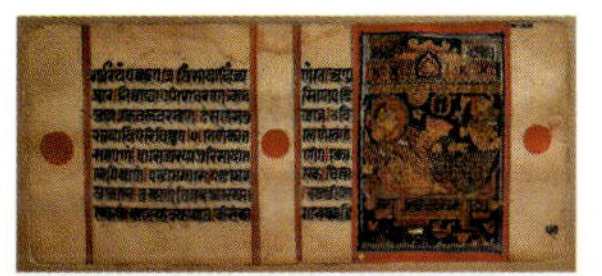

Equality of all beings is another important precept of Jainism; for the inherent *chaitanya* (attribute) of all sentient beings is the blemish-less and the infinite soul. The *acharanga sutra*, the first among the Agamas, lays special emphasis on the precept of equality. Further, the Jain ethics and practices recognises all as inherently equal with the distinction being only on account of the individual karma. This concept was equally entrenched in the order of monks and laity. Thus, it engendered a social philosophy which has influenced its followers and even the mainstream society over the centuries. Further, quite like Buddhism, Jainism too created an inclusive socio-religious platform, where distinctions of caste and brahmanical superiority had little place.

Conception of God

Jain epistemology does not consider the existence of God as a creator of the universe necessary. Rather, it emphasizes on the knowledge of seven *tattvas* or the truths (elements) with the principle of karma, governing the cyclicality of lives. Although it does believe in the existence of some divine beings, it did not consider them to be the omnipotent creator only on whose benefaction the salvation was possible While some believe Jainism to be an atheistic religion, it is often and more appropriately described as a transtheistic religion as it does not consider the necessity of a supreme being for enlightenment, but lays emphasis on the voluntary effort and right karma of the sentient being for attainment of kaivalya.

The karmic theory

The doctrine of karma in vogue in Jainism is unique too. Albeit in prominence in Hinduism and Buddhism, this theory provides a somewhat different basis of transmigration of soul by providing for bondage of the matter with soul. As per the karmic matter theory, apart from the existence of the soul and gross body, there exists the karmic body, which forms the nucleus around which the grosser body is built up. The karmic body is the basis for the worldly existence and transmigration of the soul and with its disintegration the soul attains its sublime purity or true self of *paramatman*.

The Soul and the Matter Bondage

सकाषायत्वाज्जीवः कर्मणो योग्यान् पुद्गलानादत्ते ।। 8-2 ।।

स बन्धः ।। 8-3 ।।

Sakashaayatvajeevah Karmano yogyan pudgalanadate 8-2

Sa Bandhah 8-3

The soul (sentient being) self attracts the lifeless particles of matter which are fit to turn into karma, by indulging in defilement. This is bondage.

Verses 8-2 and 8-3 Tattvartha Sutra

The building up of the karmic body happens through the accumulation of the karmic particles. Amongst the plentitude of particles pervading the universe, also exist the karmic particles, which flow unimpeded in all directions, normally without affecting the soul. But when the actions of the *jiva* are defiling, they create conditions for attraction of particles which eventually permeate the province *(pradesha)* of the soul. This causes bondage of the soul and the karmic matter, resulting in the transmigration of the soul. The prevention of ingress and removal of the existing karmic matter thus becomes crucial for salvation.

Thus, the karma in Jainism is akin to a material force as compared to the action (good or bad) in Hinduism and Buddhism, or what can be considered as psychological or metaphysical forces in the latter faiths.

JAIN SCRIPTURES

The Loss, Recompilation and Documentation of Agamas

The canonical texts of Jainism which contain the teachings of Mahavira and other Tirthankaras are contained in the scriptures called *Agamas*. These scriptures were originally transmitted orally by the Gandharas, the twelve chief disciples of Mahavira, by compiling them into sutras or texts. They were also referred as Jain Shruti or *shrut jnana* as they were a category of knowledge-texts which were 'heard'. These scriptures were not originally in written form, as the ancient tradition was of oral transmission of the knowledge from the guru (teacher) to the shishya (student). Further, possessions and attachments were not permitted in the Jain philosophy. As such, its documentation or wide dissemination was not feasible. Thus, these scriptures were passed on by oral traditions for many centuries before being eventually documented.

It is believed that after the great famine in 350 BCE, which lasted for nearly 12 years, many of the *Agamas* were lost. Subsequently, they were recompiled and eventually documented in the Jain councils.

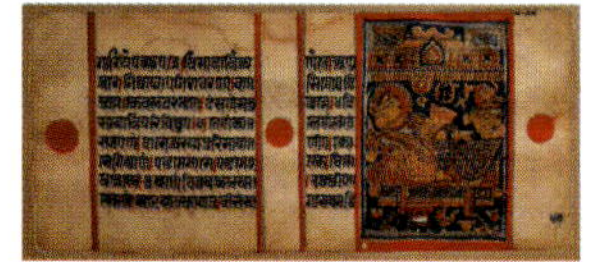

The Digambaras believe that all the *Agamas* were lost and the recompiled *Agamas* were not the authentic teachings of Lord Mahavira and are corrupted. They believe that acharya Bhutabali was the last monk who had at least partial knowledge of these texts. But the Shwetambaras hold that the *Agamas* were not lost and was recompiled and later documented. They further believe that only the 14 Purvas which were texts containing the teachings of Mahavira and earlier Tirthankaras, were lost. Thus, Shwetambaras believe the extant *Agamas* to be the teachings of lord Mahavira himself.

The Agamas

The Jain religious literature is broadly classified into Agama literature or *Agama Sutras* and non-*Agama* literature. The former contain the teachings of Lord Mahavira which was compiled by the Gandharas, the immediate disciples, into texts or sutras. These are written in *Ardha-Magadhi* a Prakrit language.

The Agamas are further classified as *Ang-Agamas* or Ang-*pravista-Agamas/Ang-Bahya-Agamas* (that which are outside of Ang-Agamas). Overall, there are 12 *Ang-Agamas* which are said to be containing direct teachings of Lord Mahavira.

The Twelve Ang-Agamas

The twelve *Ang-Agamas*, besides containing the comprehensive doctrine of Jainism, the rules of monkhood, lives of venerable saints and kings, stories and anecdotes capturing moral precepts, guidance for the lay followers, also contain a wealth of other information. These Ang-Agamas and area of coverage are briefly outlined here.

1. *Acharanga Sutra* contains the rules for discipline for the monks and conduct of the ascetic life. It also describes the penance of Mahavira.
2. *Sutrakratanga Sutra* gives a description of the Jain doctrine such as causes of bondage, destruction of Karmas etc. Further, it also contains injunctions for monks as to what is suitable and not suitable for them.
3. *Sthananga Sutra* lists the categories of knowledge pertaining to realities of nature and captures the main substances of the Jain metaphyscis. Interestingly, it is said to also include various elements of mathematical studies such as the theory of numbers, arithmetical operations, geometry, operations with fractions, simple equations, cubic equations, quartic equations, and permutations and combinations etc., adding to the diversity of domains covered by this sutra.
4. *Samvayanga Sutra* classifies objects in terms of similarities of time, place, number and so on. Besides, it also includes elements of mathematics and astronomy.
5. *Vyakhya Prajapati* or *Bhagwati Sutra* explained the realities of life and nature viz. the subtle aspects of soul matter etc. in form of catechism (questions and answers). It is said to contain nearly 36000 questions and answers which were responded to by Mahavira.
6. *Jnata Dharma kathanga Sutra* contains religious preaching in the form of stories and anecdotes which carry moral precepts.
7. *Upasaka Dashanga Sutra* which serves as a religious code for householders and lay followers.
8. *Antah Kradashanga Sutra* gives an account of 10 saints who attained salvation after immense penace and destroying their karmas.
9. *Anuttaroupa Patika Dashanga Sutra* contains the account of another 10 saints who elevated to the highest heaven (anuttara heaven) after enduring intense penance.
10. *Prashna Vyakarna* describes the five great vows *(mahavratas)* and the five worst sins which includes, killing, stealing, lying, sexual misconduct and greed.
11. *Vipaka Sutra* describes how virtue is rewarded while evil is punished by citing different stories.
12. *Drastivaada* contains five sections. These are (*a*) *Parikarma* (*b*) *Sutra* (containing tenets of philosophies) (*c*) *Prathamanuyoga* (describes history and life of saints and great kings) (*d*) *Purvagata* (describes the problem of birth, death and transmigration of soul). This also contained 14 Purvas which represented the knowledge which existed even before Lord Mahavira. (*e*) *Chulika* dealing with charms and magic. These all are believed to have been compiled from different sources and texts, post being lost.

Ang-bahya Agamas

These were the texts and commentaries on various subjects composed by the *srut kevalins*, that is those monks (acharyas) who had the knowledge of at least 10 Purvas. These were many in number and spread in different languages. *Ang-bahya-Agama* Sutras provide further explanation to the *Ang-Agama Sutras*.

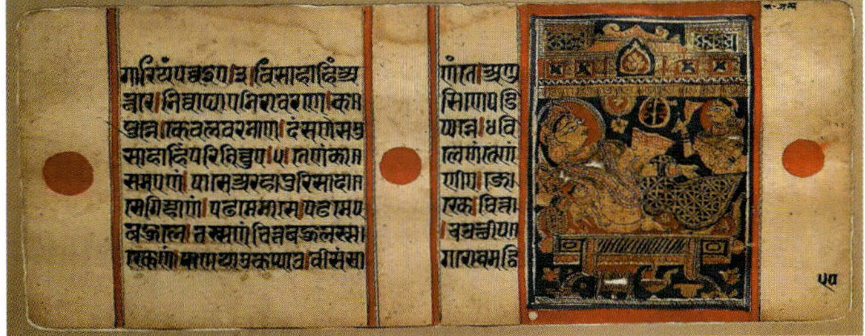

5.20: A folio of Kalpasutra depicting a miniature painting of the birth of Parsvanatha; opaque watercolour on paper; Chatrapati Shivaji Maharaja Vastu Sangrahalaya, Mumbai — photograph by Madhukar K Bhagat

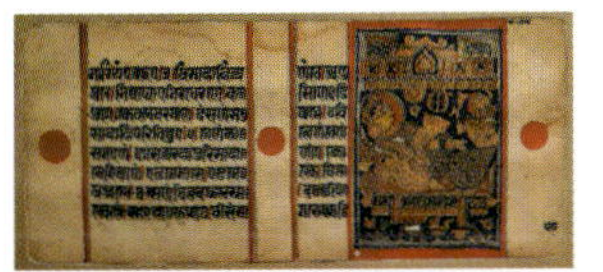

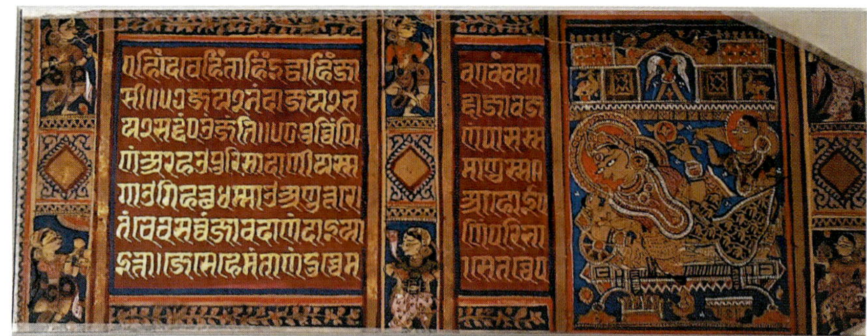

5.21: A folio of Kalpasutra depicting the birth of Mahavira; opaque watercolour on paper, 1475 CE; Sardar Vallabhbhai Patel, National Museum, Ahmedabad — photograph by Madhukar K Bhagat

The *Shatkhandagama* written by Acharya Pushpadant and Acharya Bhutabali in the Ist century CE is amongst the earliest authoritative texts of Jain Karma doctrine falling under the Digambara canon of texts.

Among the most important of the non-canonical or non-Agama texts are the *Kalpasutra*, said to be composed by acharya Bhadrabahu in around 300 BCE, and *Tattvartha Sutra*, by acharya Umaswati (also referred as Umaswami). The latter was composed in 1st-2nd century CE and is regarded highly by both the Shwetamabaras and the Digambaras alike as an authoritative text containing authentic philosophies of Jainism. It is a concise compilation of around 357 sutras (344 as per Shwetambara tradition) and enjoys the same respect in the Jain scriptural corpus as the Brahmasutra in the vedantic canon.

SECTS IN JAINISM

The Jains are divided into two sects, the Digambaras (meaning sky-clad or naked) and the Shwetambaras (meaning white-clad). The schism of Jainism into the two sects seems to have taken place in around 350 BCE. As per the Jain tradition, during the reign of Chandragupta Maurya, when there was a twelve year famine, acharya Bhadrabahu, the leading Jain muni/scholar, who had predicted the famine, had migrated to Karnataka along with a section of followers. Acharya Sthulabhadra, his pupil, had remained back, along with some other monks. But on return to Magadha, the former found differences with other Jains on the issue of wearing of clothes. Those who had remained back had started wearing white clothes. This was considered to be against the principle of *aparigraha* and against the tradition of Mahavira, who had remained naked. Later, the recompiled *Agamas* was not accepted as being the authentic *Agamas* by the group which returned back. This was the origin of the differences. It is believed that in the council of Valabhi in around 5th century CE the schism became fully entrenched, when the Digamabaras did not attend the council and Shwetamabaras adopted the recompiled Agamas as authentic teachings of Mahavira.

Difference in the Two Sects

While the Digambara sect prescribes living naked and not even having cloth as their possession, the Shwetambaras are clad in white clothes. Further, unlike the Shwetamabaras, the Digambaras do not consider the Agamas to contain the authentic teachings of Mahavira and believe that they were lost in the famine.

But apart from the above, the Digambara sect also believes that women cannot be Tirthankaras or attain salvation on account of not being able to practice complete renunciation, as they have to cover their body. This view is not held by the Shwetambaras. They accord the same status to women who have renounced the world and who are referred as sadhvis. They also believe that Mallinatha, the 19th Tirthankara, was a woman who attained salvation, and thus women are not precluded from *kaivalya*. However, Digambaras do not accept the view of womanhood of Mallinatha. Besides, there exist some other differences too between the two sects pertaining to the monastic rules and iconography.

However, the two sects do agree on basic tenets of Jainism, viz. *triratna*, *panch-mahavrata* (five vows), *ahimsa, anekantavada*, etc.

JAINISM AND SYMBOLS

In Jain philosophy, symbols occupy an important place. However, unlike Buddhism they are not representative of life or events of any of the Tirthankaras in particular, but signify abstract and metaphysical aspects, such as purity of soul, peace, well-being, wisdom, victory over carnal desire, etc.

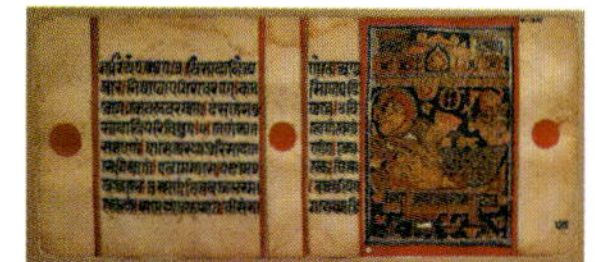

Ashtamangala

These are eight auspicious symbols of Jainism and include:

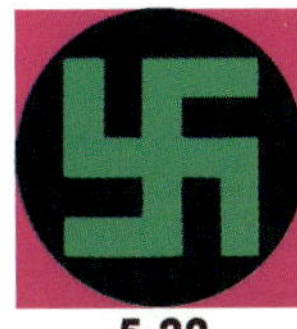
5.22

(1) ***Swastika:*** This is an auspicious symbol signifying peace and well-being. It is customarily drawn in places of worship and religious ceremonies. The four arms of the Swastika are also said to symbolise the four categories of the world (or the destiny of worldly beings based on Karma). These four categories include the heavenly being *(Deva)*, human beings *(Manushya)*, animals, birds, and plants *(Triyanch)*, and hellish beings *(Narakvasi)*.

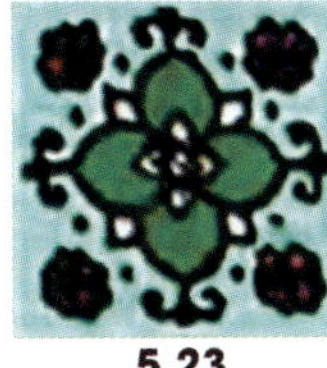
5.23

(2) ***Shrivatsa:*** It is said to be a mark on the chest of Mahavira and other Tirthankaras which signifies purity of soul, compassion, and love for all beings.

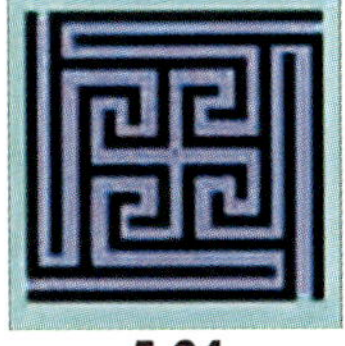
5.24

(3) ***Nandavarta:*** It is a complex form of Swastika with nine angles or corners, each representing divinity. It is indicative of higher meditative attainment.

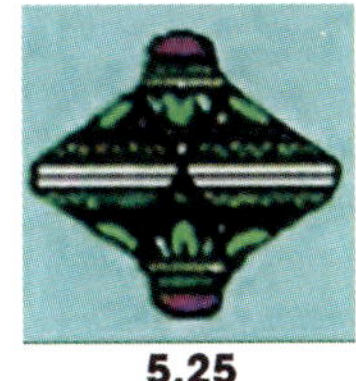
5.25

(4) ***Vardhamanaka:*** It is an earthern bowl used as a lamp, symbolic of light (knowledge) banishing darkness (ignorance).

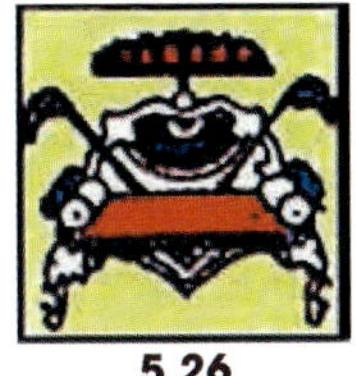
5.26

(5) ***Bhadrasana:*** It is a holy seat representing the seat of Mahavira and other venerated and liberated souls.

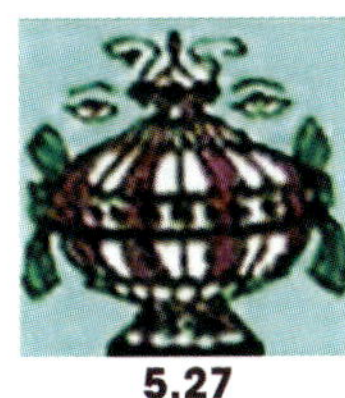
5.27

(6) ***Kalasha:*** It is a pot filled with holy water. It signifies purity and wisdom to fill our minds.

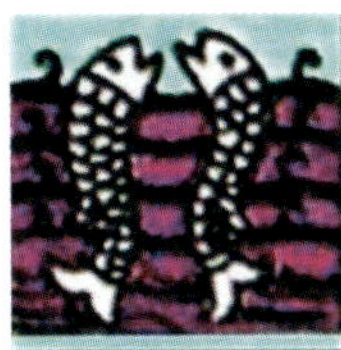
5.28

(7) ***Meen Yugala:*** It is a figure of a fish couple considered auspicious and signifying flow of divine life in the cosmic ocean. It is also said to signify victory over carnal desires.

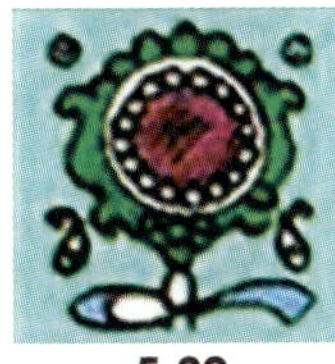
5.29

(8) ***Darpana:*** Mirror (Darpana) signifies reflection of one's true self, namely the soul.

The Jain Emblem

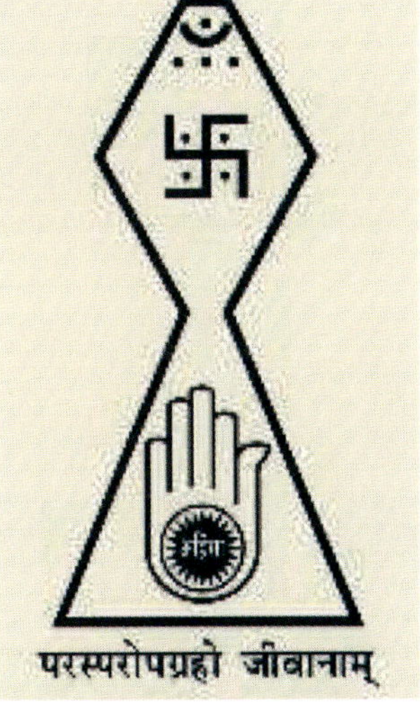

5.30: Jain emblem — Wikimedia Commons

This is a congregation of several of the Jain symbols which has been accepted and adopted by all sects. It includes:

- The emblem's outline (signifying the universe and the three worlds).
- The Swastika
- The Jain palm symbol with *ahimsa* (non-violence) inscribed in it, and the words *Parasparo Graho Jeevanaam*, which is verse 5-21 of the *Tattvartha Sutra*, is inscribed at the bottom of the emblem. It literally means that it is the function of the *jeeva*/soul (sentient being) to be mutually useful and helpful, which implies that all life is bound together by mutual support and interdependence. Thus, respect for life and others or the concepts of ahimsa and *anekantavada* are at the core of this philosophy.

JAIN COUNCILS

Historical reference of two councils is obtained in the Jain treatises. The first one took place in Pataliputra in the 3rd century BCE under the leadership of monk Sthulabhadra which led to the compilation of the *Agamas*. In the second council, held around 800–900 years later in the 5th century-6th century CE (held in Valabhi) under the auspices of Nagarjuna, twelve *Angas* and *Upangas* were compiled. However, the Digamabaras had not participated in the second council at Valabhi and the schism between the two

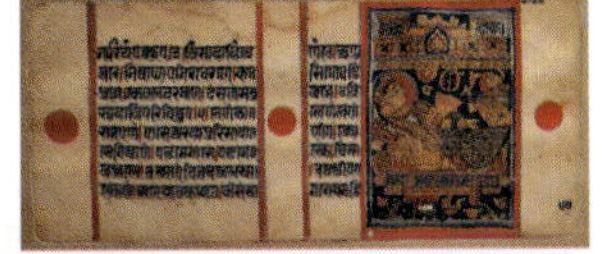

sects had thus become established. It is also believed by some schools that another simultaneous second council had taken place at Mathura.

JAIN FESTIVALS

The most important of Jain festivals are *Paryushana* and the Mahavira Jayanti (birth of lord Mahavira).

The festival of *Paryushana* also called as the *Das lakshana*, is celebrated on the 12th day of the waning moon (*krishnapaksha*) in the month of Bhadrapada. This usually falls in the months of August and September. The festival is celebrated for a period of eight days by Shwetambaras and for 10 days by the Digambaras. During this period, observation of fasting, praying and reading of sacred texts is done. The austerities are a way of removal of the accumulated karma and prevention of the ingress of more. The festival is also a time for emphasising on the five views especially on non-violence.

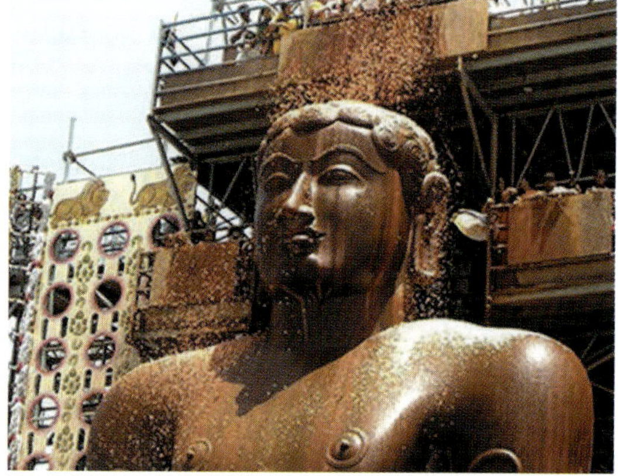

5.31: Mahamastakabhisheka of Bahubali — Wikimedia Commons

The last day of the festival is also considered as a day of atonement, which is marked by granting of forgiveness and seeking forgiveness from all sentient beings, whom they may have offended knowingly or unknowingly by any act or even in thoughts.

Mahavira *Janam Kalyanak*, or birth of Lord Mahavira, is another important festival which is celebrated on the thirteenth day of Chaitra month (March-April). This day is marked with carrying out of religious ceremonies and reading of holy scriptures. Another important festival is the day of attainment of *moksha/ kaivalya* by lord Mahavira. This is celebrated on the same day as that of the festival of Deepawali.

The *Mahamasatakabhisheka* is a unique festival which is held only once every 12 years. The festival is centered around the sage Bahubali and paying homage to him. The anointing of the 18 metre high standing statue of lord Bahubali at Shravanabelagola in Karnataka is the highlight of this festival. The next *Mahamastakabhisheka* would take place in 2030.

Namokara Mantra

The Namokara mantra is considered the most significant of all mantras in Jainism and offers obeisance to the five supreme souls or beings, or *pancha paramesthi*. It is also referred as the *Pancha Namaskara mantra, Navkara mantra* and *Namsakara Mahamangalasutra*.

णमो अरिहंताणम।

णमो सिद्धांणं।

णमो आयरियाणं

णमो उवज्झायाणं।

णमो लोए सव्व साहूणं।

एसो पंच णम्मोक्कारो, सव्व पावपणासणो।

मंगला णं च सव्वेसिं, पढ़मं हवई मंगलं ।।

I bow to all arihants* (the tirthankaras and Jinas),

I bow to all sidhas (liberated souls).

I bow to all acharyas (heads of Jain congregations)

I bow to all upadhyayas (learned scholars of Jain scriptures)

I bow to all sadhus and sadhvis (ascetics)

To these five types of great souls, I offer my prayers. May such prayers help diminish my sins.

Offering this prayer is the foremost amongst all of the auspicious benedictions.

** Arihant refer to those beings who have acquired the true and omniscient knowledge and thus have attained Nirvana or salvation. They are also called Kevalins, or those possessing Keval Jnana. However, these beings continue to remain in human form unlike the Siddhas, who are liberated souls which have already attained Nirvana and are free from the bondage of life, death, and birth. The Namokar Mantra (most important religious mantra of Jains) pays first obeisance to Arihants (as they are accessible to human beings), then to Siddhas, and then to other venerable entities.*

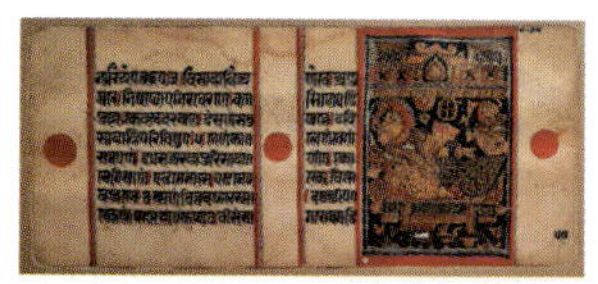

JAIN ART AND ARCHITECTURE

The temples, statues, and rock-cut architecture associated with Jainism survive to this day and throw light on Jain art and architecture. Although Jain art is restricted to religious art and architecture, yet it attained great heights and cast an important influence on the Indian art.

Jain art usually comprises the statues and carvings of Tirthankaras who are shown either seated or standing in a meditative posture and depicted naked. Images of yaksha and yakshini are seen guarding the images of Tirthankaras. Besides, the art forms usually have symbols and floral motifs. The lack of variety of subjects is more than made up in dexterity of carving, which is particularly evident in the Dilwara temple at Mount Abu (in Rajasthan), Ranakpur temple (in Rajasthan), and Palitana temple at Bhavnagar in Gujarat. The monolithic statue (18 metre high) of Bahubali at Shravanabelagola is another excellent example of Jain architecture.

The rock-cut Jain temples at Udayagiri, Khandagiri caves (in Orissa near Puri), and Ellora caves are also important landmarks of Jain architecture. Quite like many Buddhist caves, these also served as places of residences for the monks but were much simple in nature owing to emphasis on asceticism. They also lacked larger halls for congregation and community prayer.

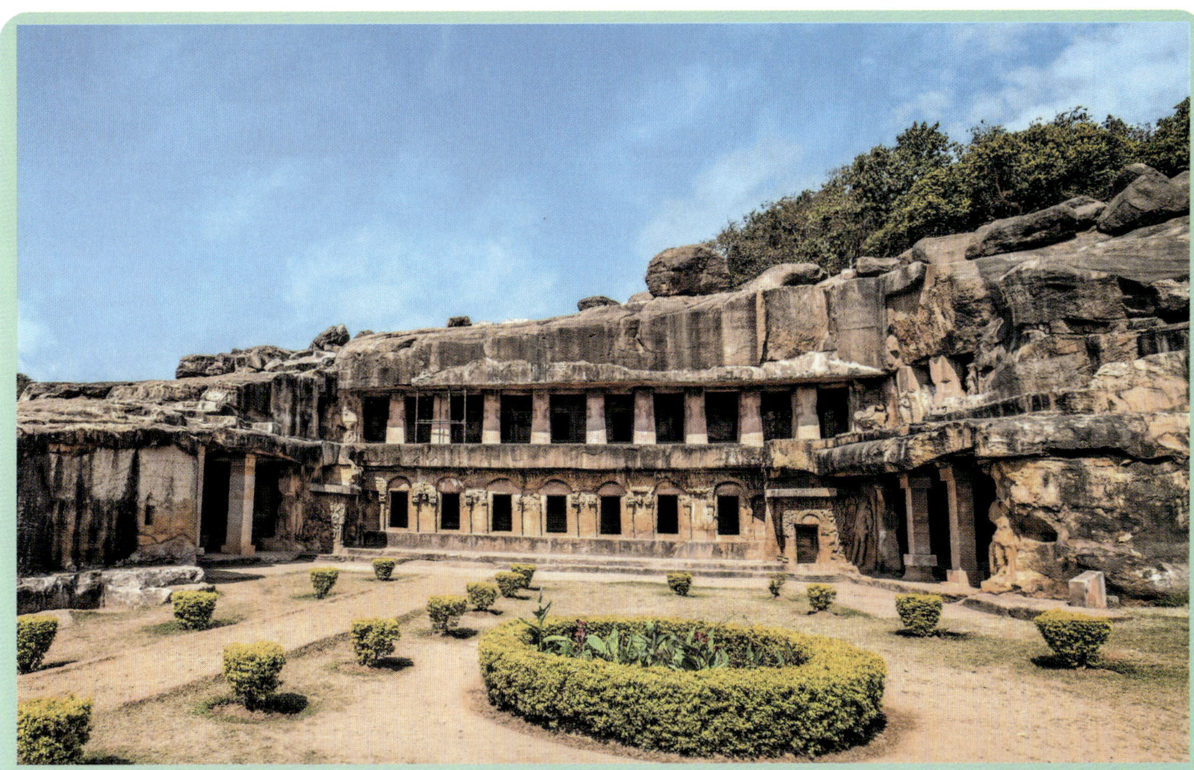

5.32: Ranigupha, Udayagiri caves, double storey Jain vihara, 1st century BCE, near Bhubaneshwar, Odisha — Courtesy, Department of Tourism, Odisha

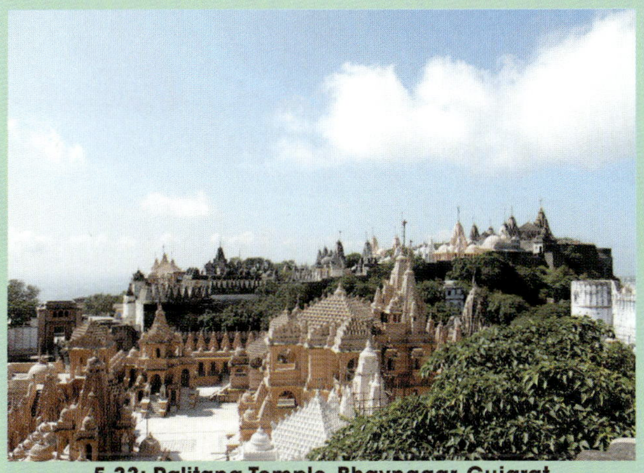

5.33: Palitana Temple, Bhavnagar, Gujarat — Wikimedia Commons

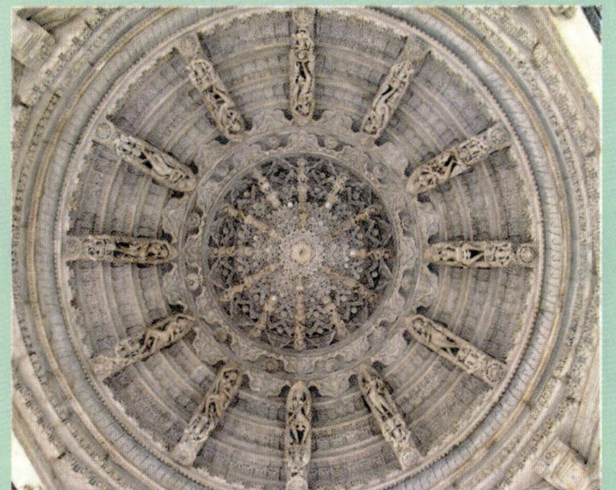

5.34: Exquisite ceiling carving at Ranakpur temple at Rajasthan — photograph by Madhukar K Bhagat

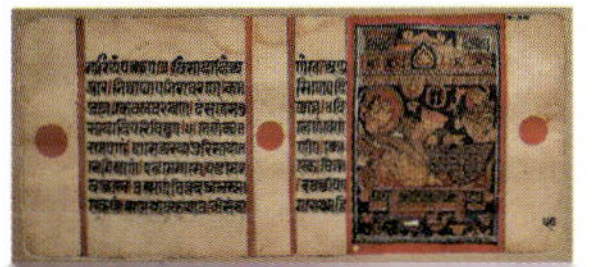

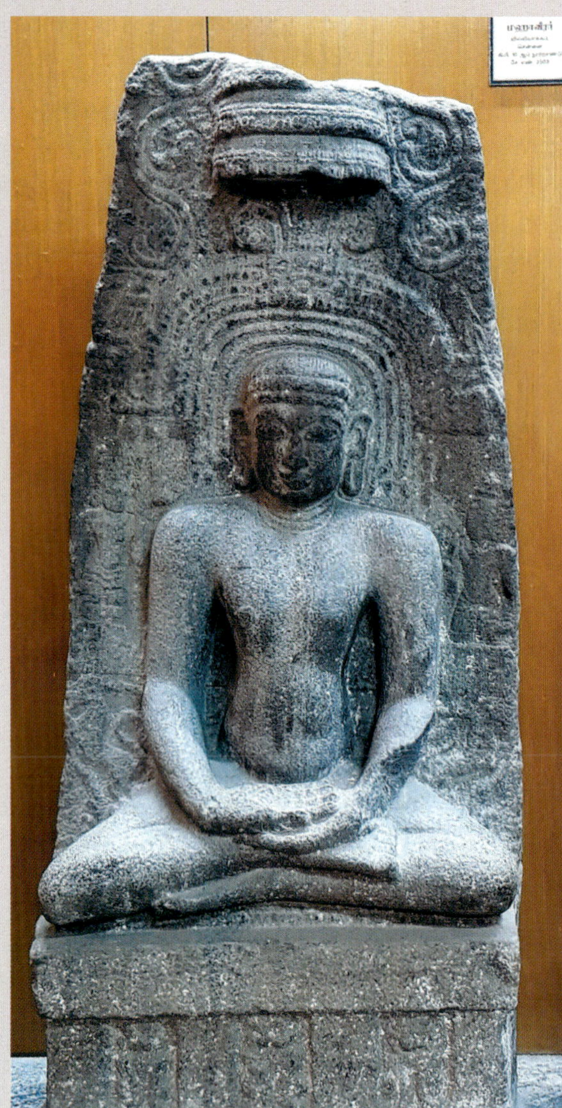

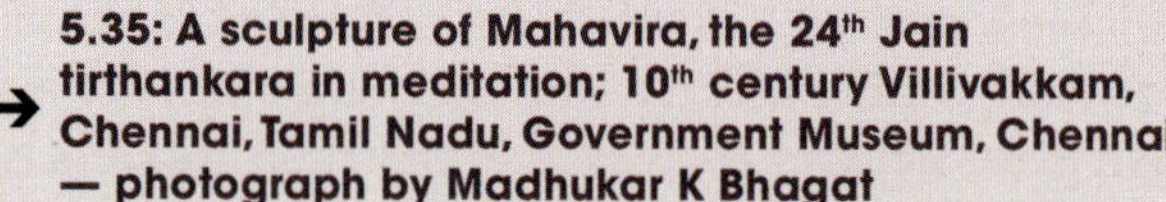

5.35: A sculpture of Mahavira, the 24th Jain tirthankara in meditation; 10th century Villivakkam, Chennai, Tamil Nadu, Government Museum, Chennai — photograph by Madhukar K Bhagat

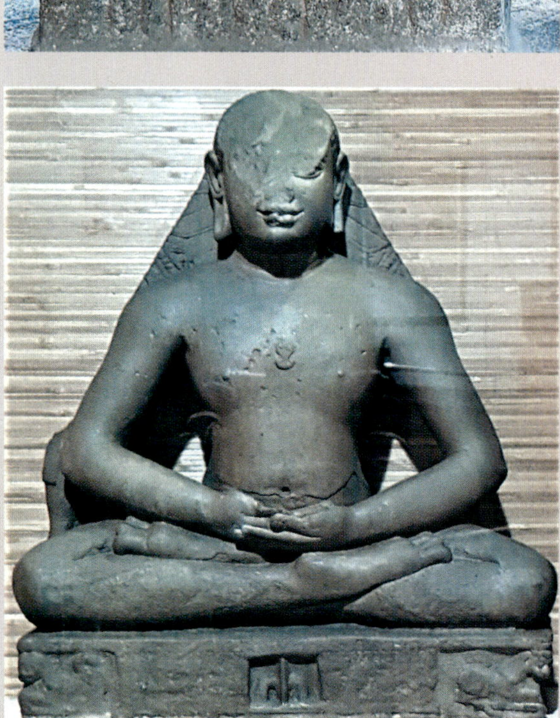

5.36: Chandraprabha, 8th Jain tirthankara, sitting in meditation, a sculpture from 4th century CE, Vidisha, Madhya Pradesh; State Museum, Bhopal — photograph by Madhukar K Bhagat

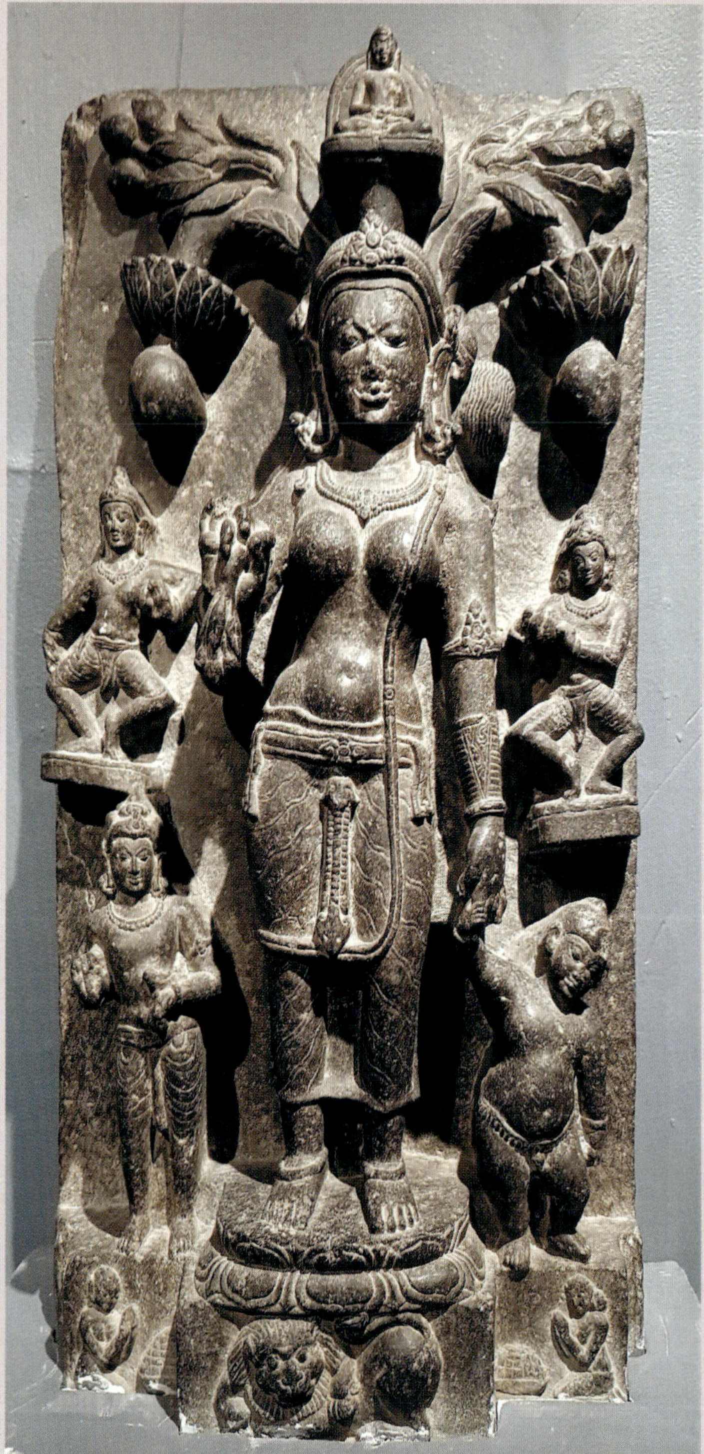

5.37: Ambika, a Jain deity, a 10th century Pala sculpture from Sundarbans, West Bengal, National Museum, New Delhi — photograph by Madhukar K Bhagat

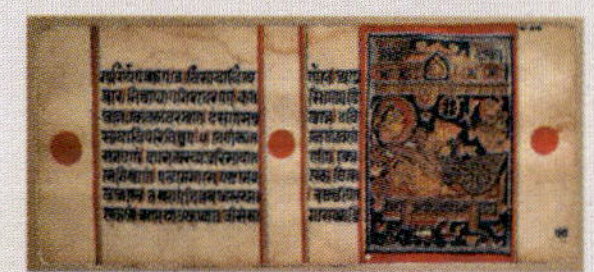

6

Tangible & Intangible Elements of Culture in Ancient India

What is art? It is the response of man's creative soul to the call of the real

Rabindranath Tagore

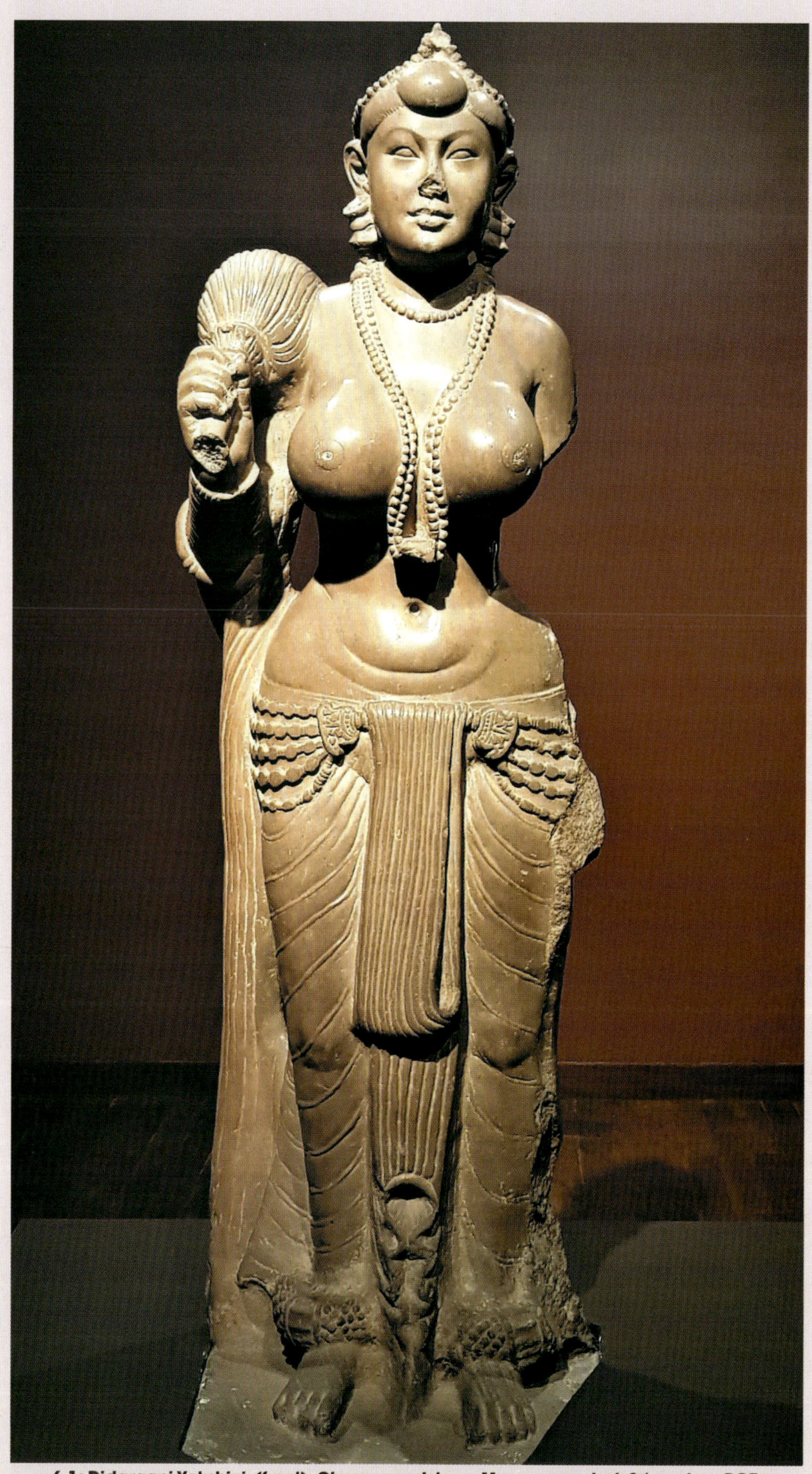

6.1: Didarganj Yakshini, (front), Chunar sandstone, Mauryan period, 3rd century BCE, Bihar Museum, Patna — photograph by Madhukar K Bhagat

AN INTRODUCTION

Art, architecture, sculpture and performing arts, are tangible elements of a culture. As the archaeologists unearth the layers of history hidden in the mounds of past settlements, and historians piece together the information gathered from the broken pieces of pottery, sculptures, ruins of palaces and innumerable artefacts, these tangible elements reveal the clues which enable the scholars to unravel piece by piece the culture and history of a civilization of a bygone era. Being visible and more readily perceivable, these are the popular, and at times, more familiar elements of culture. These are also more succinctly captured in the pages of history and galleries of museum. Besides these narratives, this chapter also brings out the evolution of some intangible elements in ancient India, including the canonical and non-canonical literature, and the disciplines of medicines, mathematics, astrology, grammar, etc.

Ancient India covers a vast period of history and multifarious subjects as well. The entire period of Indian history up to the beginning of the medieval period (1000 CE-1100 CE) falls in its purview. Many areas of culture such as the Buddhist sculpture and art, rock-cut architecture, various schools of art, pillars and capitals, coins, literature, pottery and other areas of culture too fall in its ambit. Here, a brief account is presented of the salient tangible and intangible elements of culture for the period beginning from 300 BCE (beginning of the Mauryan period) to 1000 CE–1100 CE (beginning of the medieval period). This period can be broadly subdivided into (a) the **Mauryan period** (b) the **Post Mauryan period** (c) the **Gupta period** and (d) the **Post Gupta period**.

ART AND ARCHITECTURE IN THE MAURYAN PERIOD

Since the 5th century BCE, the social landscape of India (particularly in the Gangetic plane) underwent a change, and so did the art and architecture of the period. Buddhism and Jainism, which rejected the supremacy of the Vedas and Brahmanical system, and emphasised on Ahimsa and equality, appealed to a vast section of the society and grew rapidly. The patronisation of Buddhism by Mauryan kings, particularly by Ashoka, greatly influenced the religious and political atmosphere as well as the art and culture. As such, the Mauryan art and culture bears a distinct Buddhist stamp on it, as visible in the innumerable stupas, chaityas, viharas, pillars and capitals, rock-cut architecture, cave architecture, and sculptures. All these elements of Mauryan culture are described here.

Elements of Mauryan Culture

Viharas: The viharas were **places of residence or monasteries,** of Buddhist monks, particularly for taking shelter during the rainy season (*chaturmaas*). The erstwhile kingdom of Magadha had a large number of viharas, lending it the name Bihar. Initial viharas were simple wooden structures which do not survive to this day. These structures would be having a similar plan as that of the larger houses, with an inner quadrangle, surrounded by several cells on all the four sides. As the monasteries became larger with time, they became more complex, with several adjunct structures added to it. Today, only the foundations survive at some places, with structures completely eroded.

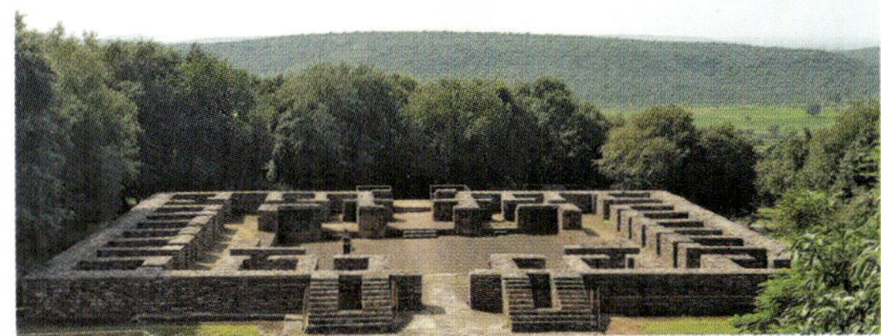

6.2: Remnants of a monastery (vihara) at Sanchi, indicating the quadrangular plan, with cells on the side — photograph by Madhukar K Bhagat

However, some of the viharas do exist in the rock-cut structures in the Ajanta, Ellora, Karle, Nasik, Bagh, Badami, and Kanheri caves, among others. Many of such viharas are seen to be having a standard or a common plan. These too would have a quadrangular court with walls flanking it. Small cells would be present around this central court. These cells would have stone beds, a raised portion of which would serve as a pillow. A small hollow in the wall of the cell would be a space for keeping an earthen lamp. Some would also have a chaitya hall nearby.

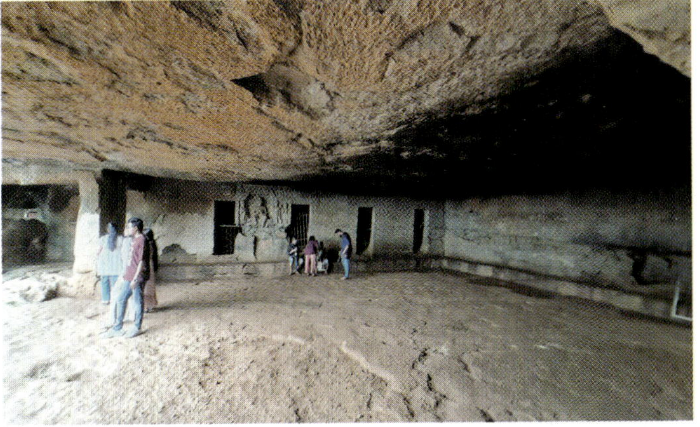

6.3: A rock-cut vihara carved inside the hill at Karla cave, Maharashtra; smaller cells/rooms are carved towards the extreme end of the vihara with the relief of Lord Buddha — photograph by Madhukar K Bhagat

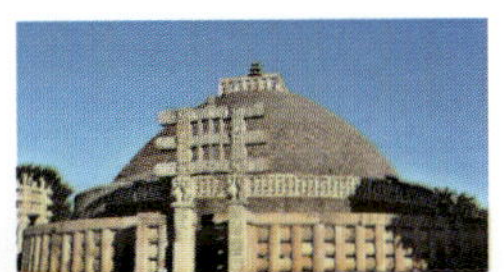

Chaityas: These were the Buddhist shrines or prayer halls with a stupa at one end of the hall, and pillars on the side of the pathway leading to the stupa. They were also community places of worship for the Buddhists. The rock-cut chaityas which exist even today are seen in **Ajanta, Ellora, Karla, Bagh, Nasik, and Kanheri** caves. Many of these were constructed in the post Mauryan period. However the chaitya at **Barabar and Nagarjuni caves** are examples of Mauryan art.

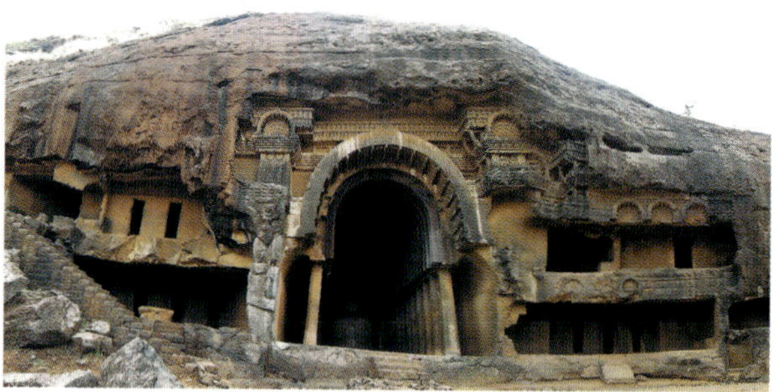

6.4: Chaitya Hall and nearby caves at Bhaja, Maharashtra; it has an apsidal hall with ribbed roof, also noteworthy is the ornate carving at the entrance of the chaitya — Courtesy, Maharashtra Tourism Development Corporation

The chaitya at **Bhaja** cave is a typical example of chaitya construction. These consisted of a hall with semicircular roof/apsidal hall. Both the sides of this hall have a number of columns which are sloping inwards. These were imitations of wooden columns. The roof, which is semicircular and barrel shaped, is having semicircular ribs. These were also features of wooden structures. The columns and walls were finely polished, which was a typical feature of Mauryan art. Thus, the hall and its structures, though cut in stone, depicted a wooden facade. The pillars were carved exquisitely and had an intricate abacus atop.

Pillars and Capitals: Pillars (stambha) and capitals are important elements depicting the Mauryan art. The object of construction of pillars was to carry inscriptions containing the edicts of kings who commissioned it. Many of the Ashokan pillars carry edicts which were teachings of Buddhist Dhamma.

The pillars of Mauryan times were **rock-cut stone pillars**. They were a single piece of stone or **monolithic pillars** unlike the contemporaneous Achaemenid pillars, which were constructed in pieces. The cutting of round pillars in hard stones reflects the skills of craftsmen of that age. The pillars were highly polished with inscriptions engraved on them. Atop the pillars, capital figures were carved, such as the lion, the bull, the elephant, etc. At the base of the capital there would be an **abacus** which would be like an inverted lotus or a bell. The pillars, lion capital of **Sarnath** (Uttar Pradesh), **Lauriya Nandangarh** (Bihar), **Vaishali** (Bihar), **Rampurva** (Champaran in Bihar), and elephant capital at **Sankisa** (Farrukhabad in UP) are well known, and belong to the Mauryan period.

Ancient Monolithic Pillars: A Marvel of Art and Engineering

The construction of these monolithic stone pillars is often considered an engineering and sculptural marvel of the ancient age, besides being an unparalleled work of art. Each of these pillars would weigh several tonnes (even up to 50 tonnes) in weight and carved from a single piece of stone (Chunar sandstone in Ashokan pillars). Their cutting and transportation from the quarries to the sites of final erection hundreds of kilometres away was an unparalleled engineering feet. As per accounts of some scholars, thousands of workmen would have been deployed for their safe transportation.

The pillars would comprise the shaft and the capital. The circular shaft itself would be 30 to 50 feet high of a single stone with slender proportions. The monolithic capital atop would have three parts (i) An inverted lotus with highly stylized petals (ii) An abacus with numerous animal motifs (iii) a crowning sculpture in the round (eg. the four lions). Working on the hard stone, carving out the highly proportionate and accurate images of the numerous animals, and bringing out the folds and delineating the curves of their bodies and lotus petals, all with a mirror-like finish of the surface, was indeed the pinnacle of art and sculpture.

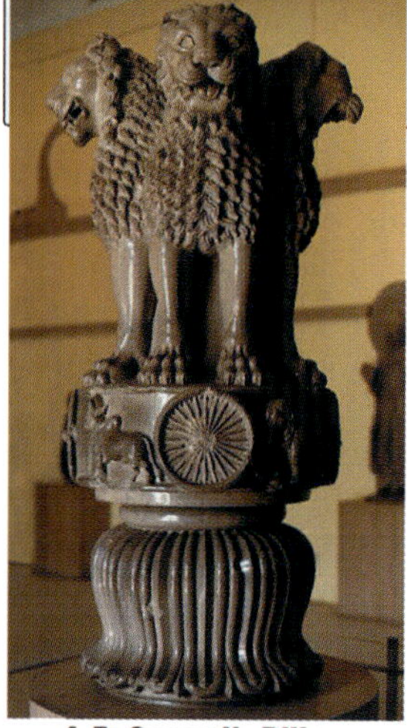

6.5: Sarnath Pillar Lion Capital — Wikimedia Commons

(i) The Sarnath Pillar: The pillar of Sarnath carrying atop the lion capital (the national symbol of India) is the most famous example of Mauryan sculpture. This lion capital (2.31 m high) consists of four parts. This includes; a bell-shaped vase covered with inverted lotus; an abacus with figures of a horse, a bull, a lion, and elephant on it; the four chakras (wheels) each having twenty four spokes; and the four lions placed back-to-back looking in the four directions.

All of these elements are symbolic, viz. the lion symbolises Buddha (a fearless roar in all directions of truth and knowledge), the chakra symbolises the turning of the wheel of law.

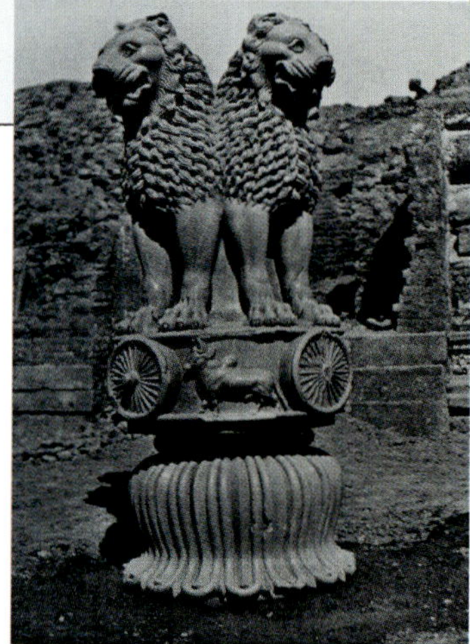

6.6: The Lion Capital on ground of excavation at Sarnath (1904-05 CE) — Wikimedia Commons

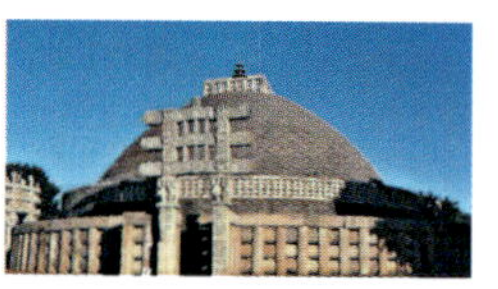

Thus, this capital symbolised the Buddha's historical delivery (at Sarnath) of the first sermon or *Dharmachakra Pravartana*. The carvings in the figures are especially exquisite. The muscularity of the lion is clearly visible. The polishing is very fine and mirror-like. The original capital also had a *Dharmachakra* (a large wheel) atop the four lions, but this was broken (and is not a part of the national symbol).

(ii) The pillar at **Lauriya Nandangarh** (3rd century BCE) is another exquisite example of Mauryan art. The pillar (9.8 m high) has a bell-shaped inverted lotus. The abacus is decorated with flying geese and a single lion atop.

(iii) Another famous example is the **Vaishali** pillar with a lion capital.

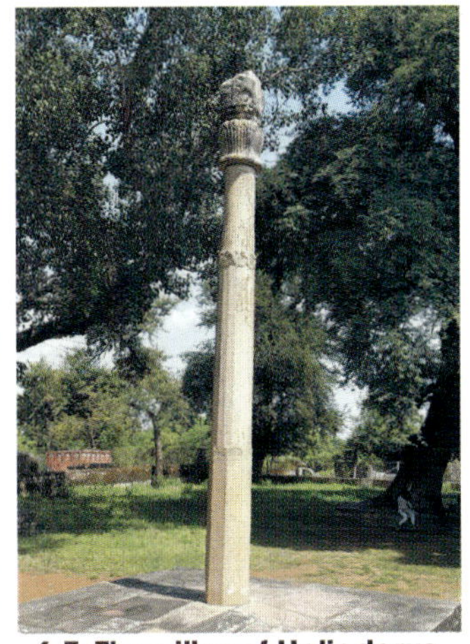

6.7: The pillar of Heliodorus, 150 BCE, Vidisha. The pillar, carrying an inscription in Brahmi was a Garuda pillar in honour of Lord Vasudeva (Vishnu), gifted by Heliodorus, a Greek inhabitant of Taxila, (as an ambassador of the Indo Bactrian king of Punjab region), to the king Bhagbhadra of Central India. — photograph by Madhukar K Bhagat

Stupa

A stupa is a hemispherical (mound shape) construction which contains holy relics or cremated remains of Buddha or other monks. Apart from the hemispherical structure, most of the stupas also have a fence around it.

Structure of a Stupa: The semicircular mound of earth is called ***anda*** which is the structure of the simplest of the stupa. This usually is made up of mud and bricks. The stupas of later period have a balcony above the *anda* called ***harmika***, which is representative of the abode of the gods. Usually, a mast also arises from the harmika. This is called a **yashti**, atop of which is an umbrella or ***chatri***. Some stupas also have a railing surrounding it which serves to separate the sacred space of the stupa. Later, stupas also had an outer circumambulatory path with railings called ***vedika*** and decorative gateways called ***torana***.

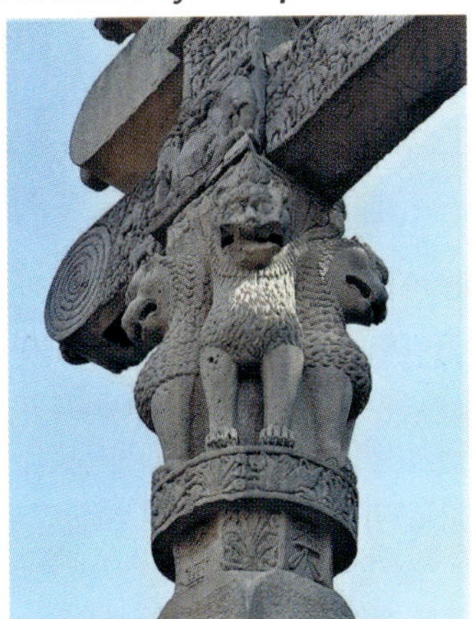

6.8: The pillar lion capital on the southern gateway of Sanchi Stupa — photograph by Madhukar K Bhagat

The Great Stupa at Sanchi was built by emperor Ashoka. With its decorative gateways containing numerous inscriptions, it is the most famous one. It is believed that the gateways and railings were built during the subsequent centuries during the rule of the Sungas and the Satavahanas. Further, the stupa was also enlarged during the latter period.

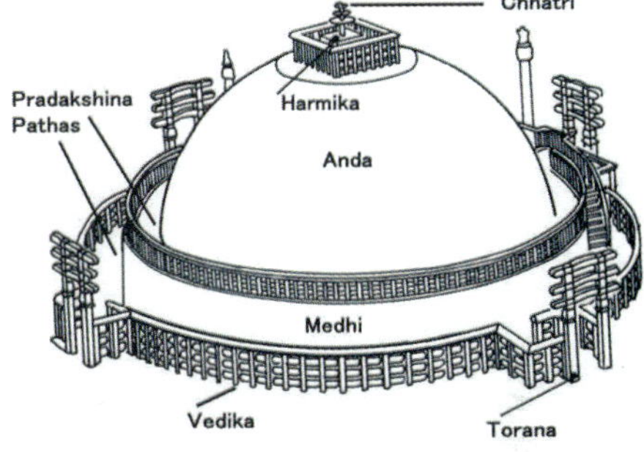

6.9: Diagrammatic representation of a stupa — Wikimedia Commons

The other famous stupas of the ancient times are **Dhamekh Stupa** at Sarnath (Uttar Pradesh), **Ramabhar Stupa** at Kushinagar (UP), **Vaishali Stupa** (Bihar), **Kesariya Stupa** (Bihar), and **Amaravati Stupa** (Andhra Pradesh). However, these stupas are not in the same good state of preservation as the stupa at Sanchi.

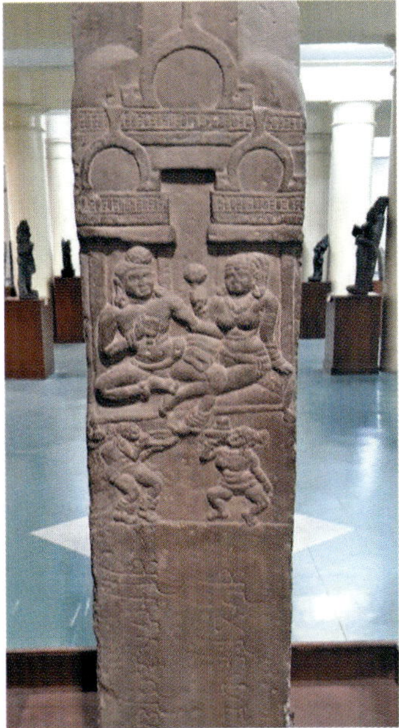

6.10: Ashokan pillar 250 BCE, with inscription in Brahmi inscript; from Gulbarga; Government Museum, Bengaluru — photograph by Madhukar K Bhagat

Sculptures

The dexterity of the Mauryan sculptures is visible in the various pillars and capitals, the stupas, and the figures on its railing and gateways, the chaityas, and viharas, etc.

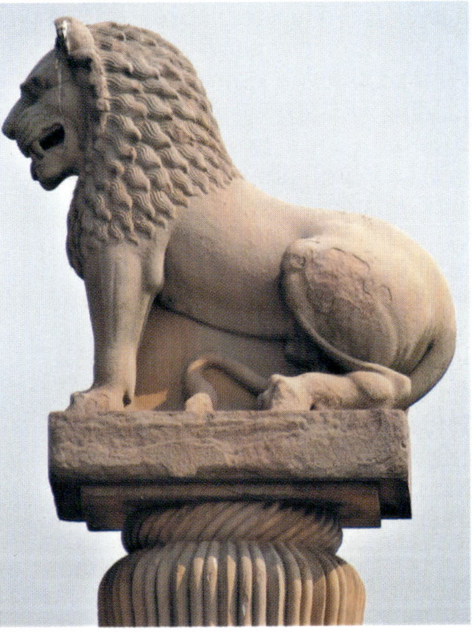

6.11: Lion Capital atop Vaishali pillar — photograph by Madhukar K Bhagat

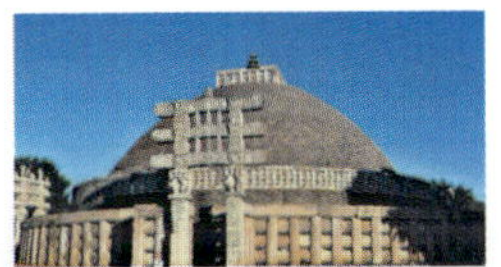

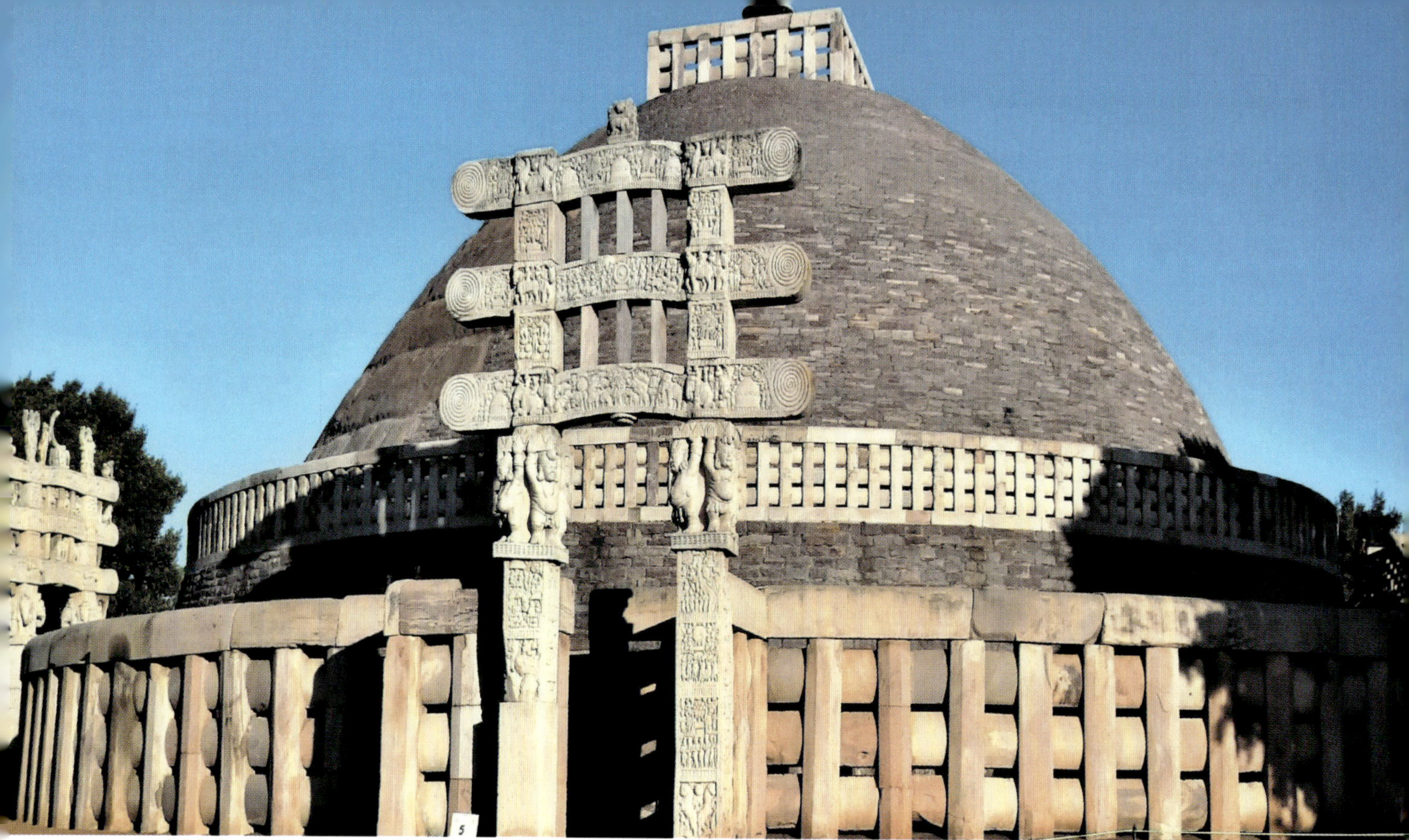

6.12: The Great Stupa at Sanchi, one of the oldest stone monuments of India — photograph by Madhukar K Bhagat

These represented the class of sculptures commissioned by the king. However, several stone statues have also been found that were not commissioned by the king, but by the governors and other rich patrons. The statues of *Yaksha* and *Yakshinis* were quite common in this category and depict the richness of Mauryan art. Some of the important sculptures are described herewith.

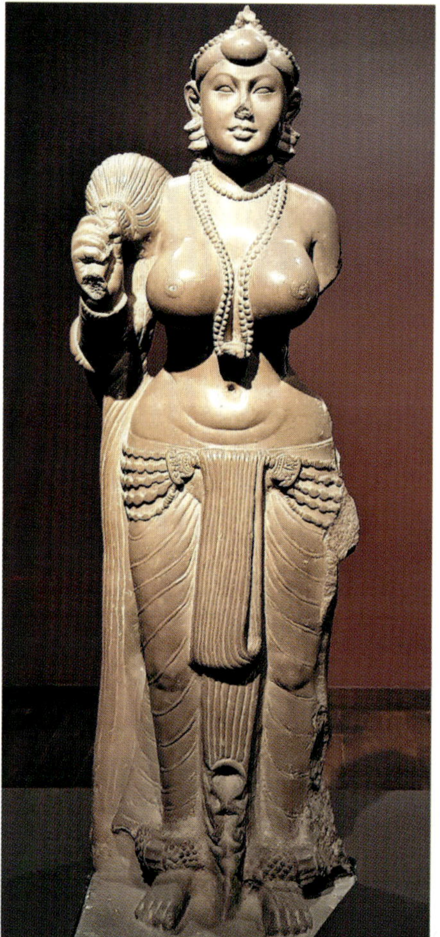

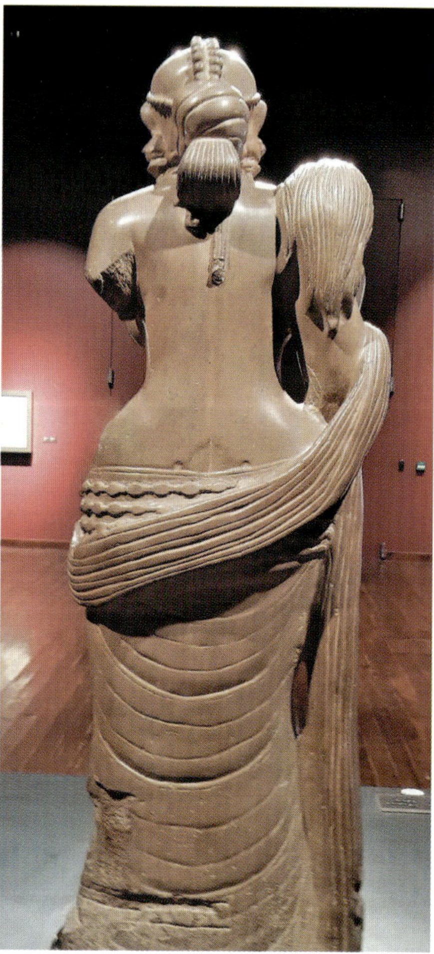

6.13 & 6.14: Didarganj Yakshini, (front and rear), Chunar sandstone, Mauryan period, 3rd century BCE, Bihar Museum, Patna — photograph by Madhukar K Bhagat

Didarganj Yakshini: This is a life-size free-standing statue of a Yakshi (discovered in Didarganj near Patna, hence the name). It is a masterpiece of a sculpture. The sandstone figure shows a Yakshi holding a *chauri* (fly-whisk). It is tall (5 feet two inches tall), well-proportioned and considered emblematic of the female body proportions. The roundness of face, muscular body, and sharp features of nose, lips, and eyes are clearly visible. The upper body is bare, with a very well-crafted necklace of beads hanging from the neck. The folds of the garment of the lower body are shown by protruding lines creating a transparent effect. This statue is presently located in the Bihar Museum at Patna.

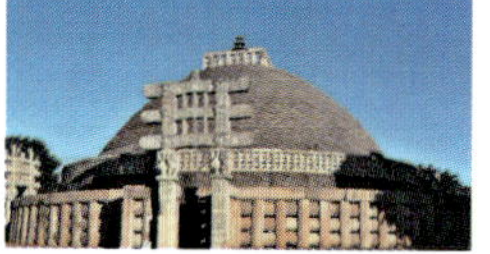

Parkham Yaksha: This is another great masterpiece of this period. It is a life size statue of Yaksha made of red sandstone found near Mathura (presently located in Mathura Museum). The muscular body and the folds of garments of the lower body are striking. However, the statue is not as well preserved as that of the Didarganj Yakshini.

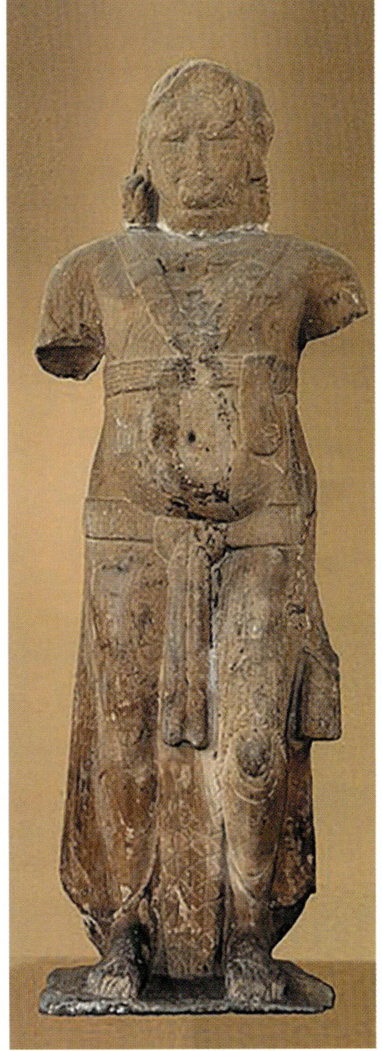

6.15: Parkham Yaksha, Mathura, 150 BCE — Wikimedia Commons

Rock-cut Elephant at Dhauli: This monumental rock-cut elephant found at Dhauli (Odisha) is another important specimen of sculpture of this period. Built by emperor Ashoka, the elephant is above a rock edict (inscribed on which is Ashoka's concern for the whole world). This place (Dhauli) is believed to be the site of the Kalinga war.

Rock-cut Caves: Rock-cut caves are important specimens of art and sculpture of ancient India. Chaityas and viharas too were built at times in rock-cut caves. They reflect the society and culture of the period. Many such rock-cut caves have been found throughout India. The example of Mauryan rock-cut cave is however limited to **Barabar and Nagarjuni** caves near Gaya (Bihar) which are the oldest surviving caves of this category. The outer facade of the Barabar cave has a chaitya arch which is semicircular. The rectangular interior hall has a circular chamber at the back. These chambers are carved out of granite rock and bear highly polished internal surface. Built by emperor Ashoka, the Barabar caves are also called the **Lomas Rishi cave** and was a centre of the followers of the **Ajivika sect**.

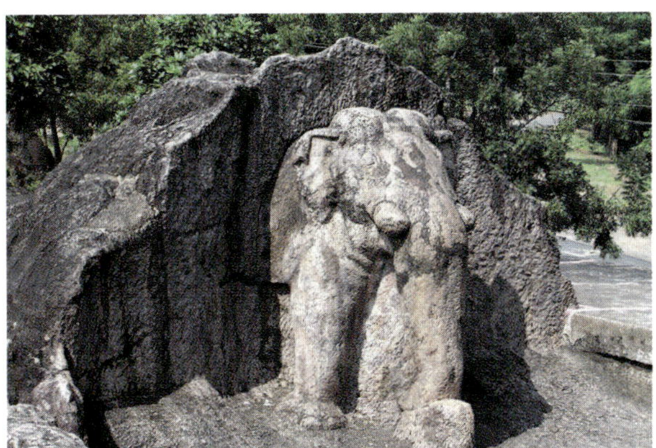

6.16: Rock cut elephant, Dhauligiri — Courtesy, Department of Tourism, Odisha

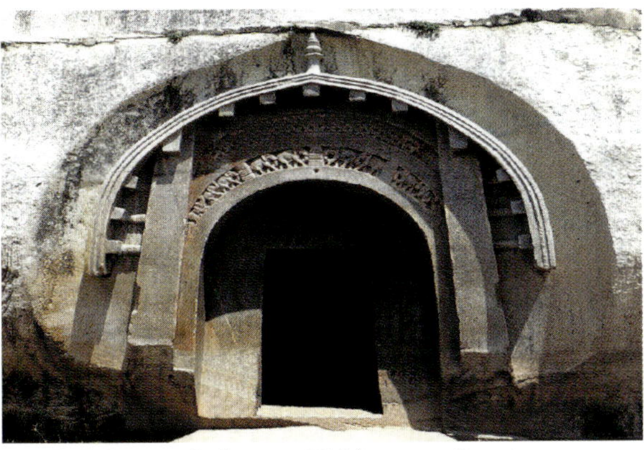

6.17: Entrance to Lomas Rishi caves, Barabar caves — Wikimedia Commons

Palaces: The Mauryan palaces were another example of the splendour of Mauryan art and architecture. The Ashokan palace, the remains of which can still be seen at **Kumhrar, Patna** (after 2250 years) had a grand 80 pillared assembly hall. All the pillars were rock-cut of 9.75 metres in height arranged in 8 rows of 10 pillars each at a distance of 4.57 metres from the other. The remains of a massive pillar of this assembly hall can still be seen at the site of the palace at Kumhrar. The pillars are believed to have supported a wooden roof. However, some scholars believe that this was not a palace, but some kind of assembly hall. Besides, a grand wooden staircase has also been discovered at Kumhrar, south of the great assembly hall. This could have been a part of the palace/adjoining city complex, and is generally believed to lead from the hall to the canal below.

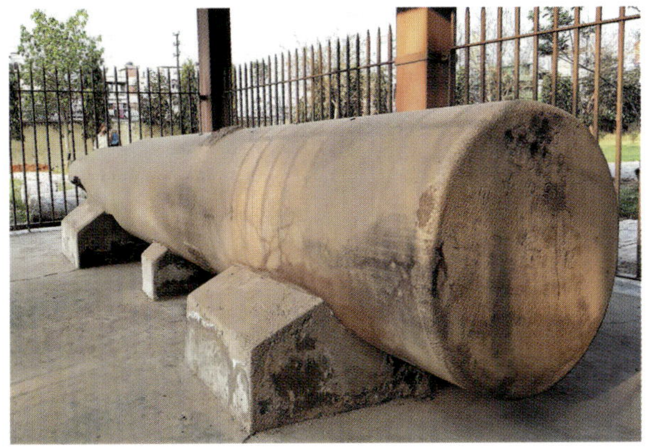

6.18: Surviving column of palace hall — photograph by Madhukar K Bhagat

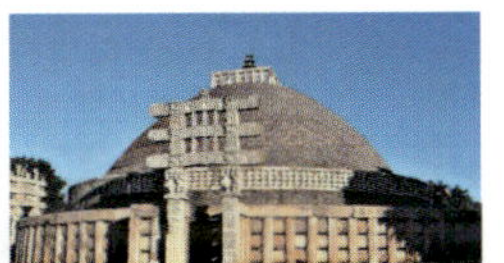

One of the significant discoveries of the Mauryan period, which reveals the magnificence of the Maurya palaces is the **Pataliputra capital** *(a capital in architecture refers to the topmost member of a column which bears the weight of the upper structure.)*. The capital was discovered near the ruins of the palace in Bulandibagh area of Patna in around 1895 CE. Historians have dated the capital to the early Mauryan period/period of Ashoka and believe that it could be a part of the famed Ashokan palace. The capital made of unpolished buff sandstone is rectangular in shape. It has the design of volutes, rosettes (in its top band) and flame palmette pattern towards the bottom. The design reflects a Greeko-Hellenistic influence. The entire capital is quite massive with a height of 1.23 metres and weighing around 900 kgs. It gives the historians an idea of the grandness of the columns and the palace itself.

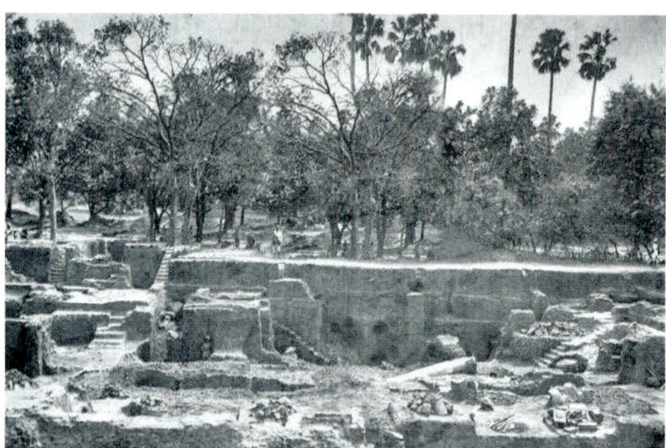

6.19: Excavation site of Kumhrar, Patna, with surviving pillar at the centre, pictures at display at exhibition hall at Kumhrar site — photograph by Madhukar K Bhagat

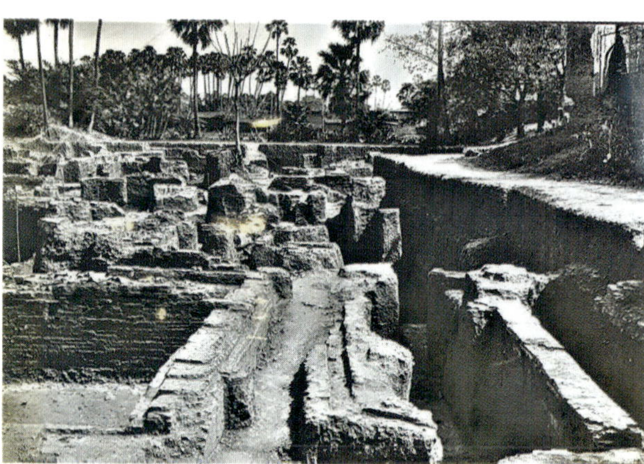

6.20: Ruins of hall with pillars at Kumhrar, pictures at display at exhibition hall at Kumhrar site — photograph by Madhukar K Bhagat

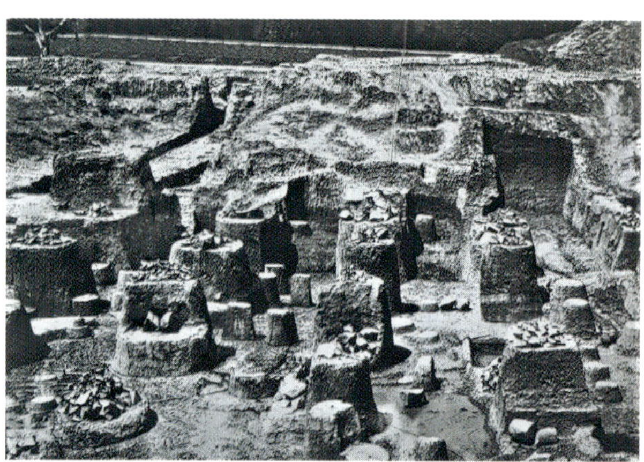

6.21: Ruins of pillared hall, Kumhrar, Patna, pictures at display at exhibition hall at Kumhrar site — photograph by Madhukar K Bhagat

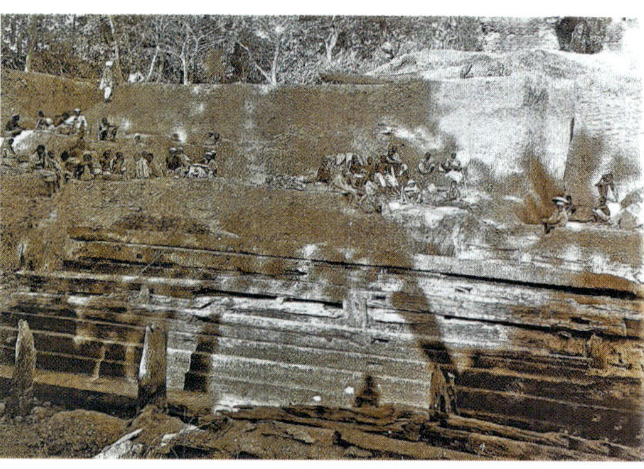

6.22: Ruins of wooden staircase, Kumhrar, pictures at display at exhibition hall at Kumhrar site — photograph by Madhukar K Bhagat

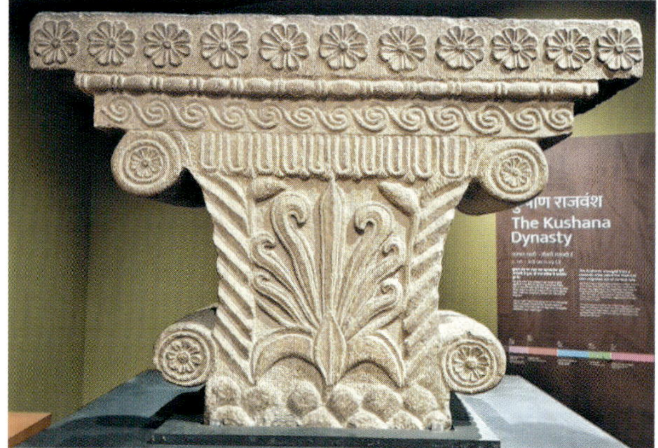

6.23: Pataliputra capital, at display in Bihar Museum, Patna — photograph by Madhukar K Bhagat

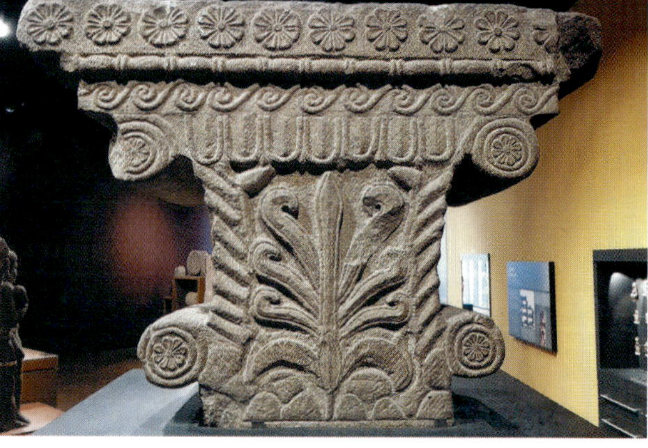

6.24: Symmetrical reverse side of Pataliputra capital — photograph by Madhukar K Bhagat

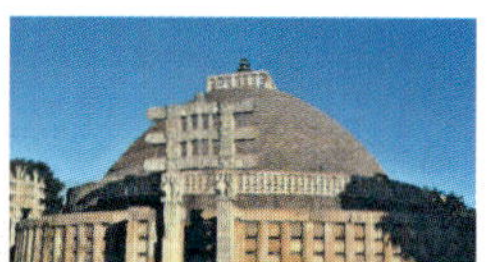

Pottery: A variety of Mauryan pottery has been found. Amongst these, the one which was of the highest quality and finish is the **Northern Black Polished Ware** (NBP). It was made of fine alluvial clay and had jet black, deep grey, or metallic steel blue hue. It had a typical lustre and was found in abundance in the Gangetic valley.

Coins: The coins in the Mauryan period were usually of silver, besides a few of copper. These were of various shapes, sizes, and weights and carried different figures as that of animals, trees, etc. The metal was first cut and the figures were then punched. These punched symbols represented either the royal insignia or the symbols of local guilds issuing it.

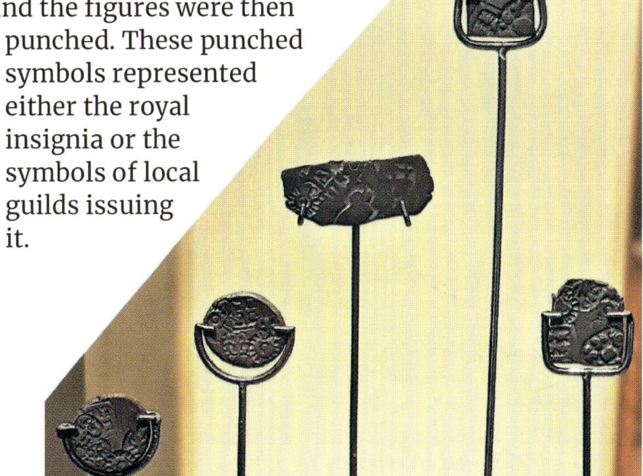

6.25: Punched marked coins, silver, 4th century BCE Kausambi, Uttar Pradesh (Bihar Museum) — photograph by Madhukar K Bhagat

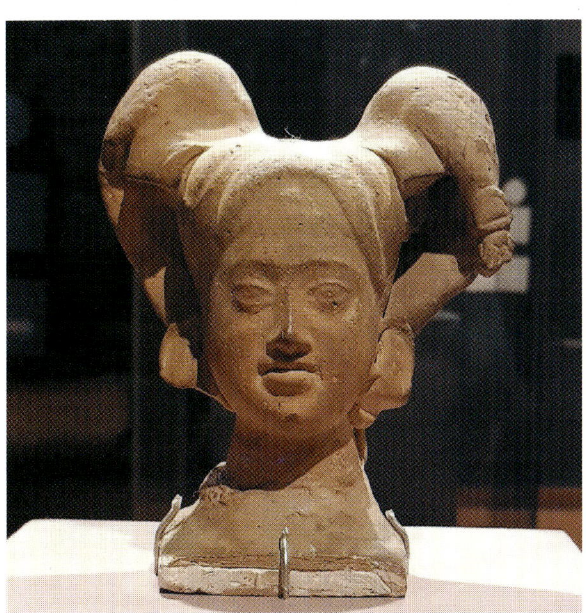

6.26: Small figurine of a smiling girl, 3rd century BCE, Maurya period, Bihar Museum — photograph by Madhukar K Bhagat

Terracotta Figurines: Besides the above, many terracotta figurines, dancing figures, smiling faces with elaborate headgears have been discovered from the Bulandibagh site at Patna. The naturalistic smiles of some of these figurines reflect the high degree of evolution of this art form, which the historians believe also to bear Hellenistic influence. Among the most famous of these are the figurines of smiling and dancing girls, which also depict an elaborate headgear.

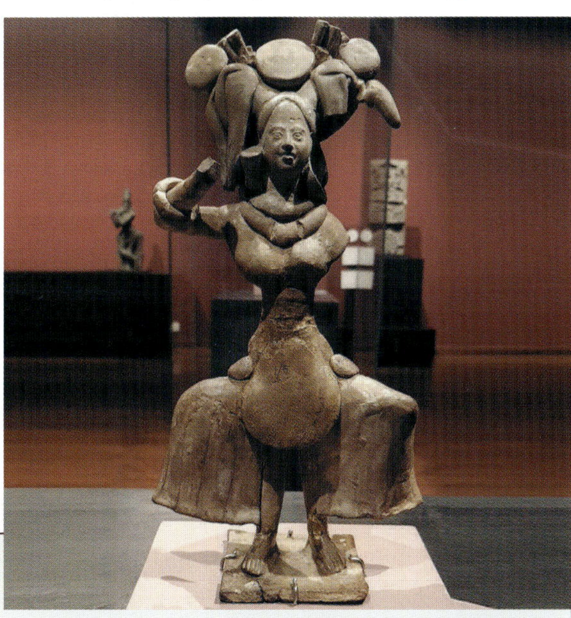

6.27: Terracotta figurine of smiling girl, Maurya period, 3rd century BCE, Bihar Museum, Patna — photograph by Madhukar K Bhagat

The Glorious Cities of Ancient India

As per the description in Buddhist scriptures, accounts of Megasthenese, Fahein and other travellers and the *Arthashastra* of Kautilya, a number of glorious and populous cities are known to have existed in ancient India, particularly since the time of Buddha. By some accounts, they may have existed even earlier. In the *Arthashastra*, Kautilya exhorts the use of stone and brick for greater durability, as against wood, the use of which was in vogue. Thus, the structures therein being largely being built of wood, mud and baked bricks, could not survive the ravages of time and ruins thereof are not evident in the excavations. Therefore, what these magnificent cities were once like, is gathered from the accounts in these manuscripts and some stone structures and pillars found of the Ashokan palace, the parts of city walls of Rajgir and other artefacts.

The typical cities would be near rivers and made of wood, while those in higher ground could be of mud and bricks. Many of these cities would have fortification, as seen from the remains of the city walls of Rajgir where large uneven stone blocks were used for building the walls. These were interspersed with gateways which were flanked by semicircular bastion and watchtowers. **Fragments of a massive wooden palisade discovered (at Bulandibagh site in modern Patna)** reveal a similar walled structure of the ancient **Pataliputra city, the capital of Ashoka.**

The reliefs of Sanchi Stupa, made around Ist century BCE to Ist century CE, depict the cities of Rajgira and Kushinagara as cities with imposing walls, as seen in the relief of the 'royal procession leaving Rajgir' and the relief titled 'war over Buddha relics'.

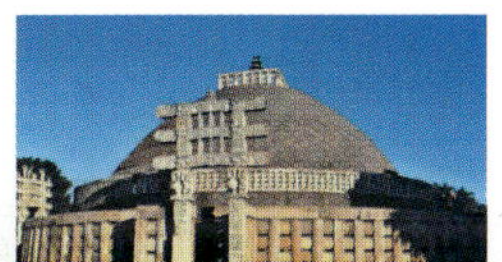

The cities were often surrounded by moats which served the purpose of defense, and was also used for discharge of the sewage. The city of Pataliputra had a similar structure. Described by Megasthenese as one of the largest cities of the world, this city was approximately 25 square kilometres and had a circumference of 33.8 kilometres. It was shaped like a parallelogram and located near the confluence of the rivers Ganga and Sone. It had an incredible 64 gates and 570 watch towers. Adrian/Arrian, a Greek historian of 3rd century CE quotes as below, in his work *Indica*, which covered the military history of Alexander in Asia.

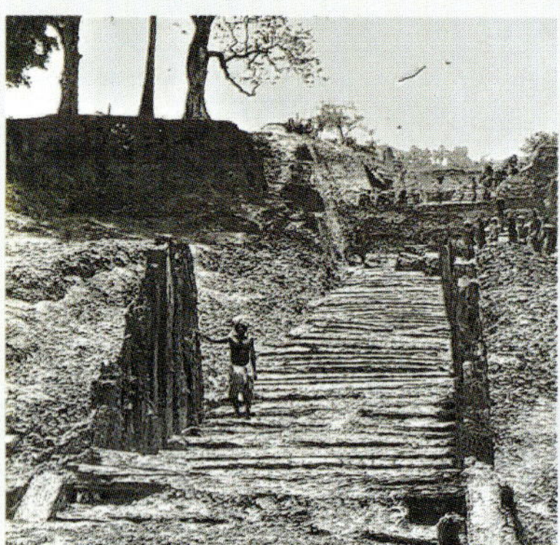

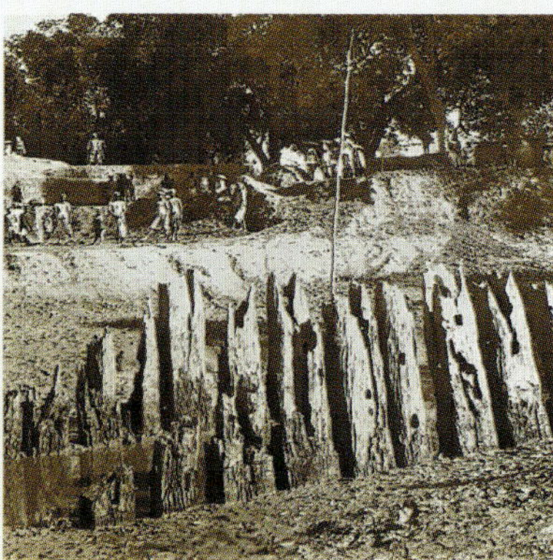

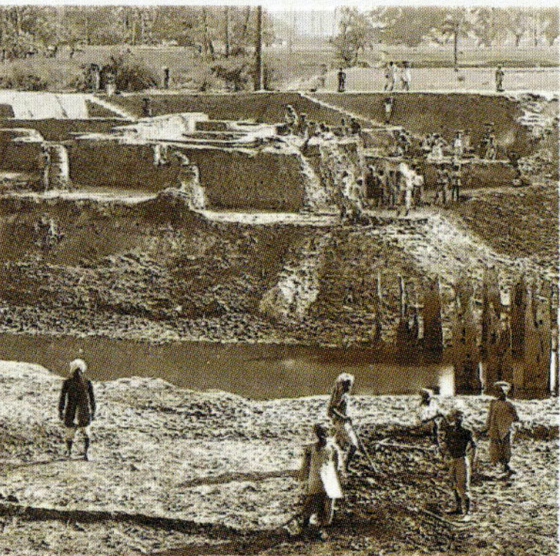

6.28, 29, 30: Remains of a massive wooden palisade of the Mauryan period at Bulandibagh site Patna; picture 1926-27 Pictures at display at exhibition hall at Kumhrar site — photographs by Madhukar K Bhagat

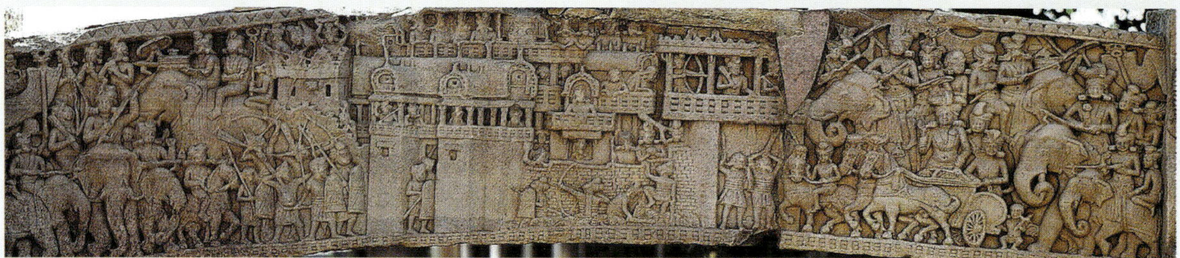

6.31: War over the Buddha's relics in city of Kushinagar, a gateway panel at Sanchi Stupa — photograph by Madhukar K Bhagat

Megasthenese says "that on one side where it is longest, the city extends 10 miles in length and that its breadth is one three quarter miles, that the city has been surrounded by a ditch in breadth 600 feet, and in depth 45 feet, and that its wall has 570 towers and 64 gates."

Strabo, another Greek historian and geographer in Ist century CE, wrote in his work *Geographia*, which presented the history of people and places in different parts of the world. He writes about Pataliputra as thus.

'At the confluence of the Ganges and of another river is situated Patlibothra, in length 80, and in breadth 15 stadia. It is in the shape of a parallelogram, surrounded by a wooden wall pierced with openings through which arrows may be discharged. In front is a ditch which serves as the purpose of defence and a sewer for the city.'

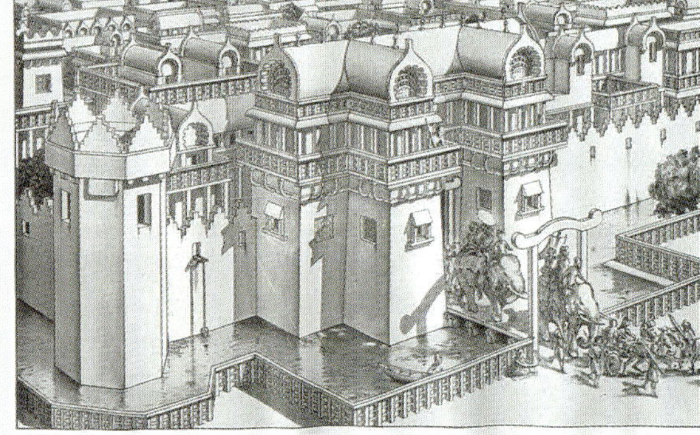

6.32: Conjectural reconstruction of the main gate of Kusinagara, circa 500 BCE; adapted from a relief at Sanchi — Wikimedia Commons

Milinda Panha, written around first century CE, contains the conversation of the Bactrian king Milinda. This treatise also gives a graphic description of the layout of an ancient city as below.

'... the city; fine and regular measures out into quarters with excavated moats and ramparts about it, with stout gatehouses and and towers, with market places, cross roads, street corners and public squares, with clean and even main roads, with regular lines of open shops, well provided with parks, gardens lakes and lotus ponds and wells, adorned with many kinds of temples of gods, free from every fault and standing in all its glory' *

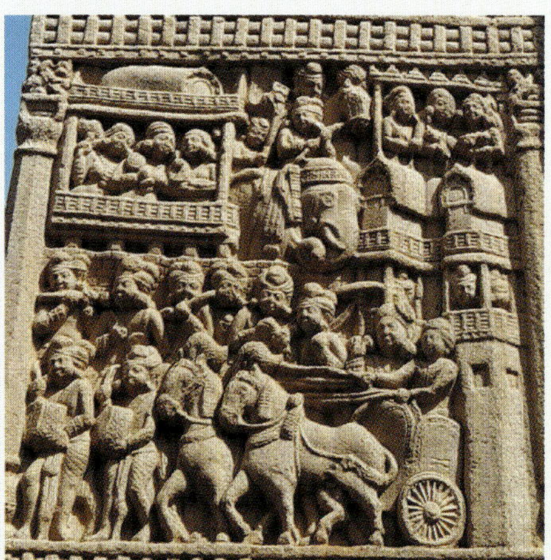

6.33: Palace and royal procession, a Sanchi Stupa panel — photograph by Madhukar K Bhagat

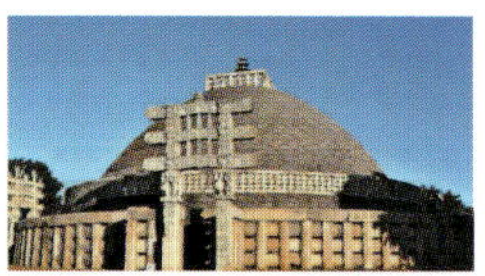

The scholars generally believe the description to hold good as a template for a class of cities of this age as gathered from the reliefs of Bharhut, Sanchi, Amaravati, and Mathura, where ancient cities of Rajgriha, Sravasti, Kapilavastu and Kusinagara have been depicted. From the various reliefs it is also seen that the buildings in the cities could have been of several storeys. The roofs of these buildings was typical wagon/ barrel vaulted (rectangular plan with arching elevation) with gables at either end. The reliefs also show presence of stairways, columns, toranas, a court in front of the building etc.

The palace could have comprised of more than one or aggregate of buildings. The most important one would have a large pillared hall supported on an elevated wooden substratum. The hall would be further subdivided into regular rows and columns by the pillars thus forming square bays. Similar structure is seen from the remains of Ashoka's palace at Pataliputra.

*Reference; 'The Age of Imperial Unity', vol 2 pg 483

ART AND CULTURE IN THE POST MAURYAN PERIOD, GUPTA PERIOD AND POST GUPTA PERIOD

Art and culture in ancient India has been deeply influenced by the political regime and its patronisation of the religious thought. While in the Mauryan period, Buddhist thought and culture was predominant, in the post Mauryan period, the Gupta period and the post Gupta period, different social religious influences dominated art and culture.

Here, a snap-shot is captured of the various regimes in the period 200 BCE to 1100 CE and their important contribution to art and culture.

Post Mauryan Period and Their Influence on Art and Culture

The Sungas: The Sunga dynasty (187 BCE to 75 BCE) founded by Pushyamitra Sunga, succeeded the Mauryan dynasty. The Sungas were a Brahmanical dynasty and this period also saw rise in Vaishnavism and Shaivism which reached its peak during the Gupta period. During the rule of Pushyamitra Sunga (and his successors Agnimitra, Vasumitra, and Devbhuti), the royal patronage shifted from Buddhism to Brahmanism. This period is known for several salient contributions to the field of art and culture.

The Mathura school of art, (a counterpart of the Gandhara school of art) flourished in this period. This was an indigenous school of art with subjects and technique which were typically Indian and had even evolved locally (see the section on Mathura school of Art). Hindu philosophy too evolved, and important works such as **Patanjali's *Yoga Sutra*** and ***Mahabhashya*** (a treatise on Sanskrit grammar) are said to have been composed during this period. Even Buddhist shrines such as the **stupas** at **Sanchi** and **Bharut** started during the Mauryan period underwent architectural expansion. Thus, all elements of culture prospered and evolved.

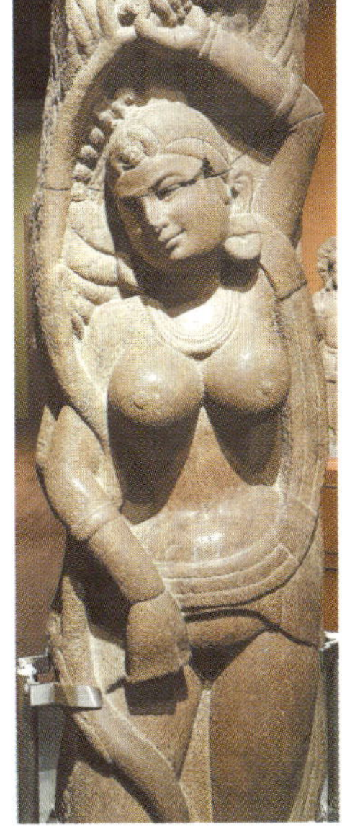

6.34: Shalabhanjika sculpture Sunga period, (Shalabhanjika, a woman considered auspicious whose touch caused flowering/ fruiting of trees) — photograph by Madhukar K Bhagat

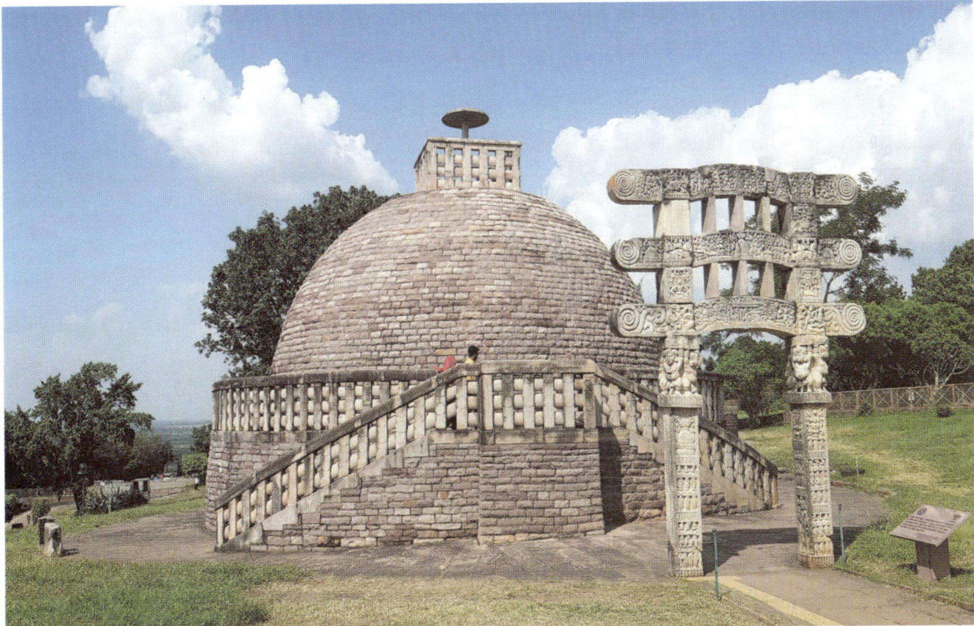

6.35: Stupa no. 3 at Sanchi. Along with the railings and its staircase the stupa was built during the Sunga period. The relics of Sariputra and Moggallana, the chief disciples of Buddha is said to have been placed in it. — photograph by Madhukar K Bhagat

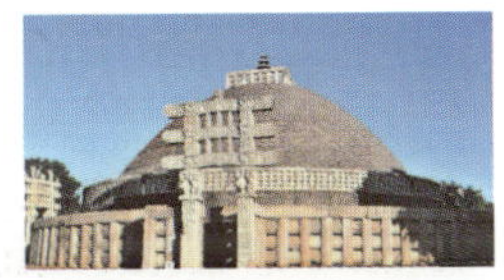

Kanva Dynasty: The Kanva dynasty (75 BCE to 30 BCE) which overthrew the Sungas was short-lived. Founded by Vasudeva Kanva, it was a Brahmanical dynasty and continued the support to Shaivism and Vaishnavism. This further pushed the Buddhist influence to Central India (from Magadha region and Northern India). This dynasty was brought to an end by the Satavahanas.

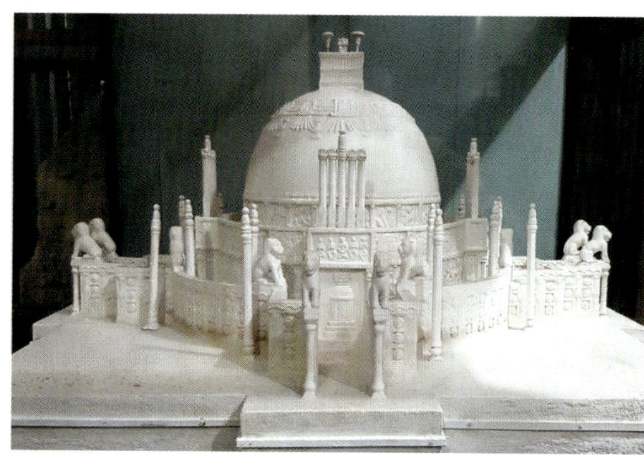

6.36: Amaravati Stupa model; Government Museum, Chennai — photograph by Madhukar K Bhagat

The Satavahana Dynasty: This dynasty came to power in the southern part of India (Deccan region) and reached its zenith under the reign of Gautamiputra Satkarni. Although they were Hindu kings (descendents of the solar dynasty—*Suryavanshi*) they were supporters of Buddhism as well as Brahmanism.

This dynasty too made some salient contributions to art and culture. The **grand stupa of Amaravati** (Andhra Pradesh) and other stupas in the Krishna river valley were built during this period. This indeed was a crowning achievement. This stupa however is now in a poor state of conservation. Further, the highly ornate gateways at the Sanchi Stupa are believed to have been started/built by them. The relief carved on these *Toranas* are a fabulous example of relief work, shedding light on numerous facets of history and culture of the period. This regime also issued its own coins with portrait of rulers, and used Prakrit in official communications, coins, etc. and as a language of administration. A singular influence of the Satavahanas was the spread of Brahmanical faith and culture to many regions in the Southeast Asia.

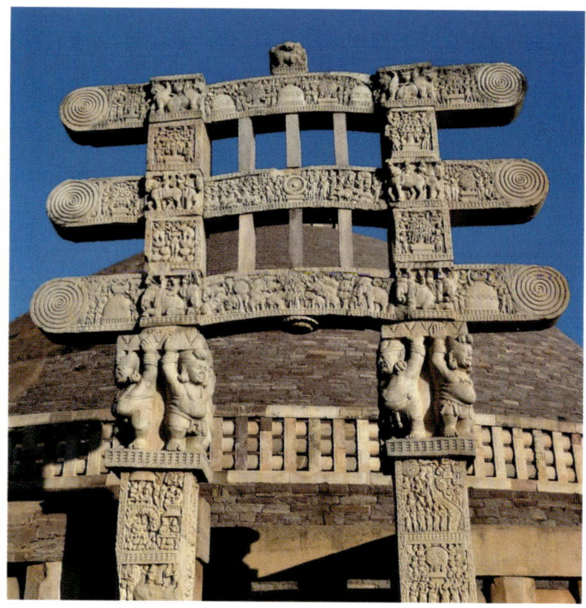

6.37: Sanchi Stupa ornate gateway (western gate) — photograph by Madhukar K Bhagat

Kushana Dynasty: The Kushana dynasty came into prominence in the northern and north western part of India in the first century CE. It also covered the present day Pakistan and large parts of Afghanistan. It was established by king Kujula Kadphises (in 78 CE). Emperor **Kanishka** was the most prominent ruler of this dynasty. The early Kushana rulers are believed to have been influenced by Hinduism and called themselves *devaputra* (son of gods). Kanishka however was a supporter of Buddhism and held the **fourth Buddhist council in Kashmir**. The reign had an important influence on Indian art and culture, particularly the rule of Kanishka. A large number of art work, figurines and sculptures which have been discovered from the Kushana period relate to Buddha or have the Buddhist influence.

A new form of Buddhism, **Mahayana sect** emerged as a consequence of the 4th Buddhist council. Mahayana was patronised by Kanishka which helped in its spread not only in India but from Gandhara to China.

The **Gandhara** as well as the **Mathura schools of art** flourished at this time. A number of large statues of Kushana rulers was found at Mathura, the most famous being the headless statue of Kanishka, all reflecting the evolution of art and sculpture.

Among the many initiatives and innovative measures was the issue of gold coins. This was done for the first time by Kushana rulers and these carried the images of the kings. Further, **the Saka Calendar** was started from 78 CE which is also adopted presently as the national calendar of India.

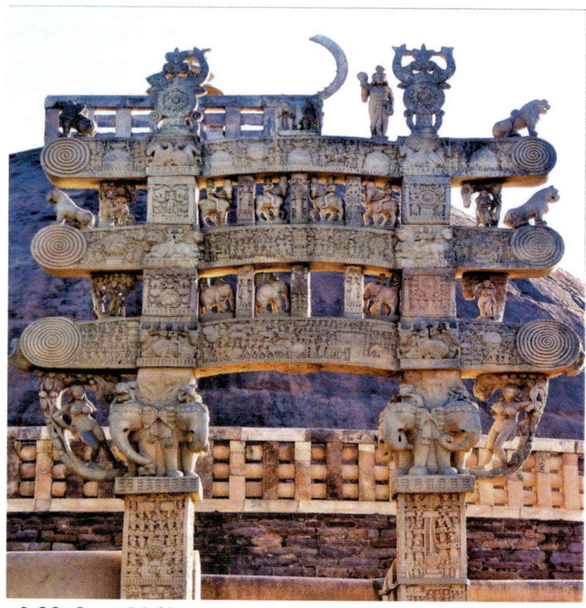

6.38: Sanchi Stupa ornate gateway (northern gate) — photograph by Madhukar K Bhagat

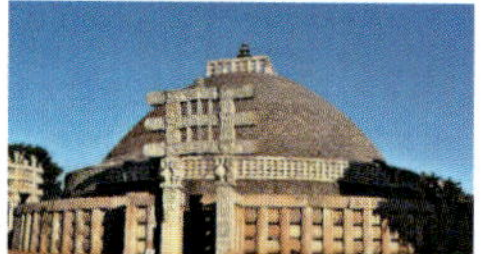

Gupta Period and Their Influence on Art and Culture

Introduction

The Gupta dynasty which flourished from 240 CE to 550 CE ushered in a new phase of growth and development in all walks of life. Historians have aptly termed it as a Golden Age of Indian history. Not only did areas of human knowledge like art, sculpture, science, technology, mathematics, astronomy, and philosophy flourished in this period, but growth of agriculture, commerce and trade coupled with sound administration and military conquests made it one of the most prominent regimes of its time in the world. Eminent scholars and litterateurs like **Kalidasa** and **Vishnu Sharma**, astronomers and scientists like **Aryabhatta** and **Varahamihira,** and other personalities like **Vatsayana**, who made notable contributions in their respective fields, prospered in this age.

A brief history of the Gupta rulers

This empire was founded by Maharaj Srigupta. **Chandragupta** I, **Samudragupta,** and **Chandragupta Vikramaditya** (Chandragupta II) were the most notable rulers of this period. Samudragupta, who is known for his great military conquests, is also referred by historians as the Indian Napoleon. He was himself a poet and musician (coins depict him playing a *veena*). The empire reached its zenith during Chandragupta II (375 CE to 415 CE) when a large part of the Indian subcontinent was directly under this empire or owed suzerainty to it. A detailed account of the Gupta period is obtained in the writings of the Chinese traveller **Faxian** (also referred as *Fahien*) who stayed in India from 405 to 411 CE. The accounts, which are the most important source of information of this age, describe a prospering civilisation, able, but mild administration, and a glorious account of the rule and the king.

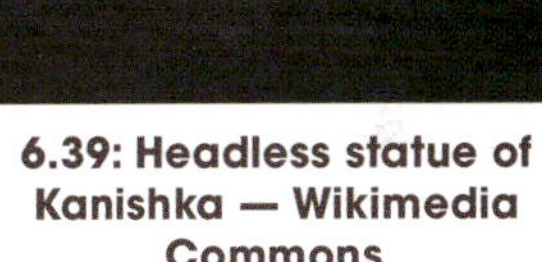

6.39: Headless statue of Kanishka — Wikimedia Commons

The Guptas were Hindu kings, and Hindu art and culture underwent resurgence in this phase. However, they were tolerant of Buddhism and Jainism and contributed to the development of a monastery at Bodhgaya.

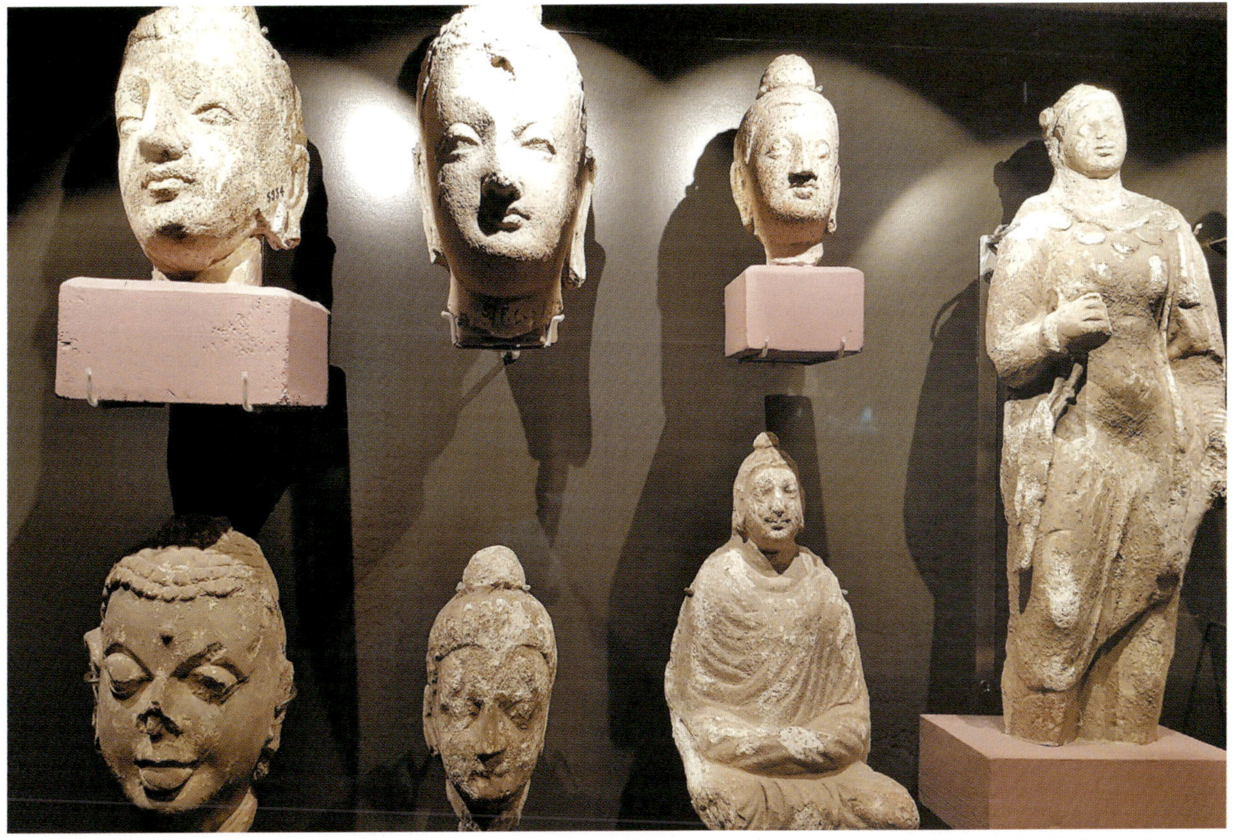

6.40: Buddha figurines and scuplture s, Kushana period, Bihar Museum, Patna — photograph by Madhukar K Bhagat

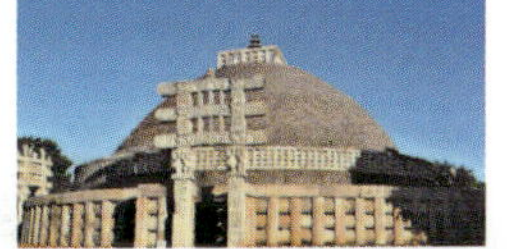

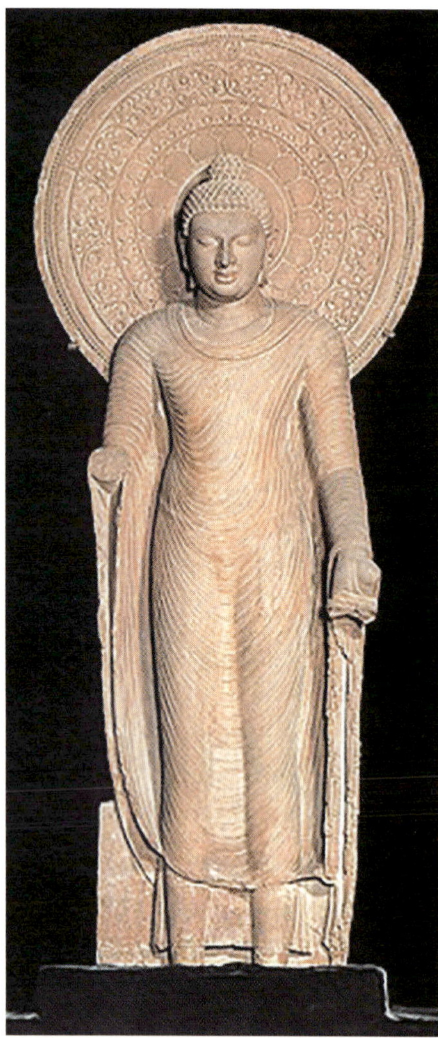

6.41: Standing Buddha from Mathura, 5th century CE, Gupta period, Rashtrapati Bhavan, New Delhi — Wikimedia Commons

Art and culture in the Gupta period

Art and culture indeed reached its zenith during this period which included Hindu, Buddhist, and Jain art with there being many notable contributions of this age.

Paintings at Ajanta – The mural paintings of Ajanta **(a UNESCO World Heritage monument)** are a contribution of this age, although, earlier the **Satavahanas,** and later the **Vakatakas,** have also contributed to it. The paintings include images of Bodhisattvas and Jatakas.

Sculptures in Gupta period – The **Dashavatara temple at Deogarh (UP)** which contains the reclining image of Vishnu is a grand example of sculpture in this age. During this phase, both the Gandhara and Mathura school of art flourished. The image of Vishnu at Mathura and seated image of Buddha at Sarnath are among the finest examples of sculpture. The sculpture of Varaha at Udayagiri caves near Vidisha (Madhya Pradesh) is another example of great craftsmanship. Further, the sculptures of *sapt-matrikas* (seven mother goddesses), standing image of Buddha at Mathura, and Buddha's bronze statue are other great examples of sculpture showing the influence of puranic Hinduism as well as Buddhism.

Temple architecture evolved during this period as seen from the **Dashavatara stone temple (Deogarh)**and the **Chaturmukh linga Shiva temple at Nachna** (Madhya Pradesh).

Cave and rock-cut sculpture flourished which is evident in the **Udayagiri Caves** and the **Elephanta Caves** (5th to 8th century CE). The latter has the famous **Trimurti** sculpture.

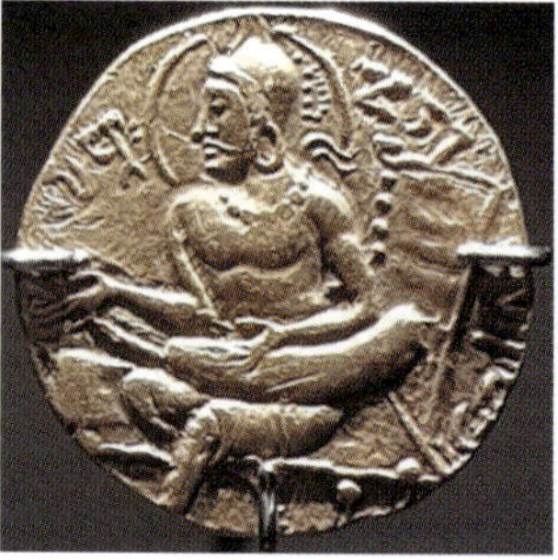

6.43: Samudragupta playing veena, gold coin, Gupta period, Bihar Museum, Patna — photograph by Madhukar K Bhagat

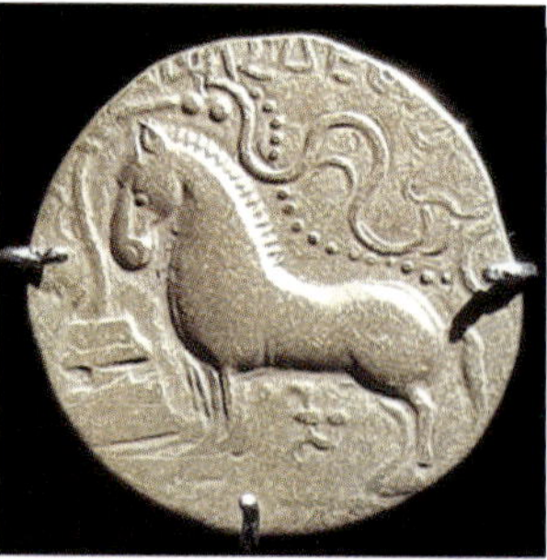

6.44: Ashwamedha yagna, gold coin, Gupta period, Bihar Museum, Patna — photograph by Madhukar K Bhagat

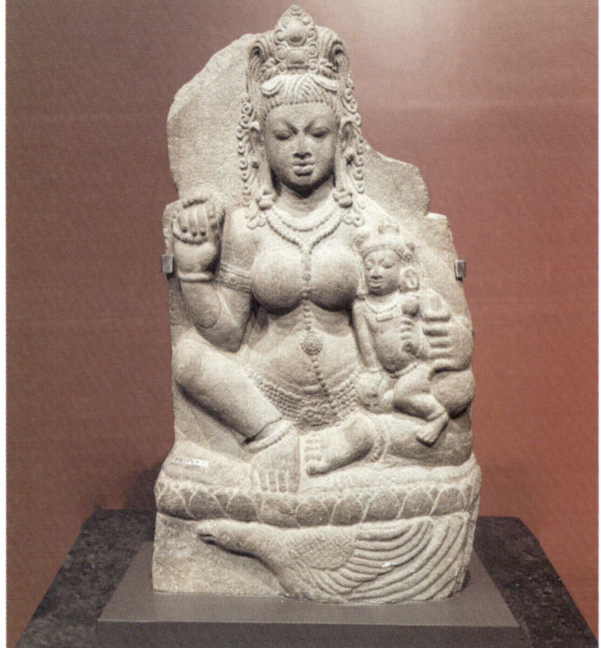

6.42: Brahmani, 6th century CE (Gupta period), one of the Sapta-matrika grey sandstone, Saraikela; current location, Bihar Museum, Patna — photograph by Madhukar K Bhagat

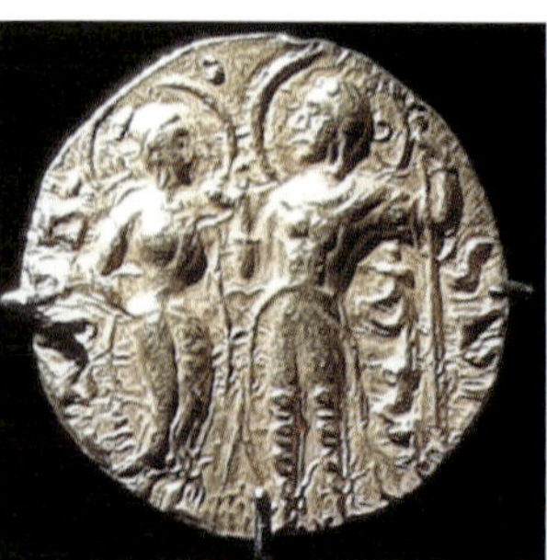

6.45: King and queen, Chandragupta gold coin, Gupta period, Bihar Museum, Patna — photograph by Madhukar K Bhagat

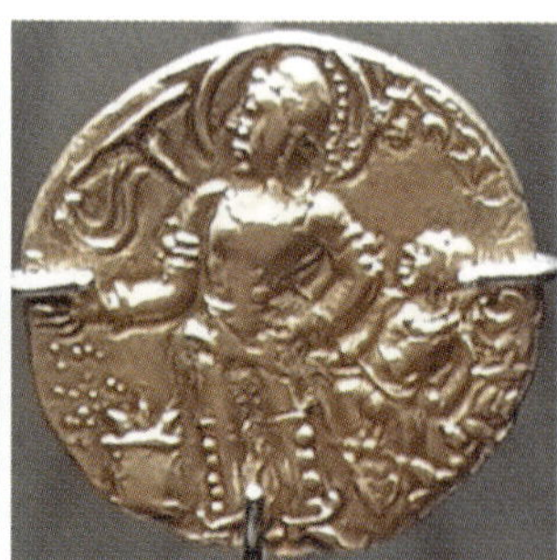

6.46: Chatradhari, Chandragupta II gold coin, Gupta period, Bihar Museum, Patna — photograph by Madhukar K Bhagat

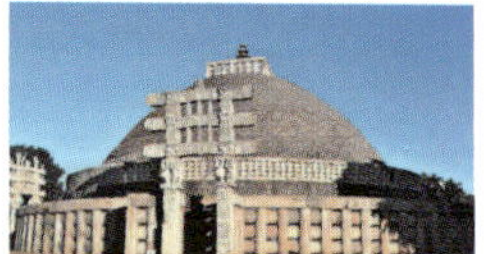

A number of **gold and silver coins** of this age have been discovered. These show images of Samudragupta, holding royal sceptre, sacrificing at the altar, holding bow, performing *Ashwamedha Yagna*, playing *veena*, etc. Coins with images of other rulers are also found.

Clothing in Ancient India

Clothing is an integral part of the culture of a society. Inherently transient in character, it is influenced by social factors, climatic conditions, evolution of techniques of weaving, use of different fabric material and changing tastes. Information as to the nature of clothing in vogue in ancient India is gathered by the historians from the images depicted in sculptures, terracotta figurines, pottery, reliefs, coins and description as contained in the numerous manuscripts such as the Vedas, the Buddhist Pitakas etc.

Clothing in ancient India is seen to have evolved over a period of time, quite like other elements of tangible culture. The Vedic literature describe general use of garment of a single cloth wrapped around the body and draped over the shoulder. However, description of garments in two parts is also given. The lower garment, often called *paridhana*, would be pleated in front and tied around the waist in various manners, while the upper garment called *uttariya* would be covered like a shawl.

In the pre-Buddhist and up to the Mauryan period, the clothing was simple, usually unstitched and comprising two parts, the lower and upper garment. The under or the lower garment would reach below the knee and typically half way up to the ankles, which is similar to wrapping of a present-day dhoti (or a sari).The lower garment would have a part wrapped around the upper part of the body or even thrown over the shoulder. The upper garment would be thrown partly over a shoulder and at times over both the shoulders. Sometimes, it would be partly twisted in folds over their head. But upper garment was often not used within the household.

Use of coloured clothes by women in the upper strata was common. The public or formal dress of higher class would also include headgear similar to turban tied as per the local custom. Ascetics would wear a single piece of cloth, often a robe, types of which is seen in statues of Buddha. These statues, particularly of the Gandhara school, even show the drapery and folds of the garment, thus indicating the way these garments were worn, especially in the period when these statues were commissioned.

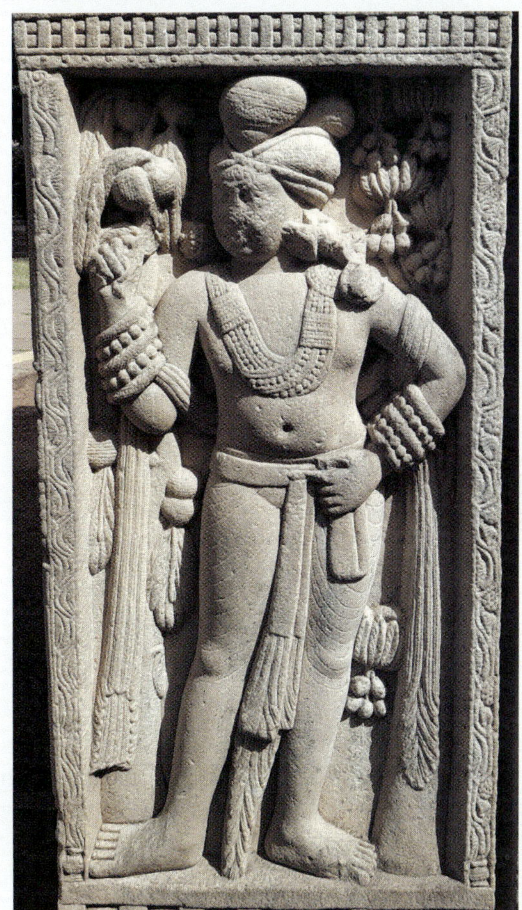

6.47: Dwarapala, or a guardian deity, at an inside panel of gateway at Sanchi stupa, also bringing out the dress of men. The lower garment, prominent headgear, thick armlet and necklace, besides upper garment flowing over left arm is seen — photograph by Madhukar K Bhagat

The differences in male and female dresses were narrower that at present. Both used dresses which comprised two pieces of clothing usually unstitched. Both also used headgear and ornaments as seen from the images of Sanchi and Bharhut stupas. However, over a period of time, the use of ornaments became lesser in men, and headgear less fashionable in women. The statue of Yakshini (Didarganj) (see fig 6.1) shows how the lower cloth (form of dhoti wrap) was worn with drapery and tied and tightened around the waist. The numerous folds of the lower cloth creating transparent effect are clearly visible and the middle band of the garment is seen falling up to the ankles. The use of a variety of jewellery such as beaded necklace, armlet, earrings etc. is also evident. Similar representation and clothing is seen in the Bharhut Yakshini image.

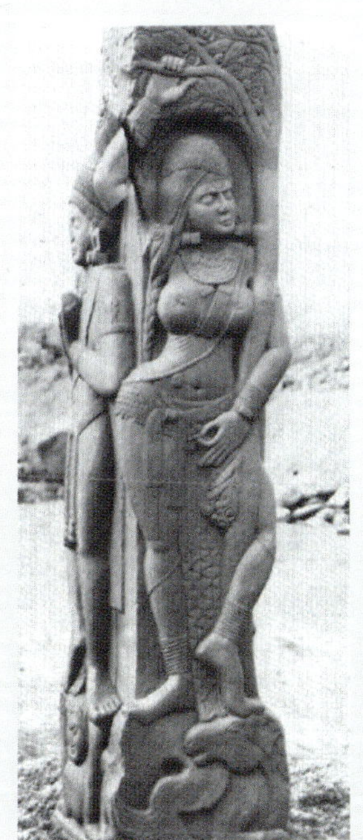

6.48: Bharhut Yakshini — Wikimedia Commons

The images of women also reveal an absence of use of any kind of veil. Some female images in these reliefs and sculptures display bare upper body with distinct images of navel and breast. Some scholars believe that this could be a depiction of women in private, or in the precincts of home, and not a public appearance where use of upper garment was a norm. Some hint at this being a mere artistic convention of the age. However, they do indicate that such bare images in art were not a taboo in ancient India, and social sensibilities, particularly in art, was different.

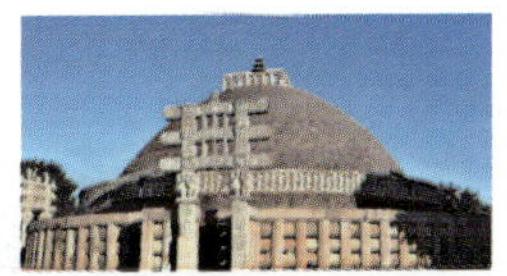

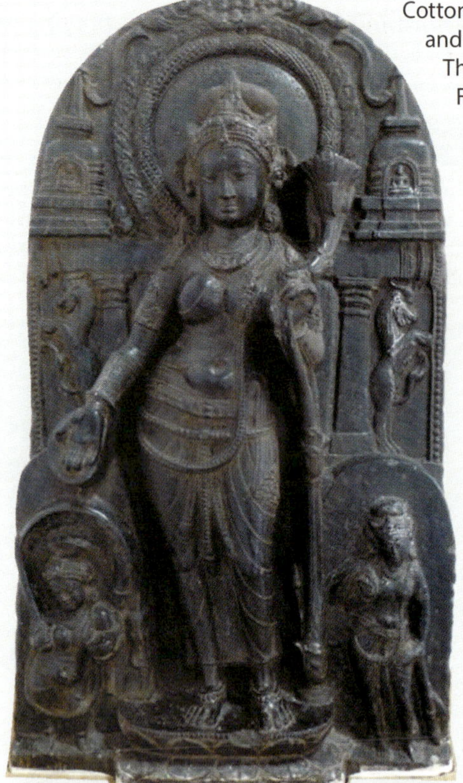

6.49: Stone sculpture of Tara (Pala school, 10th century CE) — Image depicting the folds of lower garment and use of head band, necklaces, armlet, waistband, anklet and other forms of jewellery, Bihar Museum, Patna — photograph by Madhukar K Bhagat

Cotton as a material of clothes was quite common. However, wool, linen and muslin was in demand too and even silk was well known and used. The existence of an elaborate textile industry is referred to by Kautilya. Further, the Buddhist *Vinaya* text also refer to the weaving of cloth. The *Vinaya* texts also refer to a variety of girdles for fastening clothes on waist indicating the technique of wearing these dress in practice.

Post Mauryan period, the influence of Greeks and Sycthians is also seen in the dress sensibilities. This is particularly noticeable in the Gupta period, when stitched dresses are seen to becoming more popular. The Kushan kings are seen to be wearing a big overcoat and trouser like dresses. (see the headless statue of Kanishka, Mathura school of art). Use of dress by women similar to frocks, jackets and blouses too is seen in this age. This was the foreign influence on the Indian dressing.

Use of ornaments was common. Megasthenese observes, *'in spite of general simplicity of style the Indians love finery and ornament. Their robes are worked in gold and ornamented in precious stone and they also wear flowered garments made of finest muslin*'*. (also see image of Apsara, an Ajanta cave painting, in later pages).

A description of various kinds of shoes is obtained from accounts of Nearchus, a Greek officer in the army of Alexander (quoted in *Megasthenese* by McCrindle). He describes shoes made of white leather with variegated thick soles. Even *Vinaya* texts contain description of shoes with many linings, made of a variety of leather (viz. lion, tiger, antelope, cat etc.). The shoes were of different colours and ornamented with feathers, crystal, copper, silver and even gold. Wooden shoes or shoes made of palm leaves was also in vogue in poorer people.

Reference to a variety of toiletries is also contained in *Vinaya* texts which have described the use of hair oils, combs, scents, perfumes garlands etc.

*Reference; 'The Age of Imperial Unity', vol 2 pg 574

Post Gupta Period and Their Influence on Art and Culture

The Vakataka dynasty: This dynasty (3rd to 5th century CE) was contemporary of the Guptas and flourished in the Deccan region between the Malwa plateau and the Tungabhadra river. The daughter of Chandragupta II (Prabhavati Gupta) was married to Rudrasena, a Vakataka king. The Vakatakas were Brahmin kings. They were great patrons of art and literature. Many of the viharas/chaityas were also built during this period. The paintings (in cave no. XVI) of Ajanta are said be commissioned by Vakataka king Harisena.

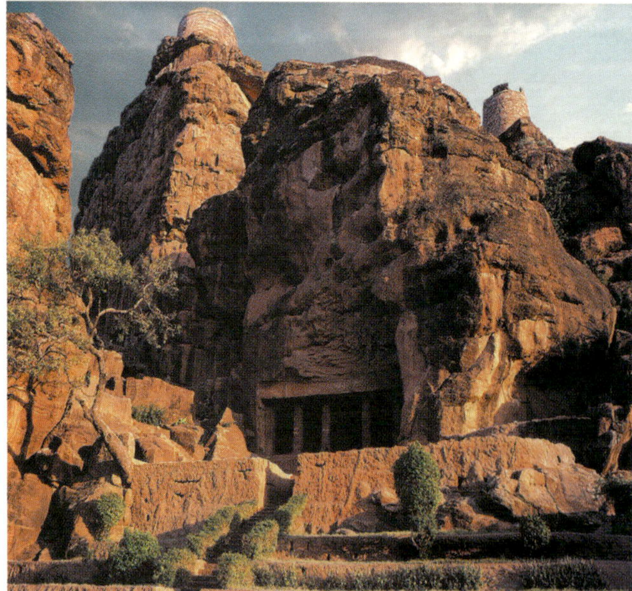

6.50: The Badami caves, famous for the rock cut statues carved in the Chalukyan dynasty, 6th century CE — Courtesy, Karnataka State Tourism Development Corporation

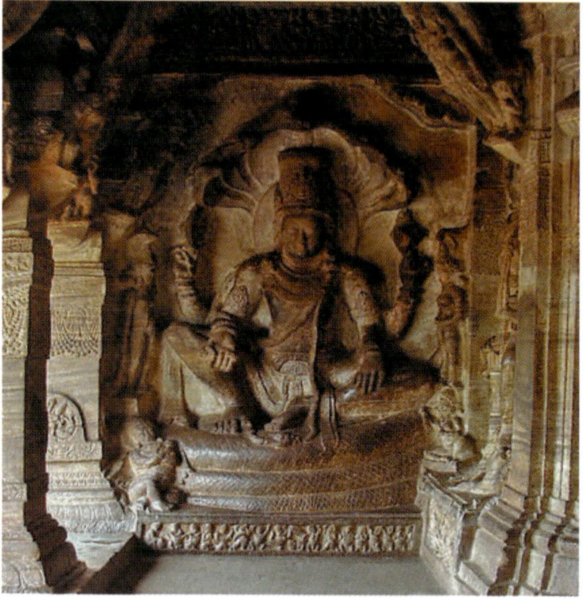

6.51: Vishnu on Shesh Nag, Badami caves — Wikimedia Commons

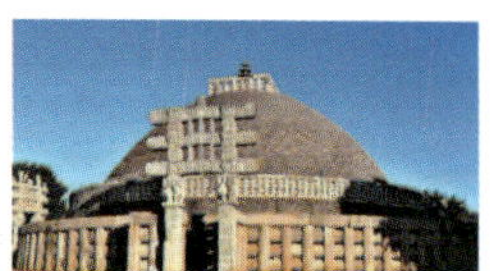

The Chalukya dynasty: The Chalukya period (6th to 13th century CE), succeeded the Vakatakas and is often referred as the golden period in the history of South India. The regime covered large parts of Central and Southern parts of India. **Pulakeshin II** was one of the most important rulers of this dynasty who halted the southward march of King Harsha. Administration, commerce, overseas trade, and art and architecture received a great boost in this phase. The **temples at Aihole** in Karnataka **(a UNESCO World Heritage site)**, **rock-cut architecture of Badami** famous for sculptures of Hindu deities (such as Shiva's *Tandava* and Vishnu as *Trivikrama*), temples of **Pattadakal (a World Heritage Site)**, and many temples of Western Chalukyas are representative of this regime.

Rani Ki Vav: A Marvel of Chalukyan Art & Architecture

Built in the late 11th century CE, Rani Ki Vav, a stepwell constructed in seven levels with over 500 major architectural panels and thousands of minor ones, is indeed a marvel of Chalukyan art and architecture. The monument, which is said to be akin to an inverted temple or a temple well, was constructed by queen Udaymati (hence its name 'Rani ki Vav' or the queen's stepwell). It was also a memorial to her late husband king Bhimadeva-1 of the Chalukya; of Solanki dynasty. The stepwell is located in town of Patan (Gujarat) and on the banks of river Saraswati. The monument also finds reference in the treatise *Prabandha Chintamani* composed by Jain monk Merutanga (in 1304 CE) where reference is made to queen Udaymati for the construction of the stepwell at Shri-Pattana.

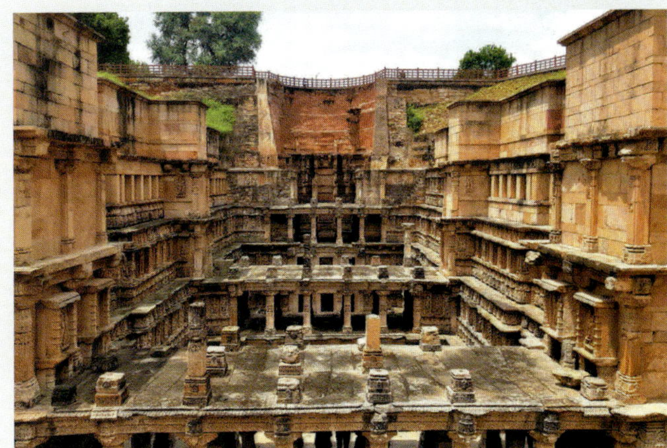

6.52: The different levels of Rani ki Vav, with architecture panel on both walls — photograph by Madhukar K Bhagat

The step-wells were one of the significant measures of water management in an area faced with water scarcity. As the underground water table dropped low in the drier months, a stepwell facilitated fetching of water through a flight of steps even from the lowest levels of the well. Rani ki Vav which is nearly 100 feet deep served this purpose, well before it was flooded in the subsequent centuries. It remained buried in silt with only the shaft of the well and a few pillars at the ground level visible, before its restoration was done in the 1980s. Today, out of the seven levels of the monument, only five survive, which are adorned with sculptures exquisitely carved in panelled niches on both walls of the stepped corridor.

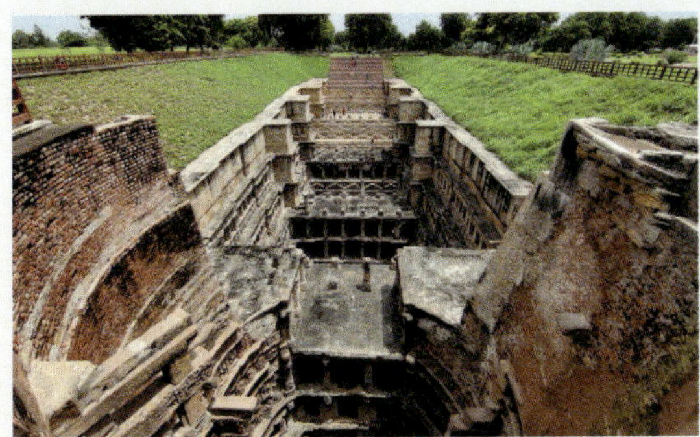

6.53: Step-well, overflow reservoir and the different architectural levels; Rani ki Vav — photograph by Madhukar K Bhagat

The sculptures depict a variety of Hindu deities including Brahma, Vishnu, Shiva, various forms of the goddess Durga and other deities. Among these the most famous and noticeable are the Dashavatara panel, lord Vishnu's twenty-four forms, Parvati's penance, twelve Gauris and eight vasus. Besides, there are also many images of celestial beings (apsaras) such as the one applying a lipstick, and the other shooing a monkey tugging

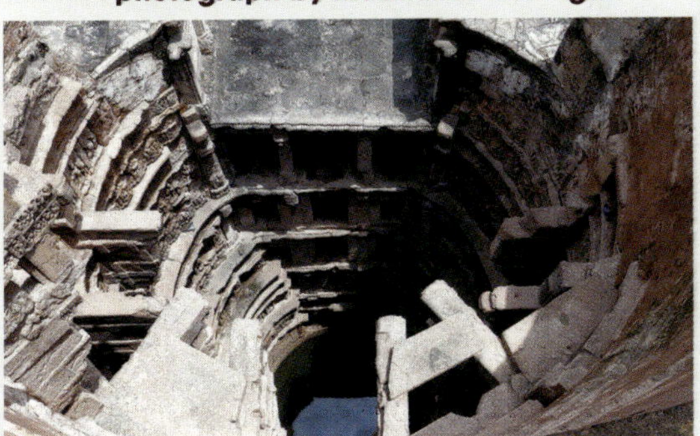

6.54: The deep step-well with water inside — photograph by Madhukar K Bhagat

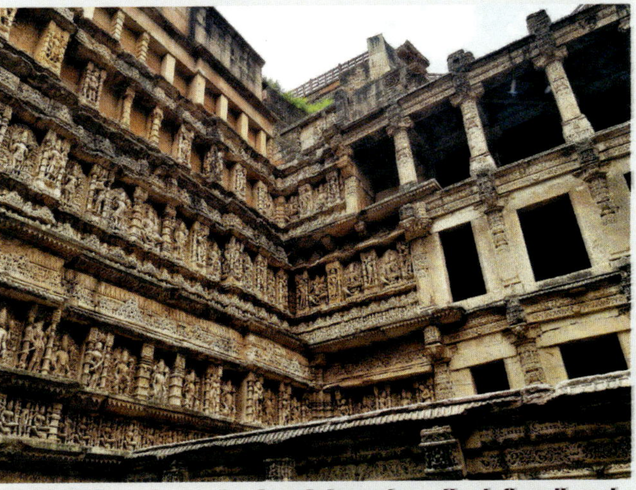

6.55: Different panels of sculpture along the left wall and the end along the well. The lower panel depicting the various forms of the goddess while the panel just above it depicting the different forms of lord Vishnu — photograph by Madhukar K Bhagat

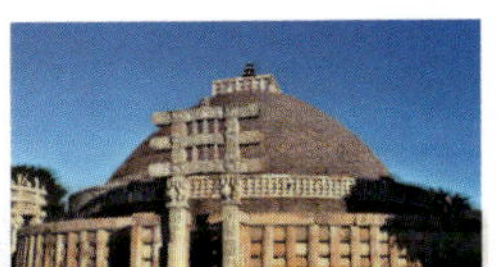

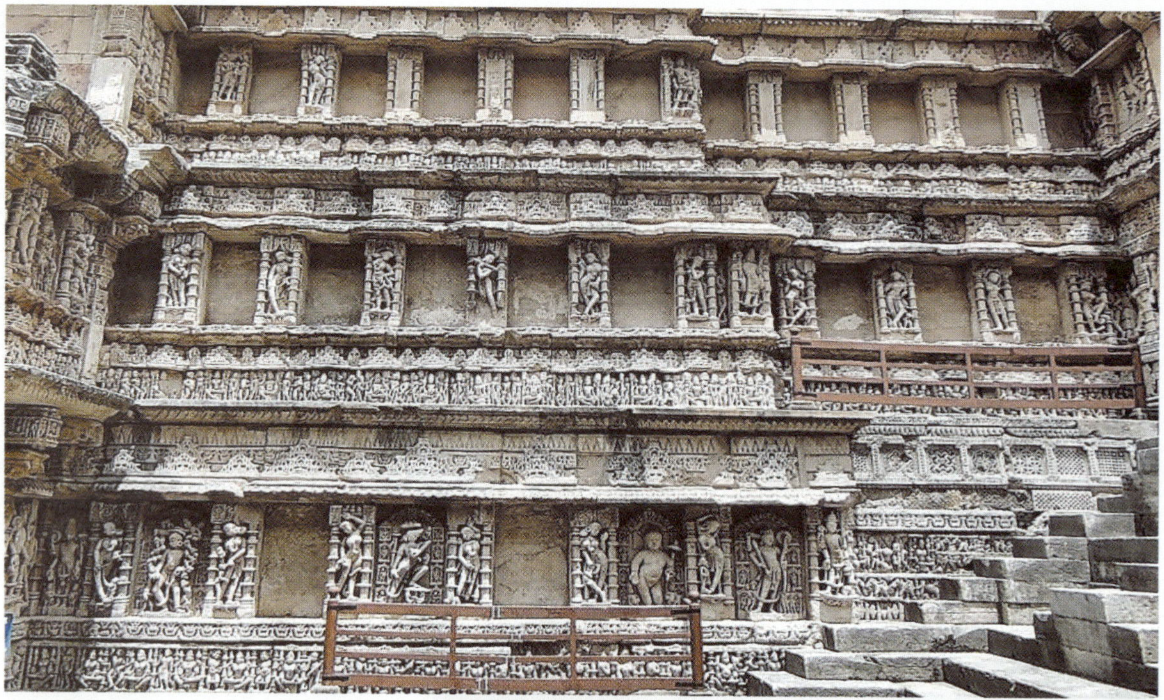

6.56: Different panels of sculpture along the right wall. Lower panel depicting different avatars of lord Vishnu. — photograph by Madhukar K Bhagat

her dress revealing her sensuous form. A nude image of a *nagakanya* (serpent maiden) with a slithering snake is another erotic image.

The monument was recognised as a **UNESCO World Heritage Site in 2014**. The image of the stepwell is also found in the back of 100 rupees note, thus underlining the historical and socio-cultural significance of the monument.

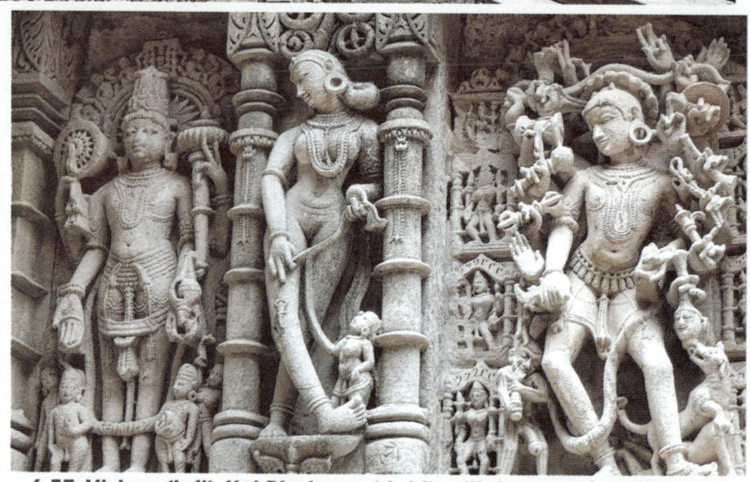

6.57: Vishnu (left) Kal Bhairava (right) with image of an apsara/ female figure in centre. A scorpion is seen climbing on the right knee of the apsara as she emerges out of water after a bath. — photograph by Madhukar K Bhagat

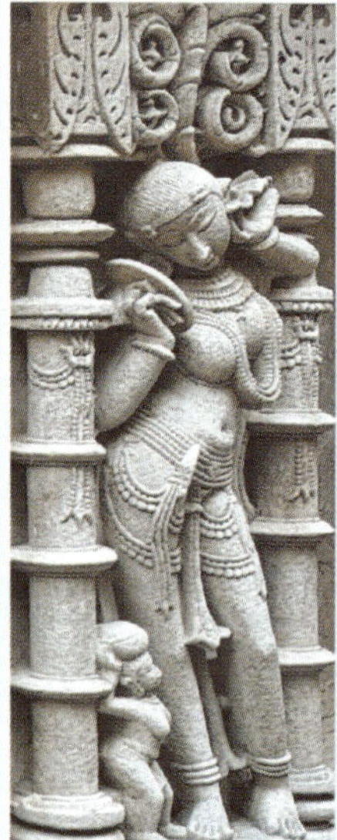

6.58: A female figure viewing a mirror

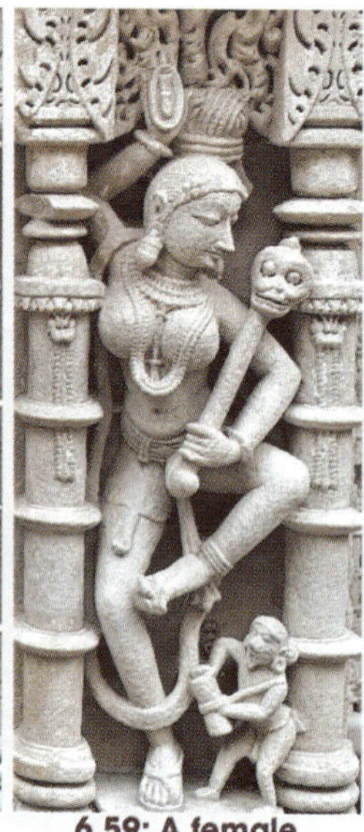

6.59: A female mendicant of certain cult with a skull club

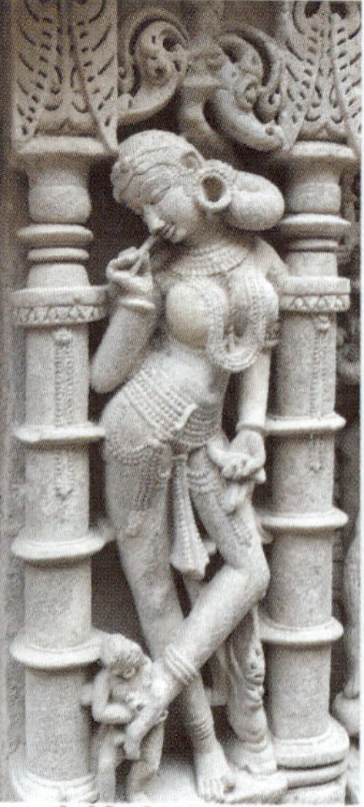

6.60: An apsara applying a product akin to a lipstick

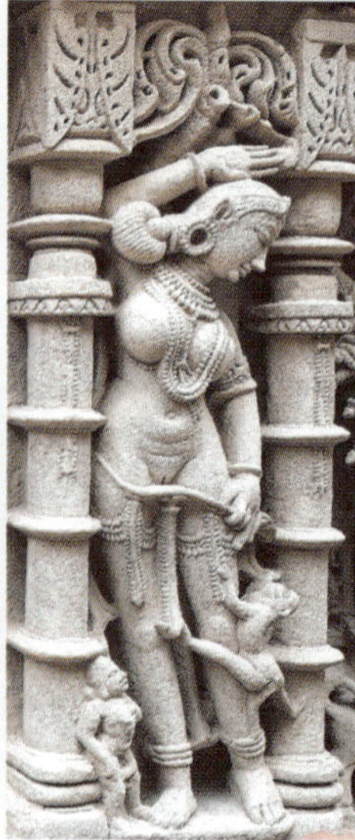

6.61: A monkey tugging at the dress of an apsara

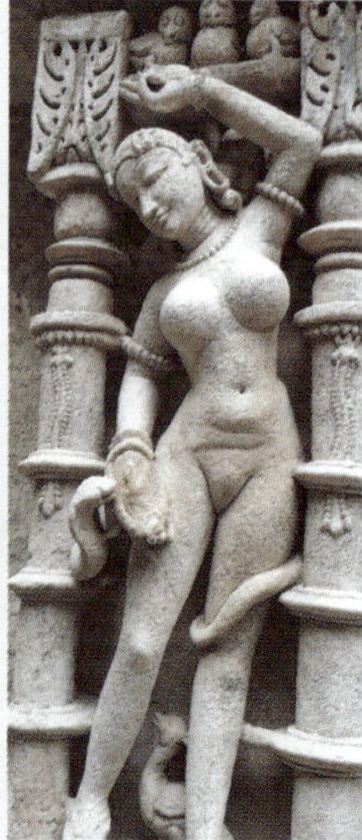

6.62: Nagkanya with a snake slithering around her body

— photographs by Madhukar K Bhagat

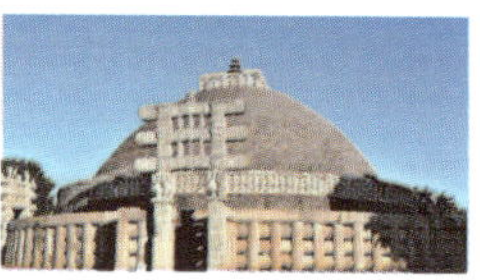

Pala dynasty: The Pala dynasty (8th century CE to 12th century CE) came into prominence in the Bengal and Bihar region. At the height of this dynasty's influence (during the rule of king Dharmapala), it brought parts of northern and north-western India under its control, though this influence was short-lived. This regime had a profound influence on art, sculpture, philosophy, etc. so much so that the Pala period sculpture was referred as a separate school of art. It was famous for its stone (black basalt) sculptures, palm leaf miniature paintings and bronze statues. The Palas were Buddhists, and subjects of art was taken from the Mahayana, Vajrayana, and Tantra form of Buddhism. The Mahaviharas of Somapura (Bangladesh), Jagaddala (West Bengal), Odantpuri (Bihar), Vikramshila (Bihar) was built during their regime. They were the patrons of Vikramshila and Nalanda universities and the latter reached its pinnacle during the rule of the Palas.

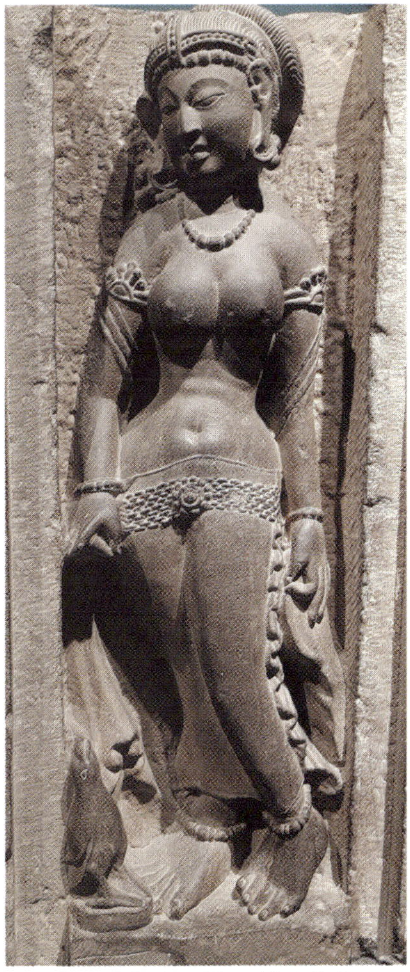

6.63: A lady with a bird, Pala sculpture in black basalt, Bihar Museum, Patna — photograph by Madhukar K Bhagat

Pallava dynasty: This dynasty flourished in South India between 6th to 9th century CE and is known for art and architecture, particularly rock-cut temples and monolithic shrines. The Pallavas were Hindu kings and built the famous temple at **Mahabalipuram** (Mamallapuram) and **Kailasanathar temple** at **Kanchipuram**. The structures at Mahabalipuram (**a World Heritage Site**) are attributed to the kings Mahendraverman-1 (600 to 630 CE) and Narasimhavarman (630 CE to 668 CE). These include rock-cut structures such as the **Pancha Rathas** (carved out of a single rock). The structure **'Arjuna's Penance'** located here is quite famous. They also include the world famous **shore temples** (which is a complex of three temples by the seashore.)

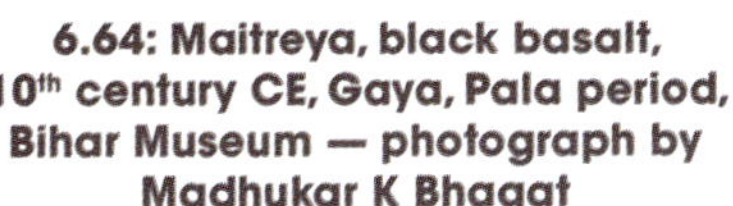

6.64: Maitreya, black basalt, 10th century CE, Gaya, Pala period, Bihar Museum — photograph by Madhukar K Bhagat

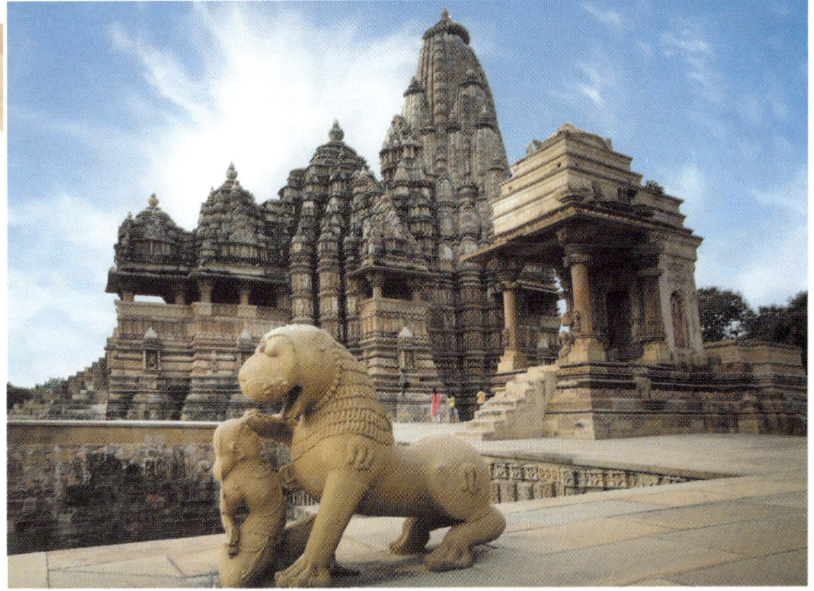

6.65: Kandariya Mahadev Temple, Khajuraho, Madhya Pradesh; an epitome of Chandela art and architecture — Courtesy, Madhya Pradesh Tourism Board

Chandela dynasty: The Chandela dynasty came into prominence in the early 10th century CE in Central India (Bundelkhand region). The Chandelas were Rajputs (*Chandravanshi*—Lunar dynasty). They are known for the construction of the Hindu and Jain temple complex in **Khajuraho** (Madhya Pradesh) which were built between 950 to 1000 CE. The group of temples are known for the dexterity in carving of erotic sculptures and figures on the temple walls. A UNESCO World Heritage Site, the most famous amongst these temples are the *Kandariya Mahadev temple, Lakshmana temple*, and *Chausath Yogini*

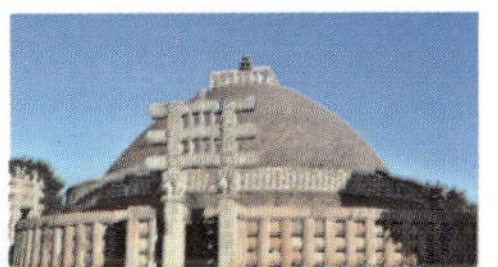

temples. Among these, the Chausath Yogini temple is the earliest of the Chandela temples and was built around 885 CE. It has 35 surviving rectangular temples in a quadrangular plan, which is quite unlike other yogini temples elsewhere which have a circular plan.

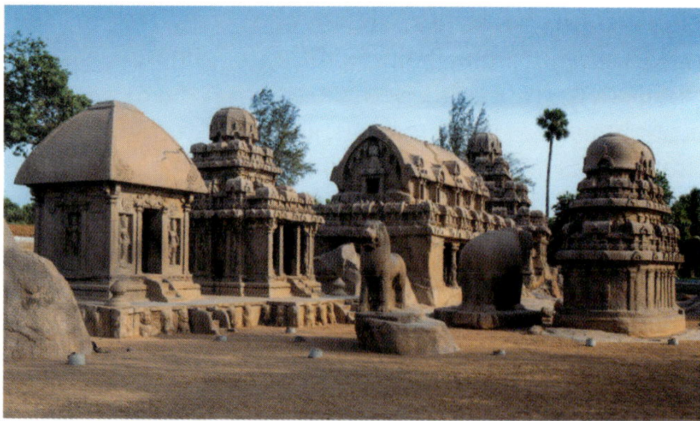

6.66: Pancharathas Mahabalipuram (Mamallapuram), signifying excellence in rock-cut art and architecture during the Pallava period — Courtesy, Tamil Nadu Tourism Development Corporation

SCHOOLS OF ART IN ANCIENT INDIA

From the 1st century CE onwards, a number of important centres of production of art and sculpture emerged in different parts of India. Each had its unique style and covered a variety of subjects. These are referred to as the schools of art. The most prominent ones were the **Mathura**, **Gandhara**, **Amaravati** and the **Sarnath** schools of art. The important schools, their salient features and creations are briefly given here.

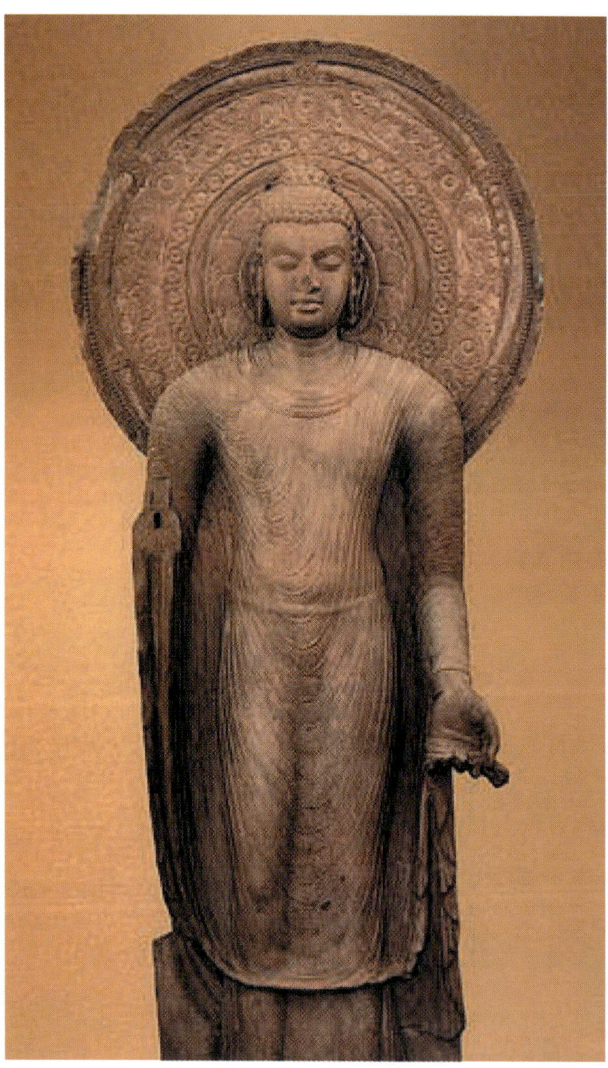

6.67: Standing Buddha at Mathura, 5th century CE, Mathura School, Gupta period, Government Museum, Mathura — Wikimedia Commons

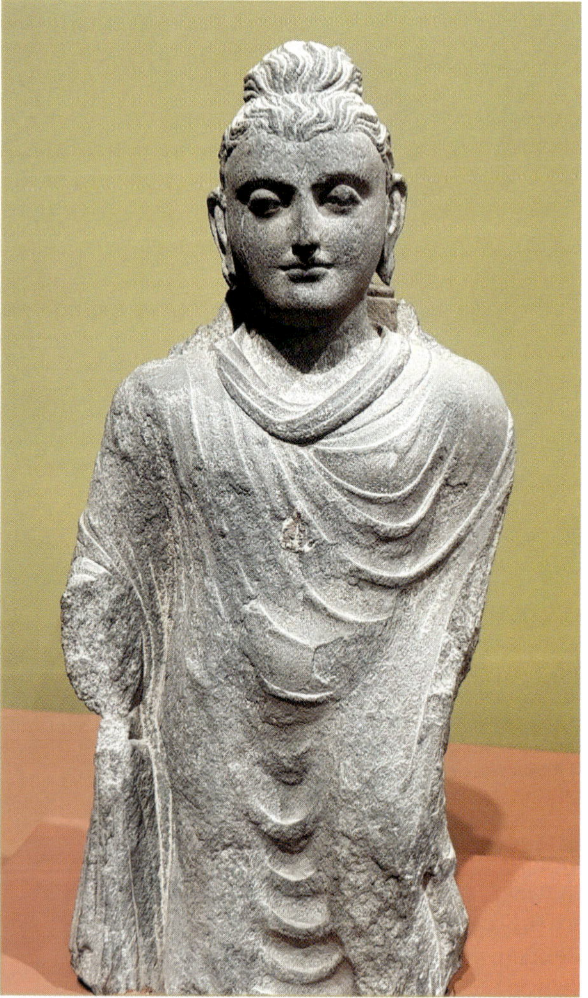

6.68: Standing Buddha sculpture, bearing a smile and exuding peace, Gandhara art, 1st century CE, Kushana period, schist (black stone), Swat Valley Pakistan, Bihar Museum, Patna — photograph by Madhukar K Bhagat

The Mathura School of Art

This school of art developed around **Mathura** region, it being the main production centre while **Kaushambi** and **Sarnath** were also important centres of art. It developed after 1st century CE, but gained in prominence during the **Gupta period** after the 3rd century CE and flourished till 5th to 6th century CE.

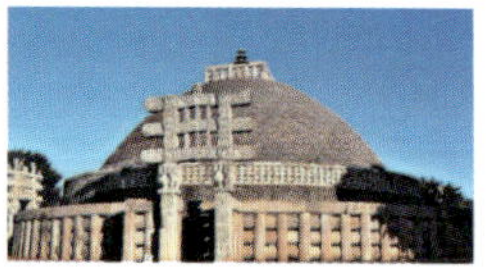

This was an **indigenous school of art**, and unlike the Gandhara school, it did not have Greek-Hellenistic influence. Subjects from **Buddhism, Vaishnavism, Shaivism**, and **Jainism** were incorporated in the sculptures. The earlier Buddhist subjects were the symbols of Buddha (viz. lotus, empty throne, etc.). But later, images of Buddha were incorporated, which were modelled around the images of the earlier *yakshas*. Thus, in the Mathura and also in the Gandhara school of art, Buddha's images first emerge in the human form. In this school the images of Buddha are either seated or standing, with a large **highly decorated halo around them**. The Vaishnavite and Shaivite images of gods are also found, which are represented by their **ayudhas** (weapons).

The images of this school have a typical boldness and are large and highly decorated. The faces are round and smiling. The features are often fleshier. However, in the images of the 4th and 5th century, the fleshiness and massiveness becomes less, and the features of body are seen to be tightened. Further, transparent quality in the robes of images of Buddha is also evident. The sculptures of this school were made in **spotted sandstone**. Important sculptures include the statue of Lord Vishnu, headless statue of Kanishka and the sandstone image of standing Buddha in *Abhayamudra*.

Gandhara School of Art

This school of art developed in north-western part of India around Gandhara. It flourished in the **Kushana** rule in the 1st century CE specially during the rule of Kanishka when it reached its zenith. The style of the Gandhara school was deeply **influenced by the Greek and Hellenistic art**. Thus, it was a confluence of Indian and Greek art traditions and is also referred as Graeco-Buddhist school of art.

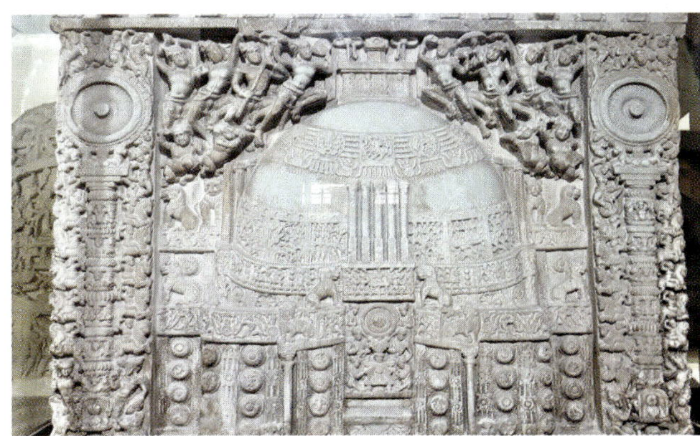

6.69: A panel depicting Stupa relief, Government Museum, Chennai — photograph by Madhukar K Bhagat

The themes were mainly Buddhist, and subjects included images of Buddha and events from his life. Images of Buddha are shown seated or standing depicting different mudras. The expression is serene. Curly hair, sharp features of eyes, ears, lips, and absence of fleshy heaviness are typical features of the sculptures. The drapery and folds of cloth create an image of transparency. High degree of craftsmanship is depicted and grey and bluish grey standstone is the material largely used in this school. However, mud, lime, and stucco has also been used. Important sculptures include the 'Meditating Buddha' (in *dhyana mudra*), 'Standing Buddha' and Bodhisattvas.

Amaravati School of Art

This school of art flourished in South India in Amaravati and other centres in Krishna and Godavari region valley, including Nagarjunakonda, Goli, and Guntapalle. Amaravati school dates back to 3rd century BCE and reached its peak during the **Satavahana period**. The school was an indigenous one, and the images had largely Buddhist subjects, though some images of Hindu gods and goddesses were also made.

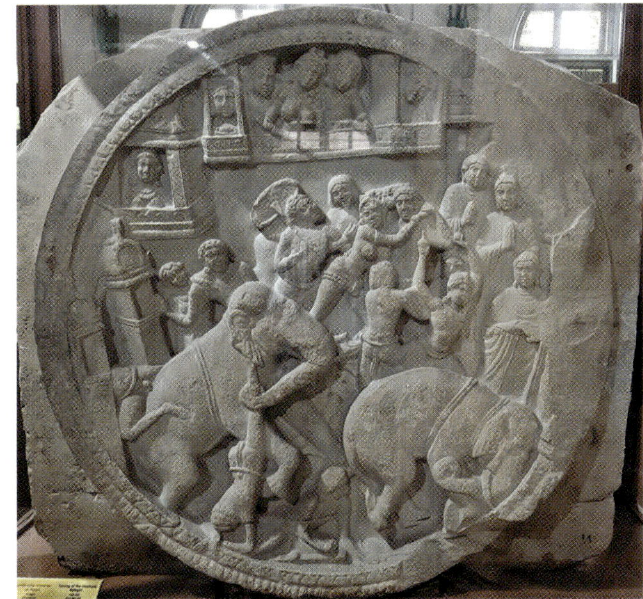

6.70: A panel depcting Buddha taming the elephant; Government Museum, Chennai — photograph by Madhukar K Bhagat

Sculptures contain images from the life of Buddha and Jataka tales in the form of narratives, viz. scenes of events in the life of Buddha (or Jataka) rather than individual images. Some images of Hindu gods are also found, viz. Ganesha, Lakshmi, and ornate bull Nandiswara. The sculptures of this school are often depicted with deep emotions, a lot of body movement, and in body postures such as *tribhanga* (three bents of the body). The images and sculptures were made usually in white, and at times, in green marble.The stupa drum slab, image of birth of Buddha (dream of Maya Devi with an elephant above her), Nandiswara, and image of Ganesha and Lakshmi are important sculptures of this school.

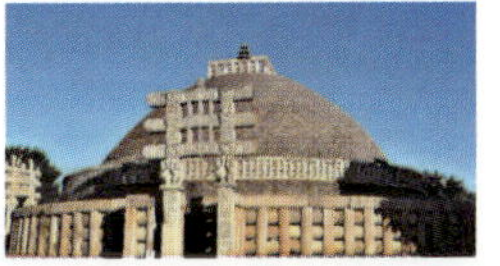

Sarnath School of Art

Sarnath (near Varanasi in Uttar Pradesh) where Buddha delivered the first sermon, developed as an important centre of Buddhist art (although Mathura was the main centre of production). This school flourished during the **Gupta period**.

Images of Buddha was the common theme in this school. These images differ from the Mathura images, as here the Buddha sculptures have **plain and transparent drapery**. Further, the halo around the head has **little ornamentation**, unlike the Mathura images of Buddha which have heavy ornamentation of the halo. The Sarnath images of Buddha are **simple** yet **sublime**. Standing figure of **ornamented Tara** (a Buddhist deity) is the best example of this school.

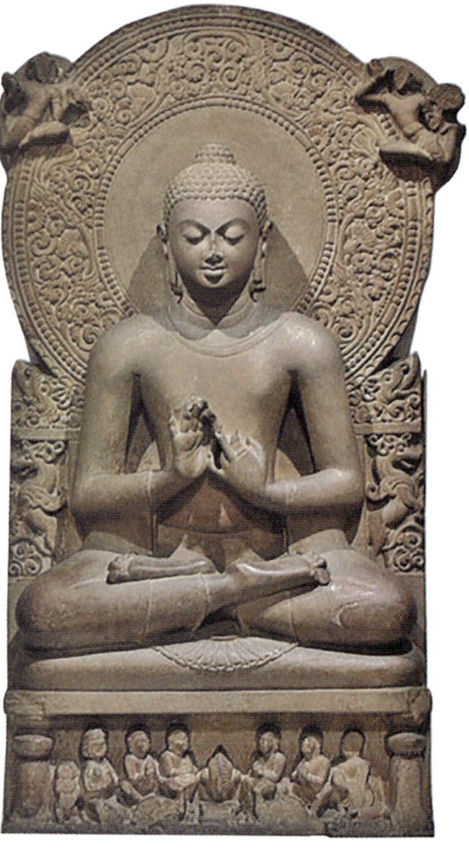

6.71: Statue of Buddha in Dharmachakra Pravartana Mudra, Sarnath — Wikimedia Commons

ROCK-CUT ARCHITECTURE

Rock-cut architecture refers to creation of structures (objects of art) by cutting and removal of stones from solid natural rock, till what is left is the structure intended to be created. This style of architecture has been an important form of religious artistic expression in India for centuries. Over 1500 known rock-cut structures survive even today, **the oldest being the Barabar Caves** of 3rd century BCE (of Mauryan period). In the post Mauryan period, hundreds of such caves were excavated. They were invariably religious in nature and a large number of them were of Buddhist origin. The Ajanta, Ellora, Bhaja, Kanheri, Karla, Elephanta, Bedse, Nashik, Pitalkhora, Junnar, (all in Maharashtra), Udaygiri, Bagh and Siddhachal (in Madhya Paradesh), Udayagiri and Khandagiri (in Odisha), Junagadh (Gujarat), Sittanavasal and Tirumalai (Tamil Nadu), Badami (in Karnataka), and Guntupalli (Andhra Pradesh) are amongst the most famous of rock-cut caves. Amongst these, **Junnar** has the maximum number of caves (more than two hundred). The subjects of the rock-cut structures varied from simple **chaitya, viharas** and **temples**, to beautiful **sculptures and paintings**. Existence of elaborate mural paintings is however a unique and noteworthy feature of Ajanta Caves.

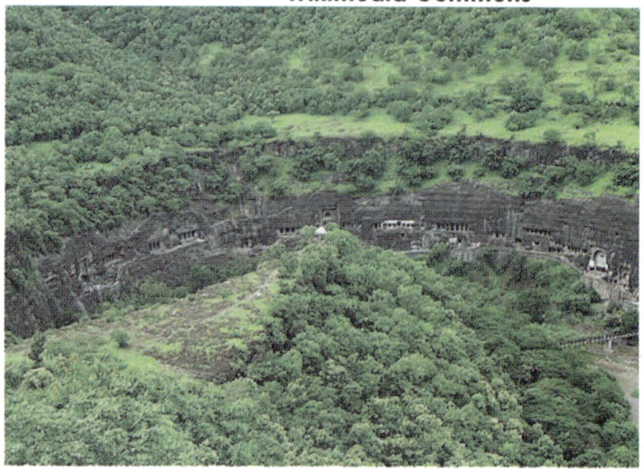

6.72: Ajanta Caves at horse-shoe bend of a rock overlooking a narrow stream — Wikimedia Commons

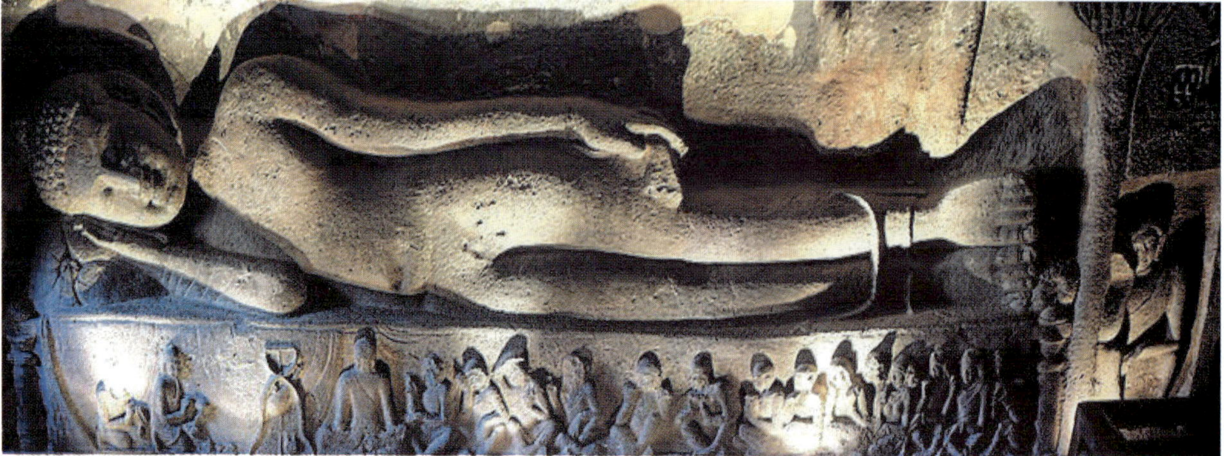

6.73: Buddha mahaparinibanna, cave 26 Ajanta — Wikimedia Commons

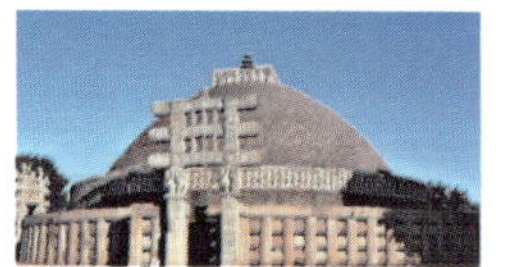

Ajanta Caves

The Ajanta Caves, a UNESCO World Heritage Site near Aurangabad (Maharashtra) is among the most famous and the most exquisite example of art of ancient India, especially of painting. The caves were discovered in 1819 (by a British hunting expedition). They are excavated in a horseshoe bend of rock surface overlooking a stream. There are 30 caves which were excavated, including one which is unfinished. Out of these, five are chaityas, while the rest are viharas.

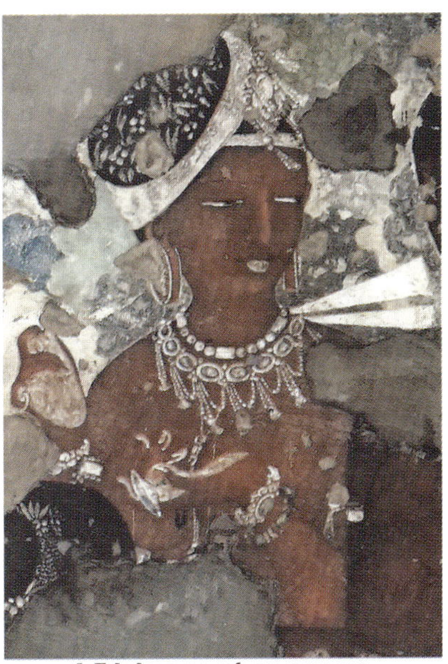

6.74: Image of an apsara — Wikimedia Commons

These caves were built from **2nd century BCE to 6th century CE** in two phases, the first phase beginning from 2nd century BCE, while the second phase was from 400 to 650 CE. The subject in all the caves are **Buddhist**. The earlier caves belong to the Hinayana phase, while the latter to Mahayana. Images of Buddha, Bodhisattvas, and scenes from *Jatakas* and *Avadanas* are included in the sculptures and paintings. The chaitya caves 19 and 26, contain elaborate, carvings with the biggest being that of **Buddha's Mahaparinibbana** (cave no. 26).

The famous **mural paintings** are found in caves 1, 2, 16, and 17. The lines of the painting are clearly defined, with body colours merging with the outline, thereby creating a volume effect. Limited colours with natural tones have been used (brown, yellowish brown, yellow ochre and greenish). The different skin colours represent multi-coloured population. The most famous painting is the one of Buddha with Rahul and Yashoda, and another is that of an apsara.

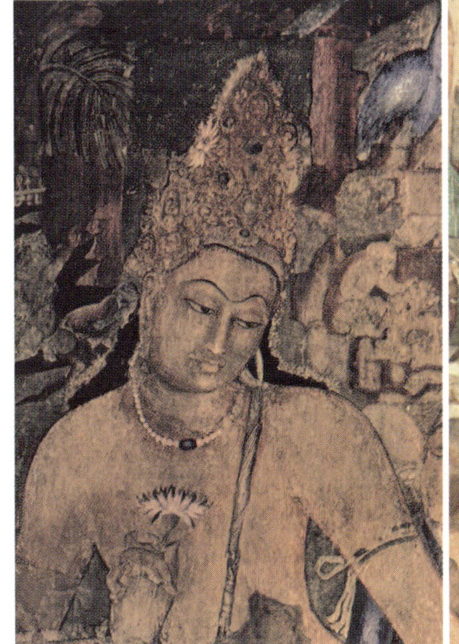

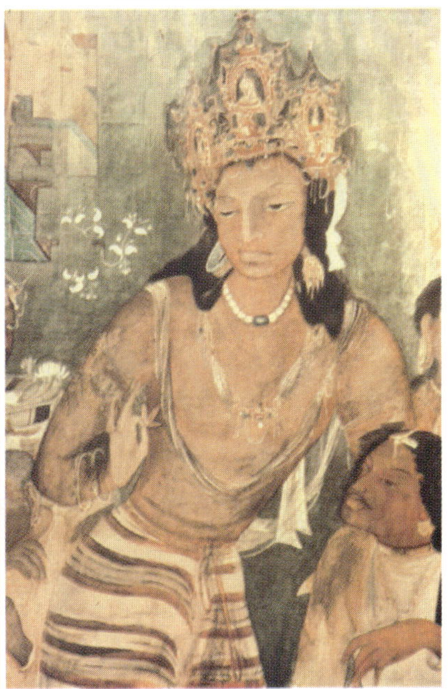

6.75 & 6.76: Boddhisatva Padmapani and Bodhisattva Vajrapani, at cave no. 1 Ajanta — Courtesy, Maharashtra Tourism Development Corporation

The paintings were done after elaborate surface preparation. Rock surface cut with chisel (with chisel marks left to help greater adhesion) was covered with a ground layer of earth mixed with rock grit, sand, vegetable fibres, paddy husk, and grass. A second layer of mud and ferruginous earth mixed. with sand, rock powder, and fine fibrous vegetable material was applied, over which a thin coat of lime wash was applied. Over this surface, bold outlines were drawn and colours were painted. These paintings are considered as murals, and not frescoes, as in these a binding agent was used, whereas in frescoes the paintings are executed when the lime wash is still wet which in turn acts as a binding agent.

Several dynasties and patrons are known to have contributed to the Ajanta Caves. These include the **Vakatakas** who were contemporary of Guptas. Varahadeva, minister of Vakataka king Harisena, was the patron of Cave no. 16. The Ajanta Cave paintings are considered unique, for they are the only surviving example of paintings which are of 2000 years and some even older.

Ellora Caves

This group of caves near Aurangabad is another UNESCO World Heritage Site and is said to be an epitome of rock-cut architecture. These 32 caves were built between 5th century CE to 11th century CE under the patronage of different dynasties, primarily the **Rashtrakutas** (**Kailasa temple** cave no. 16) and **Yadavas** (Jain group of caves).

These cave sculptures are a **confluence of Buddhist, Brahmanical, and Jain subjects**. Besides, they represent different styles of architecture and craftsmanship as guilds from Tamil Nadu, Karnataka, Vidarbha, etc. carved different caves at different points of time. Many caves are two storeys and some even

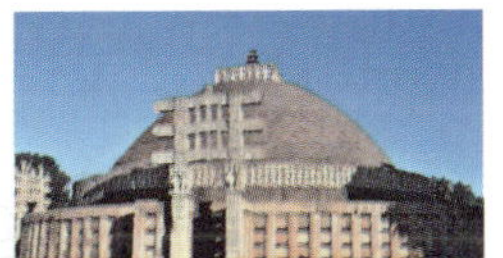

three storeys which adds to the uniqueness of Ellora. The Buddhist caves (no. 14, 15, 16, 21, and 29) contain the images of Buddha which is guarded by **Vajrapani** and **Padmapani**. Many images of **Tara** and eternal Buddhas **like Amitabha Avlokiteshwara, Vairochana, etc.** are found.

The Brahmanical caves are of Shaivism faith (image of **Gajasura Shiva** in cave no. 15), besides images of different **avataras of Vishnu** are also found in **Dashavatara** (cave no. 15).

The Jain caves (no. 32 to 34) are known for their decorative and ornate images. These are of later period (9th century CE).

The most famous creation at Ellora is the great **Kailasa temple** (cave no. 16) which is a megalith **carved out of a single piece of rock** by cutting a mountain cliff face top down making it an architectural and sculptural marvel. It is the **largest monolithic temple** which even included a courtyard. The temple is dedicated to Lord Shiva.

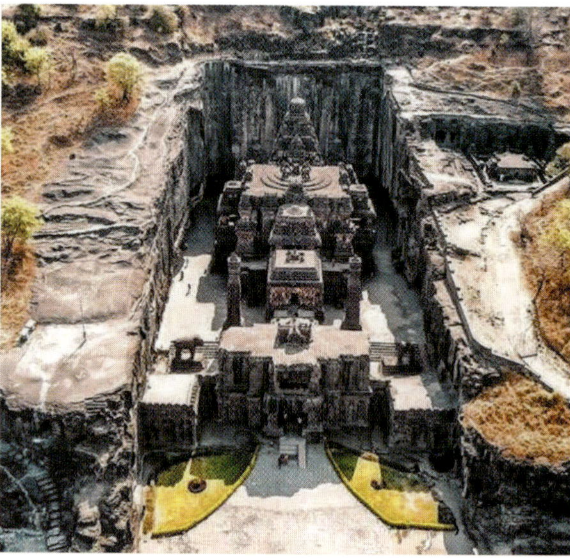

6.77: Kailash temple (Ellora cave no. 15) at Verul — Wikipedia

The temple's central shrine has a *lingam* with a roofed *mandapa*, supported by 16 pillars and a *shikhara* of Dravidian style. An image of Nandi (bull) is seen in the porch in front of the temple.

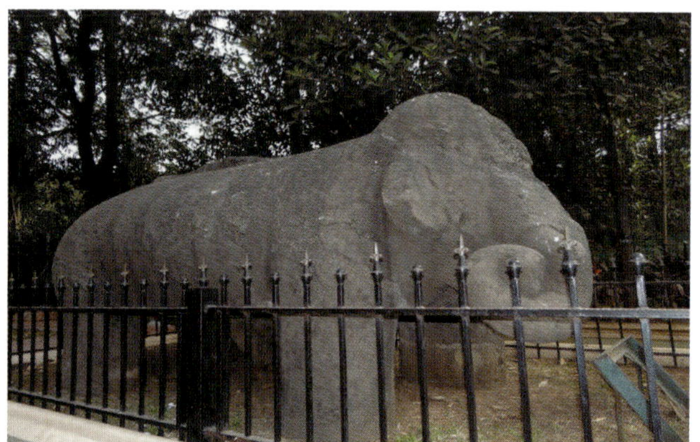

6.78: Elephant sculpture which gave the name to Elephanta Caves, now placed at Veermata Jijabai Udyan, Mumbai —photograph by Madhukar K Bhagat

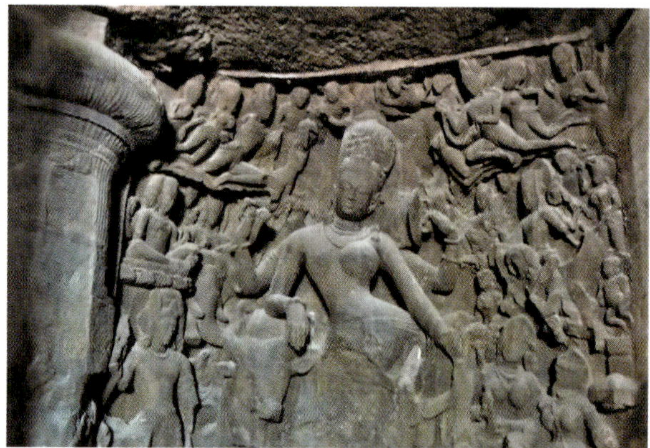

6.79: Ardhanarishwara Shiva, Elephanta Caves — photograph by Madhukar K Bhagat

Elephanta Caves

These caves located on an island near Mumbai are another great exquisite example of rock-cut architecture and is also a UNESCO World Heritage site. It derives its name from a **large stone elephant sculpture** found at the entrance.

The caves are believed to be originally a Buddhist site, but later images are of Shaivite faith. The most famous sculpture is the **Trimurti image**. The sculptures show slenderness with a unique light and dark effect. The caves are believed to be contemporary of Ellora and most sculptures are dated between 5th to 9th century CE.

However, some Buddhist stupa mounds are believed to be as old as 2nd century BCE. Many sculptures are extensively damaged, believed to be so because of the artillery practice by the Portuguese during their occupation of the island in the 16th and 17th century CE. Among other famous sculptures of Elephanta are the those of *Ardhanarishvara Shiva* and Shiva as Nataraja.

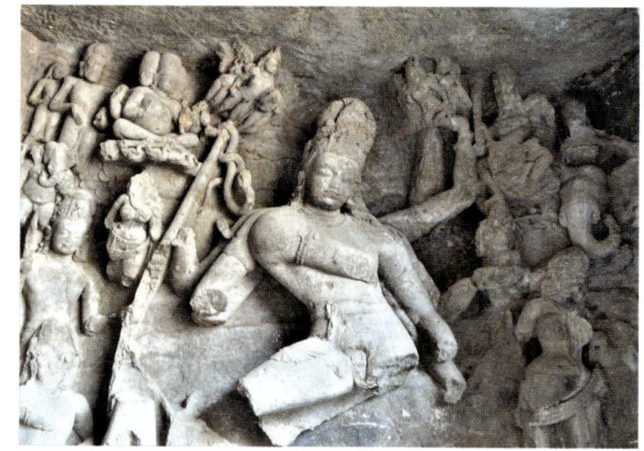

6.80: Shiva as Nataraja, Elephanta — photograph by Madhukar K Bhagat

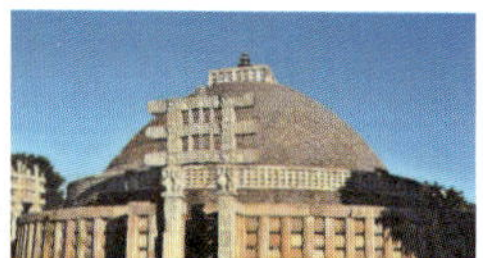

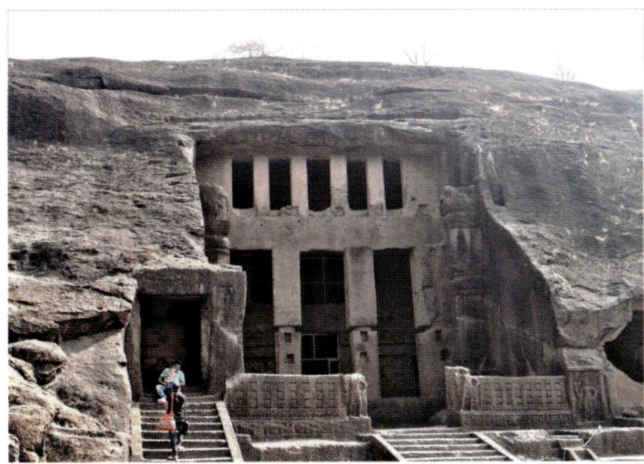

6.81: Kanheri Cave — photograph by Madhukar K Bhagat

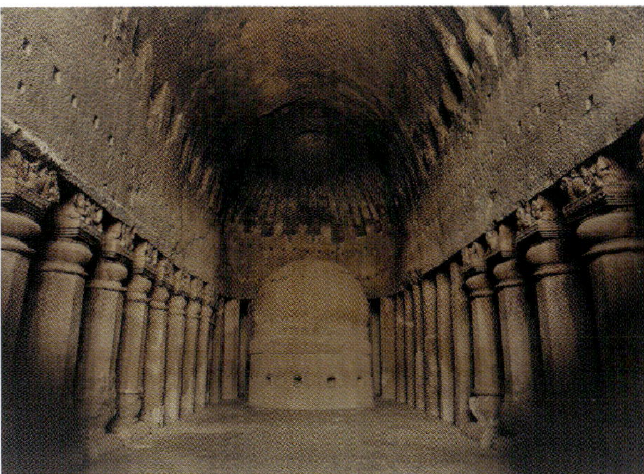

6.82: Chaitya Kanheri caves, Mumbai — photograph by Madhukar K Bhagat

Kanheri Caves

These are 108 rock-cut Buddhist caves located in Mumbai, which date from 100 BCE to 1000 CE. The caves are mostly **viharas**, which are spartan in terms of interior carvings and sculptures, and contain a stone plinth for a bed. A chaitya hall with a stupa is also present.

The images in these caves are mostly of **Buddha** and **Bodhisattvas**. The image of **Avalokiteshwara** is quite prominent.

Rock inscription in Brahmi and Devanagri script are found indicating donations from different dynasties including that from **Gautamiputra Satkarani** (Satavahana dynasty) and **Amoghavarsha** (Rashtrakuta dynasty). A unique feature of these caves was the construction of canals and cisterns which channelised rainwater into large tanks.

Karla Caves

Built from 1st century BCE to 6th-7th century CE, the Karla caves are located near Lonavala in Maharashtra and comprise 16 caves with one chaitya and 15 viharas. Its grand Chaityagriha at cave no. 8 excavated during the Satvahana period, is the biggest rock-cut chaitya hall of India. It consists of a large apsidal hall which is 148 feet in length and 45 feet high. A long front verandah of the Chaityagriha has two rows of carved pillars forming aisles. At the end of the hall is a semicircular apse where a large stupa is located. The roof the apsidal hall is barrel vaulted with ridges of stone resembling the architecture of the wooden chaityas in vogue in those days. Sculptures of Buddha, other males, females and animals such as lions and elephants, adorn the pillars of the hall and the front entrance of the chaitya cave. Other caves in the region include the Bhaja Caves, Patan Buddhist Caves, the Bedse Caves and the Nasik Caves. A unique feature of these caves was the construction of canals and cisterns which channelised rainwater into large tanks.

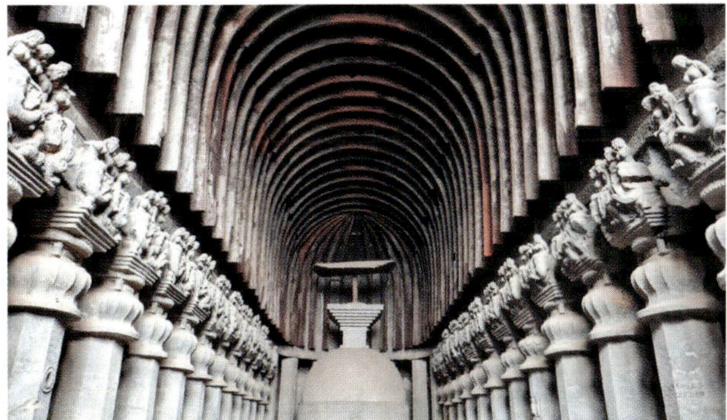

6.83: The Chaityagriha at Karla Caves, with intricate carving in pillars and vaulted ribbed roof, the largest of rock-cut Chaityagriha of India; Karla near Lonavala, Maharashtra — photograph by Madhukar K Bhagat

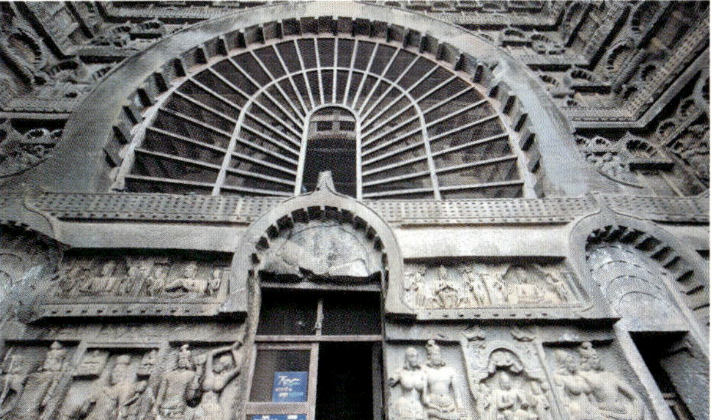

6.84: The grand entrance of Chaityagriha of Karla Caves with relief work depicting images of Buddha and other figures and intricate carvings — photograph by Madhukar K Bhagat

Nasik Caves

Buddhist caves of Uperkot

These are nearly 24 caves located near Nasik (also called Panduleni). The caves were built from the 3rd century BCE to 2nd century CE and contain subjects of **Hinayana Buddhism**.

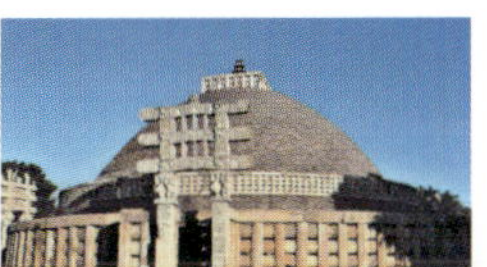

Bhaja Caves

These caves are located in Pune near Lonavala. They date to 2nd century BCE and the sculptural subjects belong to **Hinayana Buddhism**. The most prominent cave is the **Chaityagriha** (cave XII) which exhibits a wooden architecture in a rock-cut horseshoe shaped stone ceiling. The pillared verandah has a unique relief. A carving also shows a woman playing *tabla* and another woman performing dance. These caves are similar to **Karla Caves**.

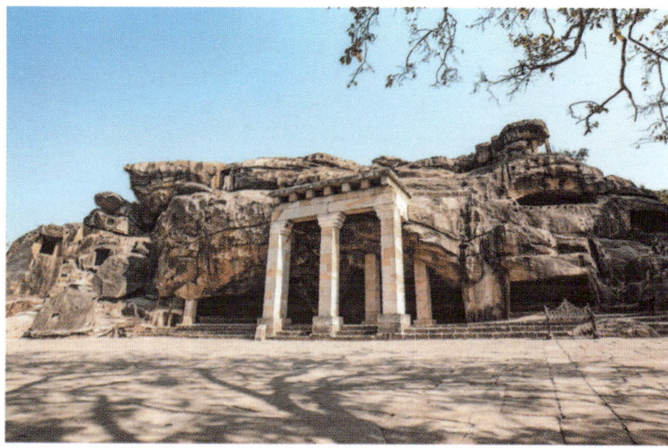

6.85: Hathigupha Udayagiri Caves, Odisha — Courtesy, Department of Tourism, Odisha

Udayagiri and Khandagiri Caves

The twin hills of Udayagiri and Khandagiri near Bhubaneswar have nearly 33 rock-cut caves (some of them natural caves also). These were built during the reign of king **Kharavela**. These caves are a **Jain complex** used as residence of Jain monks and as such, simple and spartan in architecture. The caves are notable for **Ranigumpha** which is double storeyed and also for the work relief of the 24 Tirthankaras in the **Anantagumpha**.

Guntapalle Caves

These caves are located in Guntapalle in Eluru district of Andhra Pradesh and date to the **second century BCE**. These are Buddhist caves, and quite unique, as structured stupas and viharas are excavated at one place. It has a chaitya cave which is circular. It has a stupa in the circular hall and a chaitya arch at the entrance.

Junagadh Caves

Located in Junagadh (Gujarat) and built during the 1st century to the 4th century CE, these are Buddhist caves built during different regimes. Some date to Ashoka's period, while most are of the **Satavahana** regime. The most famous are the **Uperkot Caves** which were in the form of a high citadel in three tiers.

Prehistoric Cave Paintings

Prehistoric paintings refer to paintings and rock engravings which were found on the walls of caves and pertain to the prehistoric period (that period of human history which precedes the period for which the first written or documentary account appears. These include the Paleolithic, the Mesolithic, and Chalcolithic ages). In India, a number of sites have been discovered containing numerous prehistoric rock paintings. Most important of these are Bhimbetka caves (near Bhopal), Lakhudiyar caves in Kumaon (Uttarakhand), Piklihal and Tekkalkotta in Karnataka, Kupagallu in Telangana, and Jogimara caves in Madhya Pradesh.

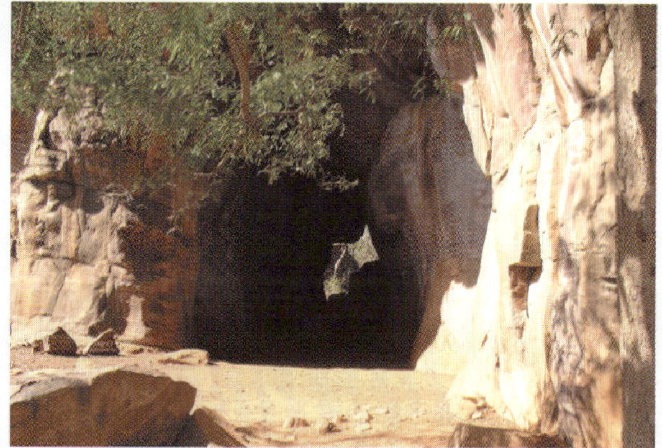

6.86: Entrance to Bhimbetka Cave — photograph by Madhukar K Bhagat

Bhimbetka Caves

Located nearly 55 kms from Bhopal (Madhya Pradesh) in Vindhya ranges, Bhimbetka site contains nearly 800 shelters, five hundred of which bear such paintings. The place draws its name from the legend of it being the sitting place of Bhima (of Mahabharata). The caves are said to be in human occupation for nearly a 100,000 years while the oldest of paintings are said to be at least 10000 years old to even 30000 years old. The images depict events in daily life of prehistoric humans, including hunting, dancing, music, animals, elephant riders, and other household scenes. These paintings have been classified into seven historical periods, the most important of which are Period-1 or Upper Paleolithic; Period-2 or Mesolithic, and Period-3 or Chalcolithic. The nature of human interaction and the paintings evolve in the different periods. The rock shelters and paintings are recognized as UNESCO World Heritage Site (2003).

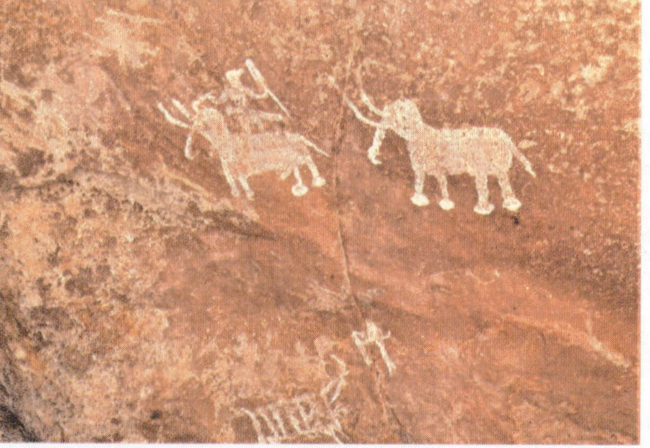

6.87: Elephants and hunting scene, Bhimbetka — photograph by Madhukar K Bhagat

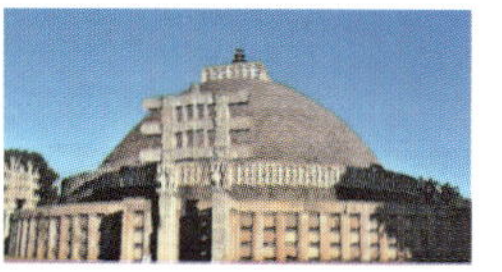

Upper Palaeolithic Paintings (40000-8000 BCE): These are linear representations of animals like elephants, tigers, rhinos, bisons, etc. Humans are shown typically as stick-like figures. The different figures are usually painted in green and dark red. Some geometric patterns are also found.

Mesolithic Period Paintings (8000-4000 BCE): Maximum number of paintings belong to this period (Period 2). The subjects are largely scenes of hunting or group hunting, with a variety of weapons such as spears, bows, and arrows sticks, etc. A large number of animals, men, women, children and even the old have been depicted. Paintings also contain images of community dancing, gathering of honey, women preparing food, etc.

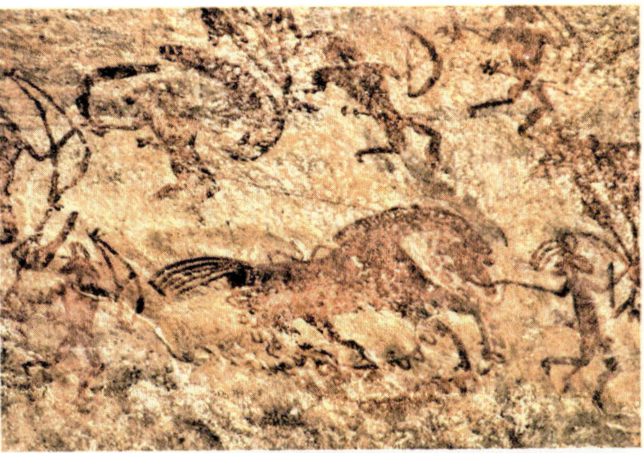

6.88: Hunting with bow, arrow and swords, Bhimbetka — photograph by Madhukar K Bhagat

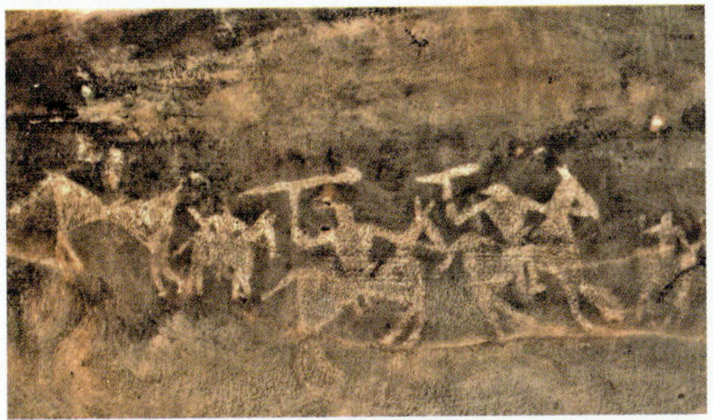

6.89: Mesolithic scene hunting with horses, Bhimbetka — photograph by Madhukar K Bhagat

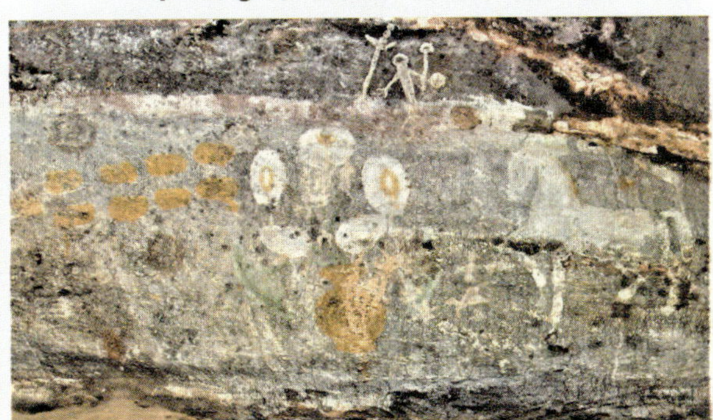

6.90: Image of horse, Bhimbetka — photograph by Madhukar K Bhagat

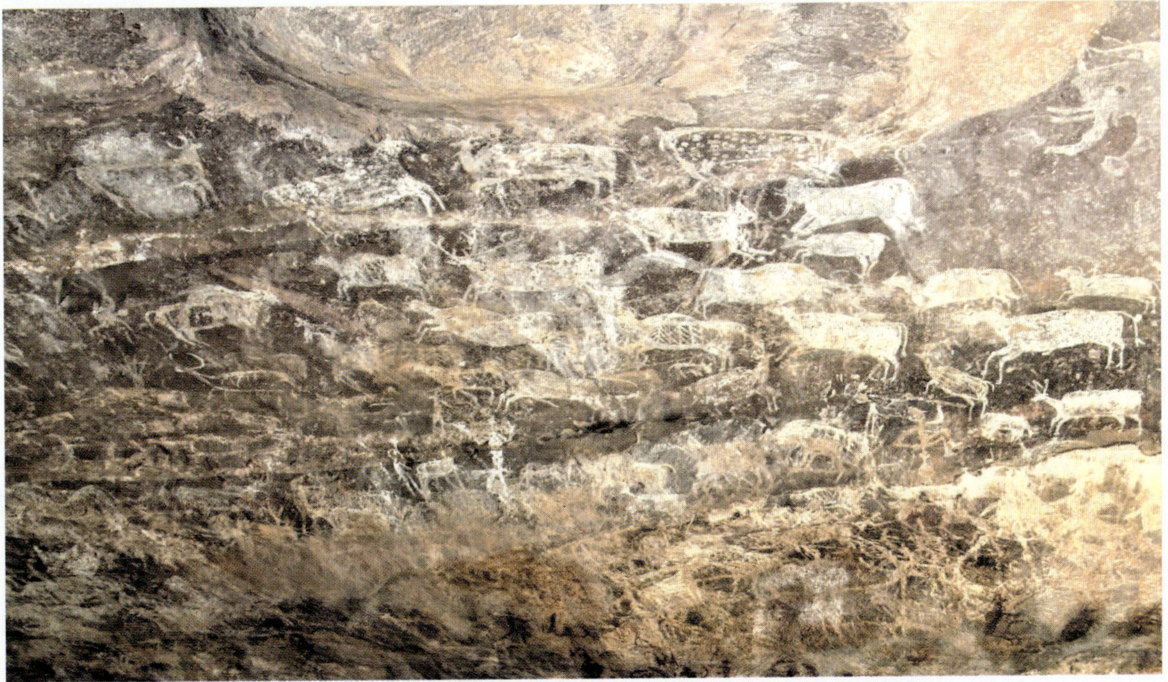

6.91: Zoo rock Bhimbetka — photograph by Madhukar K Bhagat

Chalcolithic Period: This period's (Period 3) paintings reflect further evolution of the society. They depict the exchange of the requirement of the dwellers of these caves with the agricultural communities in the Malwa plains. One rock of Bhimbetka is referred to as a 'Zoo rock' due to depiction of a large number of animals together, viz. elephant, sambhar, bison, deer, peacock, snake, etc.

Lakhudiyar Caves

Lakhudiyar literally means 'one lakh caves'. These are a group of rock caves/shelters near 20 kilometres from Almora in Kumaon Hills, Uttarakhand. The paintings are divided into three distinct categories, those of human beings, of animals, and of geometric patterns. Humans are quite distinct as they are seen to be having a stick-like appearance. Images of long snouted fox and multiple legged lizard are many. Paintings here use red ochre, white, and black colours.

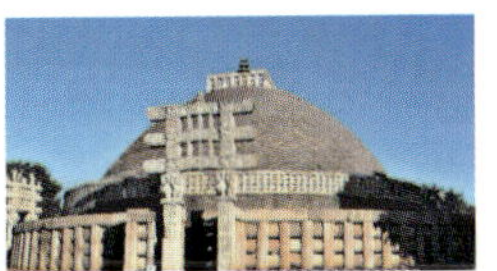

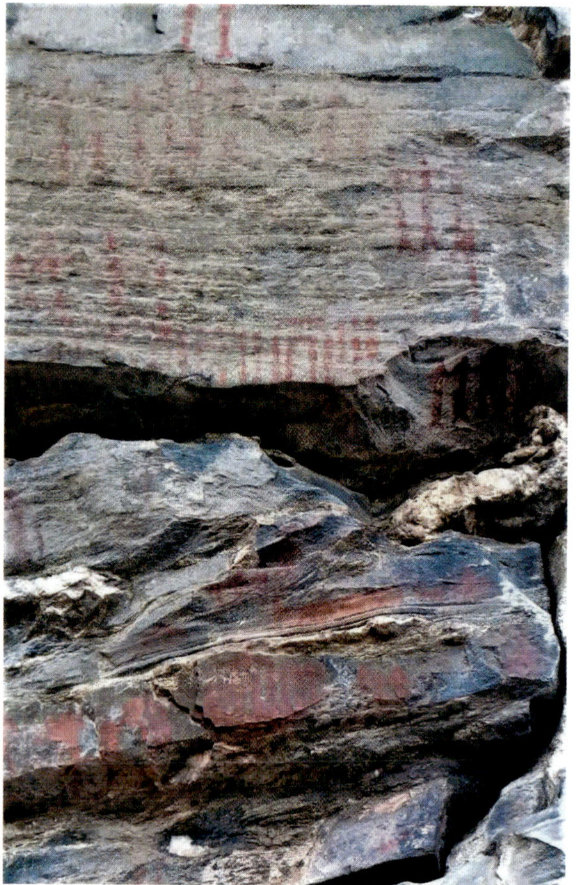

6.92: Human figures forming a chain by holding hands — photograph by Madhukar K Bhagat

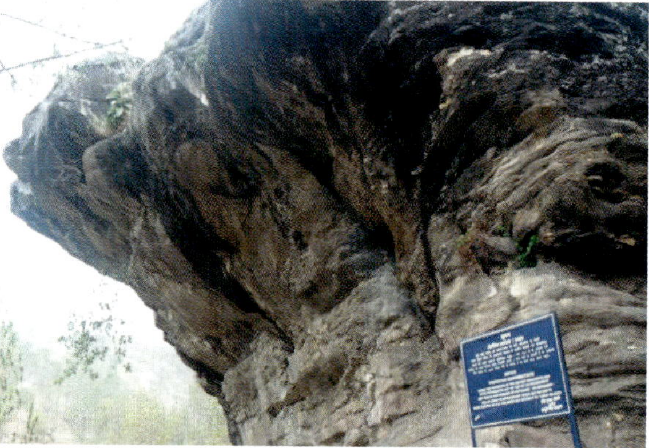

6.93: Lakhudiyar Caves outcrop — photograph by Madhukar K Bhagat

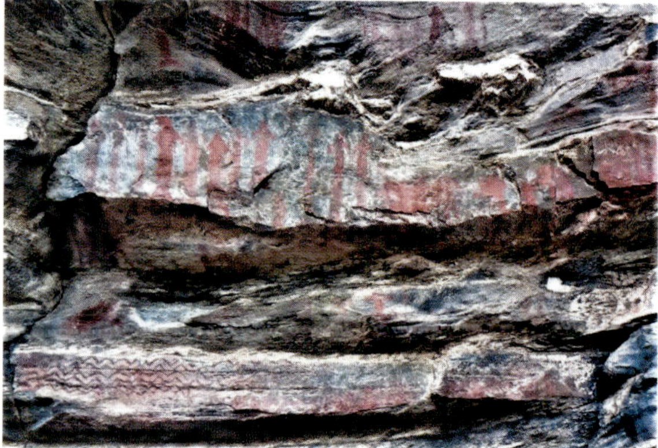

6.94: Wavy lines at bottom rock and stick like figures representing humans, Lakhudiyar Caves — photograph by Madhukar K Bhagat

EARLY TEMPLES AND ARCHITECTURE

With the rise in Brahmanism in this period and patronage of rulers like the Guptas, early temples began being constructed in ancient India. These temples would have a main deity or a central image of a god. The image narratives on the temples would contain myths from the Puranas.

The temples of this period were relatively simple in architecture especially when compared to the much ornate and complex medieval temples. They would be structures with a flat roof which was square in shape and was double storied. Temples with circumambulatory path around **garbhagriha** (sanctum) were first to develop during this phase and with passage of time the architecture evolved

Broadly, the temples could be categorised as:

Sandhara type; those without *pradakshina path* (circumambulatory pathway)

Nirandhara type; those with *pradakshina path*

Sarvatobhadra type; those which could be accessed from all the sides

Important Temples of this Age

Dashavatara temple: Located in Deogarh, this temple built in around 500 CE (in the Gupta period) is dedicated to Lord Vishnu and depicts his 10 incarnations. The temple is built in red sandstone and masonry bricks and was the first among temples with a shikhara. It is of *sarvatobhadra* type of construction which can be accessed from all sides through a flight of seven steps. The temple is

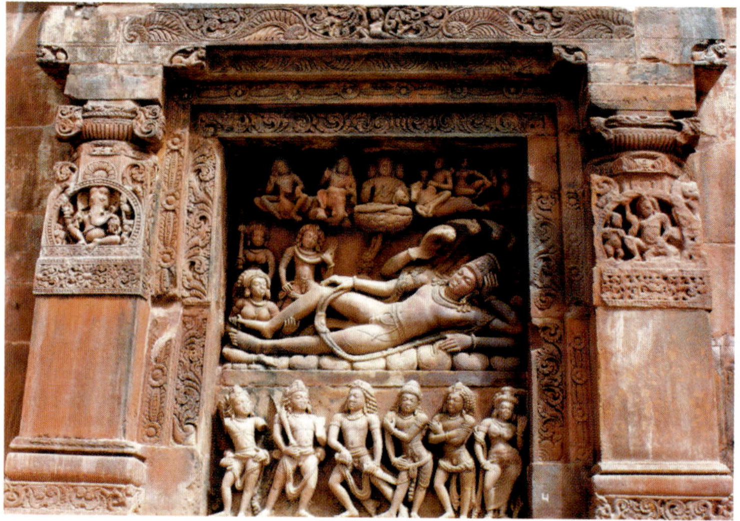

6.95: The reclining Vishnu at Deogarh; Lord Vishnu lies sheltered by Sheshnag, images of deities Brahma, Shiva and others are seen above while Trideviyan are by his side — Courtesy, Directorate of Uttar Pradesh Tourism

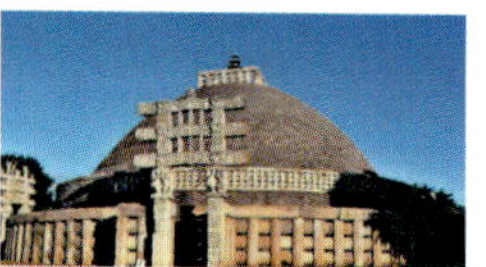

facing west which is unique, and is of *Panchayatana* style (main shrine and four subsidiary shrines at corners; see chapter 7 for temple architecture and images) and considered an epitome of Gupta style of architecture. The grand doorway of the main shrine is flanked with the two feminine images representing Ganga and Yamuna. As per accounts of some scholars the temple was built as per the third *khand* of *Vishnudharmottara Purana* which describes the design and architecture of the *Sarvatobhadra* type of temple. This temple is famous for the **reclining statue of Vishnu** on *sheshnaga* and has highly ornate decorations.

Nachna Kuthara temple: This temple, located in Nachna village (Panna in Madhya Pradesh) was built in the Gupta period in the second half of 5th century CE. It has two temples nearby, the Parvati temple (built on a raised platform with square plan) and the Chaturmukhi Linga Shiva temple which has a large linga with four faces). The Parvati temple was built around the 5th century CE, while the latter is believed to be built around the 9th century CE. Both are considered excellent examples of North Indian temple architecture.

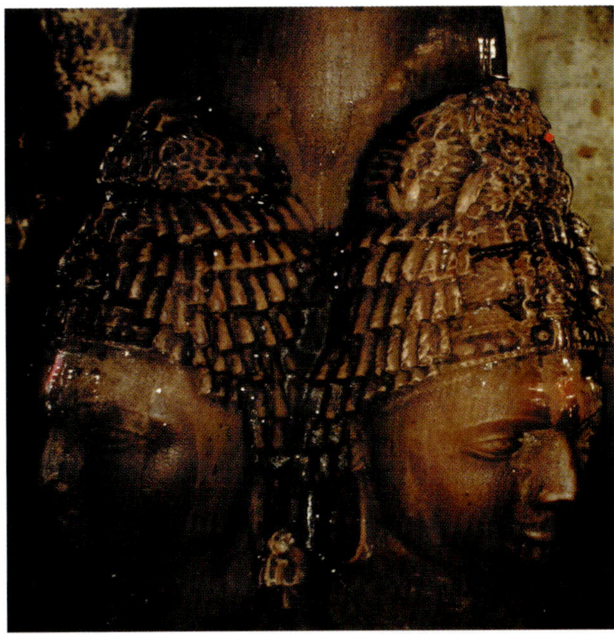

6.96: Chaumuknath at Nachna — Wikimedia Commons

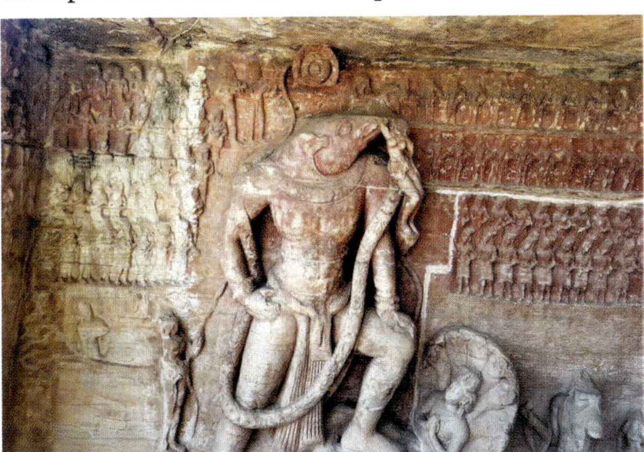

6.97: Varaha at Udayagiri Caves, Vidisha; early 5th century CE — photograph by Madhukar K Bhagat

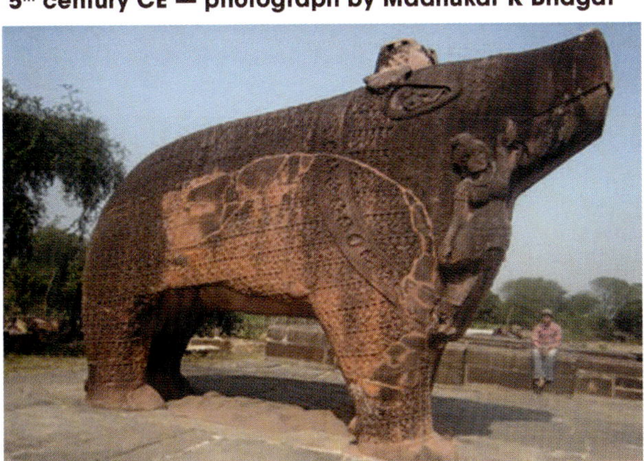

6.98: Eran Varaha — Wikimedia Commons

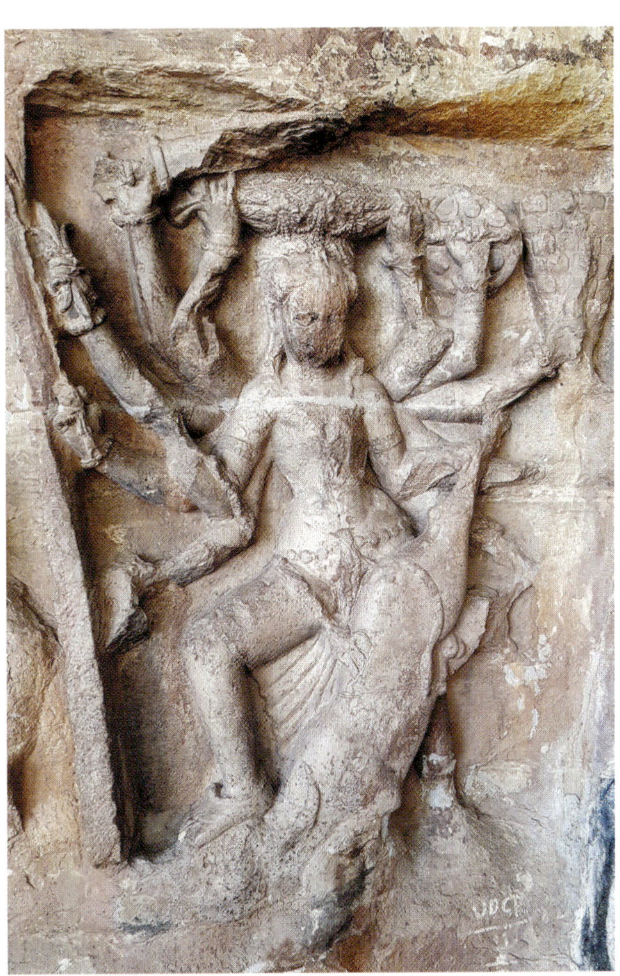

6.99: Durga as Mahishasuramardini, cave 6, Udayagiri Caves, Vidisha; early 5th century CE. — photograph by Madhukar K Bhagat

Udayagiri cave temples (Vidisha): These rock-cut cave temples (located in Vidisha, Madhya Pradesh) were built under the patronage of Chandragupta II around early 5th century CE. The entire complex of caves has rock cut sculptures reflecting prospering faiths of Vaishnavism, Shaivism and Shaktism. While one of the caves (cave 3) has an imposing rock cut image of Skanda (Karthikeya the war god) Cave 4 is known for Ekmukh-linga (Shivalinga with a face on it), thus representing the Shiva-Shakti traditions. But the most famous of the images is the **relief sculpture of lord Vishnu in Varaha avatar** (form of a boar) rescuing

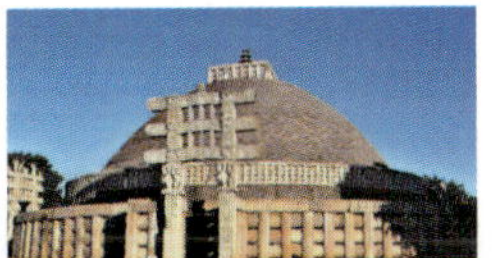

Bhumi Devi (cave no. 5) which shows lord Vishnu as varaha, lord Brahma sitting on lotus, lord Shiva sitting on Nandi, Bhumi Devi, Adityas and other gods.

Eran temple: Located in Sagar district (Madhya Pradesh), these temples were dedicated to lord Vishnu. Though largely in ruins, a mandap of lord Vishnu's temple and a large statue of Varaha (11.5 feet high) which is in red sandstone survives today. This zoomorphic image depicts lord Vishnu in *varaha avatar* rescuing Bhoomi Devi (the earth).The temple is dated to the 6th century CE. The site is also known for a *sati* temple and a number of *sati* pillars.

The Tradition of Bronze Sculptures in Ancient India

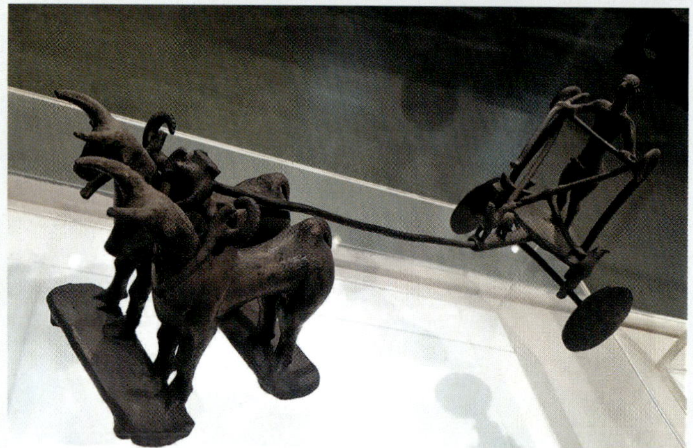

6.100: Bronze chariot Daimabad : National Museum, Delhi — photograph by Madhukar K Bhagat

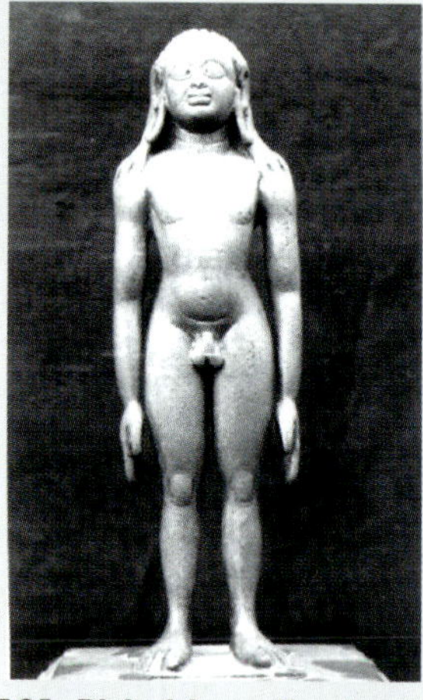

6.101: Rishabhanatha, bronze, Chausa — Wikimedia Commons

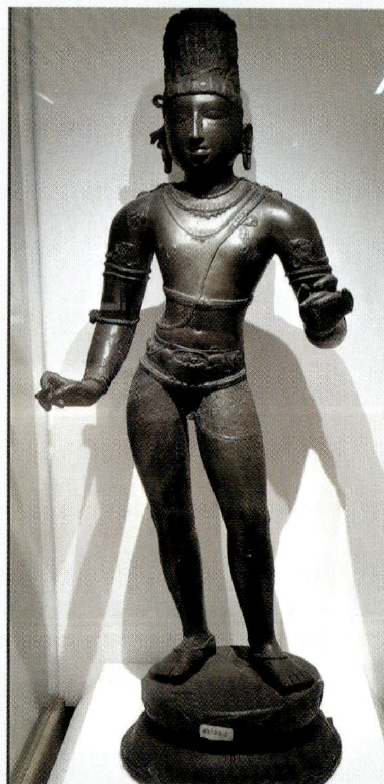

6.102: Tripurantaka Shiva, a masterpiece of early Chola bronze, 9th century CE. Tripurantaka Shiva represents the warrior form of Shiva aiming to destroy the three impregnable cities of the asuras (demons), symbolically releasing them from ignorance. National Museum, New Delhi — photograph by Madhukar K Bhagat

The tradition of bronze sculptures in India has truly been an ancient one. The discovery of a number of bronzes sculptures brings out the flourishing tradition of this art since last 4500 years. The process of casting of metals through the 'lost wax process' *(cire perdue)* was known in the Harappan Civilisation and so was the technique of making bronze, an alloy of copper, zinc and tin.

Among the earliest of the bronze sculptures discovered is the statue of the dancing girl in Tribhanga posture from Mohenjodaro, which is dated to 2500 BCE. The sculpture of a bronze chariot and other stauettes found at Daimabad (Maharashtra) dating to 1500 BCE, indicate the continuation of this tradition even in the late Harappan period in a different region. The chariot, the most significant of the bronzes, has circular wheels, a driver with elongated features and sturdy bulls at the front.

Coming to the end first millennium BCE, several sculptures of Jain Tirthankaras have been discovered at Chausa in Bihar. Commonly referred to the Chausa horde, these 17 Jain bronzes are dating to the 2nd century CE and belong to the Kushana period. Some scholars date them from 2nd century BCE to the

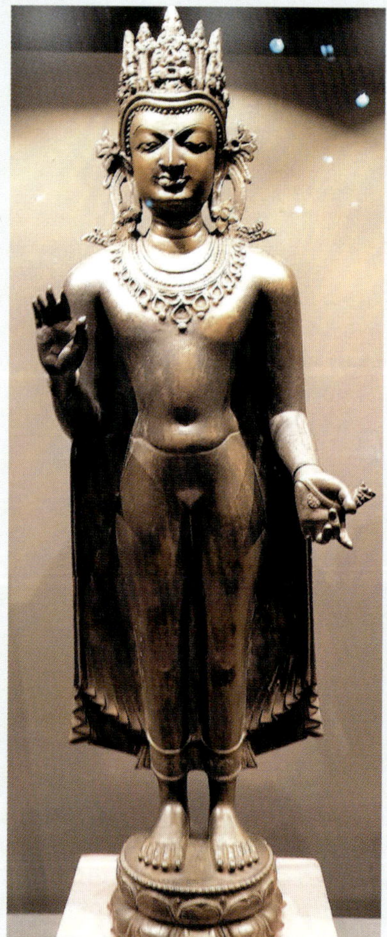

6.103: Buddha Bronze, Kukrihar Gaya, 11th century CE, Bihar Museum, Patna — photograph by Madhukar K Bhagat

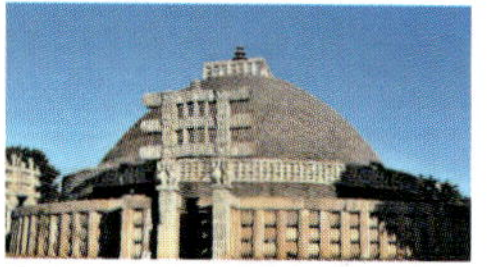

6th century CE. Notable among them is the image of Rishabhanatha, (first Tirthankara) who is identifiable by his long hair with locks up till shoulders. (This image is unlike that of other Tirthankaras who are shown having short hair). The images are reflective of the mastering of modelling of the human physique and delineating the muscles.

The ancient bronze sculptures also include several images of Buddha (particularly in *Abhaya* mudra) which were made during the Gupta and post-Gupta periods between the 5th to the 7th century CE. These are notable for the serene and youthful appearance of the Buddha and the folds of transparent drapery. Statues belonging to this period have been found at Dhanesar Khera (Uttar Pradesh). These have similar folds of drapery with drooping down curves similar to the images of Buddha in the Mathura school. The bronzes of Buddha have also been discovered at Sultanganj in Bihar which are seen to be similar to that of Sarnath school which have foldless drapery. The bronzes are also discovered at Phopnar in Maharashtra which have similarities with those of the Amaravati school. Another set of bronzes of Jain tradition were discovered at Akota, (near Vadodara) Gujarat. Besides, bronzes of Hindu gods and goddesses and Buddhist subjects were also found in Himachal and Kashmir which pertain to the 8th to the 10th century CE. Thus, the art of bronze sculptures was a continuous tradition of ancient India flourishing in different parts of the country.

ANCIENT UNIVERSITIES

The existence of several flourishing centres of study and universities in ancient India reflects the importance attached to knowledge and learning. Universities like **Takshashila, Nalanda,** and **Vikramshila,** which were important centres of learning and culture, attracted thousands of scholars, not only from India, but from China, Japan, and Southeast Asia, and as far as from Persia and Turkey. Some of these universities, their unique features, and their significant contributions to learning and culture is described below.

Takshashila University

Located in Taxila (present day Pakistan), it was the most important centre of learning in ancient India. It was founded in the 6th century BCE. It finds reference in Greek texts as a flourishing centre of learning at the time of Alexander's conquest (4th century BCE). Further, it finds glorifying reference even in Faxian's accounts. The university at its peak taught the Vedas along with 17 *shilpas* (disciplines) including Ayurveda, grammar, philosophy, and archery (other forms of warfare). Many eminent scholars and personalities associated with this university like **Chanakya** (author of *Arthashastra* and the minister of Chandragupta Maurya), **Jivaka** (physician of king Bimbisara of Magadha, who also treated Buddha), **Panini, Charaka** and **Vishnu Sharma** are also said to be associated with it.

Nalanda University

Nalanda was another great university of ancient India which flourished between the **5th century CE and 12th century CE in Nalanda (Bihar).** It was also a Buddhist Mahavihara (a revered monastery). Glorious description of this university is contained in the accounts of Faxian, Xuanzang (Chinese traveller who also studied at this university for two years) and I Tsing. The university was founded during the Gupta period by Kumaragupta-I and later patronised and supported by emperor Harsha and then the Pala kings. The university was the largest residential centre of learning with more than 10,000 scholars from different parts of India and Asia and 2000 teachers. Disciplines like Buddhism, Vedic studies, astronomy, city planning, medicine, grammar, logic, Samkhya, etc. were taught. Many eminent scholars like Nagarjuna (who propounded *shunyavaad*), Aryadeva (student of Nagarjuna), Shilabhadra (teacher of Xuan Zang at Nalanda), Dharmapala (teacher of *yogachara* discipline) and Padmasambhava were associated with it.

The ruins are spread over nearly 30 acres with eleven monasteries and six temples unearthed, apart from a trove of inscriptions, coins, sculptures, numerous stupas and other artefacts. However, several mounds which are under habitation covering 8 to 9 times of the discovered area, are still to be excavated indicating the massive spread of this centre of learning. The university flourished continuously for 800 years as an epitome of education, art, philosophy and other streams, till it was burnt by Bakhtiyar Khilji in the 12th century CE. It was accorded a UNESCO World Heritage Site status in 2016.

The Amazing Nalanda: An Account of Travellers

Deatails of the university of Nalanda is obtained from the accounts of **Xuan Zang** (Hieuen Tsang) and **Itsing** (Yizing), the Chinese travelers who visited this university. Xuan Zang (Hieuen Tsang) came to India in around 627 CE, (during the reign of King Harsha), in search of Buddhist manuscripts from Nalanda Mahavihara (particularly *Yogacharyabhumi-Shastra,* (a discourse on the stages of Yogic practices). His travel accounts of nearly 17 years, of which two years were spent at Nalanda, is documented in his work, *"Great Tang Records of the Western Region"*.

He studied under Shilabhadra, the venerable head of the university, whom he considered a teacher par-excellence in *Yogaceara.* As per his accounts, the Mahavihara was allocated the revenue of 100 villages by king Harsha for its administration. The entire establishment was surrounded by thick brick walls, with large gates, had many viharas, chaityas and other structures with adorned towers. Over hundred varied discourses would take place daily. The university had a trove of manuscripts in its rich library. On his return, Hieuen Tsang carried back to China nearly 657 manuscripts, carried on twenty pack horses.

About the erudition of the scholars, he writes in his above work;

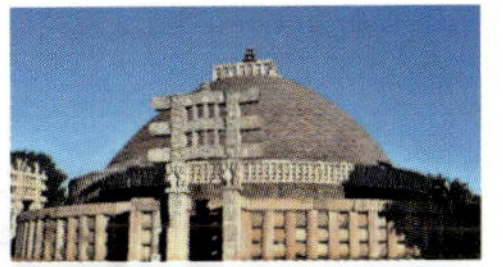

*'There are several thousand monks, all of whom are brilliant scholars of high learning; those whose virtue is esteemed by their contemporaries and whose reputation is known in foreign lands number in the several hundreds. They are pure in observing the monastic regulations and faultless in conduct according to the Vinaya rules. The monks have strict restrictions and they are all chaste and spotless, so that they are looked up to as exemplars.' They always ask for more instructions and deliberate on the abstruse theories incessantly all day long. They admonish each other day and night and extend mutual help between old and young. Anyone who did not engage in discussion of the profound teachings of the Tripitaka would be ashamed of themselves. Thus, foreign scholars who wish to win fame come here to clarify the dubious points they found in their learning before they can join the ranks of the well-reputed.**

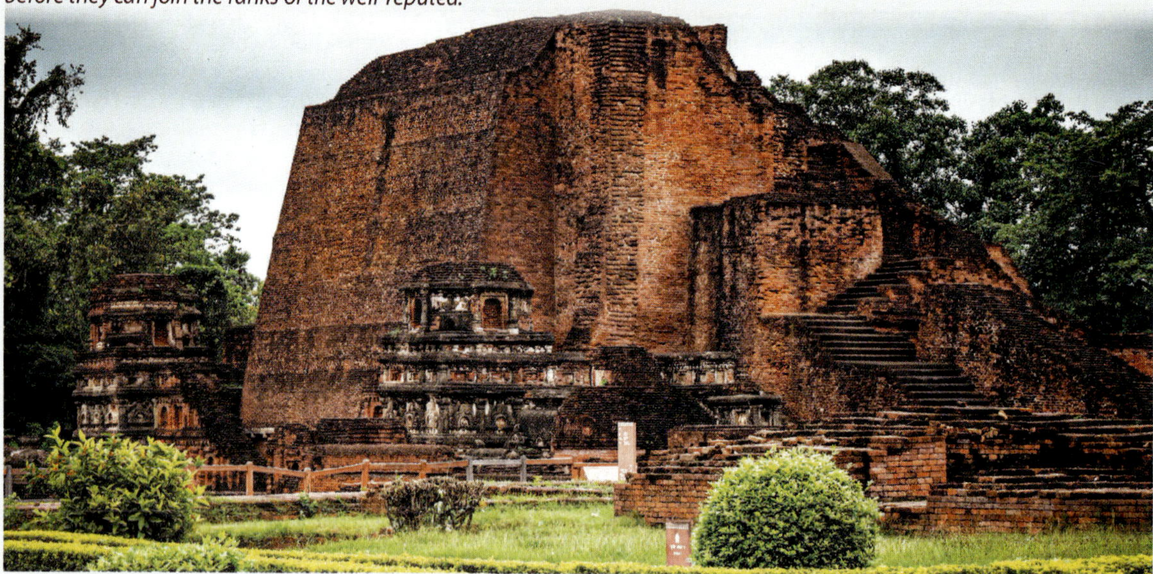

6.104: Ruins of Nalanda — Courtesy, Bihar Tourism

The university followed a unique system of admittance based on merit. Xuan Zang writes;

'Most of the people from different regions and countries who desire to enter this monastery to hold discussions are barred from entering the establishment after a preliminary interrogation by the gatekeeper. Only those who are well versed in both ancient and contemporary learning can gain admittance. The visiting students carry on debates with the resident monks, but seven or eight out of ten flee in defeat.'

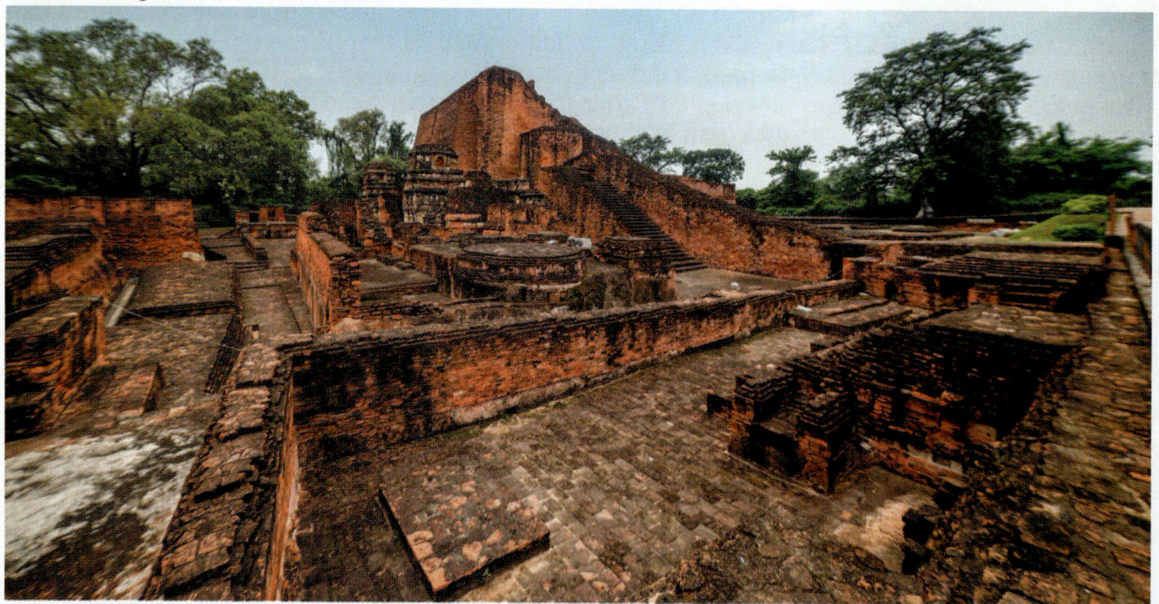

6.105: Ruins of Nalanda — Courtesy, Bihar Tourism

The magnificient architecture and great engineering skills are captured thus in a glowing account;

'Next, to the east is a great temple more than two hundred feet in height. The Tathāgata once spoke on various wonderful Dharmas at this place for four months. More than one hundred paces further to the north is a temple in which is enshrined an image of Avalokiteśvara Bodhisattva.......

To the north of the temple of Avalokiteśvara Bodhisattva is a great temple, more than three hundred feet high, built by King Bālāditya. Its size and ornamentation and the Buddha's image within are similar to those of the great temple at the bodhi tree. The stupa to the northeast is the place where the Tathāgata once expounded the wonderful Dharma for seven days, while to the northwest is a sitting place of the four past buddhas. To the south is Brass Temple, constructed by King Śīlāditya, though

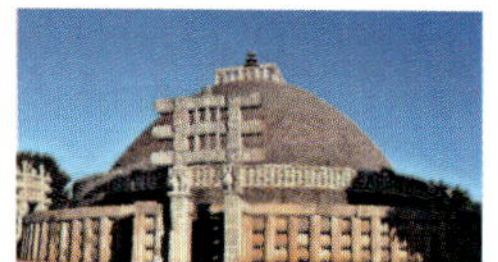

the work is unfinished. According to the drawing of the building when completed it will be one hundred feet in height. Further to the east, more than two hundred paces outside the enclosure, is a copper image of the Buddha in the standing posture, over eighty feet tall and sheltered by a pavilion as high as six stories. It was made by King Pūruavarman in olden times.'

Ytsing, another Chinese traveller who came to India in 673 CE, stayed in Nalanda for nearly 10 years. As per his accounts, the university was granted the revenue of nearly 200 villages to administer it. He gives an account of the disciplined scholarly life, existence of eight viharas and 300 cells (for the student monks). He also describes a series of rites, right from the morning gong, for ablutions and bathing of monks (in huge pools in and around the campus) to evening *chaityavandana* and other rituals. When he left Nalanda, he carried a rich haul of nearly 400 Sanksrit texts, many of which he later translated.

Vikramshila University

This university was established by the Pala king Dharmapala in the 8th century CE in Vikramshila (near Bhagalpur in Bihar). The university was a centre of Buddhist learning, particularly Mahayana and also Tantrism which had gained prominence by then. Besides, subjects like philosophy, grammar, metaphysics, logic, etc. were also taught to scholars from different parts of India and Asia. More than 1000 scholars and 100 teachers resided at the university. Among its most notable abbots was Atishi Dipankara who was the founder of the Sarma tradition of Tibetan Buddhism.

The ruins reveal the spread of the university in an area of over 100 acres, with a large square monastery enclosing a stupa in the centre. Each side of this huge monastery was 330 meters with a total of 208 cells on the fours arm of the square (52 on each side). The main stupa, made up of bricks in mud mortar, is on a raised platform and is believed to be for the purposes of worship. Attached to the south-west corner of the monastery is a large structure identified as a library. An interesting aspect of this is the presence of a range of vents in the brick wall which are believed to be a system of air-cooling/air-conditioning by use of cooled water from a nearby reservoir. This was perhaps meant to preserve perishable and delicate manuscripts.

Along with Nalanda, Vikramashila was among the two most important seats of learning and with time it even outshone the Nalanda university, the decline of which had begun. Vikramshila remained in prominence for four centuries, till it was eventually destroyed by Bakhtiyar Khilji in the 12th century CE. Indeed, the destruction of both the universities was a colossal loss of knowledge of the age. Both were great centres of eminence and gave a severe jolt to Buddhism in India.

Other Universities

As per Tibetan accounts, **Vikramshila (Bihar)**, along with **Nalanda (Bihar)**, **Jagdalla** (Bengal), **Odantapuri** (Bihar), and **Somapura** (Bangladesh) formed the five **Mahaviharas**. The latter three were also important universities/seats of learning in ancient India. It is also believed that under the Pala rule there was a system of coordination and exchange between these Mahaviharas, where certain seats of learning could have been a forte of a specific Mahavihara.

The Odantapuri university located in Biharsharif (headquarters of Nalanda district) of present-day Bihar, was founded by the Pala king Dharamapala in the 8th century CE. It was the second university of ancient India after Nalanda to be founded by the Pala kings. Information about this university, which was yet another Buddhist Mahavihara, is obtained from the Tibetan sources. As per these accounts, the university at its peak had nearly 12000 students. Like Nalanda, this Mahavihara was also destroyed at the hands of Bakhtiyar Khilji towards the end of 12th century CE.

Somapura and Jagddala Mahaviharas were also founded by the Pala kings, the former by king Dharmapala in around early 9th century CE and the latter by king Ramapala in around late 11th century CE. Both are located in present-day Bangladesh and were important seats of Buddhist thoughts and education. Somapura was another large Mahavihara whose excavated ruins are spread over 27 acres. As per the artefacts discovered and accounts of this university, it was also an important centre of the Brahmanical and Jain traditions. The site is also declared a UNESCO World Heriatge Site in 1985. Comparatively lesser information is available about the Jagaddala Mahavihara.

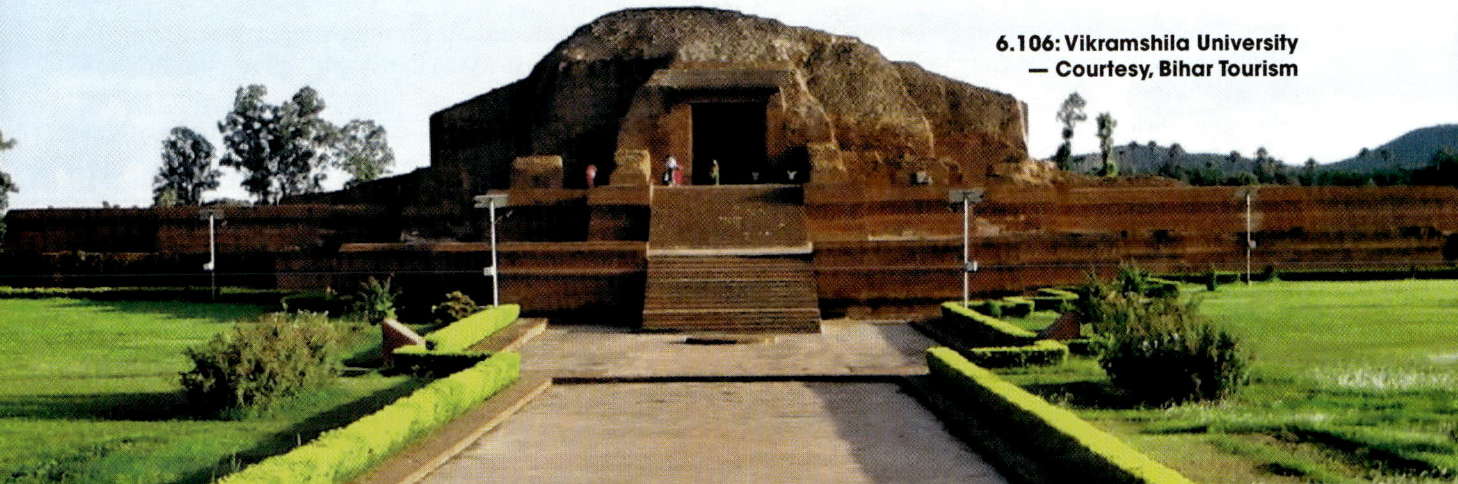

6.106: Vikramshila University — Courtesy, Bihar Tourism

Besides the above, **Valabhi University** and **Pushpagiri University**, were other important universities. The **Valabhi University** was another great centre of learning which flourished from 600 CE to 1200 CE in Valabhi, the capital city of Maitraka dynasty, in Saurashtra region (In Gujarat). Founded and patronized by the Maitraka kings, this university was an important centre of Hinyana Buddhism with nearly 6000 monks and even rivalled the Nalanda university. Besides Buddhism, the university was also known for Brahmanical studies. It was also visited by Xuan Zang and later by Ytsing. The accounts of the former give a very glowing description of the region and the university as below.

'The country of Valabhi is more than six thousand li in circuit and its capital city is over thirty li in circuit. The native products, climatic conditions, social customs, and temperament of the people are similar to those of the country of Mālava. The inhabitants are prosperous, possessing enormous wealth. More than one hundred families have each accumulated property worth one hundred kouis of coins. Many rare goods from distant places are gathered in this country. There are more than a ***hundred monasteries*** *with over* ***six thousand monks,*** *most of whom study the dharma of the* ***Hinayana Saumitiya school****. Deva temples number several hundreds and the heretics are quite numerous.'*

The **Pushpagiri University** located in Kalinga region (modern Odisha) is said to have existed from the 3rd to the 11th century CE. It too finds a reference in the accounts of Xuan Zang as an important Buddhist Mahavihara and a seat of learning which he visited. The discovery of the site at Langudi hills (Jajpur district) and excavations have happened as late as 1996 to 2006. Lesser information about this university is available as compared to Nalanda and Vikramshila.

LITERATURE IN ANCIENT INDIA

The ambit of literature is quite vast and expansive, and in its broadest sense includes religious literature as well as scientific works, poetry, as well as prose. Like other art forms, literature too flourished during the ancient period and reached its peak during the end of first millennia BCE and the Gupta period. The transmission of literature was largely oral and manuscripts (if any) do not survive (in original) to this day. The classification of ancient Indian literature can be done on the basis of languages of their composition, viz. **Sanskrit literature, Pali and Prakrit** literature, and **Dravidian literature** (in Tamil, Telugu, Kannada, and Malayalam). Literary works can also be categorised into religious literature which included the Vedic, Buddhist, and Jain literature and the non-religious, classical, and scientific literature.

The Religious Literature

The religious literature pertaining to the Vedic, Buddhist, and Jain literature is one of the earliest and richest texts in the world. The Vedic literature is said to have been composed as early as 1500 BCE to 1200 BCE, while the Buddhist and Jain literature date to a period later than 500 BCE.

Vedic Literature

The Vedic literature comprises the four Vedic texts which were written in Sanskrit, viz. the **Rigveda, Samaveda, Yajurveda**, and **Atharvaveda;** the Rigveda being the most ancient of all. Each of these had four layers, **the Samhita**, the **Brahmana,** the **Aranyaka,** and the **Upanishad**. The Vedas fall in the category of the *shrutis* or 'what was heard', and thus they are believed to be 'revealed' scriptures. The very word *Veda* is derived from the root word **'vid'** or **knowledge** or **wisdom**. Thus, Vedas were considered as scriptures containing the sum total of the knowledge of the people. Further, the word 'Vid' also refers to the knowledge which could illuminate the path in the darkness (of ignorance), eventually leading to salvation.

Historically, they are not considered the work of a single author or having origin at a one point of time. Rather, they are said to have been composed between 1500 BCE to 600 BCE. Thus, they are among the earliest works, of philosophy and diverse streams of human knowledge. As works encapsulating the highest philosophy of Advaita, they represent the epitome of cultural evolution of an epoch.

The Epics

Besides the above, the two Sanskrit epics, the **Ramayana** and the **Mahabharata** are considered to be amongst the earliest and amongst the greatest literary works. While some historians date their age to 1500 BCE to 1000 BCE, some recent researchers put their date to an even earlier period and thus, push the Vedic period to greater antiquity. However, no unanimity is reached as yet, to their age of composition. As texts, they fall in the category of Smritis or 'what was remembered', hence also considered *itihas* or 'as it happened' (literal meaning; history). Having been composed in verses, they are also considered as *mahakavya* (poetry of epic proportions). While the *Valmiki Ramayana* has around 24000 verses, the Mahabharata is believed to originally have nearly a lakh verses. Further, unlike the Vedas, a singular authorship is generally ascribed to them, with Maharshi Valmiki being considered the composer of Ramayana (an *aadi kavi*) and Maharshi Veda Vyas of the Mahabharata.

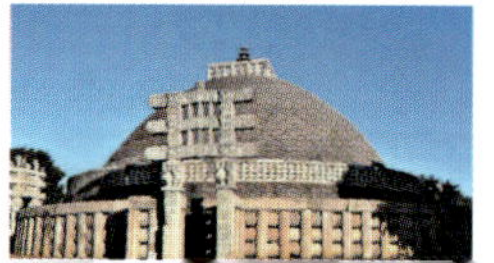

The **Ramayana**, apart from being considered a holy scripture of Hindus, a great literary composition of ancient India and a historical account of a civilization, is also considered a scripture setting the ideals and standards of a society and the very foundation for dharma. The characters, particularly that of Sri Rama inspire people of qualities worth emulation. No wonder over 300 versions of this great epic exist today in numerous languages within and outside India, making it a living cultural tradition.

The **Mahabharata**, the longest epic ever to have been composed, is an encyclopaedic account of a civilisation, its culture, philosophy, religion, ethics, customs, administration, society. Incorporating the Gita and within it the exalted philosophy of Vedanta, the Mahabharata is often considered one of the greatest epics ever and definitely the longest.

Although it is the story of the fratricidal war which often catches the popular attention, the epic is exhaustive enough to perhaps cover or touch upon every subject known to the society then. This would range from capturing the genealogy of Bharatavansha to an account of popular mythology, from the history of land to principles of administration, tenets of kingship to religious rites ethical conduct to diverse armaments and warfare strategies, arts and architecture to material sciences, etc. Even the complex topics of *Dharma, Purusharthas* etc, and those of duties of a king and a commoner are all included in its longest section *Shanthi Parva*. The perils of war, the monumental loss that the society incurs, the utmost need to make all possible efforts to avoid a war, are some crucial messages which resonate at numerous instances, making it truly a magnum opus of the literary creations of the age.

Like the Ramayana, this great epic has also been popular in different cultures over numerous centuries and many versions of it exist in India and neighbouring countries.

The Puranas

The **Puranas** which are 18 in number, too fall in the category of religious literature and are said to have been composed around fifth and fourth century BCE (See Chapter 3). Some scholars give a wider range of time for their composition from 3rd to 10th century CE. Apart from the 18 main Puranas (or Mahapuranas), 18 Upa-puranas were also composed. The Puranas are often classified in terms of the central deity around which the anthology of tales or the narration of eulogy is built. However, they contain the account of other deities, besides they invariably included five key subjects referred to as the *panch-lakshanas* (five signs) which include *sarga, pratisarga, vansha, manvantara, and vansanucharitram.* Besides being a syncretic and canonical literature which inspired Bhakti, they were also encyclopaedic in the nature and diversity of subjects. The longest *Skanda purana* carried a phenomenal 81000 shlokas (three times more than the epic *Valmiki Ramayana*).

Garuda Purana : A Canonical Text of Bewildering Diversity

The *Garuda Purana*, comprising nearly 19000 verses, primarily centres around lord Vishnu and is arranged as a dialogue between the deity, (lord Vishnu) and his *vahana* (celestial vehicle) Garuda. The purana covers an amazing range of topics including cosmology, numerous gods and their relationship, philosophies of yoga and *samkhya, moksha*, karmic cycles, rebirth and even other Upanishadic subjects. The geography of Bharatavarsha (India), account of the salient rivers, diseases and medicines, astronomy, astrology and Hindu calendar system, architecture of homes and temples, rites of passage, different virtues to be emulated, duties of king and statecraft, and even rules of grammar and genre of literature are some of the topics described in its wide array.

Sukhasya dukhasya na kopi data,
Paro dadatiti kubuddhir esa.
Svayam kritam svena phalena yujyate
Sarira he nistara yat tvaya kritam.

No one gives joy or sorrow. That others gives us these, is an erroneous conception. Our own deeds bring to us their fruits. Body of mine, repay what you have done. ***Garuda Purana***

Besides the above, the religious literature related to Hinduism composed in this period also includes the Brahmasutra, the Vedangas, the Upavedas, the Dharmasutras, the Dharmashastras and commentaries (*bhashya*) on many of the above composition, salient philosophies and doctrines (see chapter 3).

Buddhist Literature

The Buddhist canonical literature comprise the **Tripitakas**, viz. **Vinaya Pitaka**, **Sutta Pitaka**, and the **Abhidhamma Pitaka**. While the *Vinaya Pitaka* contains the rules and regulations of the monastic life and functioning of the Sangha, the main teachings of Buddhism and the sermons of lord Buddha are contained in the *Sutta Pitaka*. The **Abhidhama Pitaka** incorporates the higher metaphysical concepts and philosophy of Buddhism. Each of these further comprise grouped verses or class of verses called *Nikaya* which are akin to large sections of these voluminous Pitakas.

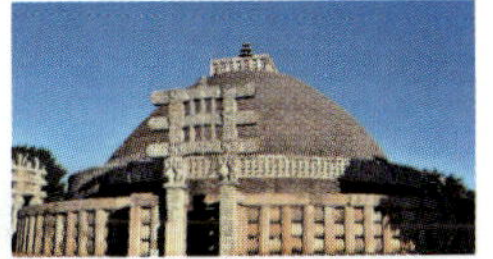

These class of texts were originally transmitted orally in the Prakrit languages, viz. Pali and others, but were translated in other languages, including Sanskrit, and subsequently to Tibetan, Chinese and others over the centuries. It is believed that they were first consigned in written form around 1st century BCE. The Buddhist religious literature is presently available in two broad canons, the Pali (corresponding to Thervada Buddhism) and the Sanskrit canon. While the Pali canon is complete, the Sanskrit Canon has certain missing texts which are retranslated from other languages viz. Chinese, Japanese where these are existent.

The *Jatakas* containing stories of previous lives of Buddha and Avadanas, were other important Buddhist literature. (See Chapter 4). *Buddhacharita* by *Ashvagosha* written in Sanskrit (in 1st century CE) is another important Buddhist literature (non-canonical) which is a biographical account of Lord Buddha in the form of an epic poem. *Mulyamadhyamika Karika* of Nagarjuna (3rd century CE) which expounds the doctrine of *Shunyavaad,* and *Yogacharabhumi sastra* (4th century CE) which brings out the central tenets of the Yogachara school are other important texts of the Mahayana Buddhism.

Jain Literature

Written in Ardha Magadhi (a Prakrit language), the Jain canonical texts are an important source of ancient literature. These are broadly classified into Agama literature or *Agama Sutras* and non-Agama literature. The former, contain the teachings of Lord Mahavira which was compiled by the *Ganadharas*, the immediate disciples, into texts or sutras. The *Agamas* are further classified as *Ang-Agamas* or *Ang-pravista-Agamas/ Ang-Bahya-Agamas* (that which are outside of *Ang-Agamas*). Overall, there are 12 *Ang-Agamas* which are said to be containing direct teachings of Lord Mahavira.

Besides the above, the canonical literature also includes the *ang-bahya* agamas which were the texts and commentaries on various subjects composed by the *srut kelvins.* These were many in number and spread in different languages. *Ang-bahya-Agama Sutras* provided further explanation to the *Ang-Agama Sutras.*

Among the most important of the non-canonical or non-Agama texts are, the **Kalpasutra** composed by acharya Bhadrabahu in around 300 BCE, and **Tattvartha sutra** by acharya Umaswati (also referred as Umaswami) in the 1st-2nd century CE.

Literature on Indian Philosophies

The six systems of India philosophy of Samkhya, Yoga, Nyaya, Vaisheshika, Mimansa and Vedanta which flourished in this period, contributed immensely to the philosophical perspective of the society and were a source of a number of profound and valued treatises.

The **Samkhya** system of philosophy which expounds the dualistic principles of the *Purusha* (consciousness/ the universal being) and *Prakriti* (the primal matter with the three basic *gunas*) was founded by sage Kapila and is considered by some scholars to be as old as the Vedic system. Its earliest extant treatise is the ***Samkya-karika*** by Ishwar Krishna. This is believed to have been composed around 4th century CE. Another treatise *Samkhya-pravachna sutra* is dated to a later period (14th century CE).

The most authoritative text of **Yoga** philosophy is Patanjali's *Yoga sutra.* Considered the foundational work on the theory of Yoga and its practice, the treatise is usually ascribed to the 4th-5th century CE, although many scholars believe it to be of earlier origin. Among the different schools of philosophy, this treatise is considered to have been the most translated one, having translations into nearly 40 Indian languages and even in Arabic and Javanese.

Nyaya-sutra by Akspada Gautama is considered to be the most important treatise of the Nyaya system, the school of logic and realism. Scholars believe the period of its composition to be from 6th century BCE to 2nd century CE.

The Vaisheshika philosophy of naturalism/empiricism, which perceived the physical world to be composed of the smallest indivisible particles (*parmanus*) and its aggregate bonds, was founded by sage Kanada. The ***Vaisheshika sutra*** also referred to as the *Kanada-sutra* (composed by Kanada), is the fundamental work of this school. The period of composition is generally considered to be 6th century BCE to 2nd century BCE.

The Mimansa or **Purva Mimansa**, was the school of ritualism, which was based on the teachings of dharma as contained in the *Samhita* and *Brahmana* layers of the Vedas. The ***Purva Mimansa Sutra*** of **Jamini** (3rd century BCE), is considered to be the most important work in this philosophical system.

The **Vedanta School** draws its philosophy from the *prasthanatrayi*, viz, the three starting points. These being, the **Upanishads**, referred to as the *smriti-prasthana*, **the Gita**, being the *shruti-prasthana* and the **Brahmasutra**, the *nyaya-prasthana.* Treatises of all these were originally composed in the Vedic period. The *Brahmasutra*, also referred as the *Vedantasutra*, is said to have been composed by **Badrayana**. Some scholars believe Badrayana to be Vyasa himself. The treatise of the *Brahmasutra* in the extant form is believed to have been compiled in the period 500BCE to 200CE, for it also contains the critique of Buddhism, Jainism and other schools of philosophy (except *Nyaya*). Over the years, a number of *bhashyas* (commentaries) have

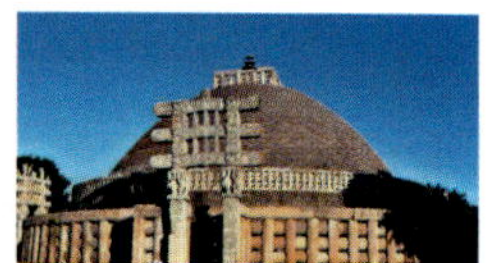

also composed on the *Brahmasutra*, particularly by different Vedantic schools and containing the essence of different schools of Vedantic thought. The most famous of these were those by Adi Shankaracharya (8th century CE, of *Advaitavaad*), Vallabhacharya (10th century CE; of *Bheda-abheda*), Ramanuja (11th century CE of *Vishistadvaita*) and Madhavacharya (13th century: *Dvaitavada*).

Classical Sanskrit Literature

The classical Sanskrit literature comprises a host of works ranging from poetry (such as epics *Mahabharata* and *Ramayana*) to dramas and prose. This form of literature flourished towards the end of the 1st millennium BCE and continued in the Gupta period. This form of literature is also referred as secular literature so as to distinguish it from the other canonical works. Notable literary figures like Bhasa, Sudraka, Ashvaghosha, Kalidasa, Bharavi, Bhatti, Magha, Vishakadatta and Dandin amongst others contributed richly to Indian literature.

Some of the important writers/poets and salient pieces of work are highlighted here.

Bhasa is amongst the earliest authors of the classical Sanskrit literature genre whose works are believed to be dating to the 4th century BCE to the 2nd century CE. Some scholars even attribute his works to the 4th century CE, closer to, but predating that of Kalidasa. Little was known about Bhasa and his works till the discovery of 13 Sanskrit plays in the early 20th century in Kerala, many of which were deployed in Koodiyatam plays. Bhasa also finds references in the works of Kalidasa, Rajashekhara and other eminent litterateurs etc. His most notable work is *Swapnavasavadatta* (Vasavadatta in dreams) based on the story of Vasavadatta the queen of legendary king Udayana.

His other works include *Pratima Natakam, Yagna Phalam and Abhisheka Nataka*, which are based on the stories and characters from the Ramayana while *Pancharatra* (the five nights), *Madhyama* (the middle one), *Duta ghatokatcha* (the envoy Ghatokatcha), *Karnabharam* (Karna's burden) *Harivamsa* (tale of childhood of Hari) and *Urubhanga* (the broken thigh: a story of Duryodhana's repentance) are based on the *Mahabharata.* His work *Charudatta*, of which only some portions are extant, later forms the inspiration for *Mrichchhakatika* of Sudraka.

Sudraka, another great litterateur of the 3rd century CE, (believed to be king Indrani gupta), is the author of three Sanskrit plays, *Mrichchhakatika*, *Vinavasavadatta* and *Padmaprabhritaka*. His most famous work is indeed the *Mrichchhakatika* (the clay cart) (also adapted into Bollywood movie *Utsav*). *Padmaprabhritaka* is a *bhana*, a short one act monologue.

Ashvaghosha, a Buddhist philosopher (1st to 2nd century CE) of the Sarvastivada school, was an eminent poet and dramatist. He is known for composition of *Buddha-charita*, an epic poem in Sanskrit, describing the life of lord Buddha. His other works include, *Sariputta-Prakarna* which captures the life and embracing of Buddhism by Sariputta and Maudgalyayana (chief disciples of Buddha). *Saundaranada,* another of his works, describes the conversion of Nanda (half-brother of Buddha) to Buddhism, so as to enable him to attain salvation.

Kalidasa, often the greatest playwright of this genre, was a poet and dramatist par excellence. He is believed to have lived in the 4th-5th century CE, during the reign of King Chandragupta II. His work *Abhijnanashakuntalam* is considered a masterpiece. The story revolves around the love of King Dushyanta for Shakuntala, the daughter of sage Viswamitra, his marriage to her in solitude, his forgetting Shakuntala, and later her recognition. *Malavikagnimitram*, which is the story of love of King Agnimitra for his exiled maidservant Malavika, and *Vikramorvashiyam*, the story of love of mortal king Pururva for the celestial nymph Urvashi, are other of his great plays. *Kumarasambhava,* a great epic poem describes the life of goddess Parvati, her marriage to lord Shiva and the birth of Kumara (Skanda). *Raghuvansham*, describing the dynasty of king Raghu is another of his great epic poems. *Ritusamhara* which gives the description of the six seasons, and *Meghadootam* which captures how a yaksha conveys the expression of his love through the cloud as a messenger, are some of his minor poetic works.

Vishakhadatta, the author of *Mudraraksha*, **Bharavi** the composer of *Kirtarjuniya*, King **Harsha** the composer of *Ratnavali*, playwright **Bhavabhuti**, **Banabhatta** the author of *Harshacharita*, poets **Magha**, **Bhatti** and **Dandin**, are some of the other great names of this genre.

Non canonical and Scientific Literature

Besides the philosophies, canonical works and great literary works, the period of ancient India witnessed exemplary works in the fields of grammar, medicine, mathematics, social economics and administration amidst others. Some of these are extant to this day and highlight the evolution of these disciplines through the ages.

Grammar: The study of grammar and its evolution is perhaps as old as the Vedas itself, with Nirukta or etymology being one of the six Vedangs (the six ancillary disciplines considered important in Vedic studies). Over the centuries, many significant contributors enriched the school of grammar but the most noteworthy contributions in ancient India being that of Yaska, Panini, Katyayayna and Patanjali.

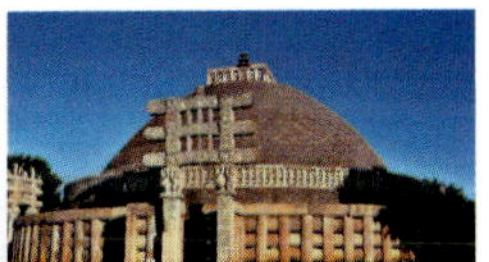

Yaska's work *Nirukta* dealt with etymology (study of root of words and their formation); this was essential for Vedic studies for proper appreciation of the words and deciphering their meaning in their natural context (Prakrit) or suffix form *(pratyaya)*. *Nirukta* itself was considered complimentary to the study of *vyakarana* (grammar), another of the six vedangs. Yaska's work (dated 7th to 5th century BCE) is thought to be the most ancient extant work, he himself quotes other grammarians, particularly Sakatayana (9th century BCE), indicating a long tradition of linguists and grammarians.

Panini's *Ashtadhyayi* is considered a seminal work of grammar. Panini succeeded Yaska and his work is dated to 6th to 4th century BCE. In *Ashtadhyayi*, he quotes nearly 10 more preceding grammarians, including Sakatyana and Saunaka, thus identifying a long tradition. The *Ashtadhyayi*, divided into eight chapters and comprising nearly 4000 shlokas gives the rules of linguistics, syntax and semantics and is considered the foundational work of Sanskrit grammar. His work later attracted many commentaries, including the famous Patanjali's *Mahabhashya*, and is also considered to mark the beginning of classical Sanskrit.

Katyayana (3rd century BCE) was the next in this lineage of grammarians. His work notes the changes in the rules of grammar since the time of Panini and also supplements Panini's work. Thus, his work was in the form of *Vartika* (a commentary and an elaboration) of the Panini's grammar.

The next monumental work was **Patanjali's *Mahabhashya*** (the great commentary) of 2nd century BCE. This commentary on Panini's work included certain supplementary rules (*ishtis*) indicating the change in grammar and evolution of Sanskrit language. It is noteworthy that Patanjali the grammarian is often considered different from Patanjali the giver of *Yogasutras.*

The next milestone in this evolution is the work ***Vakyapadiya*** by **Bhartruhari** in the 5th century CE. The work is considered to elaborate the philosophy of language and understanding the meaning of words in the contexts of the sentences.

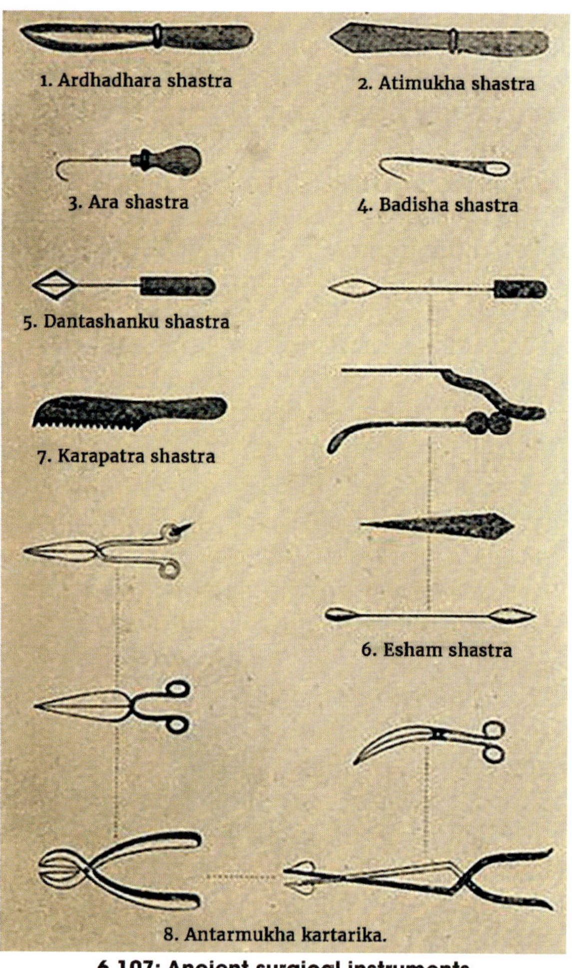

6.107: Ancient surgical instruments — Wikimedia Commons

The Chandas: Along with *Nirukta* and *Vyakarana,* another linguistic domain which saw important treatises being authored were prosody. Considered as a fundamental basis of the structure of the Vedas, prosody and verses were covered within the discipline of *chandas,* which was one of the six Vedangs. Pingala (3rd–2nd century BCE) who authored *Chandashastra* (also referred as *Chandasutra* or *Pingalasutra*) is considered to be the father of Sanskrit metrics. A work in eight chapters in the form of *sutras* (condensed verses), the work recognizes the various kind of metres and also the fixed patterns of short and long syllables, thus laying the foundation of the science of metrics. Academicians also draw an analogy with binary numbers to the use of *laghu* (small) and *guru* (heavy) in the sutra, with there being specific reference to *shunya* (zero) in it.

Bharata's *Natyashastra* is another treatise which discusses the various metres in two of its chapters (chapter 16 and chapter 32). Further, Jayadeva is another writer whose work on Sanskrit metres called *Jayadeva chandas* is widely recognized. The book in eight *adhyayas* (chapter) is in the form of sutras (condensed verses) as well as *karika* (explanatory notes of verses) in its eighth chapter. The work discusses both the Vedic and the classical metres.

Medicine: The tradition of medicine and treatises is also very ancient and draws its roots in the *Atharvaveda.* The medicinal science referred as Ayurveda was considered as an *upveda*. The ancient medicinal knowledge was documented and preserved in the form of *Samhitas*. The most famous of these were the *Charaka-samhita* and *Shushruta-samhita.*

Charaka-samhita along with the ***Shushruta-samhita***, has been the fundamental treatise of the Indian medical system. Both the texts survive to this day, though not in totality. *Charaka-samhita* is usually considered to be the older of the two, though the exact date of composition is not known. However, it is also believed by historians that the manuscript in the current form may not be the work of a single author,

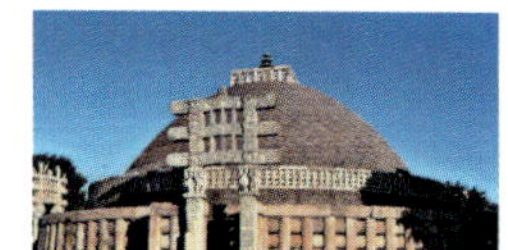

but many others, and that this discipline was taught initially by Aitreya, codified further by Agnivesa and was eventually revised and compiled by Charaka. Centuries later, some lost chapters were rewritten by Dridhabala. The treatise comprises of eight *Sthanas* (books), including 120 chapters. It covers *Sutra Sthana* (general principles), *Nidana Sthana* (pathology) *Vimana Sthana* (specific determination), *Sarira Sthana* (anatomy), *Indriya Sthana* (sensory diagnosis and prognosis), *Chikitsa Sthana* (therapeutics), *Kalpa Sthana* (pharmaceutics and toxicology) *Siddhi Sthana* (cure and treatment). It thus documents the causes and cures of diseases, and it prescribes a holistic and rational approach to medicine for which Charaka is also considered the father of Indian medicinal system.

Sushruta was a physician in around 7th to 6th century BCE in the Varanasi region. His *Samhita* is also considered to be a foundational text of the Indian system of medicine. The *Sushruta-samhita* which runs in nearly 184 chapters, documents over 1120 illnesses, nearly 700 medicinal plants and numerous other medicinal preparations based on animal and mineral sources. A unique aspect of this treatise is the detailed coverage of various kinds of surgeries, surgical instruments and procedures for which Sushruta is also considered as the father of surgery. Some of these techniques include, incision, excisions, extraction of foreign bodies, draining of fluids, alkali and thermal cauteristion, tooth extraction, removal of prostate gland, hernia surgery, cataract surgery, caesarian section, rhinoplasty, plastic surgery etc.

Another treatise on the system of Ayurveda is *Ashtanga Hridaya* by Vagbhata, believed to have been composed around 700CE. Literally meaning, the heart of the eight limbs (eight parts of the system of medicine) it captures the essence of the eight disciplines of the Ayurveda system.

Sushruta Samhita : An Amazing Account of Rhinoplasty

The constructive surgery of nose (rhinoplasty) finds a detailed description in the book-1, chapter XVI of the *Sushruta-samhita*. This book *Sutra Sthanam* is essentially a book of general principles. The meticulous elaboration of the entire procedure (and other such procedures) and post-surgical treatment is an amazing account of the advancement of the medical system even in the fields of complex plastic surgery and other advanced surgical processes.

Now 1 shall deal with the process of affixing an artificial nose. First the leaf of a creeper, long and broad, enough to fully cover the whole of the severed or clipped off part, should be gathered; and a patch of living flesh, equal in dimension to the preceding leaf, should be sliced off (from down upward) from the region of the cheek and after scarifying it with a knife, swiftly adhered to the severed nose. Then the cool-headed physician should steadily tie it up with a bandage, decent to look at, and perfectly suited to the end for which it has been employed (Sadhu Vandha). The physician should make sure that the adhesion of the severed parts has been fully effected and then insert two small pipes into the nostrils to facilitate respiration and to prevent the adhesioned flesh from hanging down. After that, the adhesioned part should be dusted with the powders of Pattanga, Yashti-madhukam and Rasanjana pulverised together; and the nose should be enveloped in Karpsa cotton and several times sprinkled over with the refined oil of pure sesamum. Clarified butter should be given to the patient for drink, and he should be-anointed with oil and treated with purgatives after the complete digestion of the meals he has taken, as advised (in the books of medicine). Adhesion should be deemed complete after the incidental ulcer had been perfectly healed up, while the nose should be again scarified and bandaged in the case of a semi or partial adhesion. The adhesioned nose should be tried to be elongated, where it would fall short of its natural and previous length, or it should be surgically restored to its natural size in the case of the abnormal growth of its newly formed flesh. The mode of bringing about the adhesion of severed lips is identical with what has been described in connection with a severed nose with the exception of the insertion of pipes. The physician, who is well conversant with these matters, can be alone entrusted with the medical treatment of a King.

Reference: Book-1 (Sutra-Sthanam) chapter XVI, Sushurta-samhita; English translation by Kunja Lal Bhishagratna, 1907

Arthashashtra, a treatise par excellence on statecraft, dealt with subjects of polity, states organization, administration, law, economy and even areas of sociology. Authored by Kautilya, it is generally believed that he was Vishnugupta or Chanakya, who was a minister in the court of Chandragupta Maurya. Thus, this treatise is ascribed to the 4th to 3rd century BCE. The work is believed to have derived from the work of previous authors and other schools, showing a long existent tradition even in this field. But soon the *Arthashastra* of Kautilya came to be regarded as the gold standard on the subject. Today, it is considered as an authoritative text on statecraft as *The Prince* of Machiavelli, authored nearly 1800 years later.

The treatise which is in Sanskrit contains both *sutras* (verses) and *bhashya* (commentary) and is divided into 15 *adhikaranas (books) in 150 chapters* and 180 *parakaranas (sections or subjects)* containing 600 shlokas. It covers diverse issues like education of princes, duties of the king, departments of state and their supervision, administration, defence of towns and establishments, civil law, criminal law, dealing with enemies of state, revenue of state, policy of state, salaries of government servants, handling of calamities (fires, floods etc.), espionage, military campaigns, corporations and guilds, and even elements of ethics and philosophy amidst many others, making it truly an encyclopedic account of the statecraft.

The invaluable manuscript seems to have been lost till it was rediscovered in the early 20th century. Later, many of its versions were discovered and a critical edition was prepared in 1960.

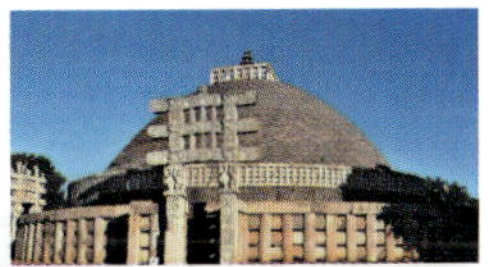

Arthashastra on Happiness and Dharma

सुखस्यमूलंधर्मः । धर्मस्यमूलंअर्थः । अर्थस्यमूलंराज्यं । राज्यस्यमूलंइन्द्रियजयः । इन्द्रियाजयस्यमूलंविनयः । विनयस्यमूलंवृद्धोपसेवा ।।

The root of happiness is dharma (ethical duties and righteousness), the root of dharma is *artha* (economy, polity, material well-being), the root of *artha* is right governance, the root of right governance is inner-restraint and victory over our own senses, the root of victorious inner-restraint is humility, the root of humility is serving the aged.

Arthashastra Sutra 1-6

Mathematics and Astronomy saw unparalleled growth in ancient India, particularly in the classical period (200 BCE to 1000 CE). Many new concepts were enunciated, including the discovery of zero and decimal system, developments in algebra, trigonometry and other disciplines in mathematics and astronomy. Many of these came to be rediscovered by the western world much later. Amongst the earliest of the mathematicians was **Baudhyayana** (900 BCE), whose sutra (*Baudhyayana sutra*) gives the approximation of square root of two and even gives the statement of theorem, now referred to as the **Pythagorean theorem**. **Katyayana** (3rd century BCE) and Pingala who were associated with grammar and metrics respectively, also made significant contributions in mathematics. Katyayana's contribution was in the field of geometry. In the sutras of Pingala, scholars recognize the presentation of what today is called the Pascal's triangle (referred to as *meruprastara* in Pingala's *sutra*). The treatise is also attributed with the description of the binary numeral system and also the presentation of the Fibonacci sequence (referred to in his sutra *matrameru*).

The most notable name among the mathematicians of ancient India is of **Aryabhata** (4th century CE). His treatise ***Aryabhatiya,*** is an exemplary work on mathematics and astronomy and covers a wide range of topics including arithmetic, algebra, trigonometry, fractions, quadratic equations, sums of power series, tables of sines etc. Another of his lost work is *Arya-siddhanta,* which finds reference in the works of Varahmihira. Aryabhata and his works are specially known for identifying 'place value system'. Some scholars also believe that concept of zero is implicit in his works. Approximation of the **value of $\pi\pi$ (Pi),** concept of **earth rotating on its own axis**, explanation of solar and lunar eclipses, are some of his other salient contributions.

Separated by just a few decades was another luminary of this age, **Varahamihira** (at times considered a contemporary of Aryabhata) who was a mathematician, astronomer and a polymath. His treatise, ***Brihat Samhita*** (literal meaning; *the great compilation*) is an extensive account of diverse subjects including astronomy, astrology, temple architecture, planetary motions, eclipses, timekeeping, mathematics, gemology, agriculture, rainfall etc. Another of his treatise, *Pancha Siddhantika*, is a compilation of the five major principles of astronomy in vogue then. He is also known for improving the accuracy of the sine tables prepared by Aryabhata and determination of the coefficients of Binomial theorem, in a form what is known today as Pascal's triangle.

Brahmagupta, (7th century CE) the author of *Brahmasphuta-siddhanta*, gave the formal rules for **computing with zero**. Another mathematician of the 7th century CE **Bhaskara-I**, wrote *Aryabhatiya-bhashya*, a commentary on the treatise of Aryabhata which is in prose form (among the oldest of prose works). He was the first to write the **numbers in the decimal system form** and use a circle for zero. Further, in another work, *Mahabhaskariya*, he has given a very close approximation formula or Sin X (a trigonometric function).

Sridhara (late 7th century) is credited with calculation of the **volume of a sphere**. **Mahavira**, a 9th century Jain mathematician and author of *Ganitsara-sangraha,* separated the disciplines of mathematics and astrology. He is also known for discovery of certain algebraic identities, formula for a combination **(^nCr)**, formula for approximation of the perimeter and areas of an ellipse and calculation of square root and cube root of a number.

The 12th century CE saw the emergence of another mathematical genius in **Bhaskara-II**. His treatise ***Siddhant Shiromani*** is divided into four parts, *Lilavati* (on arithmetic), *Bijaganita* (on algebra), *Grahaganita* (on mathematics of planetary motion) and *Goladhyaya* (on mathematics of spheres). Some of his salient contributions include, a **proof of the Pythogorean** theorem, solutions to quadratic, cubic and indeterminate equations, plane and solid geometry, properties of zero, problems of interest and computation, hypothesis of existence of two square-roots of a positive number and spherical trigonometry inter-alia many others. Scholars also believe his works include knowledge of the **principles of differential calculus** which he applied in astronomical problems and their computation. This was nearly 500 years before their discovery by Newton and Leibniz in Europe.

Besides the above, salient contributions were also made by Yativrsabha (6th century CE), Halayudha (10th century CE), Pauluri Mallana (11th century CE), and Hemachandra (12th century CE).

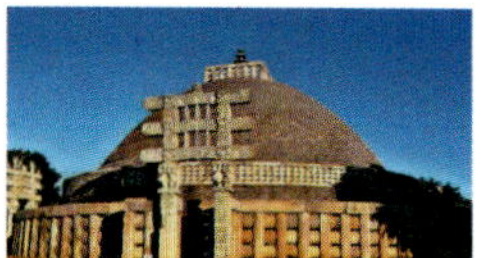

A Snapshot of Great Literary and Other Non-Canonical Works

Bhasa (4th century BCE to 2nd century CE) Date not fully certain	13 plays including *Svapnavasavadatta* (Vasavadatta in dream)
Sudraka (3rd century CE)	*Mrichchhakatika* (the clay cart); a drama
Ashvaghosha (1st to 2nd century CE)	*Buddhacharita*, an epic poem on the life of lord Buddha
Kalidasa (4th to 5th century CE)	• *Abhigyana shakuntalam* (recognition of Shakuntala); a drama • *Malavikagnimitra* (a love story of Malavika and Agnimitra); a drama • *Vikramorvasiya* (a love story of Vikrama and Urvasi); a drama • *Meghaduta* (cloud messenger); a poem • *Raghuvamsa* (about kings of Raghu dynasty); a poem • *Kumarasambhava* (birth of Kumara); a poem • *Ritusamhara* (description of six seasons); a poem
Vishakadatta (from 4th century CE to 8th century CE) Date not fully certain	• *Mudraraksha* (a play describing rise of power of Chandragupta Maurya) • *Devichandraguptam*
Bhavabhuti	*Uttararamcharita* (the later portion of life of Sri Rama); a play
Bharavi (6th CE)	*Kiratarjuniya* (Kirata and Arjuna); a poem
Magha (7th to 8th century CE)	*Sishupalavadha* (killing of Shishupala); a poem
Banabhatta (7th century CE)	*Harshacharita* (biography of emperor Harsha)
Harsha (7th century CE)	*Ratnavali* (attributed to Indian emperor Harsha); a play
Dandin (7th– 8th century CE)	*Kavyadarsha* and *Dasakumaracharita*
Jayadeva (12th century CE)	*Gita Govinda* (song of Govinda)

Other Important Treatises

Lagadha (1400 to 1200 BCE)	*Vedanga Jyotisha* (astronomy)
Baudhyayana (8th century BCE)	*Baudhayayana Sulba Sutra* (a treatise on mathematics containing Pythagorean theorem statement)
Sushruta (600 BCE)	*Sushruta Samhita* (treatise on medicine and surgery)
Charaka (300 BCE)	*Charak Samhita* (treatise on medicine)
Vishnu Sharma (date not exactly ascertained, around 3rd centuryBCE)	*Panchatantra* (compilation of stories dealing with practical wisdom in all fields of life)
Chanakya (Vishnu Gupta) (2nd century BCE)	*Arthashashtra* (a treatise on economy statecraft, administration, etc.)
Aksapada Gautama (6th to 2nd century BCE)	*Nyaya sutra* (a treatise on the Nyaya system of philosophy, a school of logic and realism)
Badrayana (5th to 2nd century BCE	*Brahma Sutra* (a treatise of salient philosophical and spiritual elements of Upanishads; also comprising one of the pillars of the vedantic philosophy)
Jamini (3rd century BCE)	*Purva Mimansa Sutra* (a treatise of the Mimansa philosophy, a school of ritualism)
Kanada (200 BCE)	*Vaisheshika* philosophy (matter composed of atom which are indivisible and eternal)
Bharata (1st century BCE to 1st century CE)	*Natyashashtra* (a treatise on dance and theatre and other performing arts)
Vatsyayana (2nd century CE)	*Kamasutra* (a treatise on love and sex)
Aryasura (4th century CE)	*Jatakamala* (34 stories of lord Buddha's previous births)
Panini (4th century BCE)	*Ashtadhyai* (treatise on Sanskrit grammar)
Patanjali (400 CE)	*Patanjali Yogasastra* and *Yoga Sutra* (196 aphorisms on Yoga)
Ishwar Krishna (4th century CE)	*Samkhya Karika* (a treatise of Samkhya philosophy)
Aryabhata (5th century CE)	*Aryabhatiya* (treatise on mathematics and astronomy)
Varahamihira (6th Century CE)	*Panch Siddhantika* and *Brihat Samhita* (astronomy and mathematics)
Narayana Pandita (9th century CE)	*Hitopadesha* (stories about animals, birds, and humans, and of wisdom and benefit to individuals and society)
Bhaskara-II (12 century CE)	*Siddhanata Siromani*, (a compendium of four works on arithmetic, algebra, mathematics of planetary motion and spheres)

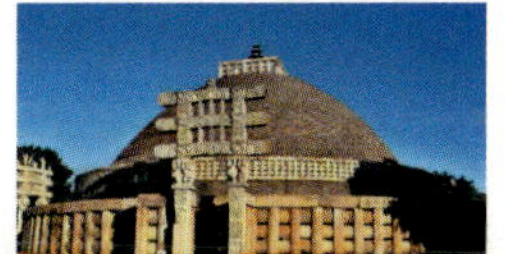

The Dravidian and the Sangam Literature

The literature composed in the southern part of India in the Tamil, Telugu, Kannada and Malayalam languages is commonly referred as the Dravidian literature. A number of great literary works were composed in ancient India, particularly in the Tamil language which is believed to be the oldest amongst the Dravidian languages.

Tamil literature: A vast body of Tamil literature was composed in the period 300 BCE to 300 CE and is referred to as **Sangam literature**. The most important treatises of this period existing today are the ***Tolkappiyam, the Pathupattu and the Ettuthogai***. The original manuscripts of these treatises were lost for centuries and were rediscovered in a Shaiva monastery in Kumbakonam only in the 19th century. The ***Pattupattu***, which is a collection of 10 long poems, can be said to be the earliest work of Tamil literature. The poems in the anthology range between 100 to 800 lines and are thus truly a substantive literary work. The most important of this collection is *the Nakkirar's Tirumurukarrupattai* (a guide to lord Murugan).

Ettuthogai or the 'collection of eight', is another poetic literary work from this period, which along with the **Pathupattu**/*Pattupattu* forms the compilation of 18 ancient great literary works. These eight anthologies are a compilation of 2371 poems, each with 3 to 40 lines. These poems are attributed to nearly 473 poets whose names can be arrived at from their works. Among these nearly 30 are believed to be women. This includes the famous poet Avvaiyar. These poets in themselves were from different parts of the region and engaged in different occupations. However, in nearly 100 stanzas the names of their authors cannot be worked out.

The poems of the Sangam period are broadly classified as *Akam* or *Agam or Aham*, meaning, 'inner' or 'love' and *Puram*, meaning 'outer' or 'public life'. These poems are of varied themes including love and emotion, worship of deities, veneration of king and his works and at times themed on war. Thus, these grand literary works were truly a reflection of the intellectual and institutional elements of the society and its culture.

During this period, *Tolkappiyam*, a work on the grammar of the Tamil language was also written. This lays the foundation of Tamil grammar. Another monumental Tamil work was the composition of the *Thirukkural* by the sage **Thiruvalluvar** which contains 1330 *Kurals*, or short couplets of seven words, each enunciating precepts to guide humanity to a noble living. The subjects of these couplets are broadly based on virtue (*aram; dharma*) wealth (*porul; artha*) and love (*inbam, kama*). Also referred as the Tamil-veda or the divine book, the *Thirukkural* is said to have been composed around 300BCE to 500 CE. However, some scholars believe the period of authorship to be around the end of the third Sangam period, while linguistically, a latter date of around 500CE is proposed.

Tamil literature is also known for the twin epics—*Silappadhikaram* and *Manimekalai*. Further, it contains a rich body of works in the compositions of Alwars and Nayanars.

Telugu literature: The Dravidian literature is also enriched by other notable works such as **Nannaya's** *Mahabharatam* (1030 CE), works of Lingayats (Virashaivas), and sage **Nachna Somanatha's** *Uttara Harivamsam*.

Kannada literature: In Kannada, *Dharmanthapurana* is a famous text written by **Madhura** on the life of the 15th Tirthankara. Another famous literary work is *Kavirajamarga* written by **Nripatunga Amoghavarsha (10th century CE).**

Pampa is also referred to as father of Kannada literature who composed *Adi Purana* and *Vikramarjuna Vijaya*. The three litterateurs **Pampa, Ponna,** and **Ranna** are also referred as *Ratnatraya* (or three gems) of Kannada literature.

Malayalam literature: The language and its literature developed in the latter half of the 1st millenia. It included works like *Kokasandesam* and *Bhasa Kautilya* (a commentary on *Arthashashtra*).

MUSIC AND DANCE IN ANCIENT INDIA

Music and dance are categorised as performing arts (along with puppetry and theatre). India has had a rich tradition of music and dance since ancient times, where it was considered as a part of *Natya*. Several ancient texts contain reference to music and dance of ancient times. Even Indian mythology attaches due importance and contains many references of these art forms.

References to Music and Dance in Ancient Texts

Reference in Samaveda and other texts: The most ancient reference to music is noted in *Samaveda*, which consisted of the hymns which were sung using notated melodies at the time of rituals. The *Samaveda* is said to contain all the seven notes of the raga *Karaharapriya* in the descending order. The earliest raga is said to be *Samagana* or *Samaraga*. The *Samaveda* has two major parts (as discussed in an earlier chapter). It includes the melody collections in the first part (*gana*) and the second part contains the verses (the *Archika*

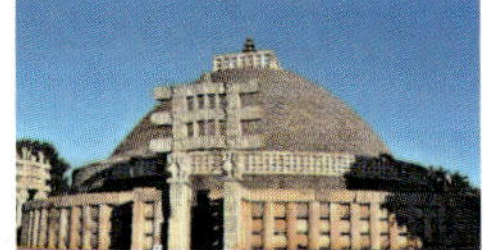

book). The melody in the first part thus corresponds to the verses in the second part. Thus, the roots of Indian music are contained in the *Samaveda*.

Reference to music is also obtained in Yaska's *Nirukta* (700-500 BCE), Patanjali's *Mahabhasya* (500-400 BCE), *Kamasutra* of Vatsyayana, and even in some places in the Buddhist *Tripitakas* which mention the occasion for music. But the most important and relevant text is the *Natya Shastra* of Bharata (200 BCE to 200 CE). The other important texts are *Dathilan* which specifies the division of octave into 22 Srutis, *Brihaddeshi* written by Matanga (9th century CE), and *Sangeet Ratnakara* by Saranga Deva (13th century CE).

Natya Shastra: A Treatise on Music, Dance and Drama

The **Natya Shastra** is the most authoritative text of this period pertaining to the performing arts. Composed by sage **Bharata,** it is said to **contain more than 6000 shlokas**.. However, scholars believe that the work is not the creation of a single person. The name 'Bharata' is itself taken to be an acronym (*Bha-Bhava, Ra-Raga, and Ta-Tal*). **Natya Shastra** is thus a compilation of the knowledge of performing arts of a whole culture.

The treatise also contains several chapters on music which delves on the octave and divides it into 22 keys or *srutis*. However, **Natya Shastra** is not a book on music alone, but a comprehensive treatise on performing arts which included music, dance, and performance. The text in this treatise is in the form of a dialogue between sage Bharata and other *munis* who seek knowledge from him about *Natyaveda* (*Natya* means performance or drama, and *Veda* means knowledge). The replies are compiled in the form of a book.

The *Natya Shastra* comprises 36 chapters each carrying a detailed description of different disciplines associated with, drama, music and dance. The first chapter *Natya* discusses the origin of drama, while in the second *Natyamandapa*, the description of the house of drama/ theatre is carried. Veneration to the gods is covered in the third, titled *Rangapuja*, while *Tandava* is the next chapter. The treatise contains separate chapters for *Purvaranga* (preliminaries of a play) *Rasa* (sentiments), *Bhava* (expression of emotional states), *Upanga* (gestures of minor limbs), *Anga* (gestures of major limbs), *Chari* and *Mandala* (movements) etc. Of special relevance are the four separate chapters on the types of musical instruments which recognise and describe stringed instruments (*tata*), hollow instruments (*susira*), time measurebeat instruments (*taala*) and covered instruments (*avanaddha*). The different types of Dhruva songs are also described in detail in a separate chapter.

Besides, subjects of prosody, metrics, diction, intonation, rules of use of language, costumes and makeup, ten kinds of play, types of character, description of roles, instrumental music (*atodya*) etc. are also comprehensively covered in it, making it an encyclopedic account of different disciplines associated with music, dance and drama.

Music in Ancient India

The ancient and Vedic music was ritualistic and devotional. *Samagana* music was popular in the Vedic period which involved chanting of hymns as per the musical notations. Subsequently, for narration of epics, a form of music called *Jattigan* was evolved. Towards the latter half of the 1st millennia BCE, *Prabandh Sangeet* (written in Sanskrit) was in vogue from which originated a simpler form of music called *Dhruvpad*. It is believed that the medieval music Drupad had its origin in Dhruvpad. Besides the *Natya Shastra*, a detailed account of the different kinds of music in vogue is contained in the *Sangitaratnakara*. The treatise discusses in detail the different types of ragas and talas and has identified seven families of talas which are further subdivided into rhythmic ratios.Thus, it incorporates the fundamentals of ancient and the medieval forms of music (and even of the classical music of modern era).

Mythological Origin of Music and Dance

As per mythology, *Om* was the first word and the primordial sound of the universe. Thus, from *Om* all music has originated. Music in the rudimentary form is said to be brought on the earth by Narada Muni who highlighted that the all-pervading sound of the universe was Naada Brahma (or Om).

Lord Shiva who is also worshipped as Nataraja (the Lord of performers), is said to be the deity of music and dance. The famous Tandava dance shows Lord Shiva holding a Damru (from which celestial beats emanate) and performing a cosmic music. Some mythological accounts also consider Lord Brahma as the fountain head of music and dance.

Dances in Ancient India

Ancient scriptures give common references to music and dance. Bharata's **Natya Shastra**, the most authoritative text on music and dance captures this art form to be in vogue right from ancient times. Referred to as the fifth Veda by sage Bharata, this treatise is said to take the **words** from *Rigveda*, **music** from *Samaveda*, **gestures** (Abhinaya) from *Yajurveda*, and **emotions** (Bhava) from *Atharvaveda*. Thus, *natya* was a combination of all of the above — words, music, gesture, and emotion. In the classical tradition as

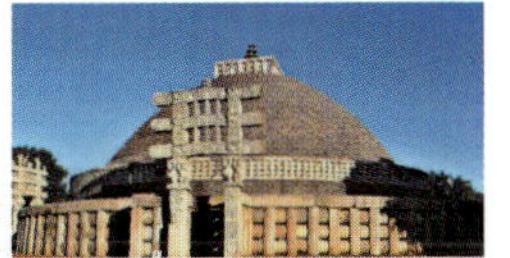

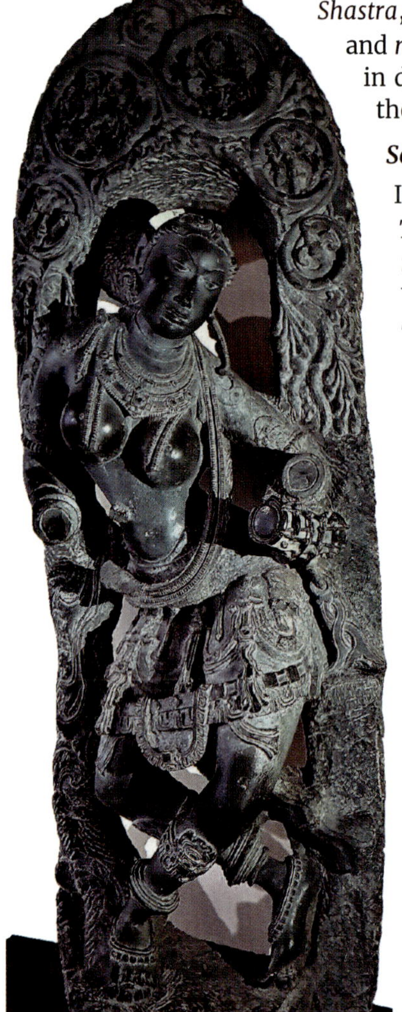

6.108: Tribhanga posture of Madanika, a dancer, 11th century Chalukya, Government Museum, Bangalore — photograph by Madhukar K Bhagat

formulated in Natya Shastra, dance and music were an integral part of performance referred to as Natya or drama. Further, in the classical dance form as per the *Natya Shastra*, the *natya* can be said to comprise three elements which are *natya*, *nritya*, and *nritta*. ***Natya*** refers to the elements of drama (not seen nowadays except in dance dramas). ***Nritya*** refers to the expression of the performer, while the ***nritta*** refers to movement of the body as per rhythm.

Some ancient dance forms

In ancient dance forms we get a reference of *Tandava* and *Lasya*. The *Tandava* is a vigorous and energetic male dance form. Out of these, lord **Shiva's Tandava** dance is more famous. *Tandava* itelf is considered to be of two types; *Ananda Tandava* and *Rudra Tandava*. While the *Ananda Tandava* is a dance of joy and bliss, the *Rudra Tandava* is reflective of lord Shiva's violent and fierce form. It is the latter dance form that the word *Tandava* is usually associated with. This is also said to be a cosmic dance in which lord Shiva is depicted with four hands and two legs balancing on a single leg in a specific dance posture. He holds a *damru* in one hand, and carries a flame in his other hand, while the remaining two are in *Abhaya mudra* (Refer to the Nataraja statue and symbolism in the chapter on Hinduism 'Bronze sculptures in medieval India'). The ***Laasya*** is a soft, graceful and feminine dance form.

Reference in different texts is also seen to the *Tribhanga* dance which is essentially a dance posture and not a dance per-se. The bronze statue of the dancing girl from Mohenjo-daro is an example of this posture (See Chapter 3). This posture has also been incorporated in several later sculptures and dances in medieval and modern times.

The *Tribhanga* (or bent thrice) is a body posture in which the performer is seen standing with the body bent {or seen to be breaking} at three positions, which are the neck, the waist, and the knee. The body is seen to be slightly but oppositely curved like an S and is considered to be a graceful and sensual posture. Paintings and sculptures also depict Krishna in this posture.

The *Natya Shastra* considered the various imaginary vertical and horizontal axes through which the body could bend viz. the *Brahmasutra*, or the imaginary vertical axis passing through the navel and dividing the body into two equal halves. Depending on the deviations and the bends that could be performed around these geomatical axes the deflections (*bhanga*) could be *samabhanga* (equal deviation from the central median) *abhanga* (minor weight shift without movement) *tribhanga* (three deflections with weight on one leg and torso jutted out as counterbalance) *atibhanga* (multiple deviations) etc. Thus, the treatise classifies the dance postures and body movements as per geometrical positioning of the body and its parts.

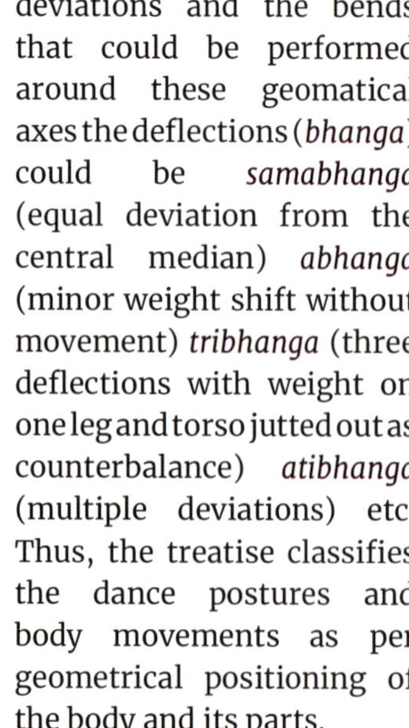

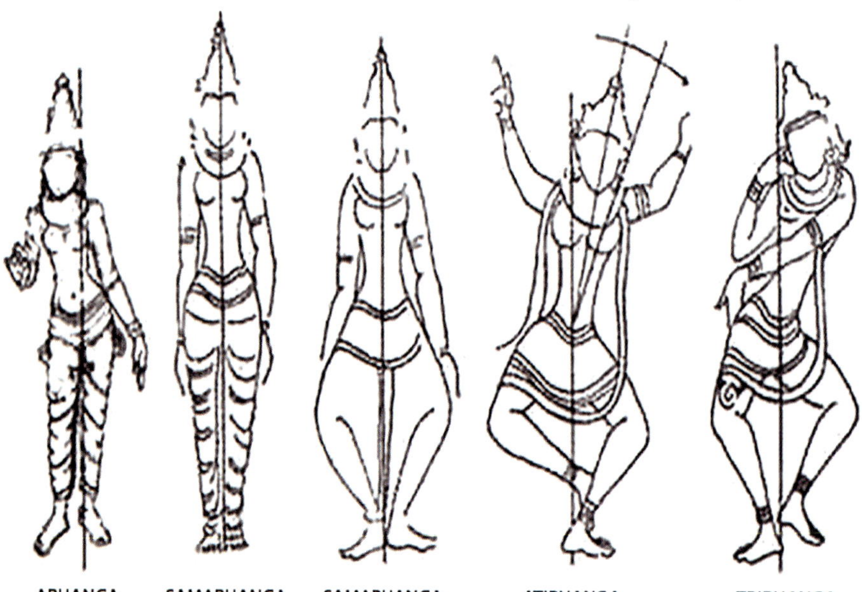

6.109: Dance postures and body movements as per Natya Shastra — Wikimedia Commons

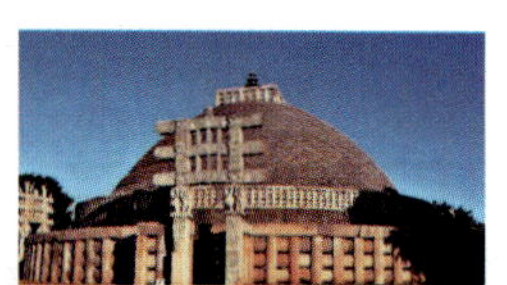

PICTURE GALLERY

Rock-cut Architecture, Sculpture and Paintings

Kailashnath temple; Ellora Caves: A rock-cut megalith and a wonder of the world

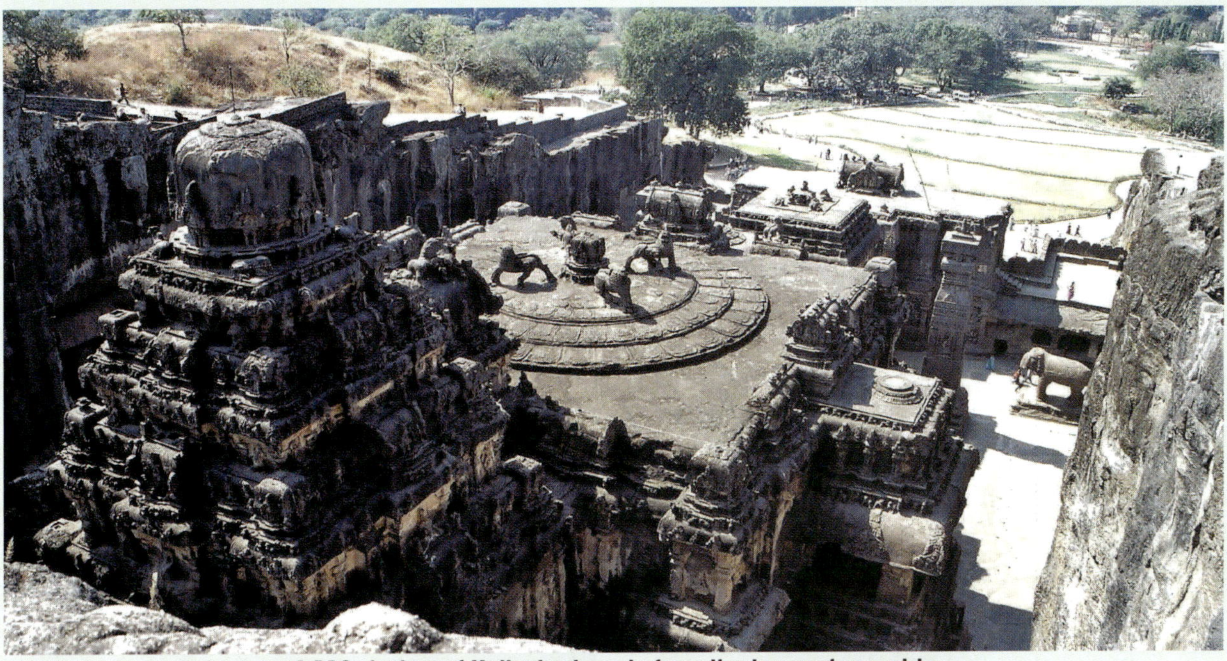

6.110: A view of Kailasha temple from the top and rear side

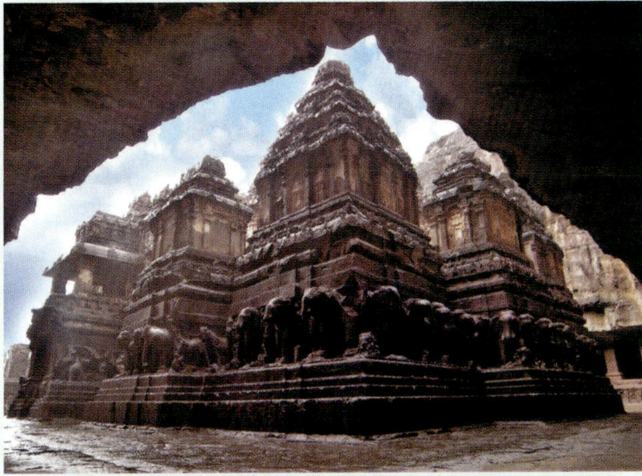

6.111: Kailashnath temple with numerous carved elephants; as viewed from an adjacent cave

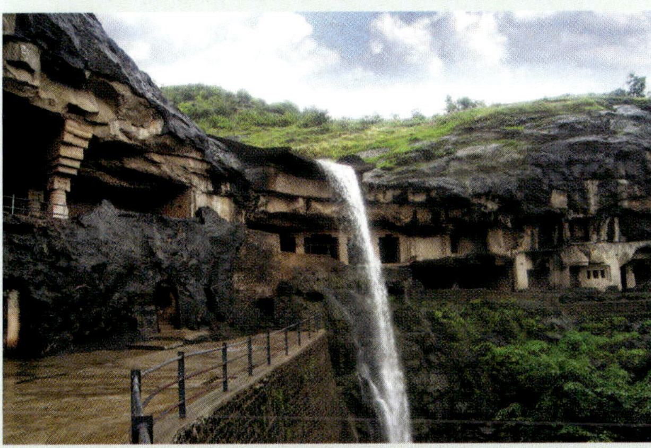

6.112: View of the Ellora Caves

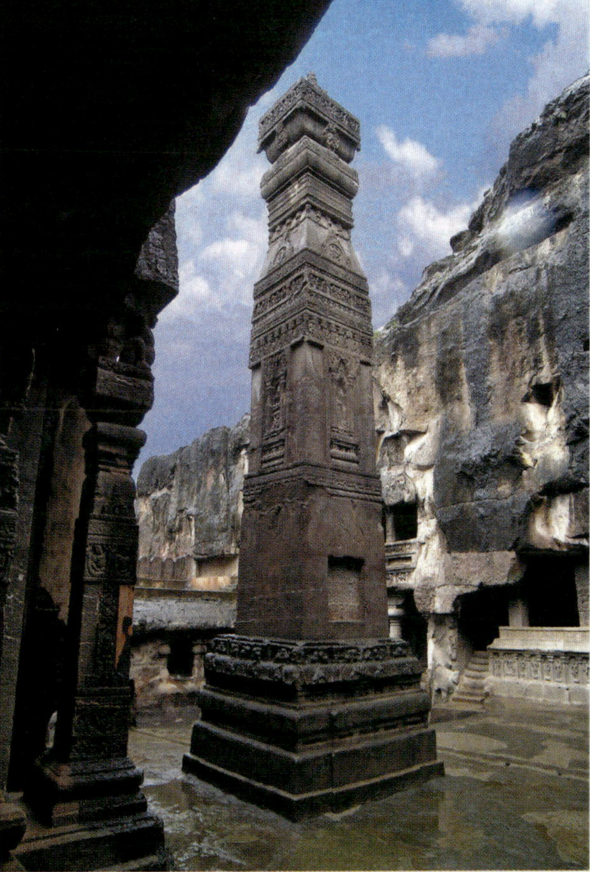

6.113: Stone victory pillar (Kirti Stambh) with intricate carvings in the courtyard of Kailashnath temple

— Courtesy, Maharashtra Tourism Development Corporation

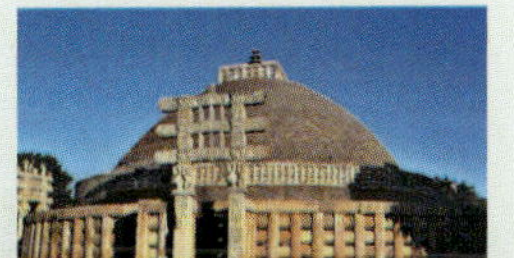

Karla Caves

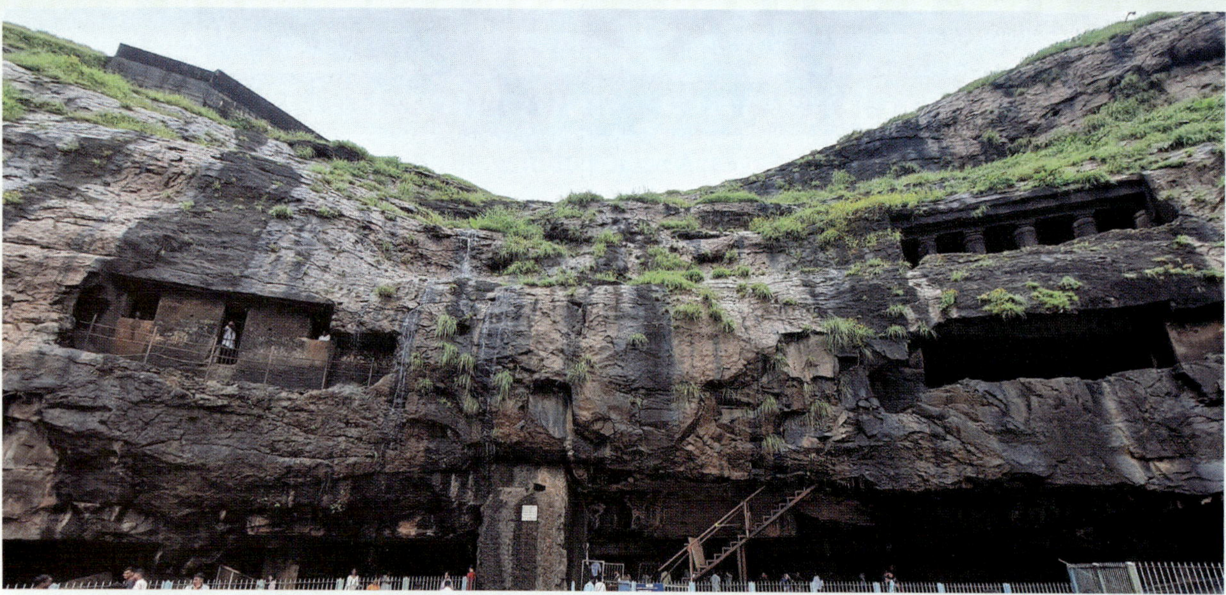

6.114: Karla Caves, an example of early rock cut architecture; viharas excavated in three levels — photograph by Madhukar K Bhagat

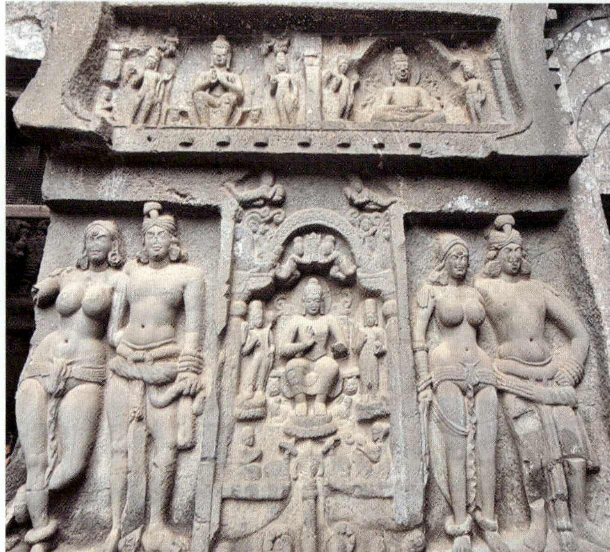

6.115: Stone carving/relief work depicting Buddha and other human figures (mithuna couple) at the entrance to the Chaityagriha at Karla — photograph by Madhukar K Bhagat

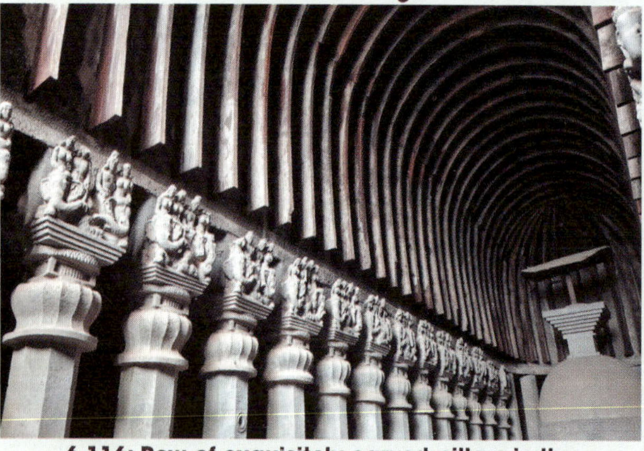

6.116: Row of exquisitely carved pillars in the Chaityagriha with lotus pillar capital adorned with human figures on elephant — photograph by Madhukar K Bhagat

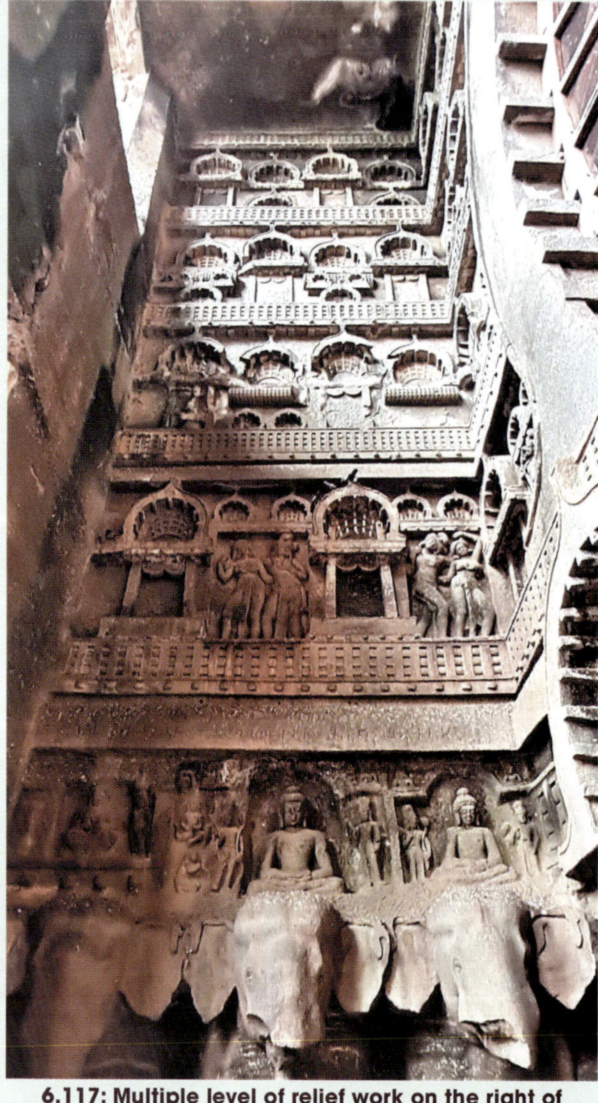

6.117: Multiple level of relief work on the right of Chaityagriha Cave entrance, depicting Buddha on elephant and other human and animal figures — photograph by Madhukar K Bhagat

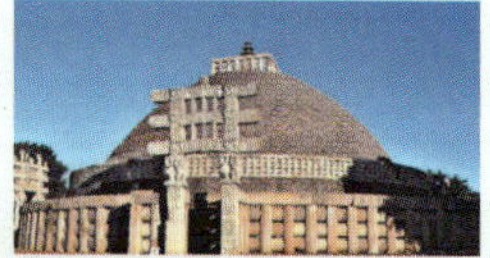

Bhaja Caves

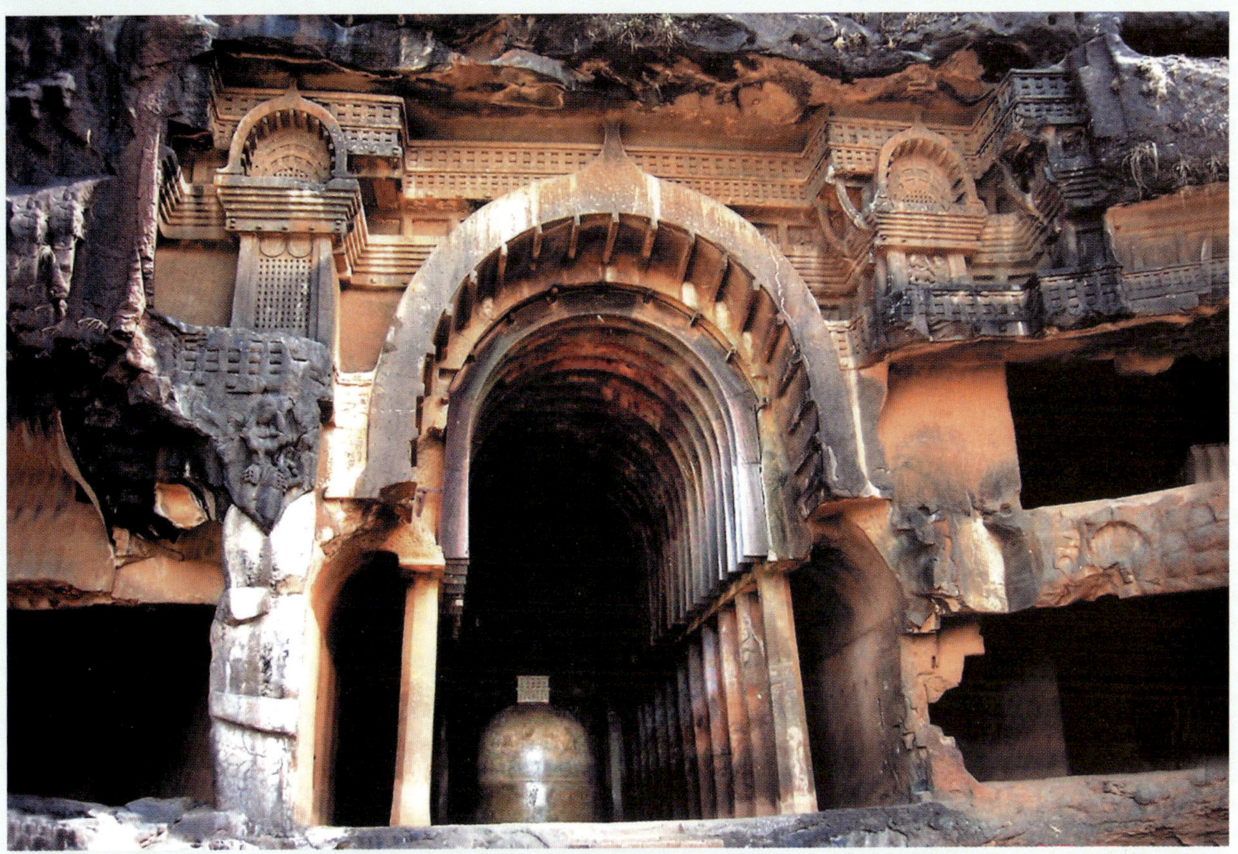

6.118: Chaityagriha at Bhaja Caves near Lonavala, Maharashtra

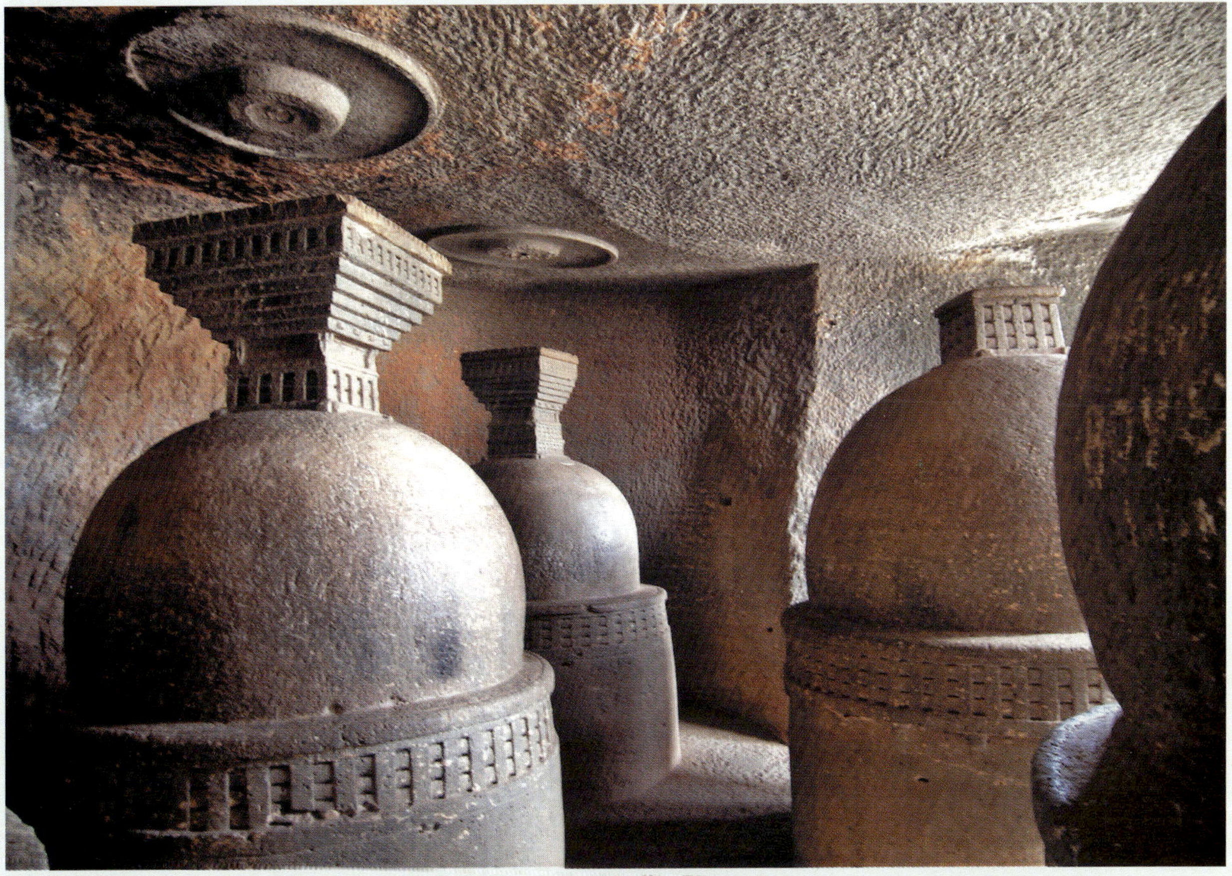

6.119: Stupas inside the Bhaja Caves

— Courtesy, Maharashtra Tourism Development Corporation

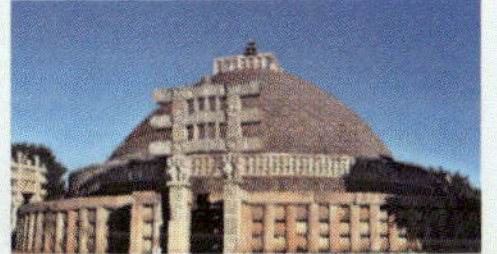

Kanheri Caves

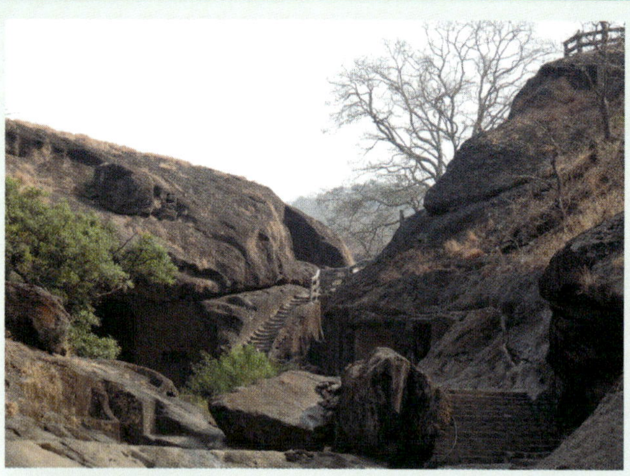

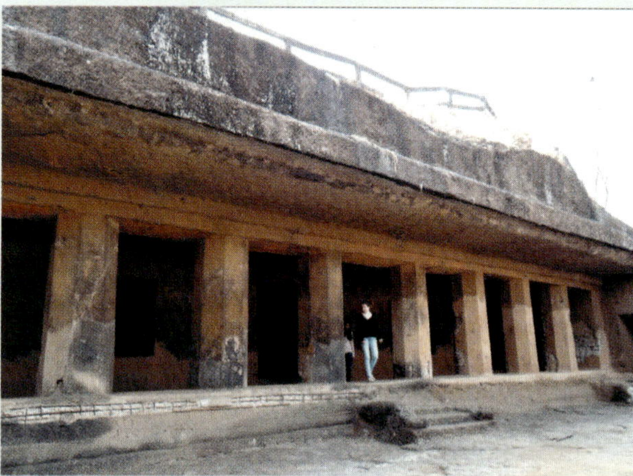

6.120: Kanheri Caves, Mumbai, rock shelters and carved out caves (left), Vihara cells at Kanheri Caves (right) — photographs by Madhukar K Bhagat

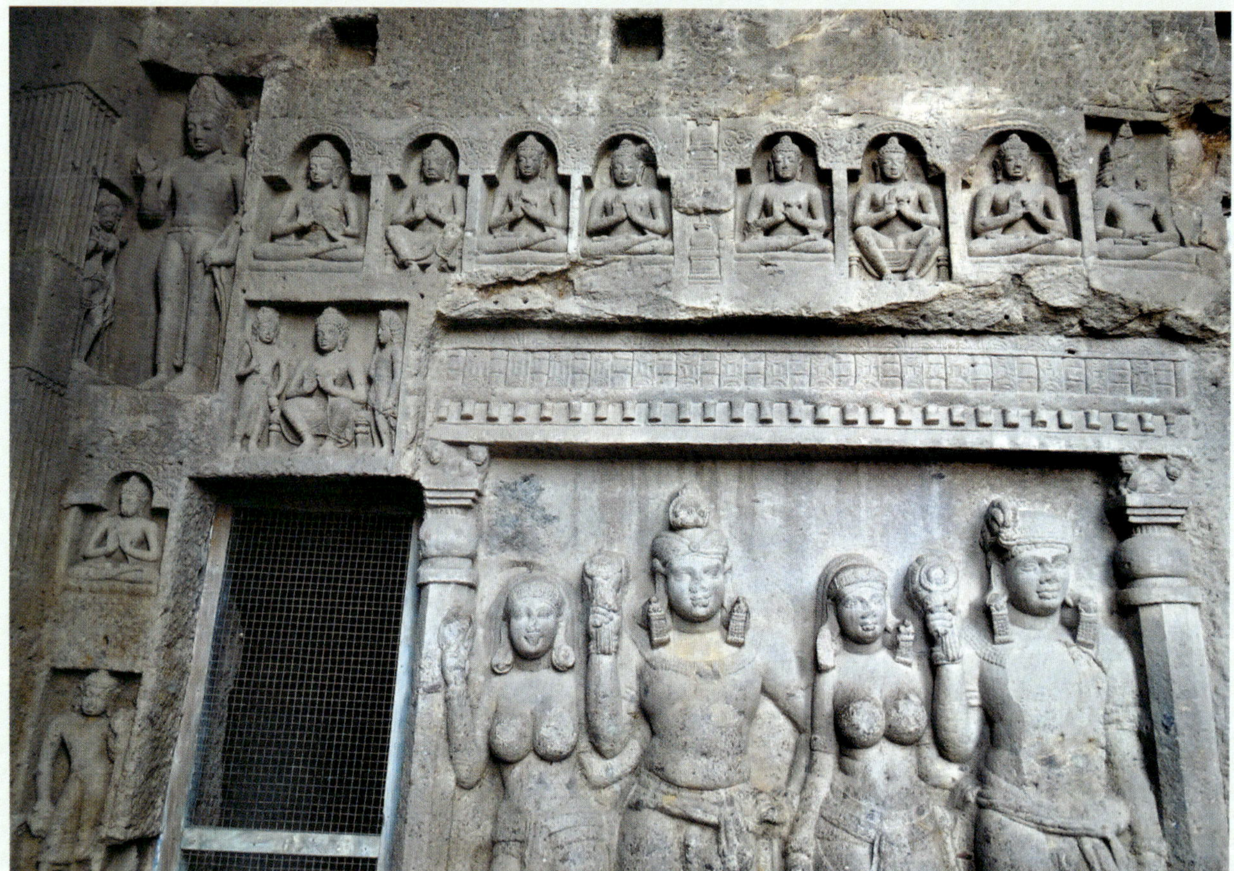

6.121: A relief carving at the Chaitaygriha entrance at Kanheri Caves; upper panel depicting Buddha in different mudras — photograph by Madhukar K Bhagat

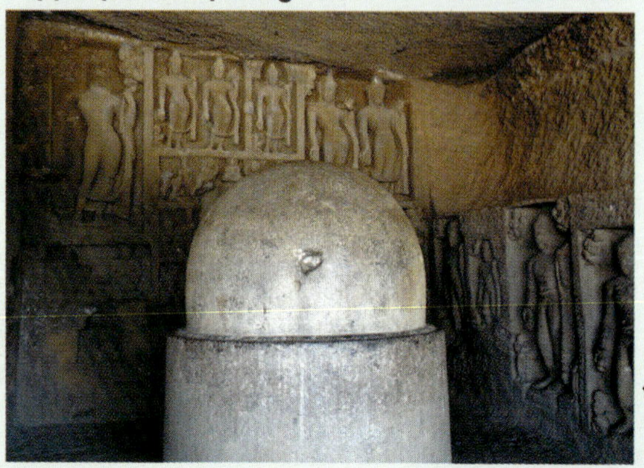

← 6.122: A stupa and relief carving depicting Buddha at Kanheri Caves — photograph by Madhukar K Bhagat

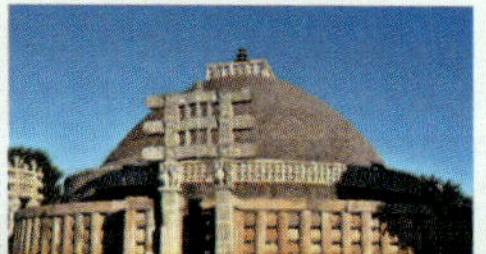

Udayagiri Caves

Udayagiri Caves in Vidisha district of Madhya Pradesh are a set of 20 caves dating from 5th century CE to 11th century which are largely Hindu and a few Jain caves. The most notable of the rock-cut sculptures of these caves is indeed the image of the gigantic Varaha lifting Bhoomi Devi. Besides there are the earliest of the images of Sheshashayi Vishnu and Lord Vishnu as Narasimha. Some of the earliest known images of deities such as Ganesha and Durga as Mahishasuramardini are also found here.

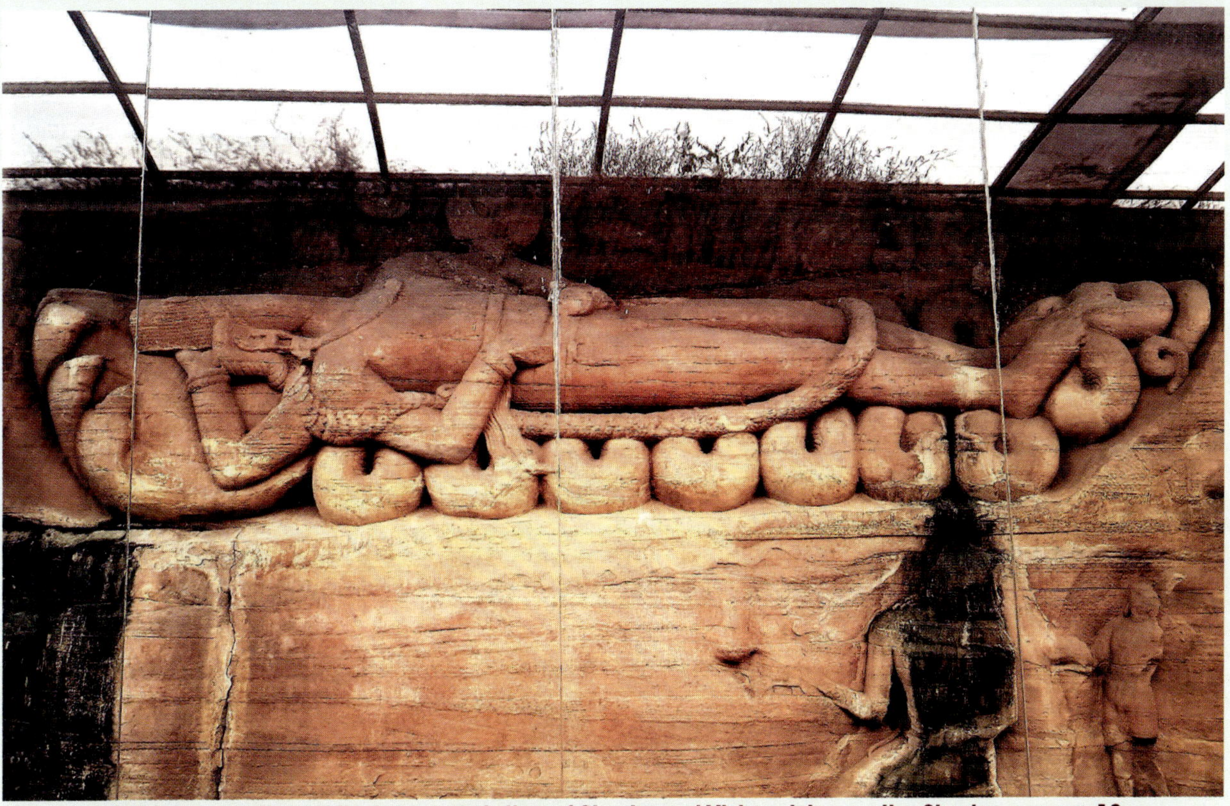

6.123: Among the earliest representation of Sheshasayi Vishnu; lying on the Sheshnag, cave 13 — photograph by Madhukar K Bhagat

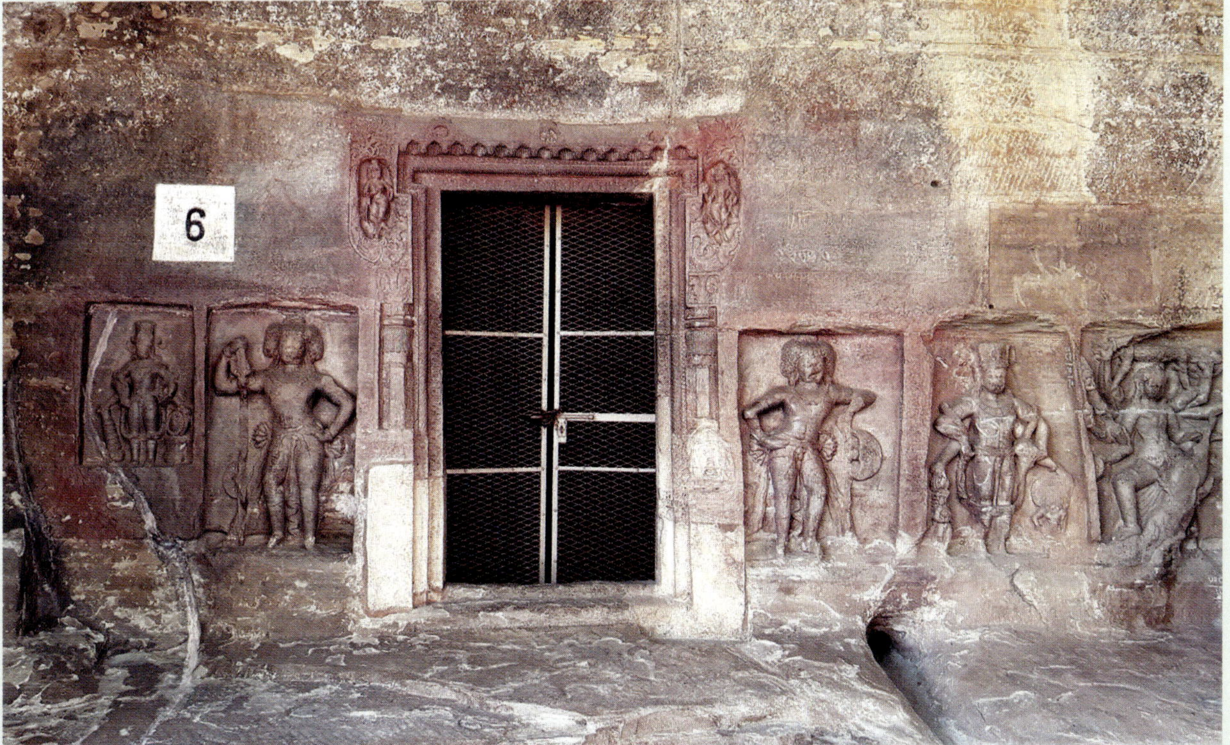

6.124: Various deities in front of cave 16. Guardians flanking the doorway with images of Vishnu and Shiva and Mahishasuramardini is also seen — photograph by Madhukar K Bhagat

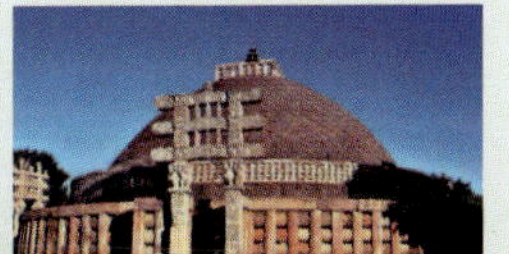

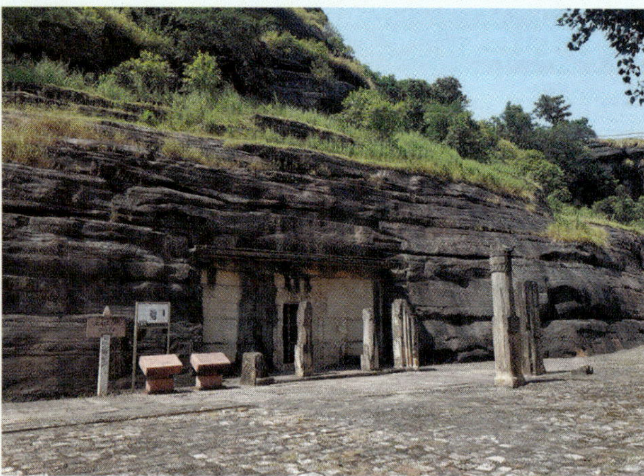

6.125: Entrance to cave 19 at the the bottom of the Udayagiri Hills, also known as the Amrit-manthan cave

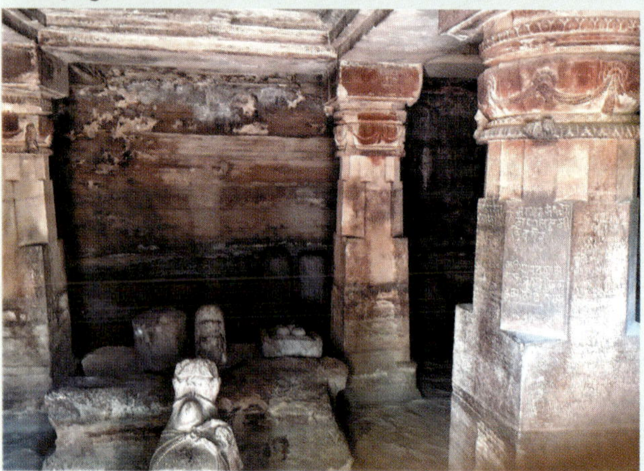

6.126: Nandi bull Shivling and Sanskrit inscription on the pillar in the interior of cave 19

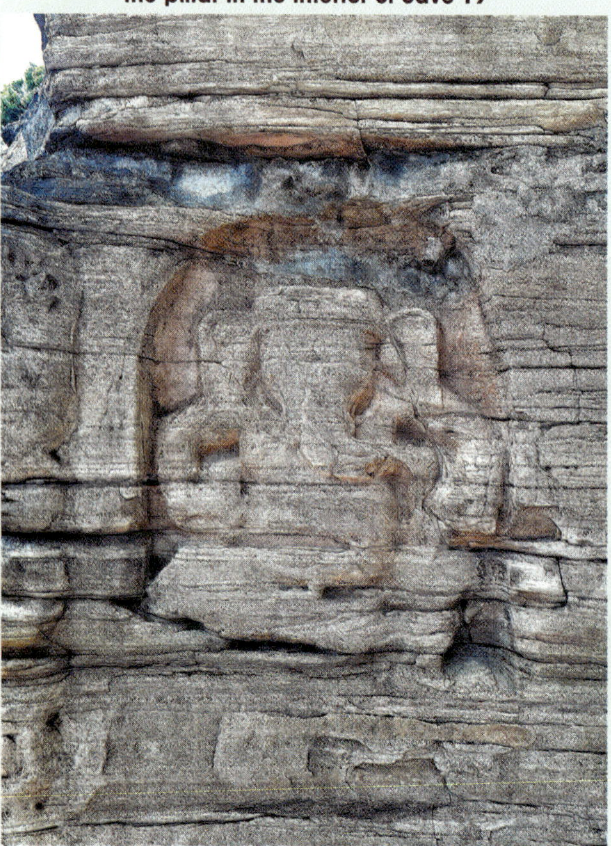

6.127: A relief of lord Ganesha; one of the earliest known images of the deity carved in a niche adjacent to the cave 17

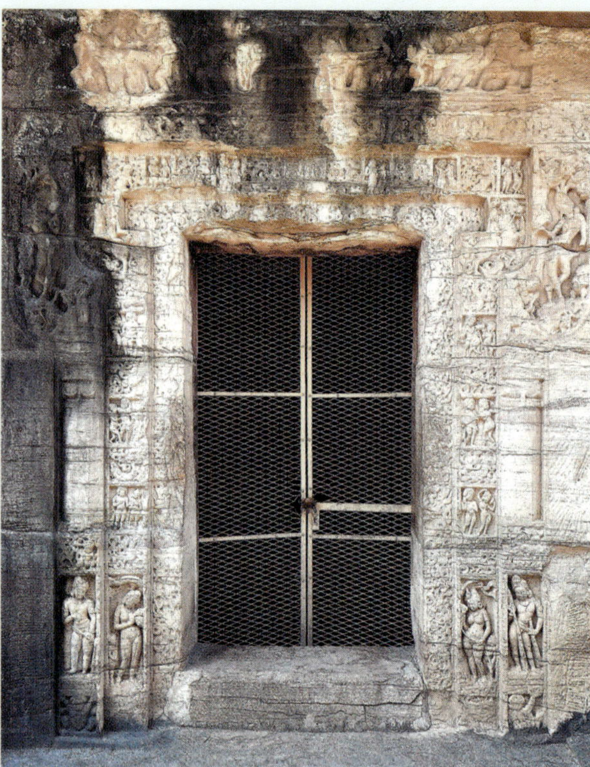

6.128: Carvings on the lintel of the doorway of the cave 19 depict scene of Amrit-manthan, while images of river goddess Ganga and Jamuna also adorn the upper part on the sides of the doorway.

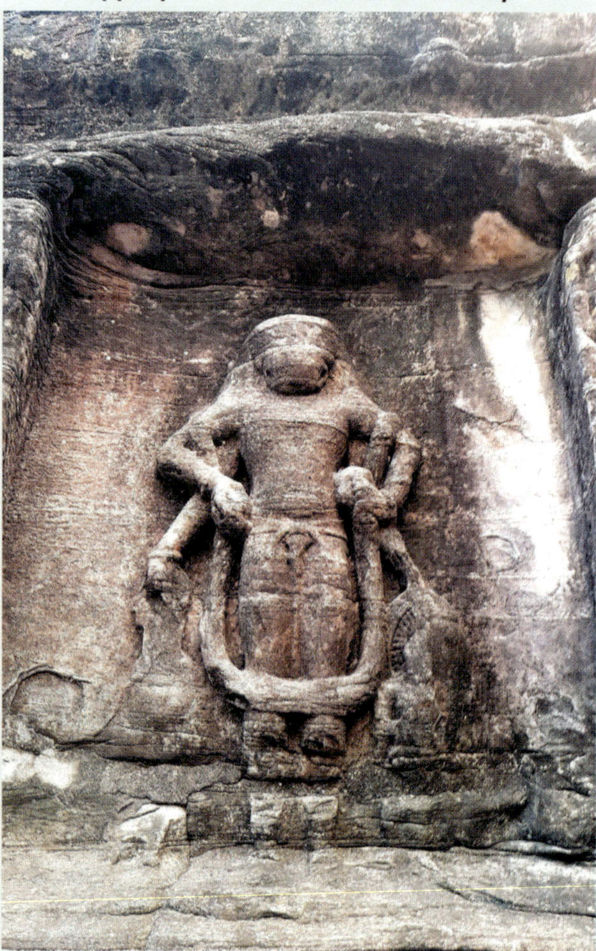

6.129: Lord Vishnu as Narasimha; among the earliest known depiction of Narasimha, in a niche near cave 12

— photographs by Madhukar K Bhagat

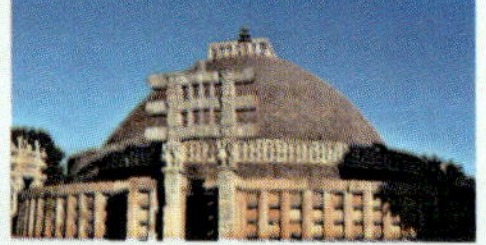

Ajanta Cave Paintings

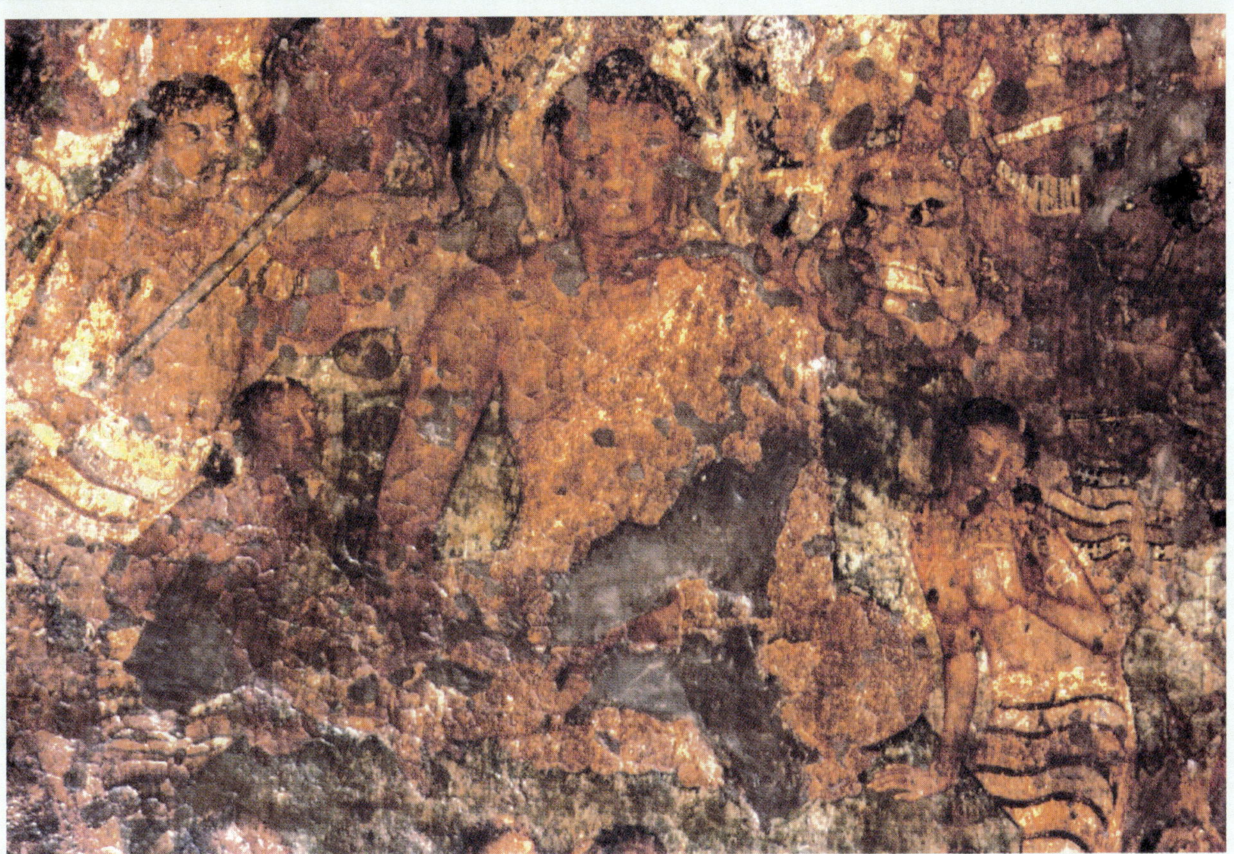

6.130: "Temptations by Mara", a painting in cave 1 depicting a resolute Buddha deep in meditation being threatened by Mara (demon) and his army with violence and also being tempted by his daughters who strike seductive postures.

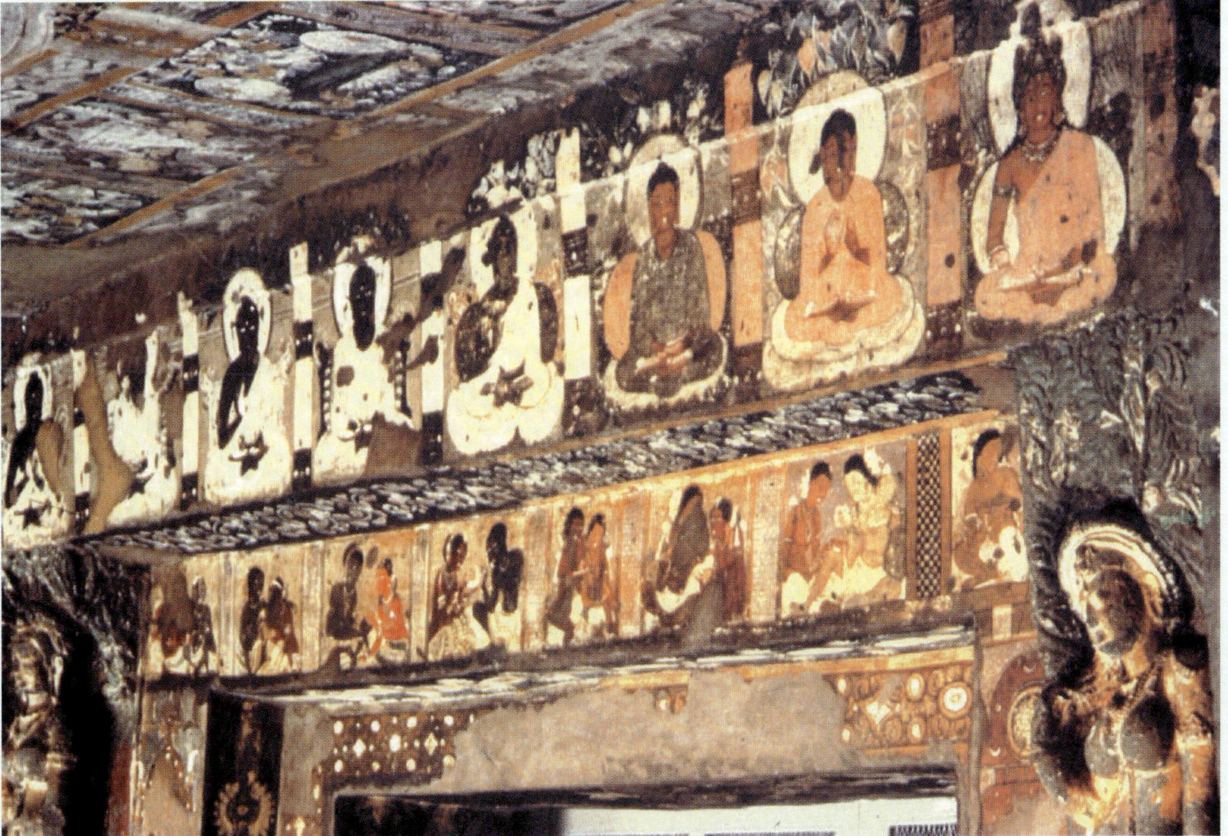

6.131: Painted doorway panel in cave 17 depicting Buddha in different mudras; and Maitreya (future Buddha) in upper panel. Different human figures are depicted in the lower panel with lifesize sculptures flanking the doorway

— photographs by Madhukar K Bhagat

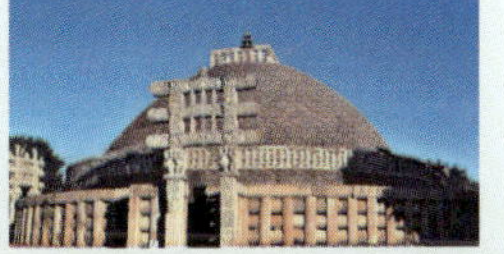

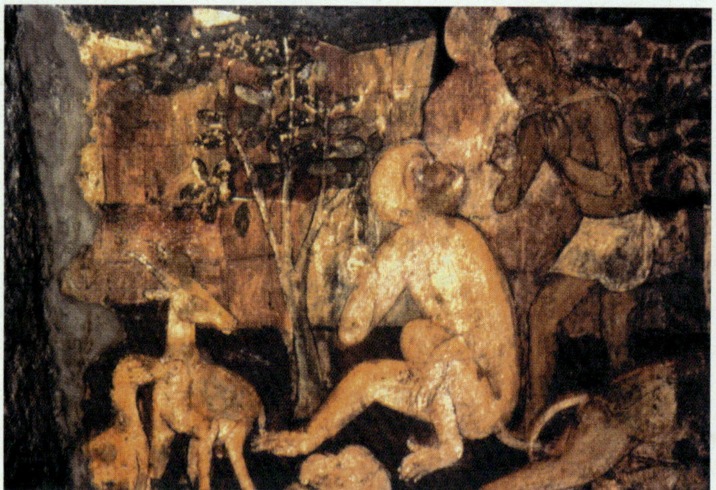

6.132: A scene from Mahakapi Jataka in cave 17. Buddha, in one of his previous births, as the leader of 80000 monkeys, saves them from the attack of a king, by forming a bridge by his body over a stream and allowing the other monkeys to cross over it while laying his life.

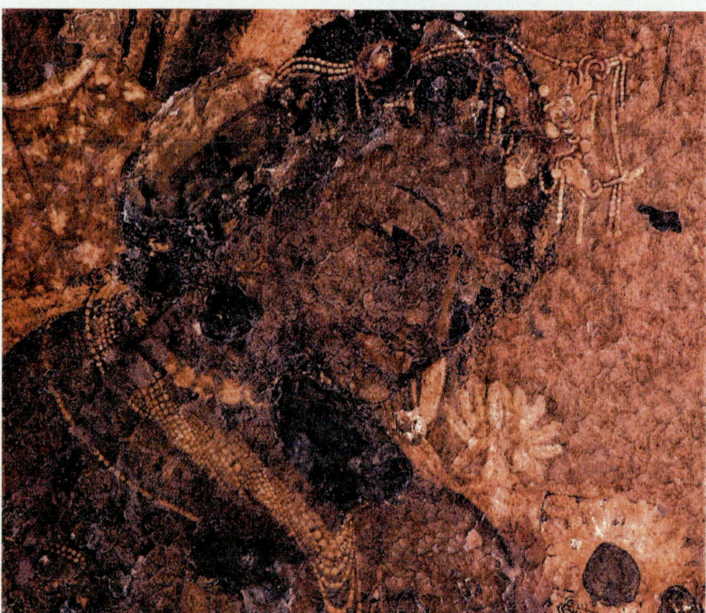

6.133: A female figure in Ajanta cave painting; poignant is the multi-stringed necklace and other jewelleries being adorned and the very fine painting of pearls and other stones

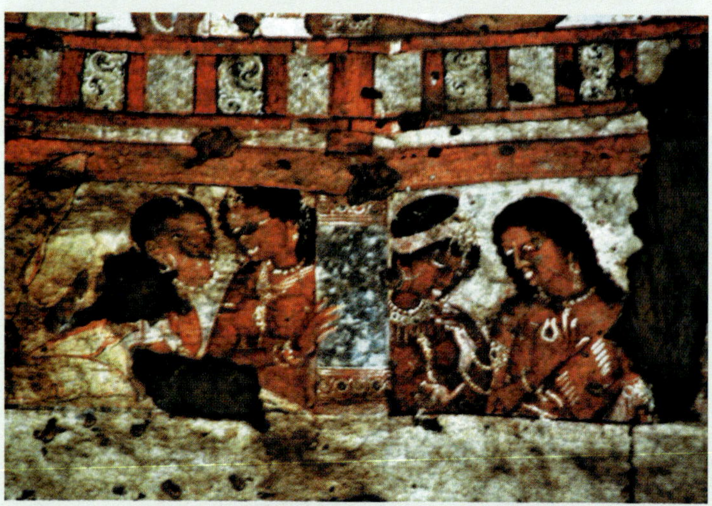

6.134: A palace scene in cave 17 depicting a royal couple in the picture frame

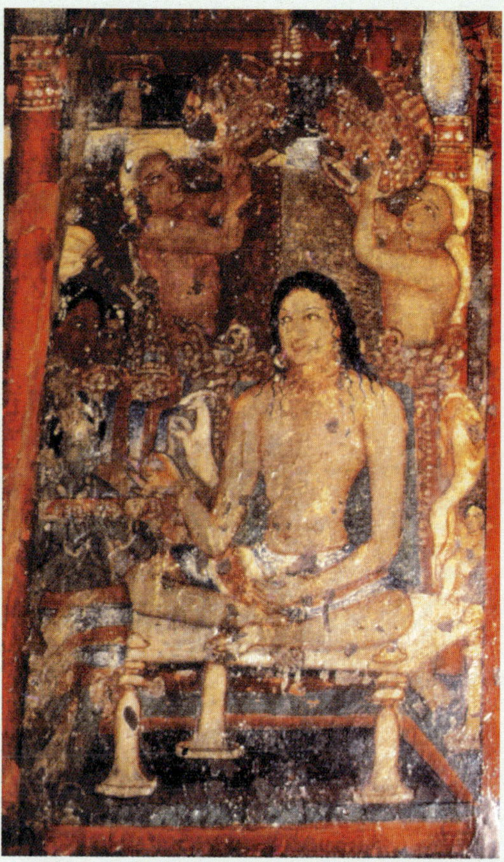

6.135: A painting of a scene from Sibi Jataka depicting ceremonial bath in a palace

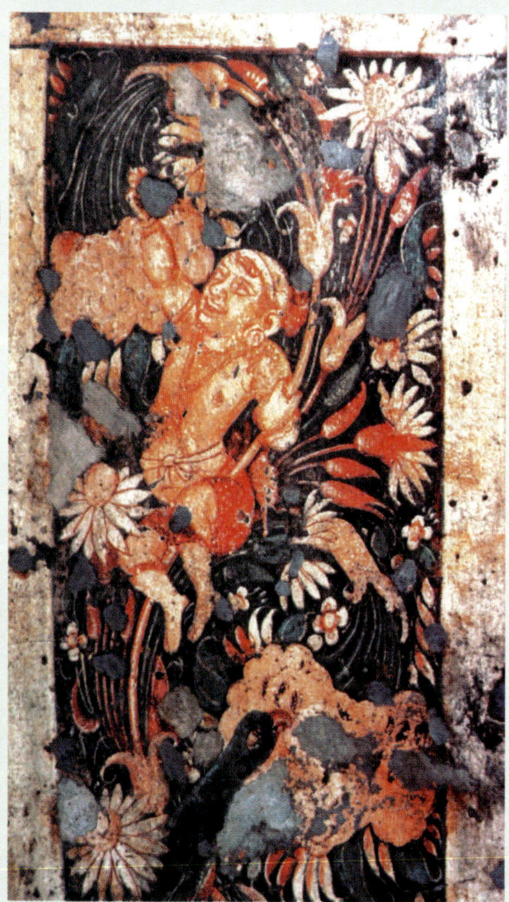

6.136: A painting in the nature of decorative work depicting a human figure akin to a clown, a bird and variety of flowers

— Courtesy, Maharashtra Tourism Development Corporation

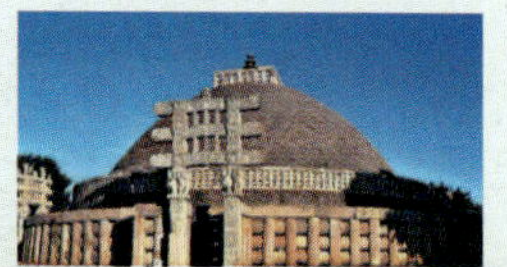

Temples in Ancient & Medieval India

Temple going is for the purification of the soul

Mahatma Gandhi

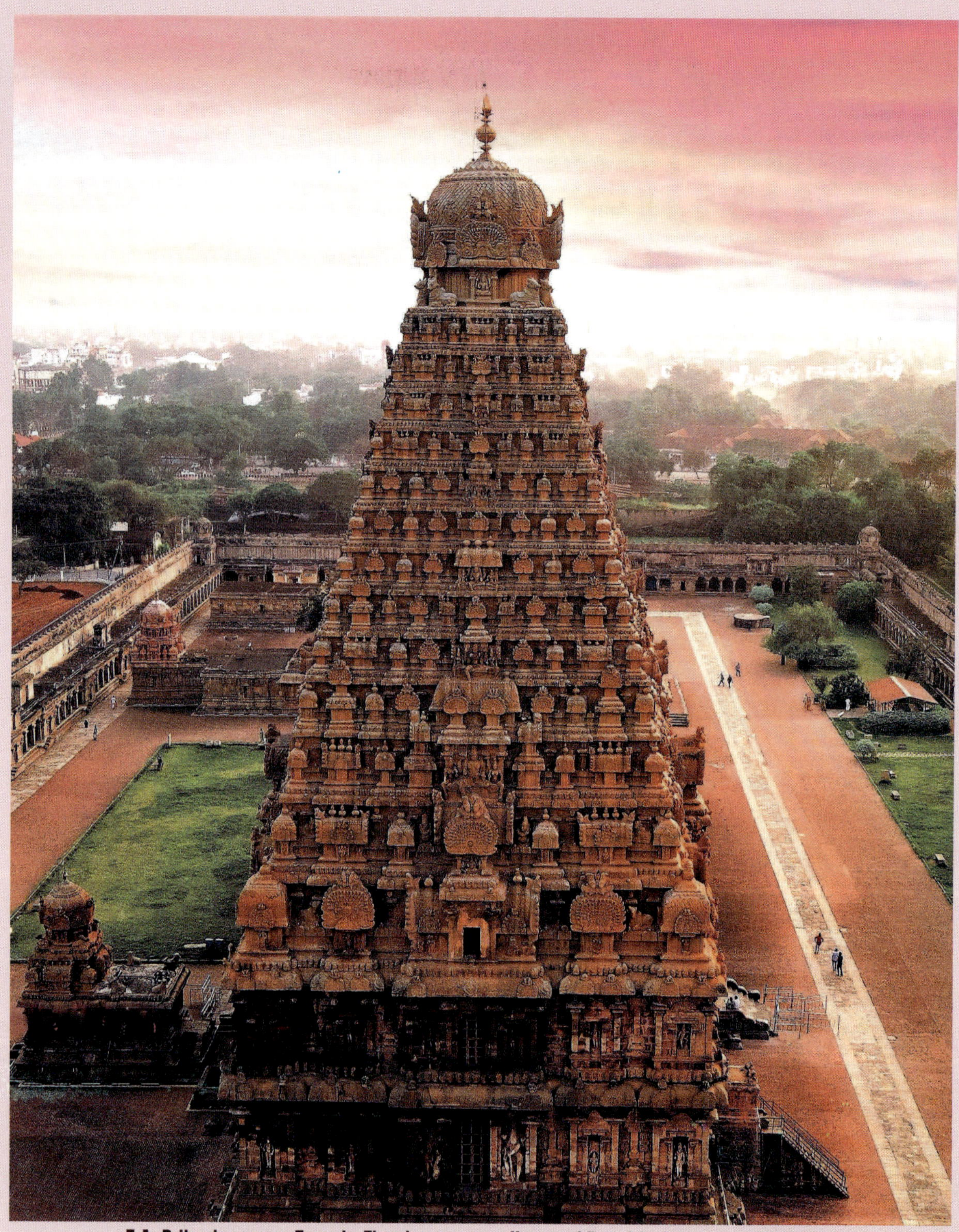

7.1: Brihadeeswara Temple, Thanjavur; an epitome of Dravida temple architecture — Courtesy, Tamil Nadu Tourism Development Corporation

AN INTRODUCTION

The temples of ancient and medieval times epitomize synthesis of the intangible and tangible elements of culture of that era. While the motivating force for many of these towering structures looming large over the centuries has been spirituality and religious faith, they are also the physical embodiment of the art, architecture, engineering and other knowledge elements of a bygone civilization. While the pyramidical *shikharas*, particularly of the Cholas and Ganga dynasties, have bewildered the onlookers with their mammoth structures that were a culmination of architectural and engineering skills, the gateways, walls and pillars of the temples often adorned exquisite carvings, sculptures, friezes from epics and even paintings, thus serving as a canvass for the artistic expression of a society.

Temples were indeed places of worship, but they were also much more. Over the years, many took the shape of large complexes and served as a centre of a host of socio-religious activities, ranging from festivals and fairs, religious and educational discourses, to socio-religious congregation and even occasional resting places for many a traveller. A number of classical Indian dances viz. Manipuri, Bharatanatyam, Odissi and Sattriya had their origins in temples, where they were an artistic means of veneration of the deity. Many of these colossal temples even served as a repository of social wealth, channelising the charity of the state and that of the individual donors and funneling it back in times of social need.

Thus, the temples played an important and at times a pivotal role in the social and cultural life of the people. The practice of building of temples itself is considered to be a predominantly *puranic* tradition with a deep regional influence, which became more popular during the Gupta period. Many of those structures which were made in stone or bricks survive to this day, telling the tale of the architectural magnificence and the crucial role these temples had in the socio-cultural milieu. Though these temples were largely of Hindu faith, many Buddhist and Jain temples were also constructed and are an important source of information about the religious faith, philosophy, art and architecture of these ages.

TEMPLE ARCHITECTURE AND ITS FUNDAMENTAL ELEMENTS

The Hindu temple architecture and sculpture are primarily documented as a subdiscipline in the treatises called the *Vastu Shastra* (the science of building and architecture) and *Shilpa Shastra* (the science of arts and crafts). Over the years, many of these *shastras* survived, albeit with their own regional variations. Most of these treatises further draw upon other fundamental and ancient treatises. The *Brihatsamhita* of Varahamihira (6th century BCE) also describes the science of architecture of temples and other buildings. Among the Puranas, the *Garuda Purana* which is often considered encyclopedic in nature, includes the subject of temple architecture inter-alia a wide range of other subjects. Further, the *Sthapatya Veda*, an upveda associated with the Yajurveda is traditionally attributed to be the origin of architecture. Mythologically, it is Maya (also known as Mamuni Maya or Mayasura), the son of Vishwakarma (the deity of engineering and architecture) who is considered to be the founder of this discipline. He is also considered to be the architect of the city of Indraprastha of the Pandavas.

Architecturally, the Hindu temples primarily had four important features viz, the *garbhagriha*, *shikhara* or *vimana*, *mandapa* and the *vahana*. In all these elements, a sense of proportion and geometry in the form of shapes such as circles, square, or curves was visible and form a key element of the temple architecture. Depending upon the shape and structure of the basic elements, the temples in India can be divided into three distinct categories:

(a) The **Nagara** style or the **North Indian** temple architecture

(b) The **Dravidian** style or the **South Indian** temple architecture

(c) The **Vesara** style containing a **mix of both** the above architectures

The Basic Features

The basic features of temples and the styles of their architecture are recognised as the *garbhagriha*, the *shikhara*/the *vimana*, the *mandapa* and the *vahana*, besides some others.

The *garbhagriha:* Literally meaning the womb-chamber, the *garbhagriha* was the sanctum where the idol of the main deity was located. In earlier times, *garbhagriha* would be like a small cubicle. However, with the passage of time the size of the sanctum grew. The rituals pertaining to the worship of the deity are performed in the *garbhagriha*.

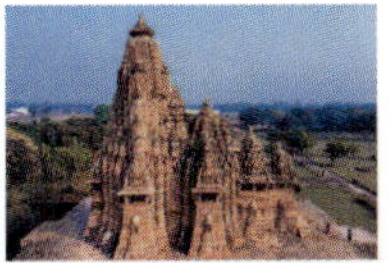

The *shikhara* and the *vimana*: Just above the *garbhagriha*, the temples have a large spire or a tower like structure. In **North Indian temples,** these spires/towers are called ***shikhara*** and they have a curving shape, while in the **South Indian temples** (Dravidian style) these are called ***vimanas***. These have a pyramidical shape and are a prominent feature in many Dravidian temples.

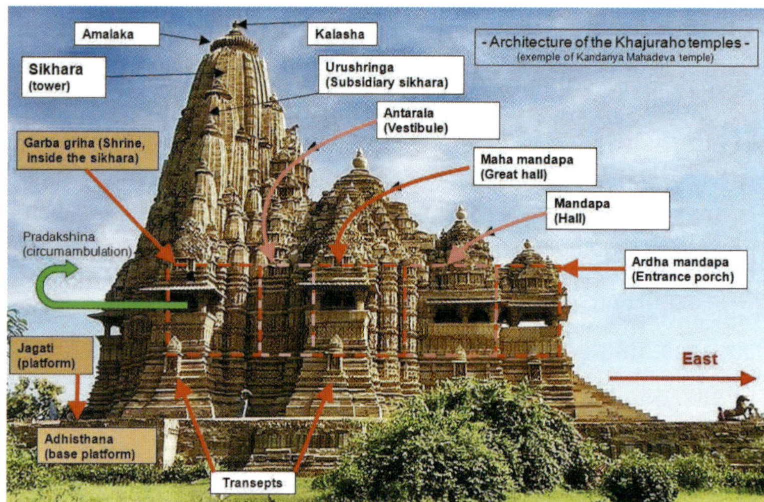

7.2: Basic features of a temple explained through the architecture of the Khajuraho temples — Wikimedia Commons

Mandapa: This refers to the colonnaded hall present before the *garbhagriha*, just inside the entrance of the temple. This provides the space for the congregation of a large number of worshippers. *Mandapa* is a typical feature of temples in Dravidian style and it may be absent in some of the smaller North Indian temples. Instead, they may have a smaller portico or a simple entrance to the temple.

***Vahana*:** The *vahana* refers to the abode of the deity. The statue of the *vahana* was present axially along with a pillar (*dhwaj*) usually in front of the sanctum (*garbhagriha*). Sometimes the *vahana* was also placed atop a pillar (*dhwaj*) in front of the *garbhagriha*.

Apart from the above main features, the temples usually have a circumambulatory path or a *parikama-path* or *pradakshina-path*. These are referred to as ***Nirandhara*** type temples. In some temples, the *pradikshana-path* is absent which are referred to as *Sandhara* type. Some temples could have access from all sides and are referred to as ***Sarvatobhadhra*** type.

Iconography and Sculptures in Temples

The study and identification of the images of the deities found in the temples is referred to as iconography. This is often based on the symbols associated with the deities, the attributes and the mythology associated with the deity. For instance, the most well recognised iconography could be the identification of a *chakra* with lord Vishnu, and a *trishul* or a snake with lord Shiva. Similarly, the U shaped *tilak* (mark on centre of forehead) is worn often by a Vaishnavite, and a *tilak* with three horizontal lines is adorned by a Shaivite.

The *veena* is symbolic of goddess Saraswati, while the lotus is associated with goddess Lakshmi, lord Vishnu and at times even with Lord Brahma. Even the *vahanas* (abode) of the deities are images signifying the deity. Thus, an image of a peacock on a temple wall is a likely association with Kartikeya (Murugan), while that of a lion, with goddess Durga. Some other non-deity specific icons could be the image of *Om* representing the divine, *swastika*– a symbol of auspiciousness etc. These invariably would have regional variations.

The temples in the Gupta period and post Gupta period had some common features in iconography. The sanctum would contain the sculpture/the image of the main deity which could be flanked with those of accompanying deities. For example,

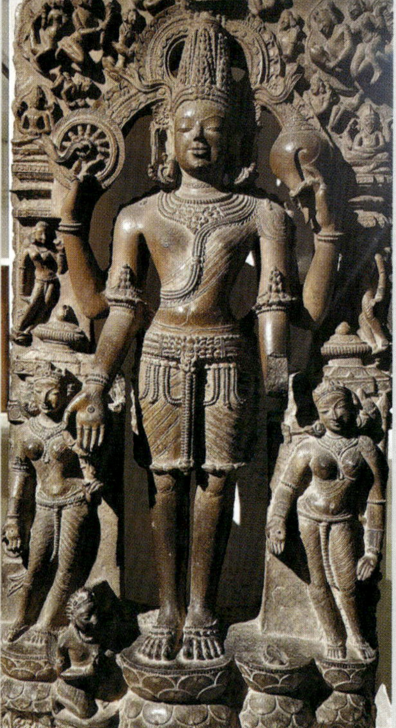

7.3: Vishnu with consorts, holding chakra (right hand) and shankh (left hand); 13th century Eastern Ganga dynasty, Konark; current location National Museum, New Delhi — photograph by Madhukar K Bhagat

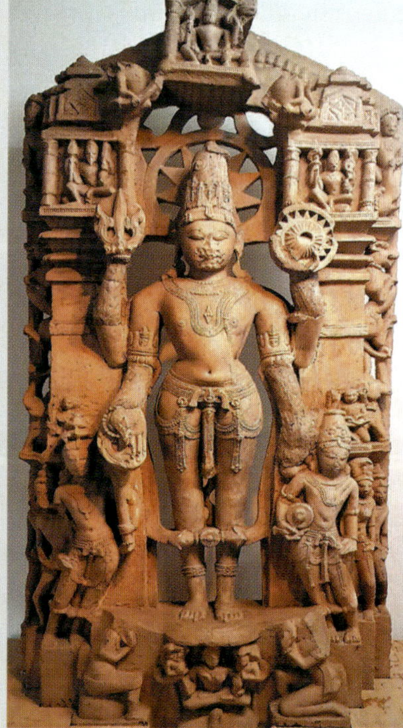

7.4: Harihar, a fusion of Vishnu and Shiva, identifiable by the trishul in the right hand and chakra in the left hand. Sculpture, 11th century CE, Mandsaur, location, State Museum, Bhopal — photograph by Madhukar K Bhagat

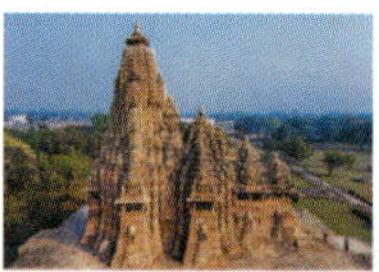

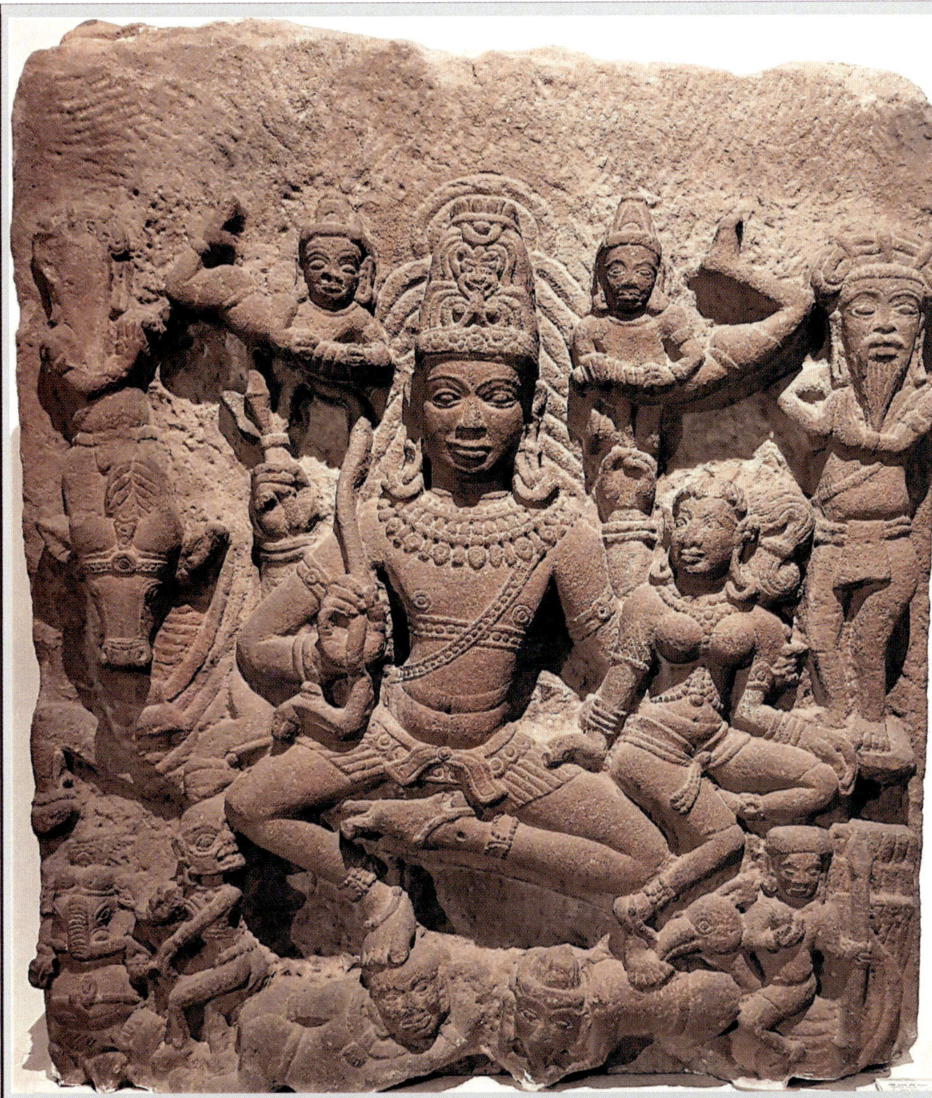

7.5: Shiva, Parvati and family: Shiva is seen seated in the centre with a snake in his right hand. Parvati is on his left. The image of Nandi (bull: vahan of Shiva) is to his right. At the left bottom corner, Kartikeya is seen seated on a peacock with a spear in his hand. Image of Ganesha is seen in the right corner. 10th century CE, Early Western Chalukya, stone relief panel; Location, National Museum, New Delhi — photograph by Madhukar K Bhagat

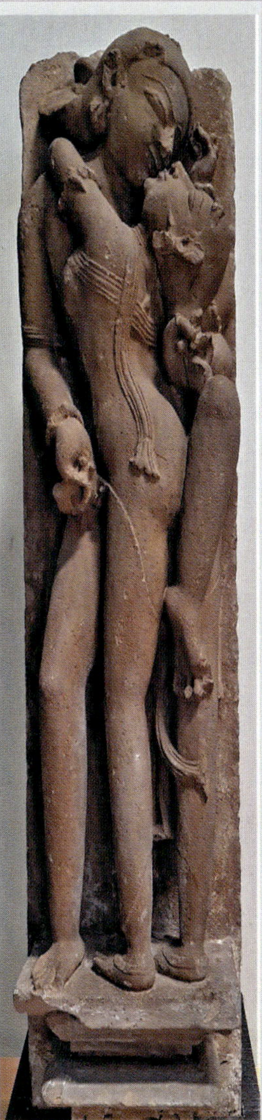

7.6: Sculpture of a Mithuna couple; 12th century CE, Khajuraho, location, State Museum, Bhopal — photograph by Madhukar K Bhagat

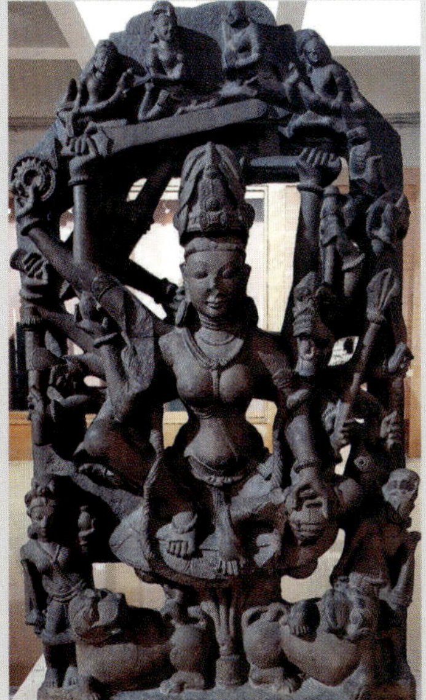

the temple of Lord Shiva could have his statue flanked with that of goddess Parvati, lord Ganesha and lord Kartikeya.

An oft repeated feature was the appearance of the images of goddess Ganga and Jamuna at the entrance of the *garbhagriha* of the Nagara temples, and of *dwarapalas* (gate keepers) at the gateways or *gopurams* of the Dravida temples. The *ashtadikpalas,* or the guardian-deities of the eight directions, would also be located on the four principal directions and the four corners on the outer walls of the *garbhagriha*. This would also be adorned with images of different forms of the main deity, or at times with that of other minor deities. Besides, the images of *yakshas, navagrahas* (the nine auspicious planets) and the erotic images of the *mithunas* (loving couple) may also be variously placed on the outer walls.

7.7: Durga holding different weapons, 11th century CE. Deity distinguishable by the vahan (mount), lion at the bottom. State Museum, Bhopal — photograph by Madhukar K Bhagat

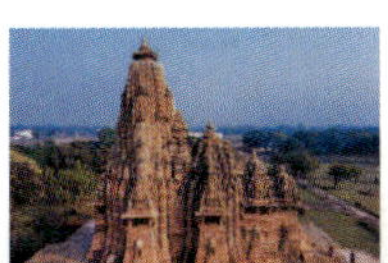

THE NAGARA TEMPLE ARCHITECTURE

The Nagara temple architecture was common in North Indian temples. This category of temple was built on a raised stone platform called *jagati*. A flight of steps would lead to the level of ***garbhagriha***. The *jagati* would have another platform called ***pithas*** over which a smaller platform called ***adhisthana*** could be present and on which the temple *garbhagriha* could be present. The temple would usually not have a boundary wall around it. Further, a gateway at the entrance (called ***gopuram*** in South India) was also absent in the Nagara style temples.

The temples would have a **singular tower** or spire above the *garbhagriha*. The spire resembled the peak of a mountain and hence is called a *shikhara*. However, in later temples, many such spires could be present. The tallest tower would however be present over the *garbhagriha* of the central deity. The *shikharas* could also be crowned (in some temples) by a stone disk called *amalaka*. Over the ***amalaka,*** a ***kalash*** could be present. This would be the topmost point of the temple. Depending on the type and shape of the *shikhara,* the Nagara temples are classified into Latina or *Rekha Prasada* type, or *Phamsana* type, or *Valabhi* type.

Latina or Rekha Prasada Temple

In such type of temples, the *shikhara* has a square base. Its walls slope upwards or curve towards inside so as to meet at a point. It is the simplest type of temple structure. (eg. temples at Khajuraho)

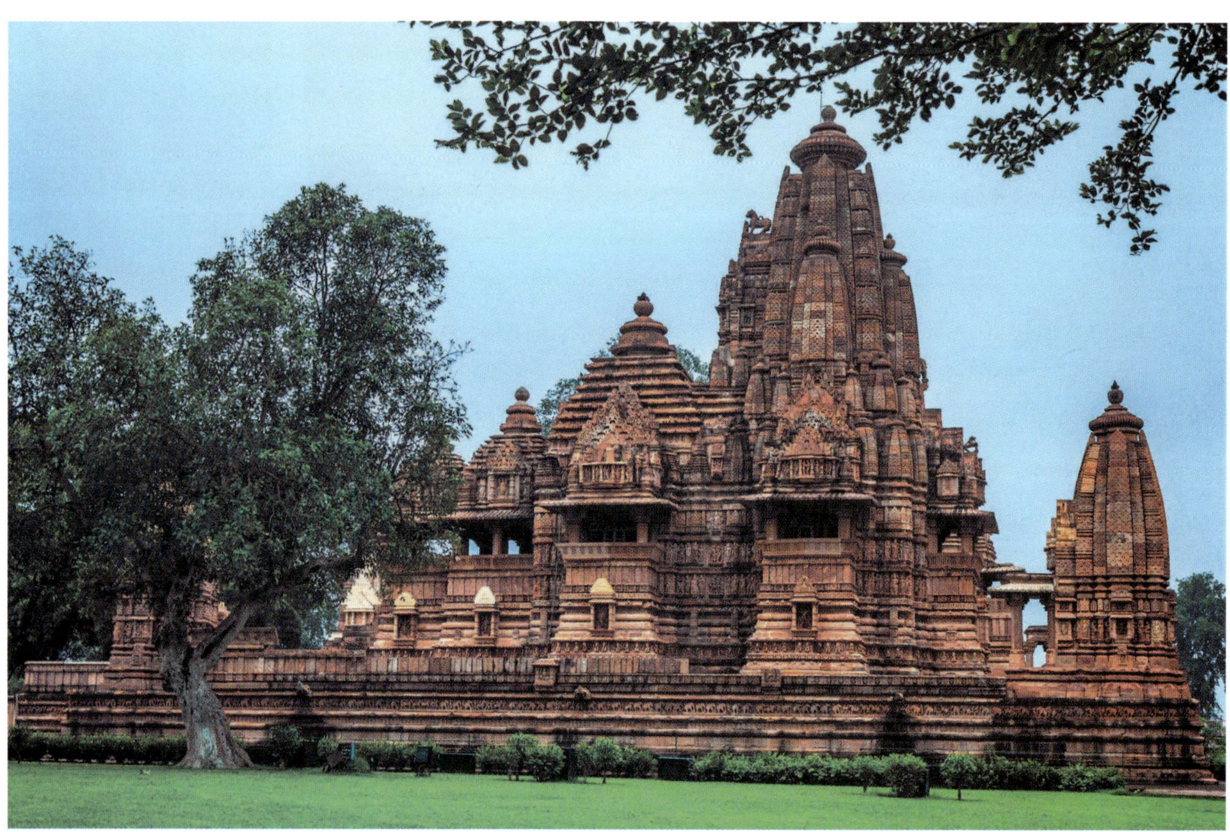

7.8: Lakshmana Temple, Khajuraho, Madhya Pradesh; a glorious example of Nagara temple architecture — Courtesy, Madhya Pradesh Tourism Board

Phamsana Type Temples

In these types of temples, the temple structure and the spire tend to be broader and shorter. The roofs of the temples consist of several slab-like structures. They rise to a single point, but the slope of the temple *shikhara* is not curved but inclined along a straight line. The *mandapa* of Lingaraj Temple at Bhubaneshwar and the Sun Temple at Konark are some prominent examples of this type. (see picture 7.9)

Valabhi Temples

In these types of temples, the ground plan is rectangular. There is a doorway on one of its longer sides. The *shikhara is* semicircular, or resembling a vaulted chamber, the edge of which is rounded. The temples of Nagara type further developed separate traits depending on the region they flourished in. These are broadly categorised as groups of temples in Eastern India, Central India, Western Indian, Southern India and the hills. Each had its own unique regional features.

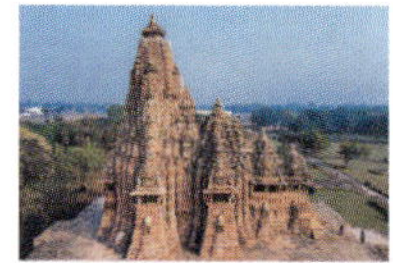

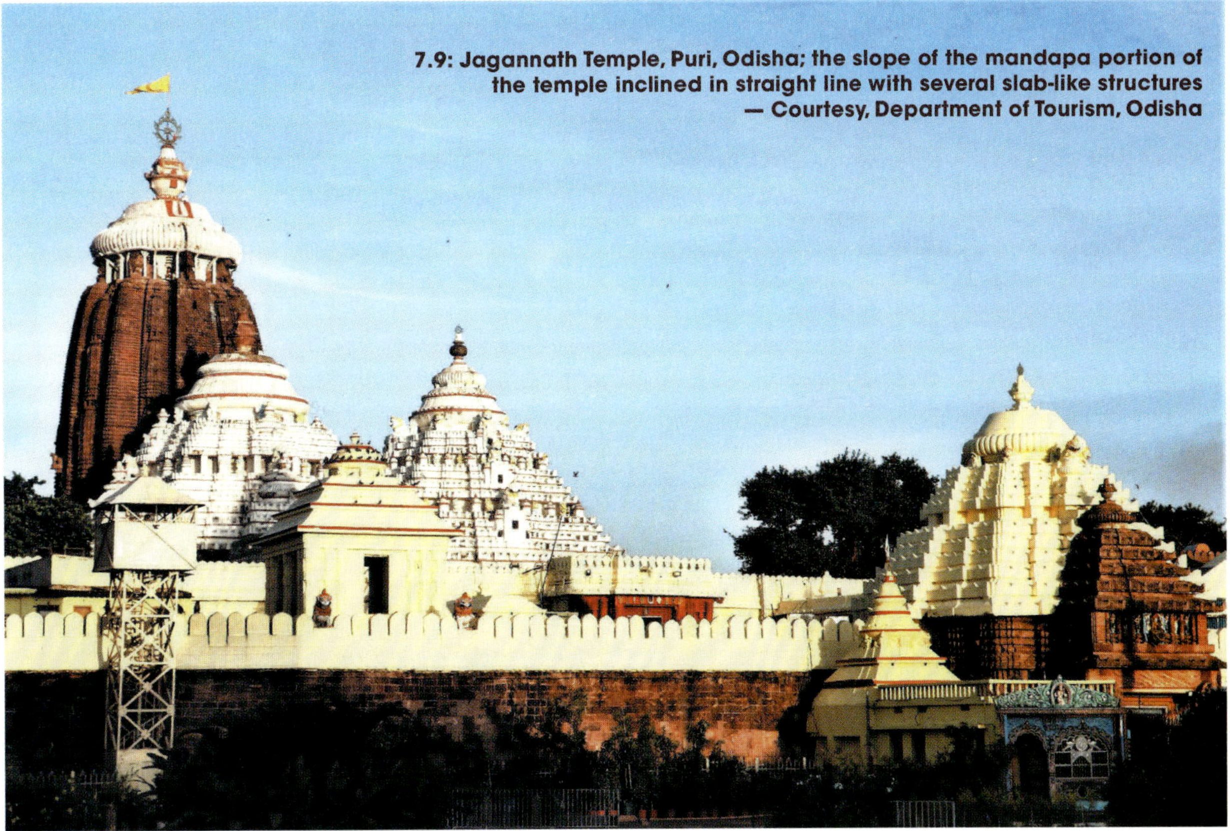

7.9: Jagannath Temple, Puri, Odisha; the slope of the mandapa portion of the temple inclined in straight line with several slab-like structures — Courtesy, Department of Tourism, Odisha

The East Indian Temples

The temples located in the eastern part of India viz. Odisha, Bengal and North East comprise this group. These were largely of the Nagara type and its subdivisions, with some showing strong local influences. The famous temples of Odisha viz. the **Sun Temple in Konark**, **Jagannath Temple in Puri** and the **Lingaraj Temple at Bhubaneswar** bear certain distinct features of the Nagara architecture, viz. the presence of the *garbhagriha*, the tall *shikhara* over it, the *mandapa* etc. But these also had some distinct features. The *shikhara* in these temples *is* seen to be composed of several slabs placed one over the other and is called *deula*. It proceeds almost vertically until the top, where it curves inwards sharply to the point of the *amalaka*. Thus, these groups of temples in Odisha are a distinct sub category of the Nagara type and its architecture is classified locally as *rekhapida*, *pidhadeul* and *khakra*.

In Bengal, the terracotta temples at Bishnupur and **Siddheshwar Mahadev** temples in Burdwan are some fine examples of East Indian temple architecture. These temples are representative of the Pala style of architecture which was the ruling dynasty of this region (8th to 11th century CE) and great patrons of art and architecture. Another important East Indian temple is the Da Parbatia Temple near Tezpur and Sibsagar Temple in Assam. The temples of this region bore the influences of the Pala style of architecture and later evolved into a local Ahom style.

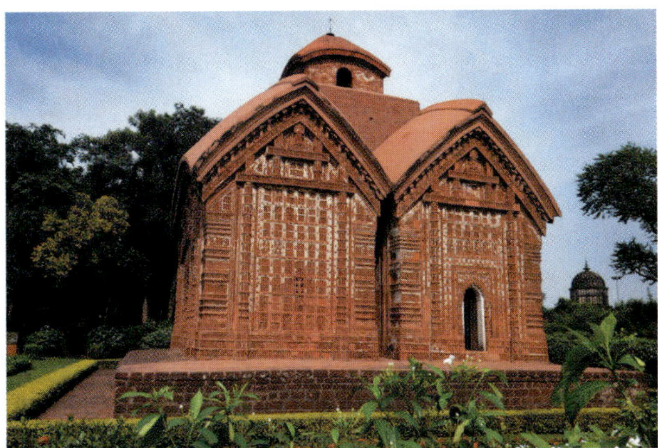

7.10: Jor Bangla Temple, Bishnupur, West Bengal: an example of Eastern India's medieval terracotta temple with poignant curved roof — Courtesy, Department of Tourism, West Bengal

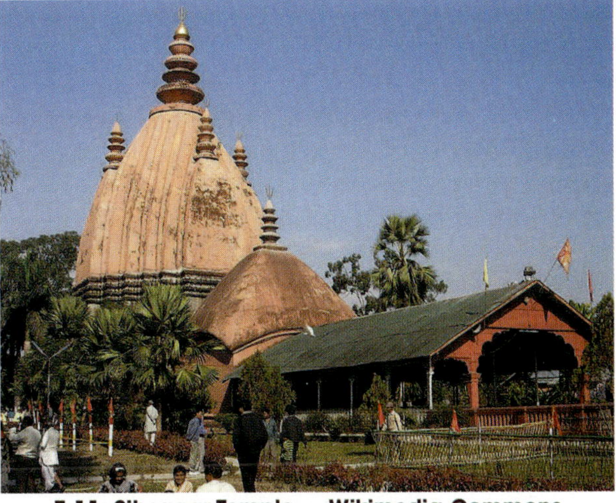

7.11: Sibsagar Temple — Wikimedia Commons

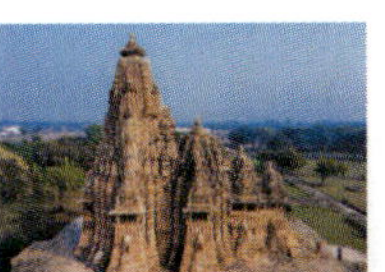

A Glimpse of Important Temples in Eastern India

The Sun Temple at Konark, Odisha

Located in the Eastern coast of India, this temple is dedicated to the Sun god. It is fashioned in the form of a gigantic **chariot of Sun god**, (Surya) **drawn by seven horses.** The temple was built by King Narasimha Deva-I of East Ganga Dynasty in 1255 CE and has a typical Odisha or Kalinga style architecture with Nagara-Phamsana *shikhara*. The traditional elements of Indian temple architecture viz, a square plan with layout of structures, sculptures and relief in geometrical pattern of square and circle can be seen here. Presently, the ruins of the temple, particularly the *mandapa* (also locally called as *Jagmohana*) survives, while the long *shikhara* (locally called *deula*) which was over 70m tall, is believed to have fallen in the 19th century (around 1837).

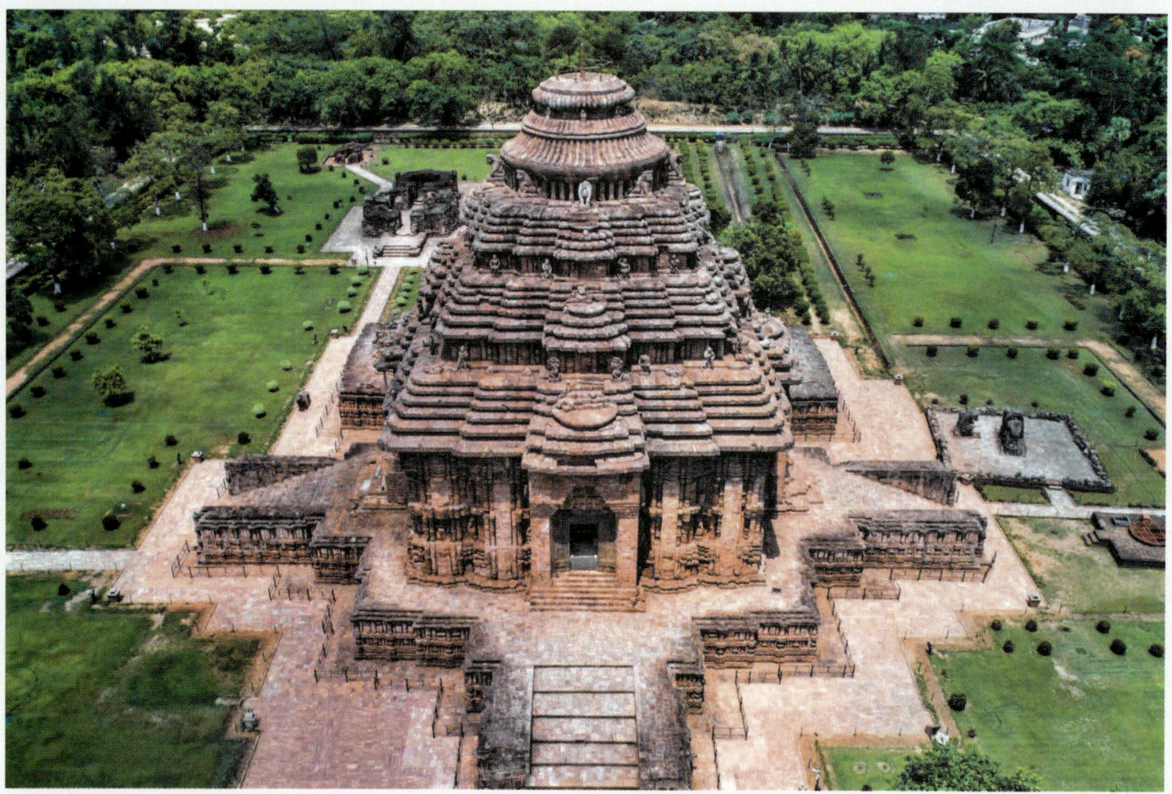

7.12: Sun Temple, Konark, Odisha; a typical Odisha or Kalinga style architecture; an aerial view depicting the geometrical layout of plan — Courtesy, Department of Tourism, Odisha

The entire temple is set on a high base and oriented towards the east so that the first rays of the Sun enter the main entrance. In fact, the whole temple structure is planned to appear as a huge processional chariot with **12 pairs of stone wheels**. Each wheel has a diameter of 9 feet, 9 inches and has eight spokes. These wheels are so designed so as to act as sundials which can calculate time to the accuracy of a minute. The twelve pairs of wheels symbolise the twelve months of a year with each month having two parts *Shukla paksha* and *Krishna paksha* (waxing and waning phases). The eight spokes represent the eight parts of the day. The seven horses pulling the chariot are said to be symbolic of the seven meters of Sanskrit prosody in which the ancient texts were composed (*Gayatri, Brihati, Ushnik, Jagati, Trishtubha, Anushtubha,* and *Pankti*). On the southern wall, a massive structure of Surya (sun god) is present which is carved in green stone.

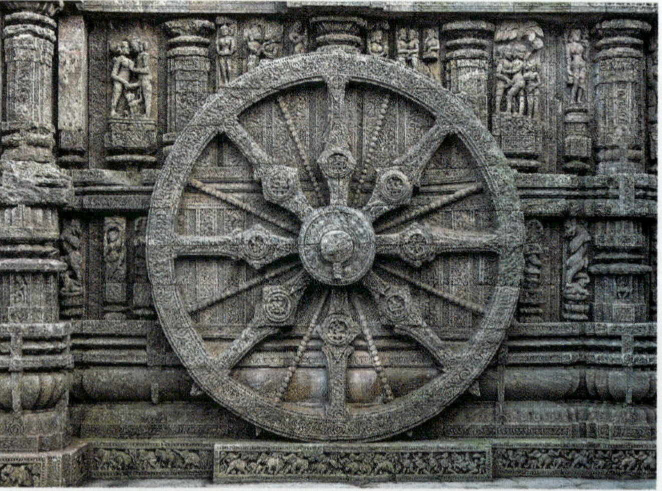

7.13: A wheel of the stone chariot engraved in the walls of the temple having 12 pair of wheels, each acting as a sundial and calculating time to the accuracy of a minute — Wikimedia Commons

The interior walls and pillars have numerous elaborate carvings in stone structures with minute detailing work. These represent a variety of images taken from daily life, animals, birds, aquatic life, friezes from scriptures and even *apsaras*, while some are erotic images of *mithunas*. The Sun Temple is recognized as a **UNESCO World Heritage Site**.

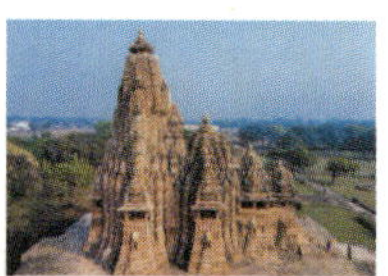

Lingaraja Temple (Bhubaneswar)

Built in the 11th century CE by king Yayati Keshri of Somavansh, it is the **largest temple of Odisha**. Some parts of this temple are believed to be built in around 7th century CE. The temple is dedicated to lord Shiva, and like the Konark temple, is east facing. The temple has **Kalinga style architecture**, with its *shikhara* of Nagara Phamsana type (a pyramidical structure with square base and sloping inwards in a straight line). It is built in Deula style and has four components, the *vimana* (which contains the *garbhagriha*), *jagmohana* (which is the assembly hall), *nata-mandir* (hall for dance and festivals), and *bhoga-mandapa* (hall of offerings).The *bhoga-mandir* hall has a pyramidical roof of several horizontal layers and has on top an inverted bell and *kalasa*. The entire temple is built in sandstone and laterite.

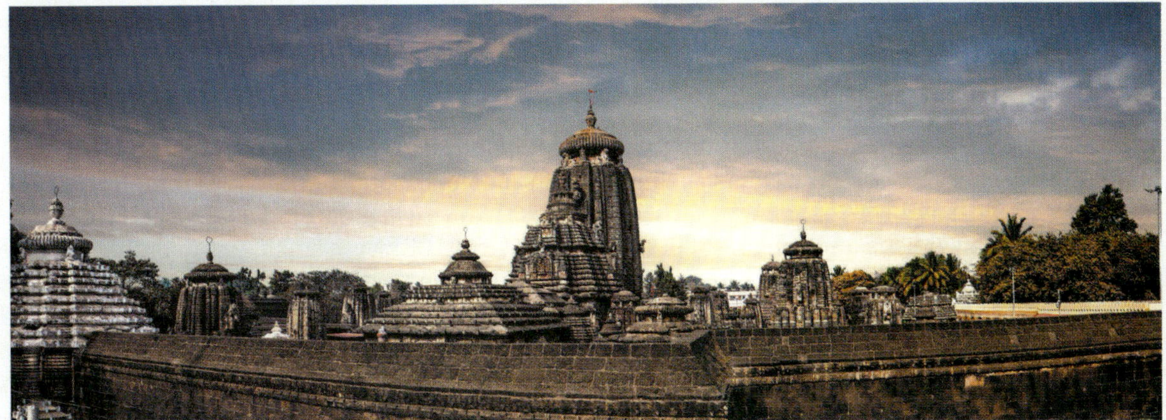

7.14: A panoramic view of the Lingaraj Temple Bhubaneshwar, Odisha — Courtesy, Department of Tourism, Odisha

Jagannath Temple at Puri

Located on the eastern coast of India at Puri in Odisha, the temple is dedicated to Lord Jagannath (incarnation of Lord Vishnu). The temple was constructed in the 12th century CE by Anantavarman Chodagangadeva of Eastern Ganga dynasty**.** The large temple complex contains over 120 temples and shrines. The main temple has four distinct structures, *Deula* (*shikhara*), *garbhagriha*, *mukhashala* (frontal porch), *nata-mandir*, and *bhoga mandapa*. The temple deities are unique; they are made of wood which is replaced every 12th year. It is one of the four *dhamas* (four divine sites) associated with the Hindu faith and is associated with the famous **Ratha Yatra** of Lord Jagannath, Balabhadhra and Subhadra, where the chariot procession brings out the temple deities in display before the people. Thus, the deity here is not only *achala* (immovable) but *chala* (movable).

Sivasagar Sivadol Temple in Sibsagar district, Assam

The temple complex was built in **1734** by the queen of the Ahom king Swargdeo Siba Singha. It comprises a group of three temples **Sivadol, Vishnudol,** and **Devidol,** (dedicated to lord Shiva, lord Vishnu and goddess Durga respectively) which are located on the banks of the Sivasagar tank. The temple has **Ahom** style of architecture. The spire of Sivadol is nearly 104 feet high and is crowned with eight feet high golden dome. The temple is made of stone and bricks. The Ahom style is also seen in Kamakhya Temple (of the 17th century) near Guwahati (Assam).

Terracota Temples of Bishnupur (Bankura district), West Bengal

These are a group of temples built by different kings of the Malla dynasty (in 17th and 18th century)**,** each having distinct features. The **Rasmancha Temple** of this group built in1600 CE is dedicated to Radha-Krishna. It has an unusually long

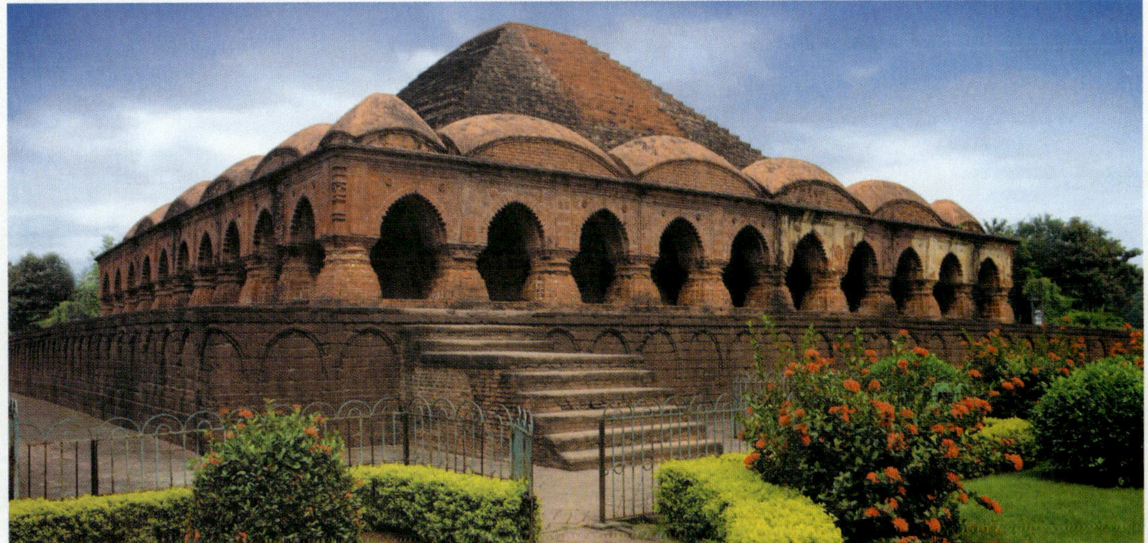

7.15: Rasmancha Temple, Bishnupur, West Bengal, a terracotta temple with pyramidical shikhar and hut-shaped curved roof turrets — Courtesy, Department of Tourism, West Bengal

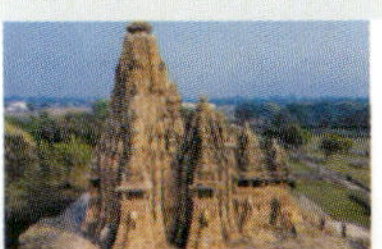

pyramid shaped *shikhara*, with a number of adjoining turrets which are hut shaped. **The Jor Bangla** Temple (built in1655) dedicated to Lord Krishna, has *chala* style of Bengal architecture. It has beautiful terracotta carvings set in walls and roofs with the shape of the roof being curving and sloping, quite unlike other temples. **The Pancha Ratna Temple** dedicated to Lord Krishna, has a low square plinth. It has an ambulatory pathway with a porch opened by three arches. It has five *shikharas*, the central *shikhara* being octagonal and the remaining being square.

Lakshmana Temple (Sirpur), Chhattisgarh: Built nearly 1400 years ago in the 7th century CE, the temple is dedicated to Lord Vishnu. Although a large part of it is damaged, yet its sanctum tower above it and the entrance door survive. The Lakshmana Temple is an excellent example of a **brick temple** and is known for its unique symmetry and exquisite carvings on pillars. Images of Vishnu on *seshnag* (*anantashaya* Vishnu) and those from Krishnaleela from the *Bhagavata Purana* are found on its walls and pillars. Further, the images of the 10 *avataras* of lord Vishnu are also found. The site also has a number of Buddhist structures, including *viharas* and statues of Buddha and Mahavira.

Central Indian Temples

This group comprises temples found in the present-day region of Uttar Pradesh, Madhya Pradesh and Rajasthan. They share a common trait viz., being built of sandstone. Some of the oldest temples belonging to the Gupta period have been found here, particularly those in Madhya Pradesh. These initial temples such as those found near Vidisha and Sanchi (built around 5th century CE) were small, with porch like modest mandapas. But later period temples display some intricate sculpture and grand designs. Examples of some of the more evolved and complex temples of this region are the **Dashavatara** Temple developed during the Gupta era, and the Khajuraho temples built under the Chandela rulers. These were marked by their ornate carvings. The latter is known for the many erotic sculptures on their walls, besides its grand construction. The **Dashavatara temple** is of **Panchaytana** style where there is a main shrine at the centre and four other smaller shrines at the four corners (making a total of five shrines).

A Glimpse of Important Temples in Central India

Khajuraho Temples, Madhya Pradesh

Comprising some of the grandest temples of Central India, the Khajuraho group of temples were built by the **Chandela kings** over a thousand years ago (950 CE to 1050 CE). Out of over 85 temples believed to have been built, nearly 25 survive to this day. The temple complex comprises a number of Hindu and Jain temples, the most famous being the **Lakshmana Temple** (dedicated to Lord Vishnu), **Kandariya Mahadev Temple** (dedicated to Lord Shiva), the **Chausath Yogini Temple,** and the **Parshvanatha Jain temple.**

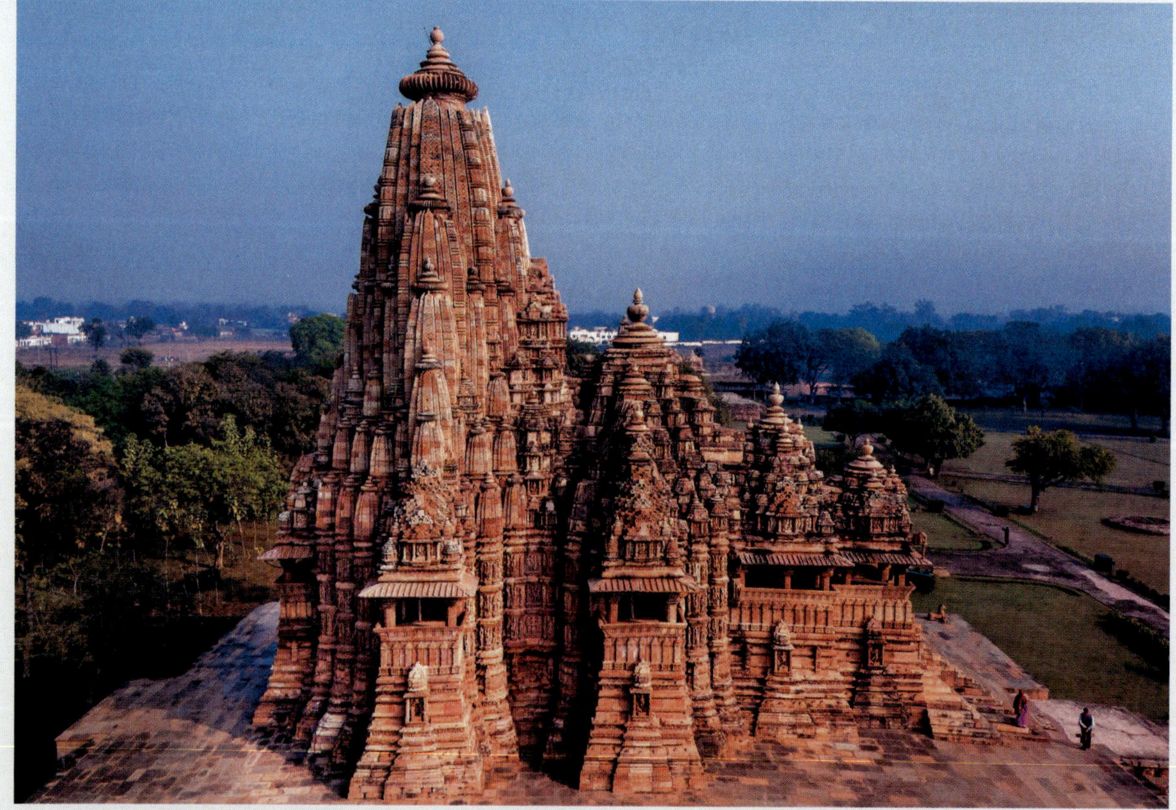

7.16: Kandariya Mahadev Temple, Khajuraho, Madhya Pradesh; highly noticeable is the intricate architecture of its multiple level shikhars — Courtesy, Madhya Pradesh Tourism Board

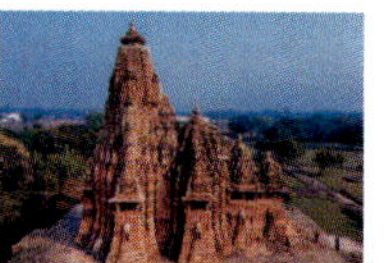

These temples are of typical Nagara style of architecture and mark the coming of age of the temple architecture, construction and sculpture. The Lakshmana temple is placed on a high platform and has five *shikharas* (Panchayatana style), with four smaller temples in the corners. All the *shikharas* rise high and are topped with a fluted disc, *amalaka* and a *kalasha*. The walls are highly decorated with numerous sculptures which are highly stylized and almost emerging in full relief (as if cut away from the adjoining stone).

Although the image of *mithunas* are generally seen in many temples, the presence of erotic carvings and sculptures on the outer and inner walls are a unique feature of these temples. In the totality of sculptures depicted in these temples, the sensuous images are albeit, a small fraction, which depict many scenes from the daily lives to even mythical stories etc. However, the presence of these erotic images signifies an equal importance attached to *kama* in human experience, along with *artha, dharma* and *moksha*. In cosmological view, these temples themselves were emblematic of the mythical mountain at the core of the cosmological realm.

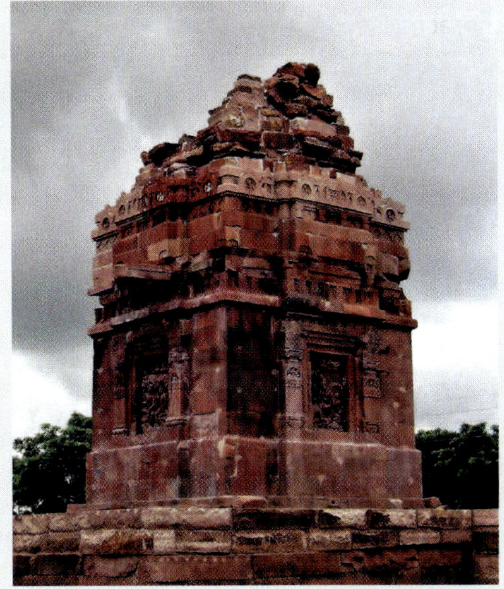

7.17: Dashavatara Temple, Deogarh, Uttar Pradesh — Courtesy, Directorate of Uttar Pradesh Tourism

The Khajuraho temple complex is recognised as a **UNESCO** World Heritage Site.

Dashavatara Temple (Deogarh District), UP

It is among the **earliest Hindu temples** which was built in the late Gupta period (in around 500 CE) and is thus a millennium and a half old. The temple is dedicated to Lord Vishnu and has the famous sculpture of **Sheshasayi Vishnu (**lord Vishnu in the reclining posture). Other important images are that of **Nara-Narayana**, and **Gajendra Moksha Vishnu.** The temple is a typical example of the Nagar temple with Panchayatana style. The main shrine has a tall *shikhara*. At the corners are also found four subsidiary shines. Architecturally, it is also a prototype of *sarvatobhadra* temple, i.e. access to temple is from all sides.

Nachna Kuthara Temple (Panna District) Madhya Pradesh

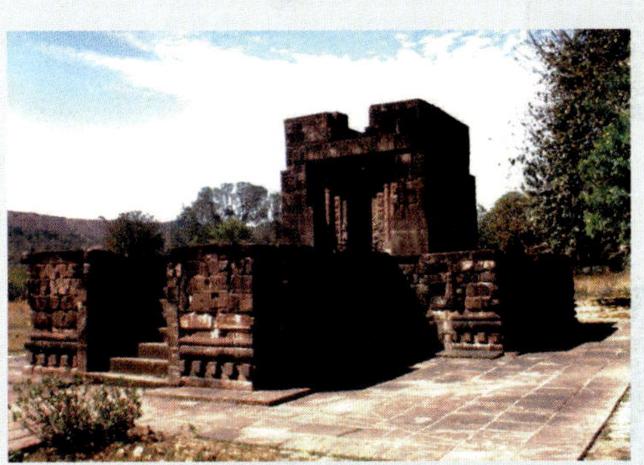

7.18: Nachna Parvati Temple — Wikimedia Commons

It is among the earliest temple structures of ancient India. The site is famous for two temples, the **Chaturmukhalinga Temple** which has a shivalinga with four faces, and a **Parvati Temple.** The latter is the older of the two, and is considered by temple experts to be built around mid-5th century CE, while the Chaturmukhalinga Temple is dated to the 9th century CE. Both the temples are built in stone. The Parvati Temple is considered to be a prototype of the North Indian temples (Nagara temples). It is built on a raised platform (*jagati*), has walls over a metre thick, with a *garbhagriha* which is almost cubical, and is considered to have had a flat roof, and faces west towards the setting sun. The doorway has images of Ganga (with river crocodile) and Yamuna (with river turtle), besides that of two *Shaiva dvarapalas* holding trident. Thus, the temple has some unique and some archetypal features.

The Temples in Western India

The temples of western India comprise those found in Rajasthan, Gujarat and parts of Maharashtra and western Madhya Pradesh. Broadly following the post Gupta architectural style, they also show strong local influences, particularly in the sculpture and material used. While sandstone has been a preferred material

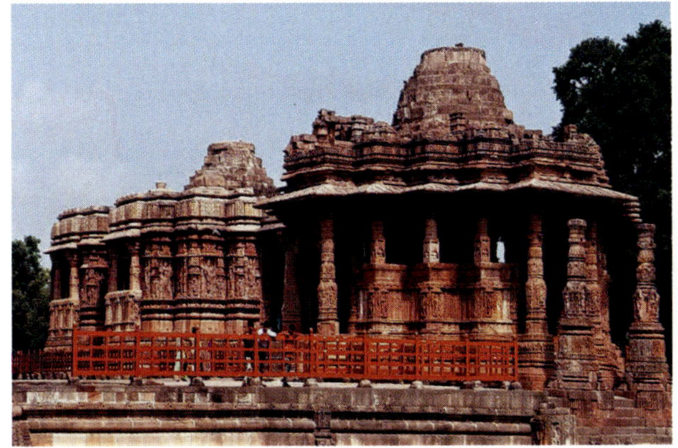

7.19: The Sun Temple, Modhera; sabhamandap/ rangamandap & gudhamandap behind it — photograph by Madhukar K Bhagat

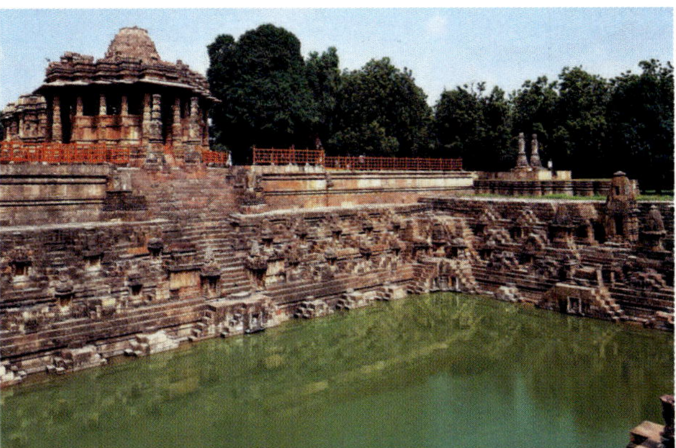

7.20: Kunda with 108 shrines at the Sun Temple, Modhera — photograph by Madhukar K Bhagat

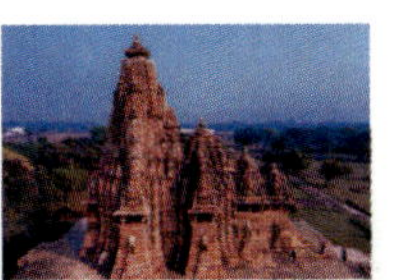

of construction, many structures in grey and black basalt are also found, which were employed around 10th to 12th century CE. Later, the use of marble as a material for sculptures made carving of intricate designs possible. It is also seen in the sculptures and carvings in the Jain group of temples at Ranakpur and Dilwara temple at Mt. Abu (in around 15th century CE). One of the grandest temples of this region is the Sun Temple at Modhera in Gujarat. This temple was built by the Solankis (Chalukyas of Gujarat) in 11th century CE, and is characterised by a massive stepped rectangular tank.

A Glimpse of Important Temples in Western India

Sun Temple (Modhera), Gujarat

Built by Raja Bhimdev–1 of the Solanki dynasty nearly a millennium ago (in around 1026 CE), the temple is dedicated to the Sun god. The temple faces east and has a unique feature, that at the equinoxes the rays of the sun shine directly on the main shrine (being built very near to the tropic of Cancer). It has a large rectangular stepped tank (*surya-kund*) which is over 100 square meters. It is one of the grandest temple tanks with 108 miniature shrines carved in between the steps in the tank itself.

The architecture, which is referred to as Maru-Gurjara style, (a Chalukyan style) is also unique as it has three axially aligned and integrated elements, viz. the **Surya kund** (temple tank), **Sabha mandap/Rangamandapa** (the assembly hall/ dance hall), and **Gudhamandapa** (the shrine hall). Each of these halls has intricately carved pillars and walls. The pillars are replete with the scenes of Ramayana and Mahabharata, while the temple walls have sculptures of Surya and other deities like Indra, Agni and Varuna adorning the corners of this octagonal structure. Besides, the external walls of the *gudhamandapa* also depict sculptures of Brahma, Vishnu and Shiva.

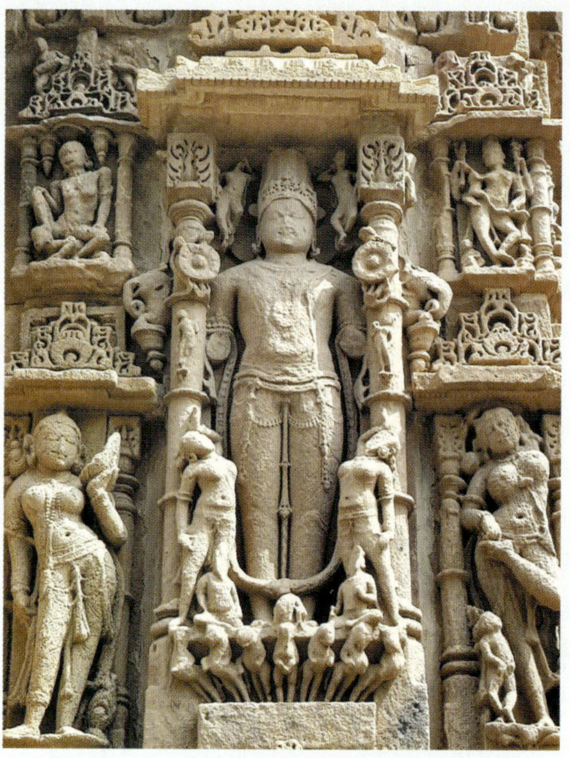

7.21: A panel on the walls of Gudhamandapa at the Sun Temple Modhera, depicting Surya with the charioteer Aruna and other deities — photograph by Madhukar K Bhagat

Dilwara Temple (Mount Abu), Gujarat: World famous for its exquisite marble carvings, this is a Jain group of temples which were built between the 11th to the 13th century CE. The style of architecture is identified with the *Maru Gurjara* type. The group comprises five set of temples**.** The most famous of it, the Vimal Vasahi temple, which is dedicated to Jain Tirthankara **Rishabhanatha** was built in 1031 CE by Vimal Shah**,** minister of Bhimadev-I, a Chalukya king. The temple is built entirely in white marble and is known for the rich and intricate carvings on the walls, ceilings, porticoes, arches and pillars. These bear images of lotus buds, petals, flowers, animals, scenes from Jain mythology, images of the Tirthankaras etc. Similar carvings are seen in the Luna Vasahi Temple dedicated to lord Neminatha. The other temples of this complex are Pittalhar temple (dedicated to Adinatha), Parsvanath temple and Mahavir Swami temple.

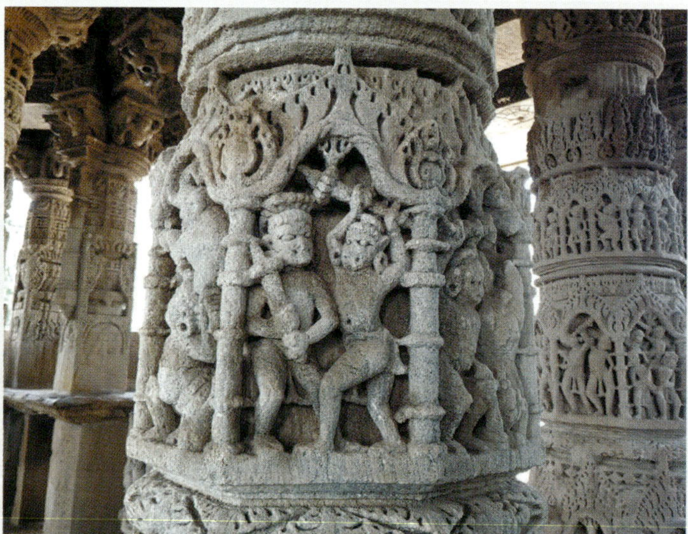

7.22: The fight of Bali and Sugriva, a scene from Ramayana depicted on a pillar in the Rangamandapa — photograph by Madhukar K Bhagat

Ranakpur Temple (Pali district), Rajasthan

Built in 15th century CE, this is also a **Jain temple** complex which is dedicated to the first Tirthankara **Adinatha** (Rishabhanatha). Like the Dilwara temples, this temple is also made in white marble and is famous for its spectacular and intricate carvings and statues. But it is also known for its architectural style (**Maru Gurjara architecture**), with the temple designed as *chaumukh* with four faces.(see also chapter 5)

Kailasha Temple (Ellora Caves, Aurangabad district); Maharashtra

The world famous Kailasha temple, a part of the Ellora Caves is the largest **rock-cut temple** carved from a single rock (monolithic

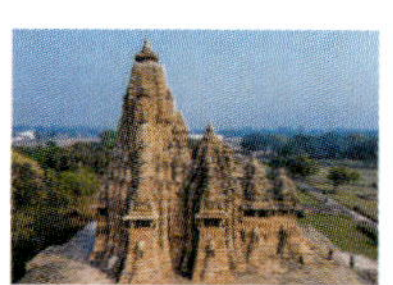

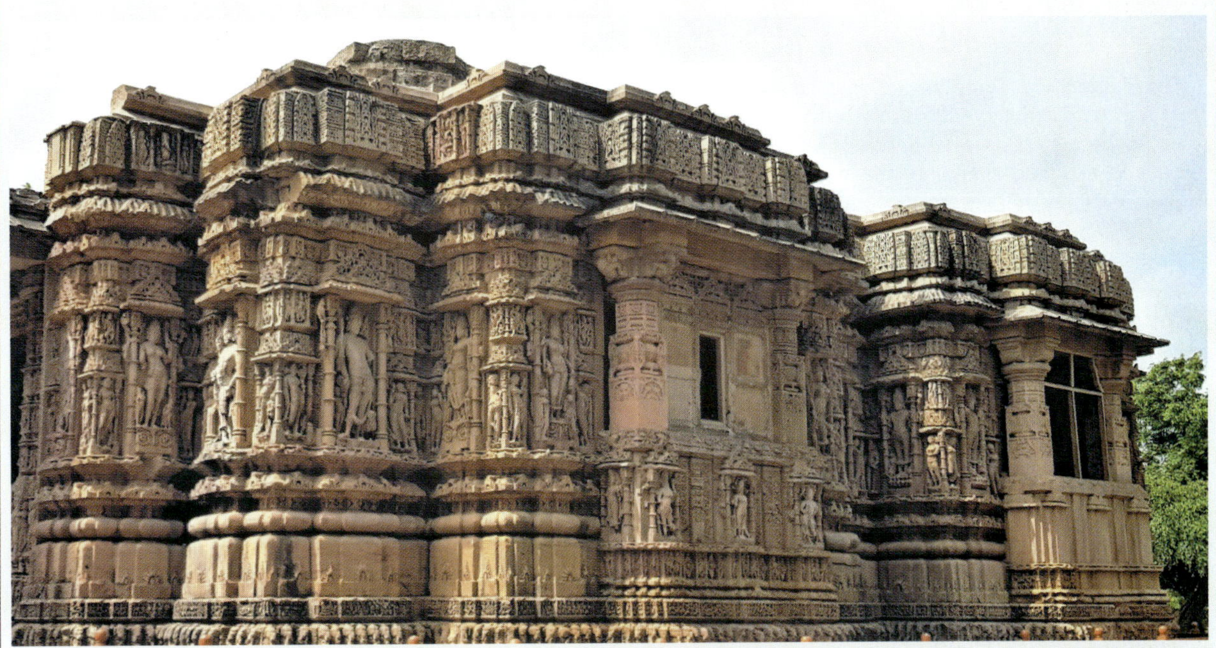

7.23: Intricate carvings of different deities on the walls of the Gudhamandapa at Sun Temple, Modhera — photograph by Madhukar K Bhagat

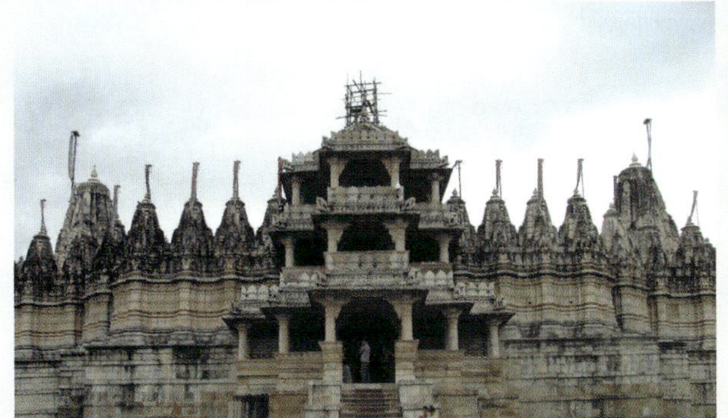

7.24: Ranakpur Temple — photograph by Madhukar K Bhagat

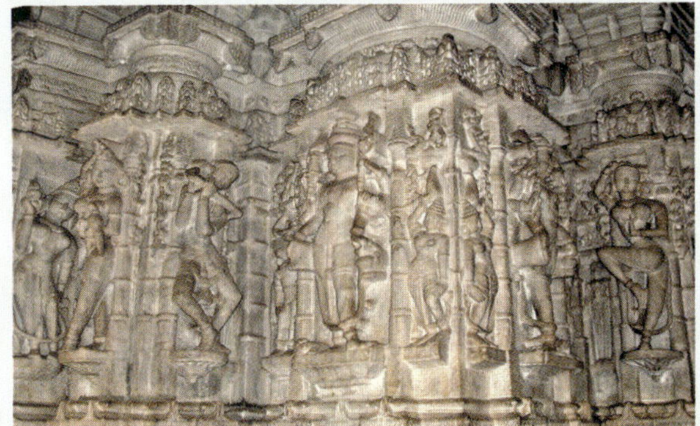

7.25: Intricate carvings in marble on columns and walls of Ranakpur Temple — photograph by Madhukar K Bhagat

structure). It is not only known for the dexterous carvings and sculptures but is indeed an amazing engineering feat for having being carved top down from a mountain. The temple was built by the Rashtrakuta king, Krishna-I in the 8th century CE and is dedicated to Lord Shiva. Quite unlike other rock cut structures which are constrained for space, the temple has a *mandapa*, a *gopuram* and even a courtyard with a statue of Nandi (*vahan*). Thus, all elements of a classic Nagara structure have been carved out of stone. The complex is recognised as a **UNESCO** World Heritage Site. (see also chapter 6)

HILL TEMPLES

Hill temples in Kumaon, Garhwal, Kashmir, and Himachal developed certain unique features of their own. The influence of various schools of architecture like Mathura, Sarnath, and Gandhara had a blending influence on the temples in this region. Further, the indigenous architecture of wooden buildings with a pitched roof was also employed. The main ***garbhagrihas*** were made in Latina/Rekha Prasada type. The *mandapa* was of older form of wooden architecture. Important temples are **Lakshana Devi Mandir** at Chamba (containing images of Mahishasura Mardini and Narasimha), **Jageshwar Temple near Almora, Champawat Temple near Pithoragarh and Pandrethan Temple in Kashmir**.

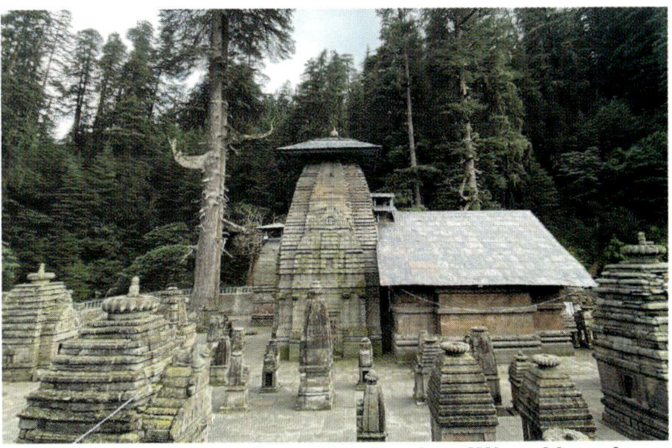

7.26: Jageshwar Temple complex, Uttarakhand. The temples' shikharas made of several cut stone slabs — photograph by Madhukar K Bhagat

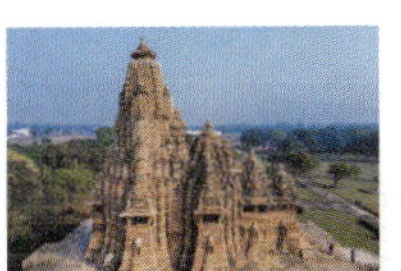

A Glimpse of Important Hill Temples

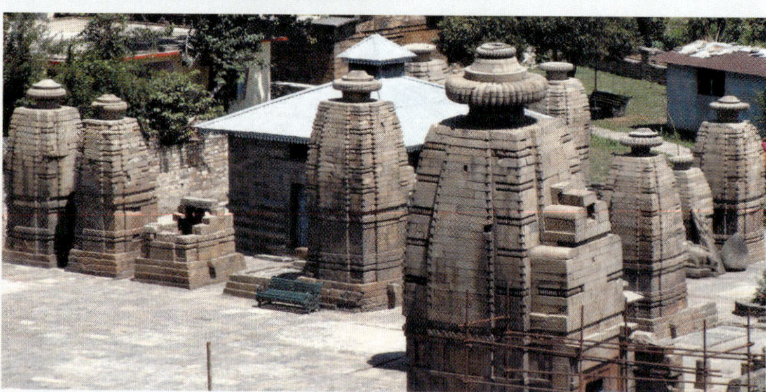

7.27: Temple complex at Baijanath, near Kausani, Uttarakhand — photograph by Madhukar K Bhagat

The Jageshwar Temples are located in Almora District of Uttarakhand. The entire complex is believed to have been built in a period spanning nearly 400 years (9th century CE to 13th century CE) and comprise nearly 124 temples. Of these, the **Mahamritunjaya Mahadev Temple** is the oldest and largest one. The **Tarun Jageshwar** is the principal temple. Both are dedicated to Lord Shiva. The temples have **Nagara** style of architecture and are made of cut stones. Some of the temples are small in size with a small cubicle of a *garbhagriha,* atop of which is a small *shikhara,* but many temples have a larger construct too. A few even have a barrel/vault shaped *vimana* showing the influence of Vesara architecture. Other fine examples of the hill temples include the **Baijnath Temple** near Kausani and the Sun Temple and other temples at Katarmal in Uttarakhand (built by Katyuri king Katarmal in the 9th century CE).

Lakshana Devi Temple in Chamba valley near Bharmour, Himachal Pradesh, is famous for the image of goddess Durga in four-armed form of **Mahishasura Mardini**. Constructed in 680 CE by Raja Meruvarman, the post Gupta period temple is one of the **oldest surviving temple** structures**.** It has Nagara style architecture and has features of old wooden architecture with richly carved entrance.

The Pandrethan Temple (Srinagar), Kashmir: This temple is said to have been built around early10th century CE and is dedicated to Meruvarddhanaswami, a form of lord Shiva. The temple is built on a plinth in the middle of a tank. Its architecture is in keeping with the old Kashmiri tradition of wooden buildings. The *shikhara* is small but pyramidical, with inner ceilings, showing carvings and a decorated gateway. The ornamentation is modest as compared to the post Gupta tradition of heavy carvings.

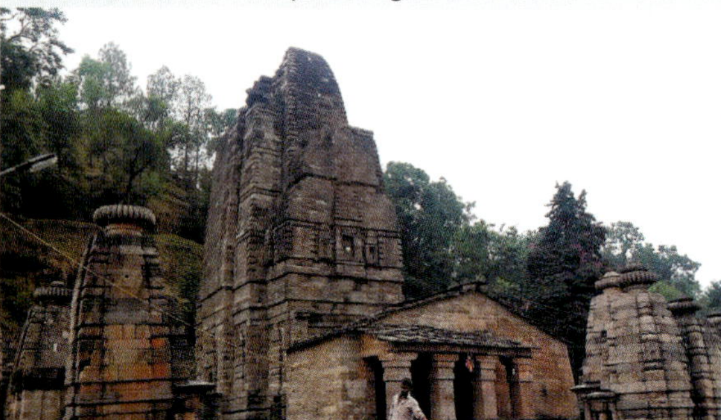

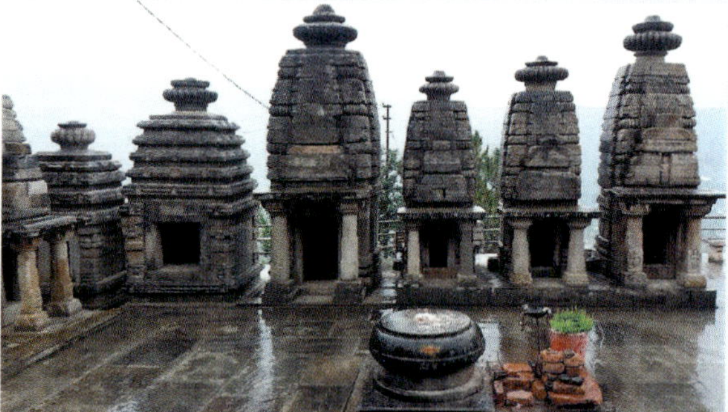

7.28-7.29: Temples at the Katarmal Sun Temple complex of the 9th century CE. Temples also include those dedicated to Shiva, Parvati and Laxmi Narayan — photograph by Madhukar K Bhagat

Ahilyabai Holkar: A Renovator and Preserver of Temples

A noble queen in the Maratha empire in the latter half of the 18th century, Ahilyabai Holkar is one of the most notable of administrators of the period, whose reign of nearly 30 years of Malwa State in central India is regarded as a phase of unmatched peace and prosperity for the region. However, Ahilyabai is often remembered in the annals of Indian history for her work of renovation and reconsecrating of many of the temples and *dharmashalas* at sacred Hindu sites which had earlier been destroyed.

Amongst the hundreds of structures reconstructed by her include the temples at **Kashi (Varanasi), Gaya, Haridwar, Somnath, Ayodhya, Mathura, Kanchi, Avanti, Dwarka, Badrinath, Rameshwaram** and **Jagannath Puri** amidst others. Besides, she built many roads connecting numerous pilgrim destinations and thus infused a new life in these temples, while preserving the religious culture and traditions of the land.

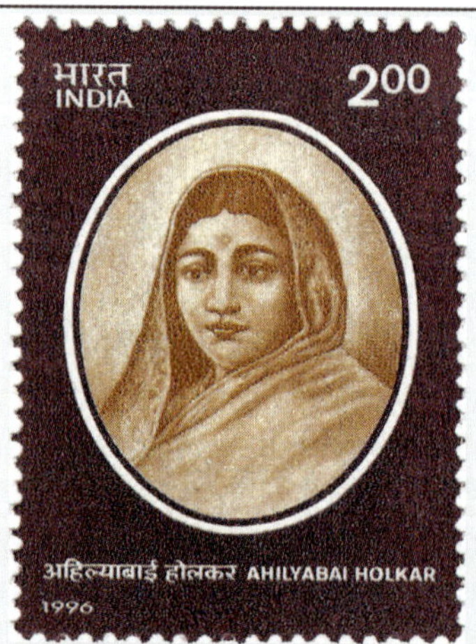

7.30: Stamp of Ahilyabai Holkar released in 1996 — Courtesy, Department of Post

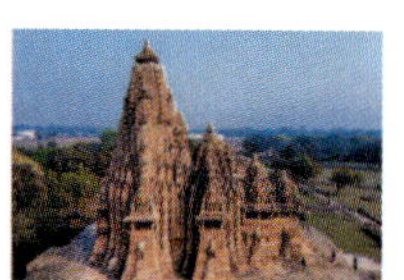

"Ahilyabai's extraordinary ability won her the regard of her subjects and of the other Maratha confederates, including Nana Phadnavis. With the natives of Malwa ... her name is sainted and she has styled an avatar or Incarnation of the Divinity. In the soberest view that can be taken of her character, she certainly appears, within her limited sphere, to have been one of the purest and most exemplary rulers that ever existed."

—John Malcolm, *A Memoir of Central India; 1820*

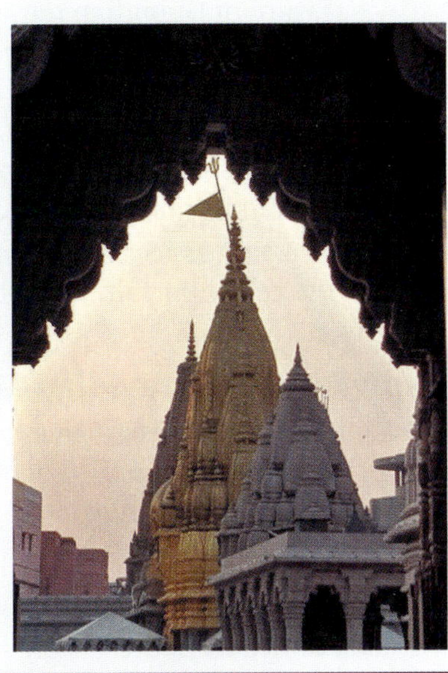

7.31: The Kashi Vishwanath Temple renovated (in around 1780 CE) by Ahilyabai Holkar — photograph by Madhukar K Bhagat

DRAVIDIAN TEMPLE ARCHITECTURE

The Dravidian style of temple architecture was popular in South India and herein the art and architecture of temple construction reached its zenith, particularly in terms of sheer grandeur and scale. Whether it was the huge *vimana* (70metre tall) of the Brihadeeswara Temple, its *shivling* which is the largest, or the breathtaking sculptures and riot of colours in the images of the *gopuram* of the Meenakshi Temple; all are unparalleled examples of art, architecture and engineering. The Dravidian temples had certain distinct features which were in stark contrast to the Nagara structures, and imparted them a separate character of their own.

The foremost visible feature was that the entire temple complex was enclosed in a **compound wall**, which is not seen in the Nagara style. This imparted it a much larger physical space and enabling a host of socio-religious activities in its precincts. At the entrance of the temple were located gateways, or ***gopurams***, which are often large and highly decorated. In the Srirangam Temple at Tiruchirappalli, there are seven concentric walls, rectangular in shape, each having a *gopuram*.

The ***vimana,*** located above the *garbhagriha,* is often like a stepped pyramid or geometrical in shape. It is not curving like the Nagara temples nor is the concept of multiple *shikharas* seen in the Dravidian temples. Further, above the *vimana* is the topmost portion which is shaped like a *stupika*. In some temples, in place of the *stupika*, an octagonal cupola-like structure may be present. This is analogous to *amalaka* and *kalasha* of the North Indian temples.

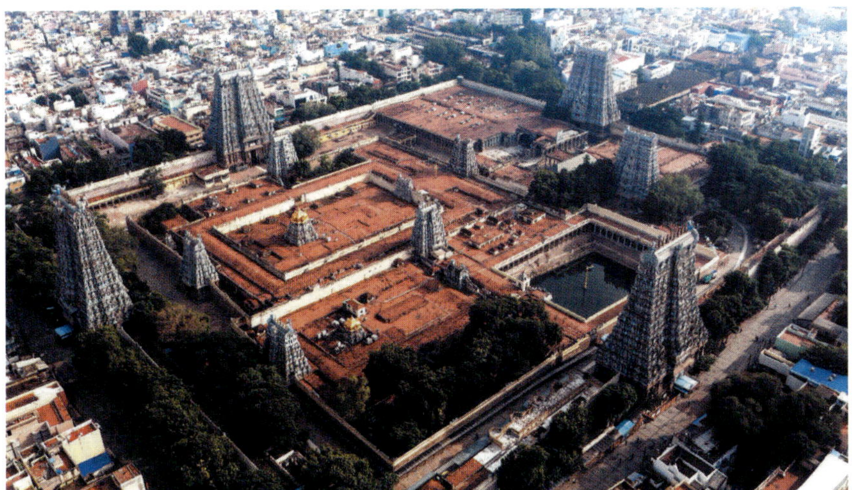

7.32: An aerial view of the Meenakshi Temple complex, Madurai, Tamil Nadu; indicating the unique features of the Dravidian temple architecture, the tall decorated gopurams, the temple enclosure wall, temple tank and a smaller vimana above garbhagriha

— Courtesy, Tamil Nadu Tourism Development Corporation

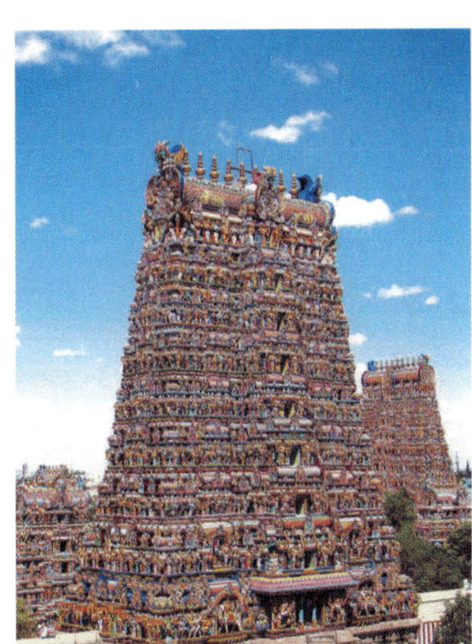

7.33: Intricately carved and beautiful gopuram of Meenakshi Temple

A distinct feature of Dravidian temples was the presence of a water tank in the temple compound. These reservoirs, apart from serving ceremonial purposes, would also be of practical utility, as the Dravidian temples with large complexes would also be centres of socio-cultural and religious activities. Another identifiable feature was the iconography of the Dravidian temples. At the entrance of the temple, images or sculptures of fierce looking *dwarapalas* (guards) would be present. This is in contrast to the images of Ganga and Yamuna, or *mithunas*, found at the entrance of North Indian temples.

Another interesting aspect is that in some temple complexes in South India where multiple *garbhagrihas* are found, the tower pertaining to the main deity may not be the largest one, rather it may even be the smallest one.

Sub-divisions of Dravidian Temple Architecture

The Dravidian temples are further subdivided into different categories based on the shape of the temples. Further, they are also classified depending on the dynasty or the group of temples of which it is a part as they carry a distinct imprint of the art and architecture of the dynasty which built or patronised it.

The classification of Dravidian temples based on shape are as follows:

- ***Kuta*** or ***Caturasra***; these were temples with square shape
- ***Shala*** or ***Ayatasra***; these were rectangular in shape
- ***Gaja-prishta*** or ***Vrittayata***; *Gaja-prishta* means 'elephant back', and it referred to temples shaped like an ellipse (*vrittayata*). These were similar to vaulted shapes of *chaityas* which have a horseshoe-shaped entrance.
- ***Vritta***; or circular shaped temples
- ***Ashtasra***; or octagonal shaped temples

Different Temple Groups in South India

Pallava architecture

The Pallavas built a number of temples in the present Tamil Nadu region. The earlier ones were rock-cut while those in the later stages were structural temples. The most famous of them is the **'Shore Temple'** at **Mahabalipuram** (now Mammallapuram). The temple is built on the shore and is facing east. It is unique as it has three shrines; the east and the west ones are dedicated to Lord Shiva and middle one to Lord Vishnu. A structure of Nandi (bull), Lord Shiva's mount lines the temple wall. Evidence of a water tank and *gopuram* is also found there.

The Pallava temples are further classified as per the rulers and the features of temples as below.

Mahendravarman group : These were early rock-cut temples constructed during the reign of king Mahendravarman-1 (7th century CE). An example of such rock cut temple is the **Tiruchirappalli Temple**.

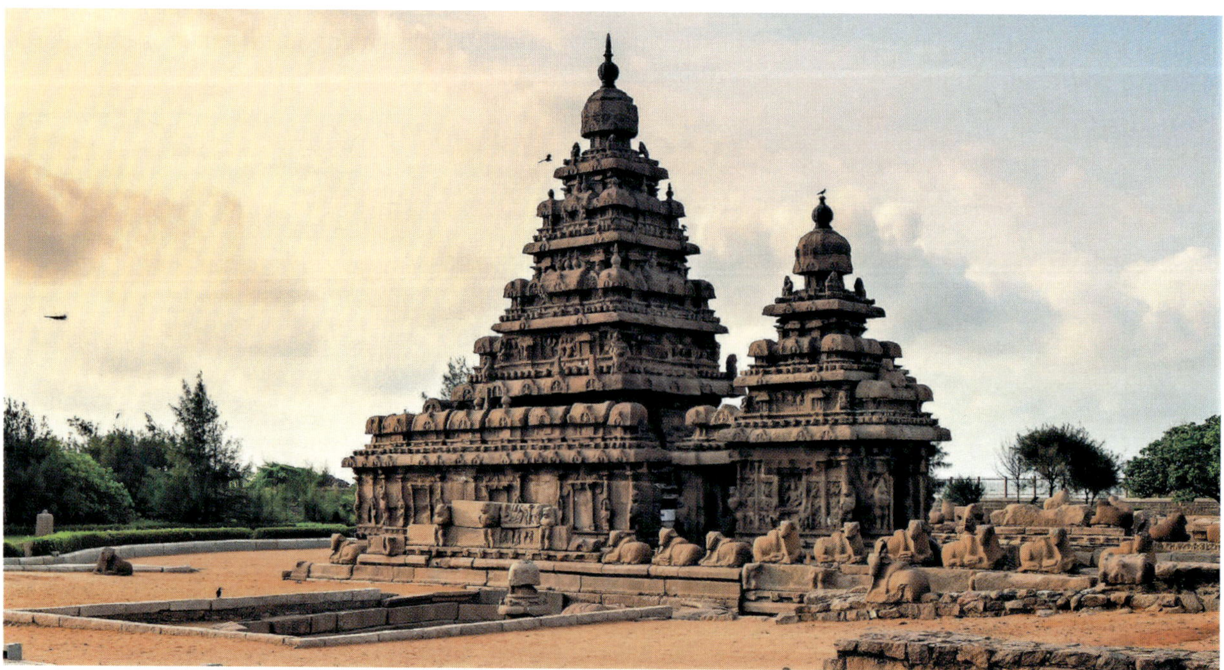

7.34: Shore Temple, Mahabalipuram, Tamil Nadu; among the prominent Pallava architectures and a glorious example of Dravida temple; visible in the foreground are a number of structures of Nandi bull, the vahana of Lord Shiva — Courtesy, Tamil Nadu Tourism Development Corporation

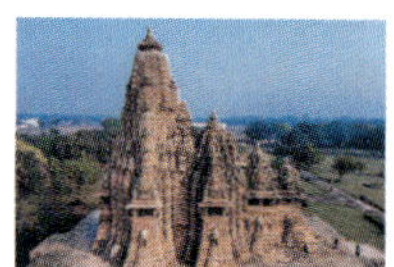

Narasimha group: These temples marked the second stage of the Pallava architecture. The temples were carved out of monolithic rocks and also had intricately carved sculptures. The *mandapa* and *pancharathas* of **Mahabalipuram** are examples of this.

Rajasimha group: Under Narasimhavarman II (also known as Rajasimha), structural temples were built. This was a marked departure from the construction of the rock-cut temples to real structural ones. **Kailasanathar Temple at Kancheepuram** and **Shore Temple at Mahabalipuram** belong to this category.

Nandivarman group: This style of architecture was common during the reign of Nandivarman Pallava. The temples were smaller but they were structural temples. Examples of this group are the Vaikunda Perumal Temple at Tirunelveli and **Mukteshwara** Temple.

Chola architecture

Like the Pallava architecture, the Chola architecture too is an important style of Dravidian temple construction. The most important temple of this group is the **Brihadeeswara Temple** at Thanjavur. Built by Raja Raja Chola in around 1009 CE (also called the **Rajarajeshwara Temple**), this is the largest and also tallest temple in India. The *vimana* of the temple is 70 m high and has a monolithic *vimana*, atop which is a massive 80 tonne octagonal stone dome, making the construction an engineering marvel. The temples of the Chola period were much grander than those of its predecessors, viz. the Pallavas, Chalukyas, and Pandyas.

VESARA STYLE AND DECCAN TEMPLE ARCHITECTURE

In the Deccan region of the country another style of temple architecture developed, which contained elements from both the Nagara style and Dravidian style and was called **Vesara style.** Thus, a hybridised style of architecture evolved and flourished. However, not all temples of the Deccan region are of Vesara style and some are completely of Dravidian style. The prominent temple architectural styles which developed are the Chalukyan, the Rashtrakuta, the Hoysala and the Vijayanagara architecture.

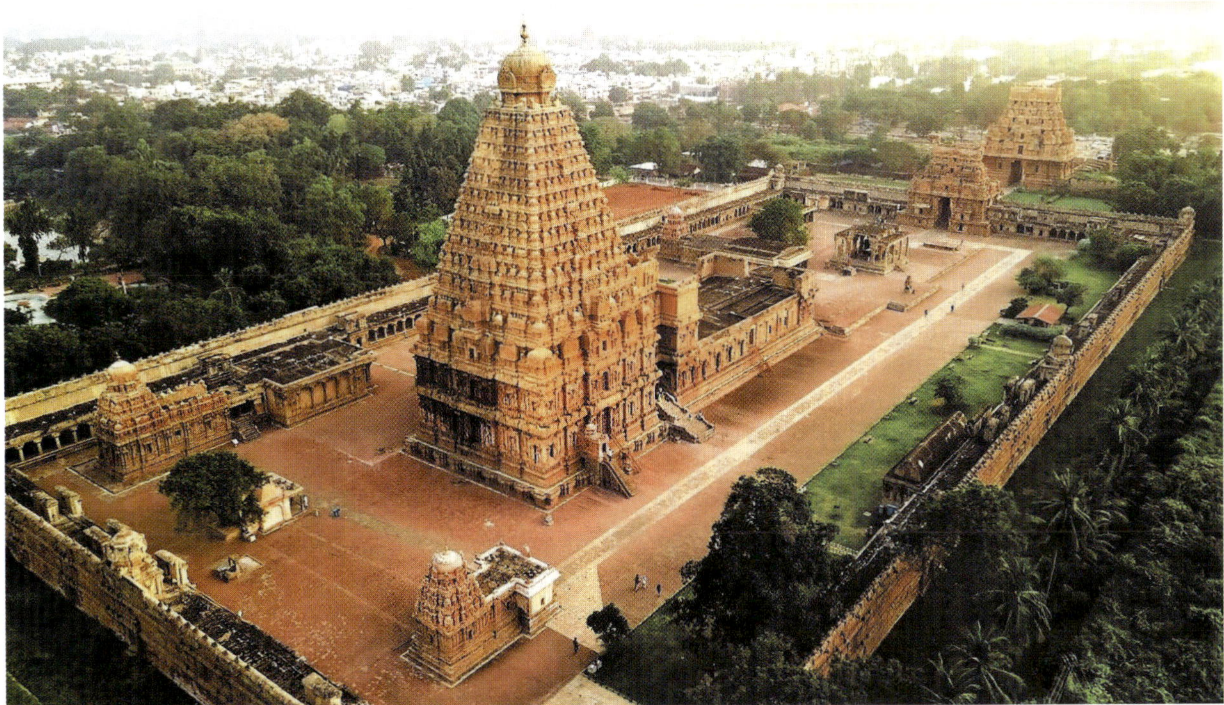

7.35: An aerial view of the Brihadeeswara Temple; Thanjavur, Tamil Nadu; seen in the picture are, temple periphery, the gopurams and the 70 metre tall vimana with a massive 80 tonne stone dome on top — Courtesy, Tamil Nadu Tourism Development Corporation

Chalukyan Architecture

The Chalukyan temple architecture gained prominence in the Karnataka region as early as the 6th century CE. While the early Chalukyan architecture was in the form of rock-cut caves, the later ones were structural temples.

These temples developed the unique **Vesara** style of architecture which can be seen in temples at **Ravan Phadi** Cave, **Durga Temple,** Lad Khan Temple (all at Aihole in Karnataka), and **Pattadakal** group of temples (Karnataka).

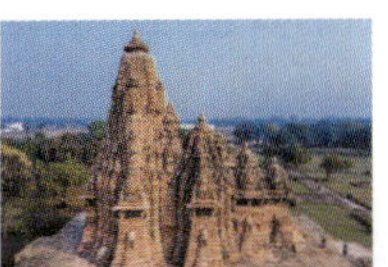

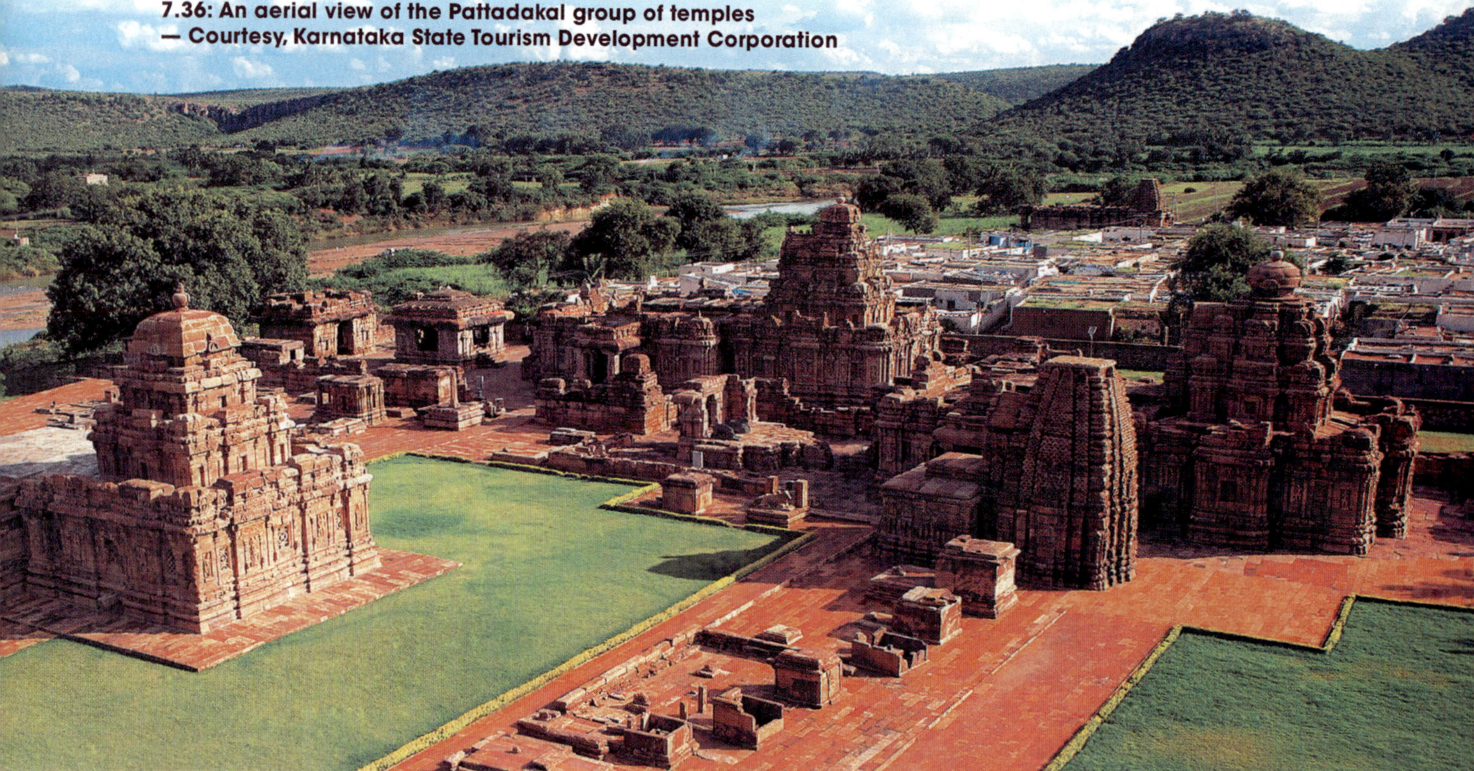

7.36: An aerial view of the Pattadakal group of temples — Courtesy, Karnataka State Tourism Development Corporation

Ravan Phadi Cave at Aihole is an earlier form of Chalukyan architecture. It is famous for the statue of **Nataraja** surrounded by *Saptamatrikas*, three of which are to the right of the statue of Shiva and four are to its left. The figures have graceful and slim bodies and long oral faces, and an extremely tall cylindrical crown.

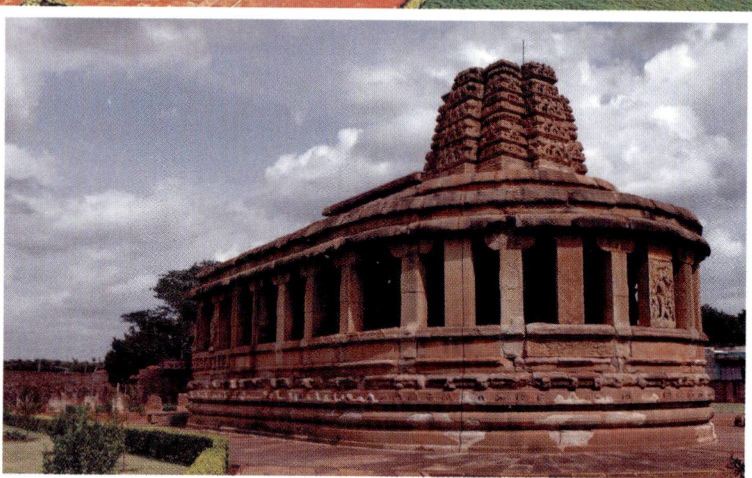

7.37: Durga Temple; Aihole — Courtesy, Karnataka State Tourism Development Corporation

The Durga Temple at Aihole has **features of Dravidian and Nagara architecture**. It also contains elements of earlier Buddhist shrines in the form of an apsidal shrine. It has a *veranda* and a *shikhara* that is similar to a Nagara one. The **Lad Khan** Temple dedicated to Shiva is amongst the oldest of Hindu temples pertaining to the 6th to the 8th century CE. It contains features of wooden roofed hill temples, but is actually made in stone. The temple is believed to be named after a commander (who stayed here for a short period) during Adil Shah's reign.

Over all, there are over 120 temples of the Hindu and Jain group which are free standing or rock cut. These date from the 6th to the 10th century CE, and have a mix of design features prompting the scholars to consider this site as the cradle of experimentation in temple architecture.

Pattadakal Temples are a group of ten temples, including a Jain temple, and are a UNESCO World Heritage Site. The temples have a mix of Dravidian and Nagara style. Some are exclusively in Dravidian and some are in Nagara style. The most famous temple is the **Virupaksha Temple** also known as Sri Lokeshwar Maha Sila Prasad built by Lok Mahadevi, queen of Chalukya king Vikramaditya II (733–44 CE).

Rashtrakuta Architecture

The Rashtrakutas came into prominence in the Deccan region in 750 CE. Their most important contribution was the **Kailashnath Temple** of Ellora. The Jain temple at Pattadakal was also built by them.

The Kailashnath Temple, dedicated to Lord Shiva, is **carved out of a single piece of rock**. Thus, it is the largest monolithic temple structure. It has Dravidian architecture, with a *gopuram*, Nandi bull statue, a complete courtyard (carved from stone), an imposing *vimana*, subsidiary shrines, staircase, etc.

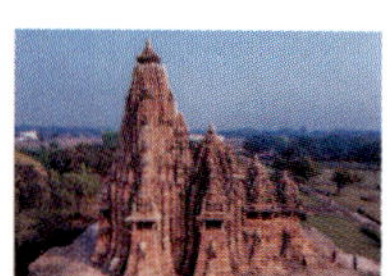

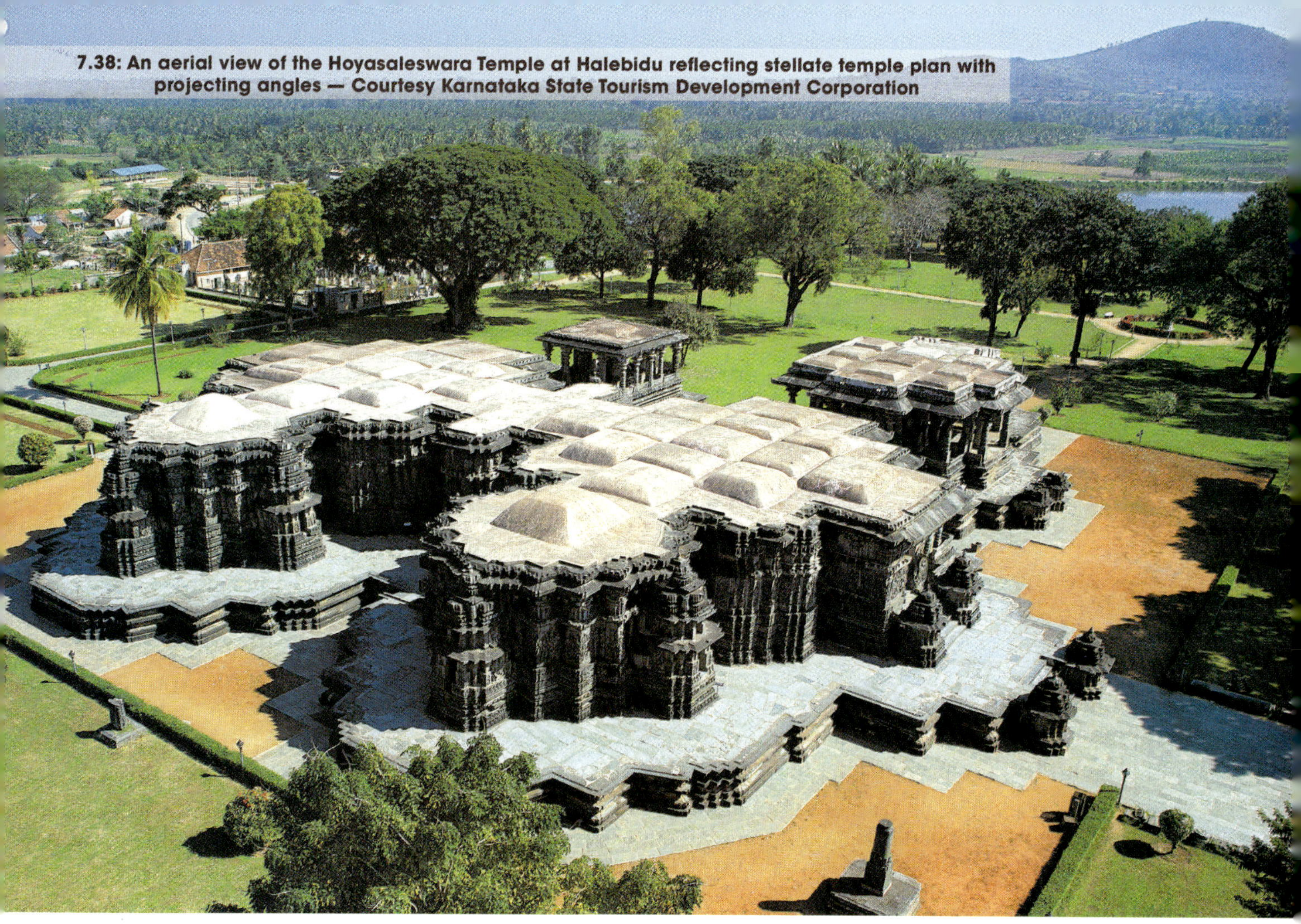

7.38: An aerial view of the Hoyasaleswara Temple at Halebidu reflecting stellate temple plan with projecting angles — Courtesy Karnataka State Tourism Development Corporation

It also houses the famous **sculpture of Ravana shaking Mt Kailasa. It is** considered as a masterpiece of Indian sculpture (see images in chapter 6).

Hoysala Architecture

The Hoysalas were in prominence in Karnataka around the Mysore region. Their reign contributed hundreds of temples, the remains of which have been found, but the most important being those at **Halebid**, Belur and Somanathapura.

The salient feature of temples of this dynasty's architecture was their increasing complexity owing to a number of projecting angles. Thus, the plan of these temples did not remain the simple square or the rectangle one, **but became more like a star, which imparts it the name of stellateplan**. Another unique feature of these temples was their construction in soapstone, a relatively soft stone. This made it possible to carve intricate sculptures visible in the finesse of jewellery of the deities carved on the temple walls.

The temple at **Halebid** (also called the **Hoysaleshvara** Temple), built in around 1150 CE, was made of dark schist stone. It is of **Vesara style** and is dedicated to Lord Shiva who is depicted as **Nataraja**. A large *mandapa* hall is dedicated to music and dance. Singular projections have been cut out from the central square plan to give it a star like appearance. The carvings on the wall are highly intricate. The panel at the bottom which carries the image of a procession, depicts hundreds of elephants, no two of which strike the same pose.

Vijayanagara Architecture

The Vijayanagara empire which came into prominence in around the 15th century CE had its capital at **Hampi**. The ruins of a number of grand structures still exist. Hampi is also recognized as UNESCO World Heritage Site.

The architecture of Vijayanagara has influence of both the **Dravidian style** as well as the **Islamic style.** *Gopurams*, which in other architectural style were usually in one side (front), were now built on all sides. Similarly, more than one *mandapa* was built. The temples walls were decorated with intricate carvings.

Important structures at Hampi include the Vittala Temple, stone chariot (at Vittala temple), Virupaksha Temple, Lotus Mahal, and Pushkarnis (water tanks).

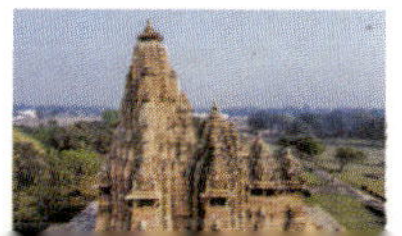

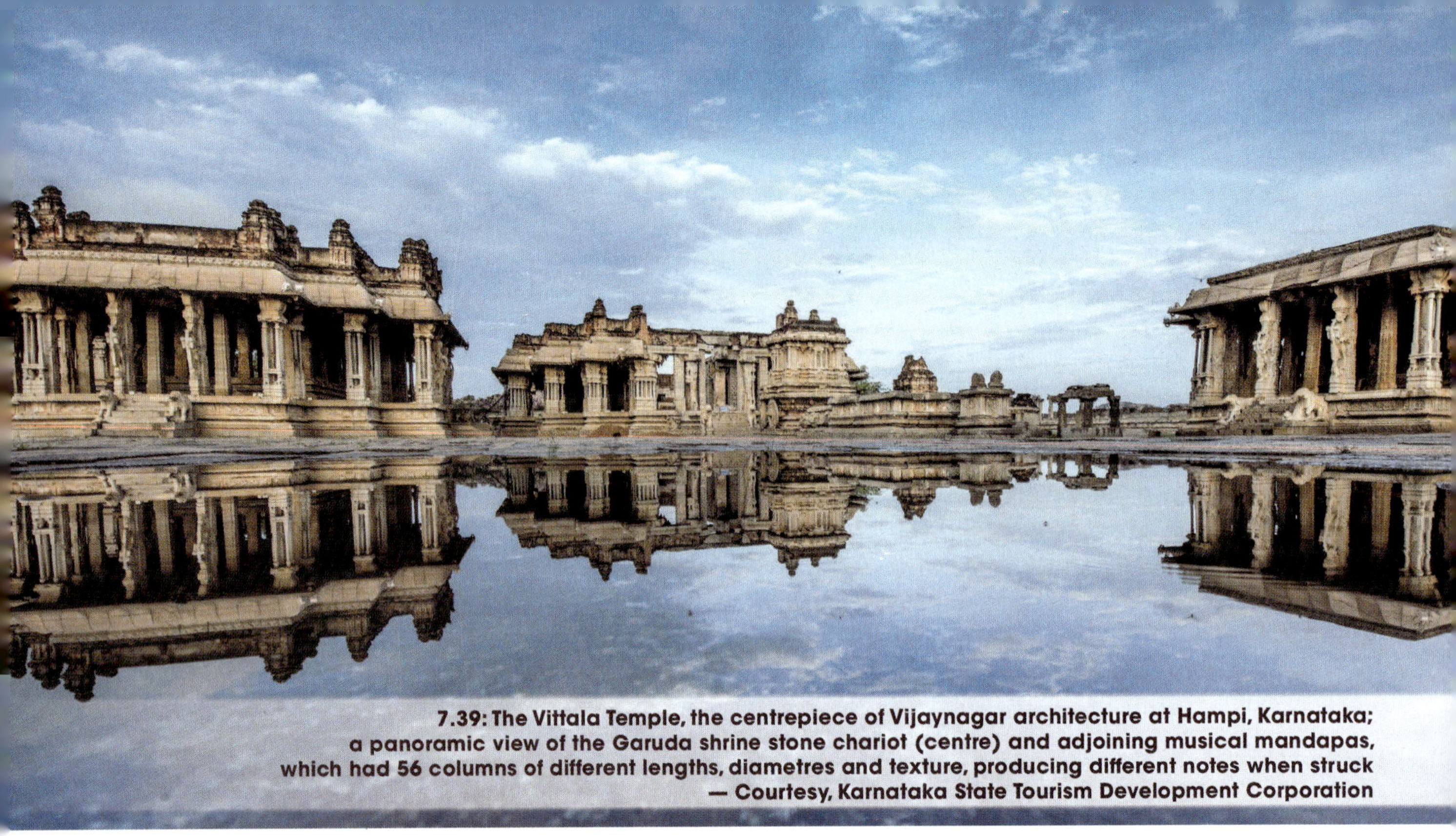

7.39: The Vittala Temple, the centrepiece of Vijaynagar architecture at Hampi, Karnataka; a panoramic view of the Garuda shrine stone chariot (centre) and adjoining musical mandapas, which had 56 columns of different lengths, diametres and texture, producing different notes when struck — Courtesy, Karnataka State Tourism Development Corporation

A Glimpse of Important Temples in Southern India

Meenakshi Temple, (Madurai); Tamil Nadu: One of the most recognised temples of Southern India, the Meenakshi Temple is unique and well known for its tall and richly carved colourful ***gopurams***. Each of its 14 *gopurams* are nearly 40 to 50 metres tall and are the most visible structures of the temple complex. The temple also has two golden sculptured vimanas under which the garbhagrihas of the main deity is present. The *vimanas* of the main deity are smaller in size as compared to the gopurams. The temple is dedicated to goddess Meenakshi, a form of goddess Parvati, and her consort, *Sundareshwar*, a form of lord Shiva. The temple complex was built by Vishwanatha Nayakar, ruler of the Nayak dynasty in the 16th century CE.

Brihadeeswara Temple: Located in Thanjavur, Tamil Nadu, the Brihadeeswara Temple is one of the largest and tallest temples of India. Built a 1000 years ago by Raja Raja Chola-I of Chola dynasty (in 1009 CE), it is a classic example of the Dravida architecture with a large *vimana*, *mandapa* hall, a huge statue of Nandi, and a *gopuram*. However, the *gopuram* is smaller than the *vimana* which is nearly 70m high. The temple is also recognised as a **UNESCO** World Heritage Site.

Gangaikonda Cholapuram Temple (Thanjavur), Tamil Nadu

Another of the great temples located in Thanjavur, it was built by king Rajendra Chola (successor of Raja Raja Chola) in the 11th century CE. Dedicated to Lord Shiva, it is a massive temple only next in size to Brihadeeshwara temple, but is considered even better than the latter in terms of quality of sculptural work. This temple with Dravidian architecture has a *vimana* which is 55 m high and nine storey high. A huge Shiva linga, 4 m high, is placed in the sanctum.

Shore Temple (Mahabalipuram), Tamil Nadu: Built during the reign of **Pallava** dynasty ruler, Narasimhavarman II in the 8th century CE, it is a set of **onshore temples** facing east towards the ocean. Of the three temples in this complex, two are dedicated to Lord Shiva and one to Lord Vishnu.

The larger temple is built with **sculpted granite rocks** on a raised platform. It is a five storied **structural temple** (and not rock-cut) with a pyramidical structure nearly 60 ft high. Along with other structures, it forms a part of **UNESCO World Heritage Site**.

Pancha Rathas (Mahabalipuram), Tamil Nadu: This group of temples were built in **7th century** CE during the reign of **Mahendravarman-1** and his son **Narasimhavarman** of the **Pallava** dynasty. Thus, it predates even the shore temple and is located at a separate monument complex from the shore temple.

The ***pancharathas*** are **monolithic rock-cut temples** and resemble and represent the five *rathas* of the Pandavas, the largest being the Dharmaraja-ratha, and the smallest one being the Draupadi-ratha. The others were Arjuna-ratha, Bheema-ratha, and Nakula- Sahadeva-ratha.

The site is famous for the bas-relief, or the large sculptural panel, nearly thirty metres long and fifteen metres high. This tableau has a large number of images, the most famous being the image of **Arjuna's penance**.

Some scholars interpret it is as the story of the descent of Ganga from heaven to earth and Bhagirath's penance for that. Along with other monuments it is a **UNESCO World Heritage Site.**

Srirangam Temple (Tiruchirappalli), Tamil Nadu

Yet another of the great Chola temples, it was built around 10th century CE. Spread in 156 acres, it is the **largest functioning temple complex in the world,** and second in size only to Angkor Vat Complex. (the latter is however not functioning as a temple.) The Srirangam Temple is a typical Dravidian style temple and has seven concentric walls

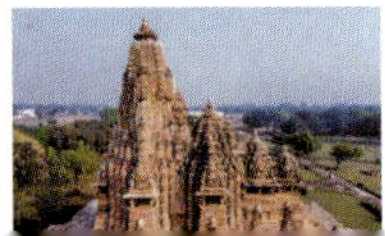

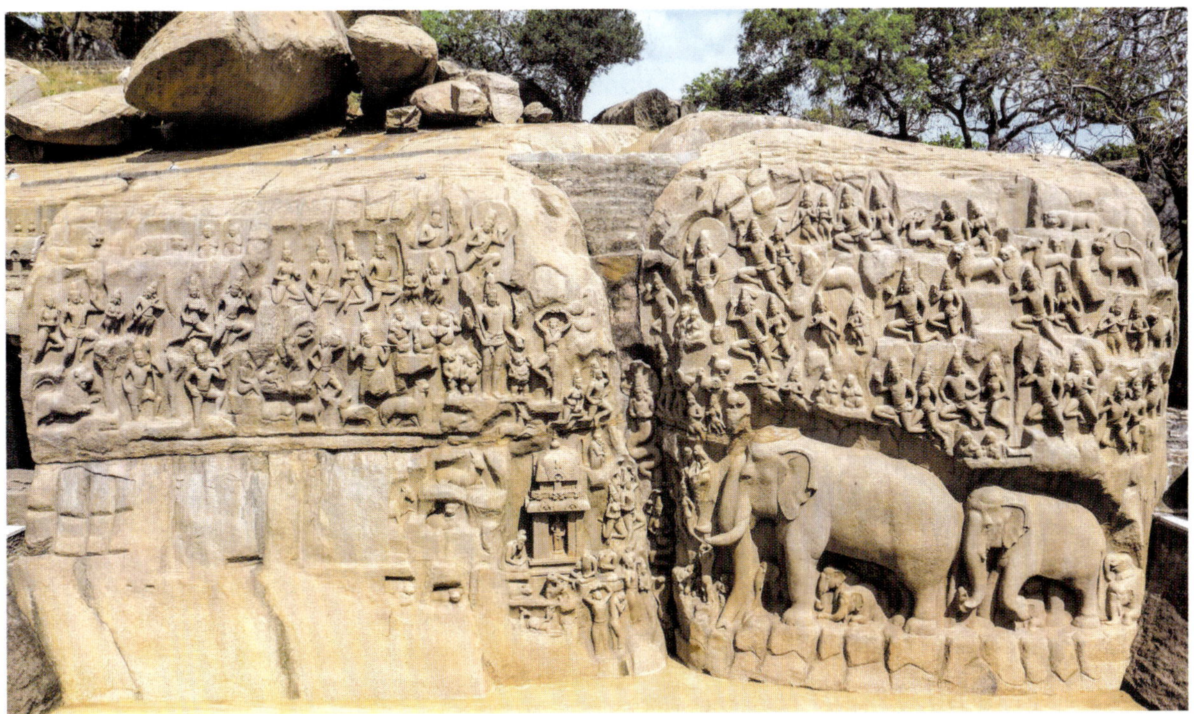

7.40: Arjuna's Penance/Descent of Ganga, bas relief Mamallapuram; Tamil Nadu — Courtesy, Tamil Nadu Tourism Development Corporation

(called *prakarams*), 21 *gopurams*, 39 pavilions, 50 shrines, and several tanks/water bodies inside. The *vimana* over the main deity Ranganathaswamy (an incarnation of Lord Vishnu), is shaped like *Om* and is **gold plated.** The temple has a 1000 pillared hall with the pillars having sculptures of various animals and other figures.

Durga Temple (Aihole), Karnataka

This temple is unique, as its plan is **oblong or apsidal** and is similar to the earlier Buddhist chaitya halls. It employs **Gajaprishta** architecture. The temple is surrounded by a circum-ambulatory verandah and has a *shikhara* similar to Nagara architecture. Thus, elements of Dravidian and Nagara style are incorporated. The temple was built around the 7th & 8th century CE by the Chalukyan kings.

Virupaksha Temple (Pattadakal), Karnataka

Built in **745 CE** by **Loka-Mahadevi,** queen of Vikramaditya-II of the **Chalukya Dynasty,** this temple is the largest temple at the Pattadakal group of monuments. It is also recognised as a UNESCO World Heritage Site. Dedicated to Lord Shiva, it has a typical Dravidian temple architecture and is famous for sculptures of **Lingobhava, Nataraja** and **Ugra Narasimha.** The temple is dedicated to Lord Shiva. It is also believed that the Kailasha Temple at Ellora was modelled as per the Virupaksha Temple.

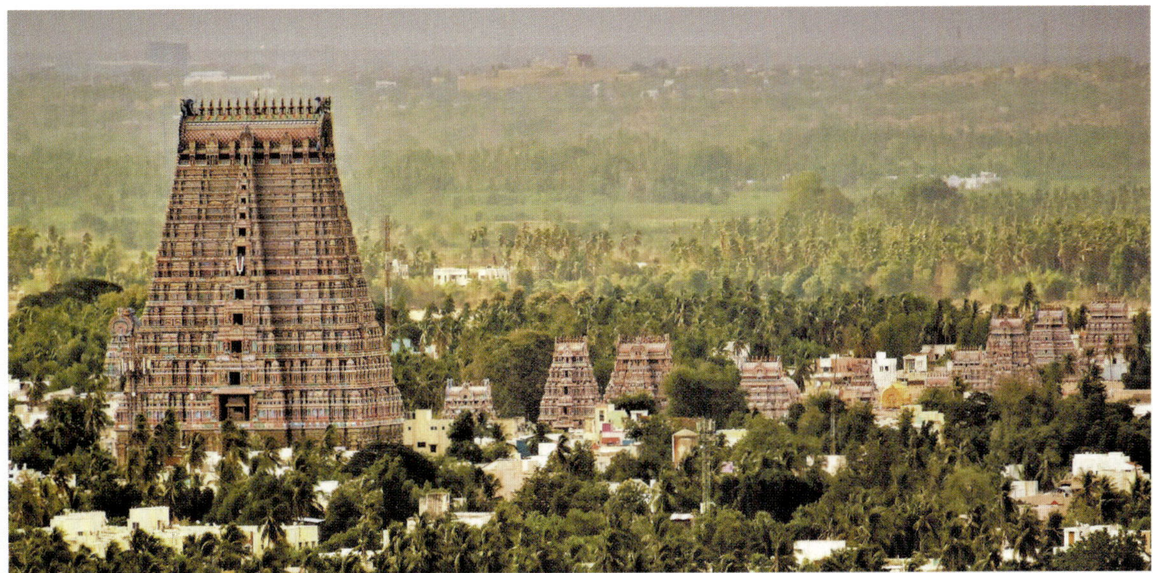

7.41: Sri Ranganathaswamy Temple, Srirangam, Tiruchirappalli; an aerial view of the temple complex and the tall, intricately carved gopurams — Courtesy, Tamil Nadu Tourism Development Corporation

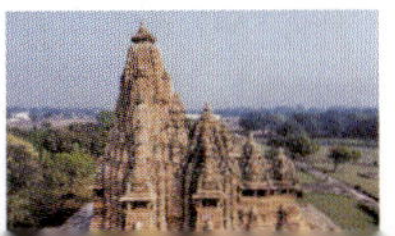

Chennakesava Temple (Somanathapura district, Mysore), Karnataka

Dedicated to Lord Vishnu, and of **Dravidian** style of architecture, this temple is unique as it has a **number of projecting angles** appearing like stars (called **stellate plan**). The material used for construction is **soapstone** (green schist) which is a relatively soft stone, making the intricate sculpture possible This is typically seen in the carving of the jewellery of the deities. The temple is built on *jagati* (a raised platform, and is *trikuta* (triple shrine). The *vimanas* have a vestibule connecting each to the main *mandapa*. The walls of the temple have scenes of Ramayana and Mahabharata depicted on them. It was built in 1268 CE under the Hoysala king Narasimha III.

Hoysaleshwar Temple (Halebid), Karnataka

Built in 1268 CE under the Hoysala king Narasimha III, the temple architecture has a mix of Dravidian and Nagara features. Thus, it has a **Vesara** temple architecture. It is dedicated to Lord Shiva, who is depicted as Nataraja. The temple has two buildings (***dvikuta vimana***), which is a plan with two shrines and two superstructures. It has a long *mandapa* (hall) for music and dance. It too has a **stellate plan** with star like projections and fine carvings.

Kakatiya Temple: Dedicated to Rudreshwara, the Kakatiya Temple (in Palampet village Telangana) is known for its distinctive *vimana* of the temple, which is made up of light weight porous 'floating bricks'. The temple complex located near Ramappa lake, comprises three temples and was built around the early 13th century. It was declared a **UNESCO World Heritage Site** in 2021.

BUDDHIST AND JAIN ARCHITECTURE

Buddhist Temples

From the 5th century onwards, a number of prominent Buddhist and Jain temples and structures were also constructed. The Buddhist structures of significance are the **Mahabodhi Temple** (Gaya in Bihar), **Nalanda University** (Bihar), **Vikaramshila University**, different Buddhist *mahaviharas*, temple at Sirpur (Odisha), etc. Important Jain temples and structures can be seen at **Ellora, Aihole, Dilwara** (Mount Abu), **Ranakpur** (Rajasthan) **Khajuraho**, and **Gomateshwara** (where the statue of Bahubali can be found).

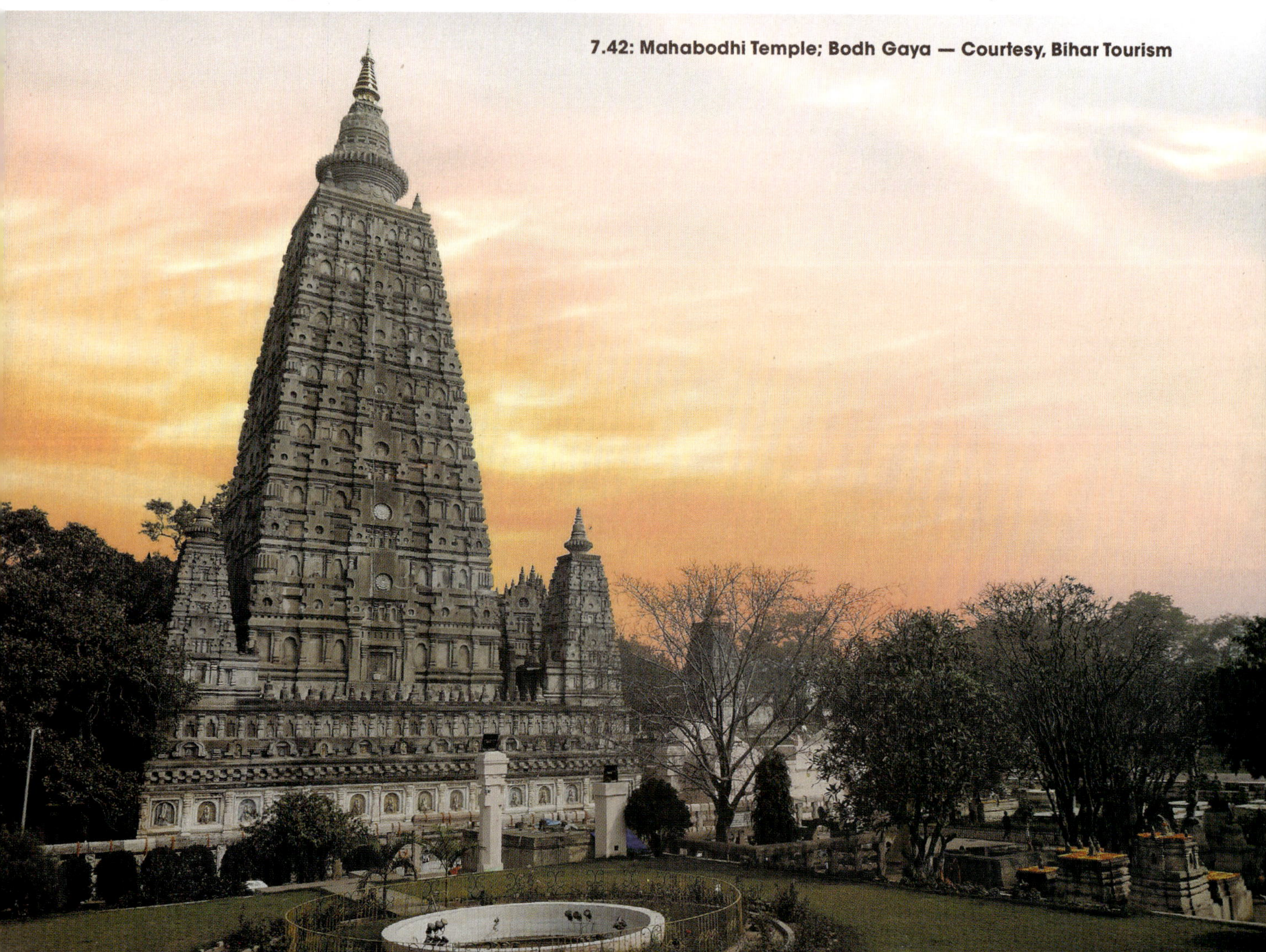

7.42: Mahabodhi Temple; Bodh Gaya — Courtesy, Bihar Tourism

Bodhgaya: It is an important Buddhist centre where Lord Buddha attained enlightenment. It has the Mahabodhi temple (located near Gaya in Bihar).The temple design is unique, as its ***shikhara* is narrow, like a Nagara** temple. However, it is **not curving**, and rises along a straight line like the Dravidian structures. Thus, it is an amalgamation of both the styles. The ***vedika*** around the temple is of around 100 BCE, while the main temple is a colonial reconstruction of the 7th century CE structure.

Nalanda University: This was a Buddhist Mahavihara which flourished from the 5th century CE to the 11th century CE. The university taught various disciplines, including all forms of Buddhism, and had more than **10000** scholars from various parts of India, China, Southeast Asia, Tibet, Sri Lanka, etc. The monastery abounds with large structures several floors high, huge courtyards, and *stupas* built in brick. A number of sculptures and statues have been found which were mainly made in stucco stone and bronze.

The art of this place can be termed as a distinct school **(Nalanda School)** which was influenced by Sarnath art. However, it had distinct features such as typical facial features, body form, and design of jewellery, clothing, etc. In 2016, it has been declared a **UNESCO World Heritage** Site.

Jain Temples

Gomateshwara

The statue of Bahubali, carved in granite stone is located at Shravanabelagola (Karnataka) and is an important **Jain** pilgrimage centre.

The statue which is nearly 18m high is the **tallest monolithic free-standing structure**. It was constructed by the **Ganga kings** (by Chamundaraya – prime minister of Ganga kings) in 10th century CE and is a reflection of the architectural marvel of the period. It is also famous for the *Mahamastakabhisheka* ceremony performed here after every twelve years.

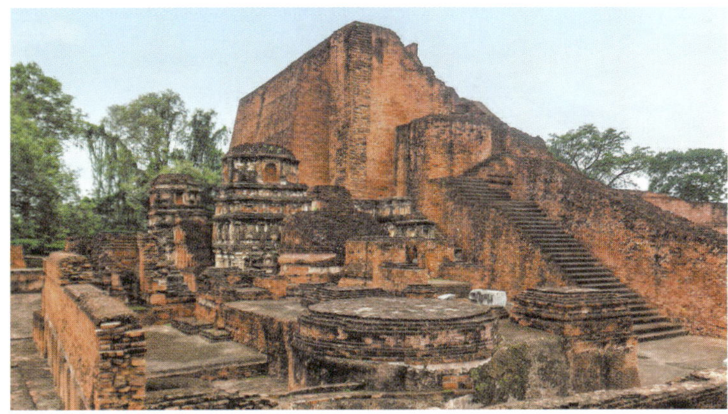

7.43: Ruins of Nalanda Mahavihara — Courtesy, Bihar Tourism

Dilwara temple in Mount Abu

It was built around the 11th to 13th century CE and is an important Jain temple dedicated to Tirthankara Rishabhanatha. It is famous for exquisite marble carvings and architecture. (see information earlier in this chapter)

7.44: Monolithic statue of Bahubali: Shravanabelagola — Courtesy, Karnataka State Tourism Development Corporation

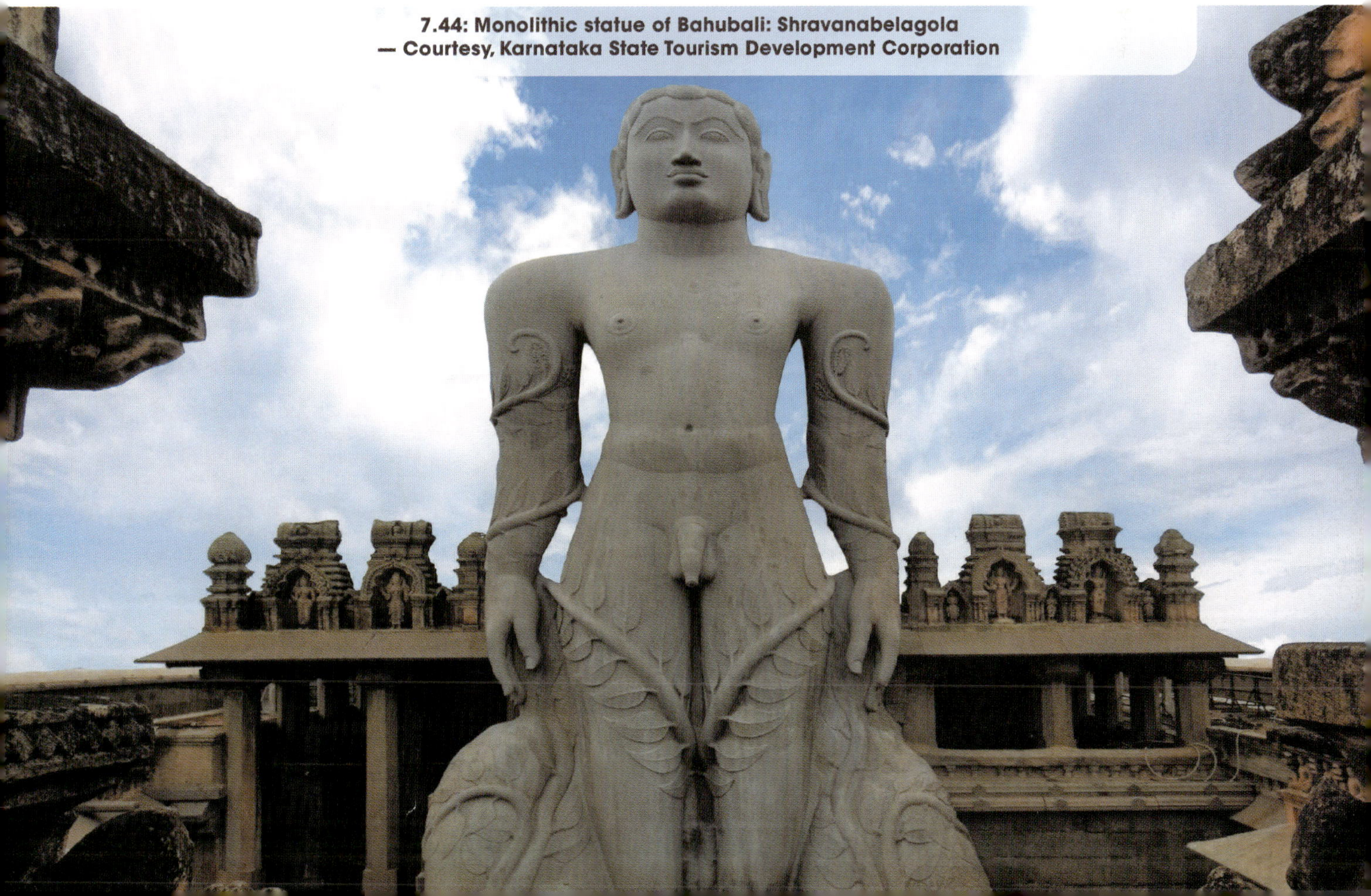

PICTURE GALLERY

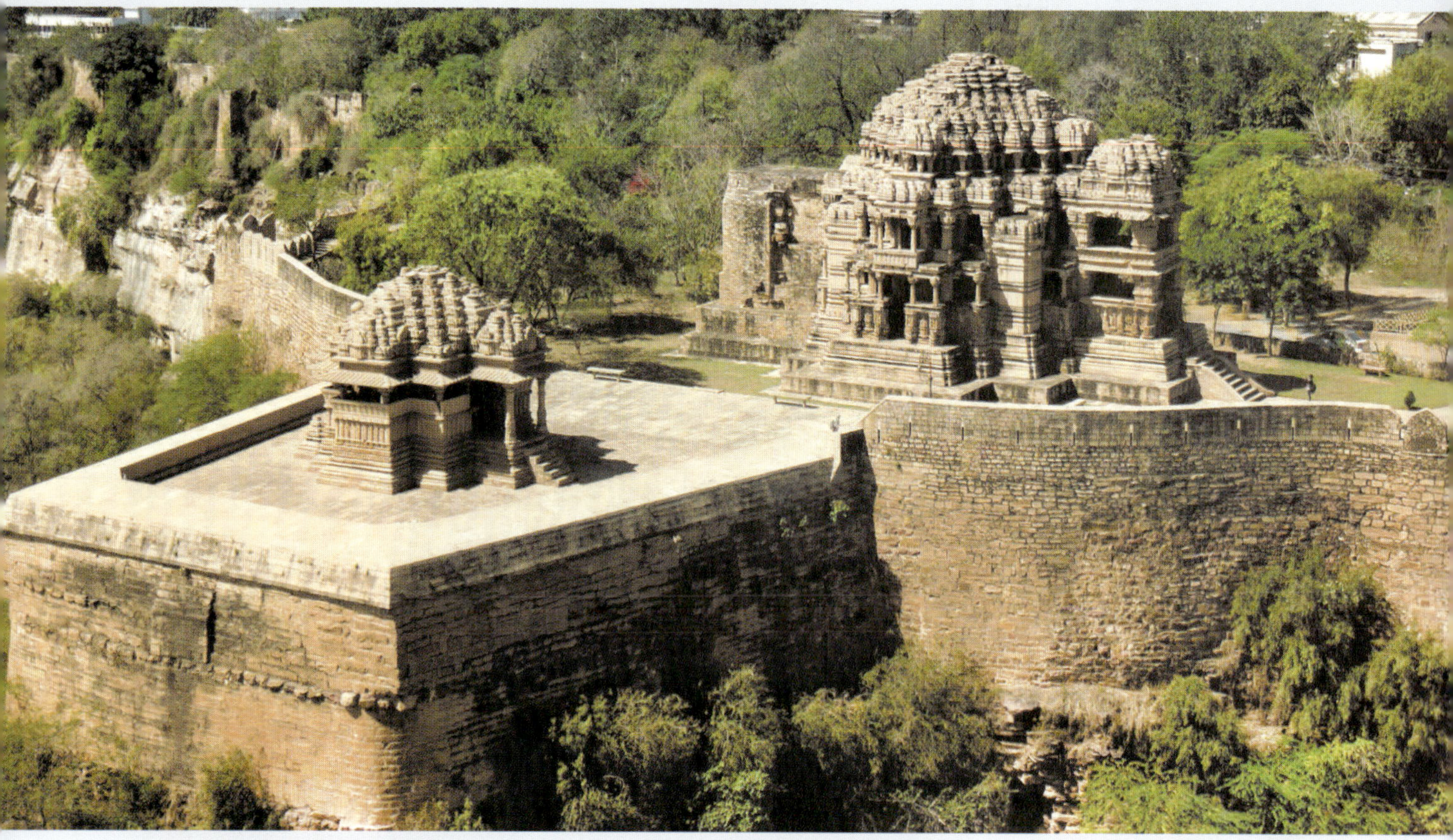

7.45: Sahastrabahu Temple, 11th century twin temples located near the Gwalior fort, Madhya Pradesh, also locally known as Sas-Bahu temple. The temple is dedicated to lord Vishnu in his form as Padmanabha. The temple has Bhumija architecture, a sub category of Nagara architecture, where the square plan keeps on rotating along a vertical axis as the temple rises. — Courtesy, Madhya Pradesh Tourism Board

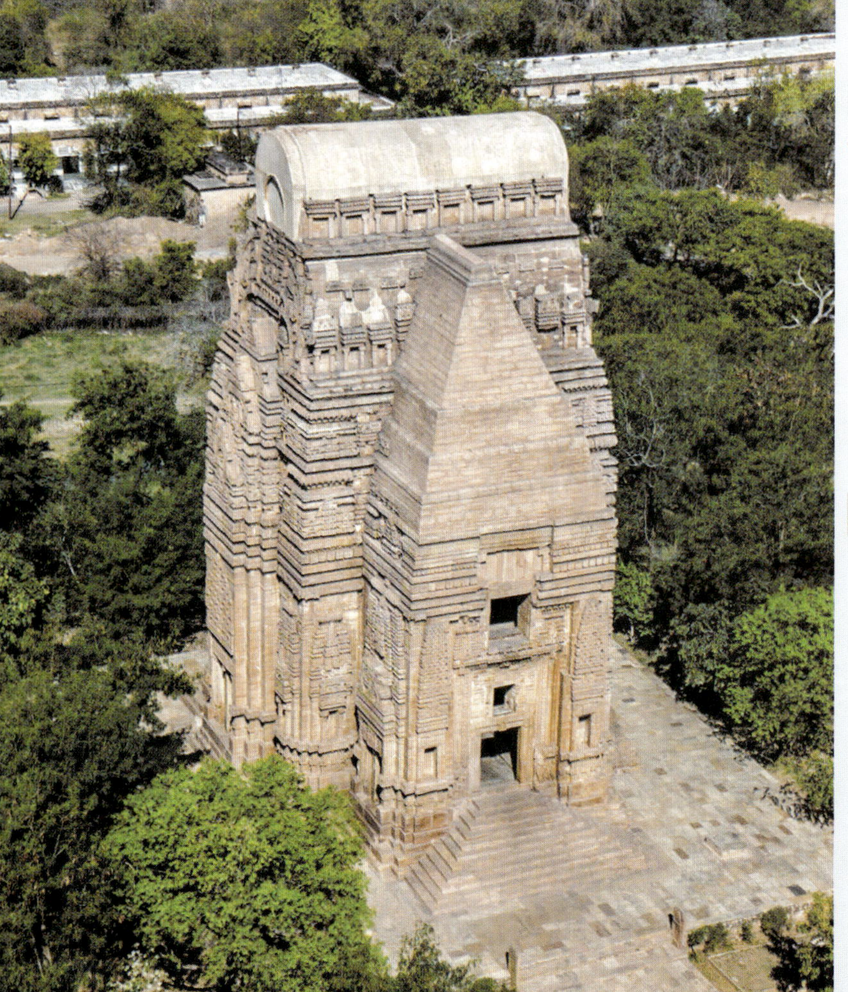

7.46: Telika Mandir also known locally as Teli Ka Mandir, an 8th-9th century CE temple dedicated to Lord Vishnu, Lord Shiva and Saptamatrikas and located in the Gwalior Fort, Madhya Pradesh. It has a rectangular plan instead of the usual square plan and is an example of Gurjara-Pratihara-Gopagiri North Indian architecture — Courtesy, Madhya Pradesh Tourism Board

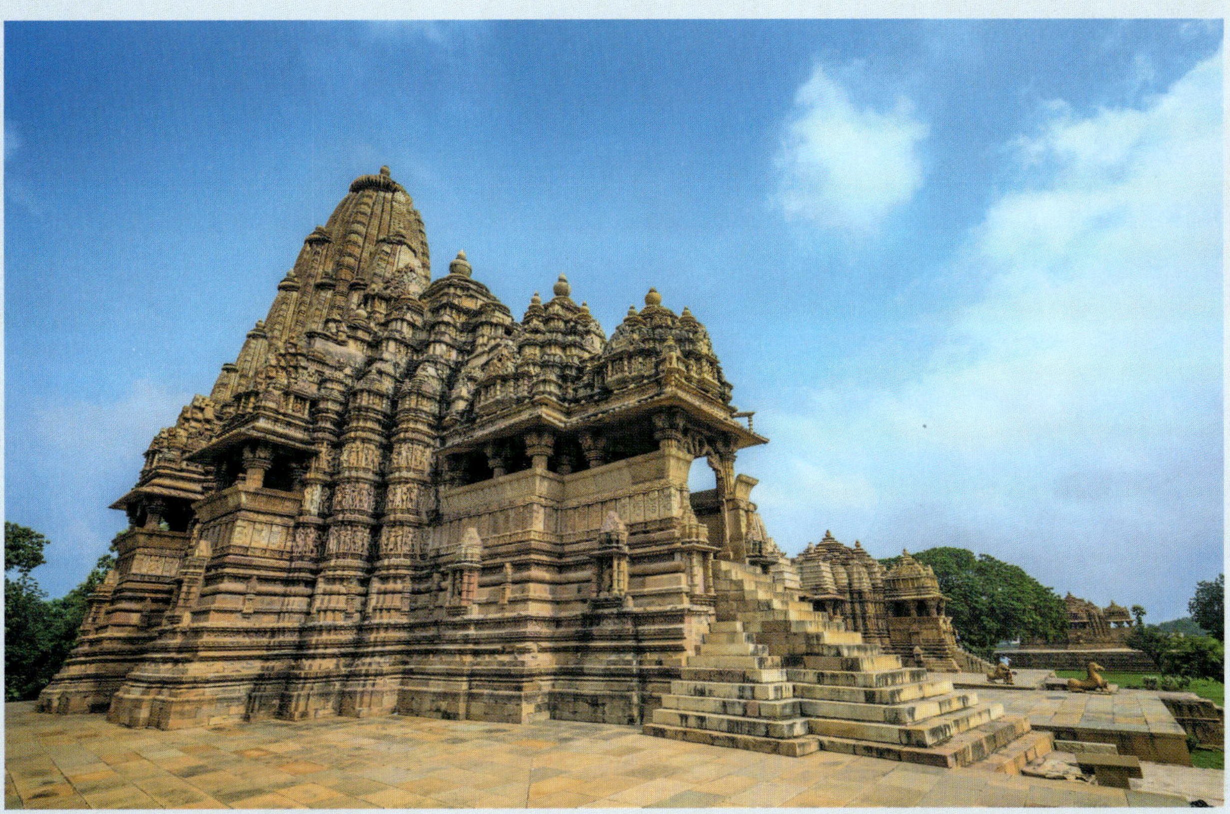

7.47: Kandariya Mahadev Temple, a view from the base of the temple — Courtesy, Madhya Pradesh Tourism Board

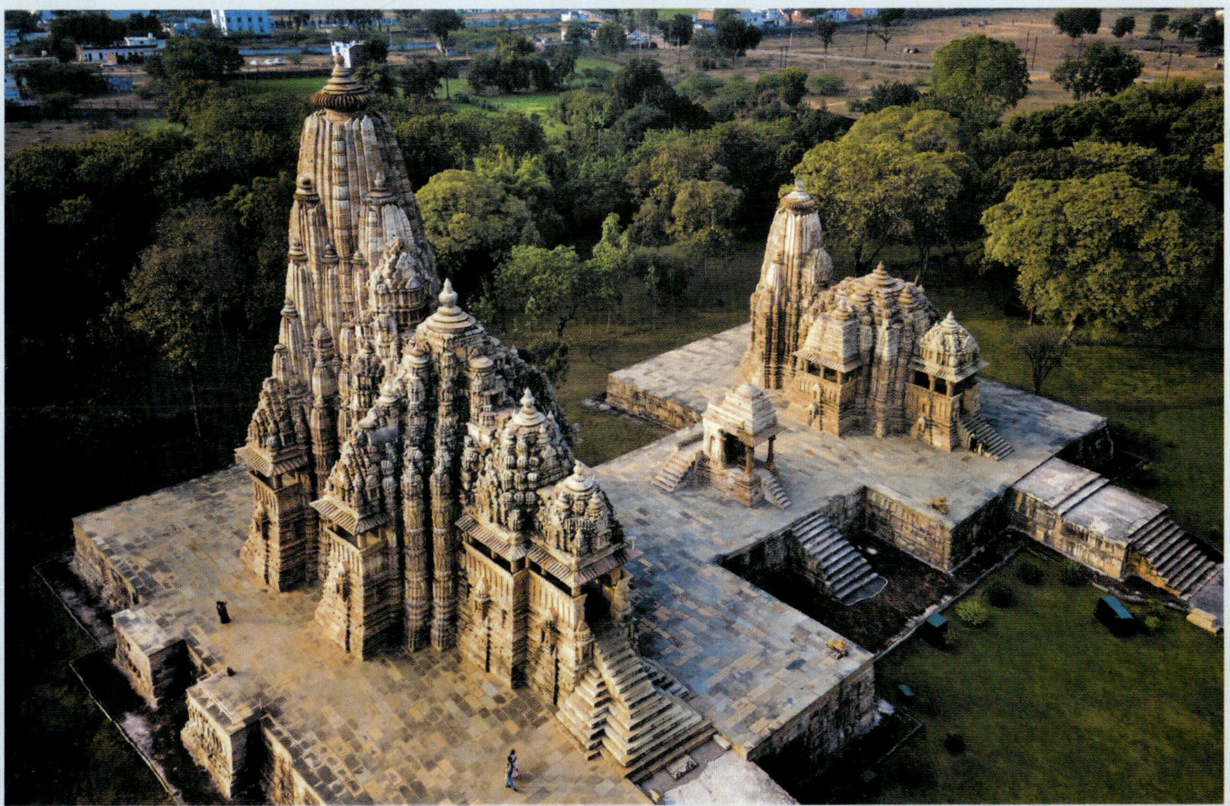

7.48: Kandariya Mahadev Temple, an aerial view indicating the temple plan, the ardha mandapa, mandapa, maha-mandapa and the shikhar — Courtesy, Madhya Pradesh Tourism Board

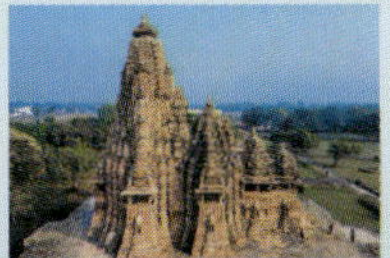

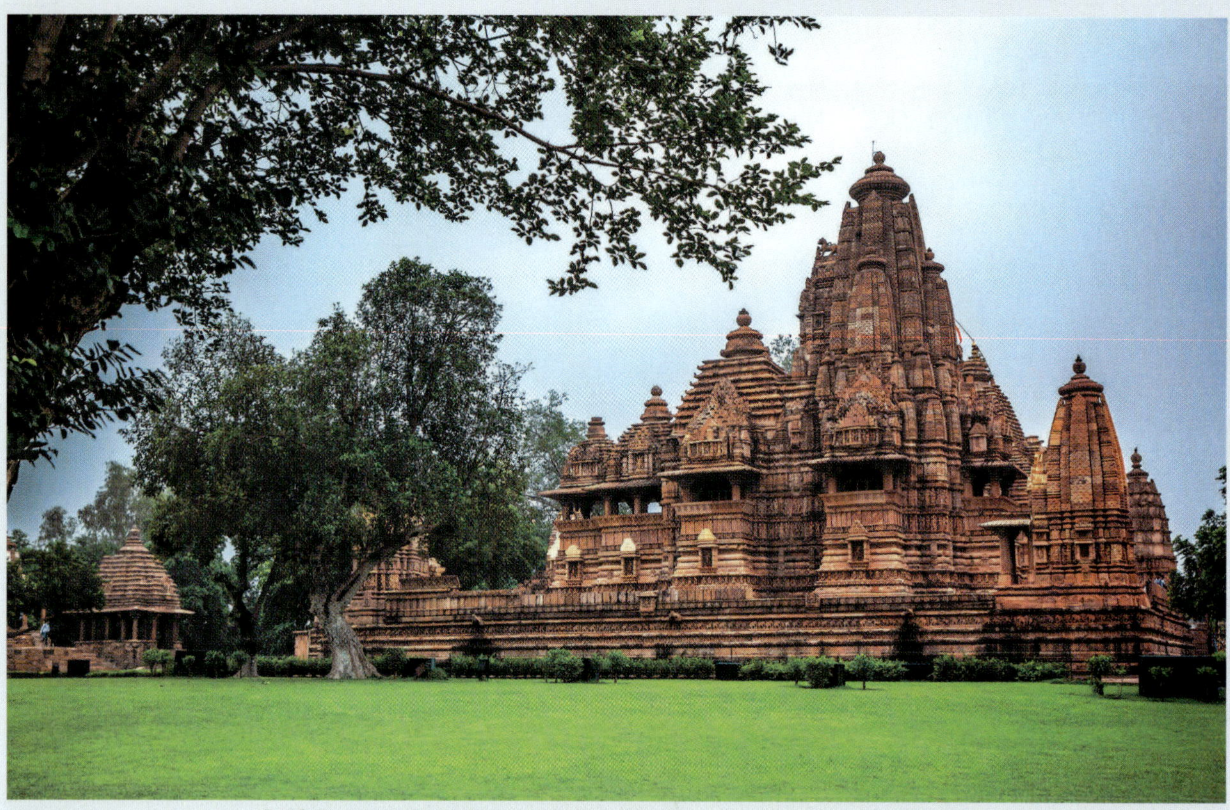

7.49: Laxman Temple — Courtesy, Madhya Pradesh Tourism Board

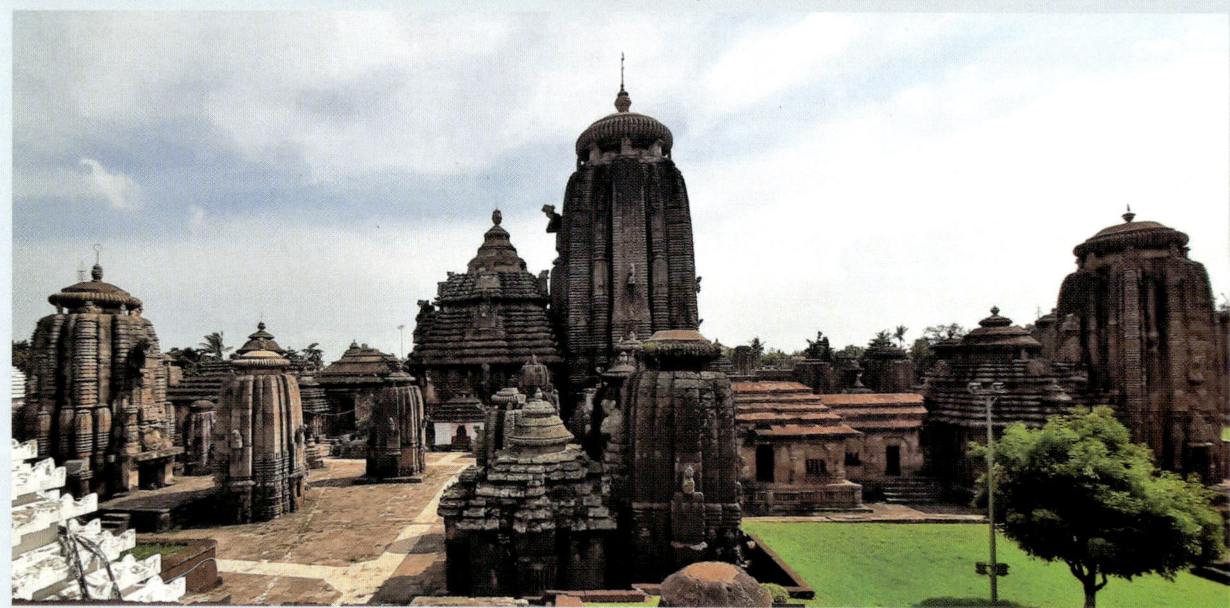

7.50: Lingaraj Temple, Bhubaneshwar; Odisha — Courtesy, Department of Tourism, Odisha

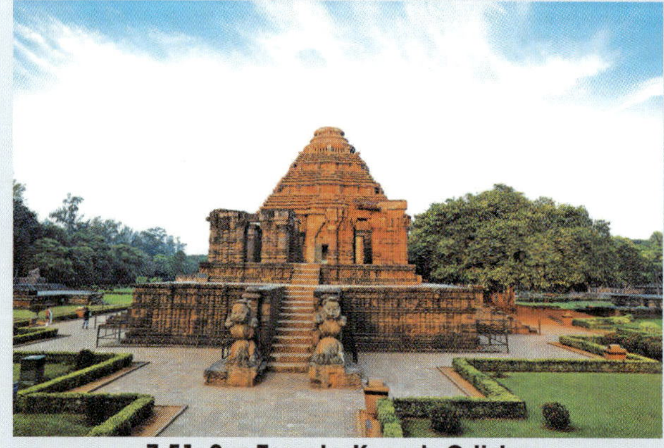

7.51: Sun Temple, Konark, Odisha — Courtesy, Department of Tourism, Odisha

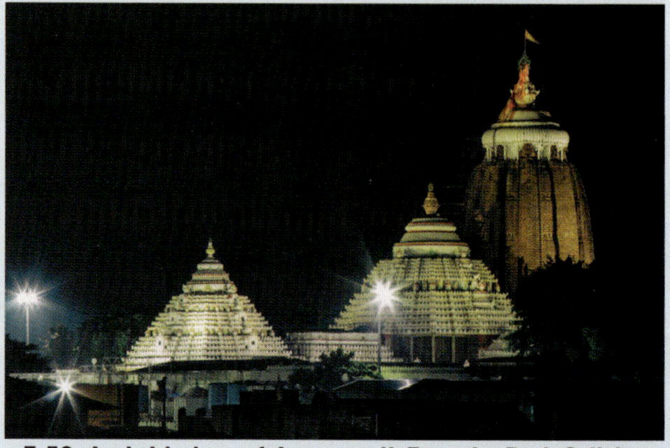

7.52: A night view of Jagannath Temple, Puri, Odisha — Courtesy, Department of Tourism, Odisha

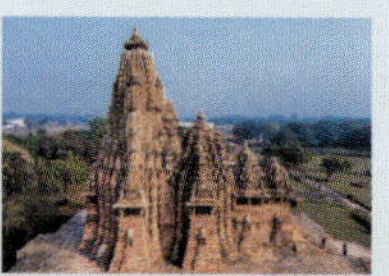

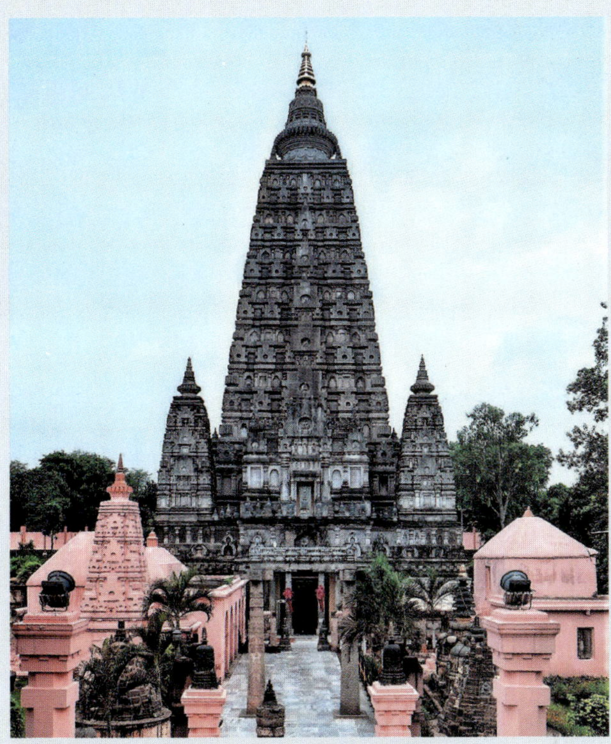

7.53: Bodh Gaya Temple
— Courtesy, Bihar Tourism

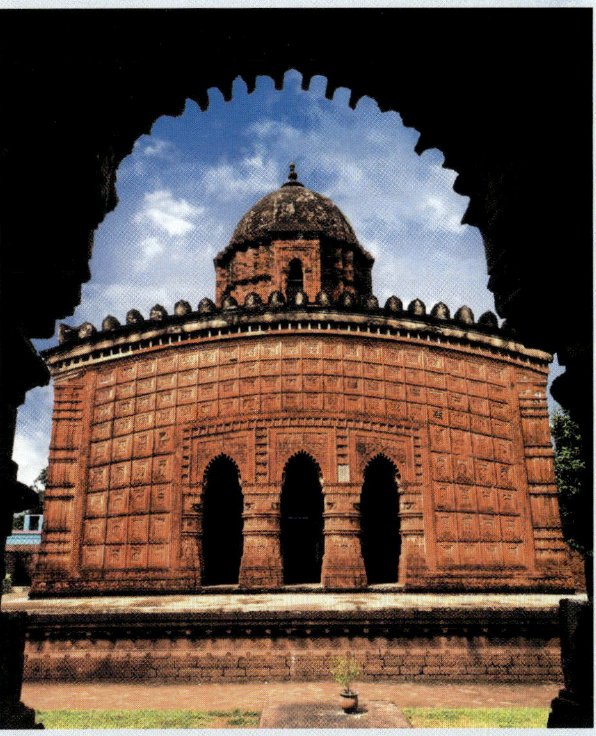

7.54: An arch framed view of Radheshyam Terracotta Temple, Bishnupur
— Courtesy, Department of Tourism, West Bengal

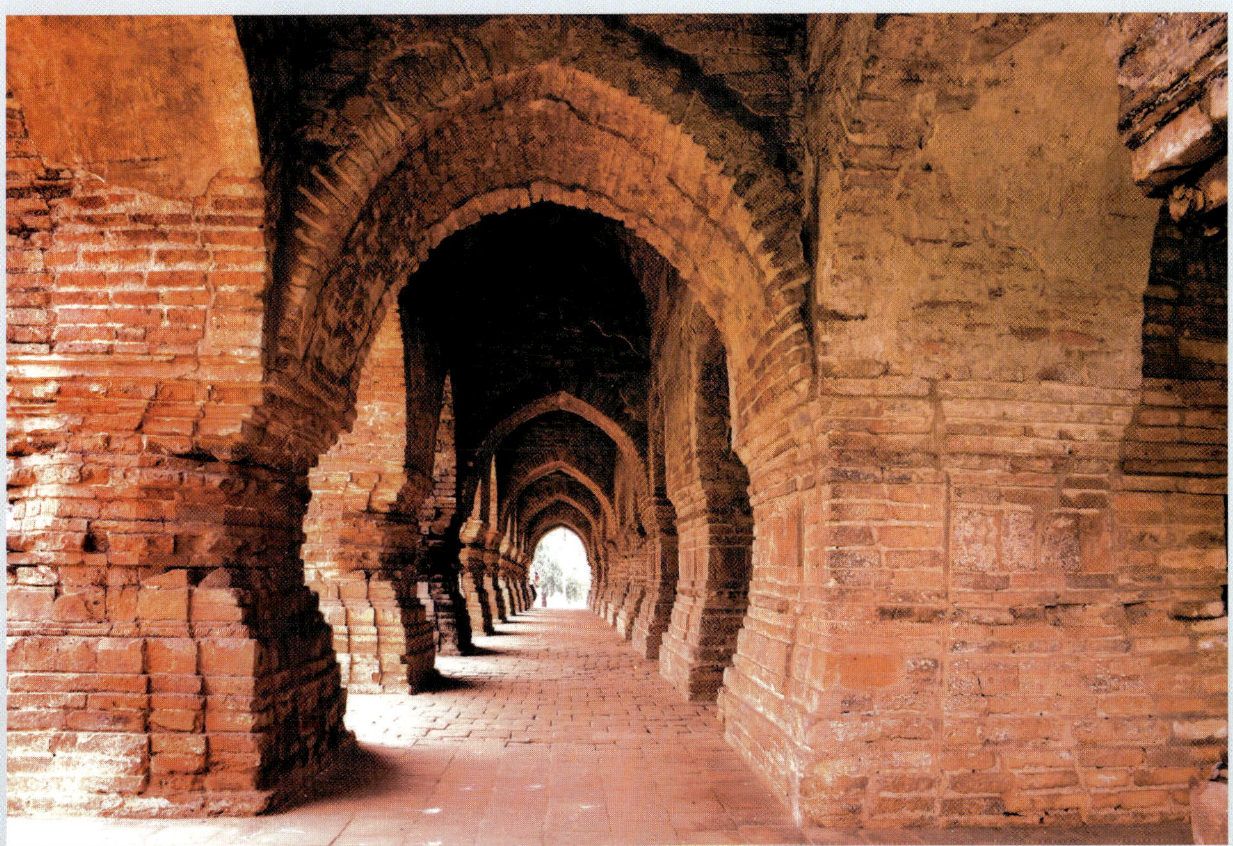

7.55: Inner terrace of Rasmancha Terracotta Temple, Bishnupur, West Bengal
— Courtesy, Department of Tourism, West Bengal

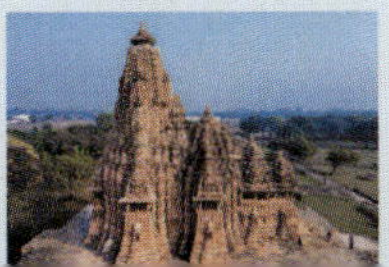

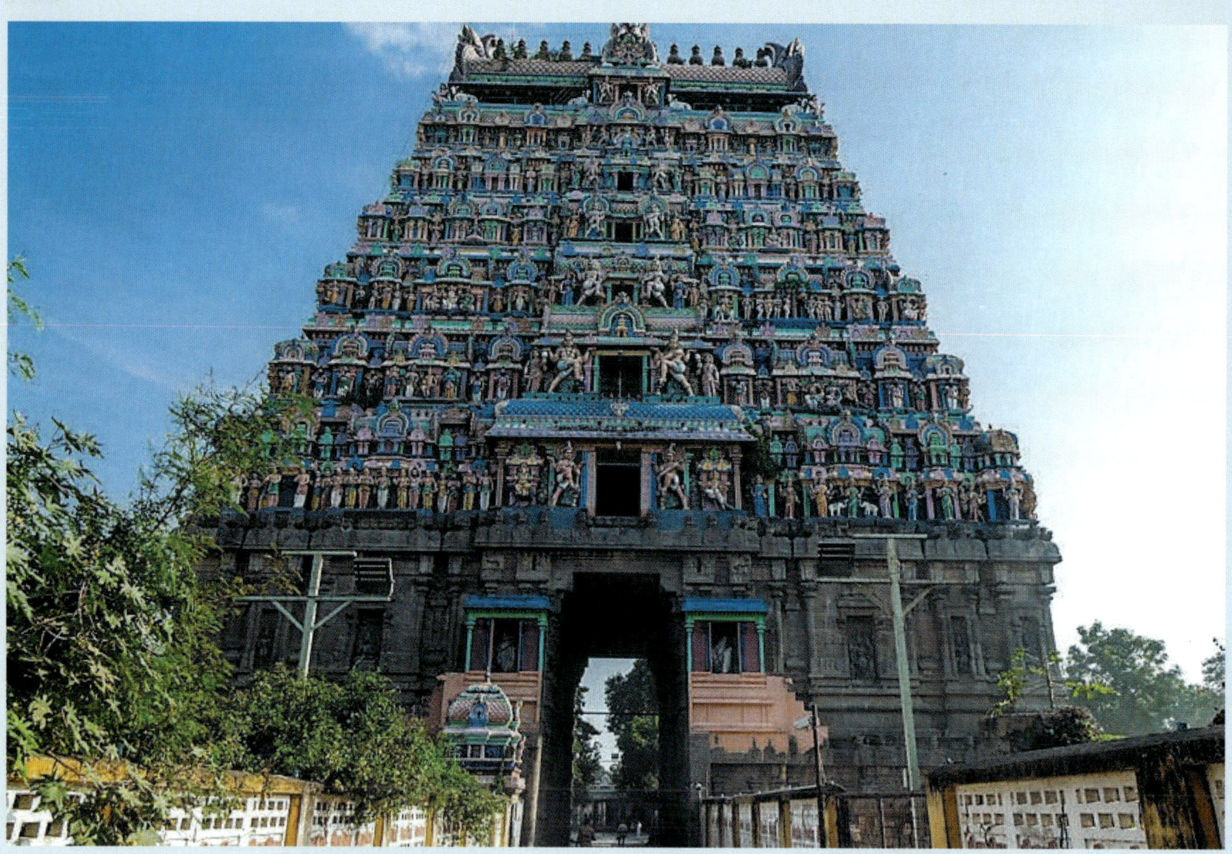

7.56: Gopuram of Nataraja Temple, Chidambaram, Tamil Nadu — Courtesy, Tamil Nadu Tourism Development Corporation

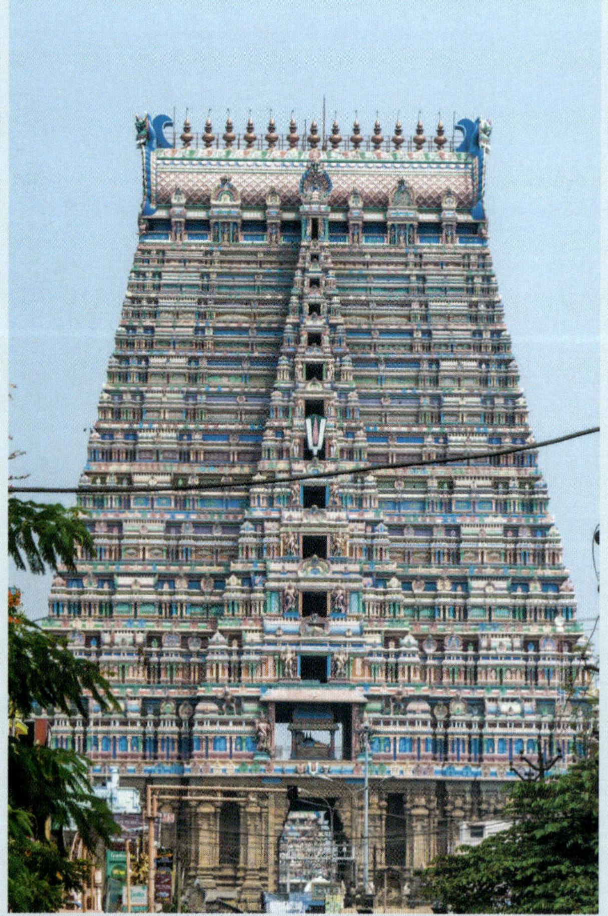

7.57: A view of the multi-tiered colourful gopuram of Ranganathaswamy Temple, Srirangam, Tiruchirappalli — Courtesy, Tamil Nadu Tourism Development Corporation

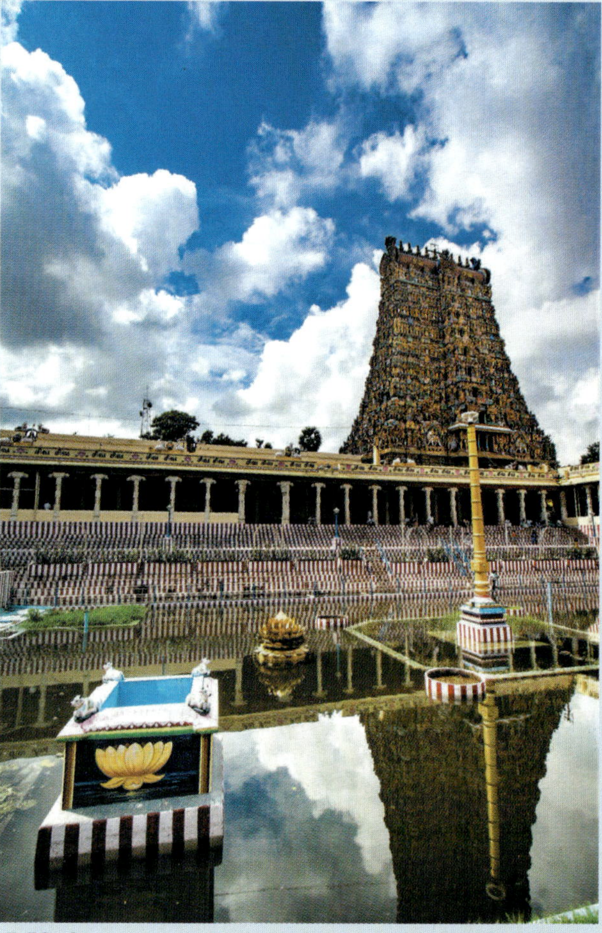

7.58: Gopuram and temple-tank at Meenakshi Temple, Madurai, Tamil Nadu — Courtesy, Tamil Nadu Tourism Development Corporation

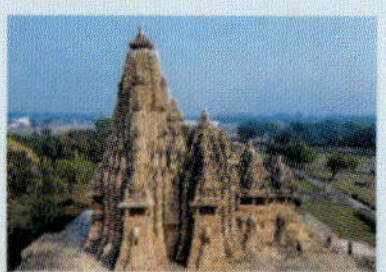

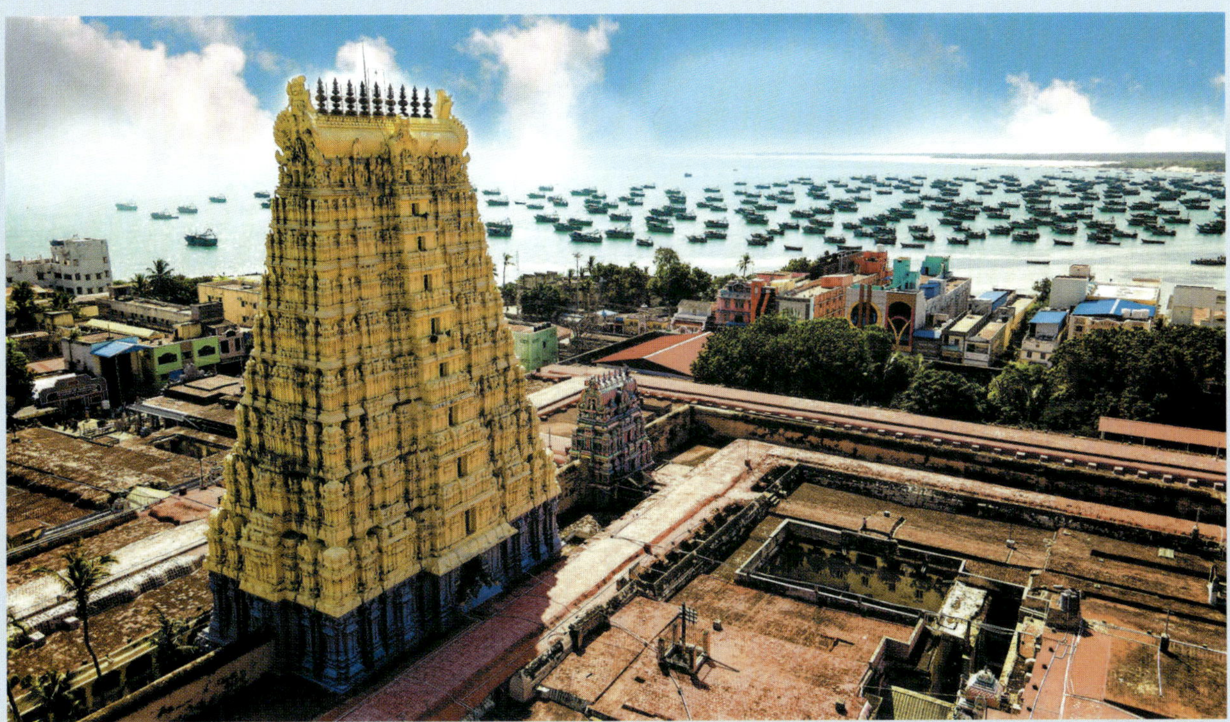

7.59: Ramanathaswamy Temple; Rameshwaram, Tamil Nadu; a 12th century Pandya dynasty temple dedicated to Lord Shiva — Courtesy, Tamil Nadu Tourism Development Corporation

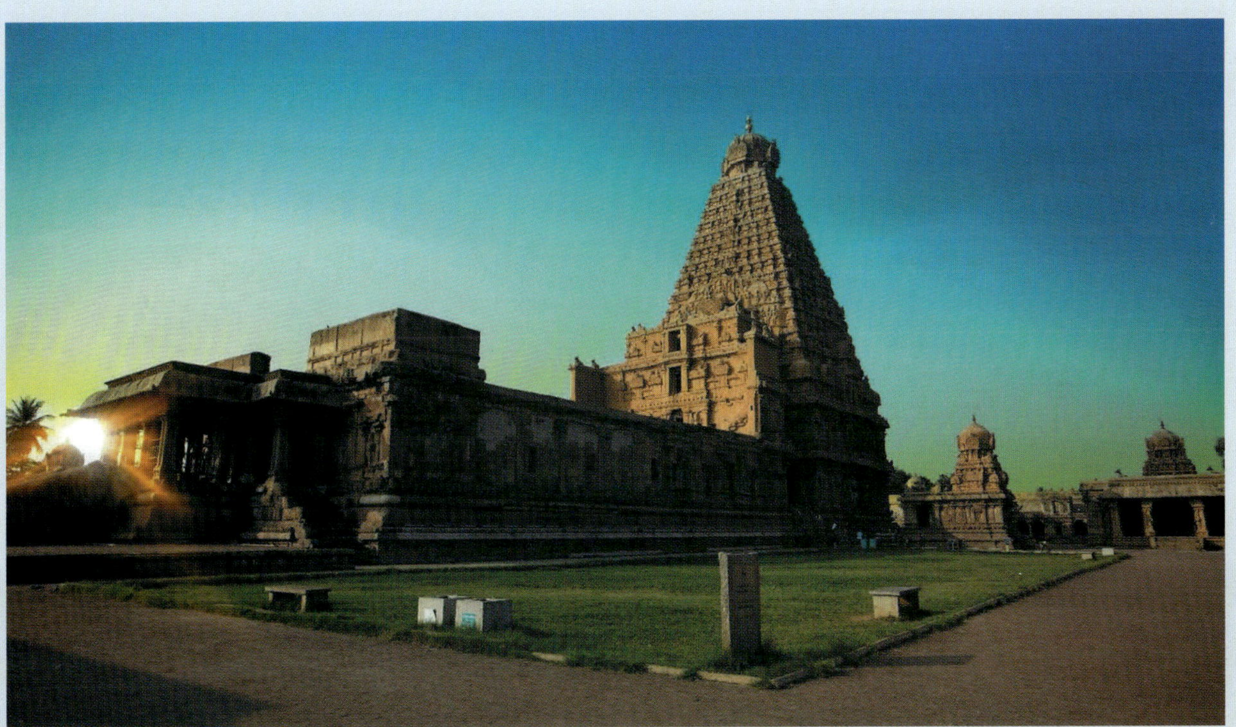

7.60: A view of sunrise at the Brihadeeswara Temple, Thanjavur — Courtesy, Tamil Nadu Tourism Development Corporation

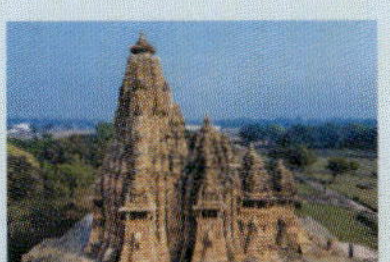

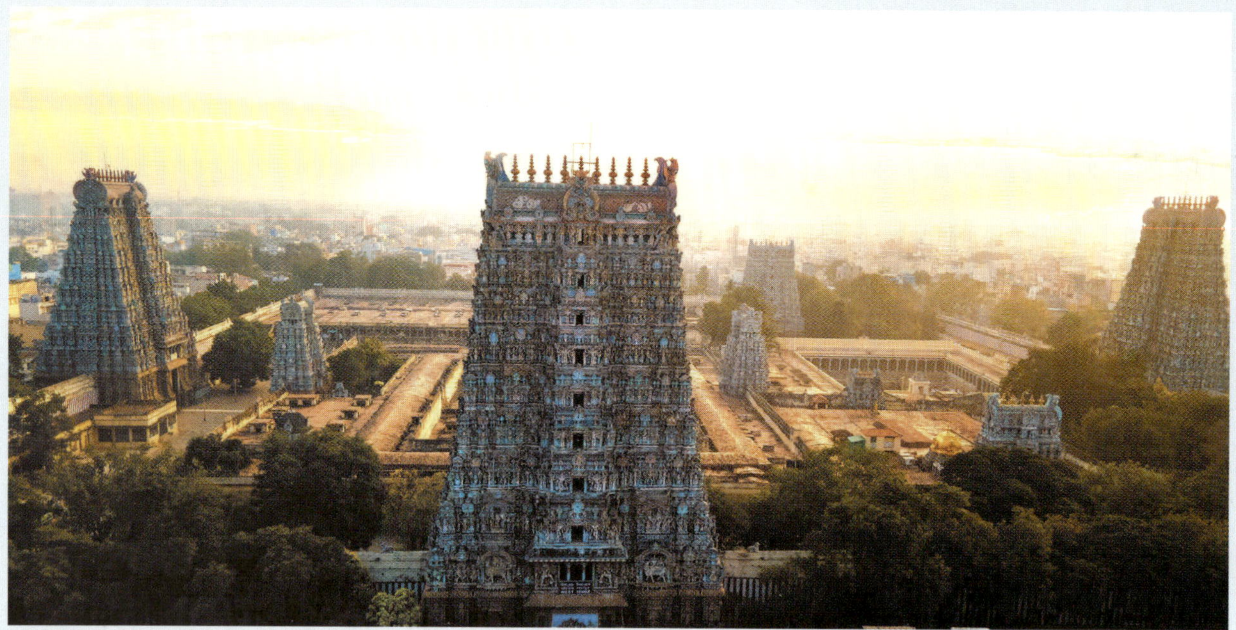

7.61: Meenakshi Temple, Madurai, at sunrise; a view of the large temple precincts and the tall gopurams — Courtesy, Tamil Nadu Tourism Development Corporation

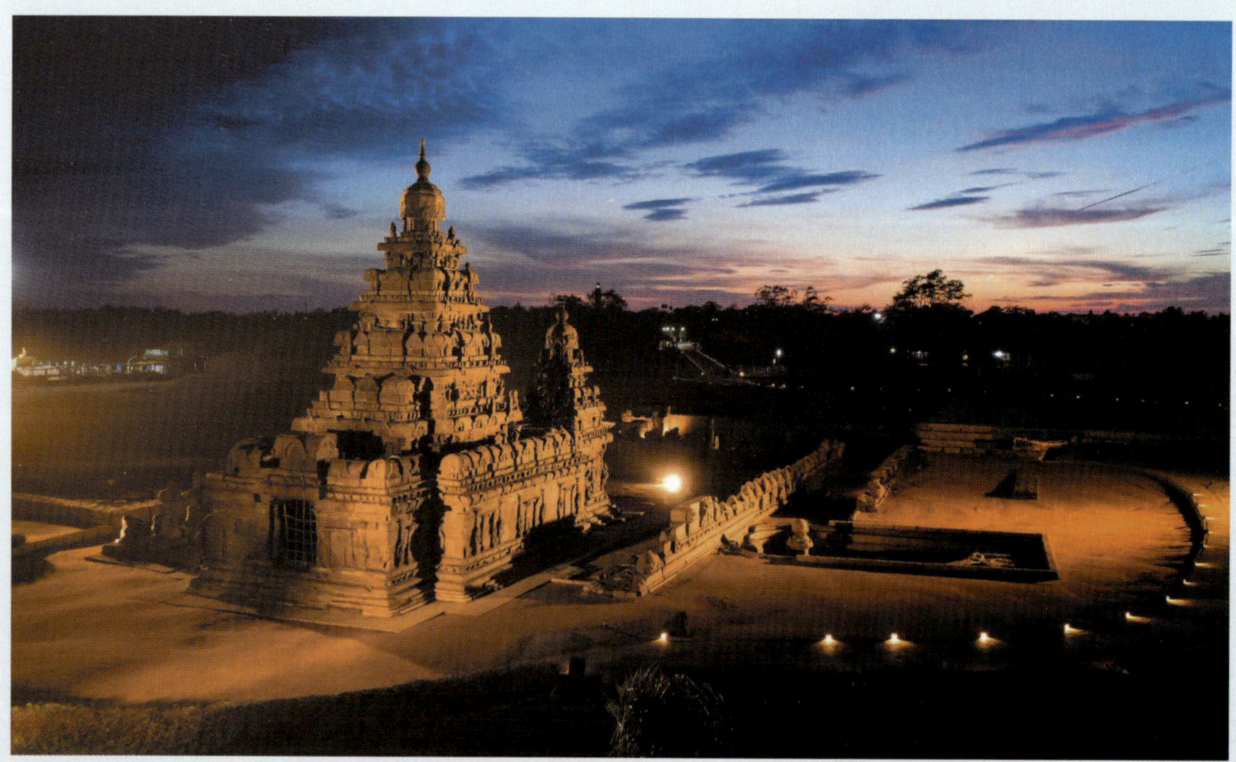

7.62: A night view of the Shore Temple Mahabalipuram; Tamil Nadu — Courtesy, Tamil Nadu Tourism Development Corporation

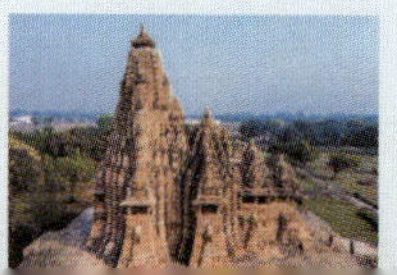

PHOTO/PICTURE CREDITS

(The numbers 1.1, 1.2, 1.3, ... etc. denotes the number of the captioned photographs.)

Chapter 1 Culture Eras: Ancient India

(*a*) **Photographs by Madhukar K Bhagat (author)** 1.1, 1.2, 1.3, 1.7, 1.9–1.22, 1.24–1.26, 1.31, 1.32

(*b*) **Links of copyright free photographs from Wikimedia/Wikipedia**

Wikimedia Commons, author Quratulain (https://commons.wikimedia.org/wiki/File:Picture_of_original_Godess.jpg) 1.5

Wikimedia Commons, author Mamoon Mengal (https://en.wikipedia.org/wiki/Priest-King_(sculpture)#/media/File:Mohenjo-daro_Priesterk%C3%B6nig.jpeg) 1.6

Wikimedia Commons (https://en.wikipedia.org/wiki/Vedic_period#/media/File:Rigveda_MS2097.jpg) 1.8

Wikimedia Commons (https://en.wikipedia.org/wiki/File:Bhagavata_Purana_(Ancient_Stories_of_the_Lord)_Manuscript_LACMA_M.88.134.4_(2_of_2).jpg) 1.23

(*c*) **Photographs with permission from museums and State Tourism Boards**

Courtesy, Directorate of Archaeology and Museums, Haryana 1.4

Courtesy, Maharashtra Tourism Development Corporation 1.27, 1.28, 1.29, 1.30

Chapter 2 The Indus Valley Civilisation and Harappan Culture

(*a*) **Photographs by Madhukar K Bhagat (author)** 2.1, 2.2, 2.4–2.8, 2.12, 2.13, 2.14, 2.16, 2.17, 2.20, 2.21–2.26, 2.28, 2.29, 2.30, 2.31, 2.34, 2.36, 2.42, 2.45, 2.48, 2.49, 2.50

(*b*) **Links of copyright free photographs from Wikimedia/Wikipedia**

Wikimedia Commons, author Avantipura7 (https://commons.wikimedia.org/wiki/File:Indus_Valley_Civilization,_Mature_Phase_(2600-1900_BCE).png) 2.3

Wikimedia Commons, author Junhi Han (file provided by UNESCO) (https://commons.wikimedia.org/wiki/File:Archaeological_Ruins_at_Moenjodaro-108221.jpg) 2.9

Wikimedia Commons, author Gaffar 772 (https://commons.wikimedia.org/wiki/File:Moen_Jo_Daro_(The_Mond_of_the_Deads).jpg) 2.10

Wikimedia Commons, author Saqib Qayyam (https://commons.wikimedia.org/wiki/File:Great_bath_view_Mohenjodaro.JPG) 2.11

Wikimedia Commons, author SMN122 (https://commons.wikimedia.org/wiki/File:Archaeological_Site_of_Harappa_by_smn121_-20.JPG) 2.15

Wikimedia Commons, author Siyajkak (https://commons.wikimedia.org/wiki/File:The_%27Ten_Indus_Scripts%27_discovered_near_the_northern_gateway_of_the_Dholavira_citadel.jpg) 2.18

Wikimedia Commons, author ALFGRN (https://commons.wikimedia.org/wiki/File:Susa_seal_with_Indus_signs.jpg) 2.19

Wikimedia Commons, author Quratulain (https://commons.wikimedia.org/wiki/File:Picture_of_original_Godess.jpg) 2.24

Wikimedia Commons, author Mamoon Mengal (https://en.wikipedia.org/wiki/File:Mohenjo-daro_Priesterk%C3%B6nig.jpeg) 2.25

Wikimedia Commons, author Royroy deb (https://upload.wikimedia.org/wikipedia/commons/a/a8/Indus_civilisation_seal_unicorn_at_Indian_Museum%2C_Kolkata.jpg) 2.27

Wikimedia Commons, author Avantipura 7 (https://commons.wikimedia.org/wiki/File:Cemetery_H_Pottery.png) 2.33

Wikimedia Commons, author Gary Todd (https://commons.wikimedia.org/wiki/File:Disha_Kaka_Boat_with_Direction_Finding_Birds,_model_of_Mohenjo-Daro_seal,_3000_BCE.jpg) 2.35

Wikimedia Commons, author Usman.pg (https://commons.wikimedia.org/wiki/File:Other_side_of_Moenjodaro_by_Usman_Ghani.jpg) 2.37

Wikimedia Commons, author Muhammad Bin Naveed (https://commons.wikimedia.org/wiki/File:Another_view_of_Granary_and_Great_Hall_on_Mound_F.JPG) 2.38

Wikimedia Commons, author Lalit Gajer (https://commons.wikimedia.org/wiki/File:DHOLAVIRA_SITE_(24).jpg) 2.39

Wikipedia/Wikimedia Commons, author Rama's Arrow (https://www.archeotravelers.com/en/2023/02/24/indian-stepwells-between-mysticism-and-engineering-prowess/) 2.40

Wikimedia Commons, author Archaeological Survey of India (https://commons.wikimedia.org/wiki/File:Kalibangan_2_Main_street.jpg) 2.43

Wikimedia Commons, author Archaeological Survey of India (https://commons.wikimedia.org/wiki/File:Kalibangan_arterial_thoroughfare,_Harappan.jpg) 2.44

Wikimedia Commons, Trish Mayo (https://en.wikipedia.org/wiki/Indus_Valley_Civilisation#/media/File:Harappan_small_figures.jpg) 2.46

Wikimedia Commons, no author attribution (https://upload.wikimedia.org/wikipedia/commons/7/71/Harappan_small_figures.jpg) 2.47

Wikimedia Commons, author Archaeological Society of India (https://commons.wikimedia.org/wiki/File:Sinauli_chariot_ASI.jpg) 2.51

(c) **Photographs with permission from museums and State Tourism Boards**

Courtesy, Directorate of Archaeology and Museums, Government of Haryana 2.32, 2,41

Chapter 3 Hinduism: A Way and View of Life

(a) **Photographs by Madhukar K Bhagat (author)** 3.1, 3.4, 3.8, 3.10, 3.17, 3.18–3.35, 3.39–3.74

(b) **Links of copyright free photographs from Wikimedia/Wikipedia**

Wikimedia Commons, from the collection Los Angeles County Museum of Art (https://commons.wikimedia.org/wiki/File:Vishnu_Discoursing_(recto),_Prince_Worshipping_and_Discoursing_(verso);_Folio_from_a_Vaishnava_manuscript_LACMA_M.72.53.27a-b_(2_of_2).jpg) 3.2

(Source/Photographer: http://collections.lacma.org/sites/default/files/remote_images/piction/ma-2792006-03)

Wikimedia Commons, author Ms Sarah Welch (https://commons.wikimedia.org/wiki/File:1500-1200_BCE_Rigveda,_manuscript_page_sample_i,_Mandala_1,_Hymn_1_(Sukta_1),_Adhyaya_1,_lines_1.1.1_to_1.1.9,_Sanskrit,_Devanagari.jpg cc by SA 4.0) 3.3

Wikimedia Commons, author Sarah Welch (https://commons.wikimedia.org/wiki/File:1200-1000_BCE,_Vajasneyi_samhita_sample_i,_Shukla_Yajurveda,_Sanskrit,_Devanagari.jpg) 3.5

Wikimedia Commons, author Sarah Welch (https://commons.wikimedia.org/wiki/File:1636_CE_Samaveda,_Sadvimsha_Brahmana,_Varanasi_Sanskrit_college,_Edward_Cowell_collection,_sample_iii,_Sanskrit,_Devanagari.jpg cc by SA4.0) 3.6

Wikimedia Commons, authors William Dwight Whitney, Charles Rockwell Lanman (https://commons.wikimedia.org/wiki/File:Atharva-Veda_samhita_page_471_illustration.png) 3.7

Wikipedia/Wikimedia Commons (https://en.m.wikipedia.org/wiki/File:Raja_Ravi_Varma,_Jatayu_vadha,_1906.jpg) 3.9

Wikimedia Commons (https://commons.wikimedia.org/wiki/Raja_Ravi_Varma#/media/File:Rama-Varuna.jpg) 3.11

Wikimedia Commons (https://commons.wikimedia.org/wiki/File:Sauti_recites_the_slokas_of_the_Mahabharata.jpg) 3.12

Wikimedia Commons (https://upload.wikimedia.org/wikipedia/commons/9/97/Bheeshma_oath_by_RRV_%28cropped%29.jpg) 3.13

Wikimedia Commons (https://commons.wikimedia.org/wiki/File:BhagavadGita-19th-century-Illustrated-Sanskrit-Chapter_1.20.21.jpg) 3.14

Wikimedia Commons (https://commons.wikimedia.org/wiki/File:Bhagavad_Gita,_a_19th_century_manuscript.jpg) 3.15

Wikimedia Commons (https://commons.wikimedia.org/wiki/File:Page_of_Text,_Folio_from_a_Bhagavata_Purana_(Ancient_Stories_of_the_Lord)_LACMA_M.82.62.1_(1_of_2).jpg) 3.16

Wikimedia Commons (https://upload.wikimedia.org/wikipedia/commons/8/89/Kali_by_Raja_Ravi_Varma.jpg) 3.36

Wikimedia Commons (https://commons.wikimedia.org/wiki/File:Raja_Ravi_Varma,_Goddess_Lakshmi,_1896.jpg) 3.37

Wikimedia Commons (https://commons.wikimedia.org/wiki/File:Saraswati.jpg) 3.38

Chapter 4 Buddhism: The Middle Path

(a) **Photographs by Madhukar K Bhagat (author)** 4.1, 4.2, 4.3, 4.4, 4.5, 4.7, 4.8, 4.10, 4.11, 4.13, 4.15, 4.16, 4.19, 4.20, 4.22, 4.23, 4.24, 4.25, 4.35, 4.36, 4.40, 4.41, 4.44, 4.45, 4.46, 4.47, 4.48, 4.50, 4.51, 4.52, 4.53, 4.54

(b) **Links of copyright free photographs from Wikimedia/Wikipedia**

Wikimedia Commons, source Chattha Sangāyana 1955 (https://en.wikipedia.org/wiki/Sixth_Buddhist_council#/media/File:Chattha_Sang%C4%81yana.jpg) 4.6

Wikimedia Commons (https://en.m.wikipedia.org/wiki/File:Siddhartha_fasting,_old_reduced-size_replica_of_original_in_Lahore_Museum,_Gandhara,_2nd-3rd_century_AD,_slate_-_Linden-Museum_-_Stuttgart,_Germany_-_DSC03816.jpg) 4.9

Wikimedia Commons (https://en.wikipedia.org/wiki/Dharmachakra#/media/File:Dharma_Wheel_(2).svg) 4.12

Wikimedia Commons, author Jean-Pierre Dalbéra (https://commons.wikimedia.org/wiki/File:Ajanta_Cave_17_Scene_of_the_Vessantara_Jataka.jpg) 4.17

Wikipedia/Wikimedia Commons, author Ethan Doyle White (https://en.wikipedia.org/wiki/File:The_Adoration_of_the_Empty_Throne.JPG) 4.26

Wikipedia/Wikimedia Commons 4.27–4.32

Wikimedia Commons, author Daderot (https://commons.wikimedia.org/wiki/File:Amitabha_of_Phat_Tich_pagoda_(reproduction),_Bac_Ninh_province,_1057_AD_DSC04844.JPG) 4.33

Wikimedia Commons, author Biswarup Ganguly (https://en.wikipedia.org/wiki/Abhayamudra#/media/File:Lord_Buddha_in_Abhaya_Mudra_-_Circa_3rd-4th_Century_CE_-_Govind_Nagar_-_ACCN_76-17_-_Government_Museum_-_Mathura_2013-02-23_5558.JPG) 4.34

Wikimedia Commons (https://en.wikipedia.org/wiki/Mandala#/media/File:Manjuvajramandala_con_43_divinit%C3%A0_-_Unknown_-_Google_Cultural_Institute.jpg) 4.42

(c) **Photographs with permission from museums and State Tourism Boards**

Courtesy, Maharashtra Tourism Development Corporation 4.14, 4.18

Courtesy, Patna Museum 4.21

Courtesy, Directorate of Uttar Pradesh Tourism 4.49

Courtesy, Department of Tourism, Odisha 4.55

Chapter 5 Jainism: The Theology and Practice of Ahimsa

(*a*) **Photographs by Madhukar K Bhagat (author)** 5.1, 5.3–5.7, 5.9, 5.11, 5.14–5.21, 5.34–5.37

(*b*) **Links of copyright free photographs from Wikimedia/Wikipedia**

Wikimedia Commons, author Jonathan Cardy (https://commons.wikimedia.org/wiki/File:Rishabhanatha_at_V%26A.jpg) 5.2
Wikimedia Commons, author Pankajmcait (https://commons.wikimedia.org/wiki/File:Sikharji_jalmandir.jpg) 5.8
Wikipedia (https://en.wikipedia.org/wiki/Ratnatraya#/media/File:In-jain-o.svg) 5.12
Wikimedia Commons, author Dayodaya (https://commons.wikimedia.org/wiki/File:Mahavir.jpg) 5.13
Wikipedia (https://en.wikipedia.org/wiki/Ashtamangala) 5.22–5.30
Wikimedia Commons, author Pushiwiki (https://commons.wikimedia.org/wiki/File:Mahamastakabhisheka_in_2006.jpg) 5.31
Wikimedia Commons, author Bhavyesh Acharya (https://commons.wikimedia.org/wiki/File:Palitana_Temple.jpg) 5.33

(*c*) **Photographs with permission from museums and State Tourism Boards**

Courtesy, Bihar Tourism (https://tourism.bihar.gov.in/en/destinations/nalanda/jal-mandir-pawapuri) 5.10
Courtesy, Department of Tourism, Odisha 5.32

Chapter 6 Tangible & Intangible Elements of Culture in Ancient India

(*a*) **Photographs by Madhukar K Bhagat (author)** 6.1, 6.2, 6.3, 6.7, 6.8, 6.10, 6.11, 6.12, 6.13, 6.14, 6.18–6.31, 6.33–6.38, 6.40, 6.42–6.47, 6.49, 6.52–6.64, 6.68–6.70, 6.78–6.84, 6.86–6.94, 6.97, 6.99, 6.100, 6.102, 6.103, 6.108, 6.114–6.117, 6.120–6.129

(*b*) **Links of copyright free photographs from Wikimedia/Wikipedia**

Wikimedia Commons, author Chrisi 1964 (https://commons.wikimedia.org/wiki/File:Sarnath_capital.jpg) 6.5
Wikimedia Commons, author Chrisi 1964 (https://en.wikipedia.org/wiki/Lion_Capital_of_Ashoka#/media/File:AshokaLions.jpg) 6.6
Wikimedia Commons, author Rohini (https://commons.wikimedia.org/wiki/File:Plan_of_Stupa_at_Sanchi_-_2.JPG) 6.9
Wikimedia Commons, author Biswarup Ganguly (https://commons.wikimedia.org/wiki/File:Yaksha_Manibhadra_-_Parkham_Mathura_circa_150_BCE.jpg) 6.15
Wikimedia Commons, author Photo Dharma from Penang, Malaysia (https://commons.wikimedia.org/wiki/File:Lomas_Rishi_entrance.jpg) 6.17
Wikimedia Commons, author, Percy Brown (1872-1955) (https://commons.wikimedia.org/wiki/File:Conjectural_reconstruction_of_the_main_gate_of_Kusinagara_circa_500_BCE_adapted_from_a_relief_at_Sanchi.jpg) 6.32
Wikimedia Commons, author Biswarup Ganguly (https://commons.wikimedia.org/wiki/File:Kanishka_enhanced.jpg) 6.39
Wikimedia Commons, author Biswarup Ganguly (https://commons.wikimedia.org/wiki/File:Standing_Buddha_Curved_or_Installed_by_Buddist_Monk_Yasadinna_-_Circa_5th_Century_CE_-_Jamalpur_Mound_-_ACCN_00-A-5_-_Government_Museum_-_Mathura_2013-02-23_5546.JPG) 6.41
Wikimedia Commons, author Cunningham (https://commons.wikimedia.org/wiki/File:CunninghamBharhut.jpg) 6.48
(https://commons.wikimedia.org/wiki/File:6th_century_Vishnu_seated_on_Sesha_in_Cave_3,_Badami_Hindu_cave_temple_Karnataka.jpg) 6.51
Wikimedia Commons, author Biswarup Ganguly (https://commons.wikimedia.org/wiki/File:Standing_Buddha_Installed_by_Buddist_Monk_Yasadinna_-_Circa_5th_Century_CE_-_Jamalpur_Mound_-_ACCN_00-A-5_-_Government_Museum_Mathura_Golden_background.jpg) 6.67
Wikimedia Commons, source Tevaprapas Makklay (https://commons.wikimedia.org/wiki/File:Buddha_in_Sarnath_Museum_(Dhammajak_Mutra).jpg) 6.71
Wikimedia Commons, source photo taken by Freakyyash (https://en.wikipedia.org/wiki/Ajanta_Caves#/media/File:Ajanta_viewpoint.jpg) 6.72
Wikimedia Commons, author Photo Dharma from Sadao, Thailand (https://commons.wikimedia.org/wiki/File:100_Cave_26,_Buddha_in_Parinirvana_(34219037182).jpg) 6.73
worldhistory.org Original image by Jean-Pierre Dalbera. Uploaded by Dola RC (https://www.worldhistory.org/image/4145/mural--ajanta-caves/) 6.74
Wikimedia Commons (https://upload.wikimedia.org/wikipedia/en/f/fc/Kailash_temple_%28Ellora_cave_no_15%29_at_Verul.png) 6.77
Wikimedia Commons, author Scram 144 (https://commons.wikimedia.org/wiki/File:The_Dashavatara,_Ellora_cave_no._15.jpg) 6.81
Wikimedia Commons, ArnoldBetten (https://commons.wikimedia.org/wiki/File:Nachna_Chaumukhnath_1999.JPG) 6.96

Wikimedia Commons, author Adarshkotia (https://commons.wikimedia.org/wiki/File:Location_of_the_Eran_boar_inscription_of_Toramana.jpg) 6.98
Wikimedia Commons, author Photo Division, Government of India (https://commons.wikimedia.org/wiki/File:Rishabhadeva,_Bronze_from_Chausa,_Bihar,_dating_from_7th_century_A.D._37644.jpg) 6.101
Wikimedia Commons, author Kaviraj Kunja Lal Bhishagratna (https://commons.wikimedia.org/wiki/File:Ancient_Hindu_text_Sushruta_samhita_shastra_and_kartarika,_surgical_instruments_1_of_4.jpg) 6.107
Wikimedia Commons 6.109

(c) Photographs with permission from museums and State Tourism Boards

Courtesy, Maharashtra Tourism Development Corporation 6.4
Courtesy, Department of Tourism, Odisha 6.16
Courtesy, Karnataka State Tourism Development Corporation 6.50
Courtesy, Madhya Pradesh Tourism Board 6.65
Courtesy, Tamil Nadu Tourism Development Corporation 6.66
Courtesy, Maharashtra Tourism Development Corporation 6.75 & 6.76
Courtesy, Department of Tourism, Odisha 6.85
Courtesy, Directorate of Uttar Pradesh Tourism 6.95
Courtesy, Bihar Tourism 6.104, 6.105, 6.106
Courtesy, Maharashtra Tourism Development Corporation 6.110–6.113
Courtesy, Maharashtra Tourism Development Corporation 6.118, 6.119
Courtesy, Maharashtra Tourism Development Corporation 6.130-6.136

Chapter 7 Temples in Ancient & Medieval India

(a) Photographs by Madhukar K Bhagat (author) | 7.3, 7.4, 7.5, 7.6, 7.7, 7.19–7.29, 7.31

(b) Links of copyright free photographs from Wikimedia/Wikipedia

Wikimedia Commons, author Tangopaso (https://upload.wikimedia.org/wikipedia/commons/6/60/Architecture_of_the_Khajuraho_temples.jpg) 7.2
Wikimedia Commons, author Aniruddha Buragohain (https://en.wikipedia.org/wiki/Sivasagar_Sivadol#/media/File:Siva_Dol.JPG) 7.11
Wikimedia Commons, author Subhrajyoti07 (https://en.m.wikipedia.org/wiki/File:Stone_wheel_engraved_in_the_13th_century_built_Konark_Sun_Temple_in_Orissa,_India.jpg) 7.13
Wikimedia Commons, author Arnold Betten (https://commons.wikimedia.org/wiki/File:Nachna_1999_Parvati-Tempel.JPG) 7.18
Wikimedia, author India Post, Government of India 7.27

(c) Photographs with permission from museums and State Tourism Boards

Courtesy, Tamil Nadu Tourism Development Corporation 7.1, 7.32, 7.33, 7.34, 7.35, 7.40, 7.41, 7.56, 7.57, 7.58, 7.59, 7.60, 7.61, 7.62
Courtesy, Madhya Pradesh Tourism Board 7.8, 7.16, 7.45, 7.46, 7.47, 7.48, 7.49
Courtesy, Department of Tourism, Odisha 7.9, 7.12, 7.14, 7.50, 7.51, 7.52
Courtesy, Department of Tourism, West Bengal 7.10, 7.15, 7.54, 7.55
Courtesy, Directorate of Uttar Pradesh Tourism 7.17
Courtesy, Department of Post 7.30
Courtesy, Karnataka State Tourism Development Corporation 7.36, 7.37, 7.38, 7.39, 7.44
Courtesy, Bihar Tourism 7.42, 7.43, 7.53

Bibliography and References

Books

General Culture and Cultural History of India

- The History and Culture of the Indian People Volume I: The Vedic Age
- The History and Culture of the Indian People, Volume II: The Age of Imperial Unity
- The History and Culture of the Indian People, Volume III: The Classical Age
- The History and Culture of the Indian People Volume IV: The Age of Imperial Kannauj
- Themes in Indian history, Volume 1: NCERT
- Living Craft Traditions of India: NCERT
- An Introduction to Indian Art, Part I: NCERT
- Indian Philosophy: Dr S. Radhakrishnan
- An Idealist View of Life: Dr S. Radhakrishnan
- The National Culture of India: S. Abid Hussain
- Bhartiya Sanskriti Ke Char Adhyay: Ramdhari Singh Dinkar
- The Cultural Heritage of India, Volume 1 to Volume 6: The Ramakrishna Mission Institute of Culture
- Indian Heritage Art and Culture: Madhukar Kumar Bhagat

Hinduism

- The Hindu View of Life: Dr S. Radhakrishnan
- Bhagavad Gita: Dr S. Radhakrishnan
- The Philosophy of the Upanishads: Dr S. Radhakrishnan
- The Essence of Hinduism: M.K. Gandhi
- Sanatana Dharma, an elementary Text-Book of Hindu Religion and Ethics
- Rig Veda: Vivek Debroy
- Rig Veda: Translation by Griffith

Buddhism

- Dhammapada: Dr S. Radhakrishnan
- The Light of Asia: Sir Edward Arnold
- The Buddha and His Teachings: Narada Mahathera
- The Dhammapada: the Buddhist Path of Wisdom; Translation by Acharya Buddha Rakhita
- The Buddha's Victory; Sangharakshita: Windhorse Publications

Jainism

- Tattvartha Sutra by Acharya Umaswami; Translation with commentary of Manu Doshi
- The Holy Kalpa Sutra: English translation by Herman Jacobi
- Jainism: Federation of Jain Associations in North America

Other Elements of Culture

- Ancient Indian literature, an Anthology, Volume - 1: Sahitya Akademi
- The Great Tang Dynasty Record of The Western Regions: An English Translation of the Accounts of Hiuen Tsang (Xuan Zang)
- Kautilya's Arthashastra; English Translation by S. Shamasastry
- An English Translation of The Sushruta Samhita. By Kaviraj Kunja Lal Bhishagratna
- The Natyashastra: translation by Manmohan Ghosh
- Rock Edicts of Ashoka: Romila Thapar

Archaeological Survey of India Booklets

- Deogarh: ASI Lucknow Circle
- Lothal: Director General ASI, Government of India
- Modhera: Director General ASI, Government of India
- Rani ki Vav, Patan: Director General ASI, Government of India
- Sanchi Museum: ASI Bhopal Circle
- Sanchi, Resurgence from Ruins: Bhopal Circle ASI

Websites

- Articles on Wikipedia
- Articles on Encyclopaedia Britannica
- Centre for Cultural Resource and Training: https://ccrtindia.gov.in/
- Gita Super Site: https://www.gitasupersite.iitk.ac.in/
- UNESCO; World Heritage Convention: https://whc.unesco.org/en/convention/

Articles in Journals and Newspapers

- *An Ancient Harappan Genome Lacks Ancestry from Steppe Pastoralists or Iranian Farmers*: Shinde *et al.*, 2019, Cell 179, 729–735 October 17, 2019
- *A note on Chariot Burials found at Sinauli district Baghpat U.P.*: Vijay Kumar: Indian Journal of Archaeology pg. 735
- *Compound specific isotope analysis of lipid residues provides the earliest direct evidence of dairy product processing in South Asia*: The Nature: 30th September 2020
- Dholavira is the most spectacular Indus Valley site in India; its demise was connected to climate change: The Times of India February 26, 2020
- *Bhirana oldest Harappan site, Rakhigarhi largest:* ASI report: Livemint 16th April 2015
- *Rakhigarhi DNA study questions Aryan invasion theory, claims author:* The Economic Times, September 2019
- *Rakhigarhi – The largest site from the Harrapan culture:* The Financial Express; November 2, 2021
- *Indus Valley had dairy production way back in the 3rd millennium BCE:* Hindustan Times Oct 25, 2020
- *Multi-grain ladoos from Harappa civilisation found during excavation at Harappan site:* Times of India Mar 26, 2021
- *The mystery of Harappan script: An enigma from the ancient world:* The Financial Express November 30, 2019